History of Martha's Vineyard

VOLUME II

REV. JONATHAN MAYHEW

BORN CHILMARK OCT. 8, 1720; DIED BOSTON JULY 9, 1776

THE HISTORY
OF
MARTHA'S VINEYARD

DUKES COUNTY

MASSACHUSETTS

IN THREE VOLUMES

VOLUME II

TOWN ANNALS

BY

CHARLES EDWARD BANKS, M. D.

ASSISTANT SURGEON GENERAL U. S. P. H. S.
(Retired)

EDGARTOWN

PUBLISHED BY THE DUKES COUNTY
HISTORICAL SOCIETY

1966

PREFACE

Having now brought forward the narrative of events from the beginning of time, through the first occupation of the Vineyard by Englishmen for a permanent residence, and presented the story of its progress as a whole to our own day, the subsequent annals of the island, under its new tenants in segregated communities, will be considered in detail. Separate histories of each township growing out of the initial settlement, commencing with Edgartown, the eldest, taking each in turn according to its chronological relations to the parent towns, will follow, and the local developments of each one be particularly treated. In order to maintain this plan, however, certain arbitrary limitations will be necessary in its application to simplify the relation, owing to the divisions of Edgartown, to form Cottage City (now Oak Bluffs); of Chilmark to form Gosnold; and of Tisbury, to form West Tisbury. Therefore, for the purposes of definite historical study of these towns, the present boundary limits of each, although at one time a part of another, will be considered as originally belonging to the later incorporated community. For example, all that relates to persons and events in the present territorial limits of Oak Bluffs, although enacted when a part of Edgartown, will be related as happening in the history of that section now called Oak Bluffs. This topographical plan will prevent duplication of statements and constant explanation of the relation of events and places to each other, and give proper credit to the scenes enacted on each one's particular soil.

In the quotations from the early records, which will be found in the text of the work in each volume, the reader may miss the familiar word "ye" a fantastic affectation of the ignorant to indicate the definite article "the," as if our ancestors were in the habit of using, or even ever used, such absurd expressions as "ye house" or "ye cow." In the early days of printing the Saxon *th* was represented by a symbol which looked like a *y* or *þ*, and when the Roman alphabet was employed exclusively there was no symbol to represent this *th* sound and the letter *y* was used as a substitute; but always pronounced as *th* and not as *ye*, as it looks. This explanation may help to correct an absurd error which is perpetuated by persons unfamiliar with the true reason for the apparent archaism.

The reader is also reminded of the differences in the calendar in the Colonial period before 1752, by which there occurred the "double dating" between January 1st and March 25th of each year. An explanation of this is given in Vol. I., pp. 489-90, and an understanding of it is required to interpret dates correctly when a double date occurs.

It has not been deemed practicable, in view of the necessity of economy of space, to supplement the Annals with long and dreary lists of town officers which have but little meaning to most people; nor to extend the details of present-day affairs to the extent of composing a business and social directory for future reference. All that can be done in such a comprehensive work as this is to bring down the narrative of events to the memory of the living. Some day in the future an historian for each principal town will be able to use the foundation I have laid as the basis for a complete superstructure in each case.

C. E. B.

ILLUSTRATIONS

ANNALS OF EDGARTOWN

ANNALS OF WEST TISBURY

ANNALS OF CHILMARK

ANNALS OF TISBURY

Illustrations

ANNALS OF OAK BLUFFS

ANNALS OF GAY HEAD

ANNALS OF GOSNOLD

ANNALS OF EDGARTOWN.

Nunnepog.

The beginnings of the history of Edgartown took place in Watertown, when, on March 16, 1641–2, the grant of township was made by the two patentees, Mayhew senior and junior, unto five of their townsmen as previously stated, and the first foundations were laid in that year when young Thomas Mayhew set foot on the shores of its "great harbour," with his companions, to consummate the title and take possession.

The identity of the passengers who came in that first shallop to Great Harbor in 1642 as companions of young Mayhew is yet an unsolved problem. We only know he came "with some other persons" and that there were "divers families," including "some of Watertown," and the records lend us no aid in the solution. Speculation may be indulged in to the extent of supposing that some of the original grantees of Watertown came to look over their deed of gift, but we know that of these only John Daggett remained to become a settler, and he may be included with the first contingent. To these we may add John Folger, John Smith (John Bland), possibly Edward Sales of Rehoboth, and their families, and—here we stop, lest speculation carry us too far.

Such was the beginning of our first settlement by the Mayhews and their associates, and little that they did in the early years of the plantation is known to us. We can picture them as busy in clearing the land east of Pease Point Way, felling timber, building houses, laying out lots, tilling the soil, and fishing in the adjoining waters.

As they landed at their future home, doubtless they were met in a questioning attitude by groups of Indians under the leadership of Tewanquatick, Sagamore of Nunnepog, for such was the Algonquian name for the place which Mayhew chose for the town site. This Indian name for the territory now comprising the present bounds of Edgartown is the only one which was attached to the sachemship of the eastern half of the Vineyard. It occurs in various forms: as Nunpauket, Nunpaug, Nunpog, and in an Indian deed of 1684 it is written Unnunpauque (Deeds I, 18), and in another of 1696, Wonnottaquan, squaw sachem of Nunpawquit, sold land situated on the east side of Watchusate neck (Ibid., I, 208).[1]

The meaning of this word is "fresh pond or water place."[2] Just what particular pond gave its character to the sachemship of Nunnepog is a matter of speculation, but it was probably the Great Pond, on the shores of which was the Mashakemmuck, or Great House of the sachems of this territory.

FIRST TOWNSHIP GRANT.

The basis of all land titles in Edgartown rests upon the original grant of the two patentees to certain individuals named in the following grant of township rights : —

> . . . . . unto John Doggett, Daniel Pierce and Rich'd Beeres and John Smith and Francis Smith with ourselves to make choice for the Present of a large Towne upon the same Terms that we have it: And also equall Power in Governm't with us, and equall Power in admission of all that shall present themselves to come to live upon any part of the whole grant of all the Islands; and wee grant also to them and their Associates with us to receive another Townshipp for Posterity upon the same Terms wee have from the Grantees.[3]

This document invested these grantees with proprietary rights in the soil, and the management thereof in a corporate capacity as townsmen, but it was not until the elder Mayhew came to live on the island that the extent of this "large Towne" was made clear, by which their rights were defined : —[4]

> This witnesseth that Mr. Mayhew the Elder and also Mr. Mayhew the Younger have freely given to the men now inhabiting on the Island namely the Vineyard, this Tract of land following for a Townshipp: namely all Tawanquatack's his Right, together wth all the Land as farr as the Easter-Chop of Homses Hole, and also all the Island called Chapaquegick, wth full Power to dispose of all and every Part of the said Land

[1]It would seem that the name had, perhaps, a more circumscribed application, for the Report of the Commissioners for the Society for the Propagation of the Gospel, made in 1698, refers to Nunnepoag as a part of Edgartown.

[2]Eliot in James III, 12, has Nunnupog, equivalent to "fresh water."

[3]New York Col. Doc. Deeds, I, 72.

[4]Ibid., III, 68.

as they see best for their own comfortable Accommodation. The Line is to goe from Tequanoman's Point to the Eastermost Chop of Homses Hole. This I doe acknowledge to bee the free Grant of myselfe and my Sonn, the day and yeare above written.

per me

Tho: Mayhew

Decem: 4 th, 1646.

There is nothing of record to show the reason for the selection of this locality as the site of the new settlement, but it offered the most natural advantages for the purpose, a safe harbor and what was quite as important, a spring of potable water convenient to the shore. As elsewhere related, it is probable that the younger Mayhew determined this selection upon his first visit, and chose the homestead site for his father and himself as a nucleus of their personal holdings on the island.

In fact, the senior Mayhew himself, in an instrument dated Dec. 1, 1642, clearly shows that on that date he had not selected all his own land. In their grant to John Daggett, Sr., the proprietors, father and son, provide that the meadow and farm shall not be selected by Daggett until the elder Mayhew had picked out similar lots for himself. The deed, however, indicates that the elder Mayhew had visited the island and had chosen his home lot, "upon the point,"[1] and Daggett was limited to a distance of three miles from "the Spring that is by the harbor in my lot."

BOUNDARIES.

The present limits of Edgartown do not comprise all the territory above described, as in 1880 the northern half of the town was set off and incorporated as Cottage City, since changed (1907) to Oak Bluffs, leaving for consideration topographically and historically the land within the following bounds:— Beginning at the middle of the inlet to Sanchacantacket Pond, and crossing the pond to the ancient landmark known as Miober's Bridge, at the head of Major's Cove; thence on a straight line to the stepping stones at the head of the Lagoon; thence on a straight line crossing the State Highway to the

[1]Dukes Deeds, I, 189.

head of Tashmoo Pond; thence returning on a straight line to the Four Town Bound; thence by nine bound-stones in a direct line southerly through the middle of Watcha Neck to the South Beach. All territory south and east of these divisional lines, including the island of Chappaquiddick, now belongs to Edgartown, and the events of historic interest connected with the people who lived within this region will be related in the annals of the town which are to follow.

SUCCESSIVE NAMES OF THE TOWN.

For the first few years after the settlement of the town, no name was formally bestowed upon it, as it was the only place upon the island inhabited by the whites and it needed no distinguishing title. In all the extant correspondence of the elder Mayhew, during that early period, his letters were uniformly dated as "Uppon the Vyneyard" or "the Vyneyard" simply, while contemporary legal instruments referred indefinitely to the "Towne uppon the Vineyard." The name of Great Harbor first appears in 1652 in the town records as the title of the settlement now comprised in the territory of Edgartown, but even ten years later in a suit prosecuted by John Daggett at Plymouth the legal entry of it was made as Daggett *versus* "the towne of the said Vinyard." As the population increased and new settlers began to occupy the territory now covered by West Tisbury and Chilmark, the necessity for a distinctive nomenclature was felt, and Great Harbor began to be applied slowly to the settlement now known as Edgartown, while the newer village was called Middletown, probably because of its location in the center of the island. This condition lasted for about twenty years when it received the title of Edgartown, which it has ever since borne. The inquiry is frequently heard "why was it called Edgartown?" because it is an unusual name. Indeed, there is but one Edgartown in the world! The Gazetteer confirms the fact that in the nomenclature of places, throughout the known world, the name of our shire town has stood alone in unique isolation for over two centuries. The source of its title has long been an object, not only of curiosity on the part of the public, but of prolonged investigation at the hands of historical students, past and present. A number of ingenious suggestions have been made, such as it might be a corruption of Egerton, a parish in England, but no answer has ever been given that could be defended on historical grounds, and indeed no really serious suggestion as to its origin has yet come to light.

THE NAMING OF EDGARTOWN.

The baptism of the town took place in New York City, at Fort James, the seat of the Provincial governor, during the important conferences held between Colonel Lovelace, the representative of the Duke of York and the elder Mayhew, in the month of July, 1671, when the entire government of the Vineyard was reorganized. These events are narrated elsewhere, and it will not be necessary to explain the details of this meeting beyond a cursory review of so much as relates to this particular topic.

"The business under consideration," read the council minutes, "was Mr. Mayhew's affayre about Martins Vineyard, etc. His Peticon and Proposalls rec'd." It was at once decided "that the Townes seated there shall have Patents of Confirmation as other Townes." On the next day a satisfactory relationship and mutual understanding had been reached; and from that time on during the remainder of the conference all was plain sailing. Mayhew had found his "Popish" master more than complaisant, and equally generous in his dealings. On the next day, July 8, it was decided to issue patents for the incorporation of the two towns on the island hitherto called Middletown and Great Harbor; and it became necessary either to adopt these names as the permanent designations or to choose others more distinctive. The latter alternative was adopted. Tisbury was selected for the settlement "formerly known by the name of Middletown," doubtless at the suggestion of Mayhew in memory of his native parish in Wiltshire; and it was now necessary to deal with the principal settlement, the chief town of the island.

We may here surmise that Mayhew, desirous of establishing and continuing the reciprocal cordiality which had been manifest throughout, requested Governor Lovelace to christen the place "formerly knowne by the name of Great Harbour." It was then the custom to honor the royal family, particularly the reigning monarch, in the bestowal of names on places in the new English possessions on this continent, as, for examples, Jamestown, Charlestown, Maryland, and later we find Williamstown and Georgetown. Whether this surmise be correct as to the initiative in this matter, the probabilities strongly point to a suggestion from Lovelace that His Royal Highness, the Duke of York, Lord Proprietor of the Provinces which included the Vineyard then in its confines, should be complimented in the selection of a name for the principal town in this new county. King Charles was childless, and besides his name was already attached to another town. The same situation obtained with relation to the Duke's name, then in use by the first settled colony in Virginia.

The children of James, as heir presumptive, would therefore become heirs apparent to the crown of England, and the eldest son in turn become King. At this date (1671) the first three children of the Duke, viz.: Charles b. 1660, James b. 1663, and Charles b. 1666 had died in infancy, and the fourth, born Sept. 14, 1667, was the only surviving son and heir to perpetuate the direct royal line. This young Prince was named *Edgar*, and bore the title of Duke of Cambridge. He would become the Prince of Wales upon his father's accession to the throne. What more natural suggestion could have been offered than that Great Harbor should exchange its indefinite name for a distinctive title in honor of the Duke's only son, Edgar, a possible future King of England? Whoever was responsible for the suggestion, it was then decreed that Great Harbor "for the future shall bee called by the Name of Edgar Towne, and by that Name & Style shall bee distinguisht and Knowne." There can be no mistake in the word. It is plainly "Edgar Towne" in the patent of incorporation.

The young Prince did not live to know or appreciate the honor intended. In fact, he was dead when his name was bestowed on our county seat, his demise having occured June 8, 1671, just one month before, a fact doubtless unknown to Lovelace and Mayhew when the choice was made, owing to the infrequency of communication with the mother country.

These, then, were the actual and supposed events leading up to the christening of our shire town, all of which have unmistakably pointed to a natural and reasonable conclusion as to the naming of Edgartown. The death of young Prince Edgar, scarcely four years old, has made him practically an unknown personage, even though of royal birth. Edgar was an uncommon name in the reigning family, that being the first use of it for many generations. Besides this, King James, his father, came to be thoroughly hated and feared in the colonies on account of his religious affiliations, and except in this instance, which was doubtless done as a stroke of policy, there was no disposition in Puritan New England to honor him or his family.

POPULATION.

The growth of population in this town prior to 1700 has to be estimated from scattered and unsatisfactory bases. We only know that at first "divers families" came, but beyond

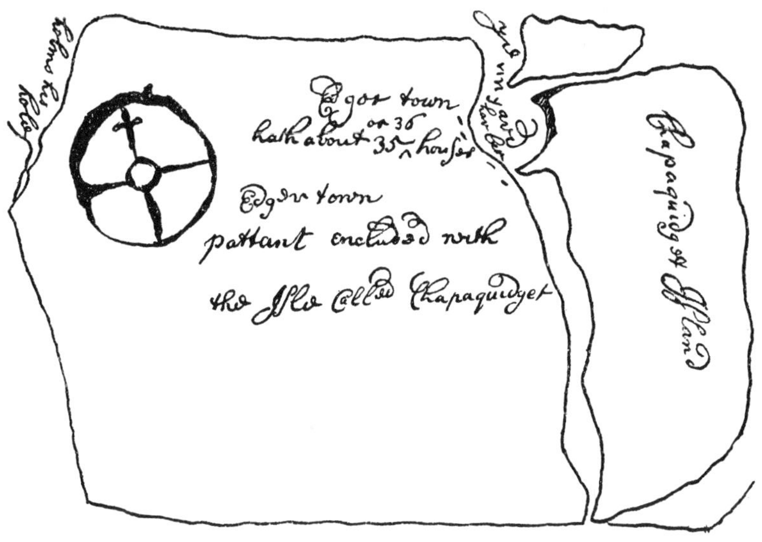

PLAN OF EDGARTOWN, 1694.

surmising how many that might comprise, we have no means of telling with any accuracy. In 1653, there were fifteen persons known to be "heads of families" who took part in a division of land, and by using five as a multiple we have an estimate of 75 souls living at that date in the town. In 1660 there were probably twenty "heads," and by the same process a total of 100 souls is obtained. In 1676 there were about twenty-seven "heads," making a total of 125 souls, a slow but steady increase. Eighteen years later, 1694, we have the first definite basis of calculation, the Athearn map of that date in which he states that there were "35 or 36 houses in the town." Census returns always show that more than one family is to be reckoned to a house, and by counting this number as forty families, and applying the same multiple we have as a result, about 200 souls living in the town in the last decade of that century. The data is not sufficient for any further accurate computation until after the middle of the next century, in 1757, when a muster roll of the company of militia in the town give us an enumeration of 182 persons able to bear arms. Using the accepted multiple, we can estimate, at this date, a total of about 900 souls then resident in this town. The first census of the Province was taken in 1765, and from this we obtain the following figures: — families 150 comprising a total of 1030 souls living in 128 houses. Of these, there were 233 males and 248 females above sixteen years of age; 234 males and 209 females below sixteen; 20 negroes (12 males and 8 females), and 86 Indians, of whom 37 were male and 49 female. At this date, Edgartown had the largest population of the three towns, about 38 per cent. of the entire country. In 1776, there were 1020 persons credited to the town in the census. The first national census of 1790 gives us an enumeration by names, and from this the following statistics are drawn: - total population, 1356 (whites), of which number there were 335 males above sixteen years, 318 below sixteen and 683 "free white" females and ten "other free persons." This leaves a balance of ten, which are assumed to be negroes.

The following figures show the population of Edgartown as enumerated in the decimal censuses of the United States from 1800 to the present time: — in 1800 it was 1226; in 1810, 1365; in 1820, 1374; in 1830, 1509; in 1840, 1736; in 1850, 1990; in 1860, 2118; in 1870, 1516; in 1880, 1303; in 1890, 1156; and in 1900, 1209.

The maximum population of over 2000 was reached in 1860, but the census of 1900 showed a decrease of 17 from that of 1800. The population had thus been practically stationary for a hundred years. The state census of 1905 showed a population of 1175.[1]

[1]Assessed valuation (May 1, 1900), $720,682.00; rate of taxation, per $1000, $15.40; number of dwelling houses, 391; number of horses, 116; number of cows, 213; number of sheep, 934; number of acres of land assessed, 11,337; number of persons assessed on property, 781.

Annals of Edgartown

Ancient Landmarks.

ALGONQUIAN PLACE NAMES.

Ahquompache, Acquampache, Aquampesha, etc. — This was the name of a neck of land sold by three Indians to Joseph Norton in 1682. (Deeds, I, 285, comp., III, 98; 119; IV, 157). And Thomas Burchard sold to Joseph Norton, May 2, 1682, "a neck called Aquampacher neck near Pahoggannot." (Ibid., IV, 36). In John Daggett's will (1673) it is written Aquampache. In a deed dated 1723, a neck "caled nonnamaset & aquampesha" is referred to. The translation of this word is "forsaken swamp or marsh."

Crackatuxett. — This place is first mentioned June 26, 1652, in the town records (p. 126). It is called "Crackatukset or Short Neck" in 1681, when Philip Watson sold two shares at Crackatuxet, "late belonging to John Bland, deceased." (Deeds, I, 255.) The letter R in this name is probably an error, as the sound of that letter ought not to appear in the Nope dialect. The appellation originally designated the outlet of the pond, now obliterated by the action of the sea. It should be written Cheke–tuk–es–et, meaning "the violent, swift, or turbulent tidal cove or estuary."

Cataama. — Simon Athearn recites (no date mentioned), that his grandfather, Nicholas Butler, gave him the "neck called Cattwama." (Town Records, 17.) It has various spellings, as Cotamy, Kuttamy, and the modern form is Katama. The same name occurs on Long Island, varied as Catawamuck, Katawamac and Ahkataamuck, (Indian fishing stations upon Long Island, pp. 54–57). It means "a crab-fishing place."

Manadoo. — In her will of June 8, 1690, Elizabeth Norton, widow, gives to her son Joseph, land at a place called "Manadoo." It is called more frequently Menada, and as such it is known at the present day. It is in the northern part of the town, on the road to Oak Bluffs.

Manequoy. — This is a neck of land, referred to in a sale from Matthew Mayhew to Thomas Daggett, dated Aug. 23, 1680, when it is called "Monequoy," and in 1719 Joseph Daggett sold to Brotherton Daggett one-third of the "short neck lying on the south side of the place between Matewase and Manequoy." (Deeds, II, 19; III, 246.) Manequoy was west from Mattakeese (Ibid., V, 38).

Mattakeset. — This was also the Indian name of Duxbury, Massachusetts. (Winsor, History of Duxbury, p. 13.) It is first mentioned in our records under date of March 23, 1646, when John Bland bought of John Pease a tract of land and meadow "lying against Mr. Blands house at Mattakeekset." The derivation of this word is not entirely apparent. It may be formed of Matta(or Mat)-auk-es-et, "at the bad place," meaning a bad or unfavorable place for canoes, or for cultivation. It may be an abbreviated form of Namat-auk-es-et, "at the sitting down, or resting place," as applied to a portage, or ferrying place; where one sits down to rest before crossing to the other side. This may have been a point where the Indians habitually crossed from Nope to Chappaquiddick. The creek which drained into Mattakeeset was called Ameshoak (the Indian word for Herring) Creek (Deeds, XI, 387).

The name Matewase (Deeds, III, 246), described as next to Manequoy, in 1719, is probably a corruption, or misspelling of Mattakeese(t).[1]

Mashakamocket–Mashacket. — The town granted to Philip Tabor, May 20, 1653, "the neck called Ashakomaksett from the bridge that is at the East side of the head of the Swamp" (p. 131). On Aug. 2, 1655, after he had removed to Rhode Island and exchanged property with Thomas Layton, this land was described as bounded on the west side by "Momanequins Neck." (Deeds, I, 325.) This name appears as Shokamackset (1655) and Mashacket (1662), which last is the modern spelling. There is a loss of the initial consonant in both of the first two forms, which is retained in the later form. The survival of the M indicates that its original form was Masha-komuk-et, meaning "at the great house," or "enclosed place;" probably referring to a palisadoed inclosure built by the native inhabitants for the Sachem's house. The Sachem of Nunnepog may have had his "great house" here. It is the equivalent of the Powhatan Machacamac, meaning "great house," Captain John Smith writes: "For presently they robbed their Machacomocko house of the towne, stole all the Indian treasure thereout, and fled into the woods as the Indians often related." (Historie, Arbers, Reprint, 538.) Eliot gives it Mishikkomukquash(pe), for "palaces."

[1]Mattakeece plain or neck is mentioned as S. S. E. from Crackatuxet. A short neck in Edgartown, bounded E. by a pond called Mattakeese and on the W. by a pond called Manaquoy is described in an early deed. (Deeds, V, 38.)

(Isaiah, XXXII, 14.) The "neck called Shackamoksett, adjoining to Quanomica on the west. . . . . to Mashackett Pond on the East," occurs in the Town Records of Edgartown (p. 13) under date of Jan. 25, 1671.

Matuhhukqussee. — In a deed of sale, from three Indians to Joseph Norton, they convey "all that neck of land called Acquampache and over a small neck of land called Matuhhukqussee." (Deeds, III, 98.)

Nonnamesset. — This appears to have been an alias for Pohoganut, or Aquampache, to which reference should be made. (Deeds, II, 32; IV, 157.) It is also a name for one of the Elizabeth Islands. In a deed, the following mention is made of this place: — ". . . . called Nonnemassett which said Nonnamessett is a neck of Land lying next and adjoining on the South of the lands in s'd Town called Aquompache." (Ibid., V, 375.)

Nashquite. — Under date of April 14, 1681, this word appears in the Edgartown Records, "a neck called Nashquite lying the Eastward of Mattakes . . . ." (p. 30). Benjamin Smith sold to Benjamin Pease, Oct. 10, 1713, six acres in Edgartown adjacent "to the plain commonly called Nashakittee." (Deeds, IV, 223.) These place names are probably identical.

Nashawamass or Nashamoiess.—This was in the southern part of Edgartown, and was one of the praying villages of the Indians. Governor Mayhew, in his will, devises land "bought of Felix at Nashowamass," which is undoubtedly the same word. It is probably a name bestowed by Governor Mayhew, especially as it designates one of his "praying towns." Rev. John Cotton called it Nashamoiess (1674), a name that has survived to the present day. Nashau–wamass means "the spirit he loves," *i.e.*, "He is beloved of the Spirit," and one of Eliot's "praying towns" had a similar derivation, viz:— Nashau–boh, "he is of the spirit." It was next to Poketapace's neck and next to Nashamoies. (Deeds, IV, 38.) Another reading is "Nashowamoiasuk" as in a deed (Ibid., I, 263). This would seem to suggest a different meaning, as Nashowa– means half or divided, seen in Nashowakemmuck (Chilmark). "Natooquan sachem of Nunpoge and of the East end of Nope Island," sold to Thomas Daggett, Sept. 10, 1688, a neck of land "called Nashamoies . . . . bounded by the cart path which is at the head of Wintucket swamp and runes South westerly to Cackatookit (?) swamp." (Ibid., III, 441.)

Pohoganut. — The first reference to this name is found in a deed, Burchard to Norton, May 2, 1682, when "Pahogg-annot is the spelling (IV, 36). The next mention is in an Indian deed, in 1684, where it is written Pahauknit (Ibid., I, 18). Again, in 1700, as Pahocknit. In 1704, in a conveyance from Joseph Norton to Samuel Smith, the following language occurs: "a cove of water on the east side of a small neck of land called Nonnamesset . . commonly called Pohoganit." (Ibid., II, 32.) This would seem to establish an alias for Pohoganut. The meaning of the word is, "at or on the cleared land," and the same word in its variations appears throughout New England, as Pokanoket, Pancanauket or Pockenocket. This was the name of King Philip's home near Mount Hope, R. I. Pahauknit was probably a planting field of the Nunnepog Indians.

Paqua. — This is a neck of land adjoining Paqua Pond, called at the present time Faqua. It is mentioned as early as 1704, under the orthography of Paquay. (Deeds, II, 52; III, 10; IV, 111.)

Quanomica. — The division of this neck of land was made in 1663 (Town Records, 109), and the name has survived in its first form to the present time. It is from Quan-amaukeag, "the long fishing place," or possibly from Quan-naumkeag, "the long eel fishing place." Either definition would apply. It appears as "Quananamack" in a deed (II, 346,) and "Quenomokey," in 1731. (Athearn Mss., Cong. Lib.) The lots on this point were numbered from the point and contained about two acres each. (Ibid., V, 141.)

Swanneck. — It is probable that this is an Indian word, and the origin of Swan Neck of modern times. The derivation may be Sowane: south, southern, and ack: land, the southern place, neck or land. It is called Swanneck in 1687 (Deeds, III, 146), and Swan Neck about same time, but it is safe to say that the name was not derived from the bird.

Sopotaminy. — This is first mentioned in the Court reccords, under date of June, 1686, when the Indian Job was adjudged to be the lawful owner of the "land, viz at Sapra-taine, in the right of his ancestors as gentlemen in an Indian way." In the Deeds it is called Sopotaminy, as above. Andrew Newcomb bought it of Job, Sept. 24, 1690 (Court Records, I). In later records it is called, "Jobs neck alias Sapotemmy" and "Sapotammy." (Deeds, I, 352; II, 81.) The etymology of this word is Sepohta-may, meaning "the extended or stretched out path," perhaps "the continuing path or road." (Massachusetts.) Simon Newcomb's Path is one of the early landmarks in the boundary line between Tisbury and Edgartown.

Wintucket. — This neck of land is first mentioned in the town records, Dec. 28, 1659, when the "first town lots" are to be divided. (p. 134.) The word is from the combination Win–ne–tukq–et, meaning "at the good tidal cove," probably referring to its advantages for landing, or protection from storms. Winnetuckquett and Winnetucksett occur in Plymouth county, and are the same words.

Wachusade–Woachet. — This was the name of a neck of land on the south side, now called "Watcha." An instrument recorded in the county records recites that a neck of land commonly "caled Woachet was divided, the East half to popmechoa & the west half to Josias alias Keetanumon the known and acknowledged sachem of Takemmy." (Deeds, I, 299.) Josias sold to Thomas Bayes, Feb. 27, 1676, certain land in Tisbury, being the neck "caled Wachusade." (Deeds, I, 309.) This is a variation of the spelling of the name. (comp., Deeds, II, 71.) It may be derived from Wadchu, "a hill," or as Eliot has it, Wad–chue–me–sik, meaning "little mountains," (Hosea, X, 8). This does not particularly apply to the lowland neck now known as Watcha, and the word may be derived from a like word, Wad–chu, "a keeper" (Eliot, Genesis, IV, 9), and refer to the fact that it was the land of some Indian keeper of cattle. In the Edgartown Town Records (p. 35), under date of Feb. 5, 1685, it was voted that Thomas Daggett should have "that neck of Land that the horse keeper Lived upon." This may be a clue to the origin of the name — Wadchusate, Horse keeper's Neck. Experience Mayhew wrote it Watshat (Indian Converts, p. 83).

Weenomset. — This was, probably, the Indian name for Felix' neck. It occurs as Wynomesett and Weenomsit, the former in 1662 and the latter in 1663. Edward Searle owned a small island, in Sanchacantacket Pond, now called Sarson's Island, described as southeast of Weenomset Neck, which applies to Felix Neck, and Sarson acquired Searles' property by purchase. The meaning of this word is, "at the place of the grape tree," or literally, "vine-berry place." There was probably a native vineyard on this neck when the whites first came to the island.

ENGLISH PLACE NAMES.

Bayes' Neck. — So-called as early as 1666 from Thomas Bayes, its first owner. Situated on the eastern shore of the Great Herring Pond.

Burying Hill. — It was so-called in 1731 (Athearn, Mss. Lib. Cong.), but it was doubtless the name which had been applied to it for years previous. The first cemetery in town was located here, to the south of Tower Hill, and it has retained the name to the present time.

Codman's Spring. — Mentioned in 1743 (Deeds, VII, 154), and so-called from Robert Codman, the early settler who had a grant of land (opposite Sarson's Island), on which a spring was located.

Eel Pond. —This pond has had other names, viz: — Gurnet Pond (Des Barres Map, 1775), and Daniel's Pond (State Map, 1795).

Felix Neck. — First mentioned in 1664 in the town records (p. 127), and named for an Indian who was living "near Sanchakantackett," as late as 1683. (Deeds, I, 259; comp., Court Records, I.) It retains the same name at the present time.

The Gurnet. — The extreme north-eastern point, or hook of beach, in the town was very early called the Gurnet. In 1660 "the Gurnetts nose" is mentioned, and in 1712, the "neck called the Gurnet" was referred to in deeds of that date. Gurnet is an obsolute or dialectal form of Gurnard, which is the name of a fish commonly called the Grunter, from the noise it makes on being landed out of the water. Hakluyt says: "the west part of the land was high browed, much like the head of a gurnard." (Voyages, II, 11.)

Jacob's Neck. — Sackonets or Jacob's neck is mentioned in a deed (Deeds, V, 323), and Jacob's neck is again referred to in 1736 (Ibid., VI, 168), located on the Great Pond.

Jones' Hill. — In 1689, Samuel Smith sold to Daniel Steward a lot of land on "Jones' Hill," next land, now or late, in the tenure of Edward Hadaway, part of the house lot of the late John Smith, deceased. (Deeds, I, 366.) It is the hill just south of Cleveland Town, and once had a windmill on its summit. Thomas Jones, an early settler, lived there and hence its name. (Deeds, XI, 926.)

Lobb's Cove. — Great Pond, Edgartown. Probably named for Ishmael Lobb, a colored man who may have dwelt there. He was baptized in 1801, at the age of 62.

Momanequin's Neck.—Philip Tabor,"now being at Portsmouth in Rhode Island," exchanged his house and lot at Shokamocket, upon the Vineyard, bounded on the side by the land of John Burchard, and on the west side by Momanequin's Neck, with Thomas Layton, Aug. 2, 1655. (Dukes Deeds, I, 325.) It was named from the "godly" Indian Momanequem. (Indian Converts, 12.)

Mortal's Neck. — This neck of land probably received its name from an Indian sachem named Peter Mortal. In the will of Towanquatuck, dated Jan. 25, 1669, this great sachem decrees that his loving friend, "peter mortall," shall be sachem "in my room." (Town Records, p. 83.) Thomas Mayhew the elder at one time owned this tract of land, and the grant of this neck to him was dated May 20, 1653. (Town Records, p. 131.) Nicholas Norton, in his will gave to his son Benjamin a piece of meadow at Mortal's Neck, April 17, 1690. (Court Records, I.) The bounds of this neck are thus given:—"S. E. and E. side by the creek that runs into Trapp's pond." (Deeds, VII, 515.) Mortal's Neck pond or Mile Brook rivulet occurs in the records. (Ibid., I, 49.)

Poketapace's Neck. — This was next to Job's Neck. A cove of water ran up between it and Nashamoiess. George Gardner of Nantucket sold land at "Poketapaces neck lying between the lands now in the improvement of Capt. Samuel Smith," in 1725. (Deeds, IV, 38.)

Sarson's Island.— This small marshy island in Sanchacantocket Pond, southeast of Felix Neck, derived its name from Richard Sarson, who bought it of its first owner, Edward Sale or Searle, before 1664. It appears on current maps erroneously as Sason's Island.

Starbuck's Neck. — The purchase in 1678, by Nathaniel Starbuck, of Home Lots 2, 3, half of 4 and 5, situated in the north-east part of the town, gave to this section the name of Starbuck's Neck, a title which it has retained to the present day. The first time it was so-called to the knowledge of the author, is in a deed dated 1735. (Dukes Deeds, VI, 169.)

Swan Neck. — Mentioned in a deed, where Namasquin an Indian dwelt in 1673. (Deeds, I, 257.) See under Swanneck.

Turkey Land. — This name appears in 1742 as belonging to "certain land on the dividing line between the neck called Mashackett & the land called the Old House Land or Turkey Land." (Deeds, VI, 276.) It may have derived this name from the planting of Turkey wheat (corn) there, although a tradition is to the effect that it was paid for in turkies.

Tower Hill.—The origin of this name is not known to the author, but it is about a century old, probably. In 1838 William Mayhew, in a disposition, refers to the "hill which is now called Tower Hill." It may have been the site of some signal tower used for maritime purposes, or a semaphore staff employed in a similar way might have been erected there.

Weeks' Neck.—The narrow strip of land between Trapp's Pond and the Sound was called Weeks' Neck.

Will Lay's Plain. — This is commonly called at the present time Willie's Plain, and is said to refer to a son of the first Nicholas Norton, named William, who lost his life there in a well which he was engaged in digging. As Nicholas Norton had no son of that name this legend must be cast aside, and the records appealed to for the true title. "Will Layes pond" is mentioned in 1716 (Deeds, III, 357); Ponit, the sachem of Homes Hole sold to Henry Luce, Feb. 4, 1717 or 1718, a tract of land bounded on the south-west by a cart path running from Chickemmoo "to the place called Will Lays Plain" (Ibid., IV, 183); and "Will lays Plain" is mentioned in 1726 (Ibid., IV, 151). It got its name from one William Lay, an Indian of Edgartown, known as Pannunnut. In his youth he lived in the family of Governor Thomas Mayhew and in later years became the principal Indian magistrate. He preached at the Indian church at Chilmark about 1690.

THE ORIGINAL "HOME" LOTS.

It seems probable that the first settlers in the town occupied lots of land by assignment of the proprietors, the metes and bounds of which do not appear of record. It was not until 1646 that the limits of the settlement were defined by the elder Mayhew and his son, at which time there may have been a dozen settlers residing eastward of the line then drawn "from Tequanomen's Point to the Eastermost Chop of Homses Hole." Naturally, these settlers arranged their home lots contiguously and the location afforded the best advantages was bordering on the harbor. Presumably, these home lots were sold to the first comers by the Mayhews, but no record of such sale exists today. Otherwise, it is not possible to see how the original patentees recovered on their investment.[1] As was the case at other settlements, the early comers here formed a body of proprietors, limited in number, who were in effect stockholders in a real estate transaction, and these original proprietors admitted others from time to time, either by an increase in their number, or by the disposal to the new man of divisions of the individual shares. A proprietor could hold more or less than one share, but its value was always based on such a fractional part of the whole, using the number of shares as the denominator. The entire area outside of the "home lots" was held in "common."

DIVISIONS OF THE TOWN LAND.

The town records afford us but little positive help on the earliest land transactions of the settlers, and the first comers seemed to acquire land without adequate written evidences of the purchase. The sparse community, where everybody knew as much about his neighbor's land as his own, needed no elaborate system of records for the protection of their titles, but a little more definite notation of such events would have saved the author many hours of study. From the scant allusions here and there, and the sequence observed in recording individual holdings in after years, it is believed that the first allotments of the common lands occurred between 1646 and 1652, and including what was termed "Dividend Lots," and the Chappaquiddick division. These dividend lots, probably the first in the point of time, varied in size from ten to forty acres and were situated in the south part of the town, bordering on the Great Pond and Katama. Their extent and bounds were carefully recorded years after by a committee of proprietors, but it was necessary for this body to rely on hearsay and private records to fix the limits of each man's property.[2]

On Feb. 2, 1652, it was voted to divide twenty acres to a man, "only those that have land already shall have so much less." [3] It is not probable that this can be identified. The first record of the action of the proprietors on this subject occurs under date of Jan. 4, 1652, when it was "Ordered

[1] "The first of us was admitted by their approbation and some purchased their Lands." (N. Y. Col. Rec. Deeds, I, 72.)

[2] There were also "thatch lots" taken up on the south shore, but when they were laid out and drawn is not known. They were used for purposes of roofing their houses and barns.

[3] Edgartown Records, I, 124.

. . . . . that all lands shall be divided by persons and estates: this is the way concluded for the present." [1] This language is somewhat obscure, but the meaning, as shown by their subsequent action based on it, is reasonably clear.

THE PLANTING FIELD.

The first known division of the "common" land was made under date of May 8, 1653, and at that time there were twenty proprietors to participate in this allotment, shown by the following record, and the list establishes the prior settlement of the persons named, viz: —[2]

Ordered that the meadows upon the pond is to be devided into twenty equal parts beginning at the path of meadow over the ware, and so to Hannah Mayhews marsh only the Pasture and Hannah Mayhew is to have that meadow that lies upon the Pastures neck: so all the rest of the meadow is to be devided into eighteen parts:

Here followeth an account of the above written Devision of meadow:

Peter Folger	1	Mr. Mayhew the	14
Lay	2	John Daggett the	15
Sale	3	Nicolas Butler the	16
Pease	4	John Foulger the	17
John Butler Jr	5	John Bland the	18
Browning the	8	Tabor the	19
Burchard the	9	Thomas Daggett the	20
Burchard the	10	Hannah Mayhew the	6
Weeks the	11	The Pasture the	7
Paine the	12		
Smith the	13		

The names in this list require some explanation as to the indentity of the individuals who only appear by surname. Lay was Edward Lay, and the others will be given in full, in order of occurrence: — Edward Searle (Sale), John Pease, Malachi Browning, Thomas Burchard, John Burchard, Thomas Paine, Richard Smith, and Peter Tabor.[3] Hannah Mayhew was the oldest daughter of Thomas Mayhew, Sr., and was then scarcely eighteen years of age, but this was the first of the large real estate holdings which she was destined to acquire and manage throughout her long and strenuous life. "The Pasture" is the phonetic disguise under which

[1]Edgartown Records, I, 125.

[2]Ibid., I, 172.

[3]It may be noted here, in this connection, that James Covel, who had been granted land the year previous, was not a proprietor at that date, to participate in the transaction.

Thomas Mayhew, Jr., is intended to be designated as Pastor, and it is one of the few instances in which he is even indefinitely referred to as a property holder in the town.

This division of "Meadow" is believed to be what was since known as "The Planting Field," which was situated on the north side of the town between Weeks' Neck and Mills' or Miles' Brook. Each lot consisted of ten acres, and a tract of two hundred acres was therefore thus allotted.

The policy of Mayhew in relation to the Indians led him to regard their rights, as is well known, but it became necessary also to protect the proprietary as a whole from the acts of individual members who wished to add to their holdings by private purchases of lands set off to the use of the Indians. Consequently, the following order was passed under date of Jan. 4, 1652:—

> No man shall procure from the Indians in any place within the town bounds any land upon Gift or Purchase upon the Penalty of Ten Pounds for every acre so purchased without the consent of the town first had.[1]

This order was necessary to guard the common interests of all against independent holdings not subject to the proprietors' control.

THE "FIVE AND TWENTY" PROPRIETORS.

The limit of eighteen proprietors did not long remain at that number after this division, and within a year the number was increased to "five and twenty." Under date of Feb. 6, 1654, the town voted that "the twenty-five lotts are to Bear Equall Charges & so are to have equal Priviledges." [2] This limit remained in force for many years and represents the number of the home lots bordering on the harbor from Pease's Point to Katama, varying in size from eight to forty acres, the largest number containing about ten acres. Thomas Mayhew and his son held the only lots of forty acres. The lots in this division, which is assumed to be the first distribution in severalty of the common property of the townsmen, were called and ever afterwards known as the lots of "Five and Twenty," and became the basis for nearly all the subsequent divisions of land in various parts of the town.

[1]Edgartown Records, I, 140. This afterward was the cause of much trouble to one of the proprietors.

[2]Edgartown Records, I, 136.

Whenever it was decided to allot in shares to the townsmen any undivided section of land, the division was made into twenty-five parts, and each of the original "Five and Twenty" was entitled to one of these divisions.[1]

The original "Five and Twenty" retained the names of their first owners for nearly a century, and long after they had passed from their possession, subsequent holders transferred them as "commonly known by the name of William Weeks his lot," or "the lot formerly belonging to Malachi Browning." In the same way the various lots in the divisions of land subsequently made were referred to as belonging to an original proprietor of one of the "Five and Twenty."

In a few cases more than one lot belonged to the same person, and the first list of proprietors of these lots contains but twenty-one names as follows:—

Arey, Richard	1	Burchard, John	1	Mayhew, Thomas, Jr.	1
Burchard, Thomas	1	Daggett, John	1	Paine, Thomas	3
Butler, Nicholas	1	Daggett, Thomas	2	Pease, John	1
Butler, John	1	Folger, John	1	Sarson, Richard	1
Bland, John	2	Harlock, Thomas	1	Smith, John	1
Browning, Malachi	1	Lay, Edward	1	Vinson, William	1
Bayes, Thomas	1	Mayhew, Thomas	1	Weeks, William	1

This list is made up and alphabetically arranged from two proprietors' drawings of Crackatuxet held on April 21, 1660, and gives the number of lots credited to each.[2]

The new names not occuring in the previous list of 1653, are Arey, Bayes, Harlock, Sarson, Smith and Vinson. Although Thomas Mayhew, Jr. and Thomas Paine had been dead for nearly three years, their estates drew on account of their original holding. This division of Crackatuxet was made after its acquisition on Oct. 4, 1659, from the sachem proprietor. The following record explains:—[3]

This record testifieth that the owners of the five and twenty lots have purchased of Towontecutt all Cracketuxett and the neck that is called Chapequeco is with all the Necks and Lands thereabouts: nothing reserved to the s'd Tewantecutt but his two shares of Commonage.

his
Witness hereunto Towon W quatuck
Thomas Mayhew mark

[1]The drawings must have been conducted after the manner of a lottery, probably by numbers placed in a box or other receptacle, as there was no regularity in the later divisions of land which fell to the original home lots.

[2]Edgartown Records, I, 156.

[3]Ibid., I, 147.

THE "LINE" LOTS.

The next division of lands held in common was known as "Lots on the Line," and it took place about 1659, the significance of the title being thus explained under date of August 22, that year in the record:—

Ordered By the town that the Line shall Run from Wintuckett four Rods to the Westward of the Great Pond By the Ox pond and so By the upper End of Goodman Weekes his Lott to John Peases Lott.[1]

It referred to a purchase line bounding rights acquired of the Indians, and was sometimes called the Old Purchase Line. It is not known, except in a few instances, who drew the original lots, as the following is but a partial list and is the only record of the allotments:—

Ordered by the town that the first eleven lots upon the line backwards from Wm Weeks fence to Wintucket are given to the first eleven houselots in town beginning at

John Peases- one	Richard Arey- one	Robert Codman- one
Wm Vinson- one	Edward Lay- one	Thomas Harlock- one
Thomas Paine- one	William Weeks- one	Thomas Bayes- one
Thomas Paine- one	Thomas Mayhew- one	

Ten acres apiece[2]

It is supposed, however, that the remaining Line lots were credited to the owners of the "five and twenty" in the same order from Main Street south as was followed in the assignment just quoted. Any other method would have been discriminating, though there were special reasons of location to warrant the assignment of the first eleven.

Later in the same year (1660) there was a more elaborate scheme of dividing the land, which is here printed in full to preserve the list of proprietors and their holdings:—[3]

Voted by the town this 22: 8: 1660 that all the lands in the town shall be devided into four parts first & afterwards these four parts every one of

[1]Edgartown Records, I, 130. In a deed of John Pease to Robert Codman it is stated that "the Line Runs from Behind the said Peases house to Quanomica." (Ibid., I, 6.)

[2]Ibid., I, 36. This record must be read horizontally, instead of by columns, and by this means the correct relations of the first eleven lots are obtained. This is an instance of the exasperating method employed by the town clerk in copying the original many years ago.

[3]Ibid., I, 147.

them into thirty seven shares of which there are thirty three and a half are now appropriated: their names are hereunder written:

John Pease	Thomas Paine or heirs which was Mr. Edward
Richard Arey	Thomas Paine or heirs given by the town
William Vinson	Thomas Mayhew Senior
Edward Lay	Thomas Mayhew jun'r or heirs
Thomas Harlock	Mallachia Browning his heirs
William Weeks	Thos Paine or heirs which was Wakefields
Thomas Bayes	Thomas Daggett which was Joshua Barnes
John Daggett	Thomas Daggett given by the town
John Smith	John Foulger or heirs
Nicolas Butler	John Butler or heirs
Mr. John Bland given by the town	John Pease was Edward Sayles
	Robert Codman given him
Mr. John Bland which was Tabors	Robert Codman was William Cases
	Richard Arey for Peter Foulger
Thomas Burchard	John Edy given him by the town
Richard Sarson	
Nicolas Norton	
John Burchard	

All these thirty one one whole share

James Covel ½ share Isaac Norton ½ share Jacob Norton ½ share
Thomas Trapp is voted not of this town.

REQUIREMENTS OF PROPRIETORSHIP.

About 1652, when a considerable number of men left the island for the purpose of settling elsewhere, the proprietors found it necessary to require a time limit of residence on grants before the grantee could acquire a full title to his land. It was seen that there would grow up a class of non-resident proprietors if some restrictions were not placed upon the holders, while the object of the grants was to secure a permanent resident population. Accordingly, when William Case was granted his lot on Nov. 11, 1652, it was provided that "this Land he is to Build upon and Live on four years att the end of which time it is his proper inheritance."[1] This, however, seemed to apply only to him, and in the course of time other "absentee landlords" developed, necessitating a general order dated April 27, 1663, covering such cases.

Whereas there was an order made at the time of entertaining of Willm Case into this town that no man should have a full inheritance in land except he did inhabit upon it the full term of four years: for as much as the same order is thought to be lost by the loss of a leaf out of the book, being

[1]Edgartown Records, I, 120.

always kept in force: this is recorded to testify it was never taken off and to continue the same in full power still: by virtue hereof and that all grants so ever are under subjection to that order and are still to be hereafter voted.[1]

DIVISIONS OF THE NECKS.

The division of the various "Necks" of land occupies considerable space in the land records of the town. On May 20, 1653, three men, Thomas Mayhew, Sr., Thomas Burchard and Philip Tabor, were selected "to devide to the Inhabitants out of all the necks so much land as thay in their Best Judgment shall see meat."[2] The principal "necks" were Crackatuxet, Quanomica, Felix, and "the little neck by Crackatuxet." It is probable that the "thatch" lots were on one of the small necks bordering on the Great Herring Pond. This committee did not seem to work with much celerity, as there is no record of a division of one of these until 1660, when Crackatuxet was laid out into twenty-five shares.[3] Quanomica was divided three years later into thirty-three shares, and in 1664, Felix Neck was divided into thirty-seven shares.

On Jan. 29, 1663, the neck called Quanomica was divided; and on April 26, 1664, the tract known as Meachemy's Field, near the Planting Field, and on the same day Felix Neck, were divided, all into twenty-five shares, but Quanomica had thirty-three (ibid., I, 109), Meachemy's Field thirty-seven (ibid., I, 128), and Felix Neck thirty-seven lots (ibid., I, 127).

The following are the new names appearing as lot owners in these three divisions: — Robert Codman, James Covell, John Eddy, John Gee, Thomas Harlock, Thomas Jones, Mistress Mayhew, as heir to Thomas Paine, her son, Nicholas, Isaac and Jacob Norton, James Pease, Mrs. Searles, Mrs. Scott, and Peter Tallman.[4]

At an unknown date, which may be assigned to the period between 1660 and 1670, the tract of land bordering on Sanchacantacket and extending south to Mills or Mile Brook, was divided into lots which took the name of Mile Brook lots. This tract is thus bounded: —

[1]Edgartown Records, I, 145.
[2]Ibid., I, 131.
[3]Ibid., I, 156.
[4]Ibid., I, 109, 127, 128.

On the south beginning at a black marked tree standing by the side of a swamp, which is the nearest swamp to the house of Mr. Thomas Harlock and running from said tree about 3 rods Southwest to a rock in the ground by the side of an old path which led to Sanchacantacket; thence about Southeast and by South continuing by said path 258 rods to a rock by the side of said path; thence Northeast 2 rods & a half to a stone set in the ground at the head of the swamp called the Cranberry or Mile Brook Swamp near the Pond; thence including all the land or ridge between the two swamps, and then beginning at a stake at the East side of Mile Brook and running thence Southeast and by South continuing by the path 20 rods to a stake stuck in the ground; thence East and by South 27 rods to a marked white oak tree; thence North and by East 30 rods to a rough white oak sapling marked near the ranging line of the land granted to Mr. Sarson. And is further bounded on the North partly by the salt water and partly by land of heirs of Matt: Mayhew dec'd.[1]

THE NEW PURCHASE.

The next division was of the "New Purchase" as it was then called. There were two great sections within the town limits of Edgartown, the "rights" of which were purchased of the Sachem representing the Indians. The first was bought very early of Tewantquatick, and consisted of all the land south of the "Line" so-called, running from Wintucket to the end of the home lot of William Weeks, as before stated. All this tract was known as "The Old Purchase," and all divisions heretofore described, excepting those of the Planting and Meachemy's Fields and the Mile Brook Lots, were in this section. On May 16, 1653, the town ordered that "Mr. Mayhew is to Purchase part of Ogissket [Sanchacantucket] Neck of the Indians," [2] and this is known as "The New Purchase," but when the transaction was completed is not of record. For many years this tract, bounded by a line drawn "from Wintucket to Myobers Bridge,"[3] called the "New Purchase Line," remained undivided, and it was not until Feb. 15, 1673 or 4 that it was allotted to the proprietors. On that date they "made choice of Justice Norton, Capt. Daggett, Isaac Norton, Mr. Benjamin Smith and Thomas Pease, according to their best Judgement for to Divide the Neck called Sachacantackett Neck." In the "Old Purchase" there were three final divisions, so-called, and in the "New Purchase" two.

[1]Edgartown Proprietors Records. There were at least thirty-eight lots in this division, and probably forty was the full number.

[2]Edgartown Records, I, 131. This is an example of the errors made by the old town clerk in his unfortunate copy. The word is Ogkeshkuppi.

[3]Ibid., I.

THE PLAIN LOTS.

The next division was of the "Plain," the largest tract held in common that was laid out up to this time, and it was surveyed and divided by Richard Sarson, Thomas Bayes and Isaac Norton into forty lots, receiving confirmation on Feb. 14, 1676 by the town. The following are the bounds of this tract: —

Beginning at a stone set in the ground on a knowl at the Southwest and by westerly end of the Great Hollow, at a place called Burchard's pond lot; said stone standing in the ranging line between the first of said Plain lots and 3d Pond lot; thence running Southwest and by west half a point westerly, one mile and seventy two rods to an old ditch near and opposite against the head of the Cove of meadow at Short Neck, Northerly from Crackatuxet; said ditch being in the ranging line between the last lot of the Plain lots and said Short Neck. Said lots running or extending in length about Southeast, southerly from said line. And is further bounded by the Common on the Northwest, northerly; and on the Northeast by Cotamy and said Pond lot; and on the Southwest by the dividend called Major Mayhew's dividend and partly by Monoquoy, and partly by Joshua Daggett's Short Neck.

And said lots is further bounded on the Southeast by Little Cotamy and partly by the sea or harbor, to the old ditch which first enclosed that land called Mattakeesett.[1]

As this division is an important one, the list of participators as recorded is herewith given to show the new proprietors as well as the old ones who still remained, twelve years later:—

THE DIVISION OF THE PLAINE.[2]

Thomas Burchard the first Lott	1 & ½ 23
Phillip Watson the	2 & 3
John Pease	4
John Gee	5
William Weekes	6
Nicholas Norton	7, 25, 19, & 34
Isaac Norton	8, 38, 39
Mr. Lawson & Simon Athearn	9th
Thomas Daggett	10, 27 & ½ 14
Thomas Trapp	11
James Pease	12 : 24
Mr. Butler	13 & ½ 37
John Butler	15 & ½ 37
Richard Sarson	16, 17 & 18
Mr. Mayhew	20 : 33 & 35

[1]Dukes Deeds, III, 498; comp., Proprietor's Records.

[2]Edgartown Records, I, 21.

Phillip Smith	21
Richard Arey	22
Thos Bayes	40 & 23
John Freeman & Joseph Norton	26
Joseph Daggett	28
Matthew Mayhew	29
William Vinson	30
Peter Jenkins & James Covel	31
Stephen Codman	32
Thomas Harlock	36 & 14

THE WOODLAND LOTS.

The next division was on Feb. 27, 1684, when a tract in the northwest part of the town, towards the Tisbury line, called the Woodland was divided into lots, being forty-two shares.[1] It is supposed the East Pine and West Pine lots are comprised in this division. There were no further divisions of common land made during the remainder of the century, and nothing occurred worth noting until Aug. 28, 1704, when an additional share was added to the "Five and Twenty."

Ordered in the meeting by the Proprietors that the lott that is put in the lot which was put in amongst the 25 proprietors which made 26 shall be made to appear between James Pease and Mrs. Ann Sarson.

At the same meeting was chosen four men to wit Major Matthew Mayhew Mr. Benjamin Smith Capt. Thomas Daggett Simon Newcomb to state and settle bounds between particular mens lands and the proprietors commons of Edgartown throughout the whole bounds of Edgartown to the end that the commons and undivided lands of Edgartown be not at all questioned or infringed upon by any person whatsoever.[2]

The following is a list of the Proprietors about this date, as given in the records:—[3]

Major Mayhew	1	Matthew Mayhew	1	Thomas Pease	2½
Joseph Ripley	½	Capt John Butler	1	Thos. Harlock	2
Samuel Smith	½	Benja: Smith	1½	Phillip Smith	½
Joseph Norton, Esq.	½	John Arey	1	Thos. Lothropp	½
Capt. Daggett	2	Andrew Newcomb	½	Isaac Norton	1
Simon Athearn	1	Anne Sarson	3	Goodwife Vinson	½
Joseph Daggett	½	John Butler Jr.	1	Joshua Daggett	½
John Coffin	1	James Pease	1½		——
					[25]

[1]Edgartown Records, I, 33.
[2]Ibid., I, 99, 100.
[3]Ibid., I, 139.

Half shares:

Isaac Norton	5	Thos. Trapp	1	Capt. Butler	3¼
Joseph Nortons (Jacob Norton)	1	Andrew Newcomb	1 &¼	Esqr Norton	¼
Thos Harlock	3	Mr. Harlock	3	Gershom Dunham (Jones)	1
Simon Newcomb	1	Justice Norton ½ his fathers ½ that was bought	2	Isaac Norton ½ Arey ½ his fathers	2
Thos. Vinson (Sachem)	1	James Pease one Codman	2	John and Charles Steward (Sarsons)	1
Mr. Dunham	1	Moses Cleveland	1	Hester Dunham	1
James Covel	1				

It is not possible to understand the arithmetic of the half shares, which amount to 31 3-4, and it is left for some future investigator to clear up the problem. Much that was clear and understood by them was either left to the town clerk to hopelessly befog in ambiguous phraseology, or else it was not recorded at all and posterity was afforded the privilege of digging out the facts by slow and laborious methods.

COMMONAGE AND FIRE-WOOD RIGHTS.

Among the privileges which were attached to the proprietorship of lots, was that of "commonage" for cattle and liberty to cut fire-wood. The record shows that in 1653 a commonage comprised feeding for eight cows, or equivalent, and the extent of a commonage as it existed in 1663 is more particularly defined: —

> Voted that a commonage is 12 great cattle or horses a man may keep upon a commonage for sheep and goats 8 for one cow or horse: it is agreed that every man that hath more than twelve great cattle or eight sheep or goats for every cow or horse that they must hire commonage of others is to be at 12 d a year for a beast and not more.
>
> Expressed by Willm Vinson, Richard Sarson, Thomas Daggett & John Edy, which judge they have commonage to spare, but that those that are overstocked do not provide commonage of such as have it then they must pay for every beast to the town one shilling an six pence that is for every beast more that they can keep upon their own with six pence over and above falls to the town in good [1]

Fire-wood rights were specifically granted as appears by a grant to Robert Codman in 1657, of a "commanage of wood." It was found necessary in 1683, to restrict the quantity taken.

[1]Edgartown Records, I, 145, 149.

Voted that every man shall have a load of wood or timber for his use for a share and he that shall have any more shall pay five shilling for every tree that shall be cut without order from the town till further order.[1]

One year later the following modification was made: —

Voted that all wood in the Old Purchase that is not layd out to be common for men to cut for their occasions.

SKETCHES OF THE EARLY SETTLERS.

RICHARD AREY.

In the early records of the Massachusetts Bay Colony the name of this settler is spelled in many different ways: Aree, Aerie, Ayre, Ary, and it is probable, for this reason, that some of his record may be lost in this variety of form.[2] The first known of him is at Salisbury, Mass., in 1646, where he was associated with Robert Codman and was sued in that year and the year following by Tristram Coffin on account of a freighting transaction in a vessel owned by Codman.[3] He was probably a mariner engaged in the coasting trade. How long he had lived in Salisbury before this is not known, nor when he removed from there. It is possible that he may have gone to Gloucester, Mass., and from thence to New London, Conn., about 1651, where "Richard Aerie who was from Gloucester, mariner," had a grant of land that year, but it was "forfeited," as he did not settle in that town.[4] Our next record of him is in the following year (1652), when he was granted a house lot in this town on Dec. 17, 1652, "Between Mr. Burchards and Thomas Daggetts." [5] This was one of the Five and Twenty situated on Starbuck's Neck, and its southern line was about at the harbor breakwater. He sold this to his old Salisbury neighbor, Robert Codman, the next year and

[1]Edgartown Records, I, 29. Dated April 11, 1682–3. See also I, 129.

[2]In the will of Robert Sole of London, 1593, mention is made of his daughter Mary Arye (Court of Husting, II, 722). Richard Ayre of Orsett, Co. Essex, deceased before 1634 is mentioned in London marriage licenses.

[3]Salem Quarterly Court Files, 1638–1647, p. 201.

[4]Caulkins, History of New London, 77. The author says of him further that he often visited the town in subsequent years, probably in his coasting business, and was there in 1667 and early in 1669. (Ibid., 250, 297.)

[5]Edgartown Records, I, 124, 125.

bought a lot still further north, of Philip Tabor, the second from Pease's Point.[1]

In 1661, he submitted to the Patentees Government, and was of the train band the next year. In 1663 he figured to some extent in the courts, being sued by William Weeks and John Daggett for debts.[2] He is recorded as participating in the divisions of Crackatuxett, Quanomica, Felix Neck and Meachemy's Field, and his purchases of two lots entitled him to two shares. The following is a record of his property: —

> The peticlceler parcells of Land of Richard Arey which he Bought of Phillip Tabor and are now in said Areys Possession, first: Ten acres of Land which is my house Lott Bounded By the Sea on the East, the Common on the West, John Peases on the North, Joseph Codmans, which was Thomas Doggetts on the South: More Two acres of Meadow Lying at Chapequideck Bounded By . . . . More one Ten acre Lott upon the Line Bounded By . . . . with a full Right of Commonage: this was Confirmed By the Town the 30 Day of Desember: 63.[3]

His second lot or share was that which originally belonged to Peter Folger, situated on Tower Hill, just north of the cemetery, and was purchased of Folger, probably about 1662, when the latter removed to Portsmouth, R. I. The following is the record of this additional property: —

> The Petickeler parcells of Land of Richard Arey which he Bought of Peter Foulger and are Now in the sd Areys Possession, first: Ten acres which (is) my house Lott Bounded By the Sea on the East, John Smith on the South, the Comon on the West, Mr. Browning and John Doggett on the North: with two acres of Meadow more or Less Beginning at the Comon wading Place on the East Runing West and Joynes to the Pastors Meadow on the West with one Ten (acre) Lott upon the Line Bounded By . . . . : with a full Right of Comonage. These Lands were Confirmed by the Town the 30th of Desember: 63.[4]

This lot was the one on which he lived, the one near Pease's Point passing into the possession of the Codman family, shortly after the date of the above record.

He testified in 1668–9 at New London, relative to a charge made against him of circulating false reports about one Thomas Stanton, concerning matters in Virginia twenty years before.

[1]Edgartown Records, I, 2. Dukes Co. Deeds, I, 319.
[2]Ibid., I, 111.
[3]Ibid., I, 2.
[4]Ibid., I, 2.

Shortly afterwards, in this same year, he was drowned on Nov. 19, with Samuel Streeter, while on a trip to Nantucket or the mainland, The inventory of his estate showed property to the value of £128-13-7, of which £40 was credited to house and land.

His wife was Elizabeth, who appears in the records several times as "Goodwife Arey," and she seems to have transacted business on her own account.[1] The following record appears under date of Aug. 30, 1663: —

> Ordered by the town that Goodwife Arey hath a commonage confirmed to her to make good that bargain which she made with Robert Pease and this commonage is given to that lot which was sold to Robert Pease.[2]

On Oct. 6, 1663, she sued William Weeks for trespass and damages due to "hoggs Ruting of Medo and spoiling of Grass" to the value of thirty shillings. In 1665, she gave testimony about the nuncupative will of John Folger, but nothing further is known of her, after that date. It is possible she may be the Elizabeth Ayre, wife of Richard Ayre, mentioned in the will of Richard Crouch of S. Giles, without Cripplegate. The testator bequeaths to his brother, William Crouch, beyond seas in New England [of Charlestown, Mass.], if same be demanded in twelve months, and by like terms indicating residence in New England, also the sum of twelve pence is given to "my sister Elizabeth Ayre." [3]

THOMAS BAYES.

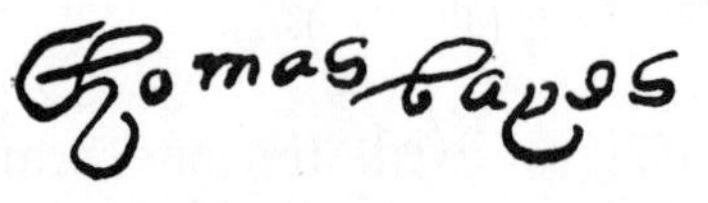

This sturdy yeoman was the Miles Standish of the Vineyard —the martial leader of the little settlement of Great Harbor. He first appeared in this country in 1636, when he signed the town Covenant at Dedham, Mass., and became a selectman in 1638. At that time he was probably a bachelor, as on Dec. 26, 1639, he married Anne Baker

[1]She sued Robert Pease in 1659 to adjust differences due on a real estate transaction. (Edgartown Records, I, 133.)

[2]Edgartown Records, I, 140: comp. Dukes Deeds, I, 319.

[3]P. C. C., Nabbs, 206. Will dated October 27, proved Nov. 29, 1660. An Elizabeth Ayre witnessed the will of Robert Pearce of Dorchester, Mass., in 1664.

in that town. Whether this was his first location in New England is not known, as he may have been of the party who removed from Watertown to Dedham.[1] Some clue to his English home is found in the following record: —

> Thomas Bayes of Dedham, carpenter, appoints Isaac Martin of Hingham his attorney to demand of the executors of — Wiseman of Barrow Apton in County of Norfolk his grand father, deceased, the legacy due to him by will. (1646) [2]

There is a registered pedigree of a Bayes family of Yorkshire, 1600–1767, and there are scattered references to persons of the name of Base, Baze, and Bayes in Norfolk County, from 1572 to 1700.[3]

Our Thomas Bayes was born in 1615, and had just reached his majority when he emigrated. As appears by the above quoted record, he was a carpenter by trade, possibly a ship carpenter. In 1648, he resided in Boston, and from the following record it would appear that this supposition regarding his trade and relations with shipping, may be well founded: —

> Thomas Bayes of Boston, carpenter, constituted Joseph Wilson of Boston his attorney to ask of all persons in Barbadoes, Christophers and any of the Carribbee Ids. Monies due him.[4]

When Thomas Bayes removed to the Vineyard is not accurately known, but he was a proprietor at Great Harbor as early as 1652, for in that same year he was chosen hog reeve for the town. In 1655 he was made a constable, and in 1656 was chosen leader of the train band. This office he filled in 1661, 1662 and 1663. These are all the recorded instances of his military leadership, but as no other person was chosen to this position in subquent years, it is probable that he continued to hold it. In 1676 he was chosen selectman, the last office filled by him prior to his death.

[1]He was convicted in 1643 of "mutinos & turbulent speaches," and bound over "to bee of good behaviour the meane while" to next Quarter Court.

[2]Aspinwall Note Book, 68. A genealogist searched the principal court in London, and the local courts, whose records are deposited at Norwich, all formerly exercising probate jurisdiction over Burgh Afton and the vicinity, for the period of 1646 back to 1630. The result was that no will of any Wiseman described as of Burgh Afton was found. Four wills of Wiseman of Co. Norfolk, 1634 to 1638, and eight wills of Wisemans of other counties, 1634 to 1645, were found. This will be a sufficient record for some descendant to follow.

[3]See Familiae Minorum Gentiorum and County History of Norfolk. Wills of Thomas Bayes, 1619, William Bayes, 1630, Thomas Bayes, 1652, are recorded in the Prerogative Court of Canterbury, Somerset House, London.

[4]Aspinwall Note Book, 145, dated 11 (9) 1648.

He lived on one of the ten-acre lots known as the "five and twenty," which had its southern boundary on Main street, and extended as far back as Pease Point way. His proprietary holdings are recorded as follows in the town records: —

This is a true Record of the Perticular percells of Land and town Rights on this Island Marthas Vineyard as followeth: which are now in the possession of Thomas Bayes & belonging to him the sd Thomas Bayes: first one house Lott being Ten acres more or less bounded by the Harbour which is Twenty Pools broad by the sea on the East, the high way as the same stands on the south the common on the West William Wix on the North with one Devident known by the name of Thomas Bayes neck bounded by the Pond on the south & west Isaac Nortons on the North Richard Sarsons on the East this being Thirty acres more or Less, with one Ten acre Lott upon the Line bounded by William Wix on the East Mr. Mayhew on the west with the Tenth Lott at Crackatuxett, with the third Lott on the adjoyning Neck, with the Thirty first lott at Quanamaca, with the Twenty fourth lott at Mechmas field, with the 19th Lott at falex neck, with two acres of Meadow adjoyning to Mrs. Blands, which was Tabors on the south, Thomas Daggets which was Barnes on the North: with all the upland adjoyning up to the old high way, some I bought of Mr. Mayhew the younger, this Land & meadow being ten acres more or Less, with the Northermost neck of Chappaquiddick for a Thach Lott, upland & Meadow being four Acres more of Less, with two acres of Meadows at Chappaquiddick lying in the great meadow, with the southermost point of the Neck at Chappaquiddick, upland & meadow being three acres more or Less, which was Cases on the North, with one full Right of Common & all other Dividable Lands in the Town Bounds, with one six & Twentieth part of fish & whale, with small shares of fish & whale: these Lands were confirmed by the Town this 19th of March 1666.

In addition to the above he owned the eastern half of Watcha Neck, which he bought of the Sachem Josias in 1676.

The death of his only son Thomas, Nov. 17, 1669, without issue, and his own death which took place between Feb. 4 and May 31, 1680, terminated this family name in the male line, but it has been perpetuated in the Norton family in every generation to the present time following the marriages of his daughters, Mary and Ruth, to the brothers Joseph and Isaac Norton. Bayes Norton is a familiar name on the Vineyard, and Bayes as a baptismal name was also used in the Newcomb family, after the marriage of Andrew Newcomb to Anna Bayes. His will was dated Feb. 4, 1679–80, and the inventory taken May 31, following. Among the personal property of this martial leader was "one gunne & loadeing staffe" and "one rapier." The total value of his estate as inventoried amounted to £214–07–06. This is a large amount for those times, and is equivalent to about $5000. His will is as follows:—

[Dukes Deeds, I, 309]

I Thomas Bayes finding myself weake in boddie but sound in memorie and understanding doe make this my last will and testament as followeth; And first my will is that my wife Anne Bayes, shall have and improve all my Estate of land and moveables, whatsoever for her comfortable subsistence, during her Naturel life provided that she continue a widdow: Secondly, I will and bequeath to Hannah Bridges, my Daughter twenty pounds after the decease of my Said wife or changing her condition of widdowhood:
Nextly, I will and bequeath to my two Daughters, Mary the now wife of Joseph Norton, and Anna the wife of Andrew Newcomb, to each of them fifty pounds, so to be understood, with what they have alreddy received of mee, with what was also received of the estate of their brother deceased; to be payed after the decease of my wife as aforesaid.
Nextly, I will and give to my daughter Ruth, wife of Isaack Norton five pounds to be payed within a year after my own decease, in Bibles and bringing up the children to reading and Education.
Nextly, when all these legacies shall be payed, according to this my will, if any estate be left, it shall be equally Devided among all my Daughters, and children of my daughter Abigall Deceased, and my will is that if any my said Daughters shall decease before they receive their portion herein willed, then it shall go to their children, and in defect of their issue, or the issue of any my beforesaid Daughter Abigall's children then such portion shall be equally devided among the surviveing.
Lastly my will is, and I do order and Request that my wife aforesaid, and Thomas Mayhew Junior, be whole executors and administrators to this my last will and testament: And in witness of this to be my last will and testament I the said Thomas Bayes, have hereunto Subscribed with my hand and put to my Seal, this fourteenth day of February in the year of our Lord one thousand six hundred seaventy and nine or eighty.

Witness.
MATTHEW MAYHEW, THOMAS BAYES, (seal).
WILLIAM WEEKES.

Nothing further is known of his wife. She was living at the date of the will, but when or where she died is not of record.

JOHN BLAND, *ALIAS* SMITH.

There is a certain air of mystery about this person, who was one of the earliest settlers at Edgartown.[1] If the town records can be trusted, he must have been here as early as the elder Mayhew, and perhaps before. The following entry

[1]A John Bland was a passenger in the ship *Globe* in 1635, aged twenty-six years. Whether the same person as John Bland of Martha's Vineyard is unknown.

in them shows that he had acquired property in the vicinity of Katama prior to 1646: —

Mr. John Bland has bought of John Pease of Martins Vineyard a parcell of Land about ten acres & two acres of medo Lying against Mr Blands house att Mattakeekset. March 23, 1646.

Mem : Mr John Bland bought of Philip Tabor March 2, 1647 all his rights that he then possessed.

He was a resident of Colchester, England, prior to his emigration to New England, and it seems that for reasons which will be explained later in this sketch, he had adopted the alias of John Smith, under which name he would in all probability successfully defy identification. He is undoubtedly the John Smith associated with the Mayhews in the first movement from Watertown, of whom we hear no more in subsequent Vineyard history, as he resumed his correct name when he established himself here. Certain it is, that there was some controversy about him and his identity as two of his early acquaintances, Nathaniel and Abraham Drake of Hampton, N. H., deposed that "he was sometimes called John Smith, but his name and his ancestors was Bland."[1] His known family consisted of Joanna his wife and two daughters, Annabel and Isabel, both married, and that his station in life was above the average of his neighbors here is evidenced by the prefix of distinction, Mr., which uniformly precedes his name in the records. His wife is given the prefix of Mistress also, and with Nicholas Butler he is the only one besides the elder and younger Mayhew so distinguished by a title which had a definite significance in those days.[2]

In 1654, John Bland was chosen one of the seven magistrates to assist the elder Mayhew in the government, but beyond this it is not known that he held any office. He participated in all the divisions of land up to the time of his death and his possessions are thus recorded in the town books: —

These are the petickelers upon the Vineyard of my Known Lands and are above Intended: Twenty acres of Land Lying near the North pond with two acres of Meadow Joyning: which Land and Meadow More or Less Bounded By the pond on the East, the Comon on the South, the Comon on the West, John Bland on the North: with Ten acres of Land Lying in the Planting feild Bounded with. . . . . . . with one Ten

[1]Deeds, I, 282.

[2]Records, Commissioners of United Colonies, II, 205, 261. For "healpfulness in Phisicke and Chirurgery att Martin's Vineyard" and "for her pains and care amongst the Indians there and for Phisicke and Surgery." His wife was paid a gratuity by the Society for Propagating the Gospel.

acre Lott upon the Line Bounded with. . . . . with two acres of Meadow Lying at Chapequideck Bounded By. . . . . . . : with a full Right of Comonage and the six and twenty part of fish.

These Lands were Confirmed By the Town the 30th of December: 63.[1]

This property he bequeathed to his wife by an instrument dated or "confirmed" Nov. 2, 1663. He died, in all probability, shortly before Jan. 6, 1668, as Mrs. Bland begins to participate in the divisions of land credited to his share in the commons from that time forth. His estate was inventoried at £355-10-0, an especially large sum for that period, and the full list of articles shows evidence of household refinement in the way of looking glasses, silver plate, table linen, books, and china, while among his stock are found horned cattle, horses, sheep, and goats. A servant, "a Lad for a Term of Time," was rated at £10, and his houses and lands were valued at £120, all of which he distributed by a will in the following terms: —

The Sixth of Jan'ry 1663: this is the Last will and Testament of me John Bland of Martens Vineyard in or Belonging to the Province of Main in New England I say made By me John Bland Delivered Into the Possession of my wife Joanah Bland this Second of November in the year of our Lord one Thousand Six Hundred Sixty and three.

In the name of God, Amen. Be it Know unto all men By these Presents and Express Partickelars that I John Bland Being in perfect memory and full understanding But Week in Body:

first I do willingly Bequeath my Body to the Earth from Whence it came When the Lord Shall Be Pleased to Call for itt and my Soul and Sperit unto God that Gave itt. Now for my Temporall Goods after my Decease as Well as Whilst I am aLive I doe wholly Give unto my well Beloved wife Joanah Bland all my houses and Lands with all my housellstuff together with all my Goods or Chattles of what Kind So Ever Giving her Most Hearty thanks for all Her Care and Gratt Love Toward me in all my needs and Nessessityes: Excepting Twenty Shillings Which I doe Give unto my Two Dafters Anable and Isable who are all the children that are aLive whome I own and Give them Twenty Shillings that is to say ten Shillings to each of them after my Decease to Be Truly paid to them at there demand: and I Do Here by these Presents make and ordain my well Beloved Wife my real and Sole Executive of this my Last will and Do apoint her to Pay my Debts and Leagecies Dated this Second of November in the year of our Lord 1663 and Confirmed By Me John Bland as witness my hand this same Second of November 63

witnesses
Thos Daggett
Richard Sarson

his
John X Bland[2]
mark

[1]Edgartown Records, I, 7.

[2]Ibid., I, 54. The signature with a "mark" can be explained upon the theory of physical inability as he was "weak in body" when it was made.

The terms of this will, by which he disowned all children except the two daughters, Annabel and Isabel, together with his dual personality as Bland and Smith, led the author into a long and finally successful search to identify him as "John Smith" prior to his migration to the Vineyard. His early appearance here, contemporary with the first coming of the Mayhews, indicated Watertown as the possible place of his settlement upon his arrival in New England. A John Smith was found there in 1630 with a wife Isabel, and this name being borne by a daughter of Bland was regarded as significant. The Watertown records contain an entry of the death of Isabel Smith, the wife, who was buried July 12, 1639, aged sixty years.[1] An examination of the Watertown land grants and estates also disclosed the fact that John Smith's homestall was contiguous to those of Jeremiah Norcross and William Barsham and that later William Barsham succeeded in 1645 to the possession of Smith's lot. It further appeared that the wife of Barsham was named Annabel and this cumulative evidence further pointed to an identity with the John Bland and his daughter Annabel, a most unusual name and therefore an aid to a solution of the problem.[2]

The connection of Jeremiah Norcross with Smith also proved to be important and convincing, practically establishing the connection between John Bland and John Smith. Norcross was a later arrival in Watertown than either Bland and Barsham, as he did not appear until 1639, with a second wife Adrian, who was the mother of our John Bland. From all the facts in the case, too numerous to rehearse, she had probably married first Bland and second Smith and third (late in life) Jeremiah Norcross, a well-to-do gentleman of a London family, connected with the parishes of S. Mary, Sunbury, Middlesex and SS. Dunstan and Sepulchre in the metropolis. He was son of Thomas Norcross, a linen draper, married his second wife, Adrian Smith, about 1630, and came to America

[1]This is a possible error as the early Watertown Records are a copy transcribed by John Sherman, who enters this explanation: "What was taken before was by Mr. Eirs and uncertaine in the transmitting." It seems that this age as given is ten years too great and may be an error for fifty years.

[2]William Barsham was of Watertown in 1630 and d. July 13, 1684. His wife Annabel signed a deed in 1678, but is not mentioned in his will dated Aug. 23, 1683. By her he had ten children, 1635–1659, and it is estimated that she was b. 1614–16, and married after her arrival in New England.

eight or nine years later.[1] The connection between Norcross and John Bland-Smith is found in the following record: —

> Mr Collens, Mr Sparhawke & goo:(dman John) Bridge are desired to heare businesses betwen John Smyth & his father Jeremy Norcros & examine accounts, & settle things if they can: if not to make report to the Courte if there be cause.[2]

This indicates a family disagreement between the son and step-father, probably about inheritances, and surely establishes the relationship of the two, and Adrian as the mother of John. It enables us to conclude that John was the son of her first marriage (Bland) and that as a boy he adopted the name of Smith at her second marriage (Smith), or was legally adopted by the second husband. In adult life, for reasons unknown, but possibly to be found in property interests, he resumed his true birth name of Bland when he came to the Vineyard.

Jeremiah Norcross returned to England after making his will in 1654, and died there three years later. In this will he bequeaths to John Smith "my wives sonne" and to Joanna Smith his wife, "one ewe sheep."[3]

Nothing has been developed to explain the reference in Bland's will to his two daughters as the only living children "whom I owne." It is inferred that he had others by the first wife, and that his second marriage to Joanna resulted in opposition from some of them which caused him to ignore them in the division of his estate.

As to the identity of this second wife, we are likewise in darkness. She was living here Aug. 12, 1680, when she sold part of her husband's estate,[4] but when and where she died is not known. The Bland property in part came later into the possession of Philip Watson, through means not of record,

[1]A manuscript genealogy of this family by Joel W. Norcross, in the library of the N. E. Hist.-Gen. Society, furnished many corroborative facts in the Bland-Smith search. This genealogy gives no authority for date of second marriage. Adrian Bland-Smith-Norcross was probably born about 1575, and was undoubtedly considerably older than her third husband. It is not believed that she returned to England with him, and may not have survived him.

[2]Record, Court of Assistants, Dec. 1, 1640.

[3]This apparently ignores the Bland connection, but in view of all the circumstances which have developed, Norcross may not have known that John Smith had reassumed his true name at the Vineyard, and it is clearly apparent that there was a family disagreement and a probable estrangement. Bland's will further corroborates this.

[4]Dukes Deeds, III, 116. This was the "Home" lot on the harbor front just south of the burying ground.

and it is surmised that he was a relative of Mrs. Bland and obtained it by gift or inheritance.[1]

Isabel Bland, the second daughter, married first about 1636 Francis Austin of Dedham, Mass., by whom she had three daughters, and second, about 1643, Thomas Leavitt of Hampton, N. H., by whom she had six children at least. Mrs. Isabel Leavitt died Feb. 10, 1698-99, aged "about 87 years."[2]

He left no known descendants on the Vineyard, and only those through the Barsham and Leavitt lines are certain descendants elsewhere.

MALACHI BROWNING.

This person was one of the Watertown contingent of first comers. He had been an owner of a home stall in that place in 1642, and probably emigrated to New England some two years before that date.[3] He was from Maldon, Co. Essex, England, a few miles distant from Baddow Magna, the home of John Pease, and Bromfield, possibly the residence of the Vincents prior to their emigration. Malachi Browning and his brother Jeremy were appointed in 1630 administrators of the estate of their sister Sarah Armestronge *als* Browninge of Maldon,[4] and in 1647, after his arrival in this country, he gave a power of attorney to a party to agree with Mr. Thomas Browning of Maldon in Essex, Clerk (*i. e.*, minister), concerning his reversionary title to lands in the Ratchford Hundred in same county.[5] These clues enabled the author to make a definite search for his family antecedents, and he had the registers of the two parishes of St. Mary, and All Saints and St. Peter searched for Browning records. The result as given below is a satisfactory solution although the name of Malachi does not appear, yet that of his brother Jeremy and

[1]A Joanna Watson was a member of the Church in Salem in 1636, but there is no evidence to associate this person with the wife of our settler.

[2]Dow, "History of Hampton," 810. Mrs. Isabel Leavitt claimed the Bland estate on the Vineyard, and filed as evidence the depositions of Nathaniel and Abram Drake of Hampton in support of her heirship as John Bland's daughter. These depositions disclosed the "Smith-Bland" situation and established the clues to his identity.

[3]On June 2, 1640, "Mr Browning for seling strong water was fined 5s witn: to ha: 2s of it." (Record, Court of Assistants, I, 282.) There was no other Browning in Massachusetts as yet come to light, and taken in connection with a subsequent entry it is entirely probable this relates to our Malachi Browning.

[4]P. C. C. Administration Book (1630), fol. 173 b.

[5]Aspinwall Notarial Records, 94.

his sister Sarah are given, and it will be noted that there is a Daniel in the list of children, and that our Malachi had a son of that name. It is probable that the family removed to another parish as no further record of the father's family is to be found in St. Mary's. Malachi was in all probability, short of absolute proof, the son of William and Dorothy (Vernon) Browning of Maldon, the record of whose family from 1581 to 1599 appears on the parish register of St. Mary.[1] By his first wife Martha, who was buried in 1583, he had two daughters, and by his second, Dorothy, to whom he was married Sept. 10, 1583, at All Saints, he had the following children baptized: —

Michael, October 5, 1584 (All Saints)
(all entries below in St. Mary's)
[Mary, ——————— bur. 23 June 1588]
Priscilla, December 5, 1587, bur. Mch. 24, 1589
Daniel, December 10, 1588
Jeremy, October 18, 1590
Mary, October 8, 1592, bur. July 29, 1593
Susan, May 12, 1594
Saree, March 28, 1597. [m. ————— Armstrong]
Anne, September 9, 1599. m. Michael Cooper, 1615
[Malachi, b. about 1601]

But if this is not convincing we have the will of William Browning of Maldon, dated April 23, 1635, then in business as a merchant of London, of the parish of S. Botolph, Bishops gate, in which instrument he mentions "Malachy Brownyng my sonne." To him he bequeaths his messuages in Maldon.[2] The will was proven a few days after its date as the testator was sick when it was drawn.

In April, 1645, he was an appraiser of an estate in Massachusetts, and he probably removed to the Vineyard during the next year or early in 1647, as on Oct. 13, 1647, he is called "late of Watertown in New England, Gent."[3] On Oct. 27, 1649, he was in Boston on legal business, in connection with his brother-in-law, Joseph Collier of London. At the same time Mrs. Elizabeth Scott was there also on similar business with her husband Robert Scott.[4] In an inventory of the estate of Adam Winthrop, 1652, there is an item of a debt due from "Mr" Browning, and a like entry under date of March 10,

[1]William was probably son of an earlier William of same parish.
[2]P. P. C. Sadler, 35.
[3]Aspinwall Notarial Records, 94.
[4]Ibid., 226.

1652-3, in an account of the estate of Robert Bulton of Boston.[1] His activities on the Vineyard were very slight. The first and only record of him is under date of May 8, 1653, when he was given a share in the planting field.[2] His homestead on which he drew this was the first lot on Tower hill, south of the "Slough" and was apparently part of a lot of which John Daggett owned the western half and Browning the harbor end. On a visit to Boston he died "at the house of Robert Scott," Nov. 27, 1653, thus terminating a short and uneventful career in New England.[3] His occupation while on the island is shrouded in obscurity, and all clues to his connection with persons on the island end in unsatisfactory threads. A "Mrs." Scott, presumably the wife of Robert, above referred to, appears in 1663 and 1664, as an owner of a share of land at Great Harbor. Conjectures as to relationship with our Browning may be easily entertained, but we are left without any recourse to confirmation as she disappears as suddenly from the scene, leaving no trace.

His known family consisted of a wife Mary, a daughter Susanna, who by her marriage with William Vinson became the ancestress of all the Vincents here, and a son Daniel. The wife was probably born Mary Collier, sister of Joseph Collier, citizen and grocer of London, who in 1648 left a bequest to "my sister Mrs. Mary Browning in New England."[4] Of the son Daniel, but few traces remain. In view of the standing of the family, an uncle perhaps a clergyman in England it is fair to presume that this Daniel may have served in a clerical capacity in the town after the decease of the younger Mayhew. The following entry in the records seems to point to that conclusion: —

February 16: 1659

Ordered by the town that what charge shall arise for the finishing of Mr. Brownings house more than the first covenant shall be paid in corne at harvest.[5]

The building of a house was usually one of the things done for ministers by towns and the "covenant" probably refers to an agreement made when he was settled. How long

[1]N. E. Gen. Register, VIII, 59.
[2]Edgartown Records, I, 172.
[3]Boston Town Records.
[4]N. E. Hist. Gen. Register, I, 58.
[5]Edgartown Records, I, 14.

he remained is not known, and like all the others connected with the first settler he disappears without leaving a trace.

Malachi Browning had a "mansion seat" a little distance south of Burying Hill fronting the harbor. In what manner it passed from his estate into the possession of Thomas Trapp is not known, but it may indicate some relationship.[1] Apparently the widow only had her "thirds," which she deeded as a gift to her grandson, Thomas Vincent.[2] The widow survived until Sept. 7, 1672, and the inventory of her estate showed property to the value of £22–7–5, which was administered by her son-in-law Vinson. Her daughter Susanna makes several references to her property rights in England, and it is presumed to relate to the estate in Essex to which the father had made claim as above related.

THOMAS BURCHARD.

Tho: Burchard

In the ship *True Love* sailing from England in September, 1635, was a family of Burchards, and from the similarity of names it is believed it was the family which later settled on the Vineyard. The husband Thomas, aged forty years, a laboring man, was accompanied by his wife Mary, aged thirty-eight and children, Elizabeth thirteen, Mary twelve, Sarah nine, Susan eight, John seven, and Ann eighteen months old.[3] In 1652 a Thomas Burchard and his son John were residents in this town, and from all subsequent records this John seemed to be his only son, as was the case of the immigrant Thomas and his only son of that name. Somewhat extended search has been made to ascertain the antecedents of Thomas, who is thought to have come from London, but no clue has yet been obtained.[4]

On May 17, 1637, Thomas Bercher was admitted as freeman by the General Court of Massachusetts.[5] and a Thomas

[1]There is a tradition that Susanna Browning sold Tower Hill for a pair of gloves or some equally trivial consideration. While nothing in the records justifies such a legend, as the Browning lot was some distance south of Tower Hill, yet there may be enough truth in the story to account for the appearance of Trapp in 1684 as owner of the ten acres.

[2]Edgartown Records, p. 82, dated July 12, 1669.

[3]Hotten, Original Lists, etc.

[4]A Thomas Burchwood, cordwainer, of St. Peter's, Cornhill, had a family of six brought to baptism 1597 to 1603, including three named Thomas, but the dates do not correspond to the family which came in the *True Love*. (Parish Registers, St. Peter's, Cornhill, London.) The name is variously spelled Bercher, Birchard, Burchard, Burchwood.

[5]Mass. Col. Rec., I.

Burchard, member of Rev. John Eliots' Church in Roxbury. Two years later, in 1639, we find a Thomas Burchard at Hartford, and no further trace of him has come to light until the year 1650, when he was of Saybrook and probably had been there some time before, as Thomas Birchard. He was Deputy to the General Court of that colony in 1650-51, and on May 15, 1651, was appointed one of a committee to go to Pequot and lay out the lands granted to Capt. John Mason's soldiers.[1]

The next record of him is under date of 1652 at Great Harbor, when "Mr. Burchards" lot is mentioned, and on May 8, 1653, two lots in the planting field are credited to "Burchard."[2] It is an arbitrary inference to assign this to him, rather than his son John, but on May 20, 1653, we are relieved of further speculation as Thomas Burchard was then chosen with Mayhew and Tabor to divide the Necks of land among the inhabitants.[3] On June 8, 1653, he was chosen as the first assistant to the chief magistrate, and on Oct. 31, 1654, "Thomas Burchard the elder" was made town clerk.[4] He was the first person who held this office in Edgartown, of whom we have record. On June 5, 1655, he was again chosen as the first assistant to the chief magistrate. On Jan. 7, 1656, he is recorded as "present" at a town meeting in Saybrook, probably as a proprietor with interests yet undisposed of, for on October 31 of that year he sold his lands in that town to his son John.[5] He was again chosen first assistant on June 23, 1656, being one of the two so elected, the number having formerly been four. but from this time on he seems to have declined in favor with the freemen or with the elder Mayhew, for this is the last time he held any office in the town and the next twenty-five years of his residence is scarcely marked by any public appearance.[6] It is noted that in the earlier records he had been called "Mr" Burchard, but that henceforth he was either Thomas Burchard or "Goodman Burchard; and in connection with this it is observed that he did not sign the submission to the Patentees Government in 1661, from which it seems clear that he had become disaf-

[1]Conn. Col. Rec., I, 221.

[2]Edgartown Records, I, 124, 172.

[3]Ibid., I. 131. One lot may have belonged to his son John.

[4]Ibid., I, 121. He was succeeded by his son two years later.

[5]Saybrook Town Book, II, 99; comp., Caulkins, "History of Norwich," p. 53. He called himself "of Marthas Vineyard."

[6]Edgartown Records, I, 120.

fected with the Mayhew regime.[1] He participated in the divisions of land from 1660 to 1676, as a proprietor, including Crackatuxett, Quanomica, Meachemy Field, and the Plains. At the Quarter Court of April 8, 1663, he was plaintiff in a suit against Thomas Jones, and on May 11, same year, had a small grant of land.[2] Besides engaging in real estate transactions during the following decade, nothing is heard from him in a public way till 1673, when he joined or probably led the opponents of the Mayhew family in the "Dutch Rebellion" of that year. His name is the first one signed to the appeal to Massachusetts, and Simon Athearn testified that Burchard was a "principal instigator" of the affair.[3] There is no record that Burchard was punished for his part in it, perhaps on account of his great age, near four score, and he apparently continued to reside in the town in quiet possession of his large landed estate for the ten years following. On May 9, 1683, he sold out a small parcel of land, and in the deed calls himself "late inhabitant upon Martins Vineyard," where he had resided the past thirty years of his life.[4] His son John had long since removed to Norwich, and the father in his old age, then eighty-eight, may have gone thither to live with his son or some of his married daughters.

The marital complications of Thomas Burchard require some explanation. There was a "Goodwife Burchard" who died in Roxbury March 24, 1654–55, and she must have been the Mary who came with him in the *True Love*.[5] His second wife was Katherine Andrews, a widow, mother of John Andrews, a linen draper of London, whom he married before 1659, and by this became related to our Thomas Trapp.[6] In several papers he refers to Trapp as "my cusen" (nephew) and "my kinsman," and it appears that Trapp was a "cousin" to Andrews. This wife was living on March 4, 1674, when she signed as witness to John Pease's will, with her husband and Thomas Trapp.[7] When she died is not known, but it

[1]Edgartown Records, I, 136, 138, 144, 147. He was a member of the Train Band in 1662, at which time he must have been about sixty-seven years of age.

[2]Ibid., I, 135, 139.

[3]Dukes Co. Court Records, I.

[4]Dukes Deeds, I, 209. No residence is stated in this deed. It was acknowledged before Richard Sarson.

[5]The Burchards were early members of Rev. John Eliot's church, and possibly she was visiting old friends there.

[6]N. E. Gen. Register, X, 87.

[7]Dukes Deeds, I, 340.

appears that a third wife named Deborah was in existence for some indefinite time, and like the first she died away from home. The records of Charlestown, Mass., contain entry of the death of "Deborah Burcham, wife of Thomas of Marthas Vineyard," under date of May 10, 1680, and that is all we know about her.[1]

It is believed that the family enumerated in the passenger list of the *True Love* represents all his children with the possible exception of a Hannah Burchard, who married in 1653 John Baldwin of Guilford.[2]

Thomas Burchard's real estate holdings began with the acquisition of the harbor lot of Richard Smith about 1652, being number five of the "Five and Twenty," which he later sold to Robert Codman. He probably resided there at first, but he acquired from several owners a tract at Katama, whereon he lived the remainder of his life here, as far as known.[3]

The following is a detailed description of the various lots, divisions, and rights owned by him in 1669:—

Upon the Vineyard anno 1669: the Lands and accomodations of Thomas Burchard: my house Lott and five acres I had of John Pease in all I Judge Eighteen acres more or Less, Bounded with the Sea on the East and the Plain on the west, Mrs. Blains Land on the North and South: my Divident Lott with my pond Lott Lying together: my pond Lott I had part of it of old John Folger and part of it I changed with Bland and his wife, a third part I took out of my Devidend Lott: both parcells I Judge to be about thirty acres more or Less, Bounded the Sea on the East and North East the East also, Mr. Butlers Land on the South and West on the plain and on the North Mr. Blands Land: thirdly att Crackatuxett two Lotts the third and fifteen with my thach Lott without Side the fence, that was Containing three acres More or Less: my Land (at) Meeshackett Containing I Judge Sixty three acres more or Less Bound with the Shrubed plain or Comon Land on the North, on the East Comon Land and Isaac Nortons Devident Lott on the South, with the fresh pond and on the west the pond and William Vincents Land: fifthly one ten acre Lott (upon the Line) within the general fence more or Less: Bounded on the South Comon Land, on the west Mr. Butlers Lott, on the north the Comon Land, on the East Thomas Butlers Lott, on the north the Comon Land, on the East Thomas Doggett his Land: Sixtly my meadow two acres more or Less which I Bought of Richard Smith Lying att poche on Chappaquidick Island, Bounded on the East towards the Sea on the South with Mr. Butlers meadow and part with the upland, Bounded on

[1]Wyman, "Genealogies and Estates of Charlestown," 154.

[2]Thomas Burchard is the ancestor of President Rutherford Burchard Hayes of Ohio.

[3]There are no records to show when or how he purchased these lots that constituted his Katama property.

the west with the upland and on the north part, a part next William Vincents meadow and a part upon the upland: two acres more or Less of meadow I had of John Burchard that the town gave him of which John Eadie hath one acre and one Remains mine Still in my Possession att this Day: I have a Shear and a half of fish & alewives att our Common Wares Called Mateckesse wherein are twenty Seven shears upon one half Divided from the heathen as also a Shear and a half of whale in our half with the Endians in the twenty Six Shears: also one Commonage and half Commonage upon all our common feeding for Eighteen neat Cattle with a purchase or Division of any of all our Common Lands.[1]

JOHN BURCHARD

The eldest and probably only son of the preceding, came to the Vineyard before his father, and is among the earliest settlers here, being fifth in priority of appearance on the records. His name occurs under date of March 27, 1651, for the first time, when his land at Meshacket is mentioned.[2] In 1656 he was chosen town clerk, probably in succession to his father, and his fine signature indicates excellent clerical ability, and an education above the ordinary.[3] His life on the Vineyard was uneventful, as far as the records furnish data, and it is probable that beyond continuing as town clerk till his departure for another place of residence he was engaged in husbandry at Meshacket. He removed about 1660-1 to Norwich, Conn., and in October, 1663, was accepted as an inhabitant of that town, where he resided the remainder of his life.[4] He was one of the original proprietors (1659) of this new settlement.

He became a prominent citizen of Norwich, serving as its Deputy to the General Court, 1671; Clerk of the Courts, 1673, and Justice, 1676. He also served as town clerk, 1661 to 1678, a period of seventeen years, almost from his first settlement there. In 1677 he was schoolmaster for the town.[5]

[1]Edgartown Records, I, 174.

[2]Edgartown Town Records, I, 124. He had lived previously at Saybrook, where he was a lot owner in 1648–9. (Saybrook Records, I, p. 1.)

[3]Ibid., I, 120. It is to be regretted that the records kept by him are not extant, in the place of the doubtful transcript made in the next century.

[4]The father, Thomas Burchard, as attorney, sold the house and land of John Burchard to Thomas Jones, July 10, 1662. (Ibid., I, 129.)

[5]Caulkins, History of Norwich, 61, 66, 73, 82, 92, 94.

His wife was Christian Andrews, whom he married July 22, 1653, during his residence here, and we may indulge the surmise that she was related to his father's second wife (Mrs. Katherine Andrews), or possibly to Edward Andrews, his neighbor at Meshacket.[1] By her he had Abigail, who married John Calkins; Mary, who married Jonathan Hartshorn; Lydia, who married ——— Raymond; Samuel, b. 1663; James, b. 1665; Thomas, b. 1669; John, b. 1671; Joseph, b. 1673; and Daniel, b. 1680, all living in 1725 in Norwich and Lebanon.[2] He died November 17, 1702.

NICHOLAS BUTLER.

For sixteen years prior to his settlement on the Vineyard, about 1651 or 1652, Nicholas Butler had resided at Dorchester, Mass., whither he emigrated in 1636 from England. The ship's list names Nicholas Butler with three children and five servants as coming from Eastwell, Co. Kent, in that year, of whom John, who came here, probably with his father, and Lydia who married John Minot of Dorchester, May 19, 1647, are two. The third child is not known, as the son Henry did not reach New England for several years after, perhaps with his mother Joyce, and therefore is not to be counted at that time. Nicholas is first mentioned in the records under date of May 8, 1653, when he participated in one of the divisions of land. Two years prior to that, on Oct. 15, 1651, he had made his "well-beloved sonne John Butler" his attorney to collect and pay debts, which may be the most probable indication of the time of his leaving Dorchester and entrusting the settlement of his affairs there to his son. When he came to the Vineyard, he was well into middle life. Though the date of his birth is not known, yet the knowledge existing of his children's ages enables us to proximately fix his birth about the years 1595–1600, and his age at fifty-five when he took up his residence at Edgartown. That he was a man considerably above the social average is shown by the number of his servants,

[1]Some family connection will be discovered, probably, between these persons and the Mary Andrews of Norwich, mother of Sarah (Post) Vincent, wife of our Thomas. Hinman states that Samuel Andrews of Hartford, Saybrook and Norwich was a brother of Christian (Andrews) Burchard. (Puritan Settlers of Connecticut.)

[2]Saybrook Records, III, 343, 419. There was a David Burchard of Norwich, 1723, who was her son probably.

the fact that his son Henry was a graduate of Harvard College (class of 1651), and this standing was at once recognized in his new home, for he became in 1653 one of the "five men to end controversies," that is magistrate. The next year he was again chosen and in 1655 he was re-elected and called "Assistant" to the chief magistrate. In all the records he is called Mr. Butler or Mr. Nicholas Butler, a use of which prefix is distinctive. In December, 1661, he was fined for absence from town meeting and "for Going away Disorderly." Beyond the usual duty on juries and an occasional trivial litigation his name does not further appear upon the town records. The following is the account of his landed possessions: —

This is a True Record of the petickeler parcells of Land of Mr. Nicolas Butler, which Lands are upon Marthas Vineyard Partickraly as followeth: first my house Lott with that Lott which I Bought of Mr. John Bland: adjoining to it is Twenty acres More or Less with one acre of Meadow I Bought of Mr. Browning, Bounded by the Sea on the East, Mr. Blands Lott on the South, the Plaine on the West, John Butler on the North: with my Divedent att Catemy forty acres, More or Less, Bounded By the Sea on the East, the Sea on the South, Mr. Blands lands on the West, the Plaine the Sea on the North North: More two thach Lotts, one Lying (at) Meshackett Bounded by John Foulger on the West, John Doggett on the East: the other Lying att Monaqua Bounded By Thos Doggett on the West, John Pease on the East: this hath four acres of upland Joyning to itt More or Less: More one Ten acre Lott upon the Line Bounded by Thomas Burchard on the East, the Common on the South, Thomas Doggett on the West, the Common the North: More Two acres of Meadow Lying att Chapequideck Bounded By the Pond on the North Lying over against my house, Mr. Mayhew the youngers Meadow on the South: this Meadow is two acres More or Less: More four Acres of Meadow to two Given to my house Lott and two I Bought of Thomas Joanse Lying on the North end of Chapequideck John Wakefield Now in Possession By his heirs Joyning to Mine is More or Less: More three acres of Meadow one Bought of Peter Foulger and Two of John Pease: this Meadow is More or Less Lying att the East End of Chapequideck Joyning and Bounded By Richard Smith on the North, By John Foulger on the South: with a full Commonage and a Six and Twentyth part of fish and whale: More three acres att Crackatuxett Bounded By Mr Mayhew the Elder and Thomas Birchard.[1]

His homestead lot was near Swimming Place Point, and consisted of twenty acres. Here he lived having as a next northerly neighbor his son John, from whom descends all of the name on the Vineyard. Nicholas Butler died Aug. 13, 1671, the day after his will was made. That he was an old

[1]Edgartown Records, I, 159.

and feeble man seems to be clearly evidenced by the curious reference to the "mark" which he used to indicate his signature, "his sight as it were Gon." The will reads as follows: —

[Dukes Deeds, I, 313]

Mr. Nicholas Butler Deceased the 13th of August in the year of our Lord one thousand Six hundred Seventy one

The Record of his will:

This doth testify that I Nicholas Butler Being at present Sound in memory doe Now by this my last will give my Estate Whatsoever that I left after I Shall be buried like a Christian wholly unto my wife Joyce Butler, uppon serious consideration for her to dispose of to hir children and my children as shee shall see good, and hereunto I praise [god] being of memorie as aforesaid Sound. I doe witness with my hand this 12th of August 1671.

This will is witnessed
by us
Thomas Mayhew
Tho' Birchard
The marke of Nicholas Norton

His sight as it were
gon
the mar X of
NICHOLAS BUTLER.

Mrs. Joyce Butler is By the worshipfull Govornour and Assistants Sitting in Court this 26th day of June 1672, admitted Administratrix & Executrix uppon the Estate of Mr. Nicholas Butler deceased.

The Inventory of the Estate.

Inprimis

To one common & half with house, fence & all priveledges	80—00—00
to fiveteen pound of pewter at 1s 8d	01—02—06
to twelve pound of pewter at 1s 2d	00—14—00
to 8 pound of pewter at 1s 6d	00—12—00
to one Silver Boule	03—07—00
to a Brass Candlestick	00—02—00
to 3 brass kettles at 1s pr pound	03—00—00
to two Iron potts, one frying pan and dripping panne	02—10—00
to one trammell, 2 payer of tonges, one payer of Andirons & Spitt	00—15—00

The inventory of the estate, amounting to £92-0-6, is remarkable for the paucity of articles which should belong to a gentleman of his standing in life. It may be that he had given his household furniture, etc., to his children during his life.

Whether his wife Joyce was the mother of all his children is placed in the doubtful category by the apparently careful way in which he refers to "her children and my children," as though she had been a widow with children or that he had children by a former wife. No allusion is made in her will to children by a former husband. She survived as Nicholas Butler's widow for eight years, and died between March 13 and Oct. 28, 1680, leaving an estate valued at £165-2-0, which she bequeathed to her descendants in the following will: —

[Dukes Deeds, I, 314.]

I, Joice Butler being through Gods blessing at present, of sound memory and understanding, doe make this my last will, and testament: Revoking all former whatsoever; and first my will is and I will and bequeath to my son Hennerie Butler, my Silver Boule and a carpet, & to each of his three sonnes, one Silver Spoone:

Nextly, I will and bequeath, to my Grandson John Butler, all the brass of the kitchen; and to my Grandson Thomas Butler one iron pottage pott, an Iron Kettle, and my bead, Beadstead, and all the furniture belonging to it, as it is in present use, as two pair of blanketts, two pillows &c— And I Give more to my Grandson John Butler, all the Bead and Beading above stairs:

Nextly, I will and bequeath, all my linnen, to be Equally devided Between my Grandchildren, John and Thomas Butler, and Mary Athearn.

And Nextly, I will and Bequeath, to my three Grandchildren aforesaid, all my Great Cattle, to be Equally devided among them, that is to say, John Butler, Thomas Butler, and Mary Athearn: Except only that my Grandson Thomas Butler, shall have two more to his part; and one heifer, before the devision set apart, which heifer I doe will and bequeath to my Grandson Samuell Minott:

And my will is, and I bequeath all my Sheep to my two Grandsons John Butler, and Thomas Butler, to be Equally devided between them:

Nextly, I will and bequeath to my Grandson Thomas Butler, my Dwelling house, with the long Table and hanging Cupboard, and to my Grandson John Butler, my cupboard, and Chest which was Joseph Butlers: and to my Granddaughter Mary Athearn, my Chest and two joint Stools: and as to my Chaires, I give the table Chaires to my Grandson Thomas Butler: the remainder of the Chaires, I leave to be Equally devided between my Grandchildren, John, and Thomas Butler and Mary Athearn.

Nextly my will is, and I doe oblige my two Grandsons John and Thomas Butler that they shall pay to my Grand Daughter Hannah Chadduck, two hundred weight of fleece wooll, yearly fivety pounds, untill it is payed which is within four years:

And as to Lands, I will and Bequeath, all my lands with the priveledges and appurtenances, to my Grandson Thomas Butler and my pewter, I will to be Devided, as my linnen as abovesaid, viz: between my Grandchildren John and Thomas Butler and Mary Athearn.

And lastly I Appoint my Grandson John Butler to be Sole Execcutor and Administrator, to this my last will, and my will is, and I doe Request my friendes Mr. Richard Sarson, and Matthew Mayhew, to be overseers that it may be performed:

And in witness of this my last will and Testament I the said Joice Butler have put hereto my hand and Seall, this thirteenth day of March, in the year of our Lord, one Thousand, Six hundred Seventy & nine, Alias Eighty

Witness	JOICE BUTLER
MATT: MAYHEW,	her I B marke
RICHARD SARSON.	

The inventory of the Estate of Mrs. Joice Butler deceased taken by Joseph Norton and Thomas Trapp Octobr : 28th : 1680.

the lands and accommodations		
a five and twentieth lot	Valued at	40—00—00
half a commonage		08—00—00
land at the Short Neck		02—00—00
two shares & halfe of Meadow not of said accommodations		12—00—00
The moveable Estate valued at 102 pd 12s		102—12—00

WILLIAM CASE.

This settler is first mentioned in the records in June, 1652, and on Nov. 11, 1652, he was granted a house lot, with the provision of four years' residence to make it "his proper inheritance."[1] This lot for many years after was referred to as "Case's" lot, though the early records fail to show how it passed from his possession. In some way Peter Tallman of Rhode Island became proprietor of a part of it. In 1655 he was sued for slander, fined for a misdemeanor, and placed under bonds for good behaviour. He was living on February 15, 1659, but must have died before July 15, 1659, and on August 22, the creditors of widow Case are given "the priviledge of Daniel Lane's bill for their satisfaction," and an inventory of his estate was returned Dec. 28, 1659, as amounting to £19-6-3.[2] This practically constitutes all that is known of him, omitting some details, and it remains to be shown whether he was related to the William Case, freeman, of Newport, 1655, and deputy from same in 1675.[3] In the next century, the first decade, there died on the Vineyard one John Case, who had received a grant of land in Tisbury, 1681, but the author has been unable to establish any connection between the two, though a son of John, named William, probably the eldest, might be suggestive of kinship.

[1]Edgartown Records, I, 120.

[2]Ibid., I, 129, 138.

[3]William Case of Newport, R. I., died in 1676, are two different men. His sons were William, settling in East Greenwich, R. I., Joseph Case, settling in Portsmouth and South Kingston, R. I., and James Case of Little Compton. His wife's name was Mary ———, maiden name unknown. She died in 1680. William of Newport is claimed to be the emigrant William Case, aged nineteen, who came over in the ship Dorset, 1635. His descendants intermarried with many of the historical families of that state.

ROBERT CODMAN.

The early spelling of this settler's name is Codnam, and the correct form is probably Codenham, which is a parish in Suffolk, England.[1] Robert Codman appeared first in Salem in 1637, with his mother, and on July 12 of that year the town granted him five acres of land for himself and five for his mother. He held a petty office that year, and was also engaged in a small law suit. In 1639 he removed to Salisbury, where he became proprietor of a ten-acre lot on the Merrimack river.[2] Codman took a wife unto himself about this time, and had a son baptized in Salem, 1641, and a second in Salisbury, 1644, but no information has yet been discovered to show whom he married.[3] His occupation was that of a mariner, and he was engaged in coastwise trading, which took him as far south as Virginia. In 1646 he is called "of Conecticot."[4] His vessel was, apparently, partly owned by the town of Salem, as the townsmen voted on Sept. 30, 1647, to authorize the sale of the "barque" Codman sailed in, as the profits belonged in part to the town.[5] Tristram Coffin sued him July 6, 1647, for the loss of merchandise which he was freighting in his vessel, and Richard Arey, late of the Vineyard, was one of the defendants with Codman.[6] This association of these two early settlers in Salem, where John Pease lived, is significant, taken in connection with their subsequent location in this town. We next find him at "Har(t)-ford uppon Conecticot river," where Robert Codnam, mariner, executed Sept. 25, 1650, a general power of attorney to his "trusty & beloved freind" Samuell Hall of Salisbury, planter, which he signed with a mark.[7] This indicates his removal

[1]In the Salem Court Records, Robert Quodnam brought suit against Henry Harwood in 1638, an instance of fantastic orthography, and Quodnam's pinnace is mentioned on the Connecticut river in 1645. There was a John Codman at Salem in 1638, but what relation he bore to Robert is not known.

[2]There was living in this latter-named town one John Stevens, Senior, who called our Codman "my brother," but as there are no records which show how this relationship came about, it is not known whether Stevens married Codman's sister or *vice versa*.

[3]Robert Codman sued Richard Cook at Salem June 30, 1640, and was defendant in a suit June 27, 1643, brought by Thomas Ruck.

[4]Aspinwall Notarial Record, 35; comp., Manwaring, "Digest of Early Wills," I, 93; History of Colony of New Haven.

[5]Salem Town Records.

[6]Salem Quarterly Court Records, 1638–1647, p. 201. Both Codman and Arey made depositions in this case before Governor Winthrop.

[7]Old Norfolk County Deeds, I, 49.

to the colony of Connecticut some time before this, probably soon after 1647, and it is of record that he had disposed of his home lot on the Merrimack to his brother John Stevens, Senior.[1]

His residence in Hartford was of short duration, and he removed down the Connecticut river to its mouth, within four years, as on June 19, 1654, Robert Codman "of Saibrooke fort. mariner" conveyed some of his Salisbury land to a resident of that town.[2] From Saybrook he removed, within a very short time, to this town, where his old neighbor, Richard Arey, was already settled, and of whom he bought the harbor lot of eight acres on Starbuck's neck, closely adjoining John Pease. On Oct. 31, 1654, Codman received a grant of land from the town, a tract of meadow near Sarson's island, in Sanchacantacket, where for nearly a hundred years, perhaps longer, there was a run of water known as "Codman's Spring."[3] His litigious habit seemed to follow him here, as on the above-named date he sued William Case for defamation of character, and Codman was found "not guilty of those aspersions which were cast upon him. . . . concerning himself and the wife of Edward Lay."[4] It is apparent that he continued his business of coastwise trading after his settlement here.[5]

In 1656, Codman made a deposition about a maritime transaction, and on Jan. 2, 1657, he was granted a commonage of wood and grazing for his cattle.[6] On June 2, 1657, he received another grant of land, and probably by this time had acquired the lot next his, to the north, which afterwards was comprised in the Codman estate.[7] He was admitted as freeman on June 5, 1660, up to which time he had drawn no shares of common land in the divisions, but on October 22 of that year he is credited with two shares, his own and "that was William Cases."[8] In 1661 he submitted to the patentees

[1]Old Norfolk County Deeds. This passed into the possession of George Martin, who is believed to be the father of George Martin of Edgartown (1683).

[2]Ibid., I, 148. The land sold was two acres, bounded east and north by the green by the meetinghouse and Isaac Buswell was the purchaser. Codman signed with a mark.

[3]Edgartown Records, I, 121; Dukes Deeds, VII, 154.

[4]It will be noted that Edward Lay was a townsman of Codman in Hartford and Saybrook.

[5]Letter, Mayhew to Winthrop, 4 Mass. Hist. Coll., VII, 36.

[6]Edgartown Records, I, 115, 129.

[7]Ibid., I, 139.

[8]Ibid., I, 147. He had acquired Case's share, probably of the widow of William Case, who died about 1659, but there is no record of the transaction.

government with his son Joseph, and both were enrolled in the train band the next year.[1] In 1663 and 1664, he participated in the divisions of Felix Neck, Quanomica, and Meachemy's Field,[2] besides being engaged with William Weeks in a law suit, as defendant in "an action of debt to the sum of twenty pounds." On June 6, 1667, he made a purchase of the lot adjoining his own from Thomas Burchard, thus making with the two bought of Richard Arey and Thomas Doggett and the one owned by his son Joseph three lots and a half on the present Starbuck's Neck.[3]

After this date he disappears from the records, and his decease is inferred thereby, probably before 1676, when Stephen Codman, his son and heir, drew a lot in the division of common land that year. The son Joseph had died also, and as representative of the respective rights of the two, perhaps by a will not now on record, Stephen, the son and brother, sold on Dec. 10, 1678, the family estate to Nathaniel Starbuck of Nantucket, and from that day to this the thirty-five acres thus purchased has been known as Starbuck's Neck.

He left no descendants of his name on the Vineyard, but in the female line through the marriage of his daughter Hepzebah with Nathan Skiff, there are numerous families who can trace back to this pioneer.

EZRA COVELL.

This person was a later settler at Great Harbor than James, but he had been living at Plymouth probably since 1635, the year he came to New England in the ship "Abigail."[4] He was then fifteen years of age, and doubtless was in the care of some person as an apprentice till he reached his majority. He bought ten acres of land and a house at Wobury Plain, Plymouth, in 1641, and as far as known, continued to live there for many years.[5] No trace of him has been discovered elsewhere until January 22, 1677, when he was granted ten acres of land near the house lot of James Covell at Meshacket.[6]

[1]Edgartown Records, I, 138, 144.

[2]Ibid., I, 109 127, 128.

[3]Dukes Deeds, I, 320.

His name appears on the list as "Cesora" Covell.

[5]Plymouth Deeds, I, 132.

[6]Edgartown Records, I, 22. In 1678 it was "voted by the town that Ezra Covell shall keep six head of neat cattle and a horse and liberty to cut fire wood on the common."

Whether this indicates relationship of the two is uncertain, but as James named one of his sons Ezra it may be assumed that they were kinsmen, perhaps brothers. Ezra Covell was a "marchant taylor," and presumably plied his trade here. He served as juror in 1677 and 1681, but nothing further of him appears of record until his death. He made his will April 29, 1696, "aged about 80 yeares," in which he mentions his wife, "formerly Abagaill Trevis," and it is more than probable that there was no issue of the marriage. He directed, in case both himself and wife "should depart the world at one time," the residue of his estate should "be bestowed in bibells or other good Bookes for the use of the children" of Edgartown.[1] The widow Abigail did not "depart the world" with Ezra and survived to become the wife of James Pease, April 22, 1706. She was probably the daughter of Richard and Grace (Clement) Trevis of Boston, b. January 8, 1662, and is mentioned in his will of May 17, 1688, as Abigail "Cove."[2] It will be seen that she was the young wife of his old age.

JAMES COVELL.

This person was one of the first comers, and received a grant of ten acres March 27, 1651, on the Meshacket Path, where he built a house and continued to live there till his death.[3] He was admitted as the proprietor of a half share in 1660, and "submitted" to the Mayhew government the next year. He was elected the drummer of the train band at the same time, and served as a juror in 1659 and 1677. His name appears in the records continuously in the drawing of lots, though there is a hiatus, 1664–1682, when it appears but once in any connection.[4] In 1687 he was granted twenty acres of land in the New Purchase, the last time his name occurs during life.[5] On August 19, 1690, administration of his estate

[1]Dukes Probate, I, 15.

[2]Suffolk Probate, XI, 379–381. The original will and papers were examined for the author, and the name "Cove" is written in a contracted form, not in the handwriting of the testator, which may account for the spelling of the name.

[3]Edgartown Town Records, I, 124. He received an additional grant of five acres in 1660.

[4]In 1682 "Mr." Covell and in 1684 "Goodman" Covell occur in the records, a differentiation hard to understand, unless one refers to Ezra Covell.

[5]This was sold by his son James to Hannah Daggett, May 23, 1694. (Dukes Deeds, I, 142.)

was granted to his son Philip, and he was then called "late desesed."[1]

Nothing is known to the author of his wife, either of her Christian or family name. He had three sons, Philip, James, and Ezra, and perhaps some daughters, but if so they are not of record. Through the children of his son James a numerous posterity resided in Edgartown during the next century, but there has been none of the name in town for a hundred years past.

There were Indians who adopted the name of Covell before 1700, and this complicates an already difficult genealogical problem to differentiate the various James Covells, senior and junior.

JOHN DAGGETT.

The published genealogy of the Doggett-Daggett family gives a full account of the English and American families bearing this name, and the reader is referred to that source for detailed information about them.[2] The name was, undoubtedly, Doggett, and some branches still retain that form of spelling, and our early New England records bear out this view. The family historian, in his review of the English origin of our John Daggett, thinks he may have been the third son of William and Avis (Lappage) Doggett of Boxford, Suffolk, baptized Nov. 4, 1602, but it may be said in criticism of this guess that the names of William and Avis do not appear in any of the immediate descendants of John for three generations, and that is an unusual omission, according to all custom and experience. The first definite knowledge we have of John Daggett is his appearance in Massachusetts as one of the large body of immigrants who came to New England with Governor Winthrop in 1630, settling first at Salem, later at Charlestown and Watertown. He was made a freeman of the colony May 18, 1631, having taken up his residence in Watertown. There he continued to live, receiving his shares in the several proprietors' divisions, until some time about 1646, when he removed to Rehoboth.

[1]Dukes Court Record, Vol. I. A Covell family resided contemporaneously on the Cape. Nathaniel Covell was among the first settlers at Eastham, before 1700, and Joseph Covell at Chatham about the same time. No connection with our family has yet been discovered, after much research of the records.

[2]"Doggett-Daggett Family in America," by Samuel Bradlee Doggett, *vide* pp. 71–76 for references to John Daggett.

Prior to that, however, Thomas Mayhew had become a townsman of his in Watertown, and when the purchase of Martha's Vineyard was made in 1641, Daggett became an interested party, as a grantee, with others of a township on this island in March, 1642. There is no evidence that he came here with the first contingent from Watertown, as his next recorded appearance is in Rehoboth, as stated, about 1646, when he was granted land in that new settlement. He remained in that town as late as the summer of 1648, but how much longer is unknown, as the next record of him is on March 29, 1651-2, when he was chosen corporal of the military company on the Vineyard. Between those dates he removed here, probably to avail himself of the rights he held in the new settlement by grant from Mayhew. He soon attained to prominence in local affairs, and on June 8, 1653, was chosen assistant to the chief magistrate to manage the business of the island, a position to which he was annually elected for the three following years. It then becomes apparent that he did not get along smoothly with Mayhew, and by 1660 he was entirely at "outs" with him. This probably arose, as elsewhere explained, from his purchase of the Indians at Ogkeshkuppe of a farm of five hundred acres without Mayhew's consent, though Doggett had been granted the choice of a farm of that size by Mayhew, in 1642, to be located not less than three miles from the governor's lot. How Daggett was fined £5000 and had to sue for his rights, will be related, and his success in retaining the "farm" was one of great humiliation to Mayhew, though the latter was clearly in the wrong. Daggett was one of the townsmen who "submitted" to the Mayhew government in 1661, and in the next two years he is recorded as plaintiff in several civil suits against his neighbors for debts or damages. The last notes of him are in the fall of 1663, as one of the subscribers to the "general fence," and early in 1665 acting as agent for the town in purchasing some fishing rights of the Sachem Tewanticut. Sometime after this he removed to Plymouth, Mass., and it is inferred that the wife of his youth and mother of his children had died here prior to that change. He married, in his old age in Plymouth, Mrs. Bathsheba Pratt, Aug. 29, 1667, probably the widow of Joshua Pratt of that town, and the record of the marriage calls him "of Martins Vineyard." It is probable however, that he had by that time removed to that Pilgrim town which ever after became his home.

Of his first wife we know nothing definite, but the author is of the opinion that the Hepzibah Daggett who signed as witness March 3, 1660, to the sale of the "Farm" from Wampamag to John Daggett was then his wife.[1] That it could not, in all probability, be the daughter Hepzibah, is based on her age at that date, seventeen years, and on the further reason that Hepzibah Daggett was then the wife of John Eddy, and would not sign as Hepzibah Daggett. The daughter was undoubtedly named for her mother, and grandchildren bore this name for John's first wife rather than in honor of the aunt.

Besides the five hundred acre "Farm" the real estate holdings of Daggett were as follows: —

This is a true Record of the pertickeler parcells of Land Now in Possession of John Doggett Inhabitant upon Marthas Vineyard: first four acres Lying at the South End of the Lott that he Sould to John Edy and of the Same Lott, Thomas Jones on the South East, the Comon on the South and on the West: Secondly one Comonage Belonging to it: third one Lott of Meadow at Sanchacantackett two acres More or Less Bounded By John Smith on the South East and Thomas Doggett meadow on the North: fourthly Two acres of meadow upon Chapequideck on the further side of the Island from the Town: fifthly one Lot at Cracketuxett Runing from one side of the Neck to the other side of it: Sixly one Lott at Quanomica: Seventhly one Lott at Meachemies his feild: and one Ten acre Lott upon the Line Bounded by John Gee his Lott upon the North East: Eighthly one Lott in Felix Neck: and Ninthly one thach Lott at Wintuckett: Tenthly one shear of alwives and a shear of whale: and Eleventhly one Seven and thirty part of the Meadow that the Town Bought of Tom Sesetom the Injain: all that Land Comonage and Preveledges were granted By the Town to the fore said John Doggett and his heirs and assigns for Ever to Injoy and are now in the possession of the foresaid John Doggett and Recorded by me

Thomas Doggett Clerk

Date May the 26th In the Year 1668.[2]

His home lot at Great Harbor was the first one south of Governor Mayhew's, and was situated on the west side of the road to the plains as it passes Tower Hill. It was apparently the west half of a lot owned by him and Malachi Browning. It is probable that this was the site of his resi-

[1]A guess may be hazarded that her maiden name was Brotherton. This appears as a baptismal name in the Thomas Daggett branch as early as 1686, and is used in the Joseph Daggett branch after the intermarriage with Thomas Martin in 1715. Brotherton Martin continued as a family name in Nova Scotia, whither this branch emigrated, until recent years. Hester Brotherton was a passenger for Virginia in the *Transport* in 1635.

[2]Edgartown Records, I, 7.

dence. He died in Plymouth in 1673, between May 17, the date of his will, and June 4, when it was probated.

[JOHN?] EDWARDS.

There are but two fragmentary traces of the person who owned one of the "Five and Twenty" lots here very early, being number eight from Pease's Point. He is referred to as "Mr Edwards" in 1660, whose share as proprietor had become a part of the estate of Thomas Paine, and this lot was mentioned in 1679 as "formerly Edwards his lot."[1] The first name of John is assigned to him as a supposition only, because our Robert Codman had business dealings in 1646 with a John Edwards "of Connecticot," and in absence of anything more definite this may stand. This is believed to be John Edwards of Wethersfield, where our Richard Smith went, and who may be the John Edwards, earlier of Charlestown or Watertown, 1640, a blacksmith.[2]

JOHN FOLGER.

One of the most distinguished Americans this country has ever produced, Benjamin Franklin, a great grandson of our early settler, made some investigations into the origin of his maternal ancestors, the Foulgers or Folgers, and concluded that they were of Flemish origin, and came to England in the time of Queen Elizabeth. John Folger, the first of the name in this country, is said to have come from Norwich, Co. Norfolk, England, in 1635, as a passenger in the *Abigail*, sailing from London, and he may have gone to Dedham, where in 1638 he was proposed at a proprietor. From the age of his son it would appear that he was born about 1590–5, and was about forty years of age at emigration. It is supposed that he brought with him his wife Merible, whose maiden name was said to be Gibbs, and a son Peter, but much of the early history of this family rests on tradition. He next appears as a proprietor of a homestall of six acres in Watertown, Mass., 1642 or 1644, both dates being given by the historian of that town.[3]

He came to the Vineyard sometime before Sept. 1, 1652, when he was chosen hog reeve.[4] He drew a lot in the Planting

[1]Edgartown Records, I, 24, 147.

[2]Lechford, Note Book, 176, 223, 225.

[3]Bond, "History of Watertown," pp. 225, 1009.

[4]Edgartown Records, I, 119.

Field division May 8, 1653, and again April 21, 1660, at Crackatuxett, but on Oct. 22, 1660, the share belonging to John Folger "or heirs" is mentioned, and it is believed this date proximately represents the time of this settler's decease.

On Jan. 29, 1663, the "Widow" Folger drew a lot at Quanomica on his share. He has left very little trace behind him to show for the twenty-five years' residence in New England, and only a nuncupative will recorded March 30, 1665, remains to give us a brief reference to his estate. This will is as follows: —

[Edgartown Records, I, 112.]

The Testemony of John Pease Sayth that Goodman Foulger said to him that his will then was that his wife should have that Estate he Left During her Life to use for her Comfortable Living : though she spent itt all for her Livelyhood : this was a Little Be Fore he Sickened and Died. This was as nigh as I can deam about a Month or six weeks afore he Sickened and Died.

The Testemony of Mary Pease the wife of John Pease, Saith she heard Goodman Folger the Elder Say upon his Last Sickness that what Estate he Left his wife should have after him Duering her Life:

The Testemony of Goodwife Arey Before the Town was: she saith that she went to John Folgers when he was sick before he died and saith she heard him say — wife to have all he had as long as she lived. Eleazer to have house and land after his wifes death. Mary to have the Cow presently and another after his wifes death. Nothing to Peter, "because he had spent or Put away so much Before."

His home lot was one of the "Five and Twenty" containing five acres, or a half share, and was situated about half way between the swimming place and the burial ground on Tower Hill. It was held by the widow and descended to Peter, who sold it to Thomas Mayehw, senior. It finally became part of the Thomas Daggett homestead. Mrs. Merible Folger (her son Peter called her Myrable) was probably deceased before 1664, when the house and lot was sold. The children of John and Merible, as far as known, are: I, Peter, b. about 1617. ?II, Ruth (signed as witness to deed of Meribell Folger, 1663), and ?III, Joanna (signed as witness as above).

PETER FOLGER.

Peter Foulger

This distinguished settler was the only known son of John and Merible Folger, and having been born about 1617, was brought by his parents to New England from Norwich, the supposed English home of this family when they emigrated. In absence of any definite facts bearing on the early life of Peter we may infer that he resided with his father at Dedham and Watertown, and came with him to the Vineyard, although our first record of Peter at Edgartown antedates that of his father by five years. This is in 1647, when he signed as a witness to a document drawn up here October 14 of that year.[1] In the years that follow the evidence from the records clearly establishes the superior ability of the son as compared with his father, for the former soon became a prominent person in the community. He had a grant of two acres of land "near the school house," where he undoubtedly taught in 1652, and in 1653 he drew a lot in the division of the Planting Field.[2] He was elected one of the assistants to the chief magistrate in 1654 and again in 1655, and about this time began the work of aiding the younger Mayhew in his missionary labor among the Indians of the island.[3] He had acquired a knowledge of the Indian tongue in conjunction with Mayhew, and was thereupon employed by the missionary with the approval of the Commissioners of the United Colonies to teach the Indian youths the English language.[4] It is believed also that he taught the village school in connection with this work. For this service he was paid at first £30 per annum, and later £25 and £20, as the funds of the Society for Propagating the Gospel would warrant.[5] He was called the "English scoolemaster that teacheth the Indians and Instructs them on Lord's day." The Rev. Thomas Prince, author of New England Chronology (1736), thus speaks of him: "an able godly *Englishman*, named *Peter Foulger*, employed in teaching the youth in Reading, Writing, and the Principles of Religion by Catechizing, being well learned likewise in the Scripture, and capable of helping them in religious matters."[6] In this capacity he was in the service of the missionary corporation from 1656 to 1661 inclusive, and was the principal assistant of the elder Mayhew after the departure of the younger Thomas in 1657 on his fatal voyage to England.[7]

[1]Suffolk Deeds, I, 86.

[2]Edgartown Records, I, 126, 172. He was chosen "hog reeve" in 1652 with his father and two others.

[3]Ibid., I, 119, 132.

[4]Records, Commissioners United Colonies, II, 167.

[5]Ibid., II, 189, 205, 218.

[6]Indian Converts, 291.

[7]The senior Mayhew wrote in 1659: "If I should be taken by death, here is hellpe that the schoolemaster (Peter Folger) who hath some languadge," etc. (Letter to John Winthrop, Jr., in 4 Mass. Hist. Soc. Coll., VII, 36.)

Peter Folger was becoming "irregular" in his orthodoxy about this time, and embracing the views of a sect then called Anabaptists by their opponents, and now known with the prefix omitted as Baptists.[1] It is probable that this was formally brought before the town for action or perhaps upon his own request to withdraw from the church. The following record under date of Oct. 4, 1659, seems to indicate a sort of dismissal from fellowship of the religious society established by Rev. Thomas Mayhew:—

> The request of Peter Folger granted touching the laying down of his creed as by the major part of the freemen and voted the same October (59).[2]

But he continued his services to the Indians, and laid the foundations of that doctrine among them which they afterwards adopted in considerable numbers before the close of that century. He was a visitor at Nantucket early after its purchase in 1660, and again in 1662, where he was a witness to land transfers. In this latter year he left the Vineyard, and removed to Rhode Island, settling first at Newport and later at Portsmouth in that colony.[3] Under date of Nov. 3, 1662, he leased a house and some land in Portsmouth, and a month later the following vote was passed in that town:—

> That day [December 3] Peter Folger late of Martins Vinyard presented to the free inhabitants of this toune of portsmouth a lease of house and land from William Corry, the Assembly doth graunt that the said peter folger shall hauld beinge amongst us during the terme of the saide lease.[4]

How long he remained in Portsmouth is not known, but it is certain that he began early negotiations for a settlement at Nantucket, for on July 4, 1663, he was granted half a share of land on that island, "on condition that he come to inhabit on Island aforesayd with his family within one year after the sale hereof. Likewise the sayd peter shall atend the English in the way of an Interpreter between the Indians and them."[5] These moves take Peter Folger out of the sphere of this history,

[1]Backus, "Church History of New England," III, 167. He joined Rev. Mr. Clarke's Society in Newport in 1675, and is considered the first of the Baptist faith on the Vineyard by that author.

[2]Edgartown Records, I, 147.

[3]Rhode Island was then a stronghold of the Baptists, under the influence of Roger Williams' teaching, and probably Folger went thither for that reason.

[4]Portsmouth (R. I.) Records, 115, 322, 325.

[5]Nantucket Records, Vol. I.

and the story of his later life belongs to our neighboring island, but it will be proper to complete briefly his personal and family record.

He married about 1644 Mary Morrill, who was said to have been attached to the household of Rev. Hugh Peter of Salem, and it is a tradition that the young people met as passengers crossing the Atlantic. Ten children were born to them, all upon the Vineyard, it is stated, except the youngest, Abiah, who became the mother of Benjamin Franklin.[1] Peter Folger died in 1690, and his widow survived until 1704.

In addition to the grants of land and shares drawn as stated above he received on Dec. 28, 1659, "ten acres of land next to Nicolas Nortons lot toward the west as the line runs," and these several lots were sold to Richard Arey before Folger left the Vineyard and became part of the Arey estate.[2] His home lot was on Tower Hill, north of the cemetery, about the site occupied by the house of the late Sol Smith Russell.

JOHN GEE.

There was a John Gee who came to this country in the *Transport* in 1635, at the age of eighteen years, but whether this man was the John Gee who appeared at the Vineyard twenty-five years later cannot be stated.[3]

The first appearance of John Gee at Great Harbor, as far as the records show, was on Dec. 23, 1661, when he submitted to the Patentee's government, but it is probable that he had been here some time before. The Boston records contain the birth of a son to him and his wife in May, 1662, so that we may conclude his residence here had lately begun and that the family remained at the former residence. Two years later he was granted land as follows on Aug. 20, 1663: —

> Voted by this town that John Gee shall have that lot and commonage which was given to Thomas Trapp: itt forfeited: which lot is ten acres upon the line and half a commonage and he to build and inhabit according to the order in fifty two.[4]

He participated in the divisions of Felix Neck and Machemys Field the next year, and on March 12, 1665, was chosen

[1] Hinchman, "Early Settlers of Nantucket," 49.

[2] Edgartown Records, I, 134; Dukes Deeds, IV, 16, VI, 416.

[3] There was a Peter Gee, fisherman, who was living at the Isles of Shoals in 1653, and was of Boston in 1667, who may have been a brother of our settler. (N. H. State Papers, XVIII, 151. Comp. Savage Gen. Dict. art. Gee.)

[4] Edgartown Records, I, 140.

"to divide the fish" caught at the town weir.[1] This seemed to be his occupation for some time, as on May 11, 1667, the town voted that "John Gee is to have three thousand of fish for orderly dividing of the towns fish every morning."[2] He was one of the five men chosen by Chief Magistrate Thomas Mayhew, in 1667, to dispossess Francis Usselton from Homes Hole Neck, and received as compensation one-sixth part of the land there which remained a part of his estate, undivided, for sixty years. Gee was "lost at sea," and is marked as deceased in the town records, Dec. 27, 1669.[3] He left a widow bearing the extraordinary name of Hazelelponah, which is a scriptural name according to Webster. She was living at the Vineyard in June, 1670, but had removed to Boston the next year, when she was received for baptism at the First Church in that town.[4] There she remained for a number of years, until Obadiah Woods, a widower and a baker of Ipswich, met her, proposed, and they mere married. William Harris of Ipswich testified that he "well remembers Obadiah Woods intermarrage with the widdow Hazelelepony Gee . . . . that sd Wood brought her from Boston, that it was the Taulk of the Times when she came to Dwell at Ipswich."[5] It does not appear what caused this "Taulk of the Times," but it may be surmised that her name was enough to excite village gossip. The late Hon. James Savage, whose monumental work on the dictionary of the early settlers of New England gave him unusual opportunities of meeting with strange names, confessed that it was unique in his experience. As might be expected, the various records spell it in a number of ways, and in later generations it was clipped to Purney! She survived her second husband, and died at Ipswich, where a stone records the last resting place of "Haselelpony Wood widow of Obadiah Wood, died Novem'r the 27, 1714 Aged 78 years,." Hence she was born about 1636, and was first a widow when thirty-three years old. John Gee had the following children by her: I, Mary b. about 1660; m. Thomas Pickering of Newington, N. H., about 1679 and d. before 1730. One daughter was named Hazelponi. II, John, b. May 27, 1662 (Boston). III, Anna, b. 1664; m. Samuel Hodgkins of Gloucester,

[1]Edgartown Records, I, 113.

[2]Ibid., I, 140.

[3]Ibid., I, 41.

[4]Sup. Jud. Court Files, No. 971; comp., Records 1st Church, Boston.

[5]Dukes Deeds, VI, 238.

Mass.; she d. July 28, 1724. IV, Martha, m. Thomas Cotes "in his life time was an Inhabitant of the Island of Marthas Vineyard"; d. before 1730. He left no known descendants on the Vineyard.

THOMAS HARLOCK, SENIOR.

In the passenger list of the ship *Assurance*, sailing for Virginia in July, 1635, may be found the name of Thomas Harlock, aged 40 years, and whether this be the person of the same name who subsequently appeared at Martha's Vineyard twenty-five years later cannot be stated with certainty, but the name is sufficiently rare to regard it as entirely probable.[1] Where he resided after his arrival in Virginia, for the next twenty years, is undetermined. Thomas Harlock is first known at the Vineyard certainly in 1658, as a witness to the sale of the Chickemmo region to Thomas Mayhew, and if the identity is to be accepted, he was then about sixty-three years of age, a few years the junior of the governor, whose daughter he married.[2] This was Bethia Mayhew, b. Dec. 6, 1636, and therefore forty years younger than her husband. This is not altogether an improbability, and as he died many years before his wife the circumstances all seem to favor the theory of this union of May and December. While 1658 is the first positive record of his appearance here, yet it is fairly inferential that he had been a resident of Great Harbor for a number of years previous. He acquired the house lot "formerly (John) Wakefields," who had left about 1652, and it may be supposed that he purchased it when the latter removed to Boston.

When he married the governor's daughter can only be conjectured. She was twenty years old in 1657, and as their son Thomas, Jr., was born about 1658 we may assume that this was the probable date of the nuptials. Harlock's home was on one of the harbor lots, number seven from Pease's Point, in the "five and twenty," proximately located between Cottage and Morse streets as shown on the map. Here were born to him "Thomas and John Harlock and their sister,"

[1]The name occurs in English records generally as Horlock, and it may be identical with Halleck and Hallock. A Thomas Harlock was of Trowbridge Co., Wilts, temp. 9 Elizabeth and a Richard Harlocke of the same county died about 1644. Widow Joan of Trowbridge, Parish of Studley, made her will in 1645, which was proved same year by Samuel Ghy. This county is apparently the home of the family.

[2]Deeds, I, 355. Dated Aug. 10, 1658.

as named in the will of their grandfather Mayhew, and referred to in the same document as "the three Harlocks."[1]

Thomas Harlock participated in the divisions of the common lands in 1660, 1663, and 1664, and received a grant in 1663 of one-half commonage.[2] His name appears on the town records continuously from 1660 to 1664 in various connections, the last time occurring on April 26, 1664, when he drew lots in the Felix Neck and Meachemys Field. After that date the name of Harlock does not reappear for twelve years (Feb. 14, 1676), when it undoubtedly refers to his son Thomas, Jr., who succeeded to the properties of the father. We may therefore place the death of Thomas, Sr., at some time not long after April 26, 1664, at which time he would have been about seventy years old.

His widow Bethia, left with two boys and possibly a girl, the oldest of whom was six or seven, probably remained on the Vineyard. Sometime before September, 1676, when Thomas was eighteen or nineteen years old, she married a second husband, himself a widower a dozen years her senior, Lieut. Richard Way of Dorchester.[3] He was a man of substance, had been an officer at the castle, and in 1674 was farmer general of the imposts. At her second marriage Bethia (Mayhew) Harlock was forty years old, and on July 13, 1677, a daughter named Hannah was born, who may be the "sister" referred to by Governor Mayhew, of whom we hear nothing further.[4] Bethia Way died four years before her father's decease (which occurred in 1682), and her Harlock children are given many special bequests in the Governor's will. It is further known that Richard Way took unto himself a third wife, Hannah (Townsend) Hall, who survived him.[5]

Of the children, the "three Harlocks," the oldest Thomas, Jr., will be the subject of a separate sketch, because of his

[1]Probate, III, 108. It is probable that Thomas and John and the unknown sister were the only issue of the Harlock-Mayhew marriage.

[2]Edgartown Records, 108, 109, 127, 156. There has been doubt expressed as to whether Thomas Harlock, Sr., ever lived in Edgartown, but this seems to be clear from the fact that his house is mentioned in 1663 (Ibid., 99), and he was a juryman in same year. (Ibid., 145.)

[3]In 1671 the first wife of Way, named Esther, was living, and it would appear that Mayhew had had business dealings with him, which explains the subsequent family connection. (Middlesex Co. Court Files, XXI, 5.)

[4]In his will Richard Way states that he had "no reason to believe any of my own children are surviving." (Suffolk Prob. Rec.) Will dated Jan. 2, 1697; prob. Oct. 28, 1697.

[5]Savage Gen. Dict., IV, 440.

prominence in town affairs during his lifetime. The sister, who is nameless, is only known through her grandfather's will, probably died in youth, as her interests do not subsequently appear in any property dealings. John Harlock seems to have been a favorite grandchild, if we may judge from the bequests in the old governor's will. Besides sharing contingently with his brother and sister in certain joint gifts of land at Chickemmoo, Kataymuch (Elizabeth Isles), and in Chilmark, he is given personally a lot on Chappaquiddick, five acres at Nashamoiess, "and all the small allotments everywhere," and as if this were not enough he was to have half of "all lots not mentioned" in his will. What became of him finally is not known, and but one record exists showing that he was here in person to make disposition of his inheritances. On May 9, 1690, he sold one half-share in common lands to John Welch, a mariner of Boston, the acknowledgment being made before Matthew Mayhew, and thenceforth disappears from view.[1] Shortly after the above date a John Harlock of Ratcliff in Stepney, Co. Middlesex, England, gentleman, was made the attorney for William Read of New England, mariner, on Oct. 2, 1691, and it is left to the reader to judge whether the Stepney John Harlock was the grandson of the old governor.[2] On May 24, 1707-8 Thomas (2d) Harlock sold property as "heir to his brother John," and this undoubtedly shows the previous decease of John.[3]

The real estate holdings of Thomas Harlock, Senior, besides the harbor or home lot, consisted of a ten-acre lot on the "line" and what was probahly his "Dividend Lot" on the plain situated just south of Jones Hill.

PETER JENKINS.

In the little settlement of "Bromigum," in Rowley Village, Mass., there lived from 1668 to 1672, one Peter Jenkins; and in 1660 one Sarah Jenkins, aged 43 years, also resided there at the last named date.[4] The woman is believed to be the

[1]Deeds, II, 46. Welch later sold this to Nathaniel Starbuck, but the date is not known (Ibid., II, 48). John Harlock's name appears as owner of one common share in the town in 1695, but this does not indicate that he resided here. Thomas also is credited with one share. (Town Records, 84.) It is probable that all of John's property went to Thomas by some blanket deed not recorded.

[2]P. C. C. Fane, 173.

[3]Dukes Deeds, VI, 115.

[4]Essex Court Rec., V, 143. Bromigum is early vernacular for Bromidgeham or Birmingham.

mother of Peter Jenkins, and that he is the person of the same name who first appears in Edgartown before 1675, when his landed possessions were recorded. In 1668, in Rowley, Peter Jenkins was indicted "for profaening the Lords day by Labouring about Bricke," which would indicate his occupation in the manufacture of that article;[1] and it is significant that he had a clay pit in this town on the property he purchased as a homestead.[2] He was born about 1644, and while a resident of Rowley led a strenuous life which frequently resulted in court proceedings;[3] and our Peter Jenkins, early in his career on the Vineyard, began and continued the same unconventional habits, which resulted in like judicial cognizance. On one occasion (1680), while on trial for disorderly conduct, he began to abuse the court (Matthew Mayhew was sitting as Assistant Justice), and on being admonished for "carrying himself in a scornful way," Jenkins "pulled of his coat saying com let me have it, let me be whipt, often itterating the same: the said Assistant bidding the Marshall carry him to Jaill, he answered, I will break it down then."[4]

The first occurrence of his name on our records is under date of Dec. 31, 1675, when there is an entry of his lands, which were situated "on the south side of Meshacket Path," and comprised ten acres as a homestead.[5] In addition to his public appearances indicated above, he served once as a juror (1680), but does not seem to have taken any active part in local affairs. His wife was named Sarah, but nothing is further known of her family, though it is a fair guess that she was the daughter of Thomas Jones, whose property he received in consideration of care and support. He was married to her before September, 1679, and had at least four known children, and a probability of more whose relationship is surmised, viz: Sarah, b. [1675]; Matthew, b. [1681]; Thomas, b. [1683]; Joseph, b. [1685]; the dates being estimated. There is no record of the death of himself or wife, nor any settlement of his estate. He was deceased before Aug. 18, 1707, when his house and lot was divided between his son Thomas

[1]Essex Court Rec., XIII, 78. His name does not appear in the land records.

[2]Edgartown Records, I, 17.

[3]Essex Court Rec., XVIII, 85, 91.

[4]Dukes Court Rec., Vol. I. June 30, 1680. The identity of Peter Jenkins of Rowley and Edgartown seems to be quite well established from these court proceedings. After 1672 there is no further record of him in Essex County.

[5]Edgartown Records, I, 17.

and Thomas Harlock.[1] It is possible that he may have died off the island, as two of his sons, Matthew and Thomas, resided in Nantucket and Boston. The name was perpetuated on the Vineyard in the line of his son Joseph until after the Revolution, when the grandsons removed to New York state. None of the name have been residents here since that time.

THOMAS JONES.

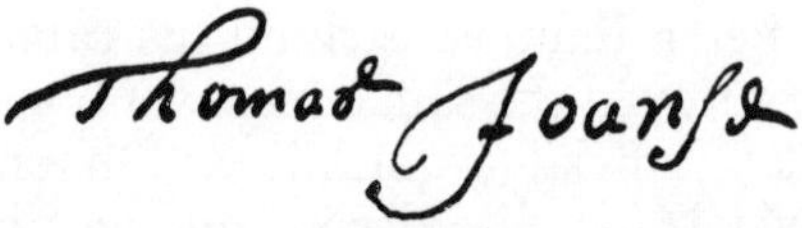

It has been impossible to identify this person among the numerous immigrants of his name, who came to New England in the great movement following the settlement of Boston. As a number of our pioneers were identified with New London, the Thomas Jones who had a lot granted there in 1651 and forfeited,[2] may be the one who is first mentioned in our records the next year as grantor of a lot "that was given him . . . . ccontaining to the estimation of four acres . . . . . in this our town called Great Harbour."[3] This indicates a prior residence of some period, long enough to acquire a title to a grant. The records show frequent appearances in court as plaintiff or defendant in suits at law, and these references indicate that he was a weaver.[4] He signed the submission in 1661, was chosen clerk of the Train Band same year, and served as juror in 1663. He joined the "Dutch Rebellion" of 1673, and signed the appeal to Massachusetts, but does not appear to have been punished therefor. In May, 1676, he transferred all his real and personal property to Peter Jenkins in consideration of care and maintenance during the remainder of his natural life.[5] How long he survived is not known, but he died before April 28, 1687, when the widow Jones is mentioned as a town pauper.[6] She was living the

[1]Dukes Deeds, II, 173. The wife of Thomas Harlock may have been a daughter of Jenkins. Her name was Hannah.

[2]Caulkins, Mss. Collections, comp., History of New London, 265.

[3]Deed Thomas Jones to William Scudder, June 4, 1652. (Edgartown Records, I, 122.)

[4]Thomas Jones, a tailor of Caversham, Oxfordshire, with wife Ann, came to New England in 1638 and lived in Hingham and Hull, where it is stated that he died about 1681. Our Thomas had a wife Ann.

[5]Dukes Deeds, II, 143. The reason for this, aside from the usual inference of age and feebleness, is not apparent. Jenkins may have been his son-in-law or a relative.

[6]The town entered into an agreement with George Martain, April 28, 1687, to keep the widow Jones. (Edgartown Records, I, 38, 40.)

next year in the same situation. It is not known that this couple had any children, and the records do not indicate any descendants.

Thomas Jones lived on the hill which bears his name, south of Cleveland Town, sometimes called Mill Hill. He owned a half share in the proprietors' divisions, which fell to Jenkins, and was later sold to Gershom Dunham.[1]

JOHN MARCHANT.

The first of this well-known family to acquire proprietary interest here was John Marchant, who had a grant of ten acres "on the right hand of Sanchacantucket cart path, near the cart path that goes to Mortall's Neck."[2] He had been before that time a resident of Yarmouth, Cape Cod, where his father, also named John, had settled between 1645 and 1648.

Marchant, as a family name, is probably of French origin, derived from "marchand," a trader or merchant, from which our English word is obtained. The name is not of very frequent occurrence in England. Thomas Marchaunt of Colchester, Essex, 1392 to 1436,[3] temp. Richard II and Henry VI, is the earliest recorded instance known to the author, and a pedigree of one family living in Sussex has been published.[4] The author found also in Wiltshire, the wills of various persons of the name from 1592 to 1674, recorded in the Prerogative Court of Canterbury,[5] while scattering references occur in other counties about the period of the early emigration to New England.[6]

The first of the name on this side of the water are two planters at Barbadoes, in 1635, William and Silas Marchant, and as the name Silas occurs quite early (1722), in our island family, the origin of the Vineyard Marchants might be looked

[1]Edgartown Records, I, 139.

[2]Ibid., I, 31.

[3]Records, Borough of Colchester, 29, 39, 43.

[4]Sussex Archæological Collections, XXV, 199.

[5]These were all original wills on file in the Bishop's Consistory Court, Sarum, at Somerset House. The testators were John, of Marlborough, March 28, 1592; John, of Tilsed, March 16, 1604; John, of East Knoyle, June 17, 1625; Thomas of Westbury Leigh, July 9, 1647; and Tristram, of Warminster, Sept. 18, 1674. A correspondent recently informed the author that there were many Marchant wills recorded at Wells, co. Somerset.

[6]There was a John Marchant of Georgeham, Devon, in 1620 (P. C. C. Soame, 45), and Walter Marchant, haberdasher, of Bristol, Gloucestershire, in 1640. (Lechford, Note Book, 209.)

for at that source.[1] The first one found in New England is John Marchant, who was admitted an inhabitant of Newport, R. I., June 2, 1638, but did not remain long there as he is found next year at Mount Wollaston, Braintree, where on February 24, 1638-9, he was granted eight acres for two heads, that is himself and another male.[2] He had brought with him a wife Sarah and a son to the new settlement, and shortly after, on Dec. 3, 1638, his wife died. Contemporaneously a William Marchant is found at Watertown in 1641,[3] and thither our John probably removed as early as 1642, and in 1645 he is mentioned as of that place.[4] Once more he removed, this time to Yarmouth, some time before 1648, as on June 7th that year he was chosen as constable for the town, an office that presupposes a residence of some duration. How long he resided there or when he died is unknown. He appears in court twice, once as plaintiff and once as defendant, and probably he was dead prior to 1670, when his son John, who by this time had married, was promoted from ensign to be lieutenant in the militia, and is called "Senior."[5]

The second John continued to reside in Yarmouth with his family, and is frequently mentioned on the records usually by his military title.[6] He was "rated" in the town in 1676, for "the late war" (King Phillip's), and was in the list of townsmen in 1679.[7] It is not known whom he married, nor the christian name of his wife, but he had taken a wife before 1648, when children are recorded to him in the Yarmouth town records beginning that date. In 1682, as above stated, he received his grant of land in this town, but whether he came here to reside is uncertain.[8] It is the author's belief

[1]The Barbadoes and other West India islands were frequent stepping stones for immigrants to New England. (Hotten, Lists of Passengers, &c.)

[2]Boston Town Records, I, 39.

[3]Savage, III, 197.

[4]Pope, Pioneers of Mass.; N. E. Gen. Register, VIII, 56. William Marchant may be the Barbadoes planter. He removed to Ipswich, where he died, Sept. 4, 1668, and is the ancestor of the Marchant family of Gloucester and other towns in Essex County. It is significant that one of the Yarmouth family went to Gloucester for a wife in 1719.

[5]Plymouth Col. Records, VII, 60; III, 36. In the natural order the elder John would not begin a military career in 1664 and be promoted in 1670, hence the belief that the first John died before the last named date.

[6]He had been made freeman June 3, 1652, and ensign in 1664.

[7]Yarmouth Town Records.

[8]There is a singular absence of records connected with this family which makes so much conjecture necessary. Taken in connection with the loss of the Barnstable County Land records, by fire, Oct. 22, 1827, when 93 volumes of deeds and three volumes of wills were destroyed, the task of piecing out the pedigree is difficult.

that he came here to live, as the grant would have been forfeited for non-residence, while it was retained as belonging to him and his estate for ten years.[1] His daughter was already living here, and three of his sons were here at this time.[2] When he died is not known, but some time before 1693 is the probable date.

The next of the name who is certainly known to have made a permanent settlement in this town is John[4], who was, in all probability, the son of Abisha of Yarmouth, though proof is lacking.[3] This John is the definite head of the Marchant family of Edgartown, and he acquired his first property here by purchase, April 8, 1707, when he bought a harbor lot, just south of Burial Hill, of Joseph Ripley.[4] He was then a young man of twenty-seven years, and had just married his first wife. In 1711, he bought the so-called "ministerial lot," and both of these were retained by him for over half a century, and descended to his sons Silas and Abisha. His life was uneventful, if we may judge from the entire absence of his name from the records, law, probate and court. Beyond serving as juror in 1722, 1730 to 1734, he attended strictly to his private affairs, and died February, 1767, at the ripe old age of 87 years.

MATTHEW MAYHEW.

Next in importance to the old governor himself, in the political life of the Vineyard, was his grandson, Matthew. He was the oldest son of Rev. Thomas and Jane (Paine) Mayhew, and was born in 1648, undoubtedly in Edgartown. Of his youth, up to the time of the death of his father in 1657, we have no knowledge, but after that unfortunate event, the widow wished to consecrate Matthew or one of his brothers to the work in which their father had acquired such an enviable reputation. Acting on the advice, presumably, of the elder Mayhew, it was de-

[1]It was sold by his son Abisha Dec. 6, 1693. (Dukes Deeds I, 393).

[2]Joseph in 1682, Christopher in 1685, and Abisha in 1693. Joseph bought five acres of William Vincent, near the cemetery, in 1698, and sold it back in 1707. (Deeds I, 140, 146.)

[3]This is the natural inference. The only other tenable hypothesis is that he was a son of the second John by an assumed second marriage.

[4]Dukes Deeds, III, 438.

termined to educate Matthew so that he might follow in the footsteps of his father. It is probable that his brother John was also to be dedicated to the same work, for in August, 1658, the governor wrote to the Commissioners of the United Colonies asking assistance for "my daughter and her 6 children," and further requesting them to "find a way to keepe two of the sonnes at schoole." The Commissioners acceeded to this request for the relief of the widow and for "Keeping her eldest son att scoole to fitt him for the worke." He must have begun these studies early in 1658, as the Commissioners' accounts for 1659 contain the following item: —

To Mr. Corlett Schoolmaster att Cambridge for . . . . . his extreordinary paines in Teaching . . . . . Mr. Mahews son about two yeares.

The young student continued his studies at Cambridge for four or five years, as shown by the following items, which are taken from the accounts of the Commissioners of the Society for the Propagation of the Gospel among the Indians of New England: —

(II, 261.)	September, 1661.	To Mr Corlett for teaching 4 Indians and Mathew Mahew	12	00	00
		To the clothing of Mathew Mahew for the yeare past.	05	00	00
(II, 277.)	September, 1662.	To the Diett and Clothing of Matthew Mahew for one year past	13	00	00
		To the Scoolmaster att Cambridge for 2 Indian youthes and Mahew	08	00	00
(II, 296.)	September, 1663.	For clothing and diet of Mathew Mahew			

A further reference shows the expectations of the Commissioners respecting the future usefulness of young Mayhew to them in their work: —

And whereas Matthew Mayhew is devoted by his parents to the worke and a considerable charge hath for his fathers sake bin expended on him; the Commissioners expect that together with his other learning hee apply himselfe to learne the Indian Language having now an oppertunitie to attaine the same, otherwise the Commissioners wilbee necessitated to consider some more hopeful way for expending the stocke betrusted in their hands.

How long he continued as a student at Cambridge is not known, but probably not beyond the dates above quoted, showing expenditures on his account. Upon his return to the Vineyard, he devoted himself to the task of learning the

Indian dialect, which he mastered successfully. In 1672, the Commissioners write as follows concerning him:—

> One whereof is the son of that Reverend and Good man Mr. Mahew deceased whoe being borne on the Iland of Marthas Vineyard and now grown to mans estate and there settled, is an hopefull young man, and hath theire Language p'fectly.

But it is evident from our knowledge of his future career, that the ministry was not his sphere. His younger brother John inherited the saintly character of the missionary, and followed the work of his father on the island as a substitute for Matthew; and doubtless the substitution was agreeable to the inclinations and temperament of both. As Matthew grew to manhood he developed business qualifications which made him useful to the aged governor, and it was in line with family custom for the eldest to succeed to the estates and temporal management of them. That he did not, however, entirely forget his obligations to the Commissioners appears from a statement of the governor in 1675, in which he says: "I praise God two of my grandsons doe preach to English and Indians Mathew sometimes and John the younger."

His first appearance in political affairs, in which he was destined to exercise such an important role for the rest of his life, was in 1670, when he was sent to New York by his grandfather to wait upon Governor Lovelace in respect to submitting to the jurisdiction of the Duke of York over the island. He was then about twenty-three years of age, and from that time he was exclusively identified with the executive management of the Vineyard and Nantucket. On July 5, 1671, when the government of the island was provided for, he was commissioned as collector of customs "in & about Martins Vineyard with places adjacent." This was the first of the offices held by him during the forty remaining years of his active life.

He was the first secretary of the General Court of the Vineyard held in 1672, and one of the assistants to the Governor. He also held at different times the office of Register of Deeds (1672), High Sheriff (1683), Judge of Probate (1697), Register of Probate (1685), besides continuous service in the office of Justice of the King's Bench. In 1682, upon the death of the aged governor, he was commissioned "in the stead of that worthy Person Mr. Thomas Mayhew his (grand) father Late Deceased to be cheife supplying the Defect by another of the Name." While not specifically designating him as governor, his functions were identical, and he is termed in the Provincial Records as "Chief Magistrate" of the island.

His administration of the public affairs of the island was not only as vigorous but equally as tactless as that of his predecessor. All the elements opposed to his grandfather continued their opposition to him and the Mayhew family. In particular, Simon Athearn of Tisbury renewed his assaults upon him as the representative of the reigning family, and these attacks, ranging over many years, often partook of a personal character. In these contests Mayhew was generally successful, as he could control the local courts and other tribunals through his political affiliations and family influence. When the jurisdiction of New York ceased and Martha's Vineyard became a dependency of Massachusetts by the charter of William and Mary in 1691, Mayhew was not favorable to the change; but bowing to the inevitable, he finally accepted with as good a grace as possible, the new order of things, and on Dec. 7, 1692, was newly commissioned as Justice of the Peace with two others of his family. He thus aligned himself with "those in authority," and maintained, ostensibly, amicable relations with his new superiors. That this acceptance was only a matter of policy has appeared in the narration of the political relations of the island with the Massachusetts authorities, immediately following the transfer.

Matthew Mayhew was a versatile man and through his early training was probably the most cultivated person, intellectually speaking, on the island in his time. He utilized his leisure moments in writing the first book relating to the island, and published it in London in 1695. Thus he has the distinction of being the earliest author in the bibliography of Martha's Vineyard. This volume gives a most interesting and authentic account of the Indian tribes of the island, their manners, customs, and the progress of religion among them. It has been quoted at length in another portion of the work, and extended reference will not be made to it here. It was customary in those days for men in all walks of life with literary aspirations, to write upon a religious topic, and when Matthew Mayhew selected as his subject and title, "The Conquests and Triumphs of Grace," and had it attested by several clergymen, it does not necessarily follow that the author was a "religious man" in the accepted sense of the word. Indeed, we have evidence quite to the contrary within a few years of his pious references to the "success which the gospel hath had among the Indians of Martha's Vineyard" and the "state of Christianity in other Parts of New England." The following amusing statements concerning his religious, or lack of religious beliefs, doubtless let us into his real opinions, rather than the stilted sentences of his published narrative. While the information came from his ancient opponent, Simon Athearn, yet he had corroborating witnesses to the conversation. The old warrior of Tisbury, under oath, made the following statements:—

> That on the 16th of March, 1697-8, major mathew mayhew, & Mr. Joseph merion com to sd. athearns house, at marthas vineyard, then sd athearn asked what newse & said he heard there wase to be a publice fast this weeke — then major mayhew pulling som papers out of his pocket, said, he would read it — and reading, made a stop — & said, what a redicolas thing is this, that thay should order a fast, for a man that thay did not know whether he was in the land of the living, or no, — sd athearn saied, you have not heard the ship is Cast away, have you? the major said no — but he did not know what security a Governor have of his life, mor then another man [1] — sd athearn said no) but hopet they were well, & said he thought the Liuetenant Governor & ye Gentillmen of the Councill did much desier his Lordship the Governor were safe a rived, and thought thay did well to pray for him — then major mayhew said, what a redicolas thing is it, when halfe the men of the Country had wrather he were hanged than ever come here to my knowledg, —

But the author of "Conquests and Triumphs of Grace" did not stop there. According to his brother-in-law, Benjamin Smith, "Major Mayhew have said viz: that ther was no such thing as fall of man for man is naturally Inclined to virtue: And that Religion is so Redicolas a thing that seaven thousand of the wisest Gentelmen in London had declared themselves to be athe(i)sts."

In addition to the above, Thomas Butler, then constable of Edgartown, is reported to "have said that when he would have shewed our most Gratious Kings most Royal proclamation, against vice and imorallity: Major Mayhew then answered & saied that he had seene it all redy And take but the Kings name from it And its fit only to . . . ."[2]

[1]This reference was to a Fast ordered by the lieutenant-governor for the safe voyage of the Earl of Bellomont, the newly appointed governor, who arrived in New York, April 2, 1698, from London. He acknowledged the efficacy of the prayers offered up for his safety in a letter to the Massachusetts magistrates. (Sewall, Diary, I, 477.)

[2]The remainder of sentence is omitted on account of its vulgarity. These depositions are on file in the Suffolk County Court Records, Case no. 4605.

Notwithstanding these imputations upon the character, loyalty, and religious sentiments of Mayhew, he had previously laid the foundations of a reputation for piety in his book, which doubtless stood him in good stead on the occasion when he had to explain these charges of "heresy and schism" before the magistrates of Boston.

He was Lord of the Manor of Tisbury from 1671 till his death. He resided in Edgartown, where he was born, and was the first citizen of the town and county for more than a generation. His home was on South Water street on the "entailed lot," but the house is not in existence. It was probably situated several rods north of the present "Old Mayhew House." He married Mary, daughter of James Skiff of Sandwich in 1674, and she died in 1690, aged forty years. He died May 19, 1710, aged about sixty-two years, leaving four surviving children.

ANDREW NEWCOMB.

This settler came to Edgartown about 1676, from the Isles of Shoals and Kittery, Maine, where he had resided for about ten years previously.[1] He was born in 1640, and probably was the son of Captain Andrew Newcomb of Boston, a resident of that town at least as early as 1663 until his death in 1686.[2] Our Andrew brought with him to Edgartown six children by his first wife Sarah, who may have deceased prior to his coming, as he married shortly after, Anna, daughter of Captain Thomas Bayes. He bought a ten-acre lot of land, Feb. 13, 1676-7, of John Daggett, and a half share of commonage formerly granted to John Freeman.[3] The death of his father-in-law, early in 1680, made him an heir to the Bayes lot on Main street, of which in right of his wife, he acquired the northern half and there made his home.

[1]Newcomb Genealogy; Comp., York Deeds, II, 162, which shows that he was a fisherman of Kittery in 1669.

[2]Boston Town Records. Captain Andrew Newcomb married in 1663, for a second wife, Mrs. Grace Rix, widow of William, by whom he had Grace, born Oct. 20, 1664. This daughter m. (1) James Butler, 1682, and (2) Andrew Rankin of York, Maine, Oct. 15, 1692, brother of Mary Rankin, the wife of Paine Mayhew of Chilmark. Captain Newcomb made his will Jan. 31, 1682-3, which was probated Dec. 8, 1686.

[3]Dukes Deeds, I, 37.

His other principal holding was Job's Neck. He became one of the prominent citizens of the town, both in civil and military affairs. He served as juror, 1677, 1680, 1681, 1700, 1703, 1704; constable, 1681; tithingman, 1693; selectman, 1693, 1694; lieutenant of the militia, 1691; and was in command of the province fortification that year by commission from the Duke's government.[1] When the Massachusetts charter of 1692 took in the Vineyard, he was proposed for the new chief justice, but the Mayhew influences were against him and he was not appointed. He died between Aug. 20, 1706, and Oct. 22, 1708, leaving a widow and nine additional children. The sons removed to Connecticut and the Cape and the family was extinct here before the close of the 19th century.

NICHOLAS NORTON.

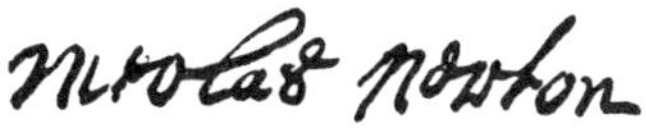

The ancestor of the numerous family of this name on the Vineyard was born about 1610,[2] probably in England, although the place of his nativity is not known.[3] It will probably be found upon investigation that he emigrated from Somersetshire, and perhaps came from the vicinity of Batcombe or Broadway in that county, and there is some reason for inferring that he was one of the party of colonists accompanying the Rev. John Hull in 1635 to New England.[4] He first appears at Weymouth, Mass., in 1637, where he married his wife Elizabeth, and in which place he maintained a residence for twenty years prior to his removal to the Vineyard.

That he was of a social station somewhat above the average appears from the fact that he kept a servant, whose "miscariages" brought the subject of this sketch into trouble in 1658 with the magistrates of Massachusetts. The following

[1]N. Y. Col. Mss., XXXVII, 230; Edgartown Records, I, 33, 37, 39, and Dukes Court Records, Vol. I. In 1688 he was indicted for taking the life of his son Andrew but the jury found no bill It was an accidental death.

[2]He testified that he was aged sixty-six years in 1676. (Dukes County Court Records, Vol. I.)

[3]There is a will of Robert Norton of Wells, Somersetshire, dated Sept. 29, 1590, who mentions his nephew Nicholas. (17, St. Barbe.) This is too early for our settler, but may be a clue to the family.

[4]Rev. Mr. Hull brought twenty families from the vicinity of Batcombe and Broadway, and in 1639 Nicholas Norton had some business dealings with one Standerwyck, a clothier of Broadway in the County of Somerset. In 1640 he had a suit at law with Parson Hull.

petition explains the case as related by Nicholas Norton himself to the General Court: —

To the Honord Genll Court now assembled the Petition of Nicholas Norton humbly Sheweth:
That whereas yor poore peti'or stood engaged to the Treasurer in the sume of five pounds to bring in his servant to a County Court held at Boston to give answer for sume miscariages Comitted, which accordingly he did, at which Court yor poore peti'ors servant was also pr'sented by the grand-Jury either for the same or for some other offences, the Court was then pleased, to deferre the Issue of the Case, & to require the Coutynuatio of the sd bond of yor poore peti'or, where upon he did agayne engage himselfe in the foresd sume to bring in his sd servant to the last Court of assistants, but in regard he was under a pr'sentment, expected to have him sent for by warrent & that wittnesses should also have bin sent for to prove the same as is usueall in case of pr'sentments, where upon yor poore peti'r, through Ignorance of the manner of Courts p'ceedinges in such Cases hath forfeited his foresd bond.
Now although yor peti'r cannot blame any but himselfe, yet is bold to Crave the favour of this Honrd Court, that the forfeiture may not be required of yor poore peti'r, but thort you would be pleased (out of yr woonted tendernes in offences which p'ceed meerely out of Ignorance, to remitt the same or so much of it as in yr wisdome you shall thinke meet, hopeing you will the rather be moved hereunto considering the great loss yor poore peti'r hath sustayned in the service of the Country in Collecting of the Country rate which he hopes is yet in yor mynds, & that the delinquent is ready when required suffer the Just sentence of the Court according to the merritt of his offences, which if the Lord move yr harts to grannt it will abundantly engage yr poore pet'r ever to pray.[1]

The Court granted his petition providing he should bring his servant to bar.

Of his life in Weymouth but little is worthy of mention. He shared in the division of lands in 1651, and was constable in 1657, an office of some distinction in those times. Two years later he was still called "of Weymouth," and in the same year his name first appears in the records of Edgartown. This may be taken as the probable date of his removal to the Vineyard. He was chosen a referee to represent the town in its controversy with John Daggett respecting his farm at Oak Bluffs.

On Aug. 22, 1659, "Goodman" Norton was granted "a Lott of forty acres of Land" and on the same day it was "ordered by the town that Goodman Norton shall have Liberty to make use of any Pond about the Ox Pond for his Trade, except the Great Ponds." It does not appear what

[1]Mass. Archives, XXXIX, 39.

trade Nicholas Norton followed, but the use of ponds suggests that he may have been a tanner. Before the end of that year, he was engaged in two lawsuits as a plaintiff and a defendant. He was sued by Henry Goss in that year and was mulcted in the sum of five shillings "for charges about the cure of Mr. Gousse's child: to pay one half in Wampam current and halfe in corne and five shillings to the constable for the Tryall about the abuse of Mr. Gousse's child." The exact nature of this suit at law is not clear from the records. In that same year he sued the Rev. Mr. Cotton, missionary to the Indians. In 1661 he was one of a committee to buy land of the Indians for the use of the town. In 1662–63 and 1669, he again appears in litigation with various townsmen, and if not a pattern in this respect, his fence was deemed the pattern and lawful standard to which others were required to conform in the maintenance of boundary fences in the town.[1] In 1666 he was forbidden by the proprietors of the fish weir from taking any fish at Mattakeesett Creek, the right to which he claimed by purchase from the sachem Tewanticut, "contrary to our patent," upon a penalty of £5 yearly so often as he disobeys the order.[2] In 1673 he joined in the "Dutch Rebellion" with others of his townsmen, and when it had collapsed he was tried and convicted. The following is the record in the case.:—

> Whereas Nicolas Norton upon Commission from the Right honorable Sr Edmond Andros Knight Governor of New York &c hath beene before the Court legally convicted of oppugning the Government established here under his Majestie wherein he acknowledgeth that he is ashamed and Sorry in his heart that he was Misled therein and hopes he shall be more careful for the future: The Court by virtue of the said Commission do adjudge the said Nicolas Norton to make a publique acknowledgment of the same at this Court and at the next quarterly Court holden at Marthas Vineyard: or to pay the summe of fifty one pounds as a fine to the Country.[3]

In 1685 he was one of a committee "chosen to make the Govenors Rate" and this is his last appearance on the town records before his death.[4]

There is no consolidated record of his real estate holdings such as was entered by others proprietors. He lived on his

[1]Edgartown Records, I, 111, 138.
[2]Ibid., I, 144.
[3]Dukes County Deeds, I, 65.
[4]Edgartown Records, I, 39.

forty-acre grant situated north of the Great Swamp and south of the present road to West Tisbury. He was an early owner of land at Sanchacantackett in the vicinity of Major's Cove, where his descendants for two centuries resided and improved that beautiful estate. These purchases were made of the Indians Wampamag or "Sam" and Thomas Sisseton, both of which are unrecorded, though it is said that the original deed from "Sam" was in existence in recent years in the hands of a descendant. It is not believed that he ever resided on this property. He also held the usual proprietor's shares in the various divisions of town lands, besides a plot of meadow land at Aquampache. At the ripe age of four score years Nicholas Norton died, leaving four sons and six daughters, at least two of whom were born in Weymouth. Following is a copy of his will dated April 17, 1690:—

[Court Records, Vol. I, 1690.]

The last will and testament of me Nicolas Norton Being very weak in body but of perfect understanding and Souend memory After my death and desent Christian burial: I give and bequest my worly good as foloeth:—

Iprimes: I give my Son Izak Norton on half Comminig as also fouer Small Shares of medow

Secondly I give my Son Benjamin Norton all my medow at Saniacantick as also my medow at Morthals neck beach from the Crick dug into the Great pond westward as also my now dwelling houes and all my land aioyning to my Sayd houes after the deces of my wife Elizabeth Norton as also my lots at quompasha with all my devided land Elsewhere: provided my Sayd Son Beniamin deliver up his now dweling houes to my now wife Elizabeth Norton with the land aioyning to the Sayd houes: to be at my Sayd wifes sole will and pleseuer to dispose of at or before her desese. as also all that medow I have from a Creek to Izak Norton Medow

thirdly. I give Moses Cleveland the Remaynder of the Sayd medow to joyne with Weeks medow also on halfe Commonidg with all prevleges belonging there untoo

fourthly I give my Son in law Thomas Wolling on halfe Commonidg with all prevelidges belonging to it with a pese of medow from Izak Norton's medow to the Creeke abofe named.

fifthly I give my Son Joseph Norton a tract of land lying at Saniacantacket joyning to the mill Creke which I bought of Mr Sam.

Sixtly I give that whole Commonidg which was Arys to my aforeSayd Son Beniamin Norton

Seventhly I give to Elizabeth Norton my wife all my Catle Coues oxen Steeres & Sheepe also all my hors kind & furder I give my Sayd wife Elizabeth Norton all my houeshold goods Beding pewter bras Iron tin wood wood as Chests trunks tables Chayers and all other things not named, also all plowes Carts Chayns yoks and all other utensells with all lumber: furder I leve my Sayd wife to give my dafter pese and my dafter wil (Wollong or Williams) and my dafter Stanbridg & my dafter Butler Something to Every one of them as much as shee sese cause: as also my dafter huxford to her my wife knows my mind

Eithly. my medow at the neck Caueled the Manado I leve to my wife Elizabeth Norton

Ninthly I doe apoynt my Sayd wife Elizabeth Norton to be my Sole Execitor and to performe my will as abof whritin.

The mark of N Nicklis
Norton

Witness
Richard Sarson
Joseph Norton.

His widow did not long survive to carry out the provisions of her husband's will. She died a few monthes after him, between June 8, the date of her will, and Oct. 8, 1690, when it was proven in Court. The following is a copy of her will:—

[Court Records, Vol. I, 1690.]

Edgartown in Marthas Vineyard June 8, 1690

The Last will and testament of me Elizabeth Norton widow I doe give to my fouer dafters named in my husbons will, five Shillins to Each of them.

I give that houes & land to Ester huxford that my Son benjamin Norton lives in and to be delevered before his Entering into mine I dwell in acording to my Said husbons will & mind he left with me to performe & I give my Sd dafter Ester huxford that pese of medow laying between Izak Nortons meadow and the medow of Moses Cleveland nere Mortols Neck. Then my will is after my death Christian buryall & funerall Rights be performed

first I give that pese or parsoll of medow laying at a place Caueled Manadoo to my Son Joseph Norton

Secondly I give to all and Every on of my gran-Children on Shillin in money to Every one of them and to be payd wthin ten days after my buriall

thirdly I give all my lands houeses medows fences Commons Cattle Sheep horses and horskind & monys with all my household goods as beding & bed furnyture with all my Chests trunks tables Chayers with all my pewter bras Iron and tin vesels with all my plews Carts Chayns yoks wedges Siths with all other things and goods that is mine to all my Sons and dafters to be Equally devided amongst them to Every on alick Equall portion and sher

fourthly I doe apoynt my Son Joseph Norton to be Execitor to this my will to pay all my depts and delever out all my legasys treuly and faythfullv acording this my mind and will.

fifthly I doe Request Richard Sarson to be overser to see this my will performed soe far as he is able: and in witnes to this my will I have put too my hand and Sele the day and yere abof whritin

Sixtly I doe Request my beloved son Izak Norton to be overser with Richard Sarson to this my will

mark
Witness here untoo The U Elizabeth Norton.
mark of
The X Johnnathan danham

gershom donham

This abof mentioned will be profed in Coart is Exepted
Court held Octobr the Eight: 1690
pr Curiam Tho Butler Clarke

Whereas by the last will and testament of Elizabeth Norton is mentioned as bequeathed to hester huxford an hous and land according to the will of Nicolas Norton left with his wife sd Elizabeth Isaac Norton

The maiden name of his wife is not known. He married her probably in Weymouth, and she must be sought for in that locality. Their descendants have constituted one of the largest families on the island from the earliest times.[1]

THOMAS PAINE.

Tho paine

This young man was the step-son of Thomas Mayhew, Senior, and was brought to the Vineyard as a boy when about fourteen. He was born Feb. 8, 1632, the son of Thomas and Jane [Gallion?] Paine of London. His father was a London merchant, who died after May, 1631, and before July, 1635, by which latter date the widow had become the second wife of the elder Mayhew.[2] Thomas Paine, the father, must have been a well-to-do business man, as he owned property outside of London, in Whittlebury, Northamptonshire, and Greensnorton, same county, which descended to the son. The latter estates were declared to be worth £140 per annum, a goodly sum in those days.[3] It was this property in part, which led the Rev. Thomas Mayhew to go to England with his brother-in-law Paine, on

[1]A century ago there were thirty-three separate families bearing this name on the Vineyard, the second largest numerically at that time.

[2]Savage states that Mayhew married the widow Paine in London. (Gen. Dictionary, III, 337.)

[3]The wife of Sir William Bradshaw had an interest in the Greensnorton property, but though Sir William "challenged some interest during his Ladyes life, yett none to the Inheritance." Mrs. Jane Mayhew went to England in 1642, "to settle her sons Rights." (Records, Commissioners of the United Colonies, II, 165; comp., Lechford Note Book, 117; Aspinwall, Notarial Record, 14, 35, 111, and Suffolk Deeds, I, 86.)

the fatal voyage, when both were lost. Young Paine became of age in 1652, and his name appears in the first division of common land in town the next year. His patrimony had evidently been invested by his parents in the purchase of land on the island, as he owned the largest number of rights in Great Harbor (three) of all the early settlers. He took no part in the public affairs of the town or island, in spite of his relationship to the proprietors, and beyond the records of his property holdings nothing about him remains to be said. He sailed for England in November, 1657, with his brother-in-law, Rev. Thomas Mayhew, and as before detailed, the ship was never heard from. He owned the home lot bounded northerly by Main street, but it is not known that he ever married, or lived on it.

JOHN PEASE.

John Pease

The relations which this pioneer bears to the legendary and actual history of Edgartown has made it necessary for the author to institute researches in the English Archives and bestow an equal amount of careful investigation of the records in New England, to establish the identity of John Pease of Great Baddow, County of Essex, England, and John Pease of Salem, County of Essex, Massachusetts. These researches have a definite bearing upon the alleged settlement of John Pease and some companions upon our island in 1632, or thereabouts, which is elsewhere discussed; and as part of the collateral evidence in this mooted question, the results of these searches must have a detailed exposition for the better understanding of the case. In no other instance has so much time and labor been spent.

In Great Baddow, as early as 1540, and doubtless a much earlier period, there lived a numerous family of the name of Pease, as evidenced by the frequent occurrence of the name in the parish registers of that place. In the entries of baptisms, marriages, and burials, this name occurs eighty-four times between 1540 and 1654, the earliest one recording the death of a daughter of Robert Pease "the Smythe." It will only concern us to consider the branch from which our John descends, and this line begins with John[2] Pease the clothier, who was the son of John[1] "the Smythe," of the same parish.

He married Margaret, daughter of Richard Hyckes, June 23, 1560, and had two children, of record, namely Robert[3] and a daughter Mary, who married Benjamin Carter in 1586. John the clothier died in November, 1612, and Margaret, his wife, deceased in the previous month.

Robert[3] Pease probably lived and certainly died in Great Baddow, where he was buried April 16, 1623, leaving a widow Margaret and several children. The following is a record of his children as taken from the parish registers. His marriage

STREET IN GREAT BADDOW, ENGLAND.

is not entered, and it is to be inferred that his wife was a resident of some adjoining parish: —

- i [daughter] bapt. Dec. 10, 1587.
- ii [son–Robert?] bapt. Oct. 28, 1589.
- iii William[4], bapt. Sept. 26, 1591.
- iv John[4], bapt. May 24, 1593, d. 1600.
- v Mary[4], bapt. Jan. 10, 1600.
- vi Elizabeth[4], bapt. Sept., 1602; m. Abraham Page.
- vii Richard[4], bapt. 4 and d. 5 April, 1607.
- viii. JOHN[4], bapt. Nov. 20, 1608.

Robert[3], the father, made his will May 10, 1613, and it was proven June 12, 1623, two months after his death. In this testament he names his wife Margaret, sons Robert[4] and John[4], daughter Elizabeth[4], and her husband Abraham Page. The widow Margaret and her family continued to reside in Great Baddow for ten years after the death of her husband. Robert[4], the elder son, had married a wife named Lydia, and two children of theirs are recorded as baptized at Great Baddow, viz:. Robert[5], April, 1630, and John[5], Feb. 11, 1631–2, both of whom will be referred to later.

The next we learn of the two brothers, Robert[4] and John[4] Pease, is when they embarked in the ship *Francis*, which sailed in November, 1634, from Ipswich, a seaport town not far from Baddow. Their names are entered as follows: John Pease, twenty-seven years; Robert Pease, twenty-seven years (doubtless an error for forty-seven, as he was about twenty years older than his brother John) and Robert Pease, aged three years, the child whose baptism we have just noted. The widow Margaret remained in Great Baddow for some time, as her name appears as witness to a bond given in August, 1636, by William Vincent of Bromfield (a Parish adjoining Great Baddow), to be paid to Abraham Page when he should come of age. This minor was a grandson of the widow Margaret, the child of Abraham Page and Elizabeth Pease, whose marriage we have stated. (The young boy was then an orphan, his father having died in 1628.) It will thus be seen that the widow Margaret and her grandson, Abraham Page, were the only ones, in all probability, left of a numerous family in this little English Parish; and we shall later hear of them both following her emigrant sons to the new world.

The ship *Francis* arrived in New England late in 1634, and landed her passengers at Boston. Where the two brothers, Robert[4] and John[4], first took up their residence is not known, but early in 1637, they were at Salem, when the land of "Robert Pease and his brother" is mentioned in the early records of that town. The considerable difference in the ages explains this form of entry in the town books. On Jan. 2, 1636–7, Robert Pease was granted ten acres, and John Pease twenty acres of land. On the 23d of April, 1638, the town granted John Pease "five acres of land next adjoining to Samuell Cominge neer unto the watermill."[1] John was concerned in a maritime transaction in October, 1638, for which he was wanted as a witness in August, 1639;[2] but he was absent from his place of abode as appears by the following record: —

[1]Salem Town Records.

[2]Lechford, Notebook, 103.

25: 4 mo: 1639:

It is ordered that wheras Mr Gervas Garford had a Cowe of John Pease for hire for a year, the tyme now being expired, and the said John Pease not returned whereupon the sd Mr Gervas requested advice from this Court wt to doe with hir: upon which the Court ordered him to keepe the Cowe untill the *p*tie shall returne upon the same tearmes he kept hir before.[1]

He may have been on a voyage to England to bring back his aged mother, as she appears for the first time in New England in that year (1639), when she was admitted a member of the church in Salem. She lived but a few years in her new home, and we may bring consideration of her to a close, in so far as her record has any bearing upon the person immediately concerned in our researches. She died in 1644 and her will, dated September 1 of that year, mentions only her grandchildren, Robert and John, the fatherless sons of her deceased son Robert. Of the elder brother Robert[4] we shall have but brief concern. He joined the Church in 1643, and on October 15 of that year three of his children were baptized. He died before his mother, the next year, as on Nov. 3, 1644, an inventory of the estate of Robert Pease of Salem, late deceased, was taken, and the widow Marie Pease appointed administratrix 3: 11 mo: 1644. Robert[5] Pease was named as the eldest son of the deceased, and John[5] Pease the second son. There were other young children by this second marriage.[1]

Thus of the Great Baddow family there were left John[4] and his nephew Robert[5], who had come over with him in the *Francis* ten years previously. The further history of these two persons is all that will now engage our attention, as both became residents of the Vineyard, the first named being the progenitor of our island family, and the latter a temporary sojourner where his uncle had previously settled. At this date (1644) John[4] Pease was thirty-six, and Robert[5] fourteen years of age. By order of the Court young Robert remained with his mother for a year, at the end of which time he applied for permission to learn a trade. In 1645 he was thereupon bound as an apprentice to Thomas Root of Salem, weaver, for the term of five years, to learn the art of linen and woolen weaving. This fact is of significance as will be shown later.

We can now return to follow uninterruptedly the further history of John Pease of Great Baddow and Salem, stopping

[1]Records, Quarterly Court, Vol. I.

[2]Files, Essex Court Records.

only to refer to a collateral incident occurring in this year (1645), which has a circumstantial relation to the subject. Abraham Page, the son of his sister Elizabeth[4], before referred to, emigrated to Boston.[1] The last reference to John Pease was under date of 1639, and related to his absence from Salem. The next recorded entry concerning him is under date of January 25, 1641–2, when Elias Stileman, Sr., appears as plaintiff in a civil suit against him, and again under date of Dec. 26, 1643, he appears as plaintiff in a civil suit against Thomas Trusler.[2] These suits indicate dealings in maritime business, and doubtless he was engaged in coastwise trading, which may account for the infrequent references to him, owing to absences on voyages. On June 18, 1644, John Pease sold to Richard Ingersoll of Salem "one house & 75 acres of Land adjoyning to the fearme whereon the said Richard dwelleth,"[3] and thenceforth his name disappears completely from the Essex County and the town records of Salem. The next appearance of his name occurs in the records of Edgartown two years later, under date of March 23, 1646–7, when he sold ten acres of land at Mattakeeset to Mr. John Bland, and we may safely conclude that following the disposal of this Salem land in 1644, he came hither with his family to settle. His eldest son James was born March 15, 1637, and this presupposes his marriage in Salem or elsewhere, and the bringing of a wife and young children to take up their life work in the island home. The identity of this wife is fully established, in the opinion of the author, but this is a view which contravenes the conclusions to be found in the published genealogical accounts of the early Peases in Salem.[4] A court record dated Nov. 3, 1635, contains the following statement: —

> Ordered that John Pease shalbe whipt & bound to his good behaviour for strikeing his mother [in law] Mrs Weston & deryding of her & for dyvers other misdemeanors & other evill carriages.[5]

[1]Savage, III, 330.

[2]Essex County Court Records.

[3]Suffolk Deeds, I, 53. This was "the one moytye of the fearme wch the towne of Salem graunted unto Frances Weston," and was probably held by Pease at this date.

[4]There are two genealogies of the Pease families. The first was compiled by Frederic S. Pease and printed in 1847, and this author adopts the legend of the landing of John Pease on the Vineyard in 1632. The second was prepared by Austin Spencer Pease and published in 1869, and is an enlarged and more critical work. This author discards the legend as improbable and advances many arguments to show the fallacy of it.

[5]Mass. Col. Rec., I, 155.

The compiler of the Pease genealogy, without any evidence cited or reason given, states that this particular John Pease was another one of the name residing in the same town. There is not a scintilla of proof that two of this name resided there 1635–1644, and the Salem records make no mention of a "Senior" or "Junior" John, which was absolutely necessary and customary for distinguishing persons bearing the same name involved in land grants or legal proceedings. Otherwise there would be inextricable confusion of titles to property. It is therefore certain that our John Pease married Lucy, daughter of Mrs. Margaret Weston, wife of Francis Weston of Salem, a fact which is of interest because of its collateral bearing on our subject. Weston was an early settler at Salem, originally a friend and supporter of Roger Williams, whom he followed in exile to Rhode Island. He was unfortunate, however, in his second marriage, as Mrs. Margaret Weston was afflicted with one of the religious whimsies of the period, and incurred the opposition of the authorities, not then famed for charity and tolerance, and she was made to sit in the bilboes for her schismatic "notions."[1] The particular doctrines she imbibed were those promulgated by Samuel Gorton, for which he and others suffered persecution and were driven from Salem to seek an asylum in Rhode Island. The nature of these doctrines is imperfectly understood now, as they were a part of the abstruse hair-splitting theological controversies of that period. Sufficient to say they were regarded as heretical by ecclesiastical authorities, and that was enough to condemn those who subscribed to them. In a few years Weston himself became a disciple of Gorton, and his step-daughter, Lucy Pease, likewise joined the sect, all of which was doubtless to the disadvantage of John Pease, socially and commercially, in orthodox Salem. In addition to this Mrs. Weston was undoubtedly unbalanced mentally, and later became of hopelessly unsound mind.[2] We are thus enabled to see the environment of John Pease, and considering the stress of the times and the religious intolerance of the period may not harshly judge his unlawful chastisement of his mother-in-law. Doubtless she deserved forcible repression, and invited it by her actions. Weston was banished in March, 1638, from the jurisdiction of Massa-

[1]Felt, Ecclesiastical Annals, I, 341.

[2]She died in 1651 in Rhode Island.

chusetts for promulgating the tabooed Gortonian doctrines, and took up his residence at Shawomet, Rhode Island, whence he continued to spread them by whatever means he could employ. The magistrates of the Massachusetts colony tolerated this defiance for five years, and then determined to silence him, by forcible measures if necessary, and place him under arrest for teaching heretical doctrines. John Pease heard of this in the fall of 1643 at Salem, and undertook to give his wife's father a warning of the approaching danger. The following account of this affair, written by Samuel Gorton himself, discloses John Pease in a highly favorable light considering all the circumstances. A letter dated Shawomet, Sept. 26, 1643, signed by Gorton and others of his sectaries, addressed to the military emissaries of Massachusetts, was sent by the hand "of one John Peise *who lived amongst them in the Massachusetts*, who having a father-in-law amongst us was willing to come and declare unto his father, out of the tenderness towards him, of the nearness of the soldiers approach, and as near as he could the end of their coming, to persuade his said father to escape for his life."[1] From this letter we glean the most convincing fact about John Pease which bears so conclusively upon his alleged settlement on this island before the coming of the Mayhews. Manifestly, he could not have been a prior settler here because as late as September, 1643, he "lived amongst them in the Massachusetts."

This expedition resulted in the seizure and return of Weston as a prisoner to Boston, where he suffered incarceration with hard labor in the Dorchester jail.[2] Doubtless this caused the wife of John Pease to consider her own safety, and shortly after her husband's return from the mission above related, she recanted her heretical views, as appears by the following records: —

> Luc(i)e Pease the wife of . . . . . Pease, p'fessing that she doth abhor & renounce Gortons opinions & confessing her fault in bloting out some things in the booke wch she brought & in showing the same before shee delivered it & p'fessing shee was sorry for it, shee was dismissed for the p'sent to appear when she shall bee called for.[3] [17 October 1643.]

[1]Simplicities Defence, London, 1647. The italics are used by the author to emphasize this important statement about John Pease. This letter was delivered to the Massachusetts Commissioners, who answered it, addressing their reply "To our friend John Peise."

[2]He died in prison before June, 1645, after a confinement of two years.

[3]Mass. Col. Records, II, 50; comp., Felt, Ecclesiastical History, I, 492.

From these facts and resulting conditions we are now able to explain why John Pease left Salem to seek a home elsewhere outside the jurisdiction of Massachusetts. The religious atmosphere was too threatening and his wife would be constantly menaced with the fear of arrest, being held under bonds by the court for the future determination of her case. Consequently, he sold his property and that of his father-in-law in the summer of 1644, and left Salem forever.

The removal of John Pease from Salem about 1644, following the arrest of his wife, the death of his mother and elder brother, is a natural effect of causes easily understood, and the appearance of a John Pease on Martha's Vineyard immediately thereafter are consecutive facts too significant to be mistaken for mere coincidences. They might be classed as such but for a further confirmation of these evidences of identity afforded us in connection with the subsequent history of Robert[5], nephew of John of Great Baddow and Salem. It will be remembered that this young lad had been apprenticed to a weaver to learn that trade. His term of service expired in 1650, and records of his residence in Salem are extant, showing that in 1652 and 1655 he was an inhabitant of that town. The next year a Robert Pease appears in Edgartown; and if anything were waiting to establish the relationship between him and the John Pease already a resident here, the following entry from the town records will furnish it: —

[[1]Edgartown Town Records, i, 138.]

February 1, 1656.

Richard Sarson will give Robert Pease 100 and half of fish every year so long as he liveth upon the Island and the same will be given him by John Burchard, Edward Lay, William Weekes, Thomas Burchard and Thomas Bays, "if the said Robert Pease doth Ingage to weave the Cloth of the town for such pay as the town can raise among them selves, except wampam."

What more natural thing could occur than this? The new settlement needed a weaver, and John Pease made it known to his nephew in Salem, and he forthwith came to continue his fortunes with an uncle whom he had accompanied from England as a boy and with whom he had been associated much of his life. Robert Pease remained here several years, but had removed before 1660. The connection between the Salem and Vineyard Peases thus seems to be established, and family tradition is not wanting, if it were needed, to substantiate this. The late Captain Valentine Pease, an aged man in 1849, stated that he had heard his father and grandfather speak of James[5] and John[5], the two eldest sons of John[4] as having lived in Salem or having come from that place. This is undoubtedly true, as these two boys must have been born in Salem, the only children (surviving at least) by his first wife.[1] Accordingly, the demonstration of the identity of John of Great Baddow, Salem, Mass., and Martha's Vineyard is left at this point for the impartial judgment of the historical student. It is a clear trail.

On March 23, 1646, John Pease sold to John Bland "a Parcell of Land about Ten acres and Two acres of Meadow" at Mattakeeset.[2] The circumstances surrounding this sale can only be surmised; whether it comprised all his property or a part of it, but the records afford us no further insight. It is probable that the former is most likely and that he left the island for Connecticut after this sale. He is next found at New London, in 1650, in connection with business matters, in which Governor John Winthrop of that colony was interested, but the historian of that town confesses that "of John Pease little is known."[3] It will be remembered that about 1645 to 1650 the new settlements at Saybrook, New London, and New Haven were being founded and were attracting hundreds from the old towns in Massachusetts and probably our John Pease was prospecting and trying his fortune on the main land. Whether at this time or later, it is known that he acquired land at Mohegan, in the town of Norwich, Conn., and on it he probably established his second son, John, Jr., and it appears that he retained it until his death, bequeathing it to this son, "with that frame of a house I set up upon some part of that land,"[4] But the island proved to be more attractive to the father, and he returned here before March 5,

[1]In another branch of the family residing here in the latter part of the 18th century, a son was christened Robert, a distinctive name in the Salem branch, in honor of a great uncle who belonged to the Salem Peases.

[2]Edgartown Records, II, 125. This is the earliest record in the town books.

[3]Caulkins, "History of Norwich," 109. This author also wrote the "History of New London," and confounds John senior and John his son, who was a settler at Norwich, on the lot granted to the father in 1659. John junior was his second son, and probably not of age.

[4]There was a land grant in November, 1659, to John Pease of seven acres on a branch of the Yantic River, now called Pease's Brook, west of Norwich, now a settlement called Bozrahville. (History of Norwich, 193.) Whether this was to John, Sr., or John, Jr., depends on the age of the latter. James, the oldert son, was b. March 15, 1637, and unless John was born by November, 1638, he would not have been able to hold property then.

1653, when he was engaged in a suit about some land with Edward Sales, of which all we know is contained in the following record: —

> The town hath ended the case between John Pease and Edward Sales thus: that the sd John Pease is to enjoy that commonage that was first given Edward Sales and the said Edward Sales hath his old right of fish still.[1]

From this and other fragmentary references it seems certain that Pease bought his property on the Vineyard of Edward Sales, whether at his first coming or on his return from Connecticut cannot be determined in the absence of any existing records.[2]

On Nov. 7, 1653, he was elected constable, the only office he is known to have held in the town. In 1658 he was one of the appraisers of the estate of John Butler, and on Feb. 15, 1659, made a deposition concerning Thomas Mayhew's "Land at home which is in controversy." At the quarterly court in September of that same year, he was sued by Richard Raines, probably a coastwise trader, and the verdict of the court was that "John Pease shall pay the Court charge and sixty weight of leafe tobacco to the Plaintiff."[3] In 1662 he had further legal trouble with Edward Sales who sued him, an outcome of their previous differences. He was a member of the train band this year. On Oct. 3, 1662, the town selected him to represent the proprietors at the Plymouth County Court, "to answare the suite of John Doged comenced against the said towne," involving title to certain granted lands.[4] In 1665 his testimony was given and is of record concerning the nuncupative will of John Folger. The following seven years contain no further references to him until 1673, when he with nineteen others of the leading residents of the Vineyard, outside of the Mayhew party, signed the celebrated appeal to Massachusetts for annexation, and joined in the "Dutch Rebellion" of that and the following year. He was one of the first to be attacked in reprisal, five days after the petition was dated. The following is the record in the case: —

[1]Edgartown Records, I, 149.

[2]Ibid., I, 120. "John Pease defendant: Lawfully bought of Edward Searles his . . . . and all his meadow & upland."

[3]Ibid., I, 140.

[4]Plymouth Colony Records, IV, 27.

John peas Being By the Govournour By his officer warned to appear to answer his misdemeanour for committing a Riott at Edgartown the Marshall Returneth answer that the warrant was by the said peas his wife taken from him and therefore he cannot Return his warrant: the said peas appearing Before the Govournour is Both person and estate Bound to answer at the next sessions of Triall held uppon the Duke his highness province and Territories for the said Riott committed and his wife for forcibly taking the warrant out of the marshalls hands.[1]

These are the only references to John Pease in the town and county records, except casual mentions not important enough for citation, with the usual drawing of lots at the regular divisions. In this connection it may be stated that he was the proprietor of one full share in the "Five and Twenty" and as such participated in every recorded division from 1653 to 1676 in the same equality with others.[2]

The following list of his property, certified to by Thomas Trapp, town clerk, shows the extent of his real estate: —

The records of the lands of John Pease the elder:

Imprimis: one house and house lot of ten acres of upland and 2 acres of meadow lying at the northermost end of the town Great Harbour, with a Cove of water on the north of the meadow and east of the harbour, the west with the land of Joseph Codman and on the South and Southeast the commons and main Island.

2d. — A dividend lying from beyond the plain containing twenty five acres more or less, called Mashakett, in the Cove of the Neck, bounded on the main pond on the South and southwest and the Pond on the south-east: the land of Thomas Daggett on the northeast: Richard Sarsons land on the west and northwest.

3d. — A little neck of land containing five acres of land, more or less, lying towards Sanchacontackett, bounded with the Salt Pond west, south and east: and with the meadow and beach on the north.

4th. — A lot of land upon Chapequideck Neck lying upon the higher land there, from water to water, cross the Neck: the harbour bounding it upon the north and on the south; the land of John Smith on the west, and William Weeks' lot on the east.

5th. — A small parcell of meadow (at) Sangacontacett in the last division there.

6th. — A share at Mechems Field, being 21st lot bounded by Robert Codman on the east and James Pease on the west.[3]

It is believed from all obtainable evidence that John Pease lived at first at Mattakeset and later, when the home lots were laid out, he drew the first one of the Five and Twenty,

[1]Dukes Deeds, I, 403. Nothing of later record shows that he suffered further in person or estate for his part in the trouble.

[2]Edgartown Records, I, 21, 109, 156, 172.

[3]From an unrecorded document furnished to the author by Miss Harriet Marshall Pease. It came from the papers of the late Jeremiah Pease, Esq.

situated at north end of town at the place ever since known as Pease's Point. It consisted of ten acres, and by inheritance and acquisition from other heirs it came into the possession of his son Thomas, who sold it in 1692 to Mrs. Hannah (Mayhew) Daggett.[1]

John Pease was twice married. It is clear that the two eldest sons — James of Edgartown and John of Monhegan (Norwich) Conn., — were issues of Lucy, the first wife, and perhaps there was a daughter or daughters. When she died is not known, nor where she is buried. His second wife bore the Christian name of Marie or Mary, and was married to him as early as 1656.[2] She was probably much younger than her husband, and calculations based on the birth of her children would place her own birth at about 1630. There is a family tradition that her maiden name was Browning, and presumably daughter of Malachi Browning of this town.[3]

It is not known when John Pease died. The last mention of him in the record is on Sept. 25, 1677, when he served as a juror,[4] at which time he was seventy years old and had already executed his last will and testament. This document is as follows: —

[Dukes Deeds, I, 340.]

March the 4th. 1674. The last willand testament of me, John Peas, husbandman and inhabitant uppon Martins Vineyard in the Town called Edgartown, I John Peas having upon good consideration and being now in some measure in good health and perfect understanding and memory though I am striken in years and Crasy in respect of what formerly; I having had two wives one formerly deceased and by her have yet two sons surviving, James Peas, & John Peas and these two sonnes James the Elder, God hath been pleased to bless him in his labours & indeavours and I have been helpfull to him so that he is verrywell to pass in his Estate farre beyond myself : I do therefore in this my last will and testament give to my Eldest Son James Peas twelve pence; My second son John Peas I have alreddy given unto and do hereby give unto him all that was given unto me at Mohegin, with that frame of a house I set up uppon some part of that land; I say I give it unto my son John Peas & his heirs forever: I having by my now living wife Mary Peas, four sonnes & four Daughters, my Sonnes Thomas Peas Jonathan, Samuell, and David and my Daughters

[1]Dukes Deeds, I, 104.

[2]Thomas Pease, the first born son of this second marriage, was born in 1657, but he may not have been the oldest child.

[3]From information furnished by Miss Harriet Marshall Pease taken from her father's papers. The note made by him states: "Red coat John's 2d wife was —— Browning daughter of —— Browning," and cites as authority Peter Pease (b., 1765), who derived it from a conversation with John Coffin (b. 1710) living contemporary with Thomas Pease (b. 1657).

[4]Dukes Court Records, Vol. I.

Abygaill Peas, Mary, Rebecca, and Sarah Peas unto these my four Sonnes and four Daughters I doe give all my landes and houseing that I have upon this Iland Martins Vineyard to be either equally devided or valued or sold or exchanged and the price thereof Equally devided to everyone of them alike and this to be performed at convenient age of them: or as my now living wife Mary shall see meet whome I make my full and whole Executrix to performe all this my last will and testament; and I give unto Mary Peas my wife all my cattle of every sort with all my household goodes whatsoever I have more or less for her use and comfort and helpfulness in bringing up my children at her disposing for Ever.
In witness hereunto my hand and seal.

John Peas.

Further I give and bequeath unto
my second son John Peas twelve pence.
Wee whose names are underwritten
are witnesses to this will and testament.
Thomas Birchard,
Kathrin Birchard,
Thomas Trappe,

His demise took place some time between September, 1677, and June 3, 1689, when his widow had already remarried, and on that date disposed of her interests in the estate of her late husband.[1] Her second marriage was to a man named Creber, probably Capt. Thomas Creber of Portsmouth, N. H., master of the ketch *John and Mary*, engaged in the coastwise trade.[2] In 1669 he was the son-in-law of John Moses of Portsmouth, and this marriage to the widow, Marie Pease, was his second.[3] She also outlived this husband, and was a widow again in 1695.[4] The date and place of her death yet remain unsolved. An Alice Shortridge, wife of Richard of Portsmouth, N. H., was the only surviving child of Thomas Crebar, late of Portsmouth (1721), deceased.[5] These facts above outlined constitute practically all our knowledge of this prominent settler, the progenitor of one of our largest and best known Vineyard families.[6]

[1]Dukes Deeds, I, 99.

[2]N. Y. Col. Mss. XXXIII, 1.

[3]York County (Me.) Deeds, II, 209.

[4]Dukes Deeds, II, 309. She disposes of land formerly belonging to Ezra Covell, but it is not known how it came into her possession.

[5]York County (Me.) Deeds, X, 226.

[6]For the purpose of collating all the scattered references to him the following memoranda are here inserted for future investigators: "James Oliver constituted Richard Hogg of Boston in New England, tailor, his attorney to demand of John Pease and Nicholas Treworgie certain monies due. 5 (12) 1648." (Aspinwall Notarial Record, 194). In the inventory of the debts due estate of David Evans in 1663, that of John Pease is classed as among those "hoped good." (Gen. Reg., XI, 345.)

RICHARD SARSON.

In May, 1635, one Richard Sarson, a tailor, embarked at London in the *Elizabeth and Ann* for these shores, and was listed as twenty-eight years of age, but what relationship he bore to the person of the same name who became so prominent in the affairs of this town, cannot be surely stated.[1] The tailor was born in 1607, while our Richard was born in 1637, and the former might have been the father, as one authority states that the elder went to Nantucket.[2] The first record of a Richard Sarson in this town is under date of Feb. 1, 1656, in connection with an agreement made by the townsmen with Robert Pease, at which time Richard Sarson and five others agreed to give Pease "two and half of fish every year so long as he liveth upon the Island."[3] As our known Richard Sarson was born in 1637 he would have been only nineteen years old on this date, not able to make a legal contract, and we may assume that it was the elder Richard who came here, bringing a son of the same name, and that he was admitted on June 2, 1657, as townsman. Otherwise we should have to concede that our later Richard was admitted as such before he was of age.[4] This hypothesis of a father and son here seems applicable to the next record of Feb. 18, 1659, when Richard Sarson was chosen as arbitrator in a land controversy, a duty to which a young man just turned twenty-one would hardly be called, and on June 7, 1659, Richard Sarson was chosen constable, an office of some considerable dignity in those times.[5] If this theory be correct, we are obliged to dispose of the elder Richard "without benefit of clergy" as there is nothing further to indicate when he died to relieve us of the doubt. There is scarcely a reference to a death or settlement of an estate on the Vineyard before 1660, and early vital statistics are entirely wanting, so that the disappearance of the elder Richard is not an unnatural conclusion to reach. As Richard Sarson

[1]Hotten, "List of Emigrants." In the same ship came Edward Seale and Jeremy Whitton, who are probably identical with the persons of those names living at the Vineyard in later years.

[2]Savage, Gen. Dict., IV, 17; comp., Dukes Deeds, I, 354.

[3]Edgartown Records, I, 138.

[4]Ibid., I, 139.

[5]Ibid., I, 142, 158.

died in 1703, he would have been ninety-seven if it were the elder of the name.[1]

After this date the younger Richard could be responsible for all the acts of which we have knowledge in the records. He took part in the division of Crackatuxett April 21, 1660, and was named among the proprietors that year.[2] He submitted to the Patentees Government in 1661, and in 1662 was one of the train band and in 1663 drew a lot at Quanomica.[3] About this time he had obtained the favor of the elder Mayhew, and on June 30, 1663, he was chosen recorder of the Vineyard Records, land court and probate "and General Assemblys," a position he held till 1668.[4] This relation resulted in a further connection of a more intimate character. The widow of Thomas Mayhew, Jr., had been in weeds for seven years, and being dependent on the charity of the Society for the Propogation of the Gospel for her maintenance, she accepted the suit of Richard Sarson, and a marriage was arranged some time after Dec. 20, 1664, when the widow disposed of her estate by gift to each of her children in anticipation of the event. She provided a loophole for herself by this clause, however: "in case this match go on betwixt Richard & I," evidently recognizing that there was uncertainty about affairs of the heart.[5] At this time the widow, Jane Mayhew, must have been about thirty-six years old, while Sarson was her junior by eight or nine years. The marriage took place, however, despite this and her uncertainty, and from that time the position of Richard Sarson was assured. By it he acquired control of the inheritances of the Paine interests descending to his wife and thus became a considerable property owner, and as stepfather of Matthew, Thomas, and Rev. John Mayhew he managed their affairs until they were old enough to look out for themselves. He became one of the governor's assistants shortly after the inauguration of the duke's government here, and remained on the bench for about thirty years, sitting with his two step-sons most of that time.[6] This spectacle gave rise to much of the discontent among

[1]Richard Sarson was witness to a deed Oct. 8, 1659. (Dukes Deeds, I, 182.)

[2]Edgartown Records, I, 147, 156.

[3]Ibid., I, 109, 138, 144. He was a juror in 1663.

[4]Ibid., 143.

[5]Dukes Deeds, I, 312.

[6]N. Y. Col. Mss., XXIV, 159; XXIX, 212; XXXIII, 95; XXXVII, 230; comp., Dukes Co. Court Records.

the people elsewhere described. On Oct. 2, 1694, he was licensed to retail liquor, not for drinking purposes, but as a convenience for the public.[1]

Richard Sarson lived on one of the "Five and Twenty" lots and his house was probably on North Water street, as the lot extended from Morse to Cottage and from the harbor to Pease Point way. This lot originally belonged to Thomas Paine, and after Sarson's death descended to Samuel his son, and thence to the heirs of Samuel, viz., Anne Belcher and Jane Little. The following is a list of land holdings: —

This Record May Sufficiently Testefy of the pertickeler parcells of Lands which followeth was Given By this Town to Searls and Sould by the Said Searls to Richard Sarson: one house Lott Being forty Poles Square with four acres of Land added to it with three acres of that Swomp Joyning to it: this Land and Swomp Near to the old School House Peter Foulger Two acre Lott on the North side, otherwise Common Round about: More one Devedent about thirty six acres More or Less Lying on the South side of the Plaine Bounded with John Peases Lands on the East, the Pond on the South, Thomas Bayes Land on the West, the Comon on the North: More an Island Lying In Sanchacantacket Pond Near the Harbour that Comes Into that Pond: with the fifth Lot at Quanomica Neck: with the thirty forth Lott att Felix Neck that Comes Into that Pond: More on(e) Lott of thach Meadow Lying at Mattecessett and Joyning to the weir Eastward. Also the Six and Twentyth part of fish and whale that Belongs to this town and with the above Mentioned pertickelers the seven and thirty[eth] part of this Town Shipp upon the Island Marthas Vineyard: with one Ten acre Lott upon the Line: also a Comonage and the Six and twentyth part of fish and whale: these Lands were Confirmed by the Town the 30th of Desember 63 and Recorded by me the same 30th of Desember 63:

RICHARD SARSON

Given to Richard Sarson By the town one half Comonage that is a half a thirty seventh part of the Lands and Comons that are undivided In this Town Bounds: with one Ten acre Lott upon the Line Being the Seventh from Quanomica: with half the thirty fourth at Meachemies feild: with half the Lott at Felix Neck.[2]

Besides this Sarson owned land in Chilmark and Tisbury. He was an owner of one-sixth of Homes Hole neck in 1667 (as one of those who helped evict Francis Usselton), but he sold it two years later.[3] When he died he owned a tract of a hundred acres at Homes Hole, bought of an Indian.

[1]Dukes Co. Court Record, Vol. I. This is a curious instance of the homely life of the Vineyard at that time when a justice of the King's bench could be seen pouring out a gill of rum for a thirsty yeoman who perchance had sat in his court a few hours before as plaintiff or defendant.

[2]Edgartown Records, I, 1.

[3]Dukes Deeds, I, 239; V, 358.

Richard Sarson died sometime before October 23, 1703, intestate, when administration of his estate was granted to Mrs. Anne Sarson, widow of his son Samuel, and Mr. Thomas Lothrop, the husband of Mehitable Sarson, only daughter of Richard.[1] An inventory of his personal effects amounted to £15-1-0, and his real estate was appraised on June 20, 1704, as follows: —

An house lot at Edgartown, formerly called Searles lot with a dividend adjoining, with 4 acres of upland & 3 of swamp adjoining	£30—0—0
One lot at planting field	24—0—0
A share of meadow, a lot on the Neck, with a whole common on Chappaquiddick	30—0—0
A hundred acres of land more or less near Cutteshmoo Spring	25—0—0
A small island in Sanchacantucket Pond, near the gut	4—0—0
One share and a half in Pocatapaces Neck	15—0—0
One share in Commons throughout the township except Chappaquiddic	30—0—0
One half share of lands in Commons in the Old Purchase	5—0—0
	£163—0—0

It is to be understood that there being several small allotments supposed to belong to the said estate the apprisement thareof is deferred by reason of uncertainty until it be better known.[2]

The homestead had been deeded to his son Samuel in 1699, and so does not appear in the estate.[3]

It is not known when Mrs. Jane (Paine) Mayhew-Sarson died, nor is there any record of the settlement of her estate. By the curious ante-nuptial document of 1664 she gave to her children her personal and real property, including the Paine homestead, whose northern boundary is the present Main street, and extending from the harbor to Pease Point way. The following is a copy of this deed of gift: —

To Matthew I give 5 pounds, which is in my fathers hand, and the hors colt: — and the half lot, which was betwixt my mother and me, with all the privileges thereto belonging,

I give unto Thomas;

and the cow called by the name of yong brown,

I give unto John,

and if any of these three die single, it shall be given to Jerusha and Jedida, unless I shall see occasion to dispose of it otherwise. This in case this match go on betwixt Richard & I.

[1]Dukes Probate, I, 16. His son Samuel had died but a short time before his father.

[2]Ibid. The appraisers were Joseph Norton, Benjamin Smith, Isaac Norton, Thomas Daggett, and James Pease.

[3]Dukes Deeds, I, 206.

That which is written in this paper I Jane Mayhew, of the Vineyard widdow, did freely give unto my children, as I have expressed in this writing bearing date this 20th of December 1664: for the confirmation hereof and of all and every of the said gifts and also to testify the premises to whom it may concern, I have hereunto set my hand, the day and year abovesaid. This writing is not to be in force except she marrieth with Richard Sarson.

Witness hereunto JANE MAYHEW.[1]

Thomas Mayhew

John Cotton

There were at least two children born to Richard Sarson and his wife Jane, namely Samuel, b. about 1667 and Mehitable who married Thomas Lothrop of Barnstable. If other children were born they died young, and the name became extinct with Samuel, whose children were daughters that grew to marriageable age. The name, however, is perpetuated in the small island in Sanchacantackett, opposite the opening or "gut" as expressed in the inventory of his estate, and is erroneously called on the charts "Sasons Island."

BENJAMIN SMITH.

Benjamin Smith

This prominent settler was a late comer, and through his marital connection with the ruling family he soon attained public office, and ever after held high places in the gift of his relatives, or through their influence. Because of his prominence for many years in the political life of the island, from his coming here, about 1684, to his death, in 1720, the author has endeavored to satisfy the desire to know something definite of his antecedents. At the end of many extended investigations, which cannot be enumerated or explained, it is necessary finally to state the presumptions based on all that has been worked out. The author therefore gives as his opinion, that he is the son of Rev. John Smith of Barnstable and Sandwich, born January, 1658-9, in the former town. All other Benjamins in New England have been traced out, and this one offers the reasonable solution as regards age, condition, and propinquity.[2] Only one confusion exists—

[1]Dukes Deeds, I, 312.

[2]Sandwich was closely connected with the Vineyard by emigration of its families, as well as with the Mayhew family by marriage. Governor Mayhew's daughter Martha had married Thomas Tupper of Sandwich, and Joseph Wing of the same town had married (in 1682) Jerusha Mayhew, elder sister of Jedidah, the wife of our Benjamin Smith.

there was a Benjamin Smith in Sandwich having children by a wife Elizabeth, 1687–1704,[1] while our Benjamin was here, and children were born to him 1685–1700. The Benjamin of Sandwich has been supposed to be the son of Rev. John, but of this, as in our case, there is absolutely no proof.[2] There were two Benjamin Smiths living in Sandwich in 1681, who were admitted as "townsmen" in that year, Shubael, John, and Benjamin "Senior," evidently the three sons of Rev. John, and Benjamin Smith, "son of Richard," so-called evidently to distinguish him from the other Benjamin. Richard Smith, the father of the latter named, was evidently in a humble walk of life. He had come to Sandwich about 1657, from Plymouth, where he is first heard of in 1643, and he was employed to keep the town cattle, and to have for his pay the use of ten acres of land and a peck of Indian corn for each creature put on the commons.[3] In 1665, he was granted three acres of bog below his house, and after that his name does not appear in the records until 1684, when he was "deceased," and on Oct. 24 that year his son Benjamin was appointed administrator of the estate.[4] In those days, social distinctions were well defined, and it is the stronger probability that Benjamin, the son of the Rev. John, would marry the daughter of Rev. Thomas Mayhew and grand-daughter of a governor, rather than Benjamin, the son of Richard, cattle keeper for the town of Sandwich.[5] It may be said in response, that our Benjamin was a "carpenter" by designation, but that does not militate against the social position of his family. A mechanical trade was sometimes specified as an occupation in early times for purposes of distinguishing individuals, especially

[1]The names of these children include Elkanah, Elisha, Peninah, Bathsheba, which are not known in the descendants of Rev. John's sons. The only names used in common are Ichabod and Ebenezer, which are found in the minister's immediate family.

[2]Benjamin Smith, son of Richard, took the oath of fidelity July 4, 1678, at Sandwich. (Plymouth Col. Rec.)

[3]Sandwich Town Records, 1659, 1662.

[4]Plymouth Col. Records, VI, 145. Richard Smith had married Ruth Bonum, March 27, 1646, and she had died before 1684, as her estate was included in the administration letters granted to Benjamin.

[5]Rev. John Smith went to New Jersey with his family and acquired property there. Mrs. Jerusha (Mayhew) Wing of Sandwich, went there also with her husband, and resided at Shrewsbury in that province. This affords a possible and probable association of the Smith and Mayhew families about the time of the marriage. It is further to be noted that Shubael Smith, the elder brother of Benjamin, came to the Vineyard later in life and spent the remainder of his days here. (1713–1734).

if they were a number of the same name.[1] There is evidence however, that he was a carpenter in fact as well as name during the earlier years of his life.

He had a grant of land in 1684 in this town adjoining a previous grant of unknown date, and it is now impossible to assign the exact time of his settlement, though it is certain that he had married Jedidah Mayhew, youngest daughter of the younger Thomas, before Feb. 8, 1683-4, and we may agree that 1683, when he was about twenty-four years of age, was the probable date, both of marriage and settlement.[2] This alliance became a career for him, and his name dots the records frequently thereafter. He was attorney for the town in 1687, 1692; commissioner as King's Attorney for the county in 1691; selectman, 1693, 1696, 1697; county treasurer, 1698, 1715; representative to the General Court, 1692, 1703; county commissioner, 1703, 1708, besides doing other less important work in town affairs up to the last years of his life. Notwithstanding his family associations it appears that he did not entirely approve of all the things that were done by his relatives in the government of the island, and in particular the head of the clan received his private condemnation, although he could not afford open opposition.[3] From this we may conclude his sense of justice was keen, even if his strength of character was not enough to apply the corrective.

Parson Homes enters in his diary under date of July 10, 1720, "Mr. Benjamin Smith of Edgartown died last week. He died suddenly, July 4, 1720, being a Monday." The gravestone records the same date, and reads further, "in the 65 year of his age." This is probably an error of the cutter of the inscription for 63, which would bring his birth to about 1658, proximately that of Benjamin, son of Rev. John of Sandwich.[4]

He left a widow Jedidah, who survived him sixteen years, and eight children, two of whom, Thomas and Ebenezer,

[1]The number of "cordwainers" (shoemakers) who appear on the records, could make shoes enough for an army. It is not to be supposed that all followed this occupation — but they were proficient in it and could do so if required. They made their own shoes.

[2]Edgartown Records, I, 99; comp., Dukes Deeds, V, 72.

[3]Simon Athearn is our authority that Benjamin Smith told him privately, "that they of Edgartown" had consulted together to have Mayor Mayhew "discarded . . . . least he should destroy the place." Athearn adds: "I once asked Mr. Benjamin Smith why some Englishmen found stealing in Edgartown & that by the Sheriffe too," were not prosecuted, and Smith confessed he "did not know." (Sup. Jud. Ct. Mss., 4605.)

[4]Edgartown Vital Records, 261, where the age is questioned by the editor as probably 63rd.

became the transmitters of his name unto this present time. Four daughters married leaders in the social and political circles of the period.

JOHN SMITH.

It is a bold task to attempt the discrimination of the various John Smiths who appeared early in New England, but as one of this name settled in the town it becomes necessary to individualize him if possible. All probabilities favor the theory that he first settled at Watertown, where he married Deborah, daughter of George and Phebe Parkhurst of that town, who was baptized in Ipswich, England, Aug. 1, 1619, and that he removed about 1644 to Hampton, N. H., at which place her aunt, Mrs. Ruth Dalton, wife of Rev. Timothy Dalton, then lived.[1] By this marriage he became later brother-in-law of Joseph Merry of Tisbury.

The earliest record found relating to him here is on June 6, 1654, when he was chosen as one of the magistrate's assistants.[2] He may be the "Smith" who on May 8, 1653, drew a lot in the Planting Field.[3] Further mention of him occurs in 1656 and 1659,[4] and in the latter year he became connected with the movement to settle Nantucket. He was a witness to the deed of conveyance of that island July 2, 1659, and later in the same year was chosen one of the ten Associate Proprietors to settle on the land in equal shares with the original purchasers.[5] Thenceforth he became active in the development of that island, although retaining his property interests here. He was of the Edgartown train band in 1662, and his name is mentioned in the town records in 1660, 1663, and 1664, either as drawing lots in the various divisions of the common land, or in other minor connections. After that it is believed he removed to Nantucket to spend his declining years.

His home lot was on Tower Hill, just north of the cemetery in that locality, and descended to his son Philip by will.

He made his will in Nantucket, but called himself "of Martin's Vineyard." He does not use any expression denoting

[1]Dow, "History of Hampton, N.H.," 979.

[2]Edgartown Records, I, 122.

[3]Ibid., I, 172.

[4]John Smith "of Martins Vin Yard" had a suit against Jonas Weed late of Southampton, L. I., in an action of debt in the Connecticut Courts 1657. (Mainwaring, Digest of Connecticut Wills, I, 113.)

[5]Macy, "History of Nantucket," 32.

"advanced years," as was a common phrase employed by the aged, and it may be assumed that he was not much beyond middle life when it was executed. It is as follows:—

I John Smith of Martin's Vineyard, being in perfect health and Soundness Both in body and Minde, doe make my Last Will and Testament this 14th day of Febua: in the year : 1670 : as followeth:—

Imprimis: I Give unto my two sonnes John and Samuell all my lands on the Iland of Nantuckett wth all privelledges thereto belonging to be equally devided between them : they paying to their two sisters Deborah and Abigaill unto either of them five pounds to be payed within one year after their Entrance and Possession thereof.

Item: I give unto my sonne phillip my land and house at Martin's Vineyard with all priviledges belonging to the aforesaid land, to be his after the decease of his mother; and in the mean time after my decease my will is that the said Phillip my sonne shall injoy two thirds of the said lands and privelledges. The true intent and meaning of this my Gift unto my sonne phillip is this : because the wise disposing hand of God hath ordered that my said Sonne at present is impotent in his understanding : that his weakness shall not alienate the lands from my familie : therefore my will is that the lands and priviledges as aforementioned shall be thus disposed : Namely : if he said phillip shall Marrie and have issue : then the lands are Given to him and his heirs for Ever : but if the said phillip shall dy without issue, then it shall at his decease fall to the next heir in the family : and farther I Give to my sonne phillip what drawing cattle are in being on the land or living aforesaid at my decease, with carts, plowes and all furniture belonging to the teame, and also two Cowes : and liberty to dwell in the house all the time of his Mothers life.

Ite: I mak Deborah my wife whole Executor of this my last will, and I desire and appoint my Loving Friends Mr. Thomas Mayhew and Isaac Robinson at the Vineyard & Mr Edward Starbuck and Thomas Macy of Nantuckett overseers of this my last will and testament : and in case one or more of these friends dy or leave the country and their places vacant, then the Survivors or Remainers shall have liberty to chuse others to supply, and are desired so to doe : for the confirmation hereof I the said Testator have hereunto set my hand the day & year above written.[1]

Witnesses John Smith
Thomas Macy Junr
Sarah Macy
Mary Starbuck.

It is not known when he died, but it was sometime before June 16, 1674, when his son John sold the Nantucket property.[2] This son returned to Hampton, N. H., where descendants resided. He was a lieutenant and by trade a cooper.[3]

The following is a list of the landed property of John Smith which he bequeathed to his son Philip:—

[1]Dukes Deeds, I, 348.

[2]Nantucket Deeds.

[3]Dow, "History of Hampton," 979.

a True Record of the Lands now in the Possession of Phillip Smith of Edgartown upon Marthas Vineyard: Desembr 27th (1676.)
Inprimus one House Lott Containing Ten acres more or Less Bounded By Thomas Harlock on the East & South the Common on the West, Richard Arey on the North: It. one Lott at the Planting feild Being Ten acres More or Less Bounded By Thomas Daggett on the East & South, Richard Sarson on the North, Joana Bland on the North: It. one Devidant at the Great Neck Bounded By the Plain on the East, Joana Bland on the South, Mr. Mayhew on the West, the Pond on the North: with the 36 Lott at Phelix Neck: 25 Lott at Meachamus feild and the 28th Lott att Quanomica with the 25th of wood Lott that was Laid out By the Ponds: on the East: Mr. Mayhews on the South, Joseph Daggett on the West and Thomas Daggett on the North: with one share of meadow at Cracketuxett Being Two acres more or Less Bounded by Thomas Daggett on the South or South East: It. one Lott at Chapequidick Neck, Mr. Mayhew on the North west, John Pease South east: It. one thach Lott Lying By Mr. Sarsons Devidant that he Bought of Thomas Mayhew: with one whole share of Commonage and one share of fish and whale and share of all undivided Lands.[1]

It is not known either when the widow Deborah died, but she probably survived till about 1686, when Philip sold the homestead to his brother Samuel, from which it is evident that the mental infirmity referred to in the father's will had been relieved, as Philip was marshal of the county at that time. Descendants through both these sons remained on the Vineyard, and now reside on the island in the tenth generation.

THOMAS TRAPP.

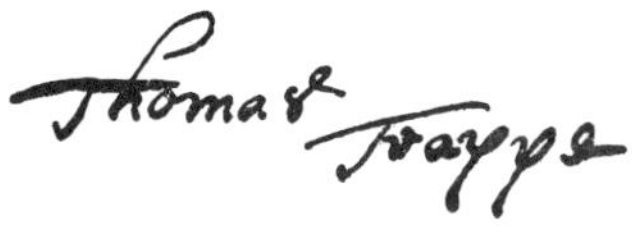

Especial interest attaches to this person, as a Trapp is one of the four legendary settlers before the coming of the Mayhews. The only Trapp positively known to have come to the Vineyard was Thomas Trapp, a late arrival (1659), who was born in 1634-5, according to his gravestone, and hence but a child at the time when alleged landing occurred. His choice of this place for a home was a natural one, probably because of the Burchards who were kinsmen of his and among the first settlers.[2] The English home of Trapp is not known, although diligent search has located

[1]Edgartown Records, I, 21.

[2]Thomas Burchard and wife Katharine speak of "cusen Thomas Trapp of Martins Vineyard," on two separate occasions.

many of his name in various parishes of Essex, the county whence came the Brownings and Peases.[1] A Thomas Trapp lived, married, and had children in Great Baddow, 1639–1659, the home of John Pease,[2] and our Thomas Trapp emigrated to New England in company with a husbandman of Purleigh, Essex, a parish only seven miles distant from Great Baddow.[3] After his arrival in this country, in 1659, he evidently came directly to Great Harbor and established a residence in this town, for he was granted a ten-acre "lot on the line" in December of that year.[4] This was north of Main street and west of Planting Field way, and he gradually increased his holdings in that vicinity northward to the pond which still bears his name. He also acquired land in the Great Swamp by purchase, and after 1670 shared in the division of the common land.[5]

He held numerous and important minor offices in the town and county. He was marshal, water bailiff and crier in 1667; juryman, 1679; deputy sheriff, 1694–1700; and town clerk, 1700 till his death. This event occurred Oct. 15, 1719, in his 86th year, and he lies buried in the old cemetery. The maiden name of his wife Mary is not known, but by her he had at least nine children who grew to adult life, five sons and four daughters.[6] These left a numerous posterity, who lived on the paternal acres until about 1800, when the last of the name had migrated, mostly to Norwich and other towns in Connecticut. The name is now extinct on the Vineyard, but is represented in the Norton and Pease families through marriage of his daughter.

[1]Trapps are to be found at this period in Ongar, Orselt, Bobbingworth, Chigwell, Greensteed, Bromfield, Great Baddow, and Good Easter, all in the county of Essex, and most of them near the home of John Pease. Doubtless a further search would definitely place Thomas Trapp in some contiguous parish. See Visitation of Essex, 1612, p. 506.

[2]Thomas Trapp, single man, of Great Baddow, married Jane Burre, Oct. 28, 1639. She was daughter of the vicar of the parish.

[3]Suffolk Co. Probate Records, X, 87, 88. This fellow passenger, Lewis Martin, died on the voyage and left all his property to John Andrews of Fenchurch Street, London, a linen draper who was a "cousen" to Thomas Trapp.

[4]He was voted "not of this town," on Oct. 22, 1660, but on Jan. 28, 1661, he is credited as owner of one lot. (Town records, I, 20, 22.) He forfeited a "lot on the line" before 1665, and it was granted to another. (Ibid., I, 35). It is certain however, that the Trapp property was in that section. (Ibid., I, 29).

[5]Edgartown Town Records, I, 20, 21. He also owned one-third of Homes Hole Neck, which he acquired by purchase, but sold same within a short time.

[6]The widow Mary Trapp survived.

WILLIAM VINCENT.

The antecedents of this early settler remain unknown to the author after much searching in this country and England. The association of the name of Vincent with the alleged landing of John Pease, before 1642, made it desirable that the Vincent should be identified. There were none of the name at Great Baddow in Essex, where John Pease lived, but in the adjoining parish of Bromfield, about four miles distant, a family of Vincents had long lived, when the Pease family emigrated to New England. One Robert Vincent, "ane ancient man" of Butlers, an estate in the parish, died in December, 1632, and the property descended to his son Robert, who married Elizabeth Godsaffe on June 28, 1633, and on the same day William Vincent of Bromfield, singleman, married Mary Burr, daughter of the vicar of the parish.[1] As our William Vincent was born in 1627, it is evident that he could not be the son of either of these persons.[2] These people, however, had dealings with our Pease family and their connections. William Vincent, yeoman of Bromfield, gave a bond in August, 1636, to pay £10 to Abraham Page (nephew of John Pease), when he comes of age, "at or in the South Porch of the Church of great Baddow." The witnesses were Thomas Burre, vicar of Bromfield and Margaret Pease, widow, grandmother of young Page.[3] When Page arrived in this country in 1645, he made Robert Scott of Boston his attorney, to collect "money from any Pson or Psons whatsoever within the Realme of England,"[4] and it will be noticed that it was at Robert Scott's house where Malachi Browning died some years later. These facts have a direct bearing upon the possible association of the Vincents with the group of people who lived in the sight of the church at Great Baddow.[5]

A William Vincent was granted a lot of land at Norwich, Conn., in 1651, but the word "forfeited" is marked against

[1]Morant, "History of the County of Essex," II, 77. The Parish Registers of Bromfield contain no Vincent entries before the marriages just quoted.

[2]He testified in 1693, aged 66 years. (Dukes Court Records.)

[3]Suffolk Deeds, I, 66. Recorded Dec. 12, 1645. This may be the William Vincent who married the vicar's daughter.

[4]Aspinwall Notarial Records, 14.

[5]There was a William Vincent, a potter, of Salem, 1636, later of Gloucester, Mass., 1643, who died in 1690, having married twice and had at least eight children, neither of whom could have been identified with this island. A William Vinson was of Providence, R.I., in 1666, but he is identified as a son of Thomas of Amesbury, Co. Wilts, baptized in 1638. (Savage, Gen. Dict., IV, 374–5; comp., Essex Antiquarian, passim.)

it, and a guess may be hazarded that this was our William, then a young man of twenty-four years, who was there at the time when John Pease was prospecting for a new location.[1] We may suppose that he returned to the Vineyard with Pease, in absence of a better hypothesis as to his whereabouts before coming to this town. His first appearance on our records is on March 15, 1655, when he bought of Robert Codman one-half of the harbor lot on Starbuck's Neck, which Arey had sold to Codman, consisting of four acres.[2] Whether he lived there is uncertain, but presumably he did, until the next year, on Feb. 18, 1656, when he bought of Edward Andrews "his house and land adjoyning to it twenty acres more or less bounded on the east side by the land of John Burchard: on the west Mamanekorn Neck: the one end butting upon the fresh pond, the other end upon the common."[3] This was at Mashakommukeset, where he afterwards resided, and it remained Vincent property for generations. Before December, 1655, he had married Susannah, daughter of Malachi and Mary (Collier) Browning, and the young couple set up housekeeping in this beautiful region, overlooking the great pond. In December, 1659, he was a juror, and in 1660, he is recorded as one of the proprietors and began to draw lots as such.[4] He submitted to the Patentee's Government in 1661, and was one of a committee appointed to evict the Indians living within the town bounds the same year.[5] He was of the Train Band in 1662, and in 1663 he was sued by William Weeks for a small debt, and with three others built the general fence for the town under contract. He was credited with owning half a lot at this time, presumably the Arey-Codman lot above referred to.[6] In 1664 he participated in land divisions, and on April 21, 1665, was chosen town constable.[7] But little is heard of him for the next ten years, except in some minor land transaction until the "Dutch Rebellion," in which he took part and was fined therefor. In 1675 he sued Peter Jenkins for debt, and four years later had a suit against sundry Indians who had detained his share of a whale and some

[1]Caulkins, "History of Norwich.

[2]Edgartown Records, I, 137.

[3]Ibid., I, 115.

[4]Ibid., I, 147, 156.

[5]Ibid., I, 144.

[6]Ibid., I, 109, 111, 140, 147. He sold this lot to Joseph Codman this year. (Ibid., I, 5.)

[7]Edgartown Records, I, 112, 127.

"Blober."[1] In 1680 he was fined for felling trees and "cutting wood for Mr. Mayhew," and in 1681 was a juror.[2] Various real estate transactions in 1682, 1684, and 1687, including further grants to him at Meshacket and Wintucket give us glimpses of his continued activity, and this brings us to May 10, 1690, when he made his will, then in his sixty-fourth year.[3] By this time he had become estranged from his only son Thomas, to whom nine years before (Sept. 16, 1681), he had sold considerable of his property including one acre "by my shop."[4] His name appears on the records in 1693, when he made an affidavit; in 1694, when he sold land at Wintucket, and on March 15, 1694–5, when he was listed as a proprietor of one share in the town.

The following is a list of his real estate holdings: —

This is a true Record of the Petickeler parcells of Land which are now In the possession of William Vinsin upon this Island as followeth: first one Neck Called Shockamockset adjoining to Quanomica on the West and so Runing by Marked Trees on the North, to Meshaket Neck on the East: and straight Down to the Pond on the South: this Neck meadow and upland Being Twenty five acres More or Less: with two acres of Land at Quanomica Being the Sixth Lott: with one acre of meadow Lying att Chapequideck Bounded By. . . . . : with the Second Lott at Felix Neck: with the Seventh Lott Mechmies feild: with a whole Right of Comonage and a sixth and twentyth part of fish and whale.

this Recorded by me the 24th of February 1663 Richard Sarson with that feild where the said Vinson fenced In Lying Near the Great Swamp Being five acres More or Less: this was Given May the Last Day: 64: with a full Right of all the allotments which Towonticut Sachem Reserved In the townshipp and was Bought of the said Sachem by Richard Sarson having Liberty by this town so to Do: the said Vinson hath paid for his part pt this foresaid purchas 2 : 8.[5]

It is probable that William Vincent lived well into 1697, at which time he was three score and ten years of age, the Scriptural limit. His will was proven in court on July 14 of that year, and an abstract of it is as follows, being the first will recorded in the probate records of the county: —

Edgartown upon Marthas Vineyard: the last will and testament of me William Vinson. . . . . . .

I do give unto my son Thomas Vinson ten shillings to be paid within ten days after my burial if he demands it of my executor: but if not de-

[1]Dukes Court Records, Vol. I.

[2]Ibid.

[3]Edgartown Records, I, 31, 33; comp., Dukes Deeds, I, 344.

[4]Dukes Deeds, I, 326.

[5]Edgartown Records, I, 2, 13.

manded within the said ten days, then my will is, and I do give my s'd son Thomas Vinson only one shilling to be paid at demand after the said ten days, at any time within an hundred year after the day of my burial: and my reasons for so doing and giving my said son Thomas Vinson no more is this, first: I have given him near forty pounds: besides he my said son Thomas Vinson hath not demeaned himself well towards me nor his mother, to our sad great grief.

I do give my wife Susannah Vinson all my whole estate, both real and personal, ...

I do appoint my said wife Susannah Vinson to be my sole executrix. . . . . . . and I do desire Richard Sarson and Simon Newcomb to do that kindness for me to see this my will performed so far as they can. . . . . this tenth day of May 1690.

The mark of W William Vinson [1]

Witnesses:
Richard Sarson
Philip Covel

It is not known whether Thomas demanded the half crown or was content to be "cut off with a shilling," which was made available to him for the entire next century. It is pleasant to record that there is evidence of the repentance of Thomas and the restoration of confidence between the aged mother and her only son in later years. The widow Susannah Vinson survived her husband a quarter of a century, and must have been very aged when she died. She made her will April 2, 1720, "being sick and weak in body," in which she gives some bedding and a "white chest with lock & key" to her grandson, Thomas Vinson, Jr., and gives all the rest of her estate to her son Thomas and his nine children.[2] It was proved May 10, 1722, and it will be safe to infer that she died a short time before that date, probably in the early part of that year. Assuming that she was twenty years old when her son was born, she was about eighty-five at her decease.

WILLIAM WEEKS.

In the parish of Staines, on the north bank of the Thames in the County of Middlesex, about fifteen miles west of London, there lived during the early part of the 17th century a family bearing the name of Atwick alias Wickes.[3] In 1638 Richard Wickes died, and his will, dated August 4, was proved November 8, that year. In it he directs his executor "to pay to my

[1]Dukes Probate Records, I, 2.

[2]Dukes Probate, I, 127.

[3]Prerogative Court of Canterbury, Soame 80.

son John Wickes now living in New England £200 at the feast of the birth of our Lord God next coming," and if he should die before its receipt the amount was to be divided equally among his minor children. This John Wickes was a friend of Samuel Gorton, and had lived at Plymouth in 1637, and later in Rhode Island at Portsmouth, on the island of Aquidneck, 1639, from whence he removed in 1643 with Gorton to Warwick across the bay.[1] His friendship for Gorton resulted in his arrest and imprisonment, but this did not last beyond a year, for on Aug. 8, 1647, his townsmen elected him a magistrate.[2] He continued to reside there till his death, at the hands of the Indians, during King Philip's war, in November, 1675, aged sixty-six years.[3]

Robert Wickes of Staines, gentleman, also left a bequest to another son reading thus: "To my son *William*, £300, as follows, £30 in three months and the remainder in three years and he to have £10 paid him every half year in the meantime, and if he should die, *or never come to claim it*, then to be divided between my sons John and Robert and their children."[4] In absence of direct proof it cannot be stated positively that this is the William Weeks whose name first appears in 1653 on the Vineyard records, but who must have been there at an earlier date to have participated at that time in a division of land. One son of Robert Wickes had already gone to New England as above stated, and it is evident that William was either going away or was absent from England, creating a doubt about his return to claim the bequest. It is a fair presumption that one brother followed the other, and as our William was a sea-faring man, and did a packet business between Rhode Island and the Vineyard, it seems that we have here a presumptive connection established for William of Edgartown.[5]

As before stated, William Weeks participated in the first recorded division of lands in this town, May 8, 1653, indicating

[1]Savage, Gen. Dict., IV, 538. It is believed he is the same person who embarked at London in September, 1635, aged twenty-six years, with a wife and a daughter Ann. His daughter Ann married William Burton of Rhode Island.

[2]The whole story may be read in Winthrop Journal, II, 140-149; Compare Mass. Col. Rec., II, 52. He must have personally known John Pease of the Vineyard.

[3]Savage, Gen. Dict., IV, 539; comp., Lechford, Note Book, 188, and R. I. Hist. Coll., II, 86.

[4]Prerogative Court of Canterbury. Lee 140.

[5]John Wickes of Rhode Island could not have been the father of our William, in all probability, as William must have been born before 1620 to take part in the business he did in later years.

a prior residence of some duration, and on April 10, 1655, was granted land "near the pines in the middle of the island." That he was married at this time is indicated by a deposition of Goodwife Weeks, dated Dec. 25, 1655, and it is probable that his children were either brought here when he settled or were born shortly after. His name occurs in 1656, 1657, 1659, and 1660, in which year on February 22, he was sued by one William Lambert. This same year he is mentioned as a proprietor of one share in the town and was elected constable. That he kept an ordinary or inn seems to be indicated by the following entry on the town records, as well as a later one to be referred to:—

> William Weeks is fined for selling of strong liquor: paying ten shillings: to Thomas Mayhew 14 s. & t(w)o bottles of liquor to the townsmen and further he doth promise for himself and family that they shall no more be sold by him or them. [28 January 1661] [1]

The next year William Weeks had some lawsuits on his hands, suing Thomas Jones for his passage from Rhode Island,[2] and in turn was sued by Jones for weaving done. In both cases he received the verdict. His name is not in the train band list of 1662, perhaps he was exempted on account of his occupation, but he took part in the division of Quanomica the next year, and was plaintiff in a number of suits against Robert Codman, Richard Arey, Nicholas Norton, and William Vinson.

His name occurs in the records each year following in minor connections till 1667, when on November 18 of that year, while making a trading trip from the Vineyard in his "vessel of 15 tunnes, laden with corn, pork, hides, tobacco, wheat, vegetables and other miscellaneous freight," he was wrecked at Quick's Hole and his vessel was seized and looted by the Indians of the Elizabeth Islands. His son William was on board, and according to the story of their experiences testified to by them they were very badly treated. "They tooke away a new hatt and a new paire of shooes from my sonne," he said, and "a suite of cloathes from me, 2 pre of shooes (and) all my tooles."[3] John Dixey "brought the deponents with his sloop out of their bondage" and carried the news to the Governor of New York, who wrote back to

[1]Edgartown Records, I, 145. His "family" must have been sufficiently grown to be included in a proceeding of this kind.

[2]This indicates that Weeks was engaged in coastwise traffic with Rhode Island.

[3]New York Col. Doc., III, 168.

Governor Mayhew to deal with the piratical Indians for their unlawful acts and require restitution of the vessel and all the stolen cargo.[1] It was not until 1671 that he had his lands recorded on the town books, and the following is a copy of his estate as then held by him: —[2]

Desember the 11th 1671 The Petickelers of the parcells of Land Granted unto William Weeks by the Inhabitance of Edgartown at the Great Harbour of Marthas Vinyard and Ordered to Be Recorded the Day above writen

one whole Comonage of the thirty seven Shears with all preveledges there unto Belonging as fish and whale: one house Lott of Twenty Poles Broad Bounded By Thomas Bayes on the South and Richard Sarson on the North Being Ten acres More or Less: to the Line Ten acres eleven Poles and a half Breadth Bounded By Thomas Bayes on the West Richard Sarson on the East: Land Bought of Peter Foulger one Neck Lying West to the Planting feild Being Eight acres More or Less: with one acre and a half of Meadow at Sanchacantackett one shear of Meadow:- one Shear at Felix Neck: another Shear at Meachemus feild: one Shear at Quanomica: one Shear at Cracketuxett: One Devidant Lying at the Great Neck Being Twenty five acres more or Less Lying betwixt Thomas Peases and Mrs Blands: with one thach Lott ajoyning Part upon my said Devidant at the Neck: at Chapequideck one Lott of three acres More or Less Bounded By John Pease on the North and young Mr. Mayhew on the South: two acres of Meadow Lying on the South East Side of Chapequideok More or Less: one acre of Meadow on the East Side of the Planting feild Lying Northward of Thomas Doggetts Be it More or Less: These all Granted By this Town and Purchased of Indians and one twenty fifth part. . . . . .

He had acquired some land at Homes Hole before the first record of it appears (Feb. 9, 1680), as that is the only way to account for his appointment on a committee in Tisbury on Jan. 16, 1678, to view every man's lot and equalize it in the matter of swamp lands.[3] It is likely he was on the committee as an outsider, with Isaac Chase and Thomas Mayhew, to deal impartially as arbitrator. The next year he was juryman at Nantucket, and was plaintiff in a suit against John Daggett for trespass.[4] In 1680 he served again as a juror, and in 1681 Arthur Biven entered a complaint against Weeks as follows: The "said Buiven caled for a gill of Rum & they brought half water and the said Weekes had no lodge-

[1]The name is spelled Weexe. Ibid., III, 169.

[2]Edgartown Records, I, p. 10.

[3]Tisbury Records, 10; compare Dukes Deeds, I, 227, where he bought land of the Sachem Ponit and I, 377, a sale of land at Homes Hole, Feb. 9, 1681, by Thomas Mayhew. This is the only reference to him in the Tisbury Records.

[4]Nantucket Records, I; Dukes Court Records, I.

ing for him nor food for his horse."[1] This complaint shows that Weeks was still keeping a tavern. The town and county records give evidence of his activities in business and litigation in 1684, 1685, and 1687, not necessary here to enumerate. He sold to Isaac Chase on July 25, 1688, his real estate interests at Homes Hole, and his last appearance on the records is another sale on December 29, same year. Between that date and Aug. 3, 1689, he had died, as his widow Mary sold the home lot and he is referred to as then deceased.[2] This sale of her interest to Simon Athearn resulted in litigation with the sons, William and Richard, who claimed ownership, and the court gave them possession.[3] There is no record of a will or administration of William Weeks' estate. His son Samuel had a grant of land in the town in 1681, consisting of ten acres on the north side of the old mill path, but he sold it in 1688 to Benjamin Smith, and is not further known as a resident here.[4]

With the death of William, Senior, the family name ceased on the island until 1710, when Joshua Weeks came here and brought the house lot formerly owned by George Martin of Edgartown and Newport. Joshua later settled in Tisbury, and his descendants resided there and in Chilmark until within recent years.

THOMAS WOLLEN.

This settler was a late comer and is another of the sons-in-law of Nicholas Norton, attracted to a residence here by one of his daughters. Where he lived before 1681, when his land is mentioned, is an unsettled question.[5] There was a Thomas Wallen or Walling of Providence (1645), who died in 1674 leaving a wife Mary and son Thomas with other children. This Thomas Junior, married in 1669, Margaret Caldwell, and he may be the one who came to this town and took a second wife, as above. He lived near the Mile Brook, on the Sanchacantacket Path as late as 1722, but nothing further is known of him. His only known son Elisha, continued the family name in Edgartown to the middle of that century.

[1]Dukes Court Records, I. June 28, 1681.

[2]Dukes Deeds, III, 41.

[3]These sons were then living in Falmouth, where children are recorded to William and another son John.

[4]Edgartown Records, I, 29. See also Dukes Deeds, I, 81, 255 and 259, where he disposes (1686) of the interest he had in his father's lot bought the year before.

[5]Ibid., I, 29.

EARLY TRANSIENT RESIDENTS.

As distinguished from the settlers who made permanent homes here, lived their lives and reared families; whose descendants developed what the pioneers had opened to the settlement of white men, there were a goodly number of transient residents who remained but a few years and then sought homes elsewhere. These men have their place in our history, but the interest in them does not call for extended notice beyond the record of their brief doings while here.

EDWARD ANDREWS.

This person was one of the early "transients," of whom we know but little. He was, possibly, a settler at Newport in 1639, later admitted as freeman at Warwick, in 1655, but before Feb. 13, 1656, he had acquired from Thomas Layton the property of Philip Tabor at Mashakommukeset, and called himself a "now inhabitant on Martin's Vineyard."[1] He had been in possession of the property but a few months when he sold it on the last mentioned date to William Vincent, and left the island, soon after in all probability. He was sued in the town court, June 24, 1656, by John Burchard. He removed to Portsmouth, R. I., and later to Warwick in the same colony. He was a shoemaker by occupation, and his wife's name was Bridget.[2]

JOSHUA BARNES.

This person was an early resident of Boston, and on Sept. 4, 1632, he was apprenticed to Mr. [William] Paine "for five years from his landing," and we may presume that he was sent over, by his parents perhaps, for that purpose.[3] Upon the expiration of his service he removed, probably, to Yarmouth, as we find him named on a committee, March 5, 1639, with Philip Tabor, to divide the planting lands in that town, and on June 1, 1641, he was entered as an applicant for citizenship.[4] In 1642 he was fined for scoffing at religion and disturbing public worship.[5] His connection with the

[1]Dukes Deeds, I, 325. He bought this after August, 1655.
[2]Austin, Gen. Dict. of R. I., 3; comp., Savage, art. Andrews.
[3]Mass. Col. Records, I, 99. William Paine was a great merchant in Boston.
[4]Freeman, History of Cape Cod, I, 135, 142, 144. II, 17, 29, 31, 36, 41.
[5]Plymouth Col. Rec.

Vineyard is of a transient nature. It is inferred that he came hither with his fellow townsman, Peter Tabor, who was here before 1647, and the date of his acquiring a lot may be placed anywhere after 1644 when the township was established. As to the location of this lot we way suppose it to be the harbor lot on Starbuck's Neck, later owned by Thomas Daggett, who had succeeded before 1660 to the possessions of Barnes.[1]

It requires some adjustment of facts to place this person as a settler at Southampton, Long Island, before 1642, as the author of the history of that town classifies him in his lists, in view of previous residence known at Yarmouth.[2] He may have gone there from Yarmouth following his court experience at Plymouth, and returned to the Vineyard to acquire a lot here. However, he finally became a settler at Easthampton in 1649, and continued to reside in that locality till his death, sometime after Sept. 13, 1696, and his descendants remained there.[3]

WILLIAM ELLISTON.

This person first appears in Edgartown, in 1663, when he was "freed" from a bond and his "master." He was plaintiff in actions for debt against Nicholas Norton in 1663 and William Weeks in 1665, and defendant in similar action brought in 1663 by the widow of John Folger. He had a lot between the "line" and "home" lots which came into possession of Isaac Norton before 1681.

JOHN FREEMAN.

John Freeman was a blacksmith, and lived here, in Cleveland Town, in 1677, but the time of his coming or going or his antecedents are not known.[4] He was fined, in 1678, for "an unseemly act in the governour's house," during a trial.

SAMUEL GOODMAN.

He served as a juror in 1684, the only time his name is mentioned.[5]

[1]Edgartown Records, I, 147.

[2]Thompson, "History of Long Island," pp. 205, 207.

[3]Chronicles of Easthampton, pp. 16, 17. Records of Southampton, II, 278, 325.

[4]Dukes Deeds, I, 37.

[5]Dukes Court Records, Vol. I.

HENRY GOSS.

He is first mentioned in 1659, when he was chosen as referee in a land dispute between John Daggett and Thomas Bayes, and the same year he sued Nicholas Norton for some dispute about a "cure" for "Gousses" child. The next year he sued the Indian Sachem Cheeshachamuck, and in 1662, accounts between him and Edward Leader are presented for trial. A John Goose was witness in 1681. Nothing is known of either of them beyond these items, and no land is credited to their name.[1]

EDWARD HATHAWAY.

In 1689, and for some time previous, this person held the tenure of the home lot at the north side of Jones' Hill. There is no record of the manner in which he acquired it nor of the disposal of it by him after the date mentioned. It may have been a forfeited grant.[2] We may suppose that this person was that Edward Hathaway, b. Feb. 10, 1663-4, the son of John and Hannah (Hallett) Hathaway of Barnstable.

EDWARD LAY.

This settler was one of the Connecticut contingent which furnished several additions to our island population between 1650 and 1660. He is first heard of at Hartford in 1640, and later at Saybrook in 1648, where he was living on the East side of the Connecticut river in the present town of Lyme. He was associated there with our Robert Codman, as appears by the following record of a court held Aug. 12, 1657:—

> The Court considering the ingagement of Edward Lay to this Jurisdiction of Robert Codmans Estate, that the said Lay should appear several years since at Hartford to answer at the Courte his abusive carriage and expressions before several of Seabrooke, which to this time he hath not attended, they order that upon the payment of £5 to the Treasr by said Codman, hee shall be free from the aforesaid seizure of Robert Codmans estate in his hands; and the said Edward Lay shall be free from the forfeiture of bond and contempt therein, which £5 being paid by Codnam for Edward Lays disappearance according to ingagement, the judge that Edward Lays estate should satisfy Codnum for the same.[3]

[1]Egdartown Records, I, 125, 130, 132, 142; Dukes Deeds, I, 90.

[2]Dukes Deeds, I, 366; II, 464.

[3]Conn. Col. Records, I, 302. He was brother of Robert and John Lay of Lyme and Saybrook. (G. R., LXII., 172.)

Edward Lay's "disappearance" from the Connecticut "several years since" is accounted for by his migration to Martha's Vineyard. He removed to this town some time prior to May 8, 1653, when he had been here long enough to be one of the proprietors and participate in the division of the Planting Field.[1] He owned at this time the sixth lot from Pease's Point, fronting the harbor and, presumably, lived there.[2] He is mentioned with his wife, whose name was Martha, in connection with a neighborhood slander case early in 1655, and on Feb. 1, 1656, is one of those who entered into an agreement with Robert Pease about his settlement.[3] In June, 1656, Lay and his wife had a case against John Pease for slander, in which he recovered damages.[4] He was fined for leaving town meeting before it was adjourned in August, 1659, and the next year, Oct. 22, 1660, is rated as a proprietor and drew lots on his share.[5] In 1661 or 1662 he removed to Rhode Island and took up a residence at Portsmouth, where he became an important citizen. He sold on Oct. 18, 1662, the following described property, which represented his real estate holdings acquired here in ten years:—

I Edward Lay inhabitant in portsmoth upon rhoad Island and in the Colonny of providence in america . . . . . .Bargain and sell unto thomas Layton (of Portsmouth) these parcells of Land with all the housin upon them first: a Lott of Eight acres of Land more or less with a Dwelling house upon the same which Land and house as all other parcells in this Deed and Sale lyeth upon the Island called Marthas Vineyard: as also I sell twenty acres of Land more or less Lying near the path Going (to) Meshackett and adjoyning to a parcell of Land of thomas Bayeses in the same Neck: as also one acre and half acre of Land Lying upon Chappaquiddick neck a Lott there be the Land more or Less and Lying between John Daggetts Land on the one side and thomas Mayhews on the other: as also ten acres of Land more of less Lying between the Land of thomas Harlock and the Land of Robert Codman Butting upon the highway to the plain: as also two acres of meadow more or Less Lying Between the land of John Pease Butting upon Mortles neck from the Sea: as also one acre of Land more or Less Lying att Crackatuxett att the going in of the next to the Land of thomas Burchards there: as also one thach Lott Joyning to peter folgers Land on the South Beach: all those above mentioned parcells of Land together with all my write of Commonage fish and whale.[6]

[1]Edgartown Records, I, 172.

[2]It was sold by him with a dwelling house on it in 1662. (Ibid., I, 98.)

[3]Ibid., I, 124, 138.

[4]Ibid., I, 114.

[5]Ibid., I, 147, 156.

[6]Ibid., I, 98.

After settling in Portsmouth, he was of the Grand Jury in 1663, Constable 1665, Deputy to the General Court 1667 and 1677, besides holding minor offices in the town. He was licensed to keep a public house in 1675.[1] His wife Martha died in 1682, and he died in 1692, aged eighty-four years. No descendants of his are known to have lived here.

THOMAS LAYTON (LAWTON.)

This person who bought the property of Edward Lay, in 1662, was from Portsmouth, R. I., where he was first settled in 1638, and in 1655 was made a freeman.[2] He is found in this town on Aug. 16, 1662, when he appears in the list of members of the train band, and a few months later he made his purchase of the Lay estate.[3] It seems probable that there is a confusion of the names Lawton and Layton in the records, as it appears there were two men of similar names in Portsmouth, Thomas Lawton and Thomas Layton. both of whom had property interests here. This Thomas Layton did not long remain here, but sold all he had purchased from Lay, as previously detailed, on June 26, 1664, when he became once more a resident of Portsmouth. He became interested with Peter Tallman of Newport in purchasing the Indian rights of Homes Hole Neck about this time, and it caused a vast amount of trouble to Governor Mayhew to disestablish the tenant whom Tallman and Layton had put there. It is here that confusion exists as to the names of Lawton and Layton. Isaac Lawton, who had married the daughter of Tallman, bought three of the shares of Homes Hole Neck and later disposed of them, while Thomas Lawton of Portsmouth, by his will of June 6, 1674, proved Sept. 29, 1681, bequeathed to his son Isaac "all rights at Marthas Vineyard."[4]

GEORGE MARTIN.

The first reference to him is under date of April 14, 1681, when he was granted "ten acres of land between the line of the ten-acre lots . . . . with the privilege of firewood and

[1]Portsmouth Town Records, passim.

[2]Savage Gen. Dict., III, 44.

[3]Edgartown Records, 98, 138.

[4]Austin, Gen. Dict. of R. I., art. Lawton. There were no "rights" belonging to a Thomas Lawton on this island, but there were speculative "rights" vested in Thomas Layton, unless some Rhode Island record contains a sale of such from Layton to Lawton.

to Live [thereon] four years."[1] The next important reference to him is as follows: Dec. 15, 1685, he was ordered to take into his possession all goods "belonging to Marget lord alias Rainer late desesed," as administrator.[2] What significance this has is not apparent by any further search, as this is the only reference to Margaret Lord. Whether she was born Lord and married Rainer, or *vice versa*, is to be construed according to facts which may develop. Neither name appears on the Vineyard Records before or after this, and where Martin got his authority is a mystery. It is possible she was Margaret, daughter of William and Jane Lord of Salem, born 1660, who on Jan. 23, 1683-84, conveyed property to her brother-in-law, and of whom no further trace is found.

On April 28, 1687, the town of Edgartown agreed with George Martin as to the keeping of "Widow" Jones, the widow of Thomas Jones. This transaction may have been without significance of relationship, a "farming out" of the town's poor.

Following this chronologically is a deposition of George Martin of Newport, under date of Sept. 18, 1690, relative to certain facts in a case then pending, together with one on same subject by Abigail Martin of Newport.[3] On Nov. 3, 1690, George Martin and Abigail, his wife, both of Newport, sold the house lot granted to him in 1681, and as far as known this ends his relation with the Vineyard.

In the second decade of the next century a Thomas Martin, or Martain, appeared at Edgartown, married and raised a family, living on the lot granted to George Martin. How he acquired it is not known, perhaps by redeeming a mortgage on it. The bounds of it were run in 1722, entered on the Proprietor's Records as belonging to Thomas Martin, "being a grant of ten acres from the town to his father, George Martin deceased."

Thomas (2) had six children recorded, of whom five were sons — Peter, Brotherton, Thomas, Lemuel, Benjamin. In 1773, Thomas (3), "gentleman," was of Lebanon, Conn., and Brotherton of Horton, Kings County, Nova Scotia. Thomas (2) was living in 1736, but died intestate before Oct. 1, 1739, when he was styled "gentleman," an unusual title on the

[1]Edgartown Records, I, 30.

[2]Court Records, Vol. I.

[3]Court Records, Vol. I; comp., Dukes Deeds, III, 126.

Vineyard records. The family name became extinct on the island in 1746, when Peter (3) died.

As to the origin of George Martin, he may have been son of George and Susanna (North) Martin of Salisbury, born 1648, several inhabitants of that town having gone to the Vineyard before 1700. Or he may be that George Martine who came to New England in the *Hannah and Elizabeth*, arriving at Boston, Aug. 10, 1679.[1]

PETER NASH.

He was the son of William Nash of Charlestown, Mass., born about 1632, and he appears to have been a mariner. The author finds him as witness to a deed of Edward Cottle in Salisbury, 1660, again at Haverhill in 1662, and a witness to a deed here in 1665 in connection with Stephen Codman.[2] Later, in 1671, he bought a ten acre lot on the "line" of Codman, which he held for many years, though probably not residing on it, and it became a part of his estate at his decease, Sept. 3, 1695, in Charlestown.[3] This lot was sold in 1709 to Thomas Trapp by Elias Brigden and wife Margaret, of Charlestown.[4]

FRANCIS NEWCOMB.

In 1681, a person of this name was granted ten acres of land "near the pond" which was later "changed," and he obtained thirteen acres adjoining the grant to Andrew Newcomb, which later became the homestead of Mr. Jonathan Dunham.[5] What relation, if any, he bore to Andrew is not known. A Francis Newcomb lived at Braintree, 1635 to 1692, and had eight children of record, but no Francis appears as his son. Our settler remained here about four years and sold his house lot on Aug. 11, 1685, and we hear no more of him on the island or elsewhere.[6]

HUGH ROE.

This person was a currier of leather residing in Weymouth as a neighbor of our Nicholas Norton, before both removed to

[1]Essex Antiquarian, IV, 137.

[2]Essex Antiquarian, II, 182; III, 108; also Dukes Deeds, I, 354. Savage finds him of Rowley, in 1660. Probably he was a mariner.

[3]The inventory of his estate included ten acres of land at Martha's Vineyard. (Wyman, Gen. and Est. of Charlestown, 696.)

[4]Dukes Deeds, III., 377.

[5]Edgartown Records, I, 30.

[6]Dukes Deeds, V, 230.

the Vineyard. How long he had lived there is uncertain, but his first wife Esther died there July 11, 1655, and he married again the following year. On Nov. 6 and 9, 1658, he sold all his property in that town; house, orchard, land, and proprietory interests in commons, and removed to the Vineyard.[1] It is more than probable that he came here with Norton, as we have found that the latter is first mentioned in our records early in 1659; and taking into account the occupation of Roe with what is known of Norton, the author thinks that both came to carry on their trade, one as a tanner and the other as a currier. He was granted a ten-acre lot on the "line" on Aug. 22, 1659, and twenty acres as a dividend at Mile Brook. It is evident that he did not show symptoms of remaining permanently, for on Oct. 22, 1660, the town voted that he "did not have right to sell or otherwise dispose of that land" granted to him.[2] Shortly after he removed to Hartford, Conn., where he was admitted an inhabitant, Sept. 2, 1661, as a currier, and in 1674 he again removed, this time to Suffolk, where he died Aug. 5, 1689, leaving a widow and several married children.[3]

EDWARD SALE (SEARLE).

This man was one of the early settlers at Great Harbor, coming here within the first decade after the younger Mayhew, and under various spellings of Sales, Sarle, Searles, Seale, and Sale his name appears in the records from 1653 to 1663 continuously. Undoubtedly, he had been here for some time prior to March 1, 1653, when there was a "case" between him and John Pease, in which it was decided "that the said Edward Sales hath his old right of fish still."[4] Whence came the settler may be determined, probably, from the following facts relative to a person or persons, bearing his name earlier in the history of the Massachusetts Bay Colony: An Edward Sale, aged twenty-four years, embarked in the *Elizabeth and Ann*, April 27, 1635, from London, and in the same vessel was

[1]Suffolk Deeds, XI, 181. The land had in part been first granted to Nicholas Norton. The deed was acknowledged June, 7, 1659.

[2]Edgartown Records, I, 147.

[3]Hampshire Probate Records, I, 267. Contemporaneously with Hugh Roe there lived, in Gloucester, Mass. (1651–1662), one John Roe, who had land once owned by Nicholas Norton in that town. John had a son Hugh born about 1640, and as the baptismal names are similar in both families it may be inferred that John was an elder brother of our Hugh.

[4]Edgartown Records, I, 149.

Richard Sarson and Jeremiah Whitton, both early residents here.[1] In 1637 he was probably a resident of Salem or Marblehead, with his wife Margaret, who in that year was tried and convicted of gross immorality and banished from the colony. At the same time "Edward Seale for his beastly drunkennes was censured to bee set in the bilboes till the end of the Court & then to bee severely whipt."[2] An Edward Seale was of Rehoboth in 1643 and his estate was appraised at £81–00–00 that year, but whether an older Edward or the same one cannot be stated with confidence.[3] The next occurrence of the name is in our records under date of February 6, 1653, when it is entered: —

> Edward Sale hath four acres added to his house lot so that it may be laid out together with least hurt to the town.[4]

This house lot was a ten-acre grant "forty Poles square," near the Great Swamp, half way between the West Tisbury road and Meshacket path. It is known to this day as the "Sarson Lot," now owned intact by Mr. Clement Norton. In May, 1653, Edward Sale drew lot number 3 in the Planting Field, and was fined for absence from town meeting.[5] On June 6, 1654, he was received as "townsman," and was elected as an Assistant to the Chief Magistrate.[6] There is no further mention of him except incidentally until 1659, when he was witness to the sale of Nantucket to the "Ten Associates" July 2 of that year,[7] and on December 2, same year, a commonage and a ten-acre lot on the line was granted to "Brother Sale."[8] In 1660 there is a further record about his lands, and on Dec. 23, 1661, he submitted to the Patentees Government.[9] He had a suit against John Pease, elsewhere referred to, in 1662, and the next year was granted the small island in Sanchacantacket, now known as Sarson's island.[10] The last

[1]Gen. Reg., XIV, 312.

[2]Court of Assistants, I, 197, 200; comp., Winthrop, "Journal," II, 349. There was a John Sayle bound out to service with his daughter Phebe in 1633 (Ibid., I, 99).

[3]Arnold, "Vital Records of Rehoboth, 910. John Daggett and Edward Seale were associated in Rehoboth.

[4]Edgartown Records, I, 131. To this was added three acres of swamp in 1654. (Ibid., 119.)

[5]Ibid., pp. 131, 172.

[6]Ibid., 122.

[7]Macy, "History of Nantucket, 20.

[8]Edgartown Records, I, 132.

[9]Ibid., 110, 144.

[10]Ibid., 108, 138.

record of him personally is under date of April 8, 1663, when he acted as a juror, and before December 30, same year, he had sold all his lands and estate in the town and thenceforth disappears from the records.[1]

Whither he went is not positively known, but again at Rehoboth is found a record that Goodman Searle was accepted as inhabitant July 3, 1663, and granted a home lot, and we may assume that he returned thither, where twenty years before an Edward Sales had lived.[2] It further appears that Jared Ingraham, son of Richard of Rohoboth, married in Boston, May 28, 1662, Rebecca, daughter of an Edward Searles, from which, in connection with the fact that Christopher Gibson of Boston speaks of "my brother Eddward Sealle," we may infer that Gibson was her uncle, and that we here have further clues to this Sales family and its descendants.[3] We may have a final view in old age of our first settler in the person of Edward Sale of Weymouth, who died before Oct. 6, 1692, when an inventory of his estate was taken, and on April 13, 1693, administration was granted to John Rogers of Weymouth.[4]

"MRS." SCOTT.

A person of this name is entered on the early records of Edgartown, as one of the proprietors of land in 1664, and is credited in the division of shares with two drawings of lots during that year.[5] This is not the first mention of her name, however, as in the previous year, when a "general fence" was to be built, the "engagers" (*i. e.*, subscribers), who were charged with the expense, are given in a list, and she appears in the following entry: "Thomas Mayhew for himself, Thomas

[1]Edgartown Records, I, 135.

[2]Bliss, "History of Rehoboth," 53. In July, 1664, "Rebeckah Sale, the late wife of Edward Sale . . . . hanged herself in her own hiered house," according to a coroner's inquest. (Plymo. Col. Rec., IV. 83.)

[3]Boston Record Com'rs Report, IX, 86; comp., Suffolk Probate, VI, 64. In his will proved in 1674 Christopher Gibson names Hannah Seale, Alice Sealle, Ephraim Sealle, and "sister Ingrham & her husband my friend Willyam Ingrham." and Jarrat (Jared) Inghram and his wife Rebecka Sealle. There is no Edward Sale, Seale or Searle in the Suffolk Deeds.

[4]Suffolk Probate, XIII, 156, 403. We are further confronted with another Edward Searle who lived in Rhode Island, at Warwick, about 1670, and married, probably as second wife, Joan White, a widow, sister of Edmund Calverly of Warwick. This Edward had a son Edward, who in 1671 married Ann, widow of John Lippit, Jr., and removed to Cranston in that colony. This Edward senior died in 1679. (Savage, Gen. Dict., IV, 45.)

[5]She drew lot 27 at Felix Neck and seven at Meachemy's Field.

Harlock, Thomas Paine 3, younger Mayhews one, Mrs. Scott one, Widow Foulger one, all in eight Lott(s)."[1] In this connection a previous entry may be of significance, a list of lot owners as defendants in a suit, 1661, which reads: "Thomas Mayhew for Myself and all Relations in the town that is eight lotts." These two entries taken together may be interpreted as a list of the relatives by marriage or blood of Governor Mayhew, then living, or owning property in Edgartown, for the first contains the name of Thomas Harlock, son-in-law; Thomas Paine, step-son; "younger Mayhews," grandchildren, and "Mrs." Scott and "Widow" Foulger (Merible, wife of John), by implication as "relatives." It is believed that the identity of "Mrs." Scott can be established, and the following facts are marshalled to indicate that she was Elizabeth, wife of Robert Scott of Boston:—

Malachi Browning and an Elizabeth Scott had legal business connected with their respective relatives in London on the same day in Boston, 27 (8), 1649, though no relationship between them is stated.[2] This conjunction would not necessarily be conclusive of anything more than accident, but for the further fact that Malachi Browning died four years later "at the house of Robert Scott," in Boston, as appears by the town records. He was probably on a visit to "Mrs." Scott when his death occurred, Nov. 27, 1653, and this association of these two incidents seems to enable us to extend the name of this lady in full to Mrs. Elizabeth Scott, the wife of Robert, a haberdasher of Boston.

Just how Mrs. Scott came into possession of a lot in Edgartown before 1664 cannot be determined, as the records give no clue. It is possible that in consideration of care during his last illness in Boston Malachi Browning bequeathed this proprietary share to her, but there remains no record of his will by which this surmise can be re-enforced. There is no record to show how Mrs. Scott's share passed into other hands.

Elizabeth Scott received a bequest of money from her grandmother, Mrs. Mary Hussey of London, some time before May 21, 1648, when Robert Scott, her husband, gave a power of attorney for collecting the legacy.[3] This might indicate that she was born a Hussey. After the death of Robert Scott,

[1]Edgartown Records, I, 147.
[2]Aspinwall Notarial Records, 226.
[3]Ibid., 147.

in February, 1654, she became the wife of John Sweete. Dorothy, wife of Nicholas Upsall, made a bequest in 1675 to her "sister, Elizabeth Sweete," who may or may not be our Elizabeth. In a deposition, 1663, Elizabeth Scott, aged forty-seven (born 1616), testified to matters in London about twenty-six years ago (1637).[1]

RICHARD SMITH.

A person of this name, born about 1617, resided here before 1652, and was the owner of a half lot, one of the Five and Twenty, the fifth from Pease's Point. He drew a lot on May 8, 1653, in the division of the Planting Field, which he sold to John Folger.[2] On June 6, 1654, he was chosen with six others "to end all controversies," and to hold Quarter Courts.[3] Previous to this, however, he had been prospecting for another settlement in Connecticut, and had received a grant in 1652 in the town of New London.[4] He had relatives also in other portions of that colony, as he speaks of "my brother Matthias Treate," who took him on a trip up the Sturgeon River, in the present town of Glastonbury. "I will show our country here," said Matthias, "it may be you will come and live here."[5] This was "30 or 40 years ago," as Richard Smith deposed in 1684, making the date of his visit 1644–1654, of which the latter is the more probable. Smith remained in the new town, or at least sold out here about that time, and ended his connection with the Vineyard.[6] Diligent effort has been made by the author and others to indentify this person in his new home and to learn more of him and his family there, as nothing is of record here to help the solution.[7] The number of Richards, Senior and Junior, in that town has proven an almost hopeless barrier to a satisfactory conclusion, and as he belongs to Wethersfield, his record after leaving the Vineyard is left to the historian of that town.[8]

[1]Pope, "Pioneers of Massachusetts," art. Robert Scott.

[2]Dukes Deeds, I, 252.

[3]Edgartown Records, I.

[4]Caulkins, History of New London, 322. He was called "of Martin's Vineyard."

[5]Connecticut Archives, Vol. III. (Personal Controversies.) Hollister *vs* Bulkeley, No. 122.

[6]He sold his harbor lot to Thomas Burchard. (Deeds, I, 320.)

[7]Particular mention must be made of the help given by Mrs. D. E. Penfield, of Vineyard descent, who has spent much time and labor in the attempt to clear up the doubts about this Richard.

[8]Stiles, History of Wethersfield, I, 299, is equally befogged with the rest who have undertaken to identify the various Richard Smiths in that town.

JOHN STANBRIDGE.

This man was a tailor by occupation, who is first heard of in Boston, 1674, on the tax list, and in 1678 he took the oath of allegiance in that town. He is found there in 1681, 1687 and 1688, but before this, probably about 1673, he had married Sarah, daughter of Nicholas Norton, which explains his connection with our island.[1] How soon he came here to live is not definitely known, possibly before 1692, when he was a witness to a deed.[2] After this he seems to have removed as in 1703 he bought property here (part of the Mayhew home lot), and is then called "late of Newport."[3] Evidently he was a roamer. He remained here for some ten years, and is mentioned in the records until 1714, when it appears that he again removed to Newport. The next record of him is in 1719, when "John Stanbridge, Taylor and wife, wich came from R. Island" were warned to depart from Boston by the authorities. This however was not followed out by Stanbridge, as he was an unsuccessful petitioner in that town for a license to retail liquor in 1723, the last we hear from him.[4] In 1731, his wife, or widow probably, entered suit in our courts against ten of her nephews by blood and marriage, alleging that they had invited her to come from Boston to Edgartown, promising maintenance, which they had failed to perform, and asking damage. The court awarded her £100 and the defendants appealed.[5]

SAMUEL STREETER.

This man was a tailor originally, settling at Gloucester and later at Nantucket. He was granted a ten acre lot on the "line" Jan. 12, 1663, is mentioned in a deed, 1665, and a short

[1]Sarah, wife of John Stanbridge, was convicted of selling rum without a license, Jan. 30, 1685-6. (Dukes Court Rec., Vol. I.)

[2]Dukes Deeds, I, 48. He was plaintiff in a suit in the Cambridge, Mass., Court 1690. (Records, Court of Assistants, I, 330.)

[3]Ibid, I, 134.

[4]Boston Town Records.

[5]Dukes County Records, Vol. II. She called herself a seamstress. It is possible that the plaintiff may be a daughter of Sarah (Norton) Stanbridge, who sues her cousins. There being no court files in the county archives of that date, the pleadings are not available.

career was terminated on Nov. 19, 1669, when he was drowned with Richard Arey between this island and Nantucket.[1]

PETER TABOR.

This person was among the earliest settlers, almost contemporaneous with Mayhew himself. He had first seated himself at Watertown, where he was made a freeman May 14, 1634, and about four years later he removed to Yarmouth, Cape Cod.[2] He remained there for an undetermined period and moved thence to Great Harbor. As he had been a townsman of Thomas Mayhew in Watertown his migration to the Vineyard after the latter had purchased the island in 1641, may be attributed to personal acquaintance with Mayhew. Taber was in Edgartown before 1647, at which time he sold to John Bland "all his Right that he then Possessed," but it is evident that Taber acquired further holdings, not recorded, as he continued to reside on the Vineyard and participated as a proprietor in all the divisions of land until 1655.[3] In this year, on May 15, "it was agreed" by the magistrates that he had been guilty of immoralities, and on Aug. 2, 1655, "Philip Taber now being at Portsmouth in Rhode Island" sold his estate on the Vineyard and thenceforth lived elsewhere.[4] He had lived here for at least nine years, but the New London records show a house lot granted to him in 1651, on which a house was built, presumably by him. This was sold in 1652 or 1653 by Cary Latham, in behalf of "my brother Philip Tabor now dwelling at Martin's Vineyard."[5]

In the "History of New London," he is mentioned as coming to that town from "Martha's Vineyard" with a body of Eastern emigrants, and was among those who "wrought at the mill dam" that year in July.[6] It is possible that he removed to New London from the Vineyard in 1651, remained a year or two, and returned to the latter place in 1653, when a land grant to him is recorded. But he had drawn lots in

[1]Edgartown Records, I, 130. Dukes Deeds, I, 354; Savage, Genealogical Dictionary, IV, 223. The late Abner Mayhew owned a book, printed in 1632, which was once the property of Samuel Streeter and containing his autograph, 1664. Its subsequent owners were Matthew Mayhew, Experience Mayhew, Joseph Mayhew, Jane Bassett and Benjamin Bassett, all of whom left their autographs inside the covers.

[2]He had a son baptized at Barnstable, Nov. 8, 1640, John, "son of Phillipp Tabor, dwelling at Yarmouth, a member of the Chh att Watertown." He was propounded as freeman, Jan. 3, 1638-9 at Yarmouth.

[3]On Oct. 14, 1647, he signed as witness at Great Harbor. (Suffolk Deeds, I, 86.)

[4]Dukes Deeds, I, 325.

[5]Caulkins, Manuscript Collections.

[6]Caulkins, History of New London, 70

August, 1651, at Edgartown, thus practically giving us conflicting dates with the New London records.

In 1656 he appears as a freeman of Portsmouth, R. I., and not long after at Providence, of which place he was a Representative in 1661. Later he was of Dartmouth (1667-8), and probably ended his days there after all these wanderings.[1] Descendants continued to reside in this latter named town during all of the next century, and probably all of the name in that vicinity can trace their lineage to him.

He was born about 1605, and married, as is stated, three times. His first wife was Lydia Masters of Cambridge. The others are not known to the author. By her, perhaps she was the mother of all his children, he had John, 1640, Philip, Lydia, Thomas, 1646, and Joseph.

During his life on the Vineyard, about nine years, his name appears frequently on the records, as grantee of sundry lots. He owned No. 2 in the "Five and Twenty" homestalls, and in 1653 acquired by grant of the town a considerable tract at Mashacket. He was one of the magistrates chosen in 1653, but was not re-elected the next year, and in 1655 was convicted as above stated and left the Vineyard.

PETER TALLMAN.

It is probable that this man came to New England in 1648, bringing "three negros" in the ship Golden Dolphin, and settled in Rhode Island.[2] He became a freeman in 1655, and in 1661 was Solicitor General of that colony. Whether he ever lived here is problematical, but it is certain that he was a land owner in 1663 and 1664, taking shares in the land divisions of those years.[3] He acquired the William Case lot, but in what manner is not known, possibly by marrying his widow. The lot is spoken of as "William Cases which is Tallmans."[4] With his son-in-law, Thomas Lawton, also a proprietor here, he bought Homes Hole Neck of the Indians about 1664 or 1667, as will be related in the annals of that place, and lost it through the opposition of Mayhew. This is his last connection with the Vineyard.

[1]Plymouth Colony Records, V, 254. No record of the settlement of his estate is to be found in the Bristol County registry. Savage states that he was also of Tiverton, but the author finds no evidence to substantiate the claim.

[2]Aspinwall, Notarial Record, 359, 370. He was an apothecary.

[3]Edgartown Records, I, 109, 127.

[4]Ibid., I, 4.

ROBERT WADE.

He was a juror here in 1681, which probably indicates residence of some duration prior to that date. He is, it may be assumed, the person of that name who was of Dorchester, 1635, Hartford, 1640, then Saybrook, and in 1669 of Norwich, showing that he was a roamer.

JOHN WAKEFIELD.

There were in New England before 1653 a number of Wakefields bearing the baptismal name of John, and the meager data respecting the John Wakefield who owned a lot here prior to 1652 does not afford any definite clue to the particular one who came to the island early and left it equally so. He was witness to a document signed here Oct. 14, 1647, in relation to a guardianship for Thomas Paine.[1] Whether he was the John of Salem and Marblehead, 1637, 1638, or the John of Plymouth, 1639, or John of Watertown, 1646, who may all have been one person having these residences in succession, cannot be satisfactorily determined.[2] Under date of Nov. 11, 1652, "the Lott that is next that which was first given to John Wakefield" is mentioned, and this tells us of his disappearance from the island before that date, and his possessions had passed either by purchase or regrant to Thomas Paine.[3] A John Wakefield appeared in Boston subsequent to this and died there about 1667, and administration of his estate was given to his widow Anne on July 18, that year.[4]

PHILIP WATSON

This settler was a late arrival in the town, coming hither from an unknown direction, about 1670, but soon attaining prominence. He became town clerk in 1671, which office he held for an undetermined period, but as late as 1686 he was still in office as such.[5] He was selectman in 1676, juror in 1681, and during the twenty years of his life here maintained the usual activities of a citizen in and out of court. It has been hinted in the sketch of John Bland that Watson may have been some "kith or kin" of Mrs. Joanna Bland, as he and his son had dealings with parts of the Bland property. Beyond this supposition there is no clue to his origin prior to

[1]Suffolk Deeds, I, 86.
[2]Savage, Gen. Dict., IV, 385; Pope, "Pioneers of Mass.," art. Wakefield.
[3]Edgartown Records, I, 120, 147.
[4]Suffolk Co. Probate.
[5]Edgartown Records, I, 13, 35, 36.

settlement at the Vineyard. No person of his name is to be found in any of the Watson family histories, nor in any of the New England settlements.[1] He may have been a recent immigrant from England [2]

He died April 28, 1690, and an inventory of his estate showed property to the value of £56–7–1, and a son Elias was recorded as "heir of Philip Watson late of Edgartown, late deceased."[3] No wife is mentioned, or known to the author. Elias remained in Edgartown as late as 1704, when he was a witness to a deed, but nothing further is known of him, whether married or having descendants.

AUGUSTINE WILLIAMS.

This transient resident was another son-in-law of Nicholas Norton, and he is first found here in 1679, as a witness, and again in 1684 and 1687 in the same connection.[4] The town records have an entry relating to him in 1681, and it may be inferred that he was a constant resident here between the earlier and later dates. Of his antecedents nothing is definitely known, but he was probably a resident of Stonington, Conn., (1663), and possibly a mariner. He married Hannah Norton (13), and had Thomas [1678], Hannah, 1680, Daniel, 1683, Bethiah, 1686, and Matthew, 1688, all recorded at Killingworth, Conn., whither he removed about the last named date. He died shortly after this, as in 1692 his widow Hannah was empowered by the General Court to sell certain property, according to a verbal bargain made by her deceased husband.[5] She was here on Aug. 17, 1692, as witness to a deed, probably on a visit.[6] She married a second time, before 1699, elder John Brown of Killingworth.[7]

[1]There was a Philip Challis in Salisbury, who was sometimes called Philip Watson Challis and had a son born in that town in 1657. (Hoyt, "Old Families of Salisbury," 89.) He was fifty-two years old in 1669, and died about 1681 in Amesbury.

[2]A Philip Watson married Margaret Seele in Nottingham, Nov. 30, 1630, according to the Parish Registers.

[3]Dukes County Court Records, Vol. I; comp., Deeds, I, 398. Thomas Harlock was appointed one of the administrators of his estate.

[4]Dukes Deeds, I, 322, 331. The Diary of Thomas Minor of Stonington speaks of delivering corn to Augustine Williams in 1680 (p. 160), indicating residence in Connecticut at that date.

[5]Conn. Col. Records.

[6]Dukes Deeds, I, 184.

[7]Killingworth Town Records. Thomas Williams, natural son and heir to Augustine Williams, deceased, deeds to his natural mother, Hannah Brown, administratrix of estate of his father, March 12, 1699. Elder Brown died in 1708, but whether she survived is not known to the author.

INCORPORATION OF THE TOWN.

Although the conditions of government for the settlements on the island, made at the time of its purchase, were presented to be "such as is now established in the Massachusetts," yet we have seen that this course was not pursued by the patentees in the general administration of its affairs as a whole, nor was it in the town of Great Harbor. In Massachusetts the towns were governed by boards of selectmen, chosen annually by the freemen, but this practice would not be countenanced by Mayhew, and there is no evidence to show that any town officers having the powers of selectmen were chosen for managing its business. John Burchard had been "chosen town Clarke" in 1656 and John Butler "chosen Constable" in 1658, and these officers were filled annually from those dates, but beyond these two necessary officials, without initiative authority, we have no town government like that "established in the Massachusetts."

When the Duke of York extended his jurisdiction over the island, this requirement, already a dead letter, became by the process null and void. As a part of New York it partook of the customs and laws of that province, and it has been seen that the ducal government did not encourage popular elections nor town meetings. The principal fruit of this political change was the incorporation of Great Harbor on July 8, 1671, under the name of Edgartown. The charter under which this town now exists is as follows: —

FRANCIS LOVELACE Esqr: one of the Gentlemen of his Maties Hon'ble Privy Chambr and Governor Genll under his Royall Highness JAMES Duke of Yorke and Albany &c of all his Territories in America: To all to whom these Presents shall come sendeth Greeting: WHEREAS there is a certaine Island within these His Royall Highness his Territoryes lyeing & being to the North West of the Island Nantuckett which said Island was heretofore Graunted unto Thomas Mayhew Senr & Thomas Mayhew Junr his Sonn by James Forrett Agent to William Earle of Sterling in whom the Government then was and by them a Proportion at the East end thereof Graunted to Severall Inhabitants Freeholders there for a Towneshipp who have made Purchase of the Indian Right, the said Towne being formerly knowne by the Name of the Great Harbour the Precincts whereof are Bounded on the East by the Eastermost End of a Small Island called Chappo-quiddick; on the South by Teque-Nomens Neck; on the North by the Eastermost Chap of Holmes Neck and on the West by a Line to bee runn between the South and North Bounds: NOW for a Confirmacon unto the prsent Inhabitants Freeholders there and their Associates in their Possession and Enjoyment of the Premises KNOW YE that by vertue of the Commission and Authority unto mee given by his Royall Highness upon whom (as well by the resignation & Assignment of the Heyres of the said William Earle of Sterling as also by Grant & Patent from his Royall Matie CHARLES the second) the Propriety & Government of Long Island, Martins Vineyard Nantuckett & all the Islands adjacent amongst other things is settled I have Given & Graunted & by these Presents doe Give Ratify Confirme and Grant unto the present Inhabitants Freeholders and their Associates their Heyres Successors & Assignes the Land whereon the said Towne is settled Together with all the Lands Soyles Woods Meadowes Pastures Marshes Lakes Waters Fishing Hawking Hunting & Fowling within the Bounds & Lymitts afore described & all other Profitts Commodityes Emolumts & Hereditaments to the said Towne & Land belonging or in any wise appertaining: the Tenure whereof is to bee according to the Custome of the Mannor of East Greenwich in the County of Kent in England in free & Common Soccage & by Fealty only. And the said Towne (which for the future shall bee called by the Name of EDGAR TOWNE and by that Name & Style shall bee distinguisht and knowne in all Bargaines and Sales Deeds Records and Writeings) shall bee held, deemed, reputed, taken & bee an Entire Enfranchized Towneship of it selfe & shall alwayes from time to time have hold & enjoy like & equall Priviledges with other Townes within the Governmt & shall in noe manner or any wise bee under the Rule, Order or Direction of any other Place but in all mattere of Governmt shall be Ruled Ordered & Directed according to the Instructione I have already given or hereafter shall give for the Good and Welfare of the Inhabitants by the Advice of my Councell: TO HAVE AND TO HOLD the said Towne with the Lands thereunto belonging with all and Singular the Appertenances and Premisses unto the said Inhabitants, Freeholders and their Associates their Heyres Successors & Assignes forever. THEY the said Inhabitants & their Associates their Heyres Successors & Assignes Yielding rendring & Paying yearly & every yeare unto his Royall Highness the Duke of Yorke his Heyres & Assignes or to such Governor or Governors as from time to time shall bee by him Constituted & Appointed as an Acknowledgment two Barrells of Merchantable Cod Fish to bee delivered at the Bridg in this Citty. GIVEN under my Hand and Sealed with the Seale of the Province at Fort James in New Yorke on the Island of Manhattans this eighth day of July in the three and twentyeth yeare of the Reigne of our Sovereigne Lord CHARLES the Second by the Grace of God of England Scotland France and Ireland King Defender of the Faith &c & in the yeare of our Lord God One Thousand six hundred seaventy & one.[1]

It will be noted that the new town was to hold its charter "in free & common soccage,"[2] according to the "custome of the Mannor of East Greenwich," county of Kent, England, which was a phrase employed in similar circumstances to describe the tenure as honorable in character, and determined

[1]New York Col. Mss. (Patents, IV, 71).

[2]Free and common soccage is to be distinguished from villein soccage. The former was definite in conditions, as by fealty and the payment of a certain nominal sum as annual rent. Villein soccage was of a base or menial quality, such as rendering labor for the proprietor, and was equivalent to what is now called copyhold tenure.

solely by fealty to the crown without service or other subordination. It was also specially prescribed that it was to be "Ruled, Ordered & Directed according to the Instructions" of the Governor and Council of New York, having at the same time "Equall Priviledges with other Townes within the Governm't" of that province.

It seemed to make but little difference with the affairs of this community whether the freemen lived under Mayhew's personal rule or under a charter. Not much remains to show that they exercised many or few "priviledges" afterward. In 1676 occurs the first indication of participation in town business. On that date, Thomas Bayes, John Pease, and Philip Watson were "put in by the town to see all orders put in execution,"[1] and this may be interpreted as three chosen or select men to administer its affairs, though they were not so designated. The title of selectmen was then a peculiar one in New England, and was not adopted by New York. In 1682, Joseph Norton and Thomas Butler were chosen "overseers," the first use of that title, and under various phraseology certain men were chosen to "act" for the town each year. We may suppose that they were equivalent to our selectmen. This title was not used until March, 1692, immediately following the consolidation of the island government with Massachusetts, under the charter of William and Mary. In 1693 they were called "townsmen", and in 1694 "overseers," but in 1696 the name "selectmen" was applied and has been borne ever since by those chosen to manage our town affairs.

ECCLESIASTICAL AFFAIRS

In considering the inception of ecclesiastical matters in the town it seems necessary to eliminate Thomas Mayhew, Jr., as originally migrating hither in a ministerial capacity. That he served the handful of people who came with him as a spiritual leader, conducting the usual weekly services and performing such other functions of a kindred character is quite within the probabilities. The necessities of the situation imposed this duty on him, which was undoubtedly agreeable to his inclinations as well as befitting his temporal leadership. But that this relation of pastor and proprietor was not regarded by the settlers as more than one of temporary expediency seems clear from the statement of Governor Winthrop in 1643,

[1]Sept. 11, 1676. Edgartown Records.

when recording the migration of "divers families" from Watertown to the Vineyard. He says: "they procured a young man, one Mr. (Henry) Green,[1] a scholar to be their minister, in hopes soon to gather a church there. He went not."[2] It is probable that this was an effort to secure a regularly educated clergyman for the little congregation of settlers, and it is scarcely probable that it did not have the sanction of both the elder and younger Mayhew, whose interests were paramount in all that pertained to the welfare of the infant colony. In consequence of the failure to secure the services of Mr. Henry Green, a continuation of the lay ministrations of young Thomas Mayhew became not only the most expedient but a mutually satisfactory arrangement. Daniel Gookin, writing in 1674, says of the young Thomas: "being a scholar and pious man *after some time* was called to be minister unto the English upon that island."[3] Rev. Thomas Prince, the New England chronologist, writing in 1723, says of Thomas Mayhew, Jr., that "soon after their settlement on the Island the new Plantation called him to the ministry among them."[4]

It may, therefore, be fairly concluded that this pastoral relation borne by the younger Mayhew was determined by accident rather than by design, and was the natural outcome of the isolated situation in which the dozen families here found themselves, unable to induce an educated young clergyman with prospects, to a far-off isle, or to offer sufficient pecuniary profit to tempt one to this seclusion. Although Johnson[5] and Gookin state that he was "called" to the "Church of Christ gathered at the Vineyard," yet for reasons above given the author doubts if he was ever ordained in the usual way by a council of ministers or regarded as more than a "teacher."

[1]Green, Rev. Henry, scholar, minister, Ipswich, freeman, May 13, 1642; was paid in 1643 for service against the Indians. Was invited to be minister at Martin's Vineyard in 1643, but "went not." He was ordained pastor at Reading May 9, 1645, and died in May, 1648. (Pope, Pioneers of Mass.)

[2]Journal, II, 152.

[3]Mass. Hist. Coll., I, 141.

[4]The Rev. Experience Mayhew in his preface to the ordination sermon preached by him at the settlement of the Rev. John Newman, in 1746, places the establishment of the Church in the year 1642, and adds: "in the same year that the first Inhabitants came to this Island your Church was gathered and a Reverend and worthy Person, (Mr. Thomas Mayhew) was ordained Pastor of it." While this distinguished grandson should be a competent witness on this point, yet writing as he did a century after the events he narrates, he is not entitled to the same credence as one writing contemporaneously like Gookin, who got his information direct from the younger Mayhew, "being well acquainted with him," as he states.

[5]Wonder-working Providence, c. 10.

FIRST MEETING-HOUSE.

It is not known when or where the first meeting-house was erected. There could not have been much demand for one of great size to accommodate the few people, and it is more than likely that services were held in dwelling houses, or perhaps the scohol-house, until such time as the settlement increased in numbers, and this temporary shelter ceased to be adequate. The "English Meeting" is referred to in 1643.[1] The first notice in the town records is under date of Feb. 6, 1653, and is as follows: —

> "Ordered By the town that upon the first day of March the town is to come together at the Pastors house to Begin to build a meeting house. The Leader is to order the Company and Set every man to his worke."[2]

Probably this first house was then built, and we may accept 1653 as the date of its erection. Thus far no clue to the proximate spot selected by the settlers for this primitive house of worship has been found. The records are absolutely silent on the subject, and it has even escaped the uncertain aid of tradition to help us fix the site. In this predicament a surmise is allowable and may pass for what is it worth. The author regards it as highly probable that this first building was placed in the acre on Burying hill, set aside for the dead in the little town. This was the usual custom in other New England towns, to set the meeting-house next the cemetery, and it may be concluded that our ancestors followed this arrangement.

DEATH OF THE YOUNGER MAYHEW.

When the young missionary left the Vineyard in the late fall of 1657 to go to England, never to return as it unfortunately proved, he left the care of the church to Peter Folger, the schoolmaster.[3] This young man had been an assistant to Mayhew in his religious work among the Indians, and was familiar with the duties devolving upon him. When the prolonged absence of the young pastor made it certain that he had been lost at sea, Folger undoubtedly served in the capacity of "teacher" or "elder" for a number of years, until about 1663, when he removed to Nantucket. He had become a

[1]Mayhew, Indian Converts, 2.

[2]Town Records, I, 125.

[3]Letter of Experience Mayhew to John Gardner, 1694.

Baptist, and it is more than probable that his departure from the settled doctrine of the Puritan sect was the cause of his leaving the Vineyard. Meanwhile the bereaved governor was searching about for a settled successor to his lost son. He sought the assistance of Governor John Winthrop, Jr., of Connecticut, in the selection, and among others endeavored to induce the Rev. Abraham Pierson of Branford to take up the fallen thread. Mr. Pierson was an A.B. of Trinity College, Cambridge, England, 1632, and had been the minister of Branford, Conn., since 1647.[1] This expectation proved futile.

MINISTRY OF JOHN COTTON.

The opportunity to secure a suitable candidate presented itself later, doubtless through the agency of Governor Winthrop. John Cotton, Jr., son of the celebrated Boston preacher of that name, was living in Wethersfield, Conn., and preaching occasionally in that town and also at Haddam and Killingworth. He was born in Boston in 1640 and was graduated at Harvard College when but seventeen years of age. Going to Connecticut soon after graduation, he pursued theological studies under Rev. Samuel Stone of Hartford. He married Joanna, daughter of Dr. Bryan Rossiter of Killingworth. His son Josiah writes as follows of the young clergyman and his bride: "He could hardly have made a more suitable Choice on account of age & other Qualifications. She was born July, 1642. And by consent of all Parties they were Married November 7, 1660. My Father remained unsettled Several years after & I suppose might preach at those Places above mentioned & elsewhere occasionally till Providence opened a Door at Edgartown or old Town on Marthas Vineyard."[2]

The young clergyman came here with his equally youthful wife about 1664–5, he twenty-four and she twenty-two years of age, bringing with them their first born child, also named John. Shortly after their arrival a daughter, named Sarah, born Jan. 17, 1665, was added to their household. Probably this was during his probationary term of preaching, customary in those times, and he proved satisfactory, as a scion of the famous Cotton family could not help proving. On Feb. 1, 1664–5, the town voted: —

[1]Savage, III, 433.

[2]Diary, Josiah Cotton, part 2, loc. cit.

"there shall be forty Pounds Raised yearly to maintain the Ministry: the way is to Rate the yearly sum By Rating of Kine, houses & Lands,"

And they supplemented this necessary preliminary basis for negotiation with a "joynt vote . . . . . for calling of Mr. Cotton to the Ministry of this Island."[1]

The town records contain his reply, short and to the point: —

"May 24, 1665. I do accept of the Call of the town so far as to continue Preaching of the gospel amongst them whilst god in his orderly Providence continues me hear."[2]

SECOND MEETING-HOUSE ERECTED.

As a regularly educated clergyman was now settled amongst them, the townsmen made immediate arrangements to build a new meeting-house to accommodate the growing population and on the same day of the acceptance of the call the following vote was passed: —

"There shall be a meeting house Built with all convenient speed: the place where the Meeting House is to be sett is at the West end of Mrs. Searles Lott upon the Common Land: the Dimentions of the house is thirty three foot long; nineteen foot in Breadth and eight foot Stud."[3]

No plan of this house remains, nor is any view of it extant. The subjoined sketch of the floor plan and elevation is presented for the purpose of indicating approximately the interior and exterior of this modest meetinghouse, whose "dimentions" did not exceed that of the ordinary dwelling of the present day. The location of this new structure can be more accurately fixed. The "Searles Lott" passed into the possession of Richard Sarson, and for over two centuries has been known as the "Sarson Lott."[4] On the east side of this lot was the "Ministerial Lot," so called, but never used as such, probably owing to the lack of settled clergymen after the death of the younger Mayhew. Near by it lived the Rev. Jonathan Dunham, when he came to assume pastoral charge here, and in the early days, when the first owner, Edward Searles, occupied it, the schoolhouse stood on adjoining land. It was therefore the intellectual centre of the town. Burial

[1]Edgartown Records, I, 110.

[2]Ibid., I, 111.

[3]Ibid., I, 111.

[4]Its present owner (1907) is Clement Norton, who derived title through the heirs of Edmund Lewis and Christopher Beetle. It is just north of "Cleveland Town."

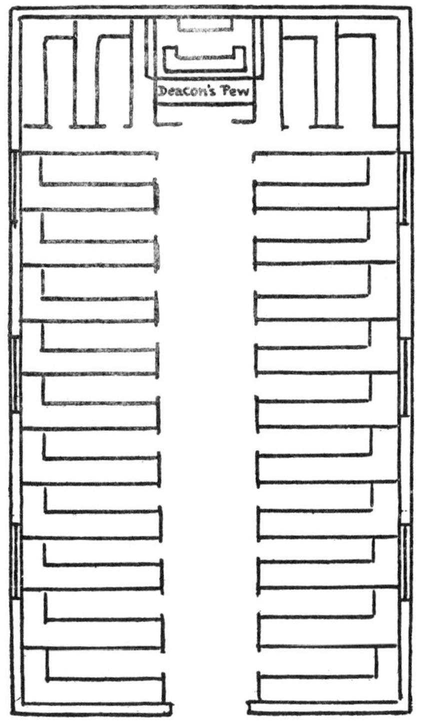

PLAN AND VIEW OF SECOND MEETING-HOUSE, EDGARTOWN.

hill was out of the way as a convienent location. The population of the town was then mostly housed between Cleveland Town and Meshacket, and this new location was intended to accommodate the majority of the settlers. It is of course hazardous to attempt locating the exact spot on the "Common Land" where they erected this second house of worship, but we can guess that it was on the old path that bounded the north side of the Sarson lot and near the great swamp.

The young clergyman immediately began to apply himself to his duties as pastor to the town and teacher of the Indian mission. Cotton Mather, his uncle, says of him: "He hired an Indian after the rate of Twelve pence per day for Fifty Days to teach him the Indian Tongue; but his Knavish Tutor having received his Whole Pay too soon, ran away before Twenty Days were out; however in this time he had profited so far that he could quickly preach unto the Natives."[1] In this dual capacity Cotton labored for over two years, when he fell under the displeasure of the old Governor. The cause of it is not known. Cotton was then twenty-five and Mayhew seventy-five years of age, and doubtless the young man refused to submit to the dictations of the elder in the performance of his duties, and a rupture resulted. The governor reported the matter to the Commissioners of the United Colonies, by whom Cotton was paid as a missionary to the Indians, and in September, 1667,

> "Mr. John Cotton appeared before the Comissioners and was seriously spoken too To Compose those allianations between him and Mr. Mayhew: otherwise it was signified to him that the Comissioners could not expect good by theire laboure wheras by their mutuall Contensions and Invictives one against the other they undid what they taught the Natives, and sundry calles (as he said) being made him by the English to other places . . . . . he was left to his libertie to dispose of himselfe as the Lord should Guid him."[2]

The young man considering his usefulness at an end promptly decided to leave the Vineyard, and on Nov. 30, 1667, removed to Plymouth, one of the places which desired his services, and there under happier conditions he served a useful pastorate for twenty years, finally removing to Charleston, S. C., in 1697, where he died two years later.[3]

[1]Magnalia Christi Americana.

[2]Records, Com. United Colonies, II, 329.

[3]Davis, Landmarks of Plymouth, 98.

INTERREGNUM, 1667–1680.

Great Harbor was again left without a pastor, and the town records do not afford any information relative to the means employed to fill the vacancy for many years. At the departure of Cotton in 1667, the young sons of Rev. Thomas Mayhew, Jr., Matthew and John, were only nineteen and fifteen years of age respectively, and of course not old enough then to fill the breach. As the Indians were then conducting two or three meetings of their own at the time and had "teachers" of their race presiding, the English would avail themselves of the services of the native preachers. Experience Mayhew says: "when there was no *English* Pastor upon the Island some of our godly *English* People very cheerfully received the Lords supper administered by him," referring to John Tackanash.[1] This was only a return for "bread cast upon the waters." It is probable also that the Governor acted in the capacity of lay pastor during such times as occasion required.[2] In this instance it was a long period. John Mayhew, who later preached at Tisbury, may have begun his ministerial work in Edgartown during this time, probably as soon as he was of age in 1673, as it is only thus that we can account for the long period between 1667 and 1680, when the next reference to religious matters occurs in the records.

THIRD MEETING-HOUSE BEGUN. PASTORATE OF

It would seem that the interregnum of thirteen years had not been fruitful for the state of religion, as on July 3, 1680, the town voted to build another meeting-house with dimensions smaller than the first. The following is the record: —

> "Voted that there should be a meeting house built of twenty foot square with four cross Galleries with ten feet stud; this house is to be finished by the last day of March next Insewing."[3]

The occasion of this vote is not clear; perhaps the second building of 1665 had deteriorated from disuse or was considered beyond repair. It is suspected however that a new candidate in the person of Mr. Deodate Lawson was preaching

[1] Indian Converts, 15.
[2] Ibid., 301.
[3] Edgartown Records, I, 24.

a probationary spell, and this action was taken to encourage his settlement. Deodate Lawson, the son of Rev. Thomas Lawson of Denton, County of Norfolk, England, was a late comer to New England. He took the oath of allegiance in 1680, and is next heard of in our records under date of May 12, 1681, as follows: —

> Voted that "Mr. Lawson hath a Call to this town and that this town will Bye him half Commodation Providing that he Lives and preaches for the Term of seven years."[1]

It is not known whether Mr. Lawson accepted or how long he preached, but it is certain that he did not stay "seven years" nor half that time. It is probable that he may have remained for a year. As a child born to him is recorded in Boston in 1682, it is probable that he had by that time severed his short connection with this town. He afterwards lived at Danvers and Scituate in a ministerial capacity, but it seems that he left the latter church in an unaccountable way.[2] The brief residence of Mr. Lawson here probably resulted in dampening the enthusiasm for a new meeting-house, and doubtless the plan to build began to languish when the new minister failed to show indications of settling down. Indeed, it would appear from the following vote passed under date of Aug. 5, 1685, that the meeting-house was begun in 1680, in accordance with the former vote, and that operations were suspended when he took his departure.

> "Voted that Thomas Daggett, James Pease Sr. & Isaac Norton are Impowered in behalf of the town to Treat with Richard Ellingham about finishing the Meeting house and to conclude with him or any others according to their Discression for finishing said House, finding Timber and all the Necessarys about the same and what they shall do In the Towns Behalf shall sattisfie and Be obliged to Perform."[3]

Whether this was "finished" on the plan laid out in 1680, of twenty feet square, is not known, but it is presumed that a larger building was found to be necessary as a new clergyman had been engaged the previous year.

MINISTRY OF JONATHAN DUNHAM.

Negotiations had been in progress during 1684 between Matthew Mayhew, as agent for the town, and Mr. Jonathan Dunham of Falmouth (Cape Cod), relative to his settlement

[1]Edgartown Records, I, 27. The earliest publication relating to Salem Witchcraft, was a little pamphlet by Deodate Lawson, issued in the summer of 1692.

[2]Deane, History of Scituate, 196.

[3]Edgartown Records, I, 35.

as pastor in this town, but the townspeople evidently tiring of the long delays which ensued passed the following vote on Oct. 27, 1684: —

Voted, "that if Mr. Mayhew cannot Prevail with Mr. Dunham the Town desire him to Treat with some other man whom he shall think fitt and is ordered to give thirty-five pounds a year."[1]

This brought the hesitating parties to the bargain to a rapid conclusion, as appears by the following statement in the town records: —

"I, Matthew Mayhew being employed by Edgar town in the year of our Lord 1684 to procure Mr. Dunham or some other Minister for them did agree with Mr. Dunham as minister of the gospell in said Town viz: to allow Thirty Pounds per annum was excepted by them which I now for there Better satisfaction do declare to said Town to have been my return to them."[2]

Jonathan Dunham, a native of Plymouth, was at this date 52 years of age, past middle life, and came to Edgartown ripe with the experiences of half a century in temporal affairs, and now chosen to be a guide in spiritual concerns. He was not an educated minister, nor a college graduate. "With toil and Pains at first he tilled the ground," his epitaph states. He had been for some time "employed in Preaching the Good word of God amongst us for our Edification," according to the statement of a committee representing the settlement at Succonnessitt [Falmouth] in 1679, but he was only a lay preacher in reality.[3] The choice however proved to be a happy one, and for a generation of years, laboring with ever increasing satisfaction to the church until he had reached the ripe age of eighty-five, this pastoral relation in our town was continued.[4] Infirmities incident to his years however, in 1711, made it necessary that he receive some assistance in his work, and on May 15th of that year, at a special town meeting, it was voted to obtain "some able minister of the Gospel to be helpful to Mr. Dunham in the ministrie." Early in 1713, the church had unanimously selected Rev. Samuel Wiswall as coadjutor, and on March 10th of that year the town unanimously voted to endorse that action in behalf of the proprietors.[5] The town

[1]Edgartown Records, I, 32.

[2]Ibid., I, 64.

[3]Sup. Judicial Court Files, No. 2110.

[4]Mr. Dunham was not ordained until Oct, 11, 1694, when he was installed as "teacher" of the church at Edgartown, ten years after his call. The pastor of the Plymouth church and Mr. Fuller came by invitation to assist at the ceremonies.

[5]Edgartown Records, I, 65, 88, 93. He was ordained that year.

voted him a salary of £30 per annum for the first year and raised this to £40 the next year, at the same time paying Mr. Dunham his regular salary, although he had "through age and other infirmity desisted preaching for the two years last past."[1] Mr. Dunham died Dec. 18, 1717, and on his tombstone the following metrical elegy is to be seen: —

With Toil & Pains at first He Tell'd the Ground
Call'd to Dress GOD'S Vine Yard & ws faithful Found
Full Thirty Years the Gospel He Did Despence
His Work Being Done CHRIST JESUS Cal'd Him Hence.

MINISTRY OF SAMUEL WISWALL.

He was succeeded by his assistant, Mr. Wiswall, then in his 38th year.[2] This pastor was the first liberally educated clergyman settled in the town, having heen graduated at Harvard as B. A. in 1701 and taken his degree of Master of Arts three years later. After this latter event he prepared himself for the duties of the ministry. He had no settled charge at first, and preached transiently as opportunities offered. Later he went on a voyage as chaplain of a large ship which was captured by the Spaniards and taken to Martinico, "where he underwent a dangerous Fit of Sickness, but God sparing his Life he returned to his Country again."[3] He preached at Nantucket for about six months before accepting the call to this town. While here he acquired the Indian tongue "with a design to do what service he can amongst that people,"[4] and labored both among the English and natives with highly satisfactory results. His ministry was uneventful, and like that of his predecessor the pastoral relations continued for over thirty years until terminated by death. He was "often infirm with respect to his bodily state," and never married, so that he might attend the work of his ministry "without Distraction." After much added labor in a season of sickness and mortality, he succumbed suddenly on the 23d of December, 1746, in the 68th year of his age.

[1]Edgartown Records, I, 102. Feb. 10, 1714-15.

[2]He was the son of "pious and worthy Parents in the Town of Dorchester," Mr. Enoch and Elizabeth (Oliver) Wiswall, and was born Sept. 2, 1679, in that town.

[3]Boston Gazette, No. 1325 (1747.)

[4]Mather, "India Christiana" (1721). Mr. Wiswall evidently was of a roving disposition, and when he first came showed symptoms of restlessness. In 1714, when Judge Sewall visited Edgartown, he was asked by Capt. Thomas Daggett to "endeavour to persuade him to stay among them." (Diary, II, 432.)

THIRD MEETING-HOUSE.

Immediately following his accession to the place made vacant by the death of Mr. Dunham, the town held a meeting to consider the necessity of repairing the old structure, which had been in use over thirty years. "After some debate," the record states, "they being sensible, or the greater part, did find the old meeting house to be too scanty for the inhabitants of this town, they passed a unanimous vote for a new meeting house."[1] With that deliberation however, which characterized all such affairs, they did not act upon this vote for a year, and on Jan. 11, 1719-20, they finally agreed with Thomas Daggett to build the new structure, which should "not contain nor cover more ground than forty feet long and thirty wide."[2] This was the third meeting-house erected in the town since its foundation. During the ministry of Mr. Wiswall he was paid a yearly salary ranging from £50 in 1718, to £100 in 1745, the latter amount being that received by him at his death.[3]

The town, on Jan. 7, 1746-7, voted to raise £150 for the ministry, and a month later a committee of five was appointed to procure a successor to their lately deceased pastor. This committee acted promptly, and in two months had secured as a candidate, a young clergyman, the Rev. John Newman, then in his twenty-seventh year, brother-in-law of John Sumner of Edgartown, and a graduate in the class of 1740 of Harvard College. He was the son of John and Mary (Marshall) Newman of Gloucester, Mass., where he was born March 14, 1716. The church had voted, on May 8, 1747, to give him a call to settle, and on May 15th the town voted to concur in the selection, and further "for an incouragement" voted him the sum of £300, for a settlement and for a yearly salary.

"The sum of two hundred and fifty pounds in the old tenor to be settled at the rate of silver money at forty six shillings old tenor the ounce and so to raise or fall as the same shall rise or fall at all times hereafter as long as he the sd Mr. John Newman shall continue in the office of the ministry among us in this town."[4]

[1]Edgartown Records, I, 75

[2]Ibid., I, 150.

[3]Ibid., I, 73, 181

[4]Ibid., I, 188.

MINISTRY OF JOHN NEWMAN.

Mr. Newman accepted this offer promptly, and the town "returned thanks for his acceptance." Elaborate preparations were made for the entertainment of the delegates from the churches which were invited to assist at his ordination, which occurred July 29, 1747, and the sum of £50 was raised to defray the expenses of entertaining the council.[1] All this seemed to be in marked contrast to the simplicity which had heretofore obtained in the history of this church, but Rev. Mr. Newman was an entirely different character from his predecessors. He was the youngest pastor who had ever occupied this pulpit, and had recently returned from the siege of Louisburg, at which place he had served as chaplain to the garrison. Being possessed of some private fortune and imbued with the commercial spirit, he entered at once into the business of shop keeping on his own account, and in maritime ventures in partnership with Mr. Sumner.[2] In addition to this he was of a "worldly" temperament, which soon begat doubts and anxieties among those who could compare him with the grave and saintly Dunham, and the studious, ascetic Wiswall. This situation had in it the elements of probable discord, and the usual factions consequent upon this grew into activity. The older and conservative church members disapproved him, and the younger element in the town became his supporters.[3]

One of the Deacons of his church, Benjamin Daggett, became a bitter enemy and circulated scandalous stories about his character. He sued the deacon in the local courts for slander in March, 1757, and recovered a small verdict with costs, from which the defendant appealed.[4] Thus vindicated,

[1]Edgartown Records, I, 190. The ordination sermon was preached by Rev. Thomas Balch, pastor of the Second Parish, Dedham, Mass, who had married his sister-in-law, Mary Sumner.

[2]An account book kept by him in Edgartown, 1747–1758, is now in existence in excellent preservation, and furnishes undoubted evidence that he did a thriving business in retail shop-keeping. He sold chintz and lawn to the women, ship chandlery, pipes and tobacco to the men. Being skilled in "phisick" and "surgery," he purged and vomited the ailing townspeople and drew their aching molars during the week, as a preparation for his spiritual prescriptions on Sundays.

[3]Letter to Rev. Thomas Foxcroft of Boston. A similar condition existed simultaneously in Tisbury, and under date of Feb. 21, 1755, Experience Mayhew wrote: "There are great Travails & Dissentions arisen in two of our churches here viz at Edgartown and Tisbury. How they will end I know not. They need the help of the prayers of others for them."

[4]Dukes County Court Records, March term, 1757.

he asked dismission from the church. The church finally acceeded to his request for severance of the pastoral relations, but the town, by a vote of 30 to 14, would not concur in July, 1758. In the following October the town reconsidered its objections, and for the "mutual good and comfort of this church and congregation doth concur with the vote of the church, and grant a dismission unto the Rev. Mr. John Newman from his pastoral or ministerial relations."[1] If these dissentions drove him from the ministry they did not drive him from the town, and like his associate in Tisbury, the Rev. Nathaniel Hancock, under similar conditions, he decided to remain rather than turn his back on his enemies. He entered into public affairs, became Justice of the Court of Sessions and Common Pleas in 1761, and was Colonel of the Militia of the county the same year. He died Dec. 1, 1763, in his forty-third year, and lies buried in the cemetery beyond Tower Hill.[2]

MINISTRY OF JOSHUA TUFTS.

The church and town, on July 10, 1759, voted to call Mr. Zachariah Mayhew of Chilmark as pastor to fill the vacancy created by the dismission of the Rev. Mr. Newman, but owing to his employment by the Society for Propagating the Gospel and "some obstructions or obstacles that were in the way," he decided not to accept the charge.[3] Another attempt was made to secure the services of a clergyman, and the Rev. Joshua Tufts, Harvard College 1736, who had been settled as pastor at Litchfield, N. H., and Narragansett Township, No. 2, was invited to assume the vacant pastorate in December, 1759. The town voted to purchase a parsonage, and made the usual provisions for his maintenance. Mr. Tufts accepted, and further provision was made "for the Removal of his family and things here and for the maintainance of his family until they may arrive."[4] But he was scarcely warmed in his seat before trouble began, and on July 9, 1760, a committee was appointed "to wait upon the Rev. Mr. Joshua Tufts and discourse with him with respect to his asking and

[1]Edgartown Records, I, 217

[2]In the same cemetery is buried the body of Mrs. Mary Newman, his mother, who died September 28, 1755, in her seventy-first year. His widow, Mrs. Hannah Newman, married Aug. 27, 1766, Jonathan Metcalf. She was five years older than Mr. Newman.

[3]Edgartown Records, I, 219.

[4]Ibid., I, 221–223.

taking a dismission from his call to the pastoral and ministerial office in this town." A sum of money was also voted him, "provided he asks and obtains a dismission."[1] His predecessor, now John Newman, Esq., was chairman of the committee of the church which reported the advisability of terminating the relations. In this report, in which the church concurred, the following recommendation was given Mr. Tufts:

> That notwithstanding some reports have been spread to the prejudice of the Rev. Mr. Joshua Tufts' character since he came to this place by which the affections of some of the people seem to be so far alienated from him that it has been thought convenient by the sd Mr. Tufts and this Church that he be dismissed from his pastoral and ministerial relation thereto: yet we hereby declare we are in full charity with the sd Mr. Tufts and hope that in some other place he may have an opportunity of improving his ministerial talents and of being more extensively useful in promoting the Kingdom & Interests of our Common Lord.[2]

The exact nature of the disaffection indicated by his involuntary exit is not known, but it may have been an echo of the troubles of his predecessor.[3]

MINISTRY OF SAMUEL KINGSBURY.

The usual town and parish committee was forthwith charged with the duty of providing a successor, and a year later Rev. Samuel Kingsbury, a recent graduate of Harvard in the class of 1759, was invited on July 15th by the church, and the town concurred, July 21, 1761, with a money offer for a settlement.[4] The town further voted him a yearly salary of £66, 13 shillings and 4 pence, and he accepted the call. He was ordained November 25th of that year,[5] and entered upon a successful pastorate which lasted for seventeen years, until terminated by his death from small pox, on Dec. 30, 1778, in the forty-third year of his age. He was the last victim of an epidemic of that disease, which had existed in

[1]Edgartown Record, I, 224.

[2]Edgarton Church Records. This report was signed by the moderator of the meeting.

[3]The town voted to reconsider the purchase of a parsonage, and devoted a portion of this money "to pay the towns debts." He was later settled at Cumberland, N. S., and died in 1766.

[4]Samuel Kingsbury was born in Dedham, Dec. 28, 1736, the son of Ebenezer and Abigail Kingsbury of tha+ town, where his ancestors had lived for four generations.

[5]The ordination sermon was preached by the Rev. Moses Adams of Roxbury, and other portions of this ceremony were taken by Reverends Andrew Boardman of Chilmark, Jacob Bacon of Plymouth, Thomas Balch of Dedham, and Abraham Williams of Sandwich.

the town for some time. Rev. Mr. Kingsbury, after a residence of two years in the town, had married, Dec. 15, 1763, Jedidah, daughter of John and Jedidah (Smith) Sumner of this town, a niece of Mrs. John Newman, and thus indentified himself with one of the leading families of the town.

During the pastorate of Mr. Kingsbury, the old meeting-house, built in 1720, and used for nearly fifty years, succumbed to the ravages of time and our climate, after many annual patchings, and on Dec. 29, 1767, the first move was made towards rebuilding, by the appointment of a committee to consider the subject and report conclusions. A change of location was advisable among other things at this time, as the centre of population in the village had moved steadily northward since the early settlement in the Mashacket region. On Feb. 2, 1768, after having voted to build a new meeting house, a committee was appointed "to agree with Deacon Matthew Norton concerning a spot of land to set or build the meeting house on as also with Mr. Matt. Mayhew concerning a way [to the land]." This arrangement was effected satisfactorily, and two weeks later, in consideration of £5 lawful money, an acre of land was purchased of Deacon Norton, and the deed passed to the church.[1] This site was described as follows: —

> The Meeting house is to be set up on the easterly part of the land that Deacon Matt. Norton purchased of Mr. Matt. Mayhew a few rods to the westward of a tract of land belonging to Thomas Vinson, on the Northwest side of the way that leadeth from Peases Point to the Plain.[2]

FOURTH MEETING-HOUSE

In order that the residents then living in the locality of South Water street might reach this new site readily, Matthew Mayhew simultaneously with Norton, deeded to the town a way one rod wide extending from Water street to the church.[3] With these preliminaries settled, the committee charged with the construction of the new house of worship, "having met and considered of the same and the bigness of sd house," made the following recommendations as to dimensions and other details concerning ways and means: —

[1]Dukes Deeds, IX, 758, dated Feb. 9, 1768.
[2]Edgartown Records, I, 292.
[3]Dukes Deeds, IX, 759, dated Feb. 9, 1768.

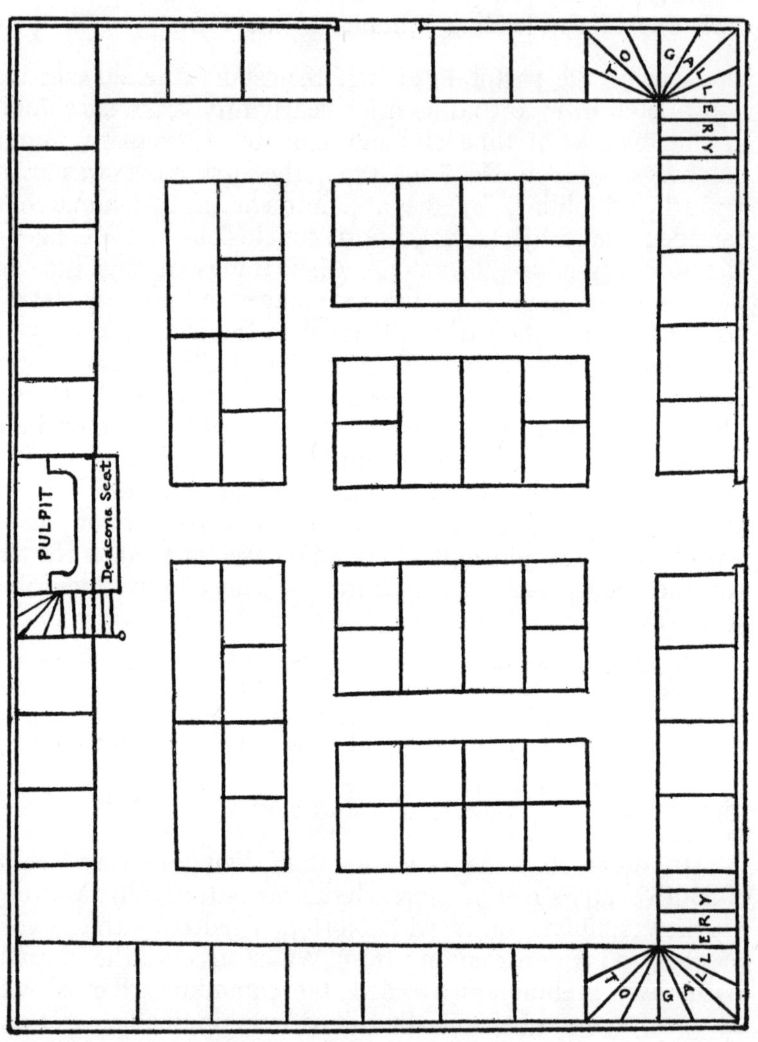

FLOOR PLAN
FOURTH MEETING-HOUSE
1769–1827

First that the meeting house be built forty-five feet wide and sixty feet long and that there shall be built in sd Meeting house ninety-seven pews sixty-four of sd pews to be set up below and thirty-three pews to be built and set up in the gallery above: The sd meeting house and pews to be built according to the plan drawn by the sd Committee.[1]

Of these pews, the one next the pulpit on the left was reserved for the ministry, and the remaining pew owners were assessed a total of £26. 36s. 8d. towards building the meeting-house. Further provisions were made for payments and forfeiture of pews, and that the town should be assessed to pay the balance of cost above the amount charged to the pews for construction. With a liberal disregard of all architectural requirements and symmetry of design, the town voted further:—

if any persons have a mind to have a window against their pews in any part of sd meeting house, and person so minded may have liberty therefor, provided that they do it upon their own cost and maintain the same, and before the outside is finished.[2]

As the work progressed, various changes in details were voted by the town, including the raising of the studding eighteen inches, "by splicing the posts," elevating the wall pews six inches above the main floor, and raising the underpinning. At length this large new structure was completed, probably about the early part of the spring of 1769, and became the fourth meeting-house erected for the worship of God in Edgartown.[3]

MINISTRY OF JOSEPH THAXTER

After the death of Rev. Mr. Kingsbury the church and town began to cast about for a successor, and on April 6, 1780, it was voted that the town should "proceed in the most expeditious manner to procure a Gospel minister to preach to the town for the space of three months." The committee who had this matter in charge procured the services of Mr. Joseph Thaxter of Hingham, as a temporary supply, some time in May following, and he began to "preach to the town."[4] Mr. Thaxter was a son of Deacon Joseph and Mary (Leavitt)

[1]Edgartown Records, I, 292.

[2]Ibid., I, 275. It is only fair to say that this vote was reconsidered later, and it was voted that these be proportioned by the carpenter. The windows in second story were to have twenty panes and those below twenty-four panes.

[3]On March 21, 1769, the selectmen were "impowered to Prime the windows of the meeting House," which wonld indicate its completion about that date.

[4]Edgartown Records, I, 321.

Thaxter of Hingham, and was born April 23, 1744, in that town. He was graduated at Harvard College in the class of 1768, and was subsequently engaged in teaching school in his native place. He had represented Hingham at the General Court, and at the outbreak of the Revolution joined the patriot forces at Concord and later at Cambridge, and was chaplain of Colonel Prescott's regiment at the Battle of Bunker Hill. At the date of his first coming to Edgartown he was in his 37th year and unmarried. After the usual "trying out" and baiting process with the new candidate, a committee was appointed to "treat" with him upon the basis of a permanent settlement. On August 10th the church unanimously gave him a call, and the town, concurring in the same manner, offered him £100 in silver at 6s. 8d. per ounce as a yearly salary. His reply is worth printing in full.

Gentlemen: Whereas the Church of Christ in this place did on the 10th of August last past unanimously invite me to settle with you in the work of the Gospel Ministry & whereas the town on the same day did unanimously concur with the Church in their choice and did then for my encouragement and support vote to pay me annually the sum of one hundred pounds in Silver money at six shillings eight pence per ounce so long as I shall continue in the office of the ministry among you. I have taken your invitation and encouragement into consideration and think your unanimity has made the call clear. Sensible of the care and trouble in which I must necessarily be involved in having all the necessaries of life to purchase wherever I can find them I most sincerely wish to avoid such cares as much as possible and therfore would propose that your agreement with me may be to give me ten cord of good oak wood, three tons of good English hay, forty-five bushels of Indian Corn, fifteen bushels of rye, eighty weight of good fleece wool, two hundred weight of large pork, two hundred weight of good beef including the proportion of tallow and two hundred Spanish milled dollars. Your compliance with these proposals will free me from such care and trouble and tend to my comfort & happiness, and I shall consider it as an evidence of your love and affection to me which I sincerely wish ever to enjoy should my proposals be agreeable and be accepted by the town. I then shall be ready to join with your committee in agreeing upon the Council and appointing the day for my solemn Seperation & introduction into work of the Gospel ministtry among you. Asking your prayers for me that I may be made a blessing unto the Church and People of God in this place I am, gentlemen, in love and affection your devoted and obedient servant in our Lord Jesus Christ.

JOSEPH THAXTER, Jr.

September 19th, 1780.

This reply was considered satisfactory, and all its requirements accepted by formal vote of the town, and agents were appointed to carry out its provisions yearly in respect to the

REV. JOSEPH ("PARSON") THAXTER

FROM MINIATURE BY FREDERIC MAYHEW

In possession of his grand-daughter, Mrs. Susan Coombs.

produce and fuel. He was ordained Nov. 8, 1780,[1] and began a distinguished pastorate under circumstances that were favorable for both parties to the contract. One exception, however, is to be noted. As he entered upon what proved to be a long ministerial service here, there arose in the town as elsewhere, those schisms in the church, which resulted in the separation of large numbers who began to follow the new doctrines preached by itinerant Baptist and Methodist preachers.[2] As time progressed, these dissenting bodies grew larger numerically, and in local influence, and were a continual thorn in his flesh. This however was but an incident in his long career of usefulness, and only the requirements of space in this volume prevent an extensive review of his life and services. "Parson" Thaxter, as he was generally known, was the last of the old school village pastors, the guide, philosopher and friend of his flock, from the cradle to the grave. He ministered to them in their physical ills as well as leading them in the spiritual paths when in health, and for forty years he was easily the most distinguished personage in Edgartown. He wore to the end of his life the cocked hat, short clothes, knee and shoe buckles, and carried the long cane familiar to the generation that lived during the Revolution. At the laying of the corner stone of Bunker Hill Monument in 1825, he was designated as the official chaplain to offer prayer, in the presence of the distinguished Marquis de Lafayette, and his venerable appearance on that occasion attracted general attention and incited public comment.[3] His prayer was reported in all the current papers of the time, and the noted Chaplain Thaxter of Prescott's regiment, then passed four score, was one of the marked figures on that memorable occasion.

The Unitarian sentiment which pervaded New England in the early part of the 19th century and penetrated the hallowed fanes of so many of the old Puritan churches, also found lodgment here under the later ministrations of Parson Thaxter, but he was affectionately regarded as a gentle heretic.

[1]The ordination sermon was preached by Rev. Timothy Hilyard, and Revs. Zachariah Mayhew, George Damon and Isaiah Mann took the other portions of this ceremony.

[2]As early as 1781, when he had just begun his work, "the religious society commonly called Annabaptists in this town" were in existence, and when Mr. Thaxter was ordained, a committee was appointed to negotiate with them as to attendance on the services.

[3]It is traditional that when passing him in the streets men and boys lifted their hats, and the women and girls made a courtesy.

He died July 18, 1827, and lies buried in the cemetery that adjoined the meeting-house on Pease Point way. In the same enclosure are buried the remains of his two wives, Mary, daughter of Robert and Desire (Norton) Allen and Ann, daughter of Samuel and Anna (Wass) Smith, together with a number of their children.

After the death of Parson Thaxter the regular services at the church were suspended, and for nine years there was only occasional supply of the pulpit by traveling or missionary preachers. In 1836, the Rev. Samuel A. Devens, a Unitarian clergyman, held services for a while, and wrote some interesting descriptive letters containing his observations of this place and the island as a whole.[1]

The following description of the ancient structure where Parson Thaxter preached, as it appeared in 1836, was written by a traveler who spent some time in the town, and published his observations in a volume of sketches of places visited by him:—

> The style of architecture — to frame a new order — is Quaker. It is situated a little out of the village and is the first object, when approaching it, that attracts attention. It is of large dimensions and without a steeple. No part of it is painted but the roof, which is of brick color. Of course with its broad paintless sides, relieved only by its reddish roof, it has a somewhat grave and sombre aspect. This specimen of antiquity rears its venerable form in the centre of an oblong enclosure of considerable extent, all of which with the exception of a path from the gate to the Church-door is occupied with graves, headstones, and monuments of various forms, dimensions and appearance. The venerable Pastor of the Town reposes in the rear of the Church just beneath the window of that pulpit in which he served his Maker for such a succession of years. A weeping willow gracefully waves over a marble monument erected by his children.
>
> The interior of the Church accords well with the exterior. All is simple and plain—in the taste of the Puritans. The front of the galleries and pulpit, with the sounding board above, and the deacons' seats below, are painted light blue. There is nought else but what wears its natural color. A neat green curtain and a cushion of the like material adorn the pulpit.
>
> At one extremity of the enclosure is a straw-colored hearse-house — neat and appropriate — recently built by a benevolent widow, daughter of the departed worthy Pastor.[2]

[1]Published in the Christian Register, 1836-7, and later in book form, Boston, 1838, 12 mo., pp.207.

[2]Devens, Sketches of Martha's Vineyard, &c., pp. 39–41. The author adds the following reference to the care bestowed by this daughter upon the old building: "This spot is the object of sacred affections — of many sad as well as sweet remembrances to her soul. Not a broken pane of glass nor a loose stone in the foundation of the old Church escapes her eye. It is never suffered to go to decay, and its hallowed precincts are swept by her own hands some three times every twelvemonth and preserved sweet and clean."

FIFTH MEETING-HOUSE

1828–1908

This relic of departed days survived the storms of about ten winters and was finally torn down, as it was becoming an unsightly object on account of disuse and decay.

FIFTH MEETING-HOUSE

The passing of Parson Thaxter also marked the end of the old church, which for nearly sixty years had been the scene of the ministrations of himself and his immediate predecessor. It had been repaired annually for many years, until further expenditures of this kind could not save it from decay, and a new structure was planned shortly before the death of Parson Thaxter. Another lot was procured on the corner of Commercial and Summer streets, and the present structure erected thereon. It was completed the year following his death, and dedicated Dec. 24, 1828, with appropriate ceremonies.

The succession in the pastoral office since the death of Parson Thaxter has been as follows: —

John H. Martyn, 1827–1831; Reuben Porter, 1832–1833; Ebenezer Poor, 1833–1835; David Tilton, 1835–1838; James Thomas, 1839–1840; Allen Gannett, 1842–1843; John S. Stores, 1843–1844; Charles C. Beaman, 1844–1846; William M. Thayer, 1846–1847; Smith B. Goodenow, 1847–1851; John E. Corey, 1852–1852; William J. Breed, 1853–1856; Nathaniel B. Blanchard, 1856–1857; Nelson Scott, 1858–1859; Stephen C. Strong, 1859–1860;[1] Edwin H. Nevin, 1860–1863; Hartford P. Leonard, 1863–1865; Benjamin T. Jackson, 1865–1867; Luther H. Angier, 1868–1869; Edson J. Moore, 1870–1874; Ephraim N. Hidden, 1874–1874; T. Frank Waters, 1875–1878; John G. Hall, 1878–1880; J. Emerson Swallow, 1881–1883; Calvin Terry, 1885–1885; Frank N. Greeley, 1885–1887; Samuel Clark, 1887–1889; Frank A. Mansfield, 1890–1890; Caleb L. Rotch, 1890–1891; Charles L. Woodworth, 1891–1892; Charles N. Gleason, 1893–1897; Duncan McDermid, 1897–1898; James Lade, 1898–1900; Charles L. Woodworth, 1900–1903; and Frederick Morse Cutler, 1903, who is the incumbent at the present time.

This historic congregation maintains the semblance of its historic past, as the parent religious organization on the island, and the worshipper at its services must have impressed on him the spiritual presence of its founders and pillars, the two Mayhews, Dunham, Wiswall, and Thaxter, as he enters this ancient temple.[2]

[1]A Rev. Mr. Fiske was temporary supply in 1860.

[2]Mrs. Newman, widow of its early pastor, presented a silver communion service to this congregation and it is still in use. She also left a fund of £333 for the benefit of derserving widows.

THE BAPTIST CHURCH

The religious body holding the Baptist doctrines in this town is an offshoot of the first association of Baptists organized in 1780 at Homes Hole. Services were held for many years in the meeting-house at Homes Hole by persons of this denomination residing in the towns of Tisbury, Chilmark and Edgartown. Most of the members from this town resided in the northern part, on the shores or contiguous to the Lagoon, and they continued their attachment to the Tisbury meeting till about 1823, when by reason of increased numbers a separate parish was organized. This was accomplished on April 16, 1823, when Elder William Hubbard and Benjamin Grafton of Boston came here and officially instituted the Baptist Church in Edgartown. Benjamin Davis was appointed first Deacon, and the following named persons constituted its membership at that date:—

Saml. Wheldon, Saml. Vincent, Zachariah Pease, Salthiel Pease, Jesse Pease, Benjamin Dunham, Matt. Allen, Thomas Norton, Henry Marchant, Thos. Coffin, Deborah Marchant, Lydia Pease, Molly Pease, Olive Vincent, Betsey Vincent, Hannah Marchant, Sally A. Pease, Sally Dunham, Ann Norton, Margaret Arey, Abigail Cook, Sophronia Norton, Louisa Norton, Ruama Coffin, Sophia Marchant, Deborah Pent, Abigail Cook, Velina Luce, Elijah Pease, Lydia A. Vincent, Jerusha Dunham, Hannah Ripley, Warren Vincent, Rev. Wm. Bowers, Charlotte Bowers, Lois Cleveland, Betsey Frisbey, Mary Cornell, Prudence Jernigan, Cordelia Coffin, Charlotte Fisher, Saml. Whelding, Hannah Norton, Marshall Luce, Puella Cleveland, Ann Covel, Nabby Crosby, Peggy Pease, Sukey Fisher, Rebecca Cleveland, Hannah Cook, Eunice Whelding, Betsey Whelding, Anna Pease, Huldah Coffin, Sally Marchant, Harriet Cleveland, Waitstill M. Pease, Saml. Pent, Betsey Pent, Mary S. Vincent, Ephraim Marchant, Velina Coffin, Charlotte Cathcart, Sophia S. Marchant, John Pease, Ambrose Vincent, Deborah Norton.

Elder Hubbard became the first pastor of this society, serving in that capacity for two years. He was succeeded by Henry Marchant [170], a native son. Services were held at first in houses, then in school buildings, and in 1811 they joined with the Methodists in the erection of a "Union" meeting-house on Winter street, nearly opposite the residence of the late Sirson P. Coffin. It was an unfinished shell of a building, provided with a regulation high pulpit, and the audience had to be content with plain board seats, without backs. This served its purpose for ten years till, finally, during the pastorate of Rev. W. W. Hall, funds were obtained for building a separate church structure for the use of Baptists solely.

A lot was procured on Maple street, and the edifice was completed in the fall of 1839. A contemporary account gives the following particulars of the dedication exercises:—

Friday, September 6, 1839, the new and Elegant Baptist Meeting house in Edgartown was dedicated to the worship of God. The Exercises of the Occasion were as follows:—Reading of the Scriptures by Rev. Henry Marchant; Reading Anthem by Rev. Mr. Hall, pastor of the Church; Introductory Prayer by Rev. James C. Boomer of Holmes Hole; Sermon and dedicatory Prayer by Rev. Mr. Neale of Boston.[1]

The following named clergymen have served as pastors of the Baptist Church from its establishment to the present time: William Hubbard, 1823-5; Henry Marchant, 1826-7; William Bowen, 1828-9; Seth Ewer, 1830-4; Jesse Pease,[2] 1834; Darius Dunbar, 1835-6; W. W. Hall, 1836-40; L. Holmes, 1840-3; A. Webb, 1843-4; S. Richards, 1844-8; C. G. Hatch, 1849-51; G. D. Crocker, 1851-3; L. Holmes, 1853-7; A. D. Gorham, 1857-60; W. W. Ashley, 1861-2; J. E. Wood, 1863-5; W. W. Ashley, 1866-7; L. B. Hatch, 1868-75; Wm. McCullough, 1876-7; Geo. D. Reid, 1877-80; Wm. W. Walker, 1881-5; H. B. Tilden, 1885-8; J. A. Bailey, 1888-9; Thos. C. Crocker, 1890-1; Fennimore H. Cooper, 1892-5; Wilber T. Rice, 1895-8; Henry D. Coe, 1898-1901; Edwin D. Richardson, 1902-4; Frederick T. Kenyon, 1904-7; W. J. B. Cannell, 1907.

THE METHODIST EPISCOPAL CHURCH

The beginnings of the Methodist Episcopal religious denomination date from the arrival of John Saunders, a negro slave from Virginia, who had become a convert to that doctrine, and held services from time to time. This was in 1787 and continued till his death eight years later. As in the case of the other schismatics from the established order, the early assemblies of persons professing this faith were combined from the several settlements on the island. Itinerant missionaries were given commission to preach to such as would gather in the towns, and the history of one is a repetition of the others in the early annals of this denomination.[3] Rev. Joshua Hall preached here in 1797; Joseph Snelling in 1798; Epaphras

[1]From paper in possession of Mrs. Wm. Pease, West Tisbury.

[2]Mr. Jesse Pease of Edgartown was ordained July 15, 1824, at the Tisbury Meeting house.

[3]It is confidently claimed that the celebrated Jesse Lee preached here in 1795 on his return from a tour in the District of Maine. It is known that he visited New Bedford and thence came to the Vineyard.

Kibby, 1799; William Beauchamp, 1800, after which for several years the supply was irregular until 1809, when a fresh start was made.

During the year last named—that of 1809—the Rev. Erastus Otis came to the island from his circuit, Falmouth. He preached his first sermon in Edgartown at a dwelling house provided by Mrs. Naomi Beecher, wife of Erastus Beecher, who was a cousin of the late Dr. Lyman Beecher. Mrs. Beecher, who had then recently removed to this place from Nantucket, and Miss Love Stewart, who a few years before had been "converted" in Maine, were then the only Methodists in the town. The preaching of Mr. Otis was of a new style—quite different, indeed, from that to which the majority of the people had been accustomed to listen—yet it found hearers, and the father of Miss Stewart and others consented to open their doors for it. During the long interlude the numbers in society on other parts of the island had been reduced by deaths, removals, and perhaps by other causes, to seven; the two named in Edgartown making the number nine in all.

Mr. Otis was remembered as a man of fine personal appearance, and of a cultivated mind. He was zealous in the Methodist cause, and finding here a field for work, he entered into it with a hearty zest. He taught a school in Edgartown for a while, still preaching there and elsewhere on the island, and his efforts resulting in frequent "revivals." On the fourth day of November of that year he formed the first "class" in Edgartown consisting of six persons. The organization took place at the house of the late Joseph Vincent, about a mile from the village. It had been for a long time one of the homes of the preachers.

The numbers increased gradually so that there was a roomful at the weekly class. Thomas Stewart, Jr., a son of the ocean, then recently "converted," soon joined and became the leader. The work spread, and another "class" was formed on the neighboring island of Chappaquiddick. It reached Eastville, where resided Joseph Linton, who with his wife came many times on foot seven miles to worship with this new sect.

The next year, 1810, Mr. Otis came by assignment, although his name was associated with that of Benjamin F. Lansford at Falmouth. He was still succesful in his work, although in the midst of it there arose a great storm of persecution in Edgartown village. The new religion, as it was called, was treated with scorn and derision by large portions of the inhabitants, insomuch that many who adhered to the new cause resorted to the outposts—the neighboring island, the Plain, and elsewhere, where they could worship in greater quietness. Instances of physical opposition to the maintenance of these meetings are known, and in common with the Baptist preachers who were then sharing the new field, the pioneer rivals of the established order of things suffered frequent personal indignities. The Rev. Mr. Otis once came to the ferry opposite the town in a heavy rain, having an appointment to attend. Such were the demonstrations of the crowd assembled on this side, laughing at Mr. Otis' condition while waiting, that they so overawed the ferryman that he did not dare to incur their anger. Mr. Otis, after waiting some time in the drenching rain, wended his way back on foot, a mile, to the nearest house. Once at an election of a representative to Congress, two men slurringly cast their votes for the "Immortal Erastus Otis." He was succeeded in 1811 by Rev. William Hinman, and the society was legally organized to comply with the state law respecting taxation for the support of the ministry. The succeeding preachers were Edward Hyde, 1812; William Frost, 1813; John W. Hardy, 1814; Benjamin Hazelton, 1815; Shipley W. Wilson, 1816; Thomas W. Tucker, 1817-18; Eleazer Steele, 1819-20[1]; John Adams, 1821-2; Francis Dane and Frederic Upham, 1823; Edward T. Taylor, 1824; David Culver, 1825 and John Adams, 1826. It is to be understood that these preachers held services at the other towns as well and were in fact assigned to the general work on this circuit. During this period the Methodists had relinquished (1822) their share in the

[1]Rev. Hebron Vincent relates the following incident: "It was during this year that while preaching on a Sunday evening, Mr. Steele lost the power of speech, through an excess of religious fervor, and stood trembling with clenched hands upon the top of the pulpit. The pulpit being but poorly secured and the side of the building—which was still unfinished within—so shook as to cause a rumbling noise, which gave rise, under a disturbed imagination, to various conjectures. A scene of great excitement ensued, most of the people leaving the house in crowded haste—causing some accidents and giving to those whom they met in their flight various answers to inquiries such as, "Earthquake"—"The power of the Lord shook the meeting house," etc. One of the men strongly prejudiced against the new cause, hearing the noise at his house—the evening being quite still—hurried to the place. On entering the church and looking up to the pulpit, he exclaimed, "Look at your preacher in fits." Putting his hand on the sides of the pulpit and feeling the trembling, he said, "Your preacher has made complete fools of the whole of you! and if you will allow me, I will take him out of the pulpit and demonstrate it to you." This the brethren present refused to consent to. This man used to tell this story a great deal, afterwards—calling the scene, "the home-made earthquake."

Union meeting-house to the Baptists, and built one for themselves on the site of the house of the late Sirson P. Coffin, Winter street. This was occupied till 1827, when it was sold to the Methodist Society of Chilmark, who took it apart and removed it to that town piecemeal.[1] Soon after a new church building was erected on Main street, which later (1843) became the present Town Hall.

Rev. Jotham Horton preached here in 1827; Thomas C. Pierce in 1828-9; Epaphras Kibby, 1830-1; John J. Bliss, 1832; John E. Risley, 1833; Joel Steele, 1834; James C. Bontecou, 1835-6; Asa Kent, 1837-8; Thomas Ely, 1839-40; Ezekiel W. Stickney, 1841; Charles Macreading, 1842-3. It was during the last named pastorate that the meeting-house on the south side of Main street was sold for a Town Hall and a new site procured on the opposite side of the street. A more commodious building was begun in 1842 and completed the next year. It was dedicated October 10, 1843, and is still occupied by the society. The following is a list of the pastors who have been assigned to this station since the present house of worship was completed: William T. Harlow, 1844-5; Cyrus C. Munger, 1846-7; Thomas Ely, 1848; Frederick Upham, 1849; Charles H. Titus, 1850-1; John B. Gould, 1852-3; William Kellen, 1854; Sanford Benton, 1855-6; William H. Stetson, 1857-8; Lucius D. Davis, 1859-60; Charles Nason, 1861; Frederick A. Crafts, 1862-3; Seth Reed, 1864-5[2]; A. W. Paige, 1865[2]-6; George W. Bridge, 1867[2]; Andrew J. Church, 1867[2]-8-9; Daniel A. Whedon, 1870-1-2; Elisha M. Dunham, 1873-4-5; Samuel M. Beale, 1876-7-8; John D. King, 1879-80-1; John O. Thompson, 1882; James H. Humphrey, 1883-4-5; Silas Sprowls, 1886; John D. King, 1887-8-9-90; Herman C. Scripps, 1891-2-3; Charles T. Hatch, 1894-5; Joseph Hollingshead, 1896-7-8-9; William H. Allen, 1900-1-2-3; George E. Brightman, 1904; Florus L. Streeter, 1905-6-7.

THE PROTESTANT EPISCOPAL CHURCH

This is a recent addition to the religious congregations in the town, and the annals of the church do not go back beyond a decade. Services had been held occasionally in houses and

[1]As an evidence of the continued antagonism of the people to this new religious body it is related that an attempt was made to upset this building by levers while the services were being held inside. The members were still called by opprobrious names.

[2]Part of that year.

public halls until about 1895, when the Bishop of the Diocese of Massachusetts placed the pastoral charge of the church in Edgartown in the care of Rev. William C. Hicks of Vineyard Haven. A weekly service was started in September of that year, and the growth of the work was such that the building of a mission church was considered necessary by the incumbent. A lot was secured on the corner of Winter and Summer streets and plans for an elaborate building were prepared. These were subsequently modified and the erection of a smaller church was begun in 1899, to be called St. Andrew by the Sea. The corner stone was laid September 7, 1899, by the Rt. Rev. Ethelbert Talbot, Bishop of the church, assisted by Rev. Andrew Gray, D.D., the missionary in charge, who had succeeded Mr. Hicks the previous year. The church was called by the shorter name of St. Andrew's, which is the legal title of the parish. It is still under the supervision of the rector of Grace Church, Vineyard Haven, who holds services alternating with those provided at that place.

QUAKERS

Notwithstanding the close proximity of Nantucket, which was essentially a Quaker community almost from its inception, our Island had very few members of this sect. In the year 1657 two itinerant Quakers visited the little settlement at Great Harbor on their return from Nantucket, where they had been on a proselyting mission. The following is their story of the reception they met with on "Martins Vineyard:"

16 August 1657.

John Copeland Christopher Holder 16th day 6th month, 1657 Martins Vineyard.

Nor did John Copeland and Christopher Holder meet with better Usuage at their hands for having been at Martins Vineyard (a Place between Rhoad Island and Plimmouth Colonẏ) and speaking there a few Words in the Movings of the Lord (who moved them to go thither) after that Priest Maho (the Governors Son) had ended his Divination in their Meeting House, they were both thrust out of the Meeting House Door by the Constable to an Indian (where were many on that Island) in order to be carried in a small Cannoo (or hollowed piece of Timber to the Mayne Land over a Sea nine Miles broad (dangerous enough for any to Pass over) having first took their mony from them to Pay the Indian; who taking the Custody of them, shewed himself more hospitable (as did the rest of the Indians) and supplied them freely with all necessaries according to what the Indians had, during the space of those Three dayes they stayed there waiting for a Calme season) and refused to take any Consideration, he who had them in

The kindness of the Indians in Martins Vineyard.

Custody saying—That they were strangers, and Jehovah taught him to Love Strangers — (learn of the Heathen ye who pretend your selves Christians) and an Opportunity presenting, set them on shoare on the Main Land.[1]

A Savory Speech of an Indian.

From this narrative it appears that there was about as little charity for Quakers on the Vineyard as elsewhere at that period. These two pilgrims who landed on the Vineyard were lucky. On the mainland they would have been whipped "at the cartes taile from towne to towne." From their own story it is clear that they purposely created a disturbance in the meeting-house, but their own story of experiences is not to be allowed to stand alone. A contemporary historian has recorded another version of the incident, and the statement of the attorney for the defendant in the case is here given in order that the reader may reach a satisfactory conclusion:

"And here I may take occasion," writes Gookin, "to mention a short but true story of certain Quakers who landing upon that island, went to some of the Indian wigwams, and discoursed with some of the Indians that understood English, as divers of them do, the Quakers persuaded and urged the Indians to hearken to them and told the Indians that they had light within them that was sufficient to guide them to happiness; and dissuaded the Indians from hearing Mr. Mayhew or reading the scriptures; and said that the ministers that preached from or used the scriptures were as Baal's priests and hirelings &c. And at last the Quakers offered the Indians some of their pamphlets and books which they always carry with them, exhorting the Indians to read them; As they would be of greater benefit to them than the bible. The Indians heard all this discourse patiently; and then one of the principall of them that could speak English, gravely answered the Quakers in this manner: You are strangers to us, and we like not your discourse. We know Mr. Mayhew that he is a good and holy man; but we know you not. You tell us of a light within us that will guide us to salvation; but our experience tells us that we are darkness and corruption, and all manner of evil within our hearts. You dehort us from using the bible, but offer your books and commend them to us; we cannot receive your counsel contrary to our own experience and the advice and exhortations of our ancient and good teachers. Therefore we pray you, trouble us no further with your new doctrines; for we do not approve it. So the Quakers not long after departed from the island; and never since have they been infested with them."[2]

In 1704 a wealthy English Quaker, who had been proselyting on Nantucket, made preparations to engage in a mission at Edgartown, but his meetings were so thinly attended that he soon became discouraged and left.[3] In 1715 another

[1]Bishop, "New England Judged," (London, 1661), p. 123.

[2] Mass. Hist. Soc. Coll., I, 141-227. Daniel Gookin's account, which was written in 1674.

[3]Journal of Thomas Story.

itinerant Quaker visited this Island and relates his experiences in Edgartown:—

"From thence (Nantucket) I went to another Island called Marthas Vineyard where I had some meetings; Being at a Place called Old-Town on a First day I found some Drawings in my Mind to go to the Presbyterian Meeting house in the Afternoon and Nathaniel Starbuck a Friend of Nantucket being with me, he accompanied me to the Meeting: I waited till the Priest, whose name was Samuel Wisell had done speaking, and then I desired Liberty to speak to the People. I directed them to the Teacher in themselves which was sufficient for them as they took heed unto it. After I had done speaking, the Priest made some Objections concerning the anointing, which I had spoken of, mentioned in the second Chapter of the First Epistle of John, and we agreed to have a Dispute the next Day at the Meeting house, to begin at nine of the clock, to which the Priest and several of the hearers came: The Things we chiefly disputed upon were concerning the Light, and the Sufficiency of the Divine anointing, the Holy scriptures and of his call to the Ministry and Maintenance not being Apostolical: The Dispute might hold near four Hours........But when I came to speak of his Maintenance and touch'd him in that tender Part he was somewhat disturbed. After the Dispute was over I went that night to a Place called Home's hole, and the next Day to the Main Land."[1]

Doubtless many persons from Nantucket who changed their residence to the Vineyard were of Quaker sentiment, and brought with them their "peculiar" doctrines. The Coffin family was a notable instance of this kind. Persons holding this belief were not accorded full civil rights and were not allowed to serve as jurors.[2] As time went on those who were attached to this belief by inheritance or family association gradually affiliated with the new sects which began to be formed on the island about the latter part of the 18th century.

There is very little evidence of religious intolerance in Colonial times on the island as shown by the number of prosecutions for neglect to attend public worships There were no cases of this kind before 1700, and the first case on record occurs in 1710, when John Steward was fined five shillings for not attending church. From that date up to 1780 there were not two dozen prosecutions for this offence, the last occurring in 1770. The fine varied from nine shillings to one pound, with the alternative of sitting in the stocks if it was not paid.

[1]Life and Travels of Benjamin Holme, p. 17.

[2]In 1763, in a civil case, Richard Coffin, Prince Norton and Samuel Coffin, who were drawn as jurors, were objected to as being Quakers. (Mass. Arch., XIV, 480.)

MILITIA.

One of the earliest entries in the town records [1651], relates to the training of the citizen for his duties as a soldier. Surrounded as they were by an alien race of scarcely civilized natives, who greatly outnumbered them, it became a matter of common prudence for the settlers to be proficient in the use of arms and accustomed to military discipline. On March 29, 1651, the following vote was passed by the town: —

> "Men shall Be Compleat in there armes the last fryday in May next if not to be fined according as the town shall think meat."[1]

This was probably the first militia organization in the town, and on the same date John Daggett senior was chosen "corperall" of the company, which we may infer was the title of the ranking officer, as the train band was numerically small. On April 1, 1653, it was voted that each man should be "complete in armes," and this was prescribed to include "a Peece a pound of powder & twenty bullets."[2] Each member of the train band was also required to provide himself with a specified number of fathoms of match. The bullets were of home manufacture. By a vote on June 8, 1653, the company was ordered to train five times more that year, and on Feb. 6, 1654, it was provided that ammunition should be kept at Mr. Mayhew's and at the leader's, and that the "leader" should appoint four training days a year. This was the name given to the commander of the town militia, and John Butler was chosen to that office on the date mentioned, for the ensuing year. The town also agreed to reimburse each man of the company for the cost of twenty-five pounds of powder, one hundred pounds of shot and twenty-five fathoms of match. Each of the twenty-five lots was required to furnish one full equipment for a musketeer, and as a penalty for failure to do militia service the following was enacted: —

> "He that wilfully neglects Trayning shall Pay five shillings and common ordinary occasions to pay three shillings."[3]

John Butler was re-elected "Leader" for the year 1655, and in 1656 Thomas Bayes succeeded him in that office.

[1]Edgartown Records, I, 122.

[2]Ibid., I, 131. The "Peece" refers to the fire-arm of that period, the match-lock musket, which preceded the flint-lock. This weapon was operated by means of a match, attached to the lock, made of flax fibre in the form of a wick, which was ignited by a hammer and flint, thus communicating with the priming charge.

[3]Ibid., I, 120.

Absence of further references to military matters for five years following leaves us without knowledge of the personnel and progress during that period. On Dec. 30, 1661, the townsmen apparently were stimulated to increased activity in martial affairs, and several laws were passed on that date as follows: —

> Voted: that there shall be six Trayning Dayes the year, that is all the six dayes between the Last of March and the Last of October to be appointed by my self and the company.
>
> All men & youths in the town are to Traine except such as are freed by the Pattentees and major part of the freeholders.
>
> Every lott that hath not a person for to train shall pay five shillings . . . . for use of the militia.[1]

On this same date the following officers of the train band were chosen: Thomas Bayes, Leader; Thomas Jones, Clerk of the Band; and James Covell, "Drumer for this yeare." The company consisted of the following named persons in 1662: —[2]

Thomas Daggett	Jacob Norton	Thomas Harlock
Richard Sarson	William Tupman[3]	John Smith
Robert Codman	John Daggett	Joseph Daggett
Isaac Norton	John Pease	Nicholas Norton
Goodman Burchard	James Pease	William Vinson
James Covell	Thomas Bayes, Jr.	Mr. [John] Bland
Thomas Jones	Joseph Codman	Richard Arey
John Eddy	Mr. [Nicholas] Butler	Thomas Layton

This list represents one man for each of the twenty-five lots, as required by town order, and it was not far from being the effective total of persons capable of bearing arms. In 1675 there were "not above 40 men" who could do military service on the Vineyard, and at the same time there were ten times that number of Indians.[4] Thomas Bayes was continued as the Leader in 1662 and 1663, but further allusions are wanting in the records for many years following these dates. Doubtless the organization of the train band was kept up with more or less interest from year to year, but the anxieties occasioned by the uprising of the Indians on the mainland during King Philip's war, 1675-6, were sufficient to stimulate the train band to continued activity.

The organization of the government under the Duke of York's regime, in 1671, made no particular provisions for

[1]Edgartown Records, I, 143.

[2]Ibid., I, 138.

[3]This name is probably an error in the old copy of our records. It may be Weeks.

[4]New York Col. Rec., Council Minutes, II, (2) 57.

a military body, and doubtless it was left to the inhabitants to deal with this question as a detail of local concern. That an organization of those "able to bear arms," was continued from year to year is evident from fragmentary allusions, though not regularly entered upon the several records. In 1684, Matthew Mayhew, in addition to his other offices, was commissioned by the Governor of New York as "Captain of the Company at Martins Vineyard," possibly a sort of general officer in charge of the combined forces.[1]

From that time till 1690 there was general peace throughout the colonies, but the symptoms of another outbreak of the Indians were plainly evident. This time they were reinforced by the French settlers in Canada, and these allies began a series of frontier massacres and depredations that continued intermittently for the ensuing half century, and some parts of New England had to be yielded back to these savage hordes. While this terrible situation was not felt on the Vineyard, by reason of its natural barrier, yet in the menaces of French sloops-of-war, on piracy bent, the islanders got some taste of the dangers to life and property which threatened their neighboring colonists on the main. In Edgartown the militia was revived, and on April 13, 1691, the following organization effected: —

> At a meeting of all the melisha in general of the town of Edgartown Left. Thomas Daggett Esq. was chosen by them their captain, by unanimous choice of them; at the same meeting Mr. Andrew Newcomb was chosen Left. at the same time, John Butler had the place of the first or eldest sargent; the same time, Moses Cleveland was chosen the second; the same time Jonathan Dunham was chosen corporal; Jonathan Pease the next corporal; the same time Mr. John Boult was chosen their ensign. This was their choice and agreement."[2]

Nothing further relating to the militia is found on the town records for many years, and we can only assume that an organization of some sort was maintained as a matter of law and custom. Enoch Coffin was Captain of the militia in 1739, and in 1757 the "Foot Company of Melitia" was under the command of Lieutenant Colonel John Norton, and comprised one hundred and twenty-one privates, with an "alarm list" of fifty-four additional. The officers of the company were Elijah Butler, Daniel Vinson, Benjamin Pease,

[1]N. Y. Col. Records. Commission dated June 5, 1684. (Vol. XXXIII.)
[2]Edgartown Records, I, 38.

and Solomon Norton, Sergeants, and Joseph Daggett and Matthew Mayhew, Drummers.[1]

In 1761 there were two companies of militia in Edgartown, the first under John Newman as Captain, Solomon Norton as Captain Lieutenant, Daniel Coffin as Second Lieutenant, and Daniel Vinson as Ensign. The second company was under command of Peter Norton, Captain, Elijah Butler as Lieutenant, and Malatiah Davis as Ensign.[2] In 1765 there were two companies of militia in Edgartown; the first under Peter Norton as Captain, Eddy Coffin as First Lieutenant, Matthew Mayhew as Second Lieutenant, and Malatiah Pease as Ensign. The second company had the following officers: Elijah Butler, Captain; Malatiah Davis, Lieutenant; and Ebenezer Smith, Jr., as Ensign.[3]

The state of the public mind for the next twenty years kept alive the military spirit, and without doubt this "Foot Company" held its organization. Early in 1776, the newly organized government formed a regiment of militia which superceded the town companies,[4] but the war resulted in other measures of a military character, which have been described in the first volume. The abandonment of the island to neutrality had the effect of destroying all military activities for many years after the Revolution.

FORTIFICATIONS.

There was a fortification in this town as early as 1691, of which Andrew Newcomb was the Commander, with a number of men enlisted to man the works; but of its size, strength, or location no evidence is obtainable.[5] It was probably situated at or near Pease's Point, the most available site from strategic considerations. Nothing further of its history is known.

In August, 1741, the General Court appropriated the sum of £700 to build in Edgartown "a sufficient Breastwork,

[1] Mass. Arch., XCV, 209. The full list of members of this company is preserved in this document. The "alarm list" indicates persons available at that time for service in the French and Indian Wars. Vide Appendix, Vol. I.

[2] Mass. Arch., XCIX, 24. There was also an Indian Military Company in Edgartown, with Enoch Coffin, Jr., as Captain, Elijah Smith as Lieutenant, and Richard Coffin as Ensign.

[3] Mass. Arch., XCIX, 25.

[4] The officers of this regiment of militia were Beriah Norton, Colonel; Malatiah Davis, Lieutenant Colonel; Brotherton Daggett and Mayhew Adams, Majors.

[5] N. Y. Col. Mss., XXXVII, 230.

a Platform & eight guns, six Pounders or others equivalent mounted & all suitable Warlike stores procured." The conditions of this grant were that "the same be maintained from time to time in good repair," and upon failure to abide by the covenant the town should repay the amount granted into the public treasury.[1] At a town meeting held in December following, the thanks of the people were tendered for the grant, and it was voted "that the fortification shall be erected and built in the most convenient place near the harbor." A committe of five[2] were also appointed, "to determine where the fortification should be built and get the work done," but the conditions of the grant were finally deemed to be disadvantageous, and a sentiment against acceptance prevailed to such an extent that a town meeting was called for March 10, 1741, when it was "voted to reconsider the vote relating to receiving the seven hundred pounds granted by the General Court" and all other votes "relating to agent & committee to draw money, build fort, get guns &c."

John Sumner, Enoch Coffin, Esq., Simeon Butler, Esq., Mr. Tristram Coffin, Ebenezer Norton, Esq., Mr. Matt. Norton, and Capt. Timothy Daggett, were chosen a committee to consider the whole affair and report to adjourned meeting.[3] This was held on March 19, 1741, and the report made by them was as follows: —

> "The committee appointed to consider and report what is proper for the town to do in the affair of the seven hundred pounds granted by the General Court to fortify the town are of opinion that the town at present should neither Except or Refuse said money on the conditions it is granted and that a Petission be prepared to the General Court representing the great advantages which will probably acrue from our harbor being well fortified in protecting and securing the vessels which will use it in times of war and praying that the s'd sum of seven hundred pounds be granted to the town, we obliging ourselves to expend the whole of s'd money in erecting a suitable breastwork procuring great guns and necessary warlike stores and whenever the town shall fail of keeping said breastwork and guns in good order and repair to return the guns and what powder and bullets are not necessarily expended to the Province or whenever s'd Province shall call for them.[4]

In accordance with this vote, a petition was prepared by a committee who represented to the General Court, that "our

[1]Acts and Resolves, Chap. 81, Vol. XII, 702.

[2]Enoch Coffin, Samuel Butler, John Norton, Joseph Jenkins and Christopher Beetle. (Edgartown Records, I, 165.)

[3]Edgartown Records, I, 170.

[4]Ibid., I, 171.

Indigent circumstances will not at present allow us to receive the s'd money upon the Terms it is granted, (fearing that the Immediate expense of procuring and providing according to the Directions of the Grant and Constant Charge of maintaining the same will exceed our ability.)" They asked that the money be allowed for the fortification, and when the town "should fail of keeping s'd Brestwork and Guns in good order and repair to return the guns and what Powder and Bullets are not necessarily expended to the Province."[1]

The General Court made answer to this proposition, in a bill prepared by William Pepperrell of the joint committee of the two houses, which was passed April 3, 1741, making provision for the purchase of "five six-pound cannon, with suitable carriages, five half bbs. of Gun Powder, a suitable number of shot & other warlike stores." The provision attached to this was that the town should "erect at their own cost & charges & (keep) in repairs a Breast Work & platform suitable for said Cannon & a house to secure the stores."[2] Whether this finally resulted in the building of a fort is not known, as there are no further references to it in the records to show expenditures for maintenance or repair.

TAVERNS.

It is probable that William Weeks was the first taverner at Edgartown, as early as 1680, though no record appears of his receiving a license as such. Under that date he was fined five shillings "for suffering disorder in his house by drunkenness & fighting." In fact, as far back as 1661, he was fined "for selling strong liquor," but neither of these entries would be conclusive that he kept a tavern, but for the following record, which in 1681 shows him to have been the proprietor of a public house:—

> The complaint of Arthur Biven against William Weeks "for taking six-pence for two amesho-ogs & said Biven caled for a gill of rum & they brought half water and the said Weeks had no lodging for him nor food for his horse."[3]

Arthur Biven was a resident of Tisbury, and had probably driven to Edgartown on court business, where he was a suitor

[1]Mass. Archives, LXII, 561, 562.

[2]Acts and Resolves, Chap. 186, Vol. XII, 742. The Captain General of the Forces of the Province was directed to carry out this law.

[3]Court Records, Vol. I. "Amesho-ogs" is the Indian word for eels.

at the March quarterly court, and the complaint against Landlord Weeks was in accordance with the laws of the times, governing the keeping of taverns. His "ordinary" was located on North Water street, about fifty rods above Main street, and it is probable that he had kept it as such long before the records above quoted. North Water street was dotted with taverns in the next century. William Weeks' next neighbor to the north was Richard Sarson, and his house and its successors became famous as taverns. Sarson had licenses to sell "strong liquor" on his premises in 1694, but that does not imply a public house kept for travelers. In 1701, his only son Samuel, who succeeded to the estate, was granted a license to keep "a publike house of entertainment," and after his death, in 1703, his widow Anne renewed this in her own name. Here the widow Sarson dispensed hospitality for a year, when she married John Worth for her third husband, and the business of tavern keeping was carried on by them for many years, in the old Sarson house. The licenses were taken out in his name. The location of this ancient hostelry was between Cottage and Morse streets on North Water. Near-by, Thomas Lothrop kept a tavern for a quarter of a century, 1715–1740, on a part of this lot. At the same time, on this same home lot, as part of her father's estate, lived Jane Sarson, successively the wife of Lemuel Little and Dr. John Sanderson. Both of these husbands took out licenses to retail liquor (1722) and to be innholders (1726); and as she took a third husband, Duncan Kelley, and they continued to reside on the property, it is probable the business was continued.

John Norton took out a license as innholder in 1715, and was given the same privilege for 34 years, from which it is assumed that he kept open his "house of publick entertainment" continuously. It was located on the Bayes home lot, just north of Main street.

In 1699, Samuel Smith, who married Hannah (Mayhew) Daggett, was licensed as innholder, and it is probable that the tavern was situated in the northerly end of the town, at Pease's Point. How long he continued to dispense hospitality to travelers is not known.

Parson Homes of Chilmark, in his diary, speaks of the tavern kept by "Mr. Hamellon" in Edgartown, under date of 1738, and the allusion is probably to James Hamellin (now Hamlin), who resided on Burying Hill, south of the old cemetery.

James Claghorn, whose residence was on the old home lot of Edward Lay (later Isaac Norton's), was licensed an innholder in 1740, an occupation which he followed until his death, ten years later. His house stood a short distance north of the Harbor View Hotel. His successor was his son-in-law, Enoch Coffin, Jr., who kept his license for ten years more.

The Kelley House of today is on the site of a hostelry that is over a century old. It is on the northerly half of the original Bayes home lot, which descended to the Newcombs and was bought of their heirs in 1743, by John Harper. He began keeping a tavern there in 1748, and was succeeded by his son-in-law, Lemuel Kelley, in 1772, and by Kelley's widow (Bathsheba Harper), in 1798. Her son, William Kelley, followed in 1801.

In 1850 it was kept by a Mr. L. Marcy and was known as the Marcy House. Today it is known as the Kelley House, and its landlord, the late William Kelley, was a descendant of the family which first gave its name to the old tavern.

On North Water street is the house in which Major-Gen. Worth, of Mexican War fame, lived when a boy. For many years this house was kept as a hotel, known as the Gibbs House, and it was at this ancient hostelry that Daniel Webster was often a guest. It was later known as the Norton House, and was built by Capt. Thomas Worth, probably about 1800. It is now in the possession of Capt. William H. Roberts, Revenue Cutter Service, as a private residence.

The following named persons were licensed innholders in the town of Edgartown by the County Court, for the years specified: — Samuel Smith, 1699-1704; John Worth, 1711-1723; Thomas Lothrop, 1715-1740; John Norton, 1715-1749; Lemuel Little, 1722; John Sanderson, 1726-1728; James Hamlin, 1733-1740; Christopher Beetle, 1734-1746; James Claghorn, 1740-1748; John Dikes, 1743-1744; George Stevens, 1743-1752; Daniel Cruttenden, 1745-1746; Bayes Norton, 1746; John Harper, 1748-1771; Enoch Coffin (succeeded James Claghorn), 1749-1759; Abner Coffin, 1751-1758; Thomas Arey, 1752-1759; Lemuel Kelley (succeeded John Harper), 1772-1787; Bathsheba Kelley (widow of Lemuel Kelley), 1798-1800, who was succeeded by William Kelley, 1801-1807; Matthew Mayhew, 1776-1787; Richard Whelden, 1782; Timothy Coffin, 1786-1787; Beriah Norton, 1798-1804; Jonathan Pease, 1800-1806.

PATHS, HIGHWAYS AND BRIDGES.

The earliest action of the town on this important subject, was under date of June 26, 1652, ten years after the settlement, when it was voted that "Mr. Mayhew the Elder and John Daggett shall lay out all highways belonging to this town." At that date it seems probable there were but two highways, exclusive of "paths," for the use of the settlers. Nearly seventy years later, another general vote was taken on this subject (Feb. 7, 1716 or 1717), "to lay out convenient highways for the use of the town." Doubtless this action was taken to establish legally the various paths and ways which had grown into accepted streets in the course of time.

Main Street.—The first street of record in this town is the present Main Street, and undoubtedly it was laid out when the home lots were divided. It separated the tenth and eleventh lots, almost the centre of the "five and twenty." The earliest reference to it is as follows:—

> Whereas there was a Controversy Between Thos. Paine and Thos. Bayes Concerning the Lott that Lyes next the high way: this Controversy is ended and the said Thomas Paines Lott is to Lye as it did Before, only a high way Between Thos. Bayes & he Two Rods wide: the Verdict of the Court.[1] [February 6, 1654.]

This street was formally laid out by metes and bounds in 1773, as a part of the road from Edgartown to Homes Hole. It was thirty feet wide from the harbor to the house of John Norton, tertia, and thirty-three feet wide from that point as the street and road then ran. In 1824, upon petition, the bounds were renewed by the Court of General Sessions, and again in 1861 the County Commissioners relocated that portion extending from the Court House to Pease Point Way, and made it thirty-three feet wide.

Pease Point Way.—This well-known thoroughfare is next in point of interest and age. It is mentioned in 1660 for the first time.[2] It extends from the harbor, at a point near the present location of the Harbor View Hotel, on the southerly side, and near to the house of the late Thomas Adams Norton, a house situated southerly of the house of Judge Braley; thence westerly by the North schoolhouse, and thence southwesterly by the cemetery, and still continuing southwesterly through what

[1]Edgartown Records, I, 119.

[2]Ibid., I, 110. It is there called three rods wide.

is known as "Cleveland town" (a few houses just out of the village), thence still southwesterly to the Great Pond. It derived its name from the point where John Pease had his house lot, and has retained it to the present day. By its windings it might indicate an Indian trail, but it is in reality the road that intersected the heads of the home lots as far as Slough Hill, where it branches off to the westward. It was the great highway which enabled the settlers to travel from the north end of the town to the Plains.

Planting Field Way.—This road intersects Pease Point Way, north of Main Street, and is of great antiquity, leading as it does to the "planting field" lots, which were laid out in 1653.

Plain Road.—This provided an outlet from the Slough, southwards, and is first mentioned in 1662, though a cart path must have been in existence for a number of years.

Swimming Place Path. — Extending from the Swimming Point towards the Great Pond this road was a necessary "cross path" in that section. Mention is first made of it in 1675.

Mashacket Path. — This old path is doubtless of greater antiquity than the first record of it would indicate (1677), and it is one of the names which has survived the two-and-a-half centuries.

Sanchacantacket Path. — After this region came into the plans for extending the area of settlement, a path was required to reach there, and it became in effect an extension of the main highway leading out of the village. It was first mentioned in 1678.

Mill Path. — The mill at West Tisbury, which was set up before that town was settled, gave the name to an old path which led from Cleveland Town to Takemmy, south of the present road. It is described in the first volume.

Wintucket Path. — This road, leading to Wintucket from the old Mill Path, is mentioned in 1708.

Mob Street. — The road or way bearing this curious name received its baptism about 1762, and retained it for many years. It ran from the "Mill Path" to the "Meeting House Way," in an easterly direction towards Tower Hill, south of Cleveland Town, and probably crossed the land once owned by David Gray. Traces of Mob Street may now be observed in this land, but in the land nearer Tower Hill frequent cultivation has obliterated all traces so that it is not possible now to find just where it ended. All that can be learned about the origin of the name is as follows: Many years ago there was a sailors' boarding-house near "Mill Hill," and near the point where "Mob Street" meets "Mill Path" there was a dwelling-house occupied by people of somewhat questionable reputation. At both houses intoxicants were sold in large quantities. The street connecting the two places was so often the scene of drunkenness and rioting that it received the name "Mob Street." This may be the correct story of its origin, unless it refers to some particular outbreak or riotous gathering of drunken sailors which occurred to give it a local significance.

South and North Water Streets. — These streets are a part of the same continuous highway, the divisional line being at Main Street. It represents practically the harbor frontage line of the home lots, and was a path or "alley" for many years, before it was formally laid out. South Water Street was called an "alley" in 1703, but this way or path had been in existence long before that date. The appearance of this locality at the time of the Revolution is thus described by Capt. Valentine Pease (born 1764): —

> "When I can first remember and for years afterwards there was a swamp near the shore below the bank extending from below the house of Matthew Mayhew, now Joseph Mayhew's, to Uriah Morse's or where the Marine Railway now is. There were then but two ways through it to the shore; one, now the termination of Main street; the other leading from the old Tavern kept by Kelley and others to the wharf now Mayhew's wharf."[1]

This street was laid out by order of the Court of General Sessions, by metes and bounds, in March, 1786, from the house of William Mayhew to the house of Enoch Coffin at its extreme north end. The width was "twenty five feet in each and every part," and this survey as approved by the Court represents this street as it now exists.[2]

Meeting House Way. — In 1768, when the new meeting house was completed on the grounds of the cemetery on Pease Point Way, the need of a public way thither from the water front was apparent, and on February 9th of that year, Matthew Mayhew made a gift to the town of a way one rod wide, extending from the harbor to the meeting-house. It is the present Commercial Street (so-called).

[1]From a statement made to the late Richard L. Pease, in 1851, when the Captain was in his 87th year.

[2]Dukes County Court Records.

Pilgrim's Alley. — The path or way leading from South Water Street, northwest to Pease Point Way, and frequently used as a "short cut" by the people who attended service at Parson Thaxter's meeting-house, was called by this quaint name. After another denomination established a place of worship in Edgartown, the people of that belief called Parson Thaxter's adherents "Puritans" and "Pilgrims," and the straight and narrow path which they trod when going to and coming from the meeting-house, "Pilgrim's Alley."

The Beach Road to Oak Bluffs was built in 1872, and rebuilt in 1902 on the Macadam plan, as a part of the state highway system.

Penny Wise Path. — There was a locality bearing this title in Edgartown as early as 1734. "Penny Wise" (a place) is mentioned in a deed from Joseph Norton to his grandson John, in that year. "Penny Wise Path" is referred to in 1735, as near the "middle line."[1] "Penny Wise Way" was described as near the road from Edgartown to Homes Hole; also near the Claypit.[2]

The "Pennywise Path" is the first road byond the homestead of the late William Jernegan, on the left side of the old Homes Hole road. It leads by the north side of the Dark woods to and by the south side of the West woods, on the West Tisbury road. A continuation of it meets Pease's Point Way at Great Pond. It was called "Pennywise Path" because it was laid out as a shorter way to Homes Hole than Pease's Point Way. But it proved to be as long if not longer than the old way, so was called Pennywise.

Tarkill (Tarkiln) Path. — There were kilns for extracting tar from wood in the Penny Wise region, and this path ran to that locality as early as 1738.[3]

Bridges. — There were no bridges in town of any importance, in construction, span or elevation. While there are a number, yet they are scarcely more than culverts over the small streams which run to the sea. A bridge at Mashacket is mentioned in 1653, again in 1676 and 1678. A couple of small bridges span Mile Brook and Menoda Creek, while a considerable pile bridge joins this town to Oak Bluffs, over the Sanchacantacket inlet.

[1]Deeds, VI, 20.

[2]"Penny Wise Swamp" is mentioned in 1743.

[3]Deeds, VI, 364.

U. S. GOVERNMENT SERVICES.

CUSTOMS SERVICE.

This branch of the national government was established in this island in 1789, shortly after the formation of the Union, and Edgartown was made the port of entry, with Homes Hole as the sub-port. There has never been a government building for the accommodation of this department, and from the beginning until about 1850 the Collector of Customs had his office in his own house. It is known that in 1799 the office was located in the 'Squire Thomas Cooke house, corner of Commercial and School streets, when the office was held by that gentleman, and his successor in 1830 transferred it to the Capt. Edwin Coffin house, North Water street. It is therefore probable that the first collector, John Pease, kept the office and records in his own residence. According to the best information now obtainable the building on the northeast corner of Water and Main streets was rented for the customs service during the tenure of Leavitt Thaxter as collector (1849-1853), and it has been occupied ever since that time by this service.

Since 1818, and probably some years before that, there has been a Deputy Collector of Customs at this port. The following is a list of these officials from the establishment of the service to the present time, with the date and term of service of each:—

COLLECTORS.

John Pease from 1789[1] to April 10, 1809.
Thomas Cooke, March 24, 1799 to April 10, 1809.
Thomas Cooke, Jr., April 10, 1809 to Feb. 20, 1830.
John P. Norton, Feb. 20, 1830 to April 8, 1842.
Leavitt Thaxter, April 8, 1842 to Sept. 16, 1845.
Joseph T. Pease, Sept. 16, 1845 to Sept. 1, 1849.
Leavitt Thaxter, Sept. 1, 1849 to May 10, 1853.
Joseph T. Pease, May 10, 1853 to May, 1855.
Constant Norton, May, 1855 to June, 1860.
Ira Darrow, June, 1860 to June 3, 1861.
John Vinson, June 3, 1861 to March 1, 1870.
Cornelius B. Marchant, March 1, 1870 to June 7, 1886.
Sirson P. Coffin, June 7, 1886 to July 12, 1890.
Charles H. Marchant, July 12, 1890 to March 7, 1895.
Abraham Osborn, March 7, 1895 to April 4, 1899.
Charles H. Marchant, April 4, 1899 to present time.

[1] He was commissioned as Collector March 21, 1791.

DEPUTY COLLECTORS

John Cooke, (indefinite), probably to 1818.
William Cooke, Nov. 18, 1818 to 1821.
Jeremiah Pease, Sr., 1821 to 1855.
Sirson P. Coffin, 1855 to 1861.
Jeremiah Pease, Jr., 1861 to 1890.
John W. Pease, May 16, 1890 to present time

THE POST OFFICE.

The mail service was established officially in 1795, when Col. Beriah Norton was appointed the first postmaster. It is probable that there was a post route to the island long before this, though the first postmaster at Homes Hole received his appointment on the same date as Colonel Norton. After the island was united with the Massachusetts Bay Colony (1691) a postal service was inaugurated under patents from the crown,[1] but the isolated position of the Vineyard prevented its participation in any of the post routes established at that early date. We may conclude that mails were brought from Boston overland to Plymouth, thence by Sandwich to Woods Hole, and delivered by ferry to the Vineyard.

In 1830 the Post office was on the corner of Water and Main streets, on the lot now occupied by the *Vineyard Gazette*, but it is not known how long it had been located there prior to this, nor when it was transferred to its present quarters. It is probable that it began the occupancy of the building opposite, where it now is, when the Custom House was installed there. The following is a list of the postmasters:

Beriah Norton, January 1, 1795; Timothy Coffin, Jr., May 20, 1819; Silvanus L. Pease, May 29, 1838; William Vinson, Sept. 28, 1846; John Pierce, Nov. 26, 1847; Jared W. Coffin, Feb. 26, 1849; Silvanus L. Pease, May 26, 1853; Jared W. Coffin, 1861; William Bradley, 1865; Jared W. Coffin, 1869; Richard L. Pease, 1877; Henry A. Pease, 1885 (present incumbent).

LIGHTHOUSE ESTABLISHMENT.

The government maintains in addition to the usual beacons, buoys and bells, two lighthouses in Edgartown for general and local maritime benefit. The first lighthouse was

[1]The conveyance of a letter from Boston to Salem, at that date, cost three pence; to Ipswich, four pence; to Portsmouth, six pence. In 1710 the postage between Boston and New York was one shilling; between Boston and any town within sixty miles, four pence. (Mass. Prov. Laws, 117, 123, 263, 420; Comp. 3 Mass. Hist. Coll., VII, 72-79.)

JARED WASS COFFIN

1823–1885

POSTMASTER OF EDGARTOWN FOR EIGHTEEN YEARS

established at the point of Cape Poge by act of Congress approved Jan. 30, 1801, and the sum of $2,000 was allotted therefor. Jurisdiction of the tract had been ceded by the State the previous year, and the title passed Aug. 10 ,1801, to the United States.[1] The tower was completed in 1802 and lasted for forty years, when the inroads of wave action on the sandy soil forced the erection of a new light-tower in 1843. This second structure survived a half century of storms and further encroachments of the sea, when in 1893 the third and present light-tower was built still further back from the tip of the cape. The first keeper was Matthew Mayhew (360), who continued in office until his death in 1834, when he was succeeded by Lot Norton (1019) who held the post about eight years.[2] Succeeding keepers have been Aaron Norton, Edward Worth, 1850-53; Daniel Smith, 1853-59;[3] George R. Marchant, 1859-65; Edward Worth, 1865; Jethro Worth, George Fisher and George Dolby.

The light was originally a fixed one, but was changed about 1885 to a revolving light.

The Harbor light was authorized by an act approved May 23, 1828, and the sum of $5,500 was appropriated for its erection about a quarter of a mile from the shore at the harbor entrance.[4] Communication with the town was maintained by boats for over a year after its completion, when the sum of $2,500 was allowed "for extending the pier on which the lighthouse is built to the shore." This bridge was built of wood and eventually cost $7,000 before it was completed;[5] and by reason of its box construction it was frequently broken by storms and ice. In 1847 the sum of $4,000 was allowed for a breakwater of rock construction, and the existing stone causeway was built on the lines as it runs to the shore today.

INDUSTRIES.

This town has never been a manufacturing centre, and but few records are to be found relating to the production of finished articles of merchandise from the raw material. The

[1]U. S. Statutes, II, 88; III, 405; comp. Mass. Laws, 1800, p. 70. The consideration was $36 for four acres. It was the twelfth light erected by the government on the Massachusetts coast.

[2]An interim appointment of Benjamin C. Smith of Chappaquiddick followed after Mayhew's death.

[3]During Mr. Smith's term the lighting power was changed from the reflector system to prisms.

[4]U. S. Statutes, IV, 282; VIII, 64.

[5]Devens, "Sketches of Martha's Vineyard," p. 18.

sea and its wealth gave a distinctive feature to such industries as grew into being here from time to time. The whale and other fisheries have constituted the chief occupation of the people from the earliest times to the last quarter of the past century. The whaling industry has already been described.[1] Second in importance were the general fisheries and the by-products of marine sea foods. In 1850 the largest single industry of this character was the oil and candle works of Daniel Fisher & Co., with a capital of $40,000 invested in the business, and the annual product for that year was 118,000 pounds of candles, 13,200 barrels of strained and refined oils. With other minor products the annual value of this business was reported to be $284,370, an industry far exceeding in direct cash income to the town the whale fishery interests. The general government was supplied with oil and candles for the lighthouses by this firm, and this business grew in importance in later years till the time of the Civil War. Whole cargoes of oil were contracted for at one time, involving values of over $100,000 at a purchase, and the industry gave employment to many men.

The general fisheries in 1850 yielded a value in product of $15,325, of which $4,500 is credited to the Mattakeeset herring fishery, the latter representing a catch of 1,250 barrels. At the present time the shell fisheries are an equally important industry, and rival in value the other sea foods collected in these waters for the metropolitan markets. It is impossible to give an accurate account of the yield, financially considered, of these several industries, but the value may be estimated by a "catch" made in the first week of January, 1908, when about 10,000 of fish were taken by five boats, having a market value of $2,000.

In the years preceding the Revolution the manufacture of salt by the process of evaporation of sea water in large wooden vats or pans was an important industry, and it was followed up as late as 1840. This business, at one time so valuable in the state, has entirely disappeared as an occupation hereabouts since the development of salt mining in other sections of the country.

Other industries allied to the above sea products, cooperage, blocks and tackling, and boat building have been in

[1]Vol. I, pp. 430-451. The annual value of the whaling business to Edgartown in 1850 was $83,267, but this was only the product of one vessel owned in the town at that time, the ship *Vineyard*. (U. S. Census Report, 1850.)

existence in the town for brief pèriods in the past, but were of ephemeral importance and are only worthy of incidental mention.[1] The only mills operated in town have been propelled by wind power and were local grist mills only. Before the days of the great manufactories of cloth the limited production of hand looms from wool was an occupation of the women in their spare hours, but of no great importance.

SCHOOLS.

The earliest mention of the subject of education in the town records occurs under date of 1652, when the "school house" is referred to, showing the establishment of schools prior to that year. Peter Folger was the first school-master, and the building where he taught was on the Old Mill path near the Sarson lot on Slough hill. He probably kept school until his departure from town in 1662, but it is not known who was his successor, nor what arrangements were in existence prior to the beginning of the next century. In 1687 Thomas Peat was "skoollemaster of Edgartown," and the school was then held in the house of Richard Arey.[2] Not until 1710 is there further reference to the subject, when a committee was chosen to procure a schoolmaster, to be paid at the rate of £30 per annum "for learning of children for to read, right and learn arithmetick," with the privilege of "taking of six scolers for the learning of Latten" outside of his school hours.[3] In 1712 Josiah Bridge, "now resident in Edgartown," was chosen schoolmaster at the rate of £25 per annum, and two years later the town voted "to hire him as reasonably as they can." In 1723 Thomas Cathcart was called "schoolmaster of Edgartown." From this time forward the records contain almost yearly reference to the subject of schools, and the manner of maintenance. Committees were chosen yearly to hire masters, and an annual appropriation was made, varying from £45 in 1738 to £60 in 1747, for the support of education. After this the amount dropped to £13 in 1750 and £8 in 1760, but this decrease may be explained by the fluctuations of the provincial currency, in old and new tenor.

[1] A spool house, erected about 1777, is mentioned in the records, but its significance is not known (Deeds, XI, 463).

[2] Dukes Court Records. The identity of this person is not established. It is possible the name should be read Peac (Pease), as the writing in the records at this date by the clerk of courts is execrable and often undecipherable.

[3] Town Records, I, 53.

The growth of the town northward, and the development of the Farm Neck settlement, necessitated, as early as 1750, the division of the school funds and separate schools for these widely separated districts. The expedient of "moving" schools was first adopted, meaning the holding of sessions alternating in time and place between the districts. In 1760 the old school-house was sold, and in May, 1765, the town voted that "there should be but one school house built in the town and no more." This was located by a vote of 14 to 8 on the "road that leadeth to the meeting house," about fifteen or twenty rods to the southward of Silas Marchant's, "a spot near the center of the inhabitants," now Cleveland town.[1] In the following month, however, two school-houses were authorized, one of which was for the northern district in Farm Neck, and £100 was voted for this combined object. Before the Revolution the town was divided into four districts.[2]

The names of the school-masters do not appear in the records, and only occasional collateral documents reveal them to us. Ichabod Wiswall, a cousin of the pastor, was one in 1746 and doubtless was such before and after this date.[3]

The growth of population in the next century necessitated new district divisions, and schools at Pohoganut, the Plains, and on Chappaquiddick were maintained in addition to those in the village. The "old red school house" of song and story, on Pease Point way near the meeting house, was a landmark and a childhood reminiscence for the older generation now living, but it gave up its primacy before 1850, and new buildings took its place in other sections. The North school was situated on Planting Field way and accommodated two grades, grammar and primary, for scholars on that side of Main Street. The South School followed in point of time, being dedicated in 1850, and was located on the corner of School and High streets. It contained what corresponds to the modern high-school grade, besides the grammar and primary. At the present time the North school

[1]Town Records, I, 245-246.

[2]The north-west section was to draw its "proportionable" share, and a committee of residents there appointed to locate the building. This arrangement was observed ever after. In 1771 Chappaquiddick was granted a separate school with "their proportion of money they pay" (Ibid, I, 295).

[3]Probate Records, III, 206. He was born in Newton, Mass., 1709, and was graduated at Harvard. He married Jerusha Norton (404) of Edgartown and died here in 1782 aged 78 years. He came of a family of teachers and ministers.

HON. LEAVITT THAXTER

FOUNDER OF THAXTER'S ACADEMY

1788–1863

has the intermediate and primary grades, and the high and grammar grades are taught in the South School.

Sometime before 1850 an additional school was built on the corner of Summer and Thomas streets, and was in operation for a number of years. The following named persons have taught in Edgartown schools, and will be remembered by the older residents: Frances E. Mayhew, Harriet R. Fisher, Caroline Arey, Emeline Marchant, Eliza A. Worth, Maria L. Norton, Eliza F. Pease, Hannah Davis, Eunice Lambert, and Emily Worth. The masters have been George A. Walton, Constant Norton, Joseph B. Gow, Richard L. Pease, John J. Leland, Smith B. Goodenow, and Henry Baylies.

THAXTER ACADEMY.

A complete survey of the subject of education in this town could not be made without devoting adequate space to the life and work of Hon. Leavitt Thaxter, a noble scion of a worthy sire. Born here, March 13, 1788, the second son of Parson Thaxter, he was trained for the duties of life by his distinguished father. Although he had prepared for Harvard College, which he entered at an early age, he did not complete the course, but was led like so many of his youthful companions by the lure of the sea, and apparently began the life of a sailor. He made a number of voyages to the East Indies, and during our second war with Great Britain, although not a belligerent, he was made a prisoner at Calcutta, and experienced the discomforts of a British prison in that climate. After several years of the seafaring life, for which he was not fitted, he turned to the work better suited to his temperament and training. Gifted with a superior mind, his father had encouraged him to use it for the benefit of others and urged the occupation of a teacher as one best fitted for his talents. A letter addressed to him by his father, bearing date New Year's day, 1819, says: "I early devoted you to God. I have spared no pains or expense to qualify you to act your part gracefully as a man and a Christian. By my advice you have devoted yourself to the instruction of youth. The office is the most important and useful in which man can be employed. That ought to be esteemed the most honorable which is the most useful; it is so in the sight of God."

He taught in several towns in the western part of this state, Leicester, Northampton, and Williamsburg, and in the latter place found a wife in the person of Martha White Mayhew (741), whose grandfather, Paine Mayhew (201), had emigrated in 1786 from Chilmark to that town. Thence Thaxter went, in 1819, to Sparta, Georgia, where he remained three or four years in charge of a large and successful academy. Returning to Edgartown in 1823, he decided to make this his permanent home, and at once engaged in teaching. With the aid and influence of his father he erected a school building for his work on the northwest corner of Davis and Maple streets, in 1825, and it was dedicated as Thaxter's Academy, November 29th, by public exercises, in which an oration was delivered by the principal.[1] Here for the best part of a long and useful life he followed the occupation of guide, philosopher, and friend of the youth of his native town. One of his pupils in an appreciative review of his career wrote as follows concerning this school and its head: —

> The school room where he presided was to those pupils who had caught his spirit and imbibed his principles, a place of delight and not an irksome prison house. Strict in his discipline, that was the place for vigorous application and toilsome study; a paradise for those thirsting for knowledge, but a hard and thorny way to the idle and obdurate. And then the recess! Indoors and out what teacher ever more sought the comfort and happiness of his pupils, or more bountifully provided for them the means of amusement.

His life however was not all devoted to this special work. He was eminently a leader of thought in all the things that make for the development of the moral and material welfare of a community, and his fellow citizens honored him with their places of public trust, until the close of his life. He was representative to the General Court (1830), senator from this district (1836,-1847), and Governor's councillor (1839). Under the National government he held numerous commissions, including judge of the Court of Insolvency, and collector of customs at this port. He was the first president of the Dukes County Educational Association (1848), and the first president of the Martha's Vineyard Agricultural Association (1858), and in this latter capacity his abilities as a practical horticulturist made him something more than a parliamentary head of this body. Not a few of the ornamental flora of

[1]This was published under the title "An Oration Delivered At The Dedication of Thaxter's Academy in Edgartown, Martha's Vineyard, November 29th, 1825. Also, A Hymn Composed For The Occasion, By Leavitt Thaxter, New Bedford, 1825." A copy is in the author's collection of the printed literature of the Island. The hymn was probably composed by Parson Thaxter.

this town now adorning the private gardens were introduced and cultivated by him, and generously given to others.

His human sympathies led him to entertain a practical interest in the remnants of the tribe of Indians living in the town, and in 1836, having been made their legal guardian, he devoted nearly twenty years' service to their welfare. Such was the confidence inspired by his execution of this apparently thankless task, that he was always after regarded by them as their trusted friend and counsellor, to whom they constantly came for advice and encouragement. This distinguished son

THE "PARSON THAXTER" HOUSE

BUILT 1784-5

HOME OF THE PARSON AND BIRTHPLACE OF LEAVITT THAXTER

of Edgartown died at his residence on Davis street, Nov. 27, 1863, in the seventy-fifth year of his age, and he lies buried beside his parents, whose name he bore with increased honor. The portrait of Mr. Thaxter, which illustrates this, now hangs in the office of clerk of courts, having been placed there as a public memorial by "a number of his former pupils." The sittings were given at their request in 1862, and the artist, Cyrus Worth Pease (1091) of this town, succeeded in painting an excellent likeness in his best style.

DAVIS ACADEMY.

Another institution for the higher grade of education was established by David Davis of Farmington, Me. He was of Vineyard ancestry, being the son of Sanford and Mary (Coffin) Davis of Eastville, born Dec. 23, 1802, and returned to this town in his early manhood. This school which prospered under his management was unfortunately destroyed by fire in 1836 after a few years of existence, but by the aid of contribution from friends and patrons here he rebuilt. This new academy building is still in existence on the corner of Maple street, diagonally opposite the building formerly known as Thaxter's Academy. Owing to ill health which followed shortly after these events, Mr. Davis was obliged to suspend teaching, but continued to reside here in the upper story of this building. The schoolroom was used by other teachers during the day and in the evening lectures, concerts and similar public meetings were held in this room, generally called "Davis Hall." Mr. Davis was a highly esteemed resident and citizen and was honored by his neighbors in 1855 by an election to the council, and when Governor Henry S. Gardiner, his chief, visited Edgartown, he was tendered a public reception in the schoolroom of his councillor. Mr. Davis died Nov. 6, 1868, at the age of 66 years, generally lamented.

MISCELLANEOUS ANNALS.

THE MASONIC ORDER.

Free Masonry had some following in this town about 1800 though no lodge was in existence here as early as that. Several residents of Edgartown were members of King Solomon's Lodge in Perfection at Homes Hole at this date and others became affiliated later with Union Lodge of Nantucket. Thomas Cooke, Benjamin Smith and John Pease were members of the former lodge, while Thomas M. Vinson, Jared Coffin, James Banning and Valentine Pease were of the Nantucket lodge. On Aug. 16, 1819, the Edgartown members just named, with three others, laid before the lodge a petition to the Grand Lodge of Massachusetts to establish an independent lodge in Edgartown, to be known by the name of "Seven Stars," and requesting Union Lodge to recommend the granting of their petition. The lodge took the following action:—

Voted:— That we recommend to the Grand Lodge of Massachusetts the following brethern to establish a Lodge in Edgartown Martha's Vinyard:—

Rt. Wor. Thomas M. Vinson to be the first Master.
Wor. Samuel Wheldon to be the first S. W.
Wor. Samuel Worthman to be the first J. W.

The Grand Lodge acted favorably upon the recommendation and the new lodge was chartered Sept. 13, 1820. The Worshipful Master, Col. Thomas Melville Vinson was not of the Edgartown family of this name, but a native of Newport, R. I., where he was born in 1784 and his military title came from service in the War of 1812 under General Samuel McComb on the northern frontier of New York.

Colonel Vinson married Hepsibah Young Marchant (160) of this town April 5, 1814, and later removed to Dorchester, Mass., where he resided until his death. He was an employee in the customs service at the port of Boston, and falling on the steps of the Custom House, March 4, 1852, received fatal injuries from which he died four days later. His widow survived twenty years, dying in Dorchester.

The Senior Warden, Dr. Samuel Wheldon (1765-1841) was a native of Edgartown where he married, but he removed late in life to Coventry, Conn. Samuel Worthman, the Junior Warden, was a transient resident, "a Scotchman by Birth," but he married here. It will be seen that the officers of the lodge were not associated by birth with this town and that fact may account for the entire absence of further knowledge concerning its existence, if it had any, after the above quoted records of its establishment

A lodge of Master Masons, under the jurisdiction of Massachusetts, was chartered June 25, 1867, by the name of Oriental Lodge, and it has been in existence for over forty years and is now in a flourishing condition. The first officers elected were: John Pierce, Worshipful Master; Grafton N. Collins, Senior Warden; James M. Coombs, Jr., Junior Warden; William L. Lewis, Secretary; and Jonathan H. Munroe, Treasurer.

The first lodge-room was over the store of Frederick E. Terrill, on North Water street, which was occupied until removal to the present room over the store of Jonathan H. Munroe on Main street. The first installation of officers, after some brief existence under dispensation, was a public ceremony held in the Methodist Church. The Grand officers of the Grand Lodge of the State were present, and installed the officers above enumerated in the presence of a large audience of interested friends.

The following is a list of Worshipful Masters to the present time: David J. Barney, Francis P. Vincent, Joseph W. Donalson, Richard G. Shute, Jason L. Dexter, James C. Sandsbury, John E. White, Zenas D. Linton, John N. Pierce, Jeremiah Pease, Elmer E. Landers, and Thomas A. Dexter.

PHYSICIANS.

The practice of medicine in the early days has been elsewhere described as carried on by the clergy, midwives, and often by lawyers. Besides those referred to the following-named persons have followed this profession in the town in the past two centuries: Solomon Bacon, 1720; John Sanderson, 1724; Daniel Crittenden, 1747; Nathan Smith,[1] 1767-1775; John Wright, 1782; Joseph Thaxter (during his ministry), John Pierce, Samuel Wheldon, W. T. S. Brackett, E. Maybury, Ivory H. Lucas, Daniel Fisher, Clement F. Shiverick, G. B. Cornell, Thomas J. Walker, Theodore P. Cleveland, and E. P. Worth.

The long services of Dr. John Pierce in this community, covering nearly half a century (1836-1879), deserve special notice. He was a native of Lebanon, Conn., where he was born Nov. 25, 1805, and he received his preliminary education in Monmouth, Maine. He was graduated from Bowdoin Medical School in 1833, and practiced for a few years in Maine prior to his settlement in this town. While there he served as surgeon to the troops called out to quell the disturbances over the northeastern boundary. During his residence here he was for eight years in charge of the U. S. Marine Hospital Service at Homes Hole, and the medical examiner for Dukes county from the establishment of that office till his death. He became a member of the Massachusetts Medical Society in 1840, and held various offices in that organization. He was a valued town official in various lines of work, a prominent Mason, and an active member and officer in the Methodist Church. He died Nov. 25, 1885.

[1] He was not of the Vineyard Smith families. He was born in 1730 and practised at Stamford, Conn., before he came here. He removed to St. John, N. B., where he died in 1818.

DR. JOHN PIERCE
1805–1885

CEMETERIES.

The first tract set apart for the last resting place of the dead was the acre on Burial Hill. It was on the home lots of John Bland and John Eddy, adjoining the harbor end, an equal part being taken from each, and probably was dedicated to its purpose before the division of lots. In 1849 it contained seventy-five stone memorials, all of slate, but this number has been reduced in the last half century by breakage and other causes.[1]

The second cemetery was a gift to the town in 1768; the donation being made by Deacon Matthew Norton, "in consideration of the love, good will and regard that he hath toward the public worship of almighty God."[2] It was an acre in extent, and was situated on Pease Point way, adjoining the lot on which the then new meeting house was being erected. It has since been enlarged by subsequent acquisitions. The first burials were in 1782, when six men of Edgartown, drowned at Gay Head, were interred in the new ground.[3]

There was a burial place at Aquampache used by the residents of that locality, some time prior to 1836, but how long it had been in existence is not known. In that year an addition was made to it by Elihu P. Norton as guardian of an estate.[4]

As happened in all communities there were private burial places used by families on their own farms or homesteads. The most important of these is the Mayhew graveyard on South Water street, in the Collins lot, just north of the old Mayhew house. This is doubtless the place where Governor Mayhew was buried, also Major Matthew Mayhew and his

[1]The list of these stones was made by Richard L. Pease in April, 1849, and published in the N. E. Genealogical Register, Vol. LI, 196.

[2]Dukes Deeds, IX, 758. Dated Feb. 8, 1768. See also deeds from estate of Rodolphus W. Coffin, April 29, 1842 (XXVII, 352) and Elijah Norton, Jan. 25, 1847 (XXXII, 150) to the town of Edgartown. In 1765 the town had voted to enlarge the old burial ground by the purchase of an additional acre.

[3]This wreck was the subject of a contemporaneous poem, of little merit except as an historical narrative. The eighteenth stanza reads as follows:—

"Six men belonged to Edgartown,
They left four widows in distress;
And parents for their sons did mourn,
And twenty-six little children fatherless."

[4]Dukes Deeds, XXVI, 7.

family.[1] Several slate stones are now standing, but being in private property in alien possession no care of this sacred spot can be bestowed on the place by an interested public.

THE OLD MAYHEW HOUSE.

The most picturesque object of interest in the town to strangers, is the ancient Mayhew homestead on South Water street. Situated on the "entailed lot," which was originally owned by the Governor, its weathered appearance, unpainted walls and huge square chimney lend aid to the common belief that it was the home of the famous head of this family. Such is not the case, however, as the first house stood about one hundred feet to the northward of the present "old" house.[2] It cannot be stated with any accuracy when it was built. The present owner, Charles Mayhew (9) (Joseph, 8; William, 7; Matthew, 6; Micajah, 5; Matthew, 4; Matthew, 3; Thomas, 2; Gov. Thomas, 1), has no definite knowledge of its age, beyond the fact that his grandfather, Deacon William (351) told him that at the age of twelve he assisted his father, Matthew (150), in shingling this house. Deacon William was born in 1748, and this shingling was therefore done in 1760, but whether he referred to the original shingles or to their renewal is not known. This date would make the building about one hundred and fifty years old now, and beyond this, guessing may add any further antiquity to it.

TOWN HALL.

The public meetings of the citizens for the transaction of town affairs were held in the church buildings at first, and in the Court Houses. Such was the custom throughout New

[1]In 1838 Deacon William Mayhew (351) in his 90th year, deposed as follows: "Gov. Thomas Mayhew and his wife according to the best of my knowledge were buried in the west corner of Grafton Norton's lot about ten feet from the street, and a little to the north-west of the graves that are now visible. I think there is a rock near the head of the graves of the said Thomas and wife; there are also several other persons buried near the same place and I believe the whole number to be eight." Excavations would probably confirm this statement of the aged Deacon, who was greatly interested in the lives of his ancestors and wished to preserve for posterity his knowledge of their place of sepulture. The eight graves would include Thomas Mayhew and wife, Matthew and wife, besides those known by existing stones. It should be a public duty to disinter these bodies and place them in a public cemetery.

[2]Information given by Mr. Charles Mayhew. He states that he had heard his grandfather, (Deacon William, 1748-1840) say that the original house stood on the site of a house built 75 years ago, and of late years when more cellar room was desired the workmen in digging came on evidences of a former building, such as bits of broken crockery, etc., and part of a wall which he is satisfied was the cellar wall of the original house.

THE OLD MAYHEW HOUSE

England in the early days, when the meeting-house was considered as much for secular as for religious purposes. When the Methodists abandoned, in 1843, their house of worship (built by them about 1828) on the south side of Main street, the town acquired it by purchase for use as a public hall. It was remodeled for the convenience of the town officials and later afforded room for the fire extinguishing apparatus of the volunteer firemen. It served these purposes for over sixty years and in 1908, by popular subscription and town grant it was enlarged at a cost of over three thousand dollars and reopened to the public Aug. 19, 1908, with appropriate dedication services. It has a stage and a new and handsome set of scenery for theatrical exhibitions.

THE VINEYARD GAZETTE.

The first newspaper to be published in Dukes County was established in this town in the spring of 1846 by the late Edgar Marchant (148). The first issue, on May 13th, was a small sheet printed on a hand press, and he was not only the editor but its printer and publisher. In 1850 it had reached a circulation of 600 copies, and by his prudent management and intimate knowledge of the wants of his patrons, he built up a weekly journal that maintained a high standard of excellence from the first with a steady growing clientele. About 1868 he sold the property and removed to Salem to continue a similar business. At the end of five years he returned to Edgartown, repurchased the *Vineyard Gazette* and continued its publication until his decease in 1878. His successor, Charles Henry Marchant, a grand nephew, has since then carried on its publication with success. It is now an eight page paper and is held in increasing favor each year by Vineyarders scattered over the world. It is a model country newspaper.

LIBRARIES.

In 1850 there was a Lyceum Library of 150 volumes and a School Library of 275 volumes for public uses. The present Public Library was established in 1892, and its collection first kept in a small room in the Pierce building, where it remained for six years. Then it was removed to a room over W. E. Marchant's store, and continued there for six years more. Mr. Andrew Carnegie, of New York, presented to the town a library building which was erected on a lot on North Water street, donated by Mrs. Frederick Warren. The building was completed for occupancy in 1904 at a cost of $5,000, and the library has grown to a collection of 2,400 volumes.

EDGARTOWN IN 1908.

The town has now been settled two hundred and sixty-six years and it may be of interest and worthy of preservation to incorporate at the close of our annals the following statistics to show its present growth from the humble beginnings at Great Harbor. From the assessors' lists the following figures regarding the valuation in Edgartown on May 1, 1908, have been furnished: Personal estate assessed, $177,530; real estate assessed, $831,810; total, $1,009,340. Total tax assessed, $18,259.67; acres of land assessed, 12,169; number of dwelling houses, 458; horses, 126; cows, 123; sheep, 95; polls, 358; residents assessed on property, 411; non-residents assessed on property, 808. Increase in assessed valuation over 1907, $83,630.

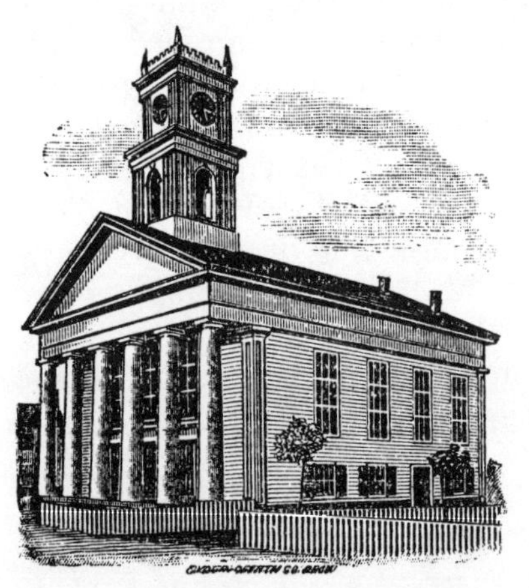

METHODIST CHURCH,
1843.

CHAPPAQUIDDICK

For the purpose of preserving the individuality of this insular part of Edgartown, it will be considered as a separate section and given special treatment. From the earliest times it has always borne the name by which it is now known. It is an Algonquian word, compounded of Tchepi-aquiden-et, which is translated as "the separated island," because it was divided from Nope by the narrow strait of water that sometimes is a continuous run and at others only a closed inlet.[1] The Massachusetts dialect requires the ending in -et, but it has become softened into -ick.[2]

While separated physically, it has always been a legal part of Edgartown since 1646, when the township grant included "also all the Island called Chapaquegick." When the whites first came here it was under the dominion of a sagamore named Pahkepunnassoo, who for many years remained an opponent of the religion brought to his people by the missionaries. Following out his plan of purchasing the aboriginal "rights" to the soil, Mayhew bought of this Indian head man, in 1653, "the Neck that lies over the river for the which land the town is to give the Sachem twenty bushels of corn a year for three years; also his son is to have two lotts when it is devided."[3] This form of quit-rent was doubtless a concession to the dignity of the chieftain, and was renewed in another form in 1663, when Mayhew agreed to pay him "one Good Goat Ram yearly or as much in Good pay as (a) Good Goat Ram should be worth......and one yarde round every whale."[4] It is significant of the scrupulous spirit which actuated Mayhew in his dealings with them, that this agreement was in effect and presumably observed as late as 1724, when the great grandson of this chief man, named Seiknout, also a sachem, commuted his quit-rent for £5 in money to the successor of the old Governor.

[1]From this changing condition Chappaquiddick is often called a neck in the early records, and such was probably its state at the settlement of the Vineyard.

[2]The pronunciation, Chabbaquiddick, now used by the older people is equally correct, as P and B are interchangeable consonants in the Algonquian dialects. The early spelling was always with a P and that is the more correct sound.

[3]Edgartown Records, I, 149.

[4]Dukes Deeds, IV, 72. In 1654 Thomas Paine was granted permission "to buy of the Indians the lot lying upon Chapequidick which hath the graves in it, provided the said Thomas Paine do not exceed the value of three bushels of corn in his pay for it."

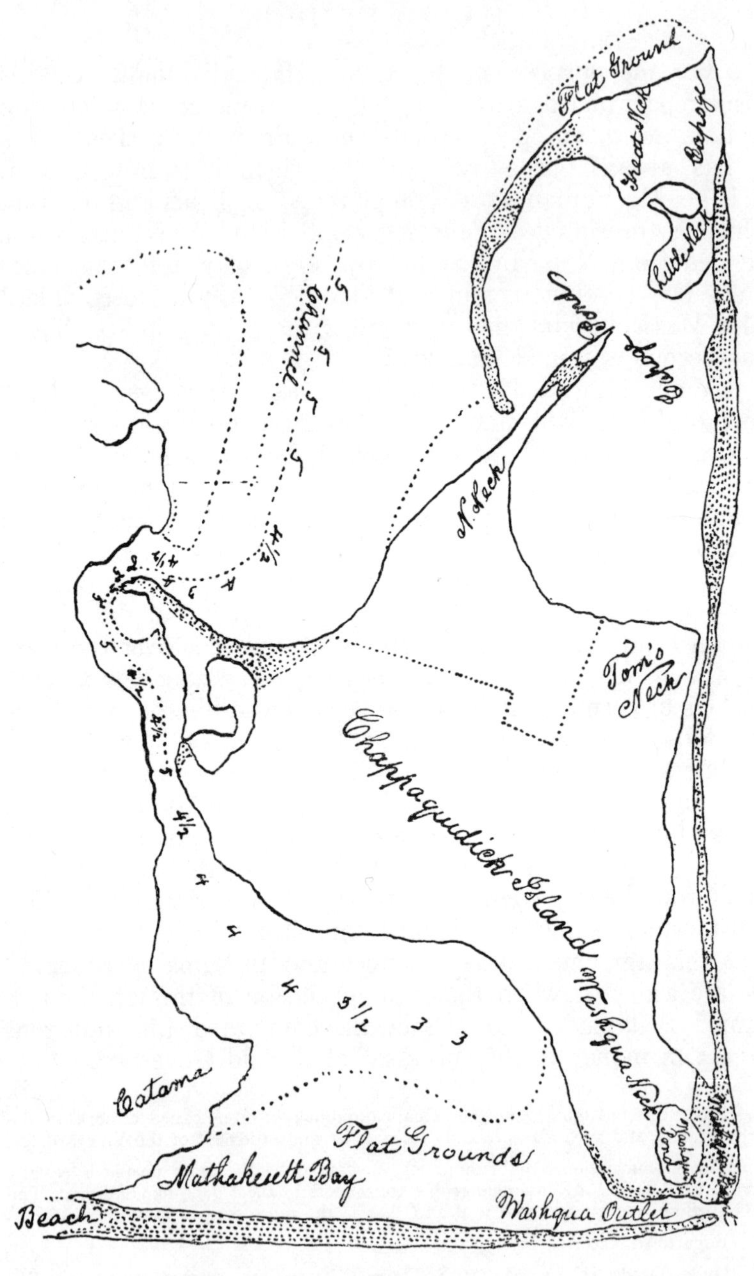

SURVEY OF CHAPPAQUIDDICK, 1795.

CATTLE AND GRAZING.

The value of this island to the settlers was its excellent grazing facilities, a place where cattle could be safely pastured without the need of fences to restrain their ranging. Each of the "five and twenty" lots had its share in the division of the land, with rights of pasturing a specified number of great cattle and small stock to a commonage. This has already been explained (p. 35) and was held as one of the most valuable rights of proprietorship. These rights of grazing were subsequently rented out by those who had no cattle. In 1703 there were nearly two hundred and fifty "great" cattle, besides sheep, entered for that year by the proprietors or their tenants. The "great" cattle, horses, oxen, cows, were taken over every fall, about October 5th and brought back in the spring, about April 25th, by the way of the Swimming place. At slack tide of low water the animals were driven in and made to swim across the "river."

Such was the extent of this business that the proprietors held annual meetings to regulate the affairs of the "separated island." Elaborate regulations were drawn up to guard against trespassing and overloading the quotas of each share, and the lists are an interesting, as well as at times amusing, evidence of their methods of conducting affairs. One puts over "one steer upon Dorcas Bayley," another "a young horse upon his grandfather Bayes" and a third "for his wifes former rights he put over 13 head."[1] To add to these complicated privileges there was great uncertainty among the proprietors themselves as to what they owned, either in severalty or in common. There had been a division of the meadows about 1668, but "the certain bounds were not known except of some particulars," and a second division was made in 1679, "which though the writings thereof are lost, yet have generally (been) improved and acknowledged."[2] Such a condition naturally caused confusion and trespassing on the lands reserved to the Indians, who lived in considerable numbers on this island, as one of their settlements.[3]

[1]Edgartown Records, I, 68, 78.

[2]Ibid., 155. "only Thomas Harlock dissents from it" as the record concludes.

[3]A portion of the land owned by the whites was fenced, and in 1700 a pound was erected by the proprietors to impound stray cattle without marks or suspected of belonging to trespassers. Field drivers were chosen to carry out the directions of the trustees. In that year Matthew Mayhew, Samuel Sarson and Jacob Norton acted in that capacity.

This reservation assigned to the Indians was on the north side of the road leading from Collop's pond eastward, and comprised all the land to the shore bordering the harbor and bay.

THE SACHEM CONTESTS HERBAGE RIGHTS.

These encroachments, as they became more flagrant, were resented by the sachem and his tribe, and the proprietors in 1708 appointed a committee "to treaty with the present Indian Sachem (Joshua Seeknout) that therein may be done as to right doth appertain, as also to make......such accord agreement and confession as they shall think meet." This plan effected a temporary truce in the hostile camp of the natives, but four years later, failing to obtain the redress which he thought due them for trespasses, he resorted to the courts and appealed to the agents of the Society for the Propagation of the Gospel. He entered a test suit against Thomas Pease and others at the October term, 1712, in an action of trespass "on the southeast part of it (Chappaquiddick) at a place called Wassaechtaack alias pocha."[1] The proprietors joined issue and appointed Matthew Mayhew and Thomas Lothrop to represent them. The sachem had for his attorney Benjamin Hawes of Edgartown and the case was tried before a distinguished tribunal. Lieutenant Governor Tailer with Samuel Sewall the Younger and Col. Penn Townsend of the Governor's Council sat in judgment on the case with the local magistrates. Sewall thus records the incident:—

> [Oct. 8, 1712.] Had a great dispute about Chappaquiddick, the Sachem appearing before us and Mr. Haws his Attorney for him. Mr. Turner plead for the English for their right in the Herbage, the Island right over against the Harbour.[2]

Subsequent suits were brought on the same grounds in March and October, 1713, and the March term of the next year against various parties.[3] At this time the old sachem, Joshua, died and was succeeded by his son, Jacob Seeknout, who took up the prosecution in behalf of his people with

[1]Dukes Court Records, 1712.

[2]Diary (printed in N. E. Gen. Register).

[3]Seeknout complained in January, 1713 of "Undue Proceedings in a Suit brought by John Norton against Nicholas and Phinehas Norton for Trespass for Driving a Mare of the said John Nortons off the said Island by Direction of the Petitioner, And in which Suit he was admitted Defendant." (Mass. Resolves, IX; appendix IV, 268; comp. Legislative Record of the Council, IX, 255.)

continued zeal.[1] The Justices required the proprietors to "give in to them a particular account of their interest and present claim" and the proprietors at once raised the sum of £100 for "the just and lawful defence of their rights." As a result of all this litigation the matter was finally submitted by agreement between Thomas Lothrop as agent and Seeknout the Sachem, Oct. 29, 1713, to the Governor, the Lieutenant Governor, Samuel Sewall, Penn Townsend and John Cushing as arbitrators. They were requested to hear and determine all their differences "and give resolve thereon." The General Court authorized these officials to act in the capacity of arbitrators as they had "manifested their willingness to undertake the compromising & Issuing of that unhappy Difference." An order was passed setting the hearings for May, 1714, "and all Quarrels & Suits depending relating to the Island are hereby stayed in the mean Time."[2] The findings were not made, however, for over eighteen months.

Under date of Dec. 19, 1715, the referees made the following decision: (1) The English should have the undisputed fee of the neck called Menechew, saving one share to the sachem; (2) The Indians should have the sole possession of the Island of Chappaquiddick for themselves and posterity, never to be sold without the consent of the Provincial government; (3) The English should have the right to mow the salt marshes (saving the "wobshaw grass" for the Indians, use in making mats), paying therefor one shilling per acre annually; (4) The winter herbage should be shared in common by both English and Indians "as stented for the number of grate catle goats and sheep between October 25 and March 25th yearly," the English paying Seeknout "the fifteenth goat and for every fatted Beast one Shilling & Sixpence" annually; and (5) the proprietors were restricted to a total of one hundred head of great cattle for grazing purposes. This decision afforded the usual loophole for the English and payment was refused to the sachem in many cases on the question of what constituted a "fatted beast." Several years more of contest followed before the end was reached. After the case was settled the Sachem sold in 1718 to Benjamin Hawes "one eight of all the herbage on Chappaquiddick that shall ever

[1]The Sachem Jacob made his last will Sept. 25, 1734, and it was probated March 5, 1735, between which dates he died. This document mentions wife Elizabeth and daughters Hepzibah and Dorcas. Samuel Norton and Thomas Lothrop were made executors.

[2]Acts and Resolves, IX, 318.

hereafter grow from the 20th of October till the 25th of March every year forever however it may be stented."[1] This was the last of the famous herbage case.

Ancient Landmarks.

ALGONQUIAN PLACE NAMES.

Capoag (*Capawack, Cape Pogue*). — The earliest known aboriginal name attached to the Vineyard. It has already been discussed and explained (Vol. I, 34-6). It applied to the pond properly and became identified with the point or cape.

Mashshachaquak. — This was "a little creek on the west side of sd Island......running to the southermost little creek that runneth out of Collops Pond" (Deeds, IV, 163; XI, 69).

Menechew. — A neck of land, "being the northermost part of the said Island" (Deeds, IV, 139, 166).

Micenuckchuwat. — The pond now known as Caleb's pond. The spelling of this name in 1726 was "Collops" and it may be regarded as the correct form (Deeds, IV, 163).

Momabhegoins Neck. — A place mentioned in 1709 (Deeds, II, 244).

Natick. —This was, in the first eighty years after the settlement, an island at the northern tip of Chappaquiddick, sometimes called Capoag island. The narrow and shallow channel which separated it from the main portion of the island was closed up during a great storm, about 1725, and it has ever since remained a part of the peninsular formation (Deeds, I, 388; IV, 153, 328; VI, 401, 520). See Great Neck.

Pocha. — This is one of the earliest place names of the island and marked the southeastern point, as early as 1665, having also an alias, Wassaechtaack. The word is derived from Pok-sha-muk, signifying "where there is a breaking in," as a pond formed by the inrush of the sea. There is a Potchey or Pochey in Eastham on the Cape.

Quamoks. — A "place called Quamoks" in 1722 was in the region of Pocha Pond (Deeds, IV, 218).

Wassaechtaack. — See Pocha.

Wasque. — The southermost point of Chappaquiddick was early called Wasque, an abbreviation of Wannasque, meaning "the ending or point." Wasqua hill is mentioned in 1742 (Deeds, VI, 401).

[1]Dukes Deeds, IV, 44; comp., IV, 204. —— where he sold a tract "excepting the grass privilege already sold."

ENGLISH PLACE NAMES.

Caleb's (*Collops*) *Pond.* — See Micenuckchuwat.

Great Neck. — After Natick Island became a part of the main island it was later called Great Neck.

Little Neck. — A small part of the original Natick was known in 1790 as Little Neck.

Tom's Neck.— This name was attached as early as 1790 and still belongs to the small neck of land on the eastern side of the island.

POPULATION.

For the first hundred years after the settlement, this island was occupied solely by Indians, and their numbers had fluctuated during and since that time, through epidemics and immigration. In 1698 there were 138 Christianized natives, perhaps two-thirds of the entire population. In 1765 about 80 were left and in 1790 there were 75, "not more than one third of whom are pure."[1] In the next century enumerations taken at irregular times give the following figures: In 1807, 65; in 1828, 110; in 1849, 84; in 1861, 74, and at the close of the last century, 7.[2]

The Des Barres map of 1781 shows twenty-three houses on the island, both English and Indian, indicating a population of about 175 of the combined races. The census of 1790 makes no separation of those resident here, but counting the families known to have lived on the island, it is estimated that about 190 constituted its population.

THE EARLY SETTLERS.

It was not until about 1750 that the whites began to take up the land for residential purposes, and it is believed that Captain Thomas Arey (35) was the first one of the Edgartown people to settle there.[3] He was born in 1716 and followed the sea in his younger days. He died in 1787 and was, in his

[1]Benjamin Bassett in 1st Mass. Hist. Coll., I, 206. The Edgartown records note the death of Bethiah Moses in 1818 aged 92 and state that she "Left only Ruth Maqud of Clear Indian about the Same age on Chappaquiddick to Survive her."

[2]Concerning their condition in 1849 an official report states: "Twenty years ago [1829] they were preeminently a degraded people, unchaste, intemperate, and by consequence, improvident; now they are chaste, not a case of illegitimacy, so far as we could learn, existing among them; temperate, comparing, in this respect, most favorably with the same population, in the same condition of life, in any part of the state."

[3]Dukes Deeds, VIII, 46, 158-9.

time, undoubtedly the largest landed proprietor of Chappaquiddick.[1] The next settler was Joseph Huxford, about 1755, and following him in probable order was Thomas Fish (31) about 1758; Henry Fish (34), Benjamin Pease, Jr. (311) about 1760; Thomas Smith (45) in 1774; Matthew Butler (53) in 1778; and about 1782, Joseph Swasey, Jr., was added to the growing white settlement. Before 1790, besides the sons of the above-named pioneers the residents of the island included Seth Dunham, Elisha Dunham, George Daggett, William Covell, John Clark, Cornelius and Ephraim Ripley, and two of the first Portuguese immigrants to our shores, Emanuel Silvara and Antony Chadwick.[2] These aliens had married two of the Fish(er) girls, Sarah (51) and Anna (61) respectively, and became identified with the church of their wives.

THE INDIAN MEETING.

Chappaquiddick was one of the "praying towns" of the Vineyard established by the Mayhews as a result of their mission work, and in 1670 Joshua Momatchegin was ordained as one of the ruling elders of the native church, gathered by the elder Thomas in his capacity of religious instructor. The converted Indians on the east side of the Vineyard were gathered into one congregation at first, but after the death of Hiacoomes in 1690 the Chappaquiddick tribe were set off as a separate body and continued under the charge of Momatchegin.[3] This elder dying in 1703 was succeeded by Jonathan Amos, who survived but three years. The condition of this church at this period is thus described: "And now the *Indians* at the said *Chappaquiddick* were in a miserable State, the *Candlestick* which had been there being *removed out of its Place.* The Place being thus *unchurched*, was filled with *Drunkards* instead of the *Good People* who had before inhabited it."[4] What became of the church organization after this date is not known. None of the maps of that century (1700-1799) show the existence of a church structure on this

[1]Council Records, No. 940 (1782). He owned or claimed not less than 250 acres bought of the Indians at various times.

[2]Chadwick was probably an adopted name as it is of English origin. Thaxter notes the death in 1820 of Anthony Chadwick, "a Portugee a state Pauper" aged 67 years. Descendants now reside in Edgartown.

[3]He was assisted by Hiacoomes and later by John Coomes, until the latter removed to "the main."

[4]Indian Converts, 34.

island and it is doubtful if there was one. The absence of records and the disappearance of the tribe contribute to our lack of information. Doubtless they were cared for by the societies which supported missionaries here. The state map of 1830 shows a meeting-house on the Indian reservation, but it is not known where it was erected nor how long it was in use. In 1860 the Indian Commissioner made the following report on this subject: "The Chappaquiddicks have no religious organization, nor have they any religious services or instruction, distinct from their white neighbors. They attend meeting at the 'Marine Church' at Sampson's hill, across the line, whenever there are services there, which is at irregular intervals."[1] These services were held by ministers of all denominations from time to time. Such is now the case. The old meeting-house has been recently repaired, and during the summer months the Edgartown clergy supply the pulpit in turn in the present century.

[1]State Senate Report, No. 96 (1861), p. 21. The Rev. John Adams in his Autobiography in 1840 tells of preaching "in the new church in Chappaquidick" (I, 420).

Annals of West Tisbury

ANNALS OF WEST TISBURY.

TAKEMMY.

The present limits of West Tisbury represent the old township of Tisbury as it was originally laid out, and the history of this town, though the latest creation in our corporate galaxy, begins actually two and a third centuries ago. West Tisbury occupying as it does the original settlement once called Middletown is therefore the historic Tisbury, though bearing a modified title. The Algonquian name of this locality was Takemmy, as it is generally written in English by the first settlers.

Taacame and Taukemy are variations of the Indian name for the territory mostly comprised in the present town of West Tisbury. Through this section flows the largest stream on the island, and this big "river" when the whites first purchased Takemmy in 1669-70 was called "Old Mill River" giving evidence that some sort of a mill had been erected there by previous settlers or residents of the island long before its purchase from the natives, possibly soon after the settlement of Edgartown. This first mill was, probably, a primitive affair, but quite sufficient for the wants of the settlers. It is possible that it was merely a large wooden mortar and pestle run by an undershot wheel, enclosed by a temporary structure.

The road leading from Edgartown to Takemmy was and is still called the "Mill Path," and the road from Chilmark running east to Takemmy was also called the "Mill Path" as early as 1664. These facts are strongly corroborative of our study of the name. The full etymology of it is Tackhum-min-eyi, of which -hum is a special affix, and implies exertion of strength, as he forces him or it after the manner expressed by the root Tack, i. e., to pound, grind, strike the object which is -min, (Grammar of the Cree, 86, 87). Min was the generic term for any small berry, nut or grain. Here it denotes the grain, par excellence, corn, (Trumbull). In the Narragansett and Massachusetts dialects Mayi, May or Meyi, signifies a path, road, which is formed from the suppositive (subjunctive) of the verb au, aui, meaning he goes to or towards (a place), with the indefinite m' prefixed, where anybody goes (Trumbull).

Hence we have Tackhum-min-eyi, with the reading "where anybody goes to grind corn," in allusion to the mill erected by the whites.

BOUNDARIES

The original bounds of Tisbury, as given in the charter of 1671 were as follows:—

neare the middle of the said Island on the south side thereof granted to several Inhabitants, freeholders there for a Towne-ship, who have made purchase of the Indian Right, the said Towne formerly known by the name of Middle-Town, the Precincts whereof are bounded on the East by the Land heretofore belonging to the Sachem Towonquateck: on the West by Nashowakemmuck: on the South by Qua-niems & a fresh Pond & on the North by the Sound:

When West Tisbury was incorporated, May 1, 1892, it was given the following division lines, as shown by the several bound marks between the towns adjoining to her limits:—

West Tisbury and Tisbury

1st. Stone monument at Makonikey near the Sound shore.
2nd. same on top of the hill at Makonikey.
3rd. same on south side of North Shore Road, near old school house site.
4th. same, top of hill, southerly from No. 2, in D. D. Norton's pasture.
5th. same in woods, westerly from outside gate of Shubael Weeks' place.
6th. same on south side of West Tisbury—Tisbury State Highway.
7th. same south-westerly from M. M. Smith's, in edge of the woods.
8th. same on easterly side of Chickamoo Path.
9th. the "four town bound."

West Tisbury and Edgartown

1st. Stone monument at the "four town bound."
2nd. same on south side of Farm Path.
3rd. same on south side of Smith's Path.
4th. same on north side of West Tisbury—Edgartown Road—old track.
5th. same on south side of Watcha Road.
6th. same on south side of first clump of woodland in Watcha.
7th. same on south side of obscure wood road in Watcha.
8th. same on south side of middle section of woodland in Watcha.
9th. same on south side of southermost woodland in Watcha.
10th. same near South Beach on the bluff.

West Tisbury and Chilmark

1st. Rock in Vineyard Sound, with a copper bolt.
2nd. Stone monument in Prof. Shaler's Place, on top of hill.
3rd. Great Rock, (Wascoseems).
4th. Stone monument in Orlin F. Davis' meadow.
5th. same on South Road at "Nab's Corner."
6th. same at southerly side of Look's brook, westerly side of road.
7th. same about four rods easterly from No. 6.
8th. same on South Beach, at the half width of the Tisbury Great Pond.

The above limits are practically those of the original township grant.

POPULATION.

West Tisbury had no known population before 1670, when the four proprietors made their first purchase of the soil and opened it up for settlement. From a computation based on the genealogies of families known to have been living here ten years later (1680) we can enumerate about 120 souls resident then. The map of Simon Athearn (1694) shows twenty-two houses in the town, and as families always exceed houses in numbers, we may reckon 25 families of five each at that date, or a total of 125 souls. Removals and the opening up of Chilmark to settlement took away in the intervening time what would be the normal increase. In 1700 there were probably about 150 people here. No further basis of computation until 1757 has been found. In a list of members of the "Foot Company" for that year, 132 men are listed for military service, and—using the accepted multiple—a total of 660 souls can be reckoned as then living in the town.

The first Provincial census of 1765 shows the following figures relating to Tisbury:—families 100, comprising a total of 838 souls, living in 110 houses. Of these there were 226 males and 233 females above sixteen years of age; 165 males and 166 females below sixteen; 9 negroes (4 male and 5 female) and 39 Indians (15 male and 24 female). Tisbury was then the smallest town, numerically, on the Island, though second excluding negroes and Indians. In the census of 1776 there were 1033 persons resident in the town.

The first federal census of 1790 gives us an enumeration by names, and from this the following statistics are drawn: total population, 1,135 (whites), of which number there were 287 males above sixteen years, 238 below sixteen, and 609

ANCIENT PLAN OF TISBURY, 1694.

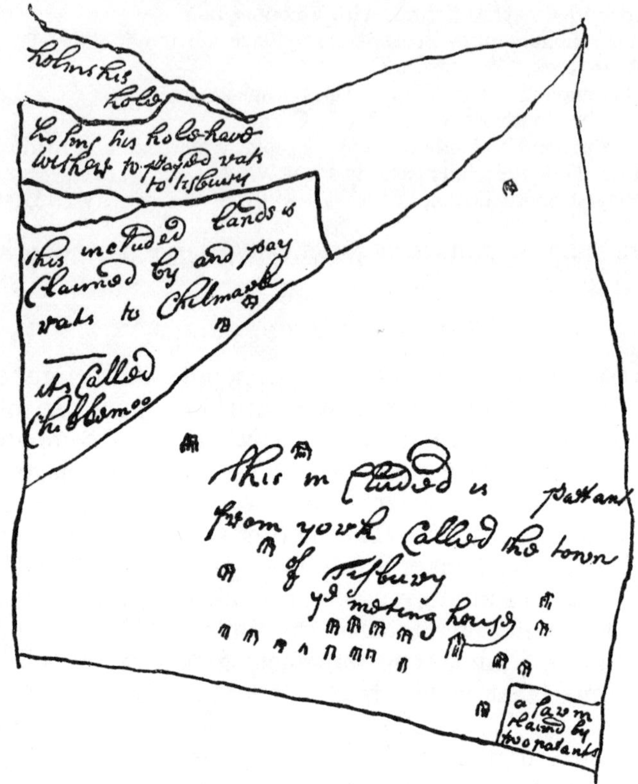

NOTE.—This interesting and valuable plan of Tisbury in 1694, is the first one of its kind known to the author, and is a part of a sketch of the entire island. It is here printed with the east to the top for the convenience of reading the written descriptions made by him on the map. These legends are as follows, beginning at the top:—

holms his hole
holms his hole have hitherto payed rat(e)s to tisbury
this included lands is Claimed by and pay rat(e)s to Chilmark
its Called Chikkemoo
this included is pattant from York Called the town of Tisbury
the meting house
a farm claimed by two patants

The plan shows two houses in the Chickemmoo district, and twenty-two houses in the town of Tisbury, besides the meeting-house, in 1694. The position of the meeting-house bears out the views of the author as to its location at that date. It was the first house of worship built, and occupied the present site of Agricultural Hall. The "farm claimed by two patants" is, undoubtedly, the Quinames property, a part of the Manor of Tisbury.

"free white" females and seven "other free persons," presumably negroes. Tisbury was then the second town in population on the Vineyard. All computations, however, do not make any distinction between the two sections (Homes Hole and West Tisbury) which then made up the whole town.

The following figures show the population of Tisbury as enumerated in the decennial censuses of the United States from 1800 to the present time: In 1800 it was 1092; in 1810, 1202; in 1820, 1223; in 1830, 1317; in 1840, 1520; in 1850, 1803; in 1860, 1631; in 1870, 1536; in 1880, 1518; in 1890, 1506; in 1900, 1149.

The population of Tisbury reached the maximum in 1850 and showed a gradual decrease to 1900, when the population was but fifty-seven above that of the census of 1800. The town of West Tisbury, which was formed from Tisbury in 1892 had a population of about 450, and the loss in the census of 1900 is thus accounted for to the parent town.

Tisbury was the first in population of the three original towns, 1860-1890 inclusive, as shown in the three decennial censuses. The state census of 1905 showed a population of 1120.

FIRST SETTLEMENT.

The settlement at Great Harbor had continued for twenty-five years to be the sole settlement on the island, but by 1666 the necessity for an extension of their territorial occupation became more apparent, and it is probable that by this date some persons had taken up land here, or occupied it for tillage purposes. Doubtless the attraction to this place was the fine water courses and the fertile meadows, which have made this the garden spot of the Vineyard. In what way the original proprietors of Tisbury were induced to invest in this territory is not known. They had no previous association with the Vineyard as land owners, nor were they connected by marriage with any of the existing families on the island. Surmises on the influences which caused them to turn their faces hither would be useless. It is sufficient to state that on the first day of July, 1668, as a result of previous negotiations, Thomas Mayhew gave authority to William Pabodie and Josiah Standish of Duxbury, and James Allen of Sandwich to enter into agreement with the Sachem of Takemmy to buy what land they wished within his bounds, and confirming previous purchases made by them. The following is the grant to the three purchasers:—

Foreasmuch as I have a grant of this Island both from the agent of the Lord Sterling, and alsoe from the agent of Sir Ferdinando Gorges, Knight, for this Island, the Vineyard, this doth witness that I, Thomas Mayhew, doe grant unto William Pabodie, Josias Standish, and James Allin, liberty to buy land, I say liberty to buy what land they can uppon this Island, within the compass of the bounds of Takemmy, of the Indian Sachims, the right owners, and to enjoy all such lands, themselves, heirs and assigns, forever, uppon the same terms and conditions, that that I have it from the Lord Proprietor: but for the people that are to be brought on, they are to bee, not only approved of by the said William Pabodie, Josias Standish, and James Allin, or the major part of them, & their heirs and assighnes, but also by mee, the said Thomas Mayhew, my heirs and assighnes; And for the government of the inhabitants that shall bee there uppon said land, it is to be carried on by myself, & the major part of the freeholders thus, that is I, the said Thomas Mayhew, cannot act without them, nor my heirs nor assignes; nor they, the said William Pabodie, Josias Standish, and James Allin, nor their heirs nor assighns, shall not doe nor act without mee, the said Thomas Mayhew, or my successors. This is also an approbation of what land they have bought alreddy, so far as concerns mee, I doe heerby allow of it, and this I doe in consideration that they, the grantees, are to pay mee six poundes, thirteen shillings and four pence, at Boston, to Captain Oliver, or Peter Oliver, at Boston. Witness hereunto my hand and seal the first day of July, 1668.[1]

THOMAS MAYHEW.

THE "FIRST PURCHASE."

It is not known what was confirmed to them in "land they have bought already," as no transfers appear of record, though it may possibly refer to purchases for the mill and a few lots within the greater territory which they soon acquired. Negotiations with the Sachem were finally consummated on Aug. 2, 1669, when in consideration of £80, four associates, James Skiffe, Jr., of Sandwich having later been admitted to partnership, received title to the following described land:—

From the mouth of Tyasquan River to the Bridge and from the Bridge in the path that goeth to the school house till it doth meet with the Bounds of Nashowakemmuck, from thence in the Bound line to the Sound: secondly from the mouth of Tyasquan to a tree in the vally by the house of papameck marked and from that tree to another tree marked tree westerly marked and from that parellell with the bound line between Nashowakemmuck and Takemmy: and also from the tree in the valley aforesaid near paapameks house in the winter 1668, it is to run Eesterly one mile and from that miles end it is to run Southerly unto the water that comes into the vally where Titchpits house and his sonnes were in the winter

[1]Dukes Deeds, I, 239.

1668 aforesaid which includes all the land or neckes westerly to Coskenachasooway.[1]

The Sachem also granted by this same deed for a further consideration of £65, all "the meadow upon all the neckes of land on the South side of the Island in his bounds." It is not possible to plot out this last indefinite territory, but the bounds of the other portion are shown in the accompanying map.

This tract of land is known as the "First Purchase," and it will be seen that it excluded the flexible "mile square" on the Sound, granted previously by Josias and Wanamanhut to the praying Indians and elsewhere described. The four partners endeavored to have this included in their grant, "but the said Josias refused to let us have any land further Eastward of the said bounds," as James Skiffe said some years later, "alledging that he had already granted it to the praying Indians."[2] It appears that the subjects of the Sachem were displeased at this purchase, by which so large a tract became alienated to the control of the whites, and as a result of the agitation the bounds of the Christian town were definitely determined in May, 1669,[3] and a written agreement about further sales was made by the Sachems and chief men, as related in the chapter dealing with the affairs of the Indian town.[4]

On June 17, 1670, about one year after the purchase, the planters finding the restrictions regarding the herding of their cattle impracticable or unnecessarily vexatious obtained from Josias an instrument in consideration of five shillings providing for a removal of this condition, in which he gave their cattle "liberty lawfully and peaceably to greas within the Commons of Tackemy without any molestation."[5] This permission of free ranging for their cattle required the marking of each man's live stock, and the methods adopted by them are described elsewhere. It is not known who, at this time, had undertaken actual residence within the "first purchase" limits. There are no records extant showing grants of land or transfers of real estate to establish priority of settlement for any person. Benjamin Church of Duxbury, the famous Indian fighter, had erected a grist mill "on the westermost brook of Takemmy"

[1]Dukes Deeds, I, 33. One of the conditions of the sale was that the English should herd their cattle, and not allow them to roam at large; a proviso inserted by them because the cattle would destroy their corn fields and squash meadows.

[2]Sup. Jud. Court Files, 4714.

[3]Deeds, I, 378.

[4]Sup. Jud. Court Files, No. 953.

[5]Town Rec., 15.

sometime before Nov. 19, 1669, when he sold it to Joseph Merry, with "one eighth part of the first purchase of land," showing that he had become interested in the speculation early. The consideration was £120 "by Bills" and the transfer was made in person. This division into eighths was probably in the nature of an undivided allotment. The later divisions were on a different basis as will be seen.

Of the four purchasers, but two became residents, or remained to settle the tract they had bought. Peabody and Standish were land speculators, the former being interested in land "booms" in Rhode Island, and the latter in lands about Norwich, Connecticut. Pabodie was the oldest partner, being 49 years of age in 1668. He had married Betty, a daughter of John Alden of the "Mayflower." He is the lineal ancestor of the author of this history, through the maternal side.

The name was early written Pabodie and so spelled by him, but it was gradually evolved into the modern form Peabody, though the early spelling has been retained by some branches.

Josiah Standish was the son of the redoubtable Captain Miles of Plymouth and Duxbury, and he had married Sarah, sister of James Allen of Braintree, and hence was brother-in-law of his partner.

James Allen was the son of Samuel of Braintree, but he was a resident of Sandwich at the time of the purchase.

James Skiffe, Junior, came from Sandwich also, and was the son of James Skiffe, of that town. Prior to his coming here he had probably resided at Sherborne, Nantucket.

THE ADDITIONAL PURCHASE.

It could not be said that there was necessity for additional land to accommodate purchasers, actual or in prospect, but for reasons satisfactory to themselves, perhaps because land was cheap, the four proprietors for the sum of fifteen shillings bought more land of Josias the Sachem, Jan. 31, 1671, which is known as the "Additional Purchase," and was thus described:—[1]

I Josias Sachem of Tackkomy do sell and Inlarge the Lotts of the English further on the East side unto the East sid of the deep woody vally in the cart way goeing to the town and so to run upon a straight line unto the mille from the marked tree & from the marked tree by papemikes field and so taking in all the Land and neckes westwardly as appeareth by trees marked on the east sid of the woody vally, by me Josias, James Allen and John Eddy.

[1]Town Rec., 15; Deeds, XXXIII 544.

MIDDLETOWN.

No formal name was adopted by the proprietors for the new settlement, as they were not yet incorporated, but it was generally known as Middletown, because of its relative position between Great Harbor and Nashowakemmuck.

Having obtained all the available property from the Sachem, the partners proceeded to the next step of admitting inhabitants and associates. It will be remembered that Thomas Mayhew reserved the right to supervise this feature of the programme and approve of all who applied for the right of admission. The following document records the first admission and the division of the land, May 20, 1671, into fifteen shares, and should be read in full:—[1]

Whereas we whose names are under writen have obtained liberty of Mr Thomas Mayhew to buy & purchas land within the bounds & limits of Taakimmy upon the Vinyard this may signifie unto men that we Willi: Pebodie Josiah Standish, James Allen and James Skiffe have made purchas of certaine Lands within the above saide bound with a purpos to people or plant the same and in order thereunto have devided the whole into twelv partes or shares payable to the charges of the whole purchas besids one lott for the mill one for a minister and one lott for John Eddy if he com according to Compacicion and further we have admitted of several persons to have thar severall shares both upland and medow land allreddy purchased or to be purchased alwayes P'vided that the parsons admited shall pay or cause to be payed their just proportion of cost and charg justly arisin thereupon unto the above named Willi Pebodie Josias Standish and James Allen or their assignes and in consideration thereof we the above named William Pabodie Josias Standish James Allen and James Skiffe doe admit of Isack Robinson, James Skiffe Sinour, Simon Athearn, Jeramiah Whitne and John Rogers to be full and joynt parcherais with and to have full Right and title to the whole with our selves: allsoe we have admitted of Thomas Mayhew Juner who is to pay five pounds to his brother Matthew Mayhew for and in consideration of a parcell of lands purchased by Willi: Pebodie Josias Standish and James Allen of Matthew Mayhew about holmes hole as may apere by a deed under his hand which parsall of land is to belong unto the whole purchas of takimmy.

May 20 1671
witness hereunto
THOMAS BONI
The mark N of
NATHANIEL BRUSTER

WILLIAM PABODIE
JAMES ALLEN
JAMES SKIFFE
JOSIAS STANDISH

This list completes the twelve shares, and John Eddy, "if he com according to Compacicion," makes thirteen; and as

[1]Supreme Jud. Court Files, No. 4974. This paper was probably drawn up in Duxbury, as Thomas Bonney and Nathaniel Brewster, the two witnesses, were residents of that town, unless they came to the island on a prospecting tour at that time.

he did settle here soon after, it raised the shares to that number. The "lott for the mill" seems never to have come into the subsequent transaction of the proprietors, as far as the writer is aware, and may be dismissed from further consideration. The number of proprietors' shares was soon increased to sixteen, at which number it stood in 1673,[1] although in 1685 Pabodie sold "one whole share or lot of land or fifteenth part" of the Takemmy purchase to Henry Luce."[2]

INCORPORATION OF THE TOWN, 1671.

We are now brought to the time and event, elsewhere described, when the elder Mayhew was summoned to New York by Governor Lovelace to arrange for the future government of the Vineyard. This was in July, 1671, and as one of the results of that journey he procured a town charter for the territory lately purchased in Takemmy. For this new settlement commonly called Middletown, he recommended to Lovelace that it be called Tisbury, in honor of the little Wiltshire parish where he was born and baptised, and whose green lanes and rolling downs filled his recollections as he was called upon to suggest a proper name for the infant town raised up under his assistance. The original charter of incorporation is still in existence among the archives of the town, the only one of the three that has survived the two and a third centuries intervening, and it is a in fair state of preservation, minus the wax seal.[3]

Under its terms the new town of Tisbury was accorded identical privileges, and the same requirements as to government were imposed as those given to Edgartown. As in the case of the other places incorporated at the same time the quit rent was two barrels of cod fish payable in New York.[4]

The inclusion of the West Chop or Homes Hole Neck in the town limits of Tisbury was a matter of subsequent arrangement, as will be seen when we deal with that precinct. It was not considered a part of the original corporate town.

[1]Deeds, II, 306.

[2]Deeds, I, 173.

[3]Printed in full in the volume of Town Records, v–vi.

[4]The present seal of Tisbury bearing representations of two barrels and codfish is an official recognition of this ancient tribute, on which our existence as a town depended.

DIVISION OF THE HOME LOTS.

Within the few years succeeding the purchase and the incorporation, the original and admitted proprietors' shares were divided and bounded. How they were assigned is not known, as no record remains touching this point, but the territory bordering on the Old Mill river, north from the Tyasquin, was selected for the location of the "home lots," and these were declared to be limited to forty acres each, measuring forty rods on the brook and "eaight skore polls" in length, east and west. This forty acres represented one share and twenty acres half a share. The location of these original lots is shown on the map accompanying this, to which reference should be made for a more particular representation. It will be seen that most of the lots were on the west side of the brook where all the prominent shareholders located, which seems to indicate that the selections made were by mutual consent rather than by lot. The only important exception is the location of Simon Athearn on the east side, without any near neighbor, a lot which he had occupied before 1672.

ADDITIONAL PURCHASES — THREE NECKS.

The proprietors of Tisbury were now in possession of all the present bounds of West Tisbury, except the Christian town and the meadows or necks eastward of Tississa to the bounds of Edgartown and to the south of the Mill path. The original purchases had taken in Great Neck, Little Neck and "the neck by John Eddys," leaving Tississa in dispute. The townsmen determined to acquire these valuable meadows and necks eastward to the bounds of Edgartown, and empowered James Allen and John Eddy to effect a purchase from the Indians. On Dec. 24, 1681, they bought of John Papameck a tract as follows:—

a certain neck of land lying within the sachemship of Takemmy, commonly called Mussoowonkwhonk, being next to Sekonquit eastward: and bounded by the uppermost end of the west cove of water: and from thence upon a square line to the vally which runs from the east cove of water: and from thence hy the said east cove of water unto the sea...... for the use and benefit of the English town.[1]

This was the neck between Long Cove and Pasqunahommons Cove. The next purchase was made of Josias the Sachem

[1]Deeds, I, 129.

on Jan. 6, 1681–2, and included Scrubby Neck and the western half of Watcha as far as he controlled, as follows:—

> a certain neck of land lying in the town of Tisbury and commonly called Wachekemmihpickquah Neck bounded with water eastward and westward: the northern bounds to begin at the line which bounds the land late sold by John Papameck to said Allen and Eddy: from thence it is to run on a straight line to the northern end of the swamp at the end of a cove which parts the said neck from a neck of land called Washusade."[1]

It was not until two years after that the remaining neck, Seconquit or Charles', was acquired. On March 29, 1683, Josias with the consent of some "parties concerned," local native magnates, sold to the townsmen this neck, which was thus described:—

> a certain Neck of land called Seconquet, known to the English by the name of Charles his Neck: bounded Westerly by a cove of water and by the Deep Bottom unto the highway: and Easterly by a cove of water called Seconquet: and from said cove upon a straight line unto the aforesaid highway.[2]

DIVISIONS OF THE COMMON LAND.

This property lay in common for several years until Oct. 19, 1687, when it was "agreed and voted by the town that the neck of land called Charles is neck shall be devided and eatch mans proportion shall be layed out as allso the medoe one the above said neck of land and the two next neckes ajoyning eastward from said neck."[3] But there was trouble and delay when this proposal was undertaken. There were Indians who claimed rights on these necks which had not been satisfied by the purchase from their Sachem, and the town left the matter in abeyance for five years, when it passed, on Feb. 2, 1692, the following vote:—

> Voted that James Allen & peter Robinson are chosen and impowered by the town of tisbury to goe and discors the Indians Steeven and Joseph Skeetup & theire company who have dwelt in Seconquit & the necks agasint And to a gree with said Indians so that the said Indians do quit Claim of said necks To the town of tisbury And yeld peasable possesion to the English as Reasonable as thay cann: to be understood to agree with Steven Joseph Skeetup sam nahommon & Joseph potobppan as Reasonable as thay Cann.[4]

It is evident that the results of the "discors" with the Indians was not productive of satisfactory results, for on July

[1]Deeds, I, 271.
[2]Ibid., I, 271.
[3]Town Records, 5.
[4]Ibid., 23.

15, 1693, the town took the following action looking to a legal defence of its rights in these necks:—

that peter robinson and John Manter be constituted and apoynted this towns Atorneys to use theire cuning in defending this towns right of the medow gras and hay on Seconquit, peanaskenamset and mossoonk-honk effetully to prevent any Indian or Indians directly or indirectly to have any improvement by Confedryce or otherwise for the space of three years: now from this day above mentioned having to themselves all the mowing grass and hay on the premisses for the term of three years afore said upon Condition that peter robinson and John manter doth make use of the law also for the defence of the premisses as the caus may require from time to time untill three yeares be expired."[1]

Ten years had now elapsed since the completion of the purchase of these necks, and from the deliberate manner in which the proprietors proceeded we may infer that they had entered upon the slow process of "freezing out" the red men by the aid of time.

The following is a record of the more important of the divisions of the common lands in the town prior to the Revolution:—

Kepegon Lots, (resurveyed)	15 March, 1699
do	27 Feb., 1700
Pine Hill Lots	15 March, 1700
Tississa	23 Feb., 1702
Charles Neck	4 April, 1707
South of the Mill Path	14 August, 1719
do do do to Watsha	15 May, 1738
Additional Purchase (31 Jan., 1671)	6 Feb., 1750
Between Indian Town and Homes Hole Road.	22 Feb.,1750-51

The last division of the properietors' "common lands" was made in in 1836.

THE ENGLISH TISBURY.

It will be interesting at this point in the story to learn something of the Old Tisbury from which our town derived its name. In 1898 the author, while on a visit to England, made a special journey to the old parish and spent two days there as guest of the vicar, the Rev. F. E. Hutchinson. While thus so favorably situated much was open to him to see and learn about the ancient places that were in existence in Mayhew's time. The church, dedicated to St. John the Baptist, is the central object in the parish, and is a venerable and curious

[1]Town Records, 25.

structure, probably six or seven hundred years old, showing in its cruciform design a composite style of architecture marking the changes and enlargements which have taken place in all these centuries. The present Vicar has extended and decorated the chancel during his incumbency. The illustrations which accompany this text show exterior and interior views of the church, and afford a much better description than can be conveyed by words of the character and appearance of the building. It still retains on its inner walls those mural ornaments and devices originally placed there when the church was erected and used in the worship of the Romish ritual, before the Reformation. The old stone font, many hundred years old, at which Thomas Mayhew was baptised still stands just within the west porch. Oaken arches, supported by grotesque figures which overhang the nave like gargoyles, tell of the antiquity of the building. On one is carved: IN THE YERE OF OURE LORDE GOD 1569: THIS PECE WAS SET UP AND IN THE 11 DAYE OF MARCH ENDED BY EDWARD BOLE THE PRAYSE BE UNTO GOD."

The name Tisbury is variously spelled in the ancient records: Tisselbury, Tisselburie, Tysbery, Tissbury and Tisburie.[1] In the Domes Day Book of William the Conqueror it is called Tisseburie. At that time it had forty ploughlands, forty villagers and fifty borderers who occupied twenty-five ploughlands. It had four mills which were taxed then; showing the early establishment of its industries, remains of the foundations of which are still extant. These mills were run by water power obtained from a pretty stream, somewhat larger than our own "Old Mill Brook," which flows through the town and is called the Noddre or Nadder. By the time of Henry III Tisbury had been erected into a manor and the grant of it *in capite* of the King was held by the Abbesses of Shaftesbury. This continued until the dissolution of the religious houses in England at the Reformation and the last Abbess surrendered it to Henry VIII. This famous king, in 1540, granted the manor to Sir Thomas Arundel, Knight, who held it until his attainder, when it reverted to the crown. King James the First, in 1608, restored it to the grandson of Sir Thomas, who was also Thomas, and made

[1]The Vicar is of the opinion that it was originally Teazelbury, so called because it was a place where woolen cloth was manufactured, and the use of the teazel in the process of raising the nap gave it a name.

CHURCH OF S. JOHN THE BAPTIST
TISBURY, ENG.

THE NAVE, S. JOHN THE BAPTIST
TISBURY, ENG.

him Lord Arundel of Wardour, by which title and in whose family the lordship of the manor still remains. Within its ancient bounds is the famous ruin of Wardour Castle so gloriously defended by Lady Blanche Arundel during the Civil War. Nearby is the new castle occupied by the present Lord Wardour, who by the way, still retains the faith of his family, the Roman Catholic, held by them for generations.

Tisbury is situated in a beautiful garden spot, a rolling country, the South Downs of England, noted for the splendid sheep raised in that section. It is probable that the early practice of raising sheep on our island was brought here through Governor Mayhew, who had been familiar with the herds that grazed on the hills of his native county and had supplied for ages the people of England with wool and mutton.

In 1886 the population was 2,445, and the present number would not differ much from that. The people are chiefly occupied in agriculture.

Ancient Landmarks.

ALGONQUIAN PLACE NAMES.

Animtissewokset. — In 1679 Josias the sachem sold to William Rogers twenty acres at a "place called in indian animtissewokset" in North Tisbury (Deeds, III, 288).

In March, 1716-17, there was a suit in ejectment brought by the Indians against Ebenezer Rogers, his son, and the tract is thus described: "a certain piece or parcel of land containing twenty acres......at a place caled by the Indians A-nimte-sawohqussuk and is bounded on the South west and North west by the fields of Issac Ompany & Job Soomannau, Ned Chamick and is the land whereon the said Ebenezer Rogerses dwelling house standeth" (Court Records). The derivation is probably from anim-tisashg-auk-es-et, meaning, "at the bad mowing place." There is another possible source, which would include the words, *sawoh* and *qussuck*, meaning, "scattered rocks," which is quite descriptive of that locality so prolific in bowlders left on the surface during the ice age.

Aushoepin. — This is the name of a cove near the lower part of Watcha neck, and Aushoepin Cove and Aushoepin Neck are mentioned in deeds as early as 1748 (Dukes Deeds, VIII, 57). In 1782 it was called Aushaven Cove (Ibid., XI, 388).

Brandy Brow. — This bluff of the bibulous name was a part of the James Skiff home lot. How it came by the appellation of Brandy Brow is not known. It is said a dram shop was once located there. From James Skiff it passed into the possession of Nathaniel Wing and then to William Parslow (1686), James Allen (1695), John Eddy (1696), and Robert Cathcart (1696).[1]

The last named died intestate and it passed to heirs, of whom Miriam[2] m. Whitten[3] Manter, whose son Robert[4] Manter came into possession. On July 3, 1765, Robert Manter and wife Elizabeth sold to Joseph Daggett, of Edgartown, for £73–6–8, "a certain tract of land & buildings whereon I now dwell in Tisbury afores'd Bounded as followeth: on the south by land Belonging to Gershom Cathcart, on the west and north By the highway; on the east by the road Leading from the highway to the house of Benjamin Manter, Esq." (Deeds, IX, 449).

On August 10, 1780, Prince Pease (who had m. Hepzibah the dau. of Joseph Daggett, heir to this part of her father's estate) of Edgartown sold to Cornelius Norton, husbandman of Tisbury for £36, "a certain Dwelling House Situate in Tisbury, being the house that was formerly Joseph Daggets together with a piece of land whereon the house stands containing one acre" (Deeds, XI, 173). Cornelius Norton retained possession till his death. He was found dead in bed March 26, 1809. He was succeeded by his son Cornelius, Jr., who in turn was followed by his daughters Damaris (n. c.m.) and Lydia. A ruined house on this bluff was a picturesque landmark until very recent years.

Cedar Tree Neck. — See Squemmechchue.

Charles' Neck. — Probably so called from one Amos Charles, an Indian of Tisbury, who may have lived there (Indian Converts, 156). It was known by that name in 1681 and its Indian designation was Seconquit.

Commaquatom. — This was a "Little pond......by the Sound" in the northwest corner of Christian town (Cong. Lib. Mss., 1737-8). Josias, the Sachem, sold to Ebenezer Rogers, April 15, 1698, a tract of 150 acres, bounded westerly by Kiphigon lots, north by the Sound, easterly by the east end of a "little pond called Com-a-quaton by the Sound" (Deeds, III, 293). In 1738 certain Indians sold to Ebenezer Rogers

[1]Dukes Deeds, I, 39, 51, 236, 200.

150 acres, bounded west by Kiphigon Lots, north by the Sound, east by the east end of a little pond called Commoquaton by the Sound (Deeds, VI, 240).

Coskenachasoo. — (1669.) Mentioned in a deed of sale to William Pabodie and his partners, to include "all the land or neckes westerly to Coskenachasooway" (Dukes Deeds, I, 33). This word is a compound term formed of Coskenuk-chice-issu, meaning "he is a stooping or staggering old man," and the way probably referred to a path leading to the wigwam of some old chief or head man living on or near the bounds of Chilmark and Tisbury, which became the bounds of Pabodie's purchase.

Duck Pond. — Jonathan Lambert sold to Samuel Luce, in 1722, a tract of land in Tisbury, bounded north by Duck pond, which lies eastwardly from the now dwelling house of widow Desire Luce, extending from the middle of said pond till it meets with the eastern corner bounds of the Indian town or "Onkokemeh" (Deeds, V, 102).

Erashog. — This is the name of a creek, which is the outlet of Great James pond. "So far as Chickamoot goes viz: to the bounds selected for Weachpoquasset which is close to the Crick caled heren Crick or Erashog Crick, just above high water mark, which is the bounds between the Christiantown and Checemoot" (Deeds, IV, 208). Erashog is the Indian word for herring, and describes this creek, which has for years been used for herring fishery.

Maanette. — (1699.) "A place called Maanette," forming the south bounds of Christian town (Sup. Jud. Court files, 72,789). This is perhaps the same as Maanexit, an Indian village in Connecticut (Trumbull, Indian Names in Conn., 28), which alludes to the establishment of a community of Christian Indians, and is defined "where there is a gathering together." This locality being in Christian town the meaning is applicable.

Mack-kon-net-chas-qua. — Included in the bounds of Christian town (1699) "and so the South bounds running westerly Mackkonnetchasqua including the field where my uncle (Pa)pamick dwelt and dyed" (Sup. Jud. Court files, 72,789). In a deed, Josias to Isaac Chase, 1682, the land is bounded to the northeast corner of a pond lying in the woods commonly called Mokonnichashquat (Deeds, I, 281). Another reading (1694) is Moconitcashtque (Ibid., I, 248). The meaning of it is "a plain field of grass" or "grassy field."

Manaquayak. — A pond in Tisbury, called sometimes "Old House Pond." In 1699 it was in a description of the bounds of Christian town, "a little eastward of a pond called Nanaquayak" (Sup. Jud. Court files, 72,789; comp. Dukes Deeds, I, 357). This word is from Nan-nau-wiy-ack, signifying a "safe or secure place." The pond or the surrounding region was held as a secure place for canoes, or else there was located an Indian stockade close to its shores, to which they could safely retreat. The terminal in its usual signification, (aki, auke, age) means "land" and the preference would be given to the allusion to the stockade.

Mattapaquattonooke.—(1669.) In the region of Christian town and part of its bounds, being a pond called Mattapaquattonooke (Sup. Jud. Court files, 72,789). There is a small pond just easterly of Obed Daggett's farm at Cedar Tree neck now called Mattaqua, which is probably an abbreviated form of this name. This name originally belonged to the tract of land adjoining, and not to the pond itself. Mat-ta-pau-quet-tah-hun-auke means "bad, broken up land," i. e. land that had been once planted or dug over. In a report of a Committee of the General Court, relative to the bounds of Christian town, the name Mattapaquaha occurs (1709). Ebenezer Rogers sold to John Lewis, blacksmith, 25 acres, part of the land sold to Rogers by Josias, and mentions "a little pond......known by the name of Mattapaquaton (Deeds, VI, 314), and there is a similar reference to Mattapaquaton, "a little pond" in 1744 (VII, 285).

Monawquete. — "A place called by the Indians Monawquete being at the Easternmost end of that Great Pond called Taukemey Pond," according to a description in 1735, probably refers to the lower end of Peanaskenamset. It means the "fertilized land," in allusion to the fact that it had been artificially enriched by the whites.

Moohow's Neck. — This is probably a name derived from an Indian of the place. Samuel Manter sold a tract of land at the North shore in 1740 called "Moohow's Neck" bounded southeast by Great James pond (Deeds, VII, 400). It is written Moohoe's Neck and there was a Little Moohoe's Neck, both being "within the bounds of a deed that Experience

Luce had of Samuel Cobb and Samuel Manter, being to the N. E. of sd Luces bounds" (Ibid., VIII, 84).

Mossoowonkwonk (*alias Mossoonkhonk*, *Mossoounkwonk*, *Mussoo-onk-sumkeh*). — This is the neck now known as Scrubby neck, and is referred to as such in deeds (II, 244, 317; III, 105, 130). An alias in the Indian tongue was Peanaskenamset (Ibid., II, 245), and another was Wachepemepquah (Ibid.).

Nepissa. — This is a pond at the north shore. In 1699 it made the northwest bound mark of Christian town, "a pond at the north shore called Pissa," (Sup. Jud. Court files, 72,789). This is the contracted form of the word, and in that form gives no indication of its meaning. In the report of the Committee on the Indian Lands in Christian town, in 1762, the full orthography appears, "the Pond called Nepisse" (Records, General Court, XXIV, appendix). It means "a little pond," — isse being the diminutive form of the locative case, the same as -es, in some names. Literally it is "the little water place." In the testimony of some Indians in 1714, relative to the meeting of the Indians when Josias gave the Praying Indians the "mile square," for a town, it is stated that "all agreed that Wonamonhoot should have all the land to the westward of a place called Neppessieh." Another form given in 1717 was Neppessoo (Sup. Jud. Court files, 72,248).

Newtown. — The name applied generally to the settlement in Tisbury in distinction to Old Town at the east end of the Vineyard. It is more particularly applied to North Tisbury and occurs as early as 1750 (Newman, Mss. Account Book, p. 82).

Nittowouhtohquay. — In the record of the landed possessions of Simon Athearn (1672) is the following entry: "fifteen acres "which lyeth at the turn of the brook on the north side of the brook, which land is caled in indian Nittowouhtohquay, & is bounded by the old mill river on the south side & a small run of water on the west" (Deeds, I, 306). In 1701 James Allen sold to Simon Athearn a parcel of land "near to a place called Nictowouhtoquoh by Wampache" (Ibid., I, 324). This land is near the present farm and mill of R. W. Crocker in North Tisbury. The meaning of the word is "land sought for use," in allusion to the desire of the Proprietors to extend their purchase to cover the territory to the east of their post line.

Nohcouwohwoothuktack. — This is by far the longest place name on the Vineyard, and is used to describe certain land on the north shore sold Dec. 9, 1703, by Josias the Sachem to Experience Luce (Deeds, III, 19). It is a boundary designation, signifying "the right hand understood tree," in allusion to some boundary mark.

Onkakemmy. — This was a pond described as "on the East side of the Indian town between the Indian line and the line of this town" (Town Records, 1711), at a place now called Okokame, or Christian Town" (Indian Converts). "At Ohkonkemme, within the bounds of Tisbury" (Report, Commissioners of the Society for Propagating the Gospel, 1698. Variations of this name are Onkkokemmo, Uncakemmo. It is derived from Ong-kone-amaug, which is defined as "beyond the fishing place," and refers probably to Ashappaquonset, as the great fishing station of the Indians on the North shore. Uncacame is a form existing in 1745 (Deeds, VIII, 71).

Papamek's Field. — This is a tract of land, which is now represented by a portion of the farm of R. W. Crocker, Esq., on the north side of the road leading to the North Shore. It was referred to in ancient documents as the field where Papameck planted and where he died.

Paul's Point. — This was probably named for "Old Paul," one of the pious Indians of Christian town, who died about 1676 (Indian Converts, p. 131).

It is mentioned in a deed of 1730 (VI, 303), and again in 1738 Ebenezer Rogers and others convey land at Paul's Point, bounded west by the Indian line; then east to the brick kiln, or run of water. The grantee was Experience Luce (VII, 400).

Peanaskenamset. — This was the Indian name for Scrubby Neck (Deeds, II, 245). In the proper orthography it should be Uppeanashkonameset. (See under Scrubby Neck.)

Pepekonnoh.—This was a small pond on Scrubby Neck. In 1715 Samuel Nahommon sold to David Paul (Indian), a tract of land on Scrubby Neck, and on the "westward side of neck, bounded southerly by the beach, westerly by Takemmy pond, easterly by the beach, untill it meeteth with a small pond caled pepekonnoh" (Deeds, III, 109).

Seconquet. — This was a neck of land "known to the English by the name of Charls his neck," as recited in a deed

(Vol. I, 271). In the town records under date of 1707, Seconquet, alias Charles' neck, is mentioned and the "thumb" was included as part of this neck (p. 42). The meaning of this is "at the mouth of a stream," or "emptying out," of which variations in the Delaware dialect are Sakunit, Sacunk and Saquit.

Seekaquatwaupog. — This is the pond between Charles' Neck and Scrubby Neck, and while the word means "the spoiled, deserted or broken-up spring," the word was used in connection with the cove that extends up between the necks in 1735.

Squemmechchue. — This was the name for Cedar Tree Neck, as appears in a deposition of Jonathan Luce, made in 1718, and this date is the earliest mention of the name Cedar Tree Neck (Sup. Jud. Court Mss., 24,769). It is derived from M'squ-mechch-auke, meaning "the red fruit land." This may refer to the cranberry, or some similar fruit or vegetable food.

Tahkenshahakket. — This was the name of a small neck of land "lying within" Scrubby Neck, on the southern side, "near or next the fence of Robert Cathcart" (Deeds, II, 60, 218).

Tequanoman's Neck. — In June, 1692, this is referred to in a document as "on the south side of the Island" (Mass. Arch., CXII, 422). It is there spelled Tickanoman. It also is referred to in the charter of Edgartown, dated July 8, 1671, as the southwest bound mark of that town. It was probably Watcha Neck.

Tiasquin. — This early Indian name for the New Mill river is of uncertain origin. This stream was crossed by a bridge, probably constructed by the settlers soon after their occupation, and it is referred to often, as in 1664, a deed from the Sachem Pamehannet to Thomas Mayhew, recites certain bounds as "from the bridge of the river called Tyasquan" (Deeds, I, 83). The Algonquian word *Tooskeonk,* means a fording place, ford or bridge, and while it may be accidental yet it can be the source of this name — the ford or bridge river. Another possible origin is Tisashg-om-(uck), "where we go to cut grass," meaning the meadows along the lower parts of this stream.

Tississa. — This was a neck of land lying between "Tyers" cove and Deep Bottom cove, and was generally known in the records as "Copeck alias Tississa" (Dukes Deeds, I, 301). It was purchased by Simon Athearn of the Indians in 1674, without the formal approval of Thomas Mayhew, and became in consequence a source of prolonged litigation (Deeds, I, 305). The meaning of Tississa is not known, but Copeck is a compound of two words, Kuppi-ack, signifying "land or a place shut in," being from the same root as Cap-o-ack. The modern abbreviation of the neck is "Sissa." John Manter sold land on Tississa, "in the Point called Sepiessa, alias Manter's Point," bounded east by Deep Bottom pond and on the west by Copeck, Sept. 17, 1736 (Deeds, VI, 137).

Wampache. — Josias the Sachem sold to Simon Athearn certain land "neer to Simon Athearns house and land at Wampache" in Tisbury, the land being Josias' "planting feild for many years," November 18, 1685 (Deeds, I, 299). James Allen sold to Simon Athearn in 1702, "a little parcel of land near to a place called Nictowouhtoquoh by Wampache," with "liberty to dig earth to use to dam the water and drown the swamps there" (Ibid., I, 324). This is believed to be in North Tisbury at or near the site of Mr. R. W. Crocker's mill, where in early days a mill formerly stood.

In the Massachusetts dialect Wompasg, or Wompasket, means a marsh, swamp or bog, a definition which seems to apply to the locality conveyed in the last-named deed. Another later form is Wampatchey, 1735 (VI, 23-4).

Waskosim's Rock.—This is the well-known landmark, now as of old forming one of the boundaries between Tisbury and Chilmark. It is first mentioned in the town records under date of Feb. 9, 1681-2, as "a place called Wasqusims," and again in 1702 as "Waskosims" (pp. 10, 274). It may have obtained its name from some Indian who had a wigwam in that vicinity.

Wechekemmipihquiah or *Wechepemepquah.* — This was one of the Indian names of Scrubby Neck, known also as Pasquanahomman's Neck, one of the planting fields of the Indians before the advent of the white settlers. The meaning of this word is "cornfield," from Wachimin, corn, and pequauke, clear place, or field. This is mentioned in a deed dated 1700 (Dukes Deeds, I, 46), under that designation, but it has had several aboriginal titles. It is mentioned in the town records, under date of 1700 (p. 35), as Pasqunahammans

Neck, and later (1743) it had been shortened to Nahamons, and at the present day it is curtailed to Homers, and the name is given to the adjoining pond. Another alias was Mossoowonkwonk (Mossoonkhonk, Mosoounkwonk, Mussoo-onksumkeh), as recorded in the County books (Deeds, II, 317, 244; III, 105, 130). Another alias was Peanaskenamset (Deeds, II, 245), occurring in 1693. In its full form this should be written as Uppeanashkonameset, meaning "a place where flags grow," or literally, "at the covering-mat place," designating a low marshy spot where the cat-tail flag (Typha Latifolia) grows in abundance. This plant was used by the natives for covering their wigwams, in making mats, baskets and such like articles, while the down which surrounds the fruit was used for the filling of cushions for the head. The same name designates other Indian localities in New England. Mossoonkhonk (1693): a field in Tisbury where meadow grass was cut and which became the subject of a dispute with the Indians as to proprietorship. Mos-soon-khonk, means "that which is sheared, or made bare" hence "a mowing meadow."

Weechpoquassitt. — This name is commonly written and spoken Eachpoquassit. It is a boundary designation, probably, as the word means, "as far the opening out," from Wekshe- "as far as, or extending to," and pocasset, "the open out or widening." Weechpoquasset was the natural boundary line between the sachemships of Takemmy and Nunnepoag, at that part of the island. It was also the west bound of Chickemmoo.

SKETCHES OF THE EARLY SETTLERS.

JAMES ALLEN.

The only one of the original purchasing proprietors of this town who remained as a settler, except James Skiffe, was James Allen, the progenitor of the Vineyard Allens now scattered over this land from Maine to California. He was the son of Samuel Allen of Braintree and Anne his wife, and was probably born in that town in 1636, the year after his father was made a freeman. Of his early years we have no knowledge, as the records of Braintree and Suffolk county are entirely silent about him, and it is more than likely that, after 1657, when he became of age, he may have removed to some other town in the colony. His sister Sarah married Lieut. Josiah Standish of Bridgewater about this time, and possibly he might be found in that town where his brother Samuel lived, or in that vicinity. About 1662 James Allen married, his wife's name according to family tradition being Elizabeth Perkins, who was born about 1644, and therefore eight years his junior.[1] It is believed that about this year he removed to Sandwich, Cape Cod, where the births of three children known to be his are recorded, 1663 to 1667, and where he probably formed his personal and business connection with James Skiffe of the same town.[2] In the summer of 1668 he was here making the preliminary arrangements with his partners and Mayhew about the purchase of Takemmy, and in the summer of 1669 the bargain with the Indians was consummated. His coming here is almost coincident with the death of his father, which occurred in Braintree in 1669, where he had been town clerk for many years.[3] By his will, dated Sept. 16, 1669, Samuel Allen bequeathed to his son James five pounds to be paid "within three years after my decease," and to his "sonn in Law Josiah Standish" he devised double that amount. James Allen's settlement here can be assigned fairly to that year, as no more births of children are recorded in Sandwich. From this time on for forty-five years he was the leading spirit in the towns of Tisbury and Chilmark, and one of the largest land holders. At one time or another he owned seven of the original home lots on the west side of Old Mill brook, besides all the dividends accruing to them, and there are no less than thirty conveyances from him recorded on the county land records. The first home lot drawn by him is thus described:—

Thes are the Lands of James allin Lieng In the tounship of tisbury one Lot containing forty 8 ackers bounded on the south by nathannil skiffs Lot and on the north by Jaremiah whittons Lot Lieng in bredeth forty 8 pols by the reiver and runeth westward from the reiver 8 skore pols in lenght with one Lot in the gret neck bounded on the est by the middel of the watar which partth the neck and on the west by goodman

[1]The printed Perkins genealogies fail to mention any Elizabeth Perkins suitable to correspond with the above facts.

[2]James Allen's sister Abigail married John Cary and lived in Bridgewater and later in Taunton. Benjamin, son of James, preached in Bridgewater after his graduation from Yale.

[3]James Allen signed as witness to a deed in Sandwich, Nov. 13, 1669 (Plymo. Col. Deeds, III, 163).

of with a sixtenth part of all undevided Lands and Meddo......to the said town the devided Lands being more or les as thay are Laid out
This is the [Record] of the Landes and inharitanc of [James Allen] in the town of tisbury[1]

This land, which is now the property of Everett Allen Davis, Esq., was doubtless the location of his residence for twenty years until his removal to Chilmark. He sold it in 1692 to John Pease, Jr., of Edgartown, whose heirs deeded it to Gershom Cathcart in 1723, and it remained many years in the possession of the latter's descendants.[2] When he removed to Chilmark is not definitely known. He began his purchases of the large estate he finally owned there early in February, 1677-8, a tract bounded south by the pond, and he is called "of Tisbury." In 1686, when making another purchase, he is called "of Nashowakemmuck," and this may be the probable date of his change of residence.[3]

His estate or home farm amounted to about 250 acres, by successive purchases, and this he gave to two of his sons before his death. Ebenezer received one half of the entire property in 1698, to be available after the decease of his father and mother,[4] and Samuel received the Keephiggon lot in 1705 near the Tisbury line.[5] Ichabod had acquired large holdings in Chickemmoo and John and Joseph were probably provided for, through their mother's inheritance. Benjamin was the youngest son and not of age till just before his father's death. This probably accounts for the absence of a will or administration on such a large and valuable estate — these ante-mortem transfers of property.

His public services were characterized by quality and not quantity. In 1675 he was an Assistant under the Mayhew regime, equivalent to a justice on the bench. How long he held this is not known.[6] Besides this he held possibly one town office and but one other county office during his long life. He was appointed on a committee "to procure a new charter" for Tisbury in 1687 (a thing that was never done), and after the inclusion of the island in Massachusetts he was one of the first three justices of the peace.[7] He was recom-

[1]Tisbury Records, 8.
[2]Dukes Deeds, I, 155; III, 446, 509.
[3]Ibid., I, 277; II, 277.
[4]Ibid., II, 41.
[5]Ibid., I, 299.
[6]N. Y. Col. Mss., XXIV, 159.
[7]Council Records, II, 207. He had served but once as a juryman in all his twenty years of residence up to this date, an unusual record. James Allen was Selectman of Chilmark in 1704, but it may have been his son.

mended for his appointment by Simon Athearn, who stated that Allen was "reputed wealthy and having such Influence in the people there," and at the same time he advised that Allen be made captain of the military company.[1] It is evident that he had no taste for arms, as he had petitioned the court two years before on the subject, as appears by this record: —

> Whereas *James Allin* of *Chilmark* did apere before the Coart in order for a *dismission from trayning:* The Coart hath granted him a dismission provided he doth apere in time of mustering: and doth help Sufficy.[2]

His standing in the community as stated by Athearn was that of a man of influence, wielding more power than if he had held a score of minor offices in the course of his life. Now he was in the most exalted one to which men in those days could aspire, a justice on the King's Bench, and in this capacity he served the people for at least six years at the Quarterly Sessions of the Peace. As the first one to hold any considerable office of honor or profit on the Vineyard since its settlement, not connected either by blood or marriage with the Mayhew family, Mr. Justice Allen had some distinction beside that of the position itself.

In 1701 he gave to the town of Tisbury its first "God's Acre" for the burial of the dead and as a location for the new meeting-house under contemplation, and within this enclosure lies his body marked with a well-preserved slate stone. His declining years were passed in Chilmark, where a large family of a dozen children were reared, married and half of them settled in homes of their own. All the daughters left the island, but seven sons have perpetuated the name of James Allen their honored father and the parent of sons who maintained his splendid reputation.

He died July 25, 1714, aged 78 years, and his wife Elizabeth survived till August 7, 1722, being of the same age at the date of her death.

SIMON ATHEARN.

Simon Athearn

Nothing less than a separate chapter would enable the author to give an adequate portrayal of the strenuous life and fruitful career of this unique character among the early settlers of the Vineyard, Simon Athearn of

[1]Mass. Archives, CXII, 424.
[2]Dukes County Court Records, July 10, 1690.

Tisbury. Amid the settings of a most peaceful and bucolic life he managed to stir up more contrary breezes than any man of his time, and was a continual thorn in the flesh of the ruling family on the island. It is a matter of regret that the author has not been able to ascertain his antecedents. Indeed, his name is unique, and nowhere has it been observed in the scores of volumes containing the records of English parishes; and a professional genealogist of London stated that he had never seen the name in his long experience. No other family of this name emigrated to New England in the 17th century, and as far as known he was the sole and first bearer of it in this country. It has been suggested that the name is of similar origin to Attwood, Att-water, Att-well, being originally Att-hern. Sewall spelled it Atturn in his Diary in 1712.

His gravestone at West Tisbury records the name Attharn and the only early English instance with a spelling approaching it — Atturn — occurring before 1600, seems to bear out this theory rather than the supposition of its identity with Atherton. It may be identical with Hathorn, now Hawthorne. But whatever the mystery attaching to his antecedents, and it covers as well his previous residence if any in this country before his appearance at the Vineyard, his subsequent life and doings after his settlement are an open book.

If the record on his tombstone is correct he was born about 1643, and the first mention of his name in the town records of Edgartown is under date of 1659, when he served on the jury. This presupposes an error somewhere; either on the gravestone or the Edgartown records, which are a transcript, not too carefully made, for he would have been at that date a minor sixteen years of age, and therefore ineligible for that duty. The occasion of his first appearance, however, on the record seems to be plausible as well as characteristic, for he spent most of the remainder of his career in court, as he had begun. He stated in a deposition that he was aged about 56 years in 1698, which carries us back to 1642. It is the belief of the author that he came to this country as a boy in the employ of Nicholas Butler of Edgartown, who was a man of property, and kept a number of servants. According to tradition he selected his future wife as she was romping with her playmates near her father's house, having about her dolls and other childish evidences that her thoughts were far away from matrimony. The girl was Mary, daughter of John Butler, and according to Judge Sewell "his wife was not fourteen when he married her." The young husband had probably taken up land at Tississa in the present limits of West Tisbury, by a purchase from the Indians before the settlement of Tisbury, contrary to the rights of Thomas Mayhew, the patentee, who had prohibited the purchase of Indian titles without his consent. Athearn thus began his long course of opposition to the Mayhews and their official control of affairs on the Vineyard. Out of this Tississa incident endless litigation arose. As soon as Peabody, Standish, Allen and Skiffe made their purchase in Tisbury Simon Athearn purchased a lot of land in 1670 and was admitted, May 20, 1671, as an associate proprietor. In 1672 his dwelling house was located on Great Neck on the east side of the Old Mill river on a lot of land comprising twenty acres. He also owned fifteen acres "at the turn of the brook" where the well-known Dr. Fisher mill property was afterwards developed. Here on his home lot were born to him and his wife nine children, all of whom married save one, and the sons maintained the high standing and distinction in Vineyard affairs that their father had set.

When in 1671 Thomas Mayhew came back from New York with town charters for Edgartown and Tisbury, a manorial grant for Tisbury Manor, and a commission as governor for life, the spirit of Simon Athearn rose within him as he saw the destinies of the island confined to the personality of one man and the government of one family. He felt that there was no place in the Massachusetts system for governors for life. The details of the abortive rebellion against this undemocratic form of government have been elsewhere related, and it will only be necessary to explain the part played by Athearn. His growing estate, comprising his sole worldly possessions, constrained him after its failure to throw himself on the mercy of the legally established government, however distasteful it may have been to him personally, rather than to accept the full consequences of his act, and seek or be driven to a new home elsewhere. So he cleared himself as best he could, as appears by the following record:—

At his Majesties court: held at Edgartown uppon Marthas Vineyard Jan: 8: 1674-5.

Simon Athearn desiring by way of petition that whereas himself was by the Authoritie Reputed one of the Ringleaders in the late Resisting of the Govourment that being lead and induced thereunto by others the Governour and Associates would so looke uppon him and Judge him accordingly and testified uppon oath that Thomas Burchard was a principall instigator of him whereby he was induced to act in the opposition of Authoritie.

The Court fined him twenty-five pounds, one half to be paid "forthwith," five pounds and ten shillings in money and seven pounds in cattle or corn. And for speaking against the fine and sentence of William Vincent he was fined ten pounds, one half "forthwith" as above and the other half in produce. "And (the Court) doe take from him his freedom during the pleasure of the Court And doe revoke the former sentence against him of sending him to New Yorke." But Athearn, though defeated, was not conquered in spirit.

"A man convinced against his will is of the same opinion still."

Before the year had expired we find him continuing agitation against the Mayhew government, as shown in a letter dated Oct. 8, 1675, addressed to Gov. Andros of New York. It is an interesting statement of the difficulties experienced by thöse not in the favor of the official circle, but is too long to be given in full.

The death in 1682 of the aged Governor removed one cause of complaint on the part of Athearn against that feature of the government of the island, the life tenure of the chief magistrate, and though no change occurred in the tenure of the Mayhew family upon the offices of the island, yet it is evident that Athearn chose to accept the inevitable conditions and bide his time. The only change in the results of his appearances in litigation after the decease of Gov. Mayhew as shown by the court records, is a series of decisions in which he is enabled to compromise or divide with his opponent. Prior to this they had all been adverse verdicts. But a new enemy soon appeared on the scene in the person of William Rogers, and he kept Athearn constantly before the court for two years. He charged him with stealing a cow the year previously and killing it privately. Athearn was non-suited. He sued him for slander and asked damages to the amount of fifty pounds. The jury returned a verdict of *non-liquet*. The next year he complained against him for stealing a black cow, but the charge was withdrawn. Athearn had evidently reached the limit of his patience, and proceeded to take the law into his own hands by personally chastising his persistent persecutor. Rogers forthwith complained against Athearn "for halling or pulling sayd Rogers by the eres and caueling him sayd William Roge and thefe with other Skurvie words in court." The court found for the defendant, though the act took place in its presence.

An amusing incident occurred at this time in which Athearn again figures as a defendant in an action for slander with damages claimed to the amount of £100. The plaintiff was Thomas Peat "Skoole master of Edgartown" and his declaration relating his grievance so dramatically sets forth the circumstances constituting the offence, that it were best told in his own language and it is here quoted:—

The plaintiff stated that he was in the house of Richard Arey on the 14th of March, 1686-7, "teaching som of his skollers then in skoolle, when in came Simon Athearn, who asked the plaintiff to give him his dafter Marys Coppy book & sum Coppys the sayd playntiffe was Ready to pleasure the said defendant, but in the entrem" the defendant was writing in his daughter Mary's book "without the liberty and privity" of the schoolmaster. The defendant "tok a pen of one of the skollers and writ in a Coppy boock som Skandloues & slandrous words......as may apere by a manniskript of the sayd defendant, which the sayd plaintiffe will produce...... in which the defendant undervalewed & disparraged the sayd plant: to his skollers, counseling them to forsak him, Rendering him to be an Idell wasting person in the way of his caulling in the very Instant that the sayd playntiffe was bisied in the performance of his Douty in his Skoole, yet was the sayd defendant so Impudent before the sayd plantiffes face, Subtilly & fox like to Record the sayd Plaintiffes name in a mock verse in the skoole."

The jury found "it a trespass for a man to com into a Skolle and take a pen of one of the Skollers in Skool & whrit in one of the Skollers books without the aprobation of the master of the Skoole," and the plaintiff was awarded twelve pence damages and costs of court. It is only to be regretted that the "mock verse" which Simon Athearn composed that day in his daughter Mary's "coppy boock" has not been preserved in order that we might enjoy a perusal of the lines which so incensed this pedagogue.

Notwithstanding all these evidences of a litigious life Athearn retained the confidence of his neighbors. He was one of the committee of the town of Tisbury to lay out sixteen shares in the new purchase in 1675. He was chosen county commissioner in 1686; constable of Tisbury in 1687; assessor in 1692; commissioner for the town (for the trial of small cases) in 1693; selectman in 1695. Such a character as the subject of this sketch is not made of the material that enters into the composition of a popular man, and although easily the first citizen of Tisbury in his day in point of energy, progressive spirit and interest in the public welfare, yet viewed from the standpoint of office-holding his true dimensions are obscured.

Athearn's possession of Tississa, which he purchased of the Indian Jude in 1674, and held without confirmation from the Lord Proprietor, or approval of the town, involved him in a long series of differences with his townsmen and litigation with a number of them on account of trespass, defamation of title and assaults. In 1678 he reached an agreement with the town concerning this neck of land by the terms of which Athearn yielded his claim to the largest part of the neck, receiving ten pounds as a return for his purchase money, out of which he was required to pay two pounds for the portion that was confirmed to him. It appears, however, that the town failed to live up to the agreement, and he felt free to act accordingly. As the neck was declared to be common lands, Athearn proceeded to acquire the shares of others from time to time; but this arrangement did not settle the contention and two years and a half later, at a town meeting, held on June 18, 1680, the following vote was passed:—

being a town mitting it was put to vott whare or no Simon Atharne shoulde have the necke......of land that liath upon the pountes of the indian necke but the towne voted that the said simon Attharne should but have his share with the reste of the inhabitants and tendred the saide simon Attharne if hee youlde sine the dedes the yould pee him the mony.

Whatever the hitch in the negotiations depended upon, it appears that the town authorities undertook to dispose of this neck of land by grants in 1683, and Athearn caused his protest to be recorded in the town book. This was immediately followed by the reciprocal protest of the townsmen against the entry of his caveat. He took this matter finally to the county court, and on June 22, 1684, the following record of the case appears:—

Simon Athearn complaineth against the Constable and overseers of the Town of Tisbury for non-payment of certain monies due by contract about a neck of land caled Copeck alias tississa.

Athearn finally acquired by one means or another the possession of the much-disputed neck.

A political change which followed several years after the death of the old Governor, the transfer by Matthew Mayhew of his manorial rights as lord of the manor to Thomas Dongan by sale, was not to the satisfaction of Athearn, but he was helpless to prevent this situation and was obliged to await the adjustment of these difficulties till a more fortunate time. It was not far off and came unexpectedly. The accession of William III brought in a government which exercised less of the ancient prerogative and seemed to give expectation to Athearn that the rights of the people would be heard and considered and that the liberality of the Prince of Orange would be reflected in his Colonial representative in New York. So when Gov. Henry Slaughter, the new appointee, arrived in New York in March, 1691, he was scarcely seated in his new office before Athearn addressed him on the condition of affairs at the Vineyard.

This letter is printed elsewhere (Vol. I, pp. 179-80), but it was not in this direction a change in the Athearn's horizon was to occur. The procurement of the new charter for Massachusetts in 1691 became the opportunity for Simon Athearn to establish himself in new relations with the authorities of the Massachusetts Bay Colony. He wrote a letter of information and advice to Sir William Phipps and recommended some of his friends for local offices, and Sir William appointed one of them to the most important office on the island. If he had aspirations for official preferment himself the following recommendation from prominent residents of the Vineyard seems to show that he was a candidate for the bench. This testimonial with its curious phraseology, is worth printing in full:—

Wee whose names under writen present our most humbel duty to your Excellency & your honnored Consesell & ar redy upon all demand or Command from your Exsellency to Sarve you with our Lives & fortine & pray for your exsellencys happines & prosperuty & for the happines & prosperity of your honoured Consell and we Count our sealfs happi that we are under the shaddow of your Exsellency & wee are willing to acquaint your Exsellency that wee were not willing to specke when the Gentlemen were here. Because that your Exsellencys orders might be setteled in Peease & quitnes now wee are willing to give your Exsellency an aCount of Mr. Simon Athearn we Looke upon him to be a well acomplish man he is no drunkerd nor no Card player nor a man that freequint tavorns but wee doe know but he may have his feialing as well as other men: for estate: few or none upon our Iland goeth beyond him & for a Justes wee Looke upon him as fit a man as any here: so wishing & praying for your Exsellencys happines & the god of paese Bles you with al Spritual Blessings & give you a hart after his owne hart that he may tack a delight in you to doe you goode & save you from all your enemies:: wee humbly beg your Exsellencys pardon in what is amisse in writing to your Exsellency & Remaine your most humbel & dutiful sarvants.[1]

This interesting document was signed by Andrew Newcomb, Joseph Norton, James Pease, Jacob Norton, John Butler, Thomas Norton, William Vinson, Thomas Wolling, Thomas Butler, Isaac Norton, Benjamin Norton, Moses Cleaveland, John Pease and Thomas Vinson. It is to be noted that no member of the Mayhew family appended his name to this testimonial.

In the meantime the Mayhews had made their peace with the new regime, and Athearn failed in his aspirations. He had to swallow his feelings as he saw the same old officials reinstated in the Vineyard courts. Thereafter he devoted his time to an agitation in favor of consolidating Tisbury and Chilmark as one township, the details of which are elsewhere narrated. Although he was representative of Tisbury at the General Court for several sessions he was unable to effect anything of personal advantage to himself or for the benefit of his town. In 1696-7 he was engaged in another litigation arising from alleged trespass on his property, and personal assaults which followed this. Voluminous papers in the case prepared by him detail the injustice he received at the hands of Richard Sarson and Matthew Mayhew, who imprisoned his son and refused to allow him an appeal to the superior court at Plymouth; Athearn states that he had been under indictment without trial for two years, on a charge of felony, and declared that there seemed to be no law by which the accused may be "discharged from such vexatious imprisonment espetially when a father-in law and his two sons are the rulle in such Infeariour Court."

It is thus that Athearn pays his respects to Richard Sarson and his stepsons Matthew and Thomas Mayhew. It is not possible to weigh the equities of this long controversy, but the recital of his grievances caused Gov. Stougton to address a letter to these justices, in which he "Signified" to them that Athearn should have the proceedings against him conducted "equal and agreeable to the Rules of Law and Justice, which is all that is expected." It must have been a strong case that induced the executive to interfere with a judicial proceeding. After the recital of all his experiences for so many years and the unfortunate results of his litigations, we may

[1]Mass. Arch., CXII, 435.

safely conclude that Athearn made a vital error in not effecting a matrimonial alliance with the Mayhew family.

The remainder of his life, as far as external evidences warrant the conclusion, was devoted to the care of his estate and the enjoyment of the declining years of an active if not a politically fruitful life. In worldly possessions "few or none upon our Iland goeth beyound him" as stated by his friends in 1692, and with extensive acres at Great Neck, Tississa, Charles' Neck, and scattering parcels of land in Chilmark, Edgartown and Tisbury, he doubtless found greater satisfaction than in the bootless campaigns he waged against the family that held sway over the island in his day and generation.

On the several visits of Judge Sewall to the island in 1702 and 1712 he mentions dining with and meeting Mr. Athearn, and again in 1714 he notes in his diary under date of April 10: "View'd Watsha Neck all over, being conducted by Mr. Simon Athearn." We thus have trace of him to within a year of his death.

He had a family of nine children — four boys and five girls — growing up about him, of whom his eldest, Samuel, remaining a bachelor until after his father's death, inherited many of the pugnacious qualities of his famous parent. His daughter Sarah was the wife of his clergyman, the Rev. Josiah Torry. His second son, Jabez, destined to lead a distinguished life on the Vineyard, had contracted an advantageous alliance with Miss Catherine Belcher. His daughter Mary became the wife of Thomas Waldron, and before Simon Athearn paid the debt of nature his latter years were doubtless made happy by the coming of grandchildren to play on his knee. He had passed three score years and ten, and on the 20th day of February, 1714-15, his earthly career was closed. The enumeration of his real and personal property disclosing, as it does, varied possessions of a man of wealth in that time, aggregating £1639, 14 shillings, 11 pence, equivalent at this time to about $50,000 is worth of the space required for its presentation. The items of tankard, cordial-cup and drinking-cup indicate that he maintained the hospitalities required of a country gentleman. Judge Samuel Sewell of Boston was a guest at his house in the spring of 1702, while on a journey to Gay Head, and doubtless sipped sack-posset from these same cups.

Not the least of the attributes of this versatile and interesting character are the helps he has given to the historian of the Vineyard in his letters regarding affairs upon the Vineyard written during the period of his political activities. They are the only documents extant dealing with the personal phases of that remote time, and the motives actuating the characters in the drama, as they appeared to him. To him also are we indebted for two manuscript maps of the island drawn before 1700, and although crude in execution and sadly lacking in typographical accuracy, yet they contain valuable information nowhere else to be found. Facsimiles of various portions of these maps appear in other portions of this work.

In the graveyard at West Tisbury carved with the gruesome emblems of mortality a slate stone tells the passing stranger where lies the mortal remains of Tisbury's first great citizen.

Probate Records, I, 50.

July 21, 1715. The estate of Mr. Simon Athearn of Tisbury late deceased prized by us the subscribers.

		£	
	The lands and building in Great Neck or homestead	600 "	
	The land in Tississa Neck	250 "	
	The land in Charles Neck	200 "	
	The land in the Oldtown or Edgartown	100 "	
	the meadow in Chilmark	60 "	
	the land at Keephegon	16 "	
	the small parcels lands between the Pine Hills	6 "	
	the Old Mill River his right of lands on the plain	2 "	
		£1234 "	
2dly	The Moveable Estate		
	one pair oxen	10. 0	
	one pair oxen	9.10	
	5 cows	17.10	
	7 cowes & calves	22.15	
	2 steers	6. 0	
	4 two year old steers	6. 0	
	2 two year old heifer & a bull	4.10	
	8 yearlings	6. 0	
	one mare and a colt	12. 0	
	6 swine	1.16	
	one mare	3. 0. 0	£ s
			99.11
3dly	112 sheep with their lambs and fleeces at £8.10s per score	47.12	
	190 sheep with their fleeces at £6 per score	57. 0	
			104.12

4thly	Money and household stuff		
	Province bills	38.16.17	
	one silver tankard	9. 0. 0	
	6 silver spoons	3.12. 0	
	one silver cup	3. 0. 0	
	one silver porringer	3. 0. 0	
	one bed with furniture	11. 7. 0	
	one do do	12. 8. 0	
	one do do	6.12. 0	
	one do do	6.10. 0	
	one do do	4.10. 0	£ s d
			92. 5. 7
5ly	his wearing apparel	12.16. 6	
	2 large Bibles	5. 0. 0	
	one do old	2. 0	
	some small books	1. 3. 0	
	4 law books	1. 0. 0	
	3 pair sheets	4.10	
	2 pair do	2. 5	
	1 pair do	2. 5	
	1 pair do	.12	
	2 pair do	1. 0	
	2 pair pillow bears	1. 4	
	5 do	.16	
	1 pair do	4	
	one carpet	6	£ s d
			33. 3. 6
6ly	4 table cloths	1. 4	
	23 napkins	2.10	
	1 cupboard cloth	.10	
	1 towel	4	
	3 cushions	3	
	1 brass kettle	2. 0	
	2 brass kettles	.18	
	3 brass candle-sticks	.13	
	1 bellmettle skillet	8	
	one iron kettle	6	
	1 chafing dish	6	
	1 spit pan & fender	1. 1	
	one warming pan	.16	
	one brass frying pan	6	
	one pair beases	.15	
	one brass gun	1. 0	
	one iron pot	.16	
	one do	.12	
	one do	. 9	
	one iron kettle	1.10	
	one do	8	
	1 cupboard	2.10	
	1 trunk	5	
	1 parcel wooden vessels	1.10	

1 Gridiron	. 6
1 pair tongs & slice	8
3 trammels	.15
box heaters & goose	3
1 pair bellows	2
old iron	1
1 pair steelyards	1. 0
1 pair worsted corns	.12
1 sword	4
1 table	1.10
1 do	1. 5
1 do	.12
1 do	. 8
1 do & form	.10
2 joint stools	. 6
1 dozen chairs	2.14
8 chairs	1.12
6 old do	.10
1 chest	. 5
1 do	.10
1 do	. 6
1 do	. 6
1 chest drawers	3. 0
1 cupboard	.12
4 pounds hops c 9	1.10
3 corn seives	. 4
1 half bushel	. 3
1 hair cloth	.12
2 bridles & saddles	1.15
1 side saddle	.15
3 seives	. 5
2 meal bags	. 6
2 sleighs & harnesses	.16
warping bars & boxes	.10
1 pair looms	1.10
3 spinning wheels	.18
1 pr. wool cards	2. 6
4 pewter platter	1.12
2 do	.12
4 do	.16
13 plates	1. 6
2 basons	. 6
4 porringers	. 6
1 cordial cup	. 5
1 tankard	. 7
1 candlestick	. 3
1 salt cellar	. 2
10 spoons	. 3. 4
3 drinking cups	. 4
2 looking glasses	1.10
mantletree furniture	. 5

60 pounds sheeps wool	2.10	
1 bushel flaxseed	. 4	
6 pound flax	. 4	
4 axes	. 8	
3 hoes	. 9. 6	
1 spade	. 2	
1 adze	. 4	
1 auger, chisel, gouge	. 6	
2 pitchforks	. 3. 6	
1 lantern	. 2. 6	
2 pudding	. 3	
1 tunnel	. 1. 6	
1 cart & wheels	2. 5	
2 cops & pins	. 7	
1 plow with irons	.16	
2 harrows	1.10	
2 rings, staple & yoke	. 6	
2 chains	.16	
1 cart rope	. 3	
1 thousand boards	2.15	
100 cedar bolts	.16	
1 beetle & wedges	. 6	
1 Grindstone	.10	
20 bush barley	3.10	
		76. 2.10
		1234.
		99.11
		104.12
		92. 5. 7
		33. 3. 6
		1639.14.11

Errors Excepted

Robert Cathcart
John Manter
Benjamin Manter

JOHN CASE

This early settler came to Tisbury from parts unknown about 1681, as the first knowledge we have of him is found in a town vote on December 16th of that year, when a home lot was granted to him on the north side of New Mill river, adjoining the Chilmark boundary line. His connection with any of the contemporary families of this name in other parts of New England has not been established.[1] He married, probably after his settlement here, Desire (13) daughter of

[1]There were several Case families in Connecticut and Rhode Island before 1700 and the indications point to the former colony as the early home of our settler. Most of his children removed there after his death.

John Manter, by whom he had eight children of record as shown by his will. His career was uneventful and scarcely any references to him appear in the town or county books. He was undoubtedly a young man, perhaps had just reached his majority when he came to Tisbury, and his death occurred in 1705 or 1706, when he was in the prime of life. His will, dated Feb. 5, 1704-5, was probated February 11, 1706, but the estate was not divided until 1720, when the minor children became of age.[1] The estate was inventoried at £105, and his son William, a weaver by trade, was made administrator in 1719, before the final settlement was effected. Descendants of this son William remained in Tisbury till about 1800, but the name became extinct here after that time.[2]

ROBERT CATHCART.

This early settler was a Scotchman and the family is said to have originated or derived its name from the Barony of Cathcart in Renfrewshire, Scotland. It is not known when he came to this country, nor when he was born. The tradition in the family is that he had been engaged in some of the numerous border or clan wars of the period, and received a wound from a bullet which he carried to his death. The first record of him on the Vineyard is in 1690 when he purchased a lot of land in Tisbury from Arthur Biven, a tract of twenty acres in the northernmost home lot on the west side of Old Mill brook.[3] He married about this time, Phebe, daughter of Thomas Coleman of Nantucket, and it is probable that the young Highlander "set up his Ebenezer" at once in the new town.[4] Here he began the occupation of innkeeper, which he followed throughout his life,[5] and in March, 1693, he was chosen town clerk, an office which he likewise held to the date of his decease. In 1696 he bought a new homestead lot on the west side of the South (Chilmark) road, just south of the Whiting estate, and in 1706 added the southern

[1]Dukes Probate, I, 24. The estate of the widow Nickerson of Yarmouth showed a debt due from John Case in 1706 (Barnstable Town Records).

[2]Members of this branch removed to Maine after the Revolution, and it is probable that the name still survives in that state.

[3]Dukes Deeds, I, 101. Dated Dec. 2, 1690.

[4]This Nantucket marriage may indicate his previous residence in that island.

[5]In 1696 his license to sell strong drink was "renewed."

half of this lot, making in all about thirty acres. Here he conducted a "shop," kept an ordinary and acted as town and proprietors' clerk until the spring of 1718 when death terminated his career.[1] His birth is estimated as in 1650, and he was therefore about 68 years of age. His widow Phebe, who was evidently many years his junior (she was b. June 15, 1674), married Samuel Athearn the following year. Five sons and six daughters of Robert and Phebe Cathcart are known, though no record of their birth exists, and while the family was prominent in Tisbury through that century, it is now extinct in the male line on the island.[2] Branches of it resided in Nantucket and western Massachusetts during the last century, and descendants may be traced throughout the United States.[3]

It is supposed that the name "Scotchman's Bridge" in West Tisbury derived its name from Robert Cathcart, who may have built it, or from one of his sons.

EDWARD COTTLE.

This early settler of Tisbury was born about 1628, and although a discrepancy exists in the records as to this point[4], it is considered more probable that this represents the date of his birth, rather than ten years earlier. He first settled in that part of Salisbury now known as Amesbury, Massachusetts. There is extant a statement made by him of his experiences there which is printed here as the best account of the reasons which caused him to move from that place:—

* * * "I the sd Edward Cottle obtained among other lands a tract called the Lion's mouth being a neck of land * * * & built a sufficient house —sd lands possessed many years, which house being providentially burnt together with my goods, I then built a small house att a place called Jamaica, w'thin same township, w'ch being burnt by the Indians (1668) & not being so able in estate as some other of my associates in said parts was necessitated to try what success I might have by removing to the south-

[1]He died between Jan. 16 and March 24, 1718. Administration of his estate was granted to the widow Oct. 1, 1719, two months after her remarriage. He died intestate, and his estate was finally divided in 1739, when the youngest child had come of age (Dukes Co. Prob., III, 121).

[2]The last member of the family to live on the Vineyard was Mrs. Ann Judson (Cathcart) Johnson, widow of Henry C. Johnson and mother of Norman Johnson of Vineyard Haven. She died in 1907.

[3]Mr. Wallace Hugh Cathcart (Salmon[6], Hugh[5], Thomas[4], Robert[3], Gershom[2], Robert[1]) of Cleveland, Ohio, President of the Western Reserve Historical Society, is a distinguished scion of this Vineyard family and a patron of this work.

[4]Essex County Court Rec., XII, 368; XIII, 72.

wardly part of New England, hopeing the Eastern parts might in time obtain a settled peace that I might then Return, to my inheritance again: but matters occuring Contrary, I purchased a small settlement at ye town of Tisbury in Dukes County afores'd, & being now grown aged & out of hopes of Ever returning" etc., etc.[1]

This interesting and valuable statement does not disclose his intermediate place of residence, before coming to Tisbury, but we learn that he removed from Amesbury with his wife Judith and a family of six or seven children and migrated to Nantucket about 1668-9, where he resided about seven or eight years.[2] At least four children of record were added to his family there, and then he probably returned to the mainland, taking up a residence at a place called "Mannamoiett." This is probably identical with Monomoy on the southeastern part of Cape Cod. He is mentioned as of that place in 1677, and on March 5, 1677-8, "Edward Cottle & his wife of Mannamoiett, for prophaning the Sabath by quarrelling [were] fined 40s—" with the alternative "to be whipt."[3] His stay there was brief, not exceeding three years.

He came to Tisbury about 1680 and is called a "freeholder" in the records as early as 1683. He was chosen one of a committee to procure a new town charter in 1687; to divide proprietors' lands in 1688; a fence viewer in 1688; a constable in 1689, and surveyor of highways in 1699. It is not known where he lived before 1688, but in that year he bought of Thomas Mayhew the eastern half of the home lot of Josiah Standish, consisting of twenty-four acres, now owned by the heirs of the late Henry L. Whiting. It is probable that this had been the site of his residence for some years prior to that date. This he sold to his son John in 1700, and his declining years were probably spent in Chilmark, perhaps with his son James, as in 1710 he calls himself a resident of that town and is so designated by others.[4] There is no record of his death either in the town or probate records. He had disposed of all his property to his son and nothing remained to be divided and made a matter of record. As he was at least 82 years old in 1710 and "grown aged" it is probable he died not long after. By his wife Judith, of whom nothing further

[1]Essex County Deeds, XXII, 201.

[2]Nantucket Records.

[3]Plymouth Colony Rec., V, 254; VII, 207; VIII, 148.

[4]Essex Co. Deeds, XXI, 231. It is quite probable that he lived in Chickemmoo, then a part of Chilmark, rather than in the present town limits of Chilmark. His son James owned land in Chickemmoo.

is known, he had fourteen children, three of whom are not of record in towns where he lived.

Edward Cottle was probably from Wiltshire. In the church at Bradford-upon-Avon in that county there is a mural coat of arms of this family, and the name is frequently found in the records there. The earliest form of the name (1250) is Cotele or Cothele, and the family was early seated at Atworth, Wilts, now called Cottles, near Melksham.[1]

JOSEPH DAGGETT.

The youngest son of John Daggett, the pioneer of the family on the Vineyard, was the only representative of that distinguished family in Tisbury. He was born about 1647[2] and is particularly noted as having married a native whom we can designate as the Pocahontas of our island. It is believed that she can be identified as the daughter of Thomas Sissetom, a Sagamore of Sanchacantacket, named Alice by the English, and that the marriage occurred some time prior to 1685, as at that date two children of this union were old enough to receive property. Presuming they were eighteen and sixteen respectively that would carry the date of assumed marriage back to 1667, when Joseph was about twenty years of age. It is doubtful if a lawful marriage was consummated. This strange fact is established by a deed on record in which "Puttuspaquin of Sanchacantacket gives to his cousins [nieces] Ellis [Alice] & Hester Daggett" a tract of land which is now known to be in the present limits of Eastville adjoining the ponds on the east bank of the Lagoon.[3] This territory is identical with a tract of land granted sixteen years before in 1669 by the sachem Wampamag to "Ales Sessetom and Keziah Sessetom......the daughters of Thomas Se[sse]tum" and probably was a gift in confirmation to the children of Alice of the property originally given to the Indian sisters.[4] It remained as an inheritance of the two half-breed Daggett girls, Alice and Esther, and was divided between them in 1698, after the latter had married Edward Cottle.[5]

Joseph Daggett was one of the first proprietors in the new settlement and his holdings are thus described:—

[1]History of the Cotel or Cottle Family by W. H. Cottell. Pamphlet, 23 pp., 1871.

[2]Deposition. Aged about 51 years in March, 1698-9.

[3]Dukes Deeds, I, 251.

[4]Ibid, VI, 412.

[5]Ibid, I, 24.

The Lands & Accomadations of Joseph Doggatt which Leieth in the Township of Takymmy or tisbury on the vineyard as foloeth One halfe house Lot which containeth twenty-five Acres Leying on the east side of the brook where his dwelling house is this present year 1673 bounded the brook on the west (& the halfe lot which James Redfield hath taken on the south) (& the halfe lot which Charls Crossthwat hath taken on the north) laid out twenty five rods in bredth by James Allen & Thomas Mayhew & Runing eight score rods Easterly from the brook being twenty five Acres mor or lesse

And halfe the sixth part of the neck by John Eddys of which; halfe the fifth lot is Joseph Doggats leying next to henery lewis his lot leying Acrosse the neck as the neck is devided to every mans lot Contained in the neck As before spoken in the order of devision of the three necks baring date february the first 1671

And the two And thirtyth part of all undevided lands whether purchesed or that may be purchesed

this is the lands And Acomadations of Joseph doggatt[1]

This property had its north boundary at the Scotchman's Bridge road on the east side of Old Mill brook, and extended half way down to the Post Office corner. Here his house stood and there played in the front yard the two half-breed children born of the romantic union, Alice (Ellis) and Esther. He maintained his residence until sometime between 1711 and 1715, when in a deed on latter date to his grand-daughter Esther Cottle, he describes himself "of Edgartown, wheelwright." There is nothing to indicate that he ended his days on his home lot in Takemmy, where he had lived so long.

His public services were of the average kind and quantity. He was surveyor of highways, 1687; committee to divide common lands, etc., 1689, 1690, 1703, 1708; selectman, 1689, 1693, 1695; pound keeper, 1690; constable, 1697; and had other small duties at various times till 1716. When he died is not known, nor the place of his burial. Equal uncertainty exists as to his Indian wife. It is probable that he was living on March 5, 1720, when as one of the proprietors of the town he executed a deed with fourteen others to a purchase of some common lands.

Of his children, Joseph,[3] the only known son, married and had issue, descendants of which are represented to-day in the lines shown under his family in the genealogical portion of this work in the Daggett, Huxford and Enoch Norton lines. Through these claim can be made of descent from the Vineyard Pocahontas, Alice Sessetom, the Indian bride of Joseph Daggett. Esther[3], the second daughter, married Edward

[1]Tisbury Records.

Cottle sometime between 1690 and 1698, and she had deceased before June 10, 1708 (Deeds, II, 184). Issue of this marriage was but one daughter named Esther, who probably married (1) a Harding (and had a son Shubael) and (2) Manasseh Kempton. It is not possible to say whether issue is now represented on the Vineyard. The oldest daughter of Joseph, Ellis[3] (Alice) left quite a record for a girl of her age and antecedents. She had three children born out of wedlock named for their presumptive fathers, Henry Luce, Samuel Look and Patience Allen. This unfortunate half-breed was made of better stuff than would be inferred from comtemplating this promiscuous progeny. She was evidently honest, honorable and thrifty, and true to her offspring. She did not live beyond middle life, as her will dated March 19, 1711, when she must have been not much over forty, was probated two months later. It is a legal condition that illegitimate children cannot inherit property, but her will devises real and personal estate to each of her children by name, and as the will was allowed and the real estate passed to the one called Henry Luce, who later disposed of it, this would seem to act as a legitimation of this anomalous family. Henry Luce so-called received his share of the property originally given by the Sachem Wampamag to Alice Sessetom; Samuel Luce was given £7, and Patience Allen the movable estate. Her father, Joseph Daggett, was named as executor, and fulfilled the trust (Probate, I, 31). Altogether it was a very creditable transaction on her part. It is not known what became of these children, but the presumption is that they became united with their Indian associates, and finally lost identity among them, if they survived to adult life.

JOHN EDDY.

John Eddy

Among the passengers for New England in the ship "Handmaid," sailing in 1630, was Samuel Eddy, who settled at Plymouth and became a resident of that town until his death. The name as spelled in the Colony records is Eedy, Eedey, Edeth, Eddy and Edy.[1] He was a tailor by trade and by his wife Elizabeth "having many children and not able to bring them up as they desire" he bound them out to

[1]Plymo. Col. Rec., II, 112, 113, 173; Deeds, II, 39, (part 2), 37.

their neighbors as they became old enough to be of service. The first of these apprentices of record is John Eddy, born on Christmas day, 1637, who was placed in the care of Francis Goulder of Plymouth, yeoman, April 3, 1645, being then under eight years of age.[1] Contemporaneously with this Plymouth family of Eddys there lived in Watertown, Mass., another family, the father of whom was John, and who also came to Plymouth in 1630 in the "Handmaid."[2]

John Eddy left Plymouth prior to 1632 and settled at Watertown, where he became a freeman in 1634 and resided there until 1684, the year of his death, being then ninety years of age.[3] By his wife Amy he had a son John, b. February 6, 1636-7, just ten months before our John of Plymouth came along, and who is the one entered as "Deced December 27: 1707" in the Watertown records.[4] It does not appear that he left any issue, as his brother Samuel in his will dated Aug 6, 1702, makes provision for the maintenance of "my brother John Eddi during his natural life."[5] It is evident that he was then without a family, in straitened circumstances and perhaps "a little distempered" mentally as his father had been. This Watertown family had the names of John, Samuel, Caleb and Benjamin, as did the Plymouth branch.

Another John Eddy lived contemporaneously with these two just mentioned, in the person of John Eddy or Eddway, carpenter of Taunton in 1660, and as John of Plymouth bought land in Taunton that year, which was bounded by John the carpenter's land, it makes a pretty good foundation for some confusion which earlier investigators did not successfully escape.[6] Whence came this John to Taunton is not known,

[1]In 1647 and 1653 his younger brothers, Zachary, aged 7, and Caleb, aged 9, were "put out" to John Brown of Rehoboth. The town records contain only the names of five children born to Samuel and Elizabeth, not enough to be called "many," so a number of others must have been born and died early.

[2]Ward, 274. There is no proven connection yet established between Samuel and John, though it is a reasonable supposition that they were near relatives. It is stated that John of Watertown, born about 1595, was son of Rev. William Eddy of Bristol, later of Cranbrook, England, who had been educated at St. Johns and Trinity Colleges, Cambridge, and received the degree of Master of Arts in 1591 at Cambridge University. The young graduate became a clergyman and received the appointment as Vicar of St. Dunstan's, Cranbrook, Kent, where he remained until his death, which occurred in 1616, after a service of twenty-five years. (Bond, Watertown, 203.)

[3]Winthrop Journal, I, 101.

[4]He had married, probably, before 1677, the date of his father's will. A bequest of £30 was made to him contingently, payable in £5 installments, annually, by his brother Samuel (Middlesex Probate, VI, 301).

[5]Middlesex Probate, XII, 454.

[6]The Eddy Genealogy makes a hopeless tangle of the several Johns, particularly the Plymouth and Taunton men.

but he is distinct from our pioneer. He may have been a half brother, or even a full brother, though bearing the same name, as there are a number of well-known instances of this double nomenclature in New England families. John of Taunton had two wives, Susanna Paddock and Deliverance Owen, and died in 1695 leaving three sons and five daughters.[1]

Having disposed of two other Johns whose contemporary life has possibly some family interest, the fortunes of our John of Plymouth will now be related. His apprenticeship with Francis Goulder terminated in 1658 and he had during that period learned the trade of a blacksmith. In what way he became attracted to the Vineyard is only a matter of conjecture, but presumably through the representations of John Daggett, senior, whose daughter he married later. Under date of Dec. 28, 1659, the following entry occurs in the Edgartown records: The town [of Great Harbor] voted "to pay the charge of the Smiths Transportation hither if he Desires: this is John Edy of Plymouth."[2] This offer made to the young blacksmith was accepted by him in the next year as we find that on Oct. 22, 1660, he was the owner of one share in the town lands "given him by the Town."

This undoubtedly marks the date of his removal hither, as from that time forth his name is found on the town and county records each succeeding year. It is quite certain that he came here in 1660 as a married man, as it is known that his wife was Hepzibah Daggett, daughter of John, and that a daughter Alice was born to them May 3, 1659. John Daggett sold to his son-in-law a homestead six acres, a portion of a ten-acre lot in that town believed to be on the "Line," but it has not been possible to identify the exact location.[3] There were born to him his first five children prior to his removal to Tisbury. Meanwhile he was attending to his smithing and qualifying as an inhabitant under the requirements. He was a member of the train band in 1662 and constable the same year. On May 11, 1663, having remained three years a town, it was voted that he should "have a lot of ten acres and a Commonage with two acres of Meadow.... the meadow lies about the pond att Miles Brook."[4] This lot was one of the "Five and Twenty," just south of the ceme-

[1]Bristol Co. Probate, I, 46; II, 20. Savage, Gen. Dict., III, 326, 328.

[2]Edgartown Town Records, I, 133.

[3]Edgartown Records, I, 4, 7.

[4]Dukes Deeds, VI, 115.

tery on Tower Hill, having a frontage of 14½ rods on the harbor. As proprietor he participated in all the divisions of land during his residence in Edgartown, and in 1667 was granted one sixth of the West Chop neck by Governor Mayhew.[1] This incident will be found explained elsewhere. At this time the project for the purchase of Takemmy was under consideration, and he entered into negotiations with the three partners for admission as a proprietor in the proposed new settlement. Accordingly he offered his lands at Homes Hole as an exchange for this right, as shown in the following document:—

Know all men by these presents that I John Eddy of the town of great-harbour upon the Vineyeard do for myself my heires and assignes sell unto William Pebody Josias Standish and James Allin I say I do sell my whole accomodations lying at Holmes his hole being on sixth part of that which was bought of the Indians by thomas Layton of Rode Island and this I do for and in consideration that the for s'd William Pebody Josias Standish and James Allin are to lett me the said Eddy have five pounds worth of Land at Takemmy at the same Rate as they bought it of the Indians provided that the sd Eddy demand it within two years after the date hereofe as also they shall let me have one Lote among them to live upon I the sd Eddy paying for it at the rate that they buy of the Indians the afores'd five pounds worths to be part of the Lote if I do not demand the Land and live upon it then to pay me five pounds at the end of the s'd 2 years the payment to made in current pay at prices current and in wittness of the premises I have hereunto set my hand this 29 of June 1669

Memorandum — that the lote mentioned is to be one whole accomodation of the town now to be setled and that if ye town be not settled then the fores'd land at holmes his hole to be returned to me the s'd Eddy in wittness to all the premises I haye set hereunto my hand the day and year above s'd JOHN EDDY[2]

Within two years, the new township being an assured success, he was granted a lot by the proprietors, on May 20, 1671, "if he com according to compacicion," and he came.[3] Thenceforth he was identified with Tisbury till the close of his life. Eight years later he sold all his Edgartown property to John Coffin, with the exception of some small divisions on the necks.[4] In 1680 he was a defendant in a suit brought by Simon Athearn for trespass and defamation, and acted as a juror later in the same year.[5] He was chosen constable of Tisbury in 1683, 1684, 1692; selectman, 1687, 1688, 1693, 1696, 1697, 1700; tithingman, 1699; besides acting in several

[1]Dukes Deeds, I, 239.
[2]Tisbury Records, p. 17.
[3]Supreme Judicial Court Files, Case No. 4974.
[4]Dukes Deeds, I, 318. Dated March 6, 1679.
[5]Court Records, Vol. I.

minor capacities on committees appointed by the proprietors or freeholders. His last public office was held in 1711, when he was chosen constable, being then in his 73rd year. He had provided for his declining years by an arrangement with his son Benjamin in 1706, by which all his property was given to this only son on attaining his majority in consideration of support during the remainder of his life.[1] But this was destined to be broken by the early death of Benjamin, May 19, 1709, in his 24th year. By a will however the son, who had married, required his wife as executrix to see "that agreement I have with my honored father and mother, John and Hepsibah Eddy touching their annual allowance shall be well and faithfully observed."[2] In the month following his death, Hannah, the widow of Benjamin, on June 4th, evidently desirous of being relieved of the support of the aged couple, transferred the entire property to John[2] Manter, grandson of John Eddy, in consideration of his assuming the "agreement between John & Benjamin Eddy about his son to the value of £9 annually for the support of John Eddy and wife living in one end of the house." The Eddy homestead property became absorbed into the Manter holdings on Dec. 20, 1710, by a deed to his grandson, the son of his daughter Hannah Manter.[3] This homestead of forty acres was located on the east side of the Old Mill brook abutting the Mill path, on which it had a frontage of 160 rods, running east, and a depth of 40 rods. During the following five years of his life John Eddy requires but little notice. He held no public office and beyond disposing of scattered property holdings to his children and others his name does not occur on the records. He died May 27, 1715, aged 78 years, and his widow died May 3, 1726, aged 83 years, both lying together in the West Tisbury cemetery, having well-preserved stones. His estate was almost all disposed of during his lifetime, except a few pieces of outlying property and personal estate which he bequeathed in an unrecorded will dated Dec. 24, 1715.

In the name of God amen: This Twenty Fourth Day of December Anno Domini 1714, I John Eddy of the Town of Tisbury in Dukes County in New England being of perfect mind & memory Yet Considering the

[1]Dukes Deeds, II, 140.

[2]Dukes Probate, I, 27. The son had probably married in Boston. His will is dated there, and after his death the widow removed to that place and remarried. A Hannah Eddy m. Thomas Cole June 22, 1710 (Boston Record Com. Reports, XXVIII, 277).

[3]Dukes Deeds, II, 203, 216.

mortallity of my Body do make & ordain this my Last will and Testament, viz: Principally and first of all I Give & Recomend my Soul into the hands of God that gave it: and my body I recomend to the Earth to be Interred in decent Christian manner att the Discretion of my Executors, and as to my worldly Estate I give & dispose the same in the following manner and form:—

Imprimis I give and bequeath to my well beloved wife Hepzibah Eddy the sole and entire use and Improvement and Comand of all and singular my reall and personall estate that I sd John Eddy shall Decease seized of in my own proper right During her Natural Life together with all my Just Dues and Debts from any person or persons whatsoever Excepting out of my personal estate one chest comonly called and known by the Name of My Chest (By the family) and which I give to my grandson Samuel Manter, and one Iron Dripping pan which I gave to my Daughter Hannah Manter.

And Furthermore

2. I give & bequeath all my household goods which may remain and be Left att the death of the sd Hepzibath Eddy my wife & all my Live or quick Stock or any moneys that may then be Due to me unto my Daughter Abigail Eddy & to her proper use and benefitt.

3. I give & bequeath to my Daughters Hannah Manter and Beulah Coffin all the lands belonging to me sd Jno Eddy Lying on the East side of the old mill Brook in Tisbury to be equally Divided between them.

4. I further give & bequeath to my Daughters Abigail Eddy all the Lands belonging to me sd Jno Eddy on the West side of the Old Mill Brook in Tisbury being Part of Two of those Lotts of Land Comonly called the Hill Lotts with all the priviledges and appurtenances thereunto Belonging And I also give to my Daughter Abigail Eddy & my Grandson Sam'l Manter all my share and Part of the Comon undivided Lands throughout the Township of Tisbury which Contains one whole share in Commons to be divided equally Between them.

5. Furthermore I give and bequeath to my grand son Sam'l Manter all that percell and tract of Land which belongeth to me sd Jno Eddy Lying in the Township of Chilmark, (which was formerly purchased by me and my son in Law John Manter of Major Matt: Mayhew of Edgarttown) to be his and his heirs ferever with all Priviledges and appurtenances thereunto belonging

And I do Constitute make and ordain my well beloved and Trusty friends Mr. Benjamin Manter of Tisbury & Mr. James Allen of Chilmark the Executors of this my Last will and Testament.

And I do hereby utterly revoke disallow and make void all and every other former wills & Testaments Legacys bequests and executors by me in any ways att any Time before named Willed and bequeathed Ratifying and Confirming this and no other to be my Last Will & Testament.

In witness whereof I Have here unto sett my hand and seal the Day and Year above written

John Eddy (seal)

Signed sealled Published and ordared by the Sd John Eddy as his Last Will and Testament in the presence of us the subscribers, viz:

Josiah Torrey
Sarah Torrey
William Case

The death of this prominent citizen and his only son without male issue before him removed the name of Eddy henceforth from our records, but it has survived as a baptismal name in several families. The following are his children:

Alice Eddy, b. 3 May 1659, m. 16 Mch. 1682-3 Benjamin Hatch, (Falmo. Rec. in Gen. Adv., III, 84).
Sarah Eddy, b. prob. 1661, m. 1 May 1681 Nathan Manter of Tisbury (problematical).
Elizabeth Eddy, b. prob. 1663, m. 11 Dec. 1683 Jonathan Lambert, (Barnstable Rec. in G. R., III, 272).
Hepzibah Eddy, b. prob. 1665, m. 9 May 1686 Moses Hatch of Barnstable, (vide Otis Gen. Notes 471).
Hannah Eddy, b. prob. 1670, m. (date unknown) John Manter of Tisbury, d. 24 Oct. 1724
Beulah Eddy, b. about 1680, m. about 1701 Enoch Coffin of Edgartown
Benjamin Eddy, b. about 1685-6, d. 27 May 1708 aet. 24
Abigail Eddy, b. about 1688, m. Thomas Trapp 18 Jan. 1716-17 and d. 14 Feb. 1717-8, aet. 29 y. 5 m.

EDWARD HAMMETT

The first of this name to reside in Tisbury came here from Taunton, at the solicitation of Matthew Mayhew, who deeded to him in 1706 a tract of land in Chilmark, "to give incouragement to Cloathing."[1] Edward Hammett was by trade a worsted comber, and took up his residence in that part of the town now known as North Tisbury. He was married in Taunton in 1704 to Experience Bowles of that place and brought his wife and one child to his new home. Here ten more children were born to him, four sons and seven daughters in all, of whom Jonathan and Robert remained on the Vineyard to perpetuate the name. The daughters married here also. Beyond doing his citizen duty as juryman occasionally, he held few public offices during his residence here. He served as constable, tithingman, and surveyor of highways, the latter for a considerable period till his death, and these compose his career as a town officer. He died March 20, 1745, in the 66th year of his age, which makes the year 1679-80 the date of his birth. His wife survived

[1]Dukes Deeds, II, 72. Nothing has been developed regarding his antecedents. There is a fantastic legend about him to the effect that his mother, a beautiful English girl was captured from a ship by some Algerian pirates and she became the consort of the chief. A son was born who bore the name of Hamid and when he grew up his mother told him the secret of his birth and bade him escape to her own people, which advice he followed. Those who wish to believe this story will probably do so. There were Hammets living in Plymouth, Newport and Boston contemporaneously with Edward of Tisbury, but no relationship between them is evident.

him. In his will dated March 16, 1744-5, which was probated on May 7th following, he mentioned all his children.[1] In the census of 1850 three families of this name lived in the town.

JONATHAN LAMBERT.

This pioneer of a numerous family came from the Cape as one of the later settlers, about 1692-3, having been previously a resident of Barnstable. He was born in 1657 and had married Elizabeth Eddy, daughter of John Eddy of this town in 1683, and this relationship was doubtless the influence which brought him here. He had served in the famous expedition to Quebec in 1690 under Sir William Phips, but after this single essay in military life he settled down on the Vineyard to follow the peaceful occupation of carpenter.[2] In 1694 he bought a tract of land bordering on Great James pond of the Sachem Josias, and ever since that date the name of Lambert's Cove has been a memorial of his residence in that region.[3] Here he lived until his death, and his sons and grandsons remained on the paternal acres until it became thoroughly indentified with the family. His life was uneventful as he was a deaf mute, and the records give but little to indicate any public activities. Two of his children were also unfortunately afflicted with congenital deaf mutism, the first known cases on the Vineyard. Sewall refers to him during his visit in 1714 to the island: "We were ready to be offended that an Englishman, Jonathan Lumbard in the company spake not a word to us, and it seems he is deaf and dumb."[4] His will, dated March 23, 1736-7, was probated Oct. 3, 1738, and his death occurred between those dates.[5] He left three sons and four daughters, the latter of whom married on the mainland. Ebenezer and Beulah, the mutes, remained single.

THOMAS LOOK.

The first of this family to settle here was Thomas, a son of Thomas Look, a collier at the Lynn Iron Works. The

[1]Dukes Probate, III, 180.

[2]He received a share in Narragansett township No. 1 (Gorham, Me.) for military service. In 1695 Jonathan Lambert, master of the Brigantine *Tyral*, was despatched to Quebec to bring back prisoners from that place. This may be our early settler.

[3]Dukes Deeds, I, 248.

[4]Diary, II, 432.

[5]Dukes Probate, III, 1. In his will he provides as follows: "considering my two Poor children that cannot speake for themselves, I Earnestly Desire that my son Jonathan and my Trusty Beloved friend David Butler, after the understanding hereof would Please as they have oppertunity to help them in any Lawful way as they shall see need."

father, born about 1622, settled in Massachusetts, whither he had come probably from Scotland to follow his trade at the newly established iron foundry at Lynn. The name Look is derived from the biblical Luke, and the first settler so spelled it. It is a name found in Scotland before 1600 among the rentallers of the Archbishop of Glasgow.[1] Thomas, the collier, became one of the original ten associates of Salisbury in 1659 who purchased Nantucket, and through this transaction his son Thomas, born June, 1646, removed to that island about 1670 and took up the share as a settler. There he married Elizabeth Bunker, and four of his six known children are recorded as born there.

The date of his removal to Tisbury may be placed about 1685-6, as he made the first purchase of land in town on Feb. 15, 1686, acquiring of Joseph Merry the valuable water and mill privilege on the Tiasquin which his descendants improved for over a century.[2] Here he spent the rest of his days, following the occupation of a miller until his death. He was a selectman in 1688 and 1695, surveyor of highways in 1689, and deputy sheriff of the county in 1699, besides the usual services as juror. He was one of four dissenters against extending a call to Rev. Josiah Torrey as minister, but the reasons for this are not known.[3]

His will, dated Dec. 4, 1725, when he was four score years of age, was signed with "his mark," probably because of infirmities or disability from illness. It was probated in January, 1726, and we may conclude that he had died in the latter part of the previous year, making some allowance for the time before the will was presented for the action of the court.[4] He called himself "miller" in this testament, and bequeathed all his property to his son Samuel and five daughters.

HENRY LUCE.

The ancestor of the largest island family left behind him fewer traces of his movements, before and after his coming to the Vineyard, than any other of the first settlers. The first record we have of him is

[1]In the next century there were several opulent merchants of the name of Luke in the city of Glasgow. It is also of record that a considerable number of Scotchmen were employed at the Lynn Iron Works (Essex Antiquarian, XII, 70). A Thomas. Lucke was a merchant of Penthurst, Co. Kent, in 1662 (Suff. Deeds, IV, 35).

[2]Dukes Deeds, I, 290.

[3]Tisbury Records, 42.

[4]Dukes Probate, II, 3.

on November 13, 1666, when he was a juror in Scituate, where he may have resided, and in 1668 he was admitted as a proprietor of purchased lands in Rehoboth.[1] The similarity of the name to Lewis, together with the varieties of spelling both names in early records, renders identification difficult. Lewis was written Luis, Luice, Lewes; and Luce appears as Lews, Lewse, Luice and Luse. The origin of the name is unknown to the author, as it is of the rarest occurrence in early English records, though the name Lucie or Lucy is well known. The Connecticut branch has a tradition that the family is of Huguenot extraction, while another statement is to the effect that it originated in Wales.[2] When he came to the Vineyard, or through what connection, is not known, but he had acquired before Feb. 1, 1671, a home lot on the west side of Old Mill river about forty rods north of Scotchman's Bridge road.[3] There is no record of the purchase, and he is not known to have been related to any of the settlers in the town. When he came here he had already married, probably in Scituate, Remember, daughter of Lawrence and Judith (Dennis) Litchfield of that town, about 1666, and had brought with him two or more children to his new home. His wife was born about 1644, and estimating him a few years older it would make 1640 as the probable date of his birth. He joined the "Dutch Rebellion" of 1673; was chosen surveyor of highways, 1675; juror, 1677, 1681, and selectman, 1687; the last recorded appearance of his name being on May 12 of that year. In March, 1689, his widow Remember is mentioned, and his death occurred between those dates. He was then a comparatively young man, but left behind him ten sons, all of whom married and seven of them begat large families to perpetuate the name. In 1807 there were 41 distinct families of Luce on the Vineyard, the largest quota of any of the island patronymics, and it has probably maintained the supremacy in the century which followed.

Besides his home lot, he owned at Great Neck, and by the several proprietors' divisions had land at Kepigon. To this he added by purchase 60 acres in Christian town border-

[1]Plymouth Col. Records; comp. Suffolk Deeds, VII, 163. The History of Scituate says he was of Barnstable (vide, p. 305).

[2]History of Windham, Conn; comp. N. E. Hist. Gen. Reg., XXXI, 415. The spelling of the name in the island records is uniformly Luce and his signature is in that form. There was a Thomas Luce in Charlestown, according to Farmer (Gen. Dictionary), who had a son Samuel b. 1644, but of whom nothing further is heard. It is probable that this was Lewis.

[3]Tisbury Records, 5. The name is spelled Lewes in this case.

ing on Great James pond. There is no record of any division of his estate among the heirs, all minors probably at the time of his death, but there are scattering references to such an allotment. The same obscurity attends the wife and widow of Henry Luce as followed him. This grand old Puritan mother of ten children was living as late as 1708, but the date of her death or burial place is not known. She left not less than 42 grandchildren, of whom twenty were boys, on the Vineyard, which is exclusive of those of the Connecticut and New Jersey branches.

JOHN MANTER.

This early settler in the town was one of the Cape Cod men. He was first known there at Eastham, when in 1657 he was admitted as a freeman, under the name of John Mantah.[1] From this, supposing him to have been at least 21 years of age, the date of his birth can be placed at 1636 or thereabouts. In 1668 he was on a coroner's jury in the case of the accidental death of Isaac Robinson, Jr., of Barnstable, older brother of our Isaac.[2]

John Manter married Martha, daughter of Bernard Lambert, July 1, 1657, who was born in Barnstable Sept. 19, 1640, and died in Tisbury Oct. 3, 1724. Eight children of record were born to them. At some date unknown, probably before 1668, he removed to Falmouth, then called Succonessit, where he acquired considerable property. He remained there until 1677, when he became attracted to the Vineyard and effected an exchange of his house and lands there on Dec. 24, 1677, with Nathaniel Skiffe, one of the early proprietors of this town. He gave Skiffe

> "my house with threescore acres of land adjoining thereunto; all other housing appertaining thereunto lying and being in the township of Sacconessit in the Collonie of New Plymouth with a whole share of meadow lying in the great marsh with a share of meadow in the little marsh which I bought of Jonathan Hatch with all my meadow lying at the Bass pond with half a town right in all undivided lands and meadows with all and singular privileges and apputrenances whatsoever thereunto belonging."[3]

In return he received the eastern half of the Josiah Standish lot on which the house of the late Henry L. Whiting now stands.

[1]The name being an unusual one was frequently misspelled in the Cape Cod records and appears as Martin occasionally.

[2]Plymouth Col. Rec., V, 7.

[3]Dukes Deeds, I, 272.

For some reason this did not suit his purpose and on May 4, 1678, he bought of Thomas[3] Mayhew the seven-acre lot on the east side of the Chilmark road, at the turn opposite the church, together with that part of a "neck of land" adjoining on the south, and east of "Merrys Field," and a half lot to the north, formerly belonging to James Skiffe, Jr. These properties remained in the family by inheritance for several generations. Two years later he sold the Standish lot to Mayhew.[1]

John Manter began early a career of usefulness in the town. He was on a committee to lay out land, Sept. 29, 1677,[2] his first recorded appearance here, and in 1679 and 1689 was chosen surveyor of highways. In 1681 he was a juror and in 1692 was appointed as Ensign in the Foot Company of Tisbury. This military instinct seemed to be transmitted to his descendants, particularly through the line of Whitten,[3] whose sons Robert and Jeremiah served in the French and Indian and Revolutionary Wars. He was chosen selectman in 1699, 1703, 1704, 1705, and had acted in behalf of the town in minor capacities previous to those dates.[3] By this time he was about three score and ten and sons had grown up about him to take his place, both destined to follow in the footsteps of their father as useful citizens.

He died probably early in 1708, as his will, dated Sept. 12, 1698, was admitted to probate May 25, 1708, and the last time his name appears in the town records is March 28, 1707, in a division of land.[4] The following is an abstract of his will:—

> To Son John all my land at "Keephegon" and all my several shares of land in the necks eastward from the Old Mill Brook, and half a common write in said town.
>
> To Son Benjamin my Dwelling house, with all my lands both meadow land and upland ajoining thereto with all out housing and fencing whatsoever thereto belonging and also half a common write in said town.
>
> All my movable estate unto his three daughters to be divided equally among them.[5]

It will be seen that Benjamin inherited the homestead, and then, after his father's death, added by purchases of his own, the entire section bounded by the Chilmark road, Mill

[1]Dukes Deeds, I, 98, 267.
[2]Ibid., II, 306.
[3]Town Records, 31, 45, 48, 50.
[4]Tisbury Records, 52.
[5]Dukes Probate, I, 19, 20.

path and Old Mill brook on the east, which constituted the Manter estate until the present century.

Mrs. Manter survived her husband sixteen years, and died at the ripe old age of eighty-four.

JOSEPH MERRY.

This prominent pioneer of Tisbury is first found as a resident of Haverhill, Mass., in 1640, where he lived with a wife named Mary until about 1654, when he removed to Hampton, N. H. There his wife died April 4, 1657, having given birth to one child of record, Joseph, b. Dec. 19, 1654. The father, Joseph, was a carpenter by trade and plied his craft in Hampton as he had done before in Haverhill. Shortly after his wife's death he bought a house and ten acres of upland in Hampton, of Thomas Coleman, Sept. 29, 1657, and at the age of 47 years found himself a widower, with possibly a child to care for in his new home. But this was not long to remain so. Emanuel Hilliard of that town was drowned shortly after this in October, 1657, leaving a widow Elizabeth, daughter of John and Phebe Parkhurst of Ipswich, England, and sister of George Parkhurst of Watertown, Mass. The young widow was then about 29 years old, and before two years had passed she entered into a marriage covenant with Joseph Merry, who was then 21 years her senior. In this agreement he gave her the house and ten acres he had recently acquired, and sometime about Dec. 13, 1659, when the covenant was dated, they set up housekeeping, and four children were born to them in rapid succession, who later spent their days on the Vineyard. This explains the curious epitaph on the gravestone of Joseph in the West Tisbury cemetery — "That being verified in him Psalms 92 14 They shall bring forth fruit in old age," a reference to his second marriage after middle life and the raising of a family.

Joseph Merry and his young family, consisting of Hannah, Abigail, Bathsheba and Samuel, born between 1660 and 1669 in Hampton, continued residence there till 1670, when in some way he became attracted to the Vineyard. If we are to credit the tradition that Governor Mayhew's first wife was a Parkhurst, possibly the sister of George of Watertown, it will be seen that Elizabeth Merry was related by marriage to the proprietor of Martha's Vineyard and thus the family connection is responsible for Merry's migration. However that be, almost as soon as the new township of Tisbury had been bought by Pabodie and his partners, Merry bought of Benjamin Church, on Nov. 19, 1669, the grist mill and its privileges "uppon the westermost Brook of Takemmy" with one eighth part of the propriety, or two shares, in the new settlement. The purchase price was £90 and Merry paid for it in whole or in part with his Hampton property, the homestead, an island of salt marsh and two shares in cow and ox commons in that town. The deeds finally passed Dec. 2, 1670, (Mrs. Merry and Nathaniel Batchelor acting as his attorneys by previous appointment), and from this it is presumed that Merry was already at the Vineyard attending to his new purchase and preparing the new home for his little family. The property purchased consisted, as laid out, of the mill on the New Mill river so long operated by the Looks, with land adjoining on the west side of the road, and about eighteen acres on the east side of the road, bounded by the river. This last lot is still known as "Merry's Field" after a lapse of two and a half centuries, though the property did not remain in the family beyond 1705. After operating the mill for five years, Joseph Merry sold that part of his estate to Tristram Coffin of Nantucket, and being then about three-score-and-ten years of age it is presumed that he devoted the rest of his life to his trade and tilling the soil. There is no record as to the location of his house, but in all probability it was in his "Field." His public services were few. He was constable in 1675, road surveyor in 1678 and 1687, and was chosen to divide common lands in 1689 and 1690. On March 2, 1677-8, the grand jury presented him "for contempt of authoritie in not obeying the summons in his Majesties Name to give in testimony" and for this he was mulcted in the sum of five shillings. In 1681 he sued Simon Athearn in the sum of £20 "for non payment of a frame of an house," but the two compromised on £7 and divided the costs. On July 12, 1689, being then about 82 years of age, he gave his homestead by deed of gift to his only son Samuel, then just entering his 21st year, and from that date on until 1701 his name appears but once in the records, when he gave some "information" about the ancient bounds of a town lot, being then in his 94th year. He passed the century mark in 1707 and died April 5, 1710, at the remarkable age of 103, undoubtedly the oldest person who has ever lived in the town. It is not known whether he survived his wife Elizabeth, as there is no record of her death nor a stone at her grave. If she survived she was 82 when her husband died. Of his children further evidences of longevity are noticeable. His daughter Abigail Pease died in her 80th year and Hannah Skiffe at 97 years.

EDWARD MILTON.

It is probable that this settler was a resident of Sandwich and prior to that may have lived in Boston, but no definite statement can be made without further evidences of identification.[1] He was one of the later settlers receiving a grant of land Oct. 2, 1701, next the minister's lot on the east side of Old Mill brook. In the spring of that year he had married Sarah Manter (17) of this town, and these dates probably indicate the time of his settlement. His name appears but few times in the records, as surveyor of highways in 1703, constable in 1715, and grand juror in 1722. In his will, dated July 30, 1731, he calls himself yeoman, "advanced in years." It was probated Sept. 11, 1733, and this last year may be taken as the date of his decease.[2] As he left no sons the name became extinct at his death, and if any descendants now live here they may trace descent through his daughter Elizabeth, who married Joseph Foster.

ISAAC ROBINSON.

The first of this family to come to Tisbury was Isaac, the second son of Rev. John Robinson, famous as the pastor of the Pilgrims at Leyden, Holland, and of Bridget White his wife.[3] "He came not to New England" writes Sewall, "till the year in which Mr [John] Wilson was returning to

[1]An Edward Milton took the oath of allegiance in Boston in 1679 and was taxed in 1681 in that town. Judge Sewall in his Letter Book refers, in four letters, dated 1687-1691, to Edward Milton as a carpenter at Sandwich, building a church there for the Indians, the first built in the English manner (Chamberlain, Historical Discourse). Experience Mayhew in "Indian Converts," refers to him and his "religious family" (p. 257).

[2]Dukes Probate, III, 3.

[3]Rev. John Robinson was a native of Lincolnshire, born about 1575. He matriculated at Emanuel College, Cambridge, in 1592, becoming a Fellow of Corpus Christi six years later. He resigned in 1604 and became identified with the Puritans or Dissenters, and fled to Amsterdam about 1608 and thence removed in 1609 to Leyden. His record as spiritual leader of the English exiles, who later became the "Mayflower" Pilgrims, is well known. He died March 1, 1625. His wife, whom he had married in Northampton, England, Feb. 15, 1603, survived, and perhaps came to New England in the fleet with Winthrop (Letter, Shirley to Bradford, March 8, 1629-30).

England after the settlement of Boston."[1] This was in 1631, and Isaac immediately settled at Plymouth, later removing to Duxbury (1634), Scituate (1636), Barnstable (1639) and Falmouth (1660). In Scituate he married for his first wife Margaret, daughter of Theophilus and Eglin (Mortimer) Hanford, June 27, 1636, sister of Rev. Thomas Hanford of Norwalk, Conn., and niece of Mr. Timothy Hatherly. By her he had five children and after her death (June 14, 1649), he married second, Mary Faunce, 1650, and four more children, all sons, were the fruit of this union.

By reason of his parentage he was a prominent man in Plymouth Colony, but later in 1669, for displaying liberality toward the doctrines of the Quakers, was disfranchised by Governor Thomas Prince. It appears that he had attended their meetings for the purpose of showing them the error of their ways, but instead of accomplishing this, became self-convicted and embraced some of their beliefs. He was restored to citizenship in 1673 by Governor Winslow.[2]

It appears that Isaac Robinson with others, in 1660, decided to leave Barnstable presumably for the Vineyard, and took letters of dismissal to the church at Great Harbor, but finally decided to settle at Falmouth.[3] How long he remained an actual resident of that town is not known, but in May, 1671, he was admitted a proprietor of the new settlement at Takemmy, and probably soon after this became identified with Tisbury. At this time he was about 60 years of age, having been born in 1610, and he was perhaps, with the exception of Joseph Merry, the oldest resident of the new settlement. In 1673 he became associated with the "Dutch Rebellion," but suffered no punishment therefor, unless the records are silent regarding him. His four sons by the second marriage, Israel, Jacob, Peter and Thomas, became residents of the Vineyard, though none of them left descendants here to perpetuate the name. Those who resided here in the next century were his descendants through his first marriage. His son Israel, baptized Oct. 5, 1651, assumed the name of Isaac in memory of an older half brother of that name who was

[1]Sewall, Diary. He came in the ship "Lyon."

[2]The old record of disfranchisement is interlined with the words:—"there being some mistake in this the said Isaac at his request is re-established." (Hist. of Falmouth, 13.)

[3]Records, Church, West Barnstable, comp. History of Falmouth. He built his house in 1661 on the neck between Fresh and Salt Ponds, Falmouth Heights (Ibid., 14).

drowned in 1668, and was ever after known by the adopted name.[1] This change made two Isaac Robinsons in the town and creates difficulties in identification of the one whose name appears on the records, but it is probable that he is the "goodman" Robinson chosen townsman in 1678, 1680, 1683, rather than the younger of the name. He had his home lot on the east side of Old Mill river, bounded on the south by the Mill path. This he sold in November, 1701, to his son Isaac, together with all his dividend lots in various parts of the town.[2] He was then over ninety years of age, but continued to reside here, presumably with one of his sons. Sewall saw him here when on a visit in 1702 and thus refers to the incident:—

"He saith he is 92 years old is the son of Mr. Robinson pastor of the ch. of Leyden, part of wch came to Plimo. * * * * I told him I was very desirous to see him for his fathers sake and his own. Gave him an Arabian piece of gold to buy a book for some of his grand children."[3]

According to tradition this scion of a distinguished family died about 1704 in Barnstable at the home of his daughter, Mrs. Fear Baker. "A venerable man," writes Prince in his Annals, "whom I have often seen."

His sons Isaac and Jacob remained in Tisbury, dying within eighteen days of each other, in 1728, while the other two brothers, Peter and Thomas, removed to Connecticut early in the 18th century.

WILLIAM ROGERS.

From his home in the neighboring island of Nantucket came William Rogers, bringing with him his wife Martha and children, Ebenezer and Experience. He had been here possibly continuously since June 29, 1669, when he signed as witness to a deed,[4] but the first positive indication of his settlement here is found ten years later in the following extract from the town records:—

It is vootted by the inhabbitants in a towne mitting that will. Rogges shall purchchis therty eakers of land of sias Sogimer for for an heritance the toune is to chuse two men to liit out and the saide rogers is to buld upon it and to live upon it fouer yeare and what the saide rogers cann purchis more it is to reteune to the toune againe[5]

[1]He signed as Israel in 1670 and 1671. Tisbury Records, 3, 4.

[2]Dukes Deeds, II, 35. This establishes the identity of Isaac Senior as the resident here, as his son Isaac was childless.

[3]Sewall, Diary.

[4]Tisbury Records, p. 1.

[5]Ibid., p. 13.

This was dated Oct. 8, 1679, and on Jan. 29, 1679-80, he bought of Josias the Sachem twenty acres within the limits of the Indian town at a place called Animtissewoksett, or Animtesawohqussuk, by the Indians.[1] There he built a house and lived an uneventful life for thirty years, troubled only by that strenuous townsman Simon Athearn, with whom he had the misfortune to run amuck. On May 26, 1685, he charged Athearn with appropriating some of his cattle, but the Court divided the number disputed and awarded half to each. He then sued Athearn for slander, but was non-suited. The next year on June 2, 1686, he returned again to the fray and charged Athearn with stealing a cow, and by the record it appears that Athearn in the presence of the court plucked Rogers "by the eres and cauelled him thefe with other Skurvie words." The jury took Athearn's view of it.

On Oct. 31, 1687, he mortgaged all his real estate to James Skiffe, an incumbrance that was later satisfied. On Oct. 13, 1699, be bought of Samuel Tilton all the latter's rights to Homes Hole Neck, which was one third, and held it during his lifetime. He occupied none of the town offices during his residence of perhaps two score years here, and as he lived almost in obscurity so he died at a date unknown to us, but somewhere prior to Feb. 9, 1714.[2]

His wife, named Martha, was daughter of Robert and Jane Barnard of Nantucket, testified in a land suit in 1696, being at that time 49 years of age, which would place her birth about the year 1647, and from this we may estimate the probable age of her husband.[3] It is supposed that she returned to Nantucket after his death, as some of her children lived on that island, and that she is the Martha Rogers whose death on Jan. 23, 1717-18 appears in the Nantucket records.

JEREMIAH WHITTEN.

According to Savage (Genealogical Dictionary, IV, 532), there came in the "Elizabeth and Ann," in 1635, one Thomas Whitten, aged 36 years, bringing Audrey aged 45, who may have been his second wife, and Jeremy aged 8 years, but he

[1]Dukes Deeds, III, 288; comp. Court Rec., 1716-17. Case, Praying Indians vs. Ebenezer Rogers. His house was near the "Red Ground" so called in 1701 (Tisbury Records, 41).

[2]Deeds, III, 170.

[3]Sup. Jud. Court Files, Case No. 4714.

does not know what became of them.[1] It can now be stated that he settled at Plymouth, where in 1643 Thomas and Jeremiah Whiton or Whitney were "able to bear arms." Before 1657 Jeremiah had removed to Sandwich as he appears that date to take the oath of fidelity. In 1660 the father gave certain property rights to his son Jeremiah[2].

The four original proprietors of Takemmy admitted, among others, in May, 1671, Jeremiah Whiten to joint proprietory rights, and if this be the Jeremy of 1635, as it undoubtedly is, our Jeremiah was forty-four years old when he took up his residence and cast his lot in the new township of Tisbury. His homestead is thus described in the records:—

> June the 27 1673 the Record of the lands And Accomadations of Jeremiah Whitin in Takymmy or tisbury on the vineyard. One house Lot which containeth fourty Acres [lying on the west side of the brook where his dwelling house] is this present year or 1673 bounded by the hey [way] And James Allens lot on the south being fourty [rods by the brook] more or less And the brook on the east And runing eight score rods in length westward being fourty Acres more or less. And the sixth part of the neck by John Eddys of [which half] the sixth and furdermost lot next the poynt is Jeremiah whitins Leying Across the neck as the neck is devided to every mans [lot], contained in the neck as before mentioned in the order of the devision of the three necks bareing dates the first of february [1671]. And the sixteenth part of all undevided lands whether purchased or to purchesse or that may be purchased
>
> This is the record of the lands And Accomadations of Jeremiah Whitin[3]

At the time of his coming here he was married to Elizabeth, daughter of John Daggett, of Watertown and the Vineyard. She was born about 1638 and two children were born to them, Thomas and a daughter Mary, b. May 1, 1666, recorded in the town book of Tisbury, though it is probable she owned some other place as her native town. Thomas died young.

Jeremiah Whitten remained in Tisbury the rest of his days, until death terminated his earthly career late in 1711. There is no record of his decease, nor of his wife's, and no

[1]With him came three Morecock children, probably belonging to his second wife by a previous marriage. They were certified by the Vicar of Benenden, Co. Kent, as to "conformity" in religion, but their names cannot now be found in the records of that parish. The name Whitten was commonly written Whitney in the Plymouth records.

[2]Thomas Whitton (Whitney) is frequently mentioned in the Plymouth records and was a juryman every year 1643-1667. He married twice after the death of the wife Audrey (before 1639), and in his will he mentions son Jeremiah and grandson Thomas.

[3]This lot was between the cemetery and Scotchman's Bridge road.

gravestones mark their last resting place. His will shows that the "aged Mother Elizabeth my wife" was living in November of that year. The daughter Mary married Benjamin Manter and the son-in-law with his wife were the beneficiaries of his estate, subject to support of the widow during her lifetime. Whitten Manter received a gun "which formerly belonged unto my son Thomas Whitten deceased" (Probate, I, 33). His estate inventoried at £283, 7s.

In his lifetime he made but little impress, if we may judge from the infrequency of appearance of his name in the town records. He was selectman in 1679, and on the committee to rearrange the town books in 1689, and this constitutes all that is known of him. The name became extinct here at his death, but that of Whitten Manter was familiar to past generations, and all the descendants of Benjamin Manter may look to him as a common ancestor.

EARLY TRANSIENT RESIDENTS

REV. BENJAMIN ALLEN.

The first college graduate from Tisbury was the youngest son of James Allen, Esq. He was born in 1689 and as the last of a large family of boys was given the benefit of a college education to fit him for the ministry. He studied theology, it is said with the Rev. Jonathan Russell, father of his classmate Jonathan, with whom he went to Yale and entered the class which was graduated in 1708, and whose daughter Rebecca Russell became the wife of his brother Ebenezer Allen of Chilmark. When Benjamin got his degree of Bachelor of Arts he was about 19 years of age, and it is supposed that he returned to his home for a while before entering upon his calling. In 1710 he was preaching for a short while at Chatham, but not as a settled minister. He appears to have been in Barnstable, though not in a clerical capacity, for he found a wife there, whom he married April 5, 1712, Elizabeth, daughter of Deacon Job and Hannah (Taylor) Crocker, born May 15, 1688, and with her he next appears at the re-settlement of Worcester, in 1715, when he remained about two years. He removed to Bridgewater where, on Aug. 17, 1717, he preached for the first time in the newly incorporated South Parish in that town, and on July 9, 1718, was ordained as its pastor, "but being an unsuccessful manager of his private secular concerns, he fell into debt, and his parish, after often relieving him, became at last weary of it, and he was dismissed by an ecclesiastical council." He preached his last sermon there on Oct. 11, 1730, and for several years he seems to have had no settled work. His next field of labor was in Falmouth, Province of Maine, a new (Second) Parish being formed in that part of the settlement known as Cape Elizabeth in 1733, and he was installed as its pastor Nov. 10, 1734, and this charge he held until his death. The installation sermon was preached by the Rev. Samuel Willard (Harv. Coll., 1723). He preached at this frontier town for twenty years, when on May 6, 1754, his death terminated a ministry that was eminently successful. The following account of him appeared in the Boston Gazette of June 25, 1754:—

> Falmouth June 13, 1754. No more Account having been given of the late worthy Pastor of the Second Church in this Town, the Rev. Mr. Benjamin Allen, I think it proper to inform the Publick, that the said Rev. gentleman died here on Monday the 6th of May last, in the 65th year of his age; and on Thursday following was honourably interr'd at the Expense of his Flock. God sent him to us in the height of his Powers and Usefulness and continued him a blessing for upwards of 20 years. He was justly accounted a Person of superior intellectual Powers, and withal a good Christian and Minister of Jesus Christ, well accomplished for the sacred office and faithful in discharge of the Trust committed to him, as well in pastoral Visits as Publick Administrations, thereby making full Proof of his Ministry, and being an Example to the Flock: His Discourses were nervous and solid, his Method clear and natural, his Delivery grave, serious and pathetick, more adapted to reach the Hearer's Hearts and Consciences, than with Words and Phrases to gratify the Fancies of the curious. He was of a healthy, strong Constitution, his Eye never dim while he lived; and tho' he used a strong Voice, yet it was easy, and without straining, and seemed not to spend for most of his Days. He was in some of his last years much impaired by Lethargick and repeated Shocks of paralytick Disorders, yet continued in his Lord's Works, till they with a Fever returning with greater Force, Nature could no longer bear up. After being last seiz'd, he continued to the tenth Day, but scarce speaking a word, much disordered in his Senses, and taking little Notice of any Thing. He was exemplary in every Relation, a kind Husband, a tender Father, a wise Counsellor and affectionate, faithful Friend. His Conversation very agreeable and entertaining; and tho' so well accomplished a Person, he was withal affable, condescending, humble and modest, never that I could observe or hear elated with Pride upon any Occasion. His disconsolate Yokefellow continues still struggling with her Infirmities, waiting for her change. He had Nine children, six of which survive him, a son and five Daughters.

The son referred to in this obituary notice was Joseph, born February 14, 1720, who is said to have matriculated at Harvard College, but was not graduated.

His eldest daughter, Hannah, married Oct. 8, 1742, Rev. Stephen Emery, Harvard College, 1730, who was born Aug. 3, 1707, and died May 24, 1782, and she died June 7, 1799. He was settled at Nottingham, N. H., 1741-8, and at Chatham, Cape Cod, from 1749 till his death. His daughter Elizabeth, born in 1716, married Clement Jordan, Esq., April 29, 1744, a prominent resident of Falmouth, and she died May 23, 1752, before her father. Another daughter, probably named Dorcas, married Tristram Jordan, Esq. in December, 1778, a prominent citizen of Saco, Maine, for his second wife, and died Dec. 19, 1781, without issue. Another daughter married Rev. Joseph Crocker, Harvard College, 1734, of the South Parish in Eastham, now Orleans. The fifth daughter married Rev. Caleb Upham, Harvard College, 1744, of Truro, Cape Cod.

ARTHUR BEVAN.

The name of this early transient was variously written Biven, Beven, Buiven, Bivens, and it probably is a Welsh patronymic. He was married when he came here but, of his antecedents prior to removal to the Vineyard nothing has been learned. He is first mentioned in 1677 in the court records, when he was fined for a breach of the peace. He was plaintiff in a suit for recovery of money due in 1680, and in the next year entered complaint against Simon Athearn for trespass and obtained judgment. What his status in the town was before 1682 is not clear, as he did not acquire property till that year. He then bought several tracts of land on the west side of Old Mill brook on the road leading to North Tisbury, including the house and home lot of Thomas West, and resided there until his removal. He was chosen town commissioner in 1688, a title which probably had the significance of selectman, but beyond this he held no public office. He sold his holdings in 1692-4, and before 1695 had removed to Glastonbury, Conn. He died there Dec. 15, 1697, leaving a widow and twelve children.

SAMUEL BICKFORD.

Before his residence in this town Samuel Bickford had lived in Salisbury and Nantucket.[1] He had married Mary, daughter of our Edward Cottle, and followed his father-in-

[1]He may have been the son of John Bickford of Dover, N. H., and the father of Jeremiah Bickford of Eastham and Yarmouth, Cape Cod.

law in his several removals hitherward as already detailed. The last record of him in Nantucket is in 1679, and in 1680 he was a witness to a document recorded here.[1] In 1681 he was called "of Tisbury" as defendant in a suit. How long he remained on the Vineyard is not known, and nothing further has been found to throw light on his residence here.

CHARLES CROSSTHWAITE.

The stay of this individual on the Vineyard was of short duration, probably not extending over two or three years, but it is not possible to determine just when he came or the time of his departure, for his name does not appear on the land records. Whence he came is unknown. He received a grant of a half lot in the town, on the east side of Old Mill brook, bounded northerly by the Scotchman's Bridge road, containing twenty-two acres, and presumably built a house thereon.

He was one of the anti-Mayhew party and in 1673 joined the ranks of the insurgents, being one of the signers of the petition to the Massachusetts authorities against the Governor. With the rest he suffered the consequences and chose to seek better social and political conditions elsewhere. On Oct. 28, 1675, he appeared before the town in meeting assembled "and acknowledged that he had made legall sale of his house landes and all Rightes and priveledges which he had in the Town of Tysburie unto Thomas Berrick" and the town at once confirmed the transfer and placed it on record.

He went thence to Boston, where by wife Judith, four children are recorded to him, George, b. 1671, probably died young; George, 1676; Charles, 1678; and John, 1680, and that is the last we hear of him. Whether he married here, or left any descendant through a daughter is not known, but the presumption is all against it.

WILLIAM PARSLOW.

This transient was another contribution to our early population from the Cape. He was born in 1660 and came here as a young man about 1685, probably from Harwich.

[1]Dukes Deeds, I, 266. In 1678 Tobias and Thomas Coleman of Nantucket sell to Bickford "an accomodation [of land] by us received of the said Samuel Bickford in a parsell of land at Mathews Vinniard as appears by our deed from him.' In 1679 Bickford conveys the same property back to the Colemans (Nantucket Deeds I, 75; II, 27). There is no record of what this property was in any of our town or county books and doubtless it has disappeared with other of the early Tisbury records.

He bought the west half of the Standish home lot in 1686 and remained about ten years, perhaps following his occupation as weaver. During this period he served as constable in 1688, his only public appearance. He removed to Harwich before July, 1696, and was living there in 1717, when his wife Susanna, daughter of Joseph Wing of Sandwich, died. She was sister of the Nathaniel Wing who was a land owner here, and of the Joseph Wing, who married Jerusha Mayhew (33) of Edgartown.

JAMES REDFIELD.

He was the son of William Redfin (Redfyne, probably same as Redfern), whose name was afterwards written in the form used by our settler. William Redfin with his wife Rebecca was first at Cambridge, Mass, in 1639, and sometime before 1653 removed to New London, Conn., where he remained until 1662, the date of his death.[1] The son James was born about 1646, probably after his parents had moved to Connecticut, and on the decease of his father was bound out till his majority to Hugh Roberts of New London.[2] In 1666 Redfield was "rated" in that town, his master having removed, and in May, 1669, he married Elizabeth How at New Haven, where he also removed about this time, as would appear by the birth of a child the next year at that place.[3] About 1671 he is found in Tisbury, where he took up a lot on the east side of Old Mill brook, near where the late Dr. D. A. Cleaveland resided. His possessions are thus described in the town records:—

The Lands And Accomadations of James Redfield which Leyeth in the Township of Takymmy or Tisbury on the vineyard as folloeth one half house Lot which containeth twenty five Acres Leying on the East side of the brook where his dwelling house is this present year one thousand six hundred seventy & three bounded with the brook on the west And Joseph doggats half Lot on the north & Isack Robinsons Lot on the South being twenty-five rods in bredth And runing in length eight score rods easterly from the brook being twenty five Acres more or Lesse And halfe the Sixth part of the neck by John Eddys of which halfe the fifth lot is James Redfields Leying on the south side of Joseph doggats halfe lot Leying Acrosse the neck as the neck is devided to every mans share Contained in the neck As before spoken in the order of devision of the three necks baring date february the first 1761

And the two And thirtyth part of all undevided Lands whether purchesed or that may be purchesed This is the Lands And Accomadations of James Redfield but to be remembred the purches not yet paid[4]

[1]American Ancestry, III, 108.
[2]Caulkins, "History of New London," and New Haven Town Records.
[3]Redfield Genealogy, passim.
[4]Tisbury Records, p. 4.

Redfield became identified with the opposition to the Mayhew regime in 1673, and was arrested and fined like the rest after the "Dutch Rebellion" had collapsed, but upon public acknowledgment of his "error," and "in consideration of his poverty," the fine was remitted.[1] It is probable that he was unable to remain under these circumstances, and his lot was forfeited, being regranted to John Tucker a few years later.[2] He returned to New Haven, where on May 8, 1674, he is called "now resident" of that town, and acted as representative of the "rebels" on the Vineyard in their further attempts to secure their rights.[3] In 1676 he was recommended as a fit man to have charge of the fort at Saybrook, Conn., and presumably he went there, as in 1683 and 1686 he had grants of land in that town.[4] His wife is believed to have died there and he is next found at Fairfield, Conn., where in 1693 he married a second time, Deborah Sturgess. By these two wives he had the following children: Elizabeth, 1670; Sarah, 1673; Theophilus, 1682; Margaret, 1694; James, 1696, none of whom remained on the Vineyard, or married here. It is supposed he died about 1723 in Fairfield.

SAMUEL RUSSELL.

This early resident was the son of George Russell of Scituate, and was connected by marriage with William Pabodie. The latter sold his home lot to George Russell, Jr., from whom it passed to Samuel his brother in a short time. It is not known whether George ever resided here, but it is certain that when Samuel came into possession of the lot he entered on it as a settler and became identified with the Vineyard. This is shown by his participation in the "Dutch Rebellion" in 1673, and as in the case of many of his associates in that affair, it resulted in his withdrawal from the island altogether. He probably returned to Scituate, and in the early part of King Philip's War fell a victim in the assault of the Indians on Rehoboth March 28, 1676, leaving two daughters, Mary and Elizabeth, as heirs to his Tisbury estate. His widow, Mary, married Cornelius Briggs, and Russell's interest in the estate, in 1683, passed to Simon Athearn by purchase.

[1]Dukes Deeds, I, 65.
[2]Tisbury Records, p. 10.
[3]N. Y. Colonial Mss., LXXV 124.
[4]Town Records, Saybrook, Vol. I.

This lot became the object of a troublesome suit in 1716, when Joseph Briggs, son of Cornelius, entered claim for the Pabodie lot, and being defeated in the local courts appealed to the Superior Court at Plymouth.

JAMES SKIFFE, SENIOR.

The father of James, Nathaniel, Benjamin and Nathan Skiffe who became settlers on the Vineyard, was himself a non-resident proprietor and his connection with the town was very brief and unimportant. However, as the progenitor of a numerous and influential family he deserves special mention aside from his original ownership of one of the first home lots. James Skiffe first appeared in New England at Lynn, Mass., about 1635 and is said to have come from London.[1] He had some association with Isaac Allerton of Plymouth, who came from London and was a passenger in the Mayflower, 1620, and "for his service Donn to Me Isaack Ollerton" he was granted land in Sandwich Jan. 14, 1636-7, which place became his permanent residence.[2] He was representative to the General Court, beginning in 1645, for thirteen years, and in 1656 was appointed to train the militia, and in various ways was a leader in the public life of Sandwich.

His interest in this town undoubtedly was of a speculative character, brought about through his son James and his acquaintance with James Allen, and was subsequent to the formation of the partnership of James, junior, with Peabody, Allen and Standish. He was admitted as a proprietor on May 20, 1671[3] and granted a full share of land. His lot was on the west side of Old Mill river, and his holdings in the town are thus enumerated:—

Thes are the Lands of Jeams Skiffe senier [in the] the township of tisbery: one lot containing forty ackers Bounded on the est By the reiver on the north By thomas wests Lot on the south By the heyway that leieth on the north sid of henery Luessis Lot and so runeth from the reiver westward fore poles in length and one Lot In the gret neck Bounded on the est by Jeans allins Lot on the west by Samuel russeles Lot with a

[1]No proof of connection with any English family has yet been discovered. A John Skiff and wife Joan lived in Modingham, Kent, England, in 1609, when the husband died.

[2]Plymouth Colony Court Orders, I, 98. It is probable that Skiffe was in the service of Mr. Allerton as the context of the grant indicates this as the reason for the grant.

[3]Sup. Jud. Court Files, No. 4974.

sixteenth part of all undevided landes and meddo the devided Landes Being more or les as thay are Laied out thes are the Landes purchused by the above named Jeams Skiff
recorded by ordor of the town: febbarary the 5: 1674[1]

This lot he gave to his son Nathan on June 15, 1675, and his quitclaim of it, when Nathan sold to Arthur Bevan, June 9, 1687, is the last record of him in connection with the town and Vineyard.

His first wife is said to have been Margaret Reaves, and he had a second wife named Mary, by one or both of whom he had the following named children:—[2]

I. James, b. 12 September 1638. Came to Tisbury.
II. Stephen, b. 14 April 1641.
III. Nathaniel, b. 20 March 1645. Came to Tisbury.
IV. Sarah, b. 12 October 1646; m. Thomas Mayhew.
V. Bathshua, b. 26 April 1648, m. Shearjashub Bourne.
VI. Mary, b. 24 March 1650; m. Matthew Mayhew.
VII. Patience,[3] b. 25 March 1652; m. Elisha Bourne.
VIII. Benjamin, b. 15 November 1655. Came to Tisbury.
IX. Nathan, b. 16 May 1658. Came to Tisbury.

It will thus be seen that through his children James Skiffe, senior, transmitted a powerful influence upon the affairs of the new settlement. His wife Mary died Sept. 21, 1673, but it is not known how long after 1687 he survived.

JAMES SKIFFE, JUNIOR.

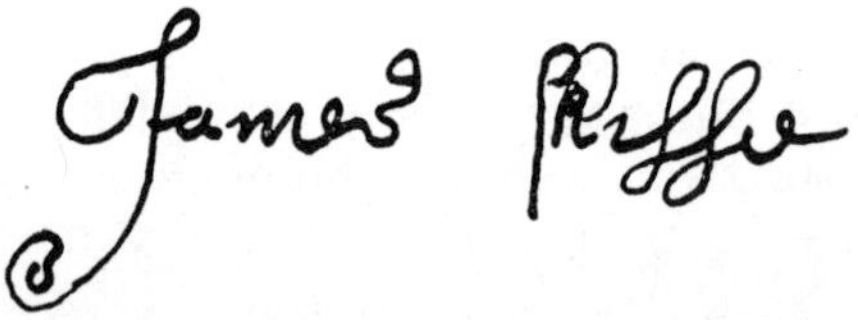

Although one of the four proprietors of Tisbury, yet his relation to the town was of a transient character. His home lot was on the west side of Old Mill brook just south of the Whiting property but how long he resided on it is not known. It passed into the possession of Nathaniel Wing some time before 1677, and it may be inferred that the participation of the Junior Skiffe in the "Dutch Rebellion" of 1673 may have been the cause of his departure. He does not appear to have been punished for it directly, but the ruling family found opportunity to reach

[1]Tisbury Records, p. 8.

[2]Sandwich (Mass.) Records. An Elizabeth Skaffe was buried at Rehoboth in 1676, possibly a daughter.

[3]This name is written Marianne, apparently, but Patience is believed to be correct.

him in other ways. Thomas Daggett entered complaint against him in 1674 for slander, in calling him "a theif, a lyer and knave and other opprobrious words," as previously related (vide Vol. I., pp. 166-7), and thenceforth his usefulness and personal safety were ended. He remained several years, the last record of his residence here being in 1677, and then removed to Nantucket. He had contracted a second marriage with Sarah, daughter of Robert Barnard of that island, in March, 1676-7, and thenceforth became a townsman there.[1] The fruit of this union was five daughters and a son, but as the latter was killed in 1723, supposedly unmarried, this line of Skiffes became extinct. The daughters married and died in Nantucket. He became a deacon of the church, and was living in 1719, when he visited Chilmark with one of his married daughters.[2] He was then eighty-one years of age, having been born Sept. 12, 1638, and his death occurred not long after. His widow Sarah survived and died in 1732.

JOHN TUCKER

This transient came to Tisbury from the Province of Maine, where he had been a pioneer in the eastern portion of that province, at Cape Annawaggon, Sheepscot Bay.[3] He was in Dartmouth, England, in 1659,[4] which was probably the region of his birthplace, and in 1662 he purchased land at Sheepscot.[5] There he resided with his family until driven off by the Indians in 1675, when he migrated to the Vineyard. His home lot was on the east side of the Old Mill river, next north of Isaac Robinson. He at once became an active citizen in the new settlement, being chosen surveyor and constable in 1675 and town clerk in 1679 and 1680.[6] But he did not long survive, as in July, 1681, Susanna, the widow of John Tucker, "late of Martha's Vineyard," is mentioned in the Plymouth Colony.[7] His son John was living in Harwich, Cape Cod, in 1716 and at that date disposed of his father's interests in Tisbury to Samuel Cobb.[8]

[1]Nantucket Records, III, 75. His previous marriage and divorce has been noted in this history (I, 474).

[2]Diary of Rev. William Homes, May 31, 1719.

[3]Dukes Deeds, I, 372.

[4]As witness to a deed. York Deeds, I, 103.

[5]Essex Deeds, LIV, 228.

[6]Town Records, 12-14.

[7]Plymouth Colony Records, VI, 65.

[8]Dukes Deeds, III, 132. Comp. Essex Antiquarian, IV, 32; VIII, 47.

ECCLESIASTICAL AFFAIRS.

The beginnings of the religious history of this town can probably be dated coincidentally with the coming of the first settlers, although there is nothing of record in the town books touching this subject until ten years after the "first purchase." As was the case at Great Harbor, there was but a handful of settlers in the early years of the town's existence, and the easiest available means of securing ministerial services and a place in which to hold them were adopted by the planters. In the division of the Takemmy purchase, made May 20, 1671, by the original proprietors, Pabodie, Allen, Skiffe and Standish, when they "devided the whole into twelve partes or shares" they provided "one for a minister."[1]

This lot had already been laid out and its dimensions and boundaries were as follows:—

> The Lands & Accomadations which belongeth to the minisstrie in takymmy or tisbury on the vineyard as foloeth
>
> One house Lot with an Adishon of low land unto the house lot the house Lot Leying on the East sid of the brook next northward unto the halfe lot once grannted unto Mr John [Bishop] upon condishon but to be remembrd, there is to be A heye way betwen this Lot And halfe Lot or there A bout most conveniant over the brooke up into the woods East And west so—this lot is to run fourty rods in bredth northward And in length Eastward eightfoor rods and the addishon of low land is all the low land betwen the lot And Simon Athearns fenc but the upland which leyeth betwen Simon Athearns lot and the lot for the minisstrie is left Common
>
> And the seventh part of the great neack as before spoken in the order of the devision of the three necks for an Inhearitanc for ever bareing date the first of february 1671 as also a sixteenth Part of all the undividedd lands and meadows lying within the bounds of said Town ship of Tisbury whether Purchased or to be purchased of the Indians[2]

MINISTRY OF JOHN MAYHEW.

The Rev. Thomas Prince, the New England chronologist, is our authority for the statement that the Rev. John Mayhew, the youngest son of the ill-fated missionary, was called to preach in Tisbury as soon as he had reached his majority. This was in 1673, when this young man, who more than any of his kindred resembled his gifted father, is described as "of great worth and usefulness and fell not short either of

[1]Supreme Judicial Court Files, No. 4974.

[2]Tisbury Records, p. 5.

the eminent genius or piety of his excellent progenitors." He had these inherited scholarly inclinations, which were early developed by the aid of his grandfather's teaching and the benefit of his father's library. As his older brothers, Matthew and Thomas, applied themselves to executive and judicial duties, the way was cleared for him as one of the co-heirs of the proprietary, to devote himself to the work of his choice.[1]

He began his ministry coincident with the establishment of marital relations. He was married in 1672 to Elizabeth Hilyard, orphan daughter of Emmanuel Hilyard of Hampton, N. H., who at the time of her marriage was a little more than seventeen years of age. She was brought to Tisbury by her mother, who had become, after the death of her husband, the second wife of Joseph Merry. With his young bride, he set up a home for himself at Quansoo, where he ever after lived, raised a large family of eight children, the eldest of whom was the celebrated Experience, and there ended his days. It appears that he was "minister of the Gospel to the inhabitants of Tisbury and Chilmark united," as testified by the epitaph on his gravestone, and it can be readily understood that such an arrangement for a joint pastorate would have been the natural plan for the two small communities lying contiguous.

THE FIRST MEETING HOUSE.

Where the services were held first, whether in Chilmark or Tisbury, is not known, but it can be surmised that the school house, frequently mentioned about that period, may have served for a time as a meeting-house. Situated as it was on the South road, near the boundary line of the two towns, it would admirably serve this purpose That a meeting-house was built before 1700 in this town seems to be a clear inference from the vote of the freeholders: "at a Leagall Town meeting [29 November, 1699] by the maiger part of the town that this meeting house shall be put in Convenient Repair." This action, however, does not seem to have been entirely satisfactory to "the maiger part" after subsequent consideration, for the next year the town expressed a determination to build a new "meeting-house."[2]

There are no church records extant covering John Mayhew's ministry and our only knowledge of his work, which

[1]Indian Converts, p. 302-306.

[2]Tisbury Records, 32, 40. The first meeting house was probably built before 1604 as there was at that date a "publique place for religious services. (Ibid, 25)

continued until his death on Feb. 22, 1668-9, a period of sixteen years, is to be found in scattered contemporary documents, from which this slender thread of facts enables us to weave an equally slender narrative of a long pastorate.

On June 17, 1679, the townsmen of Tisbury took action for the first time, so far as the records indicate, to make provisions for the support of the ministry, as expressed in the following vote:—

June the sevententh day: 1679

It is agread and ordred by the touns men of tisbury that from this day and forward that theare shall be two men chosen by this toun to rayse fiveten pounds yearly from year to year for the worck of the ministry by way of a rate apon all that shall attend the publique meteing in this place and the men to be chosen from year to year and that thay shall make the said rate according to theare best descration and shall see the said sum truely paid [1]

This provision for the support of the ministry appears to have been (in the absence of any other record) the stipend paid by the town to its minister at this date, and this small amount would equal about three hundred dollars, on the basis of comparative values at the present time. Nevertheless, this worthy and zealous man accepted this as a sufficient reward for his modestly appraised labors. It is related by a writer touching this point that although "what was allowed him was very inconsiderable indeed yet he went steadily on in this pious work and would not suffer any affairs of his own to divert him from it." In 1687 the Commissioners of the Society for the Propagation of the Gospel increased his salary by thirty pounds per annum, in consideration of his additional work among the Indians.

PASTORAL VACANCY, 1689–1701.

The death of this worthy man left a vacancy which was not filled for a number of years, and it is not known that any person regularly held services for a decade following. The oldest son of the deceased pastor, Experience, was but sixteen years old when his father died and therefore not yet ready to walk in his footsteps. As soon, however, as he became of age in 1694, the town passed the following vote:—

"at a town meeting at tisbury the 26 day of october 1694 we the Inhabitants do freely desier you Mr Experience Mayhew to Come to the

[1]Tisbury Records, 13.

publique place upon the Lords daye to teach us according to the measure and gift that god hath given you the which we hope and are perswaded will tend to the glory of god and our comfort by Jesus Christ our Lord[1]

It is supposed that the desired arrangement was effected, although there is no further reference to the subject in the records, either by payment of salary annually or in other ways. The young man was not an educated or ordained clergyman and had only been invited to "teach," which term was used to distinguish this form of ministerial supply from that of a settled pastorate. The community was not, however, entirely without opportunities of attending religious services of a regular character for coincidental with the above request to young Mayhew, the neighboring town of Chilmark had called a minister, the Rev. Ralph Thacher, to be their pastor, and it is not improbable that the people of Tisbury drove over on Sundays to his services, when no one was present to conduct them in this town. But this sort of ecclesiastical poaching on their neighbors' preserves did not satisfy the people of Tisbury and they set about the task of securing a minister who should be regularly settled.[2] It appears that they applied to the Rev. Jonathan Russell of Barnstable for advice and help in this matter, and as an expression of the gratitude of the town for his efforts in their behalf the townsmen wrote a letter to him. In it they say:—

We render you hearty Thanks for all the Christian fatherlike Care and pains you have taken for our Better Settlement: and now againe for your Care of and Advice to us[3]

At a town meeting held on May 28, 1700, the freeholders voted the sum of £20 per annum "towards the support of an orthidox Learned and pious person to be settled our ministerr who is also to Inherit for ever a valluable posesion of Lands saved for him in tisbury: being the first settled ministe: therein in tisbury." Recognizing that this amount was not a temptation to many they expressed the hope that "all such persons of honour as are concerned in power to add unto sd 20 lb. sum other way that such a minister may be able to live upon: for our poverty & other necessary charges is such that we cannot procure above 20 lb. per year."[4]

[1]Tisbury Records, 25.

[2]Three Athearn children were taken to Barnstable for baptism about this time. In November, 1699, the town voted that the meeting-house shall be put in "Convenient Repair."

[3]Tisbury Records, 35.

[4]Ibid.

Reverend Mr. Russell was asked to obtain "Mr. [Nathaniel] Stone or some other orthodox Lerned and pious person" but Rev. Mr. Stone had just been settled in Harwich and was not available. He recommended another in the person of John Robinson.

The town entered at once into negotiations with him to supply the vacant pulpit and the matter proceeded so far that at a town meeting held on July 23, 1700, it was voted "that Roberbert Cathcart shall go to barnstable a mesenger for this Town to accompany mr John Robinson over in order for setlement in the work of the ministry in Tisbury."

It was also voted at the same meeting "that mr John Robinson shall at his Comming Take up his place of Residence at Simon Atherns house."[1]

It is supposed that this candidate was the Rev. John Robinson, who settled in Duxbury two years later,[2] and not connected with the Robinson family of Cape Cod, nor with the early settlers of the name in Tisbury. There is nothing to indicate whether this minister came or preached here. If he did, he remained a very short time. On June 21st the next year a committee consisting of Ebenezer Allen and Robert Cathcart, was appointed "to prossicute the obtaining of an orthodox minister for this Town in way and manner as hath been heretofore prossicuted by this Town."[3]

SECOND MEETING HOUSE.

While this committee was engaged in this search, and before a candidate was finally selected, the town took practical steps towards building another and undoubtedly larger meeting-house to accomodate the gradually increasing population. On the same day the following vote was passed:—

> It is voted and agreed upon by the maiger part of the freeholders and other Inhabitants then met at a Leagall Town meeting that there shall be built in Tisbury a new meeting-house after the manner and dementions of the meeting-house in Chilmark and it is also voted that Simon Athern and Robert Cathcart shall agree with a Carpinter in behalf of This Town of Tisbury to build the said meeting-house as Cheap as they Can[4]

[1]Tisbury Records, 36.

[2]Winsor, History of Duxbury, 185. He was called to Duxbury on Sept. 2, 1700 but did not accept for two years. His salary in Duxbury was £60 annually.

[3]Tisbury Records, p. 40.

[4]Ibid.

Concurrent with this the town petitioned the General Court for financial assistance in the furtherance of this object. The petition was favorably considered and on June 26th of the same year the following resolve was passed:—

RESOLVED that the sum of fifteen Pounds be Allowed out of the Publick Treasury to the town of Tisbury for their Assistance in Building a Meeting House.[1]

At the town meeting held on October 2d following, much important business was transacted relating to the new meeting-house, its location and the settlement of a minister. In the first place it was voted to raise the sum of sixty pounds "for the building a new meeting-house," by assessment on the polls and estates. The location was determined by the generosity of James Allen, who on that day made a gift of land for this particular object. The brief record of this first public gift to the town is as follows:—

Know all men by these preasents that I James Allen of Chillmark do give and grant unto the Town of Tisbury an acker of Land Lying within abigall peses fence for Ever for a burying place and to set a meeting house on free from me my heires or assignes for Ever

October 2: 1701[2] JAMES ALLEN

The town accepted this donation by passing a vote that a new meeting-house should be "set upon an acker of land . . . . . which Mr. James Allen granted to this town for a buring place." This lot is the "God's Acre" on the west bank of the Old Mill river, which for two hundred years has been a cemetery for the town and here for one hundred and sixty-five years the townspeople assembled weekly for worship. The "dementions" of this building as first constructed are not now known, except that it was to be the same as the structure then existing in Chilmark. As no records of that town are extant prior to 1704 we are left without means of determining this interesting point.

MINISTRY OF JOSIAH TORREY.

Josiah Torrey.

The committee which had been charged in June previous with the duty of procuring "an orthodox minister," reported that they had secured Rev. Josiah Torrey, whom they recommended as a suitable person for settlement as their pastor.

[1]Mass. Archives, XI, 160.

[2]Tisbury Records, 40

The townsmen thereupon passed the following vote:—

Mr Josias Toary shall be the minister of Tisbury according to their former proceedings for the call and setlement of a minister in Tisbury.[1]

But this action was not unanimous. The call was passed "by the maiger part of the Inhabitants" as it appears of record, yet four of the freeholders, Thomas Look, Joseph Daggett, Edward Cottle and Zachariah Hossuet (an Indian), separately "enters his decent against the above writen vott," but the reasons therefor are not stated. Their objection may have been to his youth, for he was then scarcely entering his twenty-first year. The young clergyman was the son of Josiah Torrey, by his wife, Sarah Wilson, and was born Feb. 9, 1680, in Boston. It is believed that this was his first pastoral charge. He had graduated from Harvard College as Bachelor of Arts in 1698 and thus had received the highest education obtainable at that period. In fact all of his successors in the pastorate during the century which followed were Harvard graduates.

The Selectmen of Tisbury refused to act on the matter of raising the sixty pounds, and at a town meeting held Dec. 2 following, Simon Athearn, Robert Cathcart and Experience Luce were impowered to "assess the Town of Tisbury & precincts the said sum of Sixty Pound."[2] During the period while the new house was under construction, services were probably continued in the existing building used for the purpose. The new meeting-house was probably completed in the early part of the summer of 1702, for in July of that year the old building was sold at public auction.[3]

These are the formal records of the building of the church and beginnings of the pastorate which continued twenty-two years. Mr. Torrey, following the example of the other ministers to the English, devoted a portion of his time to missionary work among the Indians. Increase Mather, in a letter to the governor of the New England Company, under date of March 2, 1705, speaks of him as "a hopeful young man who had

[1]Tisbury Records, 42.

[2]Tisbury Records, 43. "At the same time Peter Robinson and Experience Luce were authorized to "Receive in of the people of the Town and preacincts what they are willing to allow to Mr Tory."

[3]"July 17, 1702. At a Town meeting held in Tisbury it was voted by the major part then preasant that the ould meeting house should be sould at an outcry: also it was voted that he that bid most at three times going Round should have it and at the last time of biding which was the third Time of asking on the third going Round Robert Cathcart was the bider who bid five pounds six shillings"

learned the Indian tongue, and begun to preach to them in their own language."[1]

The records covering the period of his ministry do not disclose anything to indicate other than harmonious relations between pastor and people. He was paid twenty pounds per annum with occasional arrearages until 1717, when it was voted to pay twenty-four pounds "to Gratifie & reward the Reverend Mr. Josiah Torrey for his Labour in the ministrye for the year 1716." The next year, finding themselves unable to meet this charge, they voted at a town meeting "to send a petition to the General Court for their assistance in allowing them sum Relieff in helping them to maintain their minister out of the publique Treasury."[2] Whether this was granted does not appear, but at a town meeting on August 11 following, it was voted:—

> That Mr Torrayes Salary be raised to thirty pounds per annum provided that he the said mr Josiah Torrey do accept of the same and will be obliedged to tarry with them and preach for Ever in the work of the ministrie in Tsibury[3]

Annually thereafter this amount was voted for his salary throughout the remainder of his pastorate. It is evident that he filled his office to the satisfaction of the people, although in recording his death the Rev. William Homes of Chilmark writes in his diary: "it was said that of late he had drunk too freely and too frequently of spirits."[4]

After an illness of some months, during which he had been "under a bad habit of body," he died on Saturday, Oct. 7, 1723, "in the 43d year of his age," and was buried the next evening. He married Sarah, daughter of Simon and Mary (Butler) Athearn of Tisbury, by whom he had four daughters, Sarah, Susanna, Mary and Margaret, the eldest daughter becoming the wife of Rev. Nathaniel Hancock, his

[1]In his "India Christiana," published in 1721, Cotton Mather thus speaks of Parson Torrey's labors: "The Rev. Mr. Josiah Torrey, Pastor of the English Church in Tisbury on the Vineyard, has also for many Years Past Preached as a Lecturer unto the Indians on that Island, having for that End learned their Language. He Preacheth in some or other of their Assemblies once a Fort-night, and goes frequently to their Church-Meetings, to advise & assist them."

[2]Tisbury Records, 68, 69.

[3]Ibid., 69. This indicated a firm belief that Mr. Torrey had partaken of the "Elixir of Life."

[4]That he at one time shared a barrel of rum with Paine Mayhew appears in the latter's "Commonplace Book," now in the possession of a resident of the Vineyard, according to a memorandum of a division entered therein, viz.: "in ye small cask 15 g. to be taken out for tory,"

successor in the pastorate. His personal estate was inventoried at £295–19–10 and his real estate, including the ministerial share, was equally divided in 1730 between his daughters.[1] This ministerial share was granted to Mr. Torrey in perpetuity with certain conditions Aug. 16, 1704, as shown by the following vote:—

> That all the ministers lands in Tisbury with all the priviledges there to belonging to Mr. Josiah Torry who is now minister, for an inheritance for ever: he Taking office in the work of ministrie in Tisbury & in consideration that if at any time the said ministers Lands be sould that the Selectmen of Tisbury have the Refusall in Proffer to buy said lands for the use of the Town and ministrie, for Ever.[2]

The town at the annual meeting in March, 1724, voted to raise fifty pounds for the support of a minister, and on May 20, following, Experience Luce was chosen "to go of to the main and to use all proper means to supply the town with a minister that the publick worship of God may be upheld with us."[3] It appears that a Mr. Benjamin Ruggles was a candidate in August of that year and he "proposed his willingness to abide and take office in the ministry" in the town if "encurraged with a present settlement of two hundred pounds and seventy pounds pr. annum sallery for sum time and then eighty pound per anum for the futer," but while the freeholders agreed to give the settlement named they would not agree to more than fifty pounds as a salary. Jabez Athearn and Experience Luce were chosen as a committee to treat with Mr. Ruggles and to petition the General Court and the Society for Propagating the Gospel "for sum assistance."[4]

That the town needed help would appear from the fact that it was already indebted for unpaid salary to their late pastor, and on August 10th of that year it was voted to raise £15–16–3, "to clear our Rears that was due to the Rev. Mr. Josias Torey now desesed for his Labours in the ministry." That the committee failed to come to terms with the Rev. Mr. Ruggles, probably for financial reasons, may be concluded from a vote passed Nov. 23, 1724, by which Jabez Athearn was chosen "to go over to the main" in quest of another candidate.

[1]Dukes Co. Probate Records, II, 59.

[2]Tisbury Records, 49, 50. This became the basis of a famous suit for possession as elsewhere related.

[3]Ibid., 83.

[4]Ibid., 84.

MINISTRY OF NATHANIEL HANCOCK.

The town adhered to its vote of fifty pounds per annum or a proportionate sum "to such person as shall come upon tryall: . . . . . in case there shall not be an agreement made."

Mr. Athearn secured the Rev. Nathaniel Hancock, a young man about twenty-five years of age, the son of Nathaniel Hancock of Cambridge. He was graduated from Harvard in the class of 1721 as Bachelor of Arts, and during the years 1722-3 had taught school in Woburn. He was a second cousin to the celebrated John Hancock of Revolutionary days. This was the person whom Athearn induced to come forward as a candidate. He began preaching early the next year, and on March 29, 1725, "the town having had Tryal of the abilities of the Rev. Mr. Handcock in the Ministry . . . . . and having had the approbation and advice of the reverend neighbouring Ministers," voted to call him at a salary of fifty pounds per annum with two hundred pounds as a settlement.[1] But the young clergyman was not disposed to hasten matters, and while he continued to preach regularly he kept himself free from the responsibility of a settled pastorate. He was at this time unmarried, and it may be that his mind was more or less concerned with the probabilities of a matrimonial settlement with the young Miss Torrey, who was to become his wife. On Oct. 24, 1725, Jabez Athearn and Experience Luce were chosen a committee to petition the committee on Indian affairs of the General Court, "to se whare they will alow aney incuragement to the Rev. Mr. Handcock in case he doth Learn the Indaen Langueg & preach lectures to them." In this they were not successful.[2]

On May 23, 1726, the question being still undecided the town renewed its offer for a settlement on the same terms as formerly voted. Still Mr. Hancock hesitated to commit himself, and while he continued to occupy the pulpit as a stated supply for many months, yet it was not until January 26, 1726-7, that he finally decided to accept the town's proposal. The following is his agreeing letter to the terms of settlement and salary:—

To the Church of Christ and Other Inhabitants in Tisbury:—

Having taken Under Consideration the Call you have given me to Settle in the Work of the Gospell Ministry among you as also the Pro-

[1]Tisbury Records, 86.
[2]Ibid., 87.

posalls made to me for the Encouragement Respecting my Outward Subsistence with you, Bearing Date 23 May 1726 I have at Length come to the following Thought and Resolutions, vizt:—That the offers you made to me be very low and so the Encouragement in that Regard be very slender, yet considering the smallness of the Place and how few the Inhabitants are and that what you offer may be near as much as for the Present you are able to Do for me: Having also Considered the Poor as well as others ought to have the Gospell Preached to them: Relying on the Gracious Providence of God, That God whom I Desire to serve & under him on the Justice & Generosity of the People by whom I am called, I do (you still continuing Desirous of it,) accept of your Call, both as to your offers in my Settlement & Sallery: and as I think, the call of God to serve Him in his work among you; and am content that my former answer (being not yet on Record) should become void, and be Committed to the Fire; this only with your Invitation and Proposals being Preferred and Recorded. And if what is now offered be acceptable and satisfactory to you, I Desire, in the strength of Christ, and under a Deep sense of my own Insufficiency for so Great a work, to devote myself to your Service, Resolving according to the best of my ability, & the measure of the grace of God granted unto me, to endeavor to Promot the good of your souls; Earnestly Desiring and Praying that we may be helped in our Respective Stations, so to Discharge the duties Incumbent on us that we may be Mutual Comforts one to another, here in this World, and Rejoice together in the day of the Lord. So I remain yours in the service of the Gospell.

Tisbury, 26th January, 1727.

NATHANIELL HANCOCK."[1]

The townsmen, gratified at last to have him come to a favorable decision, sent him a letter of thanks and caused all the correspondence to be spread on the records.

The ordination of Mr. Hancock took place in the following July, and the ceremonies on that occasion are thus discribed by a contemporary writer:—

July 30 1727. Being Lords day Mr Handcock preached both before and afternoon from James 2. 23 And he was called the friend of God: the discourse was not very animate yet hope it may be useful. Lord follow thy word and ordinances with a blessing. The day was fair clear and hot. On Wednesday last, being the 26th instant, Mr. Handcock was ordained Pastor of the Church in Tisbury. I preached the ordination sermon and Mr Russell and I imposed hands on him, for there was none other minister there. Mr Russell made the first prayer and I gave the Charge and made the second prayer, and Mr Russell gave him the right hand of fellowship[2]

From the remark made by the diarist as to the absence of other ministers it is supposed that reference was intended

[1]Tisbury Records, 90.

[2]Diary of Rev. Wm. Homes in Maine Historical Society Library.

to the Rev. Samuel Wiswall of Edgartown, whose failure to join in the ordination may be variously interpreted.

Again the town tried in the year following, May, 1728, to secure from the General Court "some assistance toward the Suport of the Ministry," and Jabez Athearn went to Boston for the purpose, but it is not known what were the results, if any, of his mission. The young pastor had now attained the object of his affections, and on July 16, 1729, was married to Sarah Torrey, with whom as consort he presided over the church affairs of the town for the twenty-seven following years.

THIRD MEETING-HOUSE.

The new pastor stimulated the town to provide a new house of worship, and in January, 1733, "it was voted that a New Meeting house should be built," and a committee of seven was appointed to "Determin the bigness of the meeting house & the manner of the Seats Pews & Alleys, Doors, stairs windows & Pulpit." The committee "considered & agreed upon the following Scheem:—"

> The Meeting house is to be 35 foot in length & 30 in breadth 18 foot between Joints a Double Doore on the fore side of four foot wide & a doore at Each End of 3 foot wide with forteen Pews around the walls of five foot Extent from the walls with an Alley of 3 foot wide around within the Pews: Not allowing any alley in the middle of the body of seats but allowing four Pews behind the maine body of seats of five foot forward from the Alley to be equally divided; with a Convenient Pulpit & Deacons seat: and in the Gallery four Pews in the hinder part of the front of five foot Extent from the Walls: with Suitable Stairs & Windows.[1]

Samuel Cobb was employed to construct this building in accordance with the specifications for the sum of £320, of which amount £20 was credited as the value of the old meeting house in part payment. The frame was "raised" probably in June following and the town provided an entertainment of "good wheaten cake, good Beere & Rum & Sugar," for those participating in this curious religious custom adopted by our forefathers.[2] Three men of Chilmark were chosen

[1]Tisbury Records, 95.

[2]Ibid, 97. It faced the south, having an area in front separating it from the fence. Its west side made a part of the cemetery enclosure and its east side was parallel with the road, a board fence finishing the east side of the cemetery, partly to the front and partly to the rear. It must be remembered that the road continued along its east side to the Scotchman's Bridge road, instead of turning an angle to the west as laid out about 1872.

THIRD MEETING-HOUSE, 1733-1833.

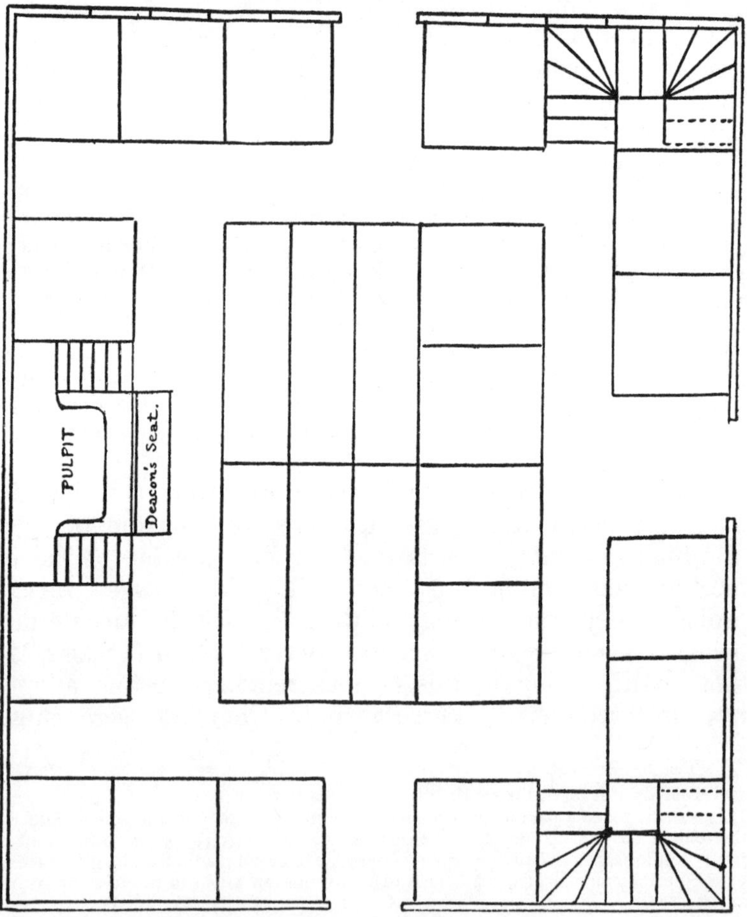

PULPIT

Deacon's Seat.

FLOOR PLAN OF MEETING-HOUSE, 1733.

as a committee to arrange the delicate question of allotments to the pews and the assessments therefor. For thirty-five years this building served its purpose as a meeting-house until the growing population had need of more room.

In 1768 it was voted "to Cut sd house in the middle and Enlarge it 15 feet and to Inlarge it 2 feet on the Back Side and to Finish all the wooden work and to Shingel the Rooff with new Shingles and to Remove the Pulpit back and to Lengthen the Galerys," and the next year it was painted "with Tarr and Oker to Preserve the Shingles." In 1771 it was plastered. In 1788 six pews were added to the accommodations for the worshippers by a rearrangement of the floor plan. Thus altered, this third house survived exactly a century as a meeting place of the religious people of the town.[1]

The pastorate of Nathaniel Hancock terminated in an ecclesiastical quarrel, the underlying reasons for which do not appear, because of the loss of the church records covering the services of himself and his predecessors also, from the beginning.[2] His salary, originally £50, was raised to £80 in 1744 and in 1747 it was made £150 old tenor, because "the fall of money & Riseing of Goods made his Sallery of but little value." The fluctuations of currency during his pastorate made continual trouble between him and the town to adjust an equitable settlement. In 1755 "severall agreved brethren of the Church . . . . obtained a Seperate Councell against their Reverend Pastor" and secured an opinion adverse to him. In February, 1756, the town voted "not to Desire sd Pastor to take a Dismission," but four months later, probably by reason of Mr. Hancock's insistence on a severance of the pastoral relation, the "Majr Part of the voters then present" (June 22) voted "to Concur with the Advice of the Late Venerable Councell." In July the church

[1]Tisbury Records, pp. 194, 270.

[2]The church records of the Torrey and Hancock pastorates were in the possession of Rev. Mr. Hancock in 1760, four years after his dismissal. The church voted that "Deacon Athearn should go to Mr. Hancock and desire him to give a record of the transactions of the Church during the ministry of the Rev. Mr. Torrey and also during his ministry" (Oct. 30, 1760). The Deacon reported that Mr. Hancock refused to give them up. What became of them is not now known, but it is traditional that they were destroyed because of the minutes they contained regarding offences committed by members of the church and the action of the officers against the offenders. The Rev. Mr. Damon began a new record book in 1760 which he continued for twenty years, but this also has disappeared, although in 1850 it was in existence. In that year, fortunately, the late Richard L. Pease made a copy of all the baptisms, marriages and funerals, and abstracted a portion of the business records. This is the only knowledge we now have of that period of the church annals, and that copy has been used by the author in the preparation of this history.

passed a vote of censure on Mr. Hancock as a result of the quarrel and this ended any further prospect of harmony.

The dismissed pastor continued his residence in town, but kept aloof from the services of the church for sixteen years, as a mark of his resentment against the vote of censure. In 1772 he petitioned for a restoration of privileges as a member. He wrote:—

> You know the terms on which I stand with respect to this church of which I am a member. I have withdrawn myself from the communion of this church now for a number of years. You have passed an act by which you have suspended me from church privileges. I own the justice of your proceedings and am desirous of being restored to your Charity. I am sensible that I have missed it greatly in withdrawing and have no other excuse to make for my conduct but this, that it has been a time of difficulty and temptation with me, which I hope the church will make due allowance for. I desire the Christian candor and forgiveness of the church.

The church on March 24th of that year, voted to accept his confession and restore him to full communion. Mr. Hancock was then over seventy years old, in poor health, and did not long survive. He became a judge of the King's Bench in 1761, sitting as a member with John Newman, who had been dismissed from the church in Edgartown. He continued to be prominent in civil affairs until his death, which occurred on September 10, 1774, in the 74th year of his age. He lies buried in the old cemetery, near the last resting place of his predecessor.

MINISTRY OF JOHN RAND.

A successor was found the next year in the person of "a Yong Gentlman as a Candidate for the Ministry, viz. Mr John Rand." He was an alumnus of Harvard in the class of 1744 and had been the college librarian (1753-5) before his coming to Tisbury.[1] At this time he was thirty years of age. On Jan. 24, 1757, a formal call was given him by the church, with the concurrence of the town, to become their pastor. A settlement of £750 and an annual salary of £350 old tenor was voted, but the candidate proposed other terms which the town thought "Rather too hard to Comply with at Present." He accepted however on May 20th, but

[1]He was born in Charlestown Jan. 24, 1726-7, the son of Jonathan and Millicent (Estabrook) Rand of that town, and related to a family of this name already resident here.

his ministry for some reason was exceedingly brief, scarcely three months. On August 12th, that same year, the pastoral relations were formally severed. He removed to Lyndeboro, N. H., and later preached at Derryfield and Bedford in the same state. He died in the latter town on Oct. 12, 1805, where he had lived for over a quarter of a century.

MINISTRY OF SAMUEL WEST.

For the two ensuing years Samuel West (55), son of Dr. Sackville West of Yarmouth, Cape Cod, a graduate of Harvard in the class of 1754, supplied the vacant pulpit, and during all this time the town, church and candidate were "dickering" about terms of settlement. He was then a young man of twenty-six and at first said "that he should Incline as Willingly to Preach at Tisbury as any other place;" but that he was not fully qualified to hold the office of minister and preacher, but "hoped with submission to accomplish that end in about the space of six weeks." Various offers were subsequently declined by him, as he insisted on the use of a parsonage.[1] This the town could not agree to, "relating to our ability" as the record reads, and matters hung thus until March 22, 1759, when he made the following reply to their last formal call:—

> I have a Tender Regard for your Spirituall & Everlasting wellfare (and) am therefore Willing to serve you as far as Godd shall enable me: But Considering the great Averseness my own Parents have Manifested about my settling here, together with my own Bodily Infermities which very much unfitt & Indispose me for studiing: for these and some other Reasons I shall be willing if the Town pleases to be Dismist from the Call you gave Me, yet if Providence should so order that the Discouragements I now labour under be Removed I shall be Ready to settle among you, In case you are not better Provided for.[2]

Although the town and church voted not to dismiss the call this reply ended his relations as candidate, and nothing further came of the negotiations. This clergyman removed to Dartmouth, Mass., shortly after, and there for nearly a half century achieved widespread fame as the pastor of the church in that place. He was a man of great intellectual ability, of marked individuality bordering often on eccentricity and in the annals of the pulpit at that period he was easily

[1]Tisbury Records, pp. 159-169.
[2]Ibid., p. 170.

a leading character. He died Sept. 24, 1807, at Tiverton, R. I. After the departure of Mr. West the town sought the services of Rev. Zachariah Mayhew of Chilmark, the missionary, but he declined the call and Mr. William Whitwell, Jr., "now Resident at Mr Zachariah Mayhews," was asked in September, 1759, to fill the vacancy, but beyond preaching for a few weeks the negotiations were dropped.

MINISTRY OF GEORGE DAMAN.

Early in 1760 the usual committee on candidates reported a success in their search for a new minister, in the person of George Daman of Dedham. He was the son of John and Elizabeth (Metcalf) Daman of Dedham, where he was born July 7, 1736, and had just graduated in the class of 1756 at Harvard College. On June 16, 1760, he was given a unanimous call by town and church to become their pastor. This he accepted on July 30th following, "not for the sake of Filthy Lucer," as he replied to them, but because he felt the call was "the Mind & Will of Christ the Great Head of the Church."[1] Mr. Daman was ordained as pastor Oct. 1st of that year. In the terms of settlement the town agreed to pay him a gratuity of £1000 and a yearly salary of £400, and at once set about providing a parsonage for his use. The town bought for this purpose of Samuel Cobb, a tract of land on the west side of Old Mill brook, with an old house and buildings thereon, now known as the Whiting homestead. The house was repaired, broken windows glazed, rooms plastered, the barn shingled and the premises made ready for the new minister, under an agreement that the settlement of £1000 should be relinquished by him in consideration of the use of a parsonage.[2]

His ministry covered the troublous times of the pre-Revolutionary period, and lasted throughout the war, when the financial situation was so greatly affected, and the people of Tisbury, like all other towns on the Vineyard, suffered from the business depression as a result of the struggle for independence. His salary was often in arrears, and payments were made in the depreciated currency of the times. In 1767 efforts were made to increase his stipend and enlarge and

[1]Tisbury Records, 175-6. He was dismissed from the church of Dedham on Sept. 14, 1760 (Records, First Church, Dedham).

[2]Tisbury Records, 177-8. This property was valued at £2000 in the depreciated currency of the time. It was made ready for occupancy in 1762 and he signed a waiver in that year (ibid., p. 182).

THE WHITING HOMESTEAD, WEST TISBURY.

repair the church, but both proposals failed. This created discontent on his part and a committee was chosen "to goe and Treet with the Revend Mr Damon Consarning his uneseness." Ten years later, 1777-8, arrearages had again piled up and a compromise was made upon partial payment, and the town further agreed to "Cut and Cart Ten Cord of Wood to sd Mr Damans Dore for his fireing the Ensuing Winter."[1] This temporary shift was repeated the next year and he offered to relinquish his salary for one year if the town would give him title to the parsonage and guarantee payments for the future. This was not favorably received by the townsmen and various alternative offers were made by them to pay his salary in Spanish milled dollars, silver bullion, "or in other specia." He was also to be allowed to preach in Edgartown "one Quarter Part of the year for his Own profitt," and another quarter in the Homes Hole district, until the time when his stipulated salary should be regularly paid.[2] The remainder of his pastorate was a repetition of the same financial deficiencies, continually growing larger and at last a committee of Chilmark and Edgartown men were chosen by himself and the town as referees "to Settle what Mr Daman should have Considering him a Sufferer with his People since the war by reason of the fall of monney." The arrangement effected by this arbitration appears to have been satisfactory, and might have resulted in his indefinite retention, but at this juncture the new society of Baptists had been formed at Homes Hole and they refused to pay their share of the ministerial taxes. This was the "last straw" and on the 2nd of March, 1781, he made formal request to the church for his dismission from the pastoral office. In his letter he recited the difficulties of his position for several years past as above related, claiming that "he did not in six years and a half scarcely receive his usual small support for one year and a half." He added that "nearly one half the town always appeared opposite to every thing that was proposed and some of them some of the foremost men for ability."[3] The church on March 28th voted his dismission, and gave him a handsome "letter of recommendation." He removed to Woodstock, Vt., after his dismission and died there in December, 1796, aged 60 years. His wife was Dinah Athearn (47), whom

[1]Tisbury Records, 226.
[2]Ibid., 230.
[3]Church Records.

he married here Oct. 14, 1762, and by whom he had three sons and four daughters.

The town concurred with the church in his dismission and then spent several months in a contest with him over his unpaid salary for past services. They voted "to Hire out the Personage to the Highest bidders" and instructed a committee "to Treat with the People of Chilmark about Hireing Some Person to Preach by Turns as they shall agree." What arrangement was finally made is not known, but religious interest was evidently at a low ebb in Tisbury at this time. For three years the records are silent on all church subjects.

MINISTRY OF ASARELAH MORSE.

This clergyman became a candidate for the vacant place in July, 1784, and in the fall of that year he was formally invited to become the pastor. He was born Jan. 27, 1745, a graduate of Harvard in the class of 1767, and had held a pastoral charge in Nova Scotia at Granville and Annapolis, about 1771; and at the time when invited here he was a resident of Harwich, Cape Cod.[1] Mr. Morse was at that time forty years of age with a family, his wife, Hepsibah Hall, being a member of the church in East Yarmouth, Cape Cod, at the time of her marriage. He accepted the call Oct. 26, 1784, and was ordained as pastor December 1st following.[2] His salary was fixed at £70 yearly with the use of the parsonage, after it should be repaired for his occupancy. His ministry continued till the close of that century and was characterized by uninterrupted harmonious relations between pastor and people. During his term of service the important subject of the support of the clergyman by taxes levied on the town had become acute, beyond amicable settlement. The Baptists of Homes Hole had continued to refuse payment of their share and in 1793 the town offered as a compromise that Mr. Morse should preach in that precinct "in proportion to the taxes they may pay towards the Minesters Sallery." This ecclesiastical shuffle was not satisfactory to the Baptists, who wished for preachers of their own doctrines, and in 1794 the town agreed to join with the inhabitants of Homes Hole,

[1]Tisbury Records, 251. In 1790 Mr. Morse petitioned the County Court for naturalization, as he had "moved out of the jurisdiction of the state into Nova Scotia some time before the late war" (Dukes Court Records, Oct., 1790).

[2]Church Records.

in a petition to the General Court, that all residents east of Savage's Line be incorporated as a separate parish for purposes of church taxation.[1] This was the beginning of the final settlement of an important and exceedingly delicate religious question which had vexed the people of the two extreme sections of the town and marked the separation of church and state matters in Tisbury. In the last year of the century, Mr. Morse asked and obtained his dismission from the pastoral office, after about fifteen years' service.[2]

SUCCESSION OF PASTORS, 1800–1900.

After an intermission of two years the Rev. Nymphas Hatch was elected to fill the vacancy, and on Oct. 7, 1801, was ordained. He held the charge for eighteen years, and on June 26, 1819, received his dismission. At the close of this pastorate the flock had become almost decimated through secessions to the new sects, the Baptists and Methodists.[3] In asking for his release after years of depression and discord, due to the numerous withdrawals, he wrote: "You have long witnessed and no doubt with much regret, the great diminution of our church by deaths, by emigration and by seceders. You are my witnesses of the opposition and may I not add variegated discouragements which I have had to encounter during my ministry."[4] Five male members only remained loyal to the old organization to consider this solemn situation — Joseph Look, Jonathan Smith, Malachi Luce, Timothy Athearn and Ephraim Luce—and they granted his request.

He was followed by Josiah Henderson in 1822, who remained four years. His agreement included the "use of the Parsonage, for Feedage and Tillage and $100 for one year, together with all that may be obtained by subscription, contribution or otherwise." The line of succession as given below includes all those ordained or installed, and those who supplied the pulpit for a year or more: —

[1]Tisbury Records, 274, 299.

[2]Mr. Morse died April 25, 1803, four years after his dismissal.

[3]Not less than forty persons withdrew during Mr. Hatch's pastorate to join the Baptist society alone; how many became Methodists is not known.

[4]Church Records. About 1817, during his ministry, assessments ceased and voluntary contributions became the method of supporting the ministers.

Joshua Payson, 1827-30; Timothy Davis, 1831-32; William Marchant,[1] 1834-35; Ebenezer Chase,[2] 1835-42; John Walker, 1843-47; Henry Van Houton, 1849-50; Lot B. Sullivan, 1851-52; Samuel Cole, 1852-59; William H. Sturtevant, 1859-77; John W. Hird, 1878; Frank L. Bristol, 1879; John H. Mellish, 1880-82; A. M. Rice, 1882-86; J. R. Flint, 1887-89; Richard T. Wilton, 1889-92; Horace Parker, 1892-98; R. C. Moodie, 1898-1904; Haig Adadourian, 1904-07; Charles G. Fogg, 1907 (present incumbent).

FOURTH MEETING-HOUSE.

The old meeting-house, which for a hundred years had resounded to the preaching of Hancock, Daman, Morse, Hatch, Payson and Davis, reached its limit of usefulness in 1833 and was considered beyond repair or remodeling. A new structure was authorized by the church and completed that year. The old building was torn down and the fourth meeting-house erected on the spot hallowed by the associations of the past. There it remained until 1865, when it was reremoved to its present location, next Agricultural Hall, and the site previously occupied by it became a part of the old cemetery enclosure.

METHODIST CHURCH.

The development of this denomination in old Tisbury dates from about 1815, when the itinerant preachers, assigned to the Vineyard, with station at Edgartown or Homes Hole, visited the western part of the island in search of converts. The earliest follower of this sect was Mrs. Mary (Chase) Lambert, and about 1820 she invited Rev. Eleazer Steele, then at Edgartown, to come to this part of the island and preach the new religion. This he did and succeeded in forming a "class" at the North Shore. Among the first converts was Captain Thomas Luce, who had lost his sight at sea, while using the spy-glass against a bright sun; David Nickerson, then a young man residing in West Tisbury,[3] and George

[1]The church records speak of him as "a missionary now here."

[2]"Reformation" John Adams, the Methodist parson of Homes Hole said of Mr. Chase in 1842: "his note preaching I think has been a lullaby" (Autobiography, 495).

[3]The following story of a "remarkable Providence," which happened to young Nickerson is related by the chronicler of this denomination: He was accustomed to read his bible after retiring to bed; the weather being cold, and he having no accommodations for a fire in his room. One night he dropped asleep without extinguishing his light. What was his astonishment on awakening, to find that his candle had burned down, having somehow caught his bible and burned the cover to a crisp, caught the bed-clothes and burned them and the bed all round his head. The fire had then gone out of itself, without so much as scorching a hair of his head. It was considered a miraculous preservation.

Weeks, who afterwards became a noted preacher, exhorter and assistant on the circuit.

The services were held in the houses of the members of this denomination, for they were few in numbers and unable to support a regular ministerial supply or to build a house of worship. Among the earlier preachers to this "class" at the North Shore before 1850 were, William Barstow, Caleb Lamb, Mark Staple, "Reformation" John Adams and Micah J. Talbot. In 1845 the present existing chapel at Lambert's Cove for the use of this sect was built and dedicated, and has been a regular station in the Vineyard district ever since.

The following list of ministers represents the successive assignments to this society by the Southern Conference since 1857. Prior to that date the ministers of Chilmark or Homes Hole were given oversight of this mission.

L. C. McKinstry, 1857; Joseph Hunt, 1858-9; Benjamin Haines, 1860; Jason Gill, 1861-2; Isaac B. Forbes, 1863; David Cook and G. A. Silfverston, 1864-5; James Dixon, 1867-8; Wm. T. Miller, 1869-70; Lawton Cady, Wm. A. Cottle and R. F. Macy, 1871; R. F. Macy and C. G. Downing, 1872; Moses Brown, 1873; Charles Stokes, 1874-5; T. B. Gurney, 1876-7; A. B. Bessey, 1878; E. H. Hatfield and J. B. Hamblin, 1879; J. B. Washburn, 1880-2; J. S. Fish, 1883-5; J. B. Washburn, 1886-7; James A. Wood, 1888-90; C. P. Flanders, 1891-3; F. D. Sargent, 1894; Walter A. Gardner, 1895; Chauncey W. Ruoff, 1896.

BAPTIST CHURCH.

The beginnings of this church here were marked with much ill feeling, caused by the refusal of the adherents of the new sect to pay the legal tax for the support of the standing order. This in addition to the resentments caused by their withdrawal from the old church, engendered much bitterness. Early in 1800 John Davis, a leading man in the new sect, as well as a prominent citizen, was arrested for non-payment of the ministerial tax and being found guilty and refusing still to pay, was sent to jail. This act aroused great excitement in all circles and the Court, recognizing its tactical error, speedily released him. Not so the members of the old church. A parish meeting was called for May 13, 1800, to consider the action of the Court in discharging Davis from prison. Ezekiel Luce, Benjamin Allen and Cornelius Dunham were chosen a committee to inquire into the matter and they reported that Davis should not have been released until he had paid his tax, and the church voted to enter a protest against this action. This occurrence did more than anything else, in all probability, to promote the schism and enlist sympathy for the new denomination.[1]

The annals of this denomination are fragmentary and date from about 1805, when there were probably a dozen residents of this town, who had joined the society previously gathered at Homes Hole, and began holding meetings at the private houses of the members. Many proselytes from the ancient congregation worshipping in the old meeting-house were made, and such was the growth of the new society that in 1820 they arranged with the authorities for the use of that building on alternate Sundays; and the next year they were so flourishing and the old church so feeble and without a pastor, that it was practically given up to Baptist preachers most of the time. The earliest known members were John and Benjamin Davis, Hugh and Jonathan Cathcart, John Hancock, Prince Rogers, William Rotch and Belcher Athearn. The first "teacher" was the Rev. Abisha Sampson, who led the new flock for about four years. His success was marked and in that period, 1807-1812, the notices of withdrawal from the old church numbered nearly thirty adults. They included Russell Hancock, Patience Allen, Mary Allen, William Athearn, Solomon Athearn, Elijah Athearn, Matthew Manter, Jeremiah Manter, Samuel Crowell, Matthew Manter, Jr., Jeremiah Crowell, Nathan Clifford, Lot Rogers, Jacob Clifford, William Ferguson, Stephen Clifford, Ephraim Dunham, Jr., Robert Rogers, Henry Athearn, James Luce, Ephraim Harding, John Athearn, James Cleveland, Clifford Dunham, Abigail Dunham, George Manter, Athearn Manter, Melatiah Norton, Edmond Cottle, Shubael Merry and Warren Cleveland.[2]

FOUR CORNERS BAPTIST MEETING HOUSE.

The first house of worship built by this denomination was located on the road to Middletown near the Scotchman's Bridge road and was completed about 1820-1 for occupancy. It was a branch of the Homes Hole church and so remained

[1]October 7, 1801 the old church voted to release from further obligations, all Baptists whose ministerial taxes were unpaid, including that of John Davis for 1799 which caused his arrest.

[2]Tisbury Records, 344-392.

until May 19, 1832, when by mutual agreement the West Tisbury congregation was recognized as an independent parish. Rev. Mr. Harris of Barnstable preached a dedicatory sermon June 4, 1832 in celebration of this event. The first minister was Jesse Pease (397) of Edgartown who remained until 1828, when he was succeeded by Seth Ewer, both of whom had had charge of the church at Homes Hole. He remained till 1835 when Jesse Pease returned and preached three years. Cyrus Miner followed, 1841-3; Charles C. Lewis, 1844; Cyrus Miner, 1845-7, whose pastorate was the last in this meeting house. It was sold and is now doing duty as a barn on the Whiting estate.

MIDDLETOWN BAPTIST MEETING-HOUSE.

The second house of worship for this sect was built in the village of Middletown in 1847, and has existed to the present time with a fairly complete record of regular services for over half a century. In 1852 the members in the village of West Tisbury seceded to form a new society. The succession of clergymen who have ministered to this church is as follows: —

O. T. Walker, 1847; —— Bray, 1850; Bartlett Pease, 1851; —— Dennison, 1852; Stephen A. Thomas, 1853; C. R. Northrup, 1861; William Hurst, 1863; Thomas Atwood, 1865; John Sawyer, 1866; —— Blake, 1869; H. P. Watrous, 1871; C. R. Nichols, 1876; —— Goff, 1878; —— Terry, 1881; —— Maury, 1883; Willard Packard, 1885; —— Hatfield, 1889; —— Vinal, 1891-3.

Since that time services have been irregularly maintained, though temporary supplies have maintained the organization through these periods, notably by Mrs. George Hunt Luce of West Tisbury. Rev. O. W. Kimball is the present pastor.

WEST TISBURY BAPTIST MEETING-HOUSE.

As a result of a church feud the members of this denomination living in the old village of West Tisbury seceded from the Middletown society in 1852, and aided by popular subscription the meeting-house now standing on the Edgartown road was built. Rev. Jesse Pease was the leading spirit in the enterprise and was its first pastor, remaining five years. The next minister was Bartlett Mayhew and later William

A. Cottle. This society never flourished after the death of Mr. Pease and its existence as a church organization has been a precarious one. The Middletown pastor in later years has supplied both churches at times, but the old church is now practically defunct and the building out of commission.

MILITIA.

The town records are singularly lacking in allusions to military affairs and references to such matters can only be found in scattering documents in other depositaries. It seems that this town combined with Chilmark in maintaining a "Foot Company," and the first reference to it occurs in 1692, when it was under command of Benjamin Skiffe as Captain, Isaac Chase as Lieutenant and John Manter as Ensign.[1] Skiffe continued as Captain as late as 1709, and in that year Paine Mayhew of Chilmark was commissioned as Lieutenant of the combined company.[2] In 1746 Sergeant Jacob Robinson and Ensign Gershom Cathcart are mentioned, showing continuous organization of the local company. In 1749 Cathcart is called Lieutenant.[3] In 1757 the following officers were in command of the town militia, and by that time the military union with Chilmark had terminated: — Gershom Cathcart, Captain; Thomas Look, Joseph Merry, John Luce and Ransford Smith, Sergeants; Thomas Butler and Joseph Cathcart, Drummers. In 1761 there were two companies in the town, as a probable result of the French and Indian Wars of that period, of which the first was under command of Peter Norton as Captain, Benjamin Allen as 1st Lieutenant, Stephen Luce as 2nd Lieutenant, and Josiah Hancock as Ensign. The second company was under command of Thomas Waldron as Lieutenant, and Noah Look as Ensign.[4] There were in addition two Indian companies in the town, the first under command of Eliakim Norton as Captain, with Thomas Allen, Lieutenant, and Bernard Case,

[1]Mass. Arch., CXII, 424. Simon Athearn recommended that James Allen be commissioned as Captain in the place of Skiffe, and Peter Robinson as Lieutenant in the place of Chase, who was the Quaker and "will not take an oath."

[2]The original commission is in possession of Miss Eunice G. Mayhew of Edgartown.

[3]Town Records, 126, 138.

[4]Mass. Arch., XCIX, 24. Captain Peter Norton was promoted to be Major of the County Regiment in the place of Benjamin Manter, who had been made a general officer in the regiment. Eliakim Norton succeeded Peter Norton in command of the first company.

Ensign; and the second under command of David Butler as Captain, with Noah Look as Lieutenant and William Foster as Ensign. In 1765, the peace having been established, there was but one company thereafter in the town; and on that date it was commanded by James Athearn as Captain, Noah Look as Lieutenant, and Russell Hancock as Ensign.[1] Particulars are wanting for details of military matters until the time of the Revolution, when such interests became merged in the general county organization. It is probable that Nathan Smith, who had seen active service in the previous wars, was a leading spirit in the foot company of Tisbury before the Revolution. The part played by this town in that great national struggle has been related. Since then the martial spirit has not been manifest in the organization of parading companies of citizen soldiery in times of peace. It is doubtful if any such existed; but if so, they were short lived and no records remain to tell the tale.

TAVERNS.

Contemporaneous with Isaac Chase at Homes Hole, Robert Cathcart became a taverner in the present village of West Tisbury. In 1701 he was licensed "to keep publike house of Entertainment," and for many years after, probably till his death about 1719, "Kithcarts," as it was called, was one of the well-known hostelries of that day. It was located on the west side of Old Mill river, not far from the store now occupied by S. M. Mayhew & Co. A diary of the visit of the famous Judge Samuel Sewall to the Vineyard in 1702, describes the local taverns he patronized on his journey. After embarking at Wood's Hole, he says: —

> Have a good passage over in little more than hours time. Refresh at Chases; from thence rode to Tisbury. First man I speak with is Joseph Daggett: he tells me Kithcart keeps an Ordinary: we go thither, the daylight being almost spent. Mr. Robinson's son helps us and bears company awhile.

In 1722 Samuel Cobb and Samuel Athearn were licensed as inn-holders, the latter probably to fill the void left by the death of Cathcart. Cobb lived on the lot now occupied by the post office, his land extending to the brook. As he married Isaac Chase's daughter, the instinct for tavern keeping came to him by marriage, and it is probable that he continued the

[1]Mass. Arch., XCIX, 25.

business through his long life. He died in 1786. Samuel Athearn married the widow of Cathcart and doubtless continued the business at the old tavern made famous by his predecessor. He was called in 1722 a "shopkeeper," and it is probable that her house was a combination residence, inn and general "store."

On the opposite side of the road from the old Cathcart House stands the building known in 1850 as "the Travelers Home," then kept by William Athearn, and in later years called the Tyasquin House.

The situation of West Tisbury has been such that there has been no demand for taverns in its limits, as transient travelers were infrequent visitors to the centre of the island and such as came were guests of private individuals.

The following named persons were licensed Innholders in the town of West Tisbury by the County Court for the years specified: —

Robert Cathcart, 1701-1716; Samuel Cobb, 1722-1767; Samuel Athearn, 1722-1724; Gershom Cathcart, 1737-1772; Wilmot Wass, 1739-1752; Shubael Nickerson, 1749-1752; Shubael Cottle, 1759-1770; Ebenezer Rogers, 1776; James Manter, 1777-1780; Ezekiel Luce, 1780-1784; William Case, 1786-1787; James Cook, 1787; Jabez Luce, 1803.

INDUSTRIES.

The natural topography of the Vineyard does not favor the employment of water-power, because there are no large streams on the island, and the fall of water in the small brooks is not sufficient to develop considerable horse-power. The value of a mill privilege was recognized by every community in the settlement of New England, and Tisbury was the only town on the island able to profit by her natural advantages. Thomas Mayhew, Sr., in a letter to John Winthrop of Conn., Aug. 6, 1651, says, "we here have greate want of a mill and there is one with you that I here is a verry ingenuous man about such work . . . . . now these are to intreate you if possible you can dispense a while with him that you would be pleased to doe it & wee shall rest much obleidged unto you for it." Whether anything came of this is not recorded, nor is it known what kind of a mill was contemplated, as there is no water-power in Edgartown. It is probable that it resulted in the erection of a mill on the large brook flowing

OLD MILL ON THE TIASQUIN.

THE VIEW SHOWS THE ANCIENT TYPE OF UNDERSHOT WHEEL.

through Takemmy, which continued in operation till the power on the Tiasquin was utilized about 1668 by a new and improved structure.

The mills of the early days on the island were all operated by the under-shot wheel, as there was not sufficient fall of water to use the other form. The under-shot wheel was set directly in the running stream or placed close to a sluice leading from the dam. The water was admitted by a gate at the bottom of the dam. The wheel, made of wood securely ironed, had stays projecting from its rim, upon which stout planks, called floats, and also palettes, extended along its length.

MILL INTERESTS — OLD MILL RIVER.

The mill privilege on Old Mill river, the larger and more valuable, seems to have been unused for nearly a century after the "first purchase," as we have no record of a mill on that stream until 1760, except that it was a site "where a mill anciently stood." It is probable that the first mill erected there before the white settlement was a crude affair, and that it had fallen into decay. The erection of a mill on the Tiasquin in 1668 or 1669 seems to warrant such an inference, as there could be no urgent business requiring the capacity of two mills so near together. We are reduced to such speculations for want of a definite allusion to the continued existence of a mill on this stream in any records of property transfers covering this ancient site. The location of the mill was on the Josiah Standish home lot, which after several transfers came into the possession, in 1688, of Edward Cottle, and by him was sold in 1700 to his son John. The early death of John in 1705, leaving a widow and three young children, prevented any development of the property and the estate was not divided till 1726, when Sylvanus, the oldest son, attained his majority.

At what time the mill was erected cannot be told, but Sylvanus in a deed dated August 11, 1760, sold to Samuel Cobb his dwelling house, barn "and my Mill with every utensil &c."[1] A month later, Manter disposed of his half of this mill to Barnard Case, July 26, 1765,[2] and on Sept. 11, 1769, Cobb sold his moiety to Rev. George Daman for £24, who

[1]Dukes Deeds, IX, 51.

[2]Deeds, IX, 457.

thus combined the work of grinding out sermons and corn for the parishioners of his flock. But this association of material and spiritual garnering of wheat and separation of the chaff, lasted only a brief time, for the parson sold his interest to Case on Jan. 10, 1770,[1] and thereafter, till his death, Barnard Case operated the mill. By his will, he bequeathed it in 1792, to his sons William and James, to he held in equal shares,[2] the latter of whom parted with his half Feb. 7, 1797, to Cornelius Dunham.[3] This share passed from Dunham to Samuel Hancock, May 19, 1802,[4] and seven years later, July 12, 1809, to David Look.[5] Look had purchased, two years previously, William Case's share, March 18, 1807, and thus became the sole proprietor of the two grist mills on the Old and New Mill rivers.[6] But he did not intend to enter into competition with himself as a grist miller by this purchase, for he utilized the power for carding wool by machinery, and further enlarged its usefulness by adding looms for weaving woolen cloth. For a quarter of a century under his ownership, the click of the shuttle and the noise of the treadles and looms responded to the swish of the water in the mill-race. After his death, in 1837, the property was managed by his widow for eight years, when she sold it for $1800 to Thomas Bradley, June 12, 1845,[7] who continued the business of manufacturing woolen cloths.[8] On May 27, 1859 Bradley sold this to Henry Cleveland for $3000,[9] and on Nov. 3, 1874 it passed into the hands of the late Thomas G. Campbell for a consideration of $1700.[10] It is now a part of the Campbell estate and its use as a woolen mill ceased in a few years.

Farther up Old Mill river, where Dr. Daniel Fisher built his grist mill, another power was available and was early ulitized. This property belonged to Simon Athearn originally and descended to sons and grandsons. When a mill was erected

[1]Dukes Deeds, X, 124.

[2]Dukes Probate, VIII, 244.

[3]Dukes Deeds, XIV, 276.

[4]Ibid., XIV, 350.

[5]Ibid., XVIII, 50.

[6]Ibid., XV, 265.

[7]Deeds, XXX, 525.

[8]Seven hands were employed and the annual production was 7000 yards of Satinet, 9000 yards of Kersey and 6000 pounds of rolls, of the total value of about $10,000 (Census, 1850).

[9]Deeds, XXXVIII, 558.

[10]Ibid., LVII, 320.

there is not known, but the brook shows the remains of an old dam, and the grist mill of Ezra Athearn is mentioned in 1792. It had doubtless been in operation many years before that.

TIASQUIN RIVER.

Benjamin Church of Duxbury built the first grist mill in this town about 1668, "which mill standeth uppon the westermost Brook of Takemmy," a speculative venture in common with that of his townsmen, Pabodie and Standish. He sold it Nov. 19, 1669 for £120 to Joseph Merry of Hampton, together with one eighth part of the first "purchase." Merry operated this as a grist mill until March 5, 1675, when he disposed of it to Tristram Coffin, Sr., of Sherbourne, Nantucket,[1] from whom it passed into the possession of Jethro Coffin of Mendon, his grandson. The last named sold the "corn or grist mill" July 5, 1715, to Thomas Look, who resided on the property and had been operating the mill in behalf of the owner.[2] Thomas Look, who was then nearing three score and ten, held this mill but three years, when "for love and good will" he transferred it, Aug. 7, 1718, to his son Samuel.[3] The son continued the business of grinding the grist that came to his doors for thirty years, when he in turn "for love and affection" sold it to his youngest sons, Noah and Job, Jan. 29. 1748.[4] The two brothers followed in the footsteps of their forbears until Nov. 14, 1763, when Job disposed of his moiety to his older brother Elijah.[5]

The business was then carried on by the new proprietors until May 7, 1777, at which date Elijah purchased Noah's interest[6] and thenceforth conducted the mill alone, until his death, Jan. 29, 1800, at which time it passed by inheritance to his sons, Robert and Elijah, Jr.[7] On Sept. 4, 1804 Elijah, Jr. sold his interest to his cousin David (the son of Job), and on June 19, 1805 Robert sold his right and title to the same person.[8] David Look kept the mill running for over thirty years until his death, April 28, 1837, when his widow

[1]Deeds, I, 337.
[2]Ibid., III, 199.
[3]Ibid., III, 338.
[4]Ibid., VIII, 9.
[5]Ibid., IX, 477.
[6]Ibid., X, 444.
[7]Prob. Rec., IX, 55.
[8]Deeds, XV, 29, 276.

succeeded to the business and kept it in operation during a long widowhood and until near the end of her life. She died Jan, 15, 1877, and David N. Look, a grandson of Robert, bought it of her executors. For two centuries its wheel had turned to the flow of the Tiasquin river.

Of this time it had been in the possession of the Look family for one hundred and fifty-six years, which is almost an unprecedented record of continuity of occupation in the succeeding generations of one family. The last proprietor closed its career as a mill soon after coming into possession, removed the building and converted it to other uses.

The second mill built on this water-course before 1850 was set further up the stream and was owned by Matthew Allen. It came into the possession of his son-in-law, Captain George Luce, who rebuilt the property about 1860 and operated it for twenty years or more as a grist mill.

EDUCATIONAL.

One of the first landmarks in the town was a building designated in 1669 as "the school house," situated on the path that now is known as the South road, near the Chilmark line. The time of its erection could not have been much earlier than that date, unless it was one of the places where the Indian youths were taught by the younger Mayhew as a part of the missionary work. No actual reference to a school in the town appears in the records until nearly seventy years after this date, and we are left in doubt as to the existence of a public school during this time. In 1675 Simon Athearn bewailed the lack of "a scool master to teach our children." There were, perhaps, at that date fifty children of school age in the town, and we cannot suppose that the absence of any records on the subject means that educational matters had no part in the life of the people. In 1724 James Smith "late of Tisbury, schoolmaster," is mentioned in the court records in a suit, and from this casual reference we may conclude that the teaching of the youth was then a private business arrangement among the parents whose children needed instruction. The first action of record taken by the town was in 1737, when a committee was appointed "for Considering & Settling a schoole." This language indicates that no public school system was then in existence. The committee made the following recommendations: —

"The aforsd schoole to be held & keept in Tisbury near the house of Whitten Manter seven months & a half in a year from the time of its Commencing.

2: To be kept & held att Checemmoo near the Common Road betwixt the Dweling houses of David Butler & John Cottle eleven weeks next Ensuing the aforsd Terme.

3 The Remaining part to Compleat a year, to be keept at some Convenient place at Homeses hole:[1]

The town accepted the report and voted "that there should be a schoolehouse built forthwith as Conveniently may be & to stand at the Easterly corner of Whitten Manters field in sd Tisbury which is to be Twenty feet in length & Sixteen feet in breadth six foot & an half between joints which is to be built & finished suitable for such a use having a Chimney to itt."[2] Fifty pounds were appropriated for this building and "a schoole master Provided for that End to Teach children & youth to Read & Write &c."

As far as our knowledge goes this was the beginning of the public school system in Tisbury. From this time forward the yearly disposition of the subject of schools became a matter of quite regular record, and this confirms the above conclusion. The large area of the town, sparsely settled, in three separated village districts, turned the question of teaching children into an inevitable annual quarrel about the time and places where the school sessions should be held. It began almost immediately after the above plan was inaugurated and the townsmen resorted to the usual committee of outsiders to settle the difficulty. Samuel Bassett, Ebenezer Smith and Tristram Coffin of Chilmark and Edgartown were asked to determine whether the school should be "fixed" or "moving" and to devise plans for either method.[3] The latter alternative was recommended and a moving school, to be held seven months in West Tisbury and five months each year at Lambert's Cove, was agreed upon by the town.[4] At this time Samuel Draper, a native of Boston, was employed as school

[1]Tisbury Records, 101. The house of Whitten Manter was next north of the old cemetery. The school house at Chickemmoo was near the turn of the North Shore road at Lambert's cove.

[2]Ibid., 103. In 1739 "a house of 14 foot square Conveniently finished for that use," was built at Lambert's cove at a cost of £30, "together with (what) might be gathered by free Contribution."

[3]Ibid., 107.

[4]Ibid., 112. No arrangement seems to have been made for the convenience of Homes Hole at this time.

master and continued in that service about forty years. His salary was 150 Spanish milled dollars at fifty shillings apiece, or in goods.

In 1748 a redistricting of the town was made for school purposes as follows:—

> In the first place to be keept at homeses hole two months begining at the first begining of the school & then at the School hous at Chickemmo for three months, and then at the place Called Kiphigan that is all to the northward & North westward of the River or Runs of water from Chilmark line to Waksha so on Including Timothy Luces for two months & then at the School house in Tisbury near the meeting house for the space of five months.[1]

This plan lasted ten years. In 1758 the school-house near the cemetery was removed to the west side of the road "near about opposite to a pair of barrs of John Luces near the Dividing Line between sd John Luces Land & the Land of Mercy Luce or her family." This was on the road leading to Middletown, about half way between the two villages. Another decade almost passed during which the old plan was followed, until 1765, when a revision of the "moving" school plan was determined upon. In that year the town left the question to "Squire Jeams Athern Mr Maletiah Davis (of Edgartown) and abijah Athern to Purfix a Place Wher It Should Be Cept," for seven months of each year. The spelling and writing in the records just quoted imply the need of considerable schooling, but we are to learn that in 1768 the town abandoned its work in this line and was indicted at the County Court for neglecting to provide school facilities.[2] Abijah Coye was the next schoolmaster, following Samuel Draper. He came to Tisbury about 1762, married Judith Luce and was first employed in 1770 "to keep the Town Chool the yeare In Suing." In 1776 and 1777 the teaching was done by Henry Young[3] and in 1778 by Ebenezer Skiffe (105), afterwards an attorney-at-law.[4] Fifteen years later (1783) the town again fell under the indictment of the grand jury for

[1]Tisbury Records, 129. There were no school-houses at the first two named districts and the people resident therein were required to provide suitable "house-roome" during the sessions assigned to them.

[2]Town Records, 200.

[3]Ibid., 293. There were two persons of this name resident in West Tisbury at that time, Levi and Henry, and it is not possible to say which one served as teacher, but the latter is believed to be the one.

[4]Ibid., 226.

neglect of her schools, and on several occasions after that the records disclose the same discreditable failure.[1]

In 1792 a redistricting of the town for school purposes was devised by a committee selected from the various sections. Four districts were laid out, substantially as follows: 1st, all residents south of the Old Mill brook, including a line drawn southeast from the turn of the brook in North Tisbury to the bounds of Edgartown; 2nd, all residents north of this brook to the Sound as far as Christiantown; 3rd, Chickemmoo; 4th, Homes Hole. The sum of £60 was raised "to Support a Lawful School in Tisbuary" and the committee above named was further directed to "devide the Monney already raised......according to the Number of Children in Each District Sett forth as above Males from Twenty one year old and under, and Females from Eighteen years old and under."[2] In 1793 the school appropriation was increased to £70, and after this certain persons in each district were chosen to arrange equitable divisions of these funds raised by taxation. This was probably the beginning of the office of school committee in the town. In 1801 these persons were specifically chosen "to provide for and Superintend the Schools in the several School districts."[3] After this time they were annually elected to attend to these duties.

The first school census of record, in 1821, shows that there were 255 children in attendance in the three districts now comprised in the bounds of West Tisbury. In 1825 the number was 262 and in 1835 it had fallen to 248 pupils, while in 1870 a further decrease to 124 shows the losses in the town's population. The annual appropriation at this period was $200, or less than one dollar for each child. In 1870 the amount spent averaged about $8.75 each, while in 1900 the total school expenses amounted to nearly $3,000 for sixty scholars, an average of $50 each pupil. This most creditable record must demonstrate the gain in the last century in the estimation of the townsmen of the importance of their public school system.

[1]Indictments were presented against the town in 1783, 1792 and 1793 for these neglects. In 1787 the town refused to vote any money for schools (ibid., 248, 260, 285, 290). As late as 1810 the town was indicted for the failure to maintain a school (ibid., 353).

[2]Ibid., 286. These districts remained practically the same for the next twenty-five years.

[3]Ibid., 314.

DUKES COUNTY ACADEMY.

In 1797 a movement was started to establish an Academy in this county for the higher education of selected pupils, and Rev. Asarelah Morse, Edmund Cottle and Peter West were chosen in Tisbury "to Join the other Commites that are or may be Chosen in Dukes County for to Consult about the Establishment of an academy."[1] Nothing definite resulted from this early effort, as far as known, but the seed thus sown bore fruit in the next century. During the term of David Look as Representative to the General Court (1830-1835), he secured from the State an appropriation of $3,000 for a County Academy to be located in this town.[2] It was completed about 1833, and was located on a commanding site next the Congregational church.[3] The original building was sold about 1850 and became the dwelling house of the late Obed Nickerson.

Leavitt Thaxter was the first teacher and he was followed by Robert Coffin. The following list comprises the successive pedagogues to the merging of the institution into the town school system:—

M. P. Spear, 1840; W. S. Butler, 1846; T. D. Blake, 1847; J. P. Washburn, 1848; Henry Baylies, 1850; F. N. Blake, 1852; Robert McGonigal, 1854; J. W. Allen, 1855; S. W. Matthews and G. B. Muzzey, 1856; Bartlett Mayhew, 1857; Atwood Severance, 1858; Henry M. Bishop, 1859; C. R. Parker, 1861; Simon W. Hathaway, 1862; J. G. Leavitt, 1863; I. N. Kidder, 1864; C. G. M. Dunham, 1865; N. C. Scoville, 1866; Wm. B. Allen, 1867; Moses C. Mitchell, 1869-72; J. T. Merrick, 1876; E. A. Daniels, 1877; G. H. Calver, 1879; F. E. Perham, 1880-2; P. R. Kendall, 1881; S. S. Sanborn, 1884; Addie Weeks, 1886; James Richmond, 1887; J. R. Flint, 1888; Mary C. Humphrey, 1889; Amy S. Rhodes, 1890; Ella W. Bay, 1891; Edna Merrill, 1892 and Lena B. Carlton, 1893.

About 1850 a new building was erected and remained in use about twenty years, when it was found to be unsuited for the requirements of its growing patronage. After serving as an "annex" to its successor it was sold and now exists as a carriage house.

[1]Tisbury Records, 305.

[2]The grant was conditioned upon the contribution of a like amount by the citizens, which was done.

[3]The grave stone of David Look records the fact that "thro' his influence a grant of Three Thousand Dollars was obtained from the state." He died April 28, 1837 aged 70 years.

In 1869-70, during the service of Moses C. Mitchell, and largely through his efforts, a new building was erected with funds in the treasury and added contributions of the citizens, and on Nov. 1, 1870 was ready for occupancy. The General Court, in April, 1871, appropriated $5,000 towards this new building, almost the last grant of this kind made by the legislature, and thus the academy fund was reimbursed.

Since 1894 the town and academy have merged their interests in educational matters. A grade equivalent to a High School curriculum is provided, in addition to the grammar and primary grades.

THE PUBLIC LIBRARY.

In the autumn of 1890 the late Professor Nathaniel S. Shaler proposed the establishment of a public library in the town, and Rev. Caleb L. Rotch canvassed this section of the Vineyard for the purpose of obtaining financial aid in starting such an institution. Encouraging results were obtained, and on Dec. 29, 1890 a meeting of persons interested was held to perfect a temporary organization. Rev. Mr. Rotch was chosen president, with a secretary, treasurer, executive committee, and Dr. Lyman H. Luce as librarian. This meeting selected the name of "Dukes County Library Association," adopted a constitution and made arrangements for quarters in the Dukes County Academy. Books were purchased with the funds subscribed, many were donated by friends, and from this time until July, 1892 the library was operated in that building. Sanderson M. Mayhew succeeded Rev. Mr. Rotch as president in 1891 and in May, 1892, it was voted to purchase "Mitchell's School" for a library building. This was accomplished by the aid of outside subscriptions, and the exterior and interior fitted up for the special purposes of a public library.[1] The association in 1893 became incorporated under the name of "West Tisbury Free Public Library," and Everett Allen Davis was chosen its first president. At this time it had 1100 volumes and at the present time about 2500 have been accumulated.

AGRICULTURAL SOCIETY.

The Martha's Vineyard Agricultural Society, founded in 1858, has its headquarters in this town. The Hon. Leavitt Thaxter was its first president, and a fair was held that year,

[1]Up to May, 1895 there had been subscribed by friends the total of $1063, to found and maintain the library.

Henry L. Whiting

the exhibits being displayed in the Academy. In 1859 the Agricultural hall was built, next the church lot and annual fairs have been held ever since in this large and commodious structure.

PATHS, HIGHWAYS AND BRIDGES.

The layout of the first roads in town, the Mill road, the Scotchman's bridge and the road leading from Nashowakemmuch to North Tisbury, is not of record. The earliest reference to a road is found under date of 1699, when a way "of about 3 Rods broad" from the Old Mill brook to the Sound, was laid out, "between the Ministers Lot & Israel Luces Lott to & for the generall use of those interested...... & to no other." This road had no real existence elsewhere and probably was never staked out. "Ways" and "Paths" were in existence and in common use, without legal acceptance by the town, from the earliest times. Their course changed at the convenience of the people in driving their carts through the woods and over the hills.[1] Most of them were closed "by Gates and Bars" until within the last hundred years.[2] Those roads which have some definite history are as follows:—

Mill Path. — The first road in town was the "path" leading from Edgartown to the Old Mill brook. It has already been described (vol. I, p. 460). It was the "great road" of the settlement and a part of the county system of highways.

School House Path. — Contemporary with the Mill path and a continuation of it from the brook to the Chilmark line, was this highway, now the south road. Both of these were old Indian trails.

Scotchman's Bridge Road. — This was the first highway mentioned in the records, as early as 1671, and was doubtless laid out when the home lots were plotted. It was originally the road midway of the lots running east and west the entire section.

Homes Hole Path. — This road led from the Mill path on the east side of the Old Mill brook to Homes Hole, following very nearly the present road over the plain. It is first

[1]An example of this is to be found in the following record of a layout in 1741: "both sd ways meet Each other at the old way that before Lead from sd Hametts house: the aforesd new way being Cleared of the wood that Grew upon itt by sd agents by Consent of the Owners of the Land."

[2]The map of Des Barres (1781), which was the best map of the Vineyard up to that date, shows but one road in West Tisbury, the way leading from Chilmark to the old church and on past the cemetery.

mentioned in the records in 1700, but doubtless it was in existence long before that.

Meeting-House Way.—A path leading west from the School House path (South road), at a point where the Congregational meeting-house now stands, to the head of the home lots, existed before 1700 and has continued to the present day. It was a "way" used by residents of the Kephigon section to reach the first meeting-house.

The Back Road.—In 1726 there was a formal layout of the road bounding the west headline of the home lots. It began at the meeting-house way and extended to the Scotchman's Bridge road. In 1741 this way continued northward to intersect in Middletown the road on the east side of the brook that led to Christiantown.

Pow-wow Hill Way.—Starting from the Homes Hole path, about sixty rods north of Scotchman's Bridge road, and running along parallel to the brook, a way two rods wide was laid out in 1700 to the present village of Middletown.

Lambert's Cove Road.—This was a way laid out in 1751 by the owners of land as a combination of the North Shore road from West Tisbury village, and it was provided that it should extend through Chickemmoo, "towards the North-east as may be best for Conveniancie of Said Road and as may be Leaste for Dammage on each Mans Land untill it comes to goe thro Saviges Line." It then intersected the Homes Hole path near its present junction. In 1770 there was a petition to the Court reciting the need of a road in this section to connect Tisbury and Homes Hole. It is probable that it had never been accepted.

THE U. S. GOVERNMENT SERVICES.

But one branch of the general government has a representation in the town, the Post Office Department. A mail service was doubtless in operation for a considerable time prior to the establishment of a local office here, and it is probable that it was served through the Homes Hole office until 1828, when it was established as an independent mail station. The first postmaster was Willard Luce, who was commissioned Jan. 25, 1828, and the office was designated as Tisbury. The next year it was changed to West Tisbury, and Mr. Luce continued in office for twenty-three years. He was succeeded in 1851 by William A. Mayhew for a short term, and in sequence the office was held by Joseph B. Nickerson, Caroline W. Nickerson (his widow) and Mrs. Phebe L. Cleveland.

The office has been continued for over fifty years in its present location on the corner of the Edgartown and Vineyard Haven roads.

PHYSICIANS.

Rufus Spalding was the earliest practitioner of medicine in this town before 1800, and he lived in a house opposite the post office. Here was born his son, Rufus Paine Spalding, distinguished in later life as a member of Congress from Ohio and a judge of the Federal Court. Dr. Spalding removed to Homes Hole about 1805 and later to Connecticut. Dr. T. J. E. Gage came about 1837, remaining ten years, and a Dr. Philbrick about 1845, living opposite Agricultural hall, followed. Dr. W. H. Luce succeeded to the practice of Dr. Gage and remained here throughout his long life. His son, Dr. Lyman H. Luce, formerly in practice in Falmouth, took up his father's work and continued until 1892, when a mortal disease terminated his career. Dr. C. D. N. Fairchild came from Fairhaven about 1893 and still practices here. Dr. D. A. Cleaveland, until his death in 1903, had practised here at intervals, having been settled elsewhere for a considerable period of his professional career.

CEMETERIES.

In 1782 the town voted that James Athearn should "Examine the Records of this Town county or the Registree of Probate and See wt Land Said Town has Reserv'd for a Bureying Place." It is not known what he found, but besides a few private places of interment there are only two public enclosures in the town.

Old Cemetery. — The first burying place owned by the town was the "acker of Land" donated by James Allen in 1701, and with several subsequent enlargements it continues to be used for this purpose at the present day, a record of over two centuries.

Lambert's Cove.— There is a cemetery on the North Shore near the John Look place which has been used for public interments for more than a century. The oldest stones in it bear date of 1771, and the land was probably set apart for a burial place about that date, though there are no records of its acquisition by the town, nor is it known how it was dedicated to such uses.

DIVISION OF THE TOWN.

In 1850 the village of Homes Hole had outgrown in population the western section of Old Tisbury and was gradually developing at the expense of the smaller settlements in the rest of the town. The interests of these two portions of the town were not homogeneous — the one was a compact village with a maritime and manufacturing population, and the other was chiefly devoted to agriculture and fishing.[1] Several miles

THE RUFUS SPALDING HOUSE.

BIRTHPLACE OF HON. RUFUS PAINE SPALDING, M. C., (1798)

of "ragged plain" separated West Tisbury, Homes Hole and North Tisbury, and the inevitable jealousies and disagreements arose between the village and the town regarding improvements to roads, school facilities and the proper balance of appropriations. This became more and more acute as the village of Homes Hole thrived and grew and demanded modern streets, sidewalks, fire protection, lighting, water supply and all the requirements of a compact settlement. The farmers of the western section were outnumbered in town meetings, and chafed under the load of enforced taxation for those things which they could not utilize. Each year these troubles became accentuated and would be temporarily composed under some form of truce between the two parties. It was a case of the

[1]In 1850 Homes Hole had 259 polls to 153 in the rest of the town.

offspring outstripping the parent, for the older men could remember the time when the "Hole" was an insignificant part of Tisbury town. They remembered, too, that Governor Mayhew in his original grant of West Chop to Tisbury in 1673, had in view its ultimate separation as a distinct corporation. It was to be a part of Tisbury he wrote "until the said necke of Land be a particular township." Early in the decade of 1880-90, the farmers of West and North Tisbury began to agitate for this separation decreed by history and topography. Each year the subject was discussed with much spirit and considerable acrimony at times, as the people of the village of Vineyard Haven objected to a division. In 1890, after much political agitation, a petition was sent to the General Court by the people of West Tisbury asking for a division of the town, but it was referred to the next session. In 1891 the General Court enacted a permissive bill for division, provided it should be accepted by a majority vote of the townsmen at either of two meetings called for the purpose at Vineyard Haven and Middletown.

At the first meeting, held in the former village, the proposal failed by a vote of 115 yes to 161 no; and at one of the largest town meetings ever held the second test vote, 150 yes to 204 no, resulted in its final rejection. The people of West Tisbury renewed the contest the next year, and it was decided by the General Court in favor of the petitioners without use of the referendum. It became a law April 28, 1892, when signed by the Governor, William E. Russell, and the new town of West Tisbury celebrated its victory by a torch-light procession and a jubilation meeting at Agricultural Hall.[1]

THE NEW TOWN AT THE PRESENT TIME.

The first town officers, elected May, 1892, were the following: William J. Rotch, Horatio G. Norton, Edwin A. Luce, Selectmen; George H. Luce, Horatio G. Norton, Edwin A. Luce, Assessors; George G. Gifford, Clerk; Sanderson M. Mayhew, Treasurer; Ulysses E. Mayhew, David Mayhew, Frank L. Look, School Committee; Richard Thompson, Walter G. Cottle, Constables; Henry H. Lovell, Auditor; James F. Cleaveland, Collector of Taxes; Henry L. Whiting, William J. Rotch, Cyrus Manter, Cemetery Committee.

[1]The leading spirit in this movement was William J. Rotch of West Tisbury and the satisfactory results which have followed the years of bickering between the two sections, justifies the wisdom of his contentions during the campaign.

This village is now about two hundred and forty years old, and the town sixteen years in its independent standing. Its material progress and present prosperity, as indicated by the following statistics taken from the assessors' books, May 1, 1908, shows in contrast to the lone mill of 1669 on the ancient stream of Taakemmy: Personal estate assessed, $155,373; real estate assessed, $379,414; total, $534,787. Total tax assessed, $2429.14, with about $700 additional, which is appropriated from other income. Acres of land, 12,821; dwelling houses, 190; horses, 125; cows, 164; neat cattle, 40; sheep, 685; fowl, 2589.

WASKOSIM'S ROCK

AN ANCIENT BOUND MARK OF WEST TISBURY AND CHILMARK.

CHRISTIANTOWN.

MANITOUWATTOOTAN, THE PRAYING TOWN. 1660.

The beginnings of Christiantown carry us back to the year 1659, when according to the evidence of Josias, the sachem, "there was only Known but four Praying Indians in my Sachimshipp Whose names was Pamick my uncle and Nonoussa and Tahquanum & Poxsin." In the winter of 1659-1660, continues the sachem, "I gave one mile square of land unto my uncle Pamick Nonoussa, Tachquanum & Poxsin of Taukemey to be a township for them."[1] It is believed that Papamick, the well-known Indian of Takemmy is meant as the uncle of Josias, to whom the grant was made, as "Papamek's Field" was one of the bounds of this tract.[2] This grant was laid out to these four Christianized natives for a "praying town," so-called, and the condition of the grant provided "That the Praying Indians should give Twenty Shillings every yeare to me Their Sachim," but it appears that in after years this ceased to be observed by the grantees, through death and removal.[3] There was no formal record of this transaction, and it obtained a standing in the knowledge of men through common report, that this square mile of land at the North Shore, in the bounds of Takemmy, had been set apart for the sole use of these converts. This arrangement lasted for about a decade.

When Thomas Mayhew, the elder, on July 1, 1668, gave permission to William Pabodie and his partners "to buy what they cann uppon this Island within the compass of the bounds of Takemmy, of the indian sachims, the right owners," the rank and file among the natives did not relish the idea of their sachem selling territory, which belonged to them, to a new lot of "pale-faces." Already the eastern half of the Island had been alienated by Tequanomin to the settlers of Great Harbour, and when the prospectors for a new township came to the fertile meadows of Takemmy, in 1668, and began to negotiate with Keteanummin, alias Josias, the sachem, for the purchase of that land, the discontent was openly expressed. It came to the knowledge of Mayhew, and it was

[1]Dukes Deeds, I, 357.

[2]Experience Mayhew calls one of the Indians Pockqsimme (Indian Converts, 73).

[3]Dukes Deeds, IV, 173. The date of the agreement was February 23, 1658, probably 1658-9.

determined to appease them in some way. The land desired by Pabodie and his associates was known to them as being valuable, and they would not derive any benefit from the sale of it by the sachem. However, Josias sold to Pabodie the tract known as the First Purchase on Aug. 2, 1669, as elsewhere described, and was negotiating with the buyers for the sale of more territory. There were constant quarrels between the sachem and the angry braves of Takemmy, and Mayhew called a general meeting of the natives to hold a "pow-wow" over the matter. It was held early in March, 1669-70 and one of the earliest settlers of Tisbury has left on record his recollections of the matter. The deponent is Joseph Daggett, who, as a young man, was a witness of the proceedings. He was able to understand the native language and frequently acted as interpreter for the town. His evidence is as follows:—

The Testimony of Joseph Daged aged 51 years or there abouts testifieth & Saith, that about 28 or 29 years agoe [1670-1671] I was at a Meeting of the Indians at Tacamy and there was a great quarrell between the Indians and Josias commonly called Sachim for that he the sd Josias had Sould so much land to the purchasers of Tisbury in so in so much that mr Thomas Mayhew Esqr deced who was then present had very much adoe to quiet the Indians untill at length sd Josias did agree to and oblige him Self that he would Sell no more land with out the Consent and approbation of a Certain number of Indians who were then named & Confirmd as Trustees for and in behalfe of the sd Indians: [1]

This agreement, made at that time, is as follows:—

It is absolutely agreed by us Thomas Mayhew, Kiteanumin, Tichpit, Teequinom(in) Papamick and Joseph, and wee doe hereby promise for our heirs and successors that all the lands in Takemmy that is not sold unto the English shall remain unsold for the use of the Indians of Takemmy and their heirs forever; except the said Thomas Mayhew, Kiteanumin, Tichpit, Teequinomin, Papamick and Joseph their heirs successors doe all and everie one of them consent to the sale thereof of any part of the same.

This agreement was made with the consent and approbation of most of the inhabitants at a meeting held the 15th day of March (1669-1670).

Further it is agreed that noe person that buyeth any land except it be of all the aforenamed trustees shall enjoy the same; and whosoever shall presume to sell land without the consent of the trustees, shall be liable to be fined att the will of the major part of the trustees.

Witness our hands the day and year above written:

[1]Superior Judicial Court Mss., No. 3834. The date of this deposition is March 3, 1698-9.

Further the old custom about elwifes is to bee observed.

	THOMAS MAYHEW	
	KITEANUMIN	his mark
This is an absolute agreement	TICHPIT	his mark
Witness	TEEQUINOM	his mark
THOMAS MAYHEW	PAPAMICK	his mark
	JOSEPH	his mark

This is to testify that Keteanummin hath noe power to sell any more land; but hath made a publique promise that all the land unsold is to remain for the Indians of Takemmy forever, except he hath sold not half already: yet not then may he sell till one half be sold.

Witness my hand this 29th (March) 1669. He doth not by this exclude himself.

THOMAS MAYHEW[1]

The last codicil, if it may be so termed, attached to this agreement by Mayhew is thus explained, in part, by Joseph Daggett, in the same deposition. He states that when the agreement about the trusteeships and the powers under which they held these relations to the Indians and to "each-other was Concluded and Effected," he says:—

I went away from the Meeting but have often been Informed that at the same Meeting the sd Josias confirmed a Grant of a certain tract of land which adjoyneth to the Northern line of the purchased Township of Tisbury for a Christian Town or for the Settlemt for the praying Indians and that ever since the sd Meeting it hath generaly been esteemed to be the Indians and called by the name of the Indian Town.[2]

The motives which actuated the elder Mayhew and the sachem Josias may, or may not, have been altruistic. It looks like a bone thrown to snarling dogs to keep them quiet. Accordingly, to satisfy the discontented, it was decided by the governor and the sachem to renew the old grant of a "mile square," formerly given to Papameck and his fellow converts so that the praying Indians should always have a place by themselves, which they could call their own. The governor testifies:—

Josias and Wannamanhutt Did in my Presence give the Praying Indians a Tract of Land for a Town and Did Committ the Government Thereof into my hand and Posteritie forever: the Bounds of the said Land is on the North sid of (the) Island bounded by the land called Ichpoquassett and so to the Pond called Mattapaquattonooke and into the

[1]Superior Judicial Court Mss., No. 953; comp. Dukes Deeds, I, 402.
[2]Ibid., No. 3834.

Island so far as Papamaks fields where he Planted and now Plants or soes: it is as broad in the woods as by the Seaside.[1]

A supplemental agreement was drawn up several months later to provide for the defect of a proper succession, in case the "Praying Indians" should recant, die out or leave. Accordingly the following document was drawn up on Jan. 9, 1670:—

Agreed by myself and Keteanummin that the town Manettouwatootan in Taukemey Shall Remain forever in the possession of the Praying men—That is Thus: That if the Inhabitance Turn from god his Ways Other Praying Indians of Taukemy shall have their land If there Be Anny: If not Then other Praying men of this Island: Further Keteanummin Saith That When 20 Families are settled in this town it shall be enlarged with Land the same say I it is fitt itt should: This Town for the Governent of it was put by the Sachims Keteanummin and Wanamanhut into the hands of Thomas Mayhew and his posterity for ever: The meaning is If all do forsake the Worship of God They shall loose their Predecessors Land.[2]

Thirty years later Josias, then an old man, confirmed this grant and amplified the description of the boundaries in a deed, dated Aug. 26, 1699, as follows:—

Bounded on the north by the North shore and bounded on the East by Ichpoquassett the black water, and so to run southerly in the bound line Between Taukemy and Chickemoo land, untill it come to a little Eastward of a pond called Manaquayak and bounded on the south from that mile end near the Pond called Manaquayak, and so to the south bounds runing westerly Mackkonnetchasqua including the field where my uncle Pa(pa)-mick Dwelt and Dyed and so the south bounds to Come to a Place called Maanette and from that mile end Bounded on the West to a Pond at the north shore called Pissa: so this mile square of land Lyeth in Taukemmy on the north east corner of my Sachemship.[3]

Ten years after this, owing to some disputes about the territory in the possession of the remnants of these "Praying Indians," and in response to a petition of the town authorities, a committee, appointed by the General Court, consisting of John Otis and William Bassett, made a re-survey of the tract in October, 1709 and defined the bounds as follows:—

Beginning att the Stake standing on the Easterly side of the Ware att the beach att of neare the place Caled Itchpoqueassett and thence Runing westerly by the sea or Sound untill it come to a Stake standing att the

[1]The date of this paper is May 28, 1669, probably written shortly after the meeting above referred to, and written down for permanent record (Dukes Deeds, I, 378).

[2]Superior Judicial Court Mss., No. 72789. This was signed by Thomas Mayhew and Ketanummin (his mark), and witnessed by a number of Indians.

[3]Dukes Deeds, I, 357.

East corner of Mattapaquaha pond by the fence, and thence Runing up Southerly on a Streight line to a great Rock, extending Easterly unto a stake with stones about it standing on the plain land over against the house in which Robert Luce now dwelleth, and thence Runing down a streight Line to a marked tree with stones about it standing att the head of the pond caled Great Jameses Pond at Itchpoqueassett pond and thence down on a streight Line across the s'd pond unto the first mentioned stake standing on the beach.[1]

ALIENATION OF LAND TO THE ENGLISH.

From contemporary documents, it is certain that Josias adhered to the compact which he had made with the braves of his tribe. James Skiffe gives testimony of this in a statement made thirty years after. In it he says: —

> We the said purcjasers (of Takemmy) desired of said Josias to let us have our bounds and limits to extend further Eastward........ but the said Josias refused to let us have any land further Eastward of said bounds, alledging that he had already granted it to the praying Indians; and the next year after when we the said purchasers were about to purchase another parcel of Land of the said Josias in Tacomy the Indians who then dwelt on the said Tacomy were much displeased at Josias for inclining to sell any more land and would not consent thereto untill Josias did confirm the remainder to them the said Indians.[2]

Joseph Daggett gives similar testimony as to the general observance of the conditions by the whites, when he says that those "imployed to buy lands of the Indians by and in behalfe of the Town of Tisbury have refused to buy any lands there as concluding properly belonging to the Christan Indians."[3] But Josias was not above the temptations which beset human nature, especially the simple nature of the red man. He never embraced the Christian religion, and as a consequence failed to be embalmed among the "good men" in Mayhew's Indian Converts." Indeed, Mayhew goes out of his way to give him a doubtful certificate of respectability. "Of him I can give no very good character," says the author of that volume of praise for all sorts and conditions of converted natives. In an explanation of his predicament, in his old age, he says: —

> Now long since my uncle Pamick Dyed and his sons are dead Nonoussa and Taquanum and Poxsin are all dead and they never Pay'd me my fifteen pounds:—so the Praying Indians Being Dead and Removed and

[1] Mass. Archives, CXIII, 534. Report of Otis and Bassett, 1709.
[2] Superior Judicial Court Mss., No. 4714.
[3] Ibid., No. 3834.

forsook that place so I had Nothing as they had Promised That the Praying Indians should give Twenty Shillings every yeare to me Their Sachem ans Being grown old and Poor not able to work Proposed to sell the land to the English for my maintenance.[1]

So he began to sell, first to Simon Athearn, on Nov. 10, 1674, a tract of land, which became, in after years, the origin of a famous law-suit which extended over many years, and was the occasion of many exciting encounters, due to alleged trespass. It will be, therefore, well to have a copy of this deed for reference:—

......this parcel of land that I have now sold lyeth by Wampache with there corners almost three square bounded on the south and south west and west sides with the land I sold to William Peaboddie and his friends and it is bounded on the north and by west side through marked trees one old dead tree with a forked toppe and one white oak butt standing by a crook of the brook of water and one old tree standing on the north side of a little bushy swamp and so this line do runne west norwest and east south east until it come to the land I sold to William Peaboddie and his friends on both ends......[2]

The sale of this land by Josias gave rise to prolonged litigation in subsequent litigation with abutting owners, perhaps owing to the usual indefinite description of its bounds, and in order to settle the controversy, Richard Sarson and Matthew Mayhew were chosen arbitrators by the litigants. The two arbitrators, who could not be called friendly to Athearn, on account of the family and political differences in the past, nevertheless made an award, in the following terms, entirely in his favor:—

In the Controversy left to the arbitrament of us Between Simon Athearn & the Town of Tisbury concerning a tract of land bought by said Athearn neer William Rogers his land we award as followeth, viz:— that the said Simon Athearn shall enjoy said land and that the other proprietors or sharers in said townshipp shall be each of them allowed and allotted as much land as said purchase and one eight more in the two necks and half last purchased, and what it may want if there be not sufficient, to be made up to each man out of the next land that shall be purchased: before he hath any allotment, having the land aforesaid witness our handes this 24th of December 1682.[3]

This certainly left Athearn in full and quiet possession of this tract.

[1]Dukes Deeds, I, 357.

[2]Ibid., I, 302.

[3]Superior Judicial Court Mss., No. 4974.

The next purchase was made by William Rogers, twenty acres, Jan. 29, 1679,[1] and on Jan. 13, 1686, another tract was sold to Arthur Bevan, adjoining the Rogers purchase on the east.[2] This latter transaction caused considerable unfavorable comment, and Bevan "tendered to the Town of Tisbury at a Town Meeting some land which he had bought, which land was a part of s'd land which s'd Josias had barred him self from selling without the approbation of the Trustees afores'd and the Town refused to Meadle with it for the Reasons aforesaid (viz) that they looked at it to be Indians Town."[3] But Josias put on record his justification for these sales, in which he states:—"Having sold som of the Land to Isaac Chase and to John Manter and others, for which Mr. Mayhew Witt(nessed) the Deed, and Mr Mayhew concented That I might sell it now."[4] After this the old sachem made four more sales, before his decease, to the following named persons: To Henry Luce, on Feb. 3, 1687, of sixty acres;[5] to Experience Luce, on Dec. 9, 1693, of sixty acres;[6] to John Lambert, on May 17, 1694, of sixty acres,[7] and to John Manter, on Aug. 17, 1694, of forty acres.[8]

These continuous sales incensed the members of the tribe and there arose, as William Parclow of Tisbury testifies, "a great Contest between Josias Indian Sachim and the Christian Indians, so called, about the Title of some lands called the lands of the Christian Town." This was "sometime in or about the year 1688." He continues: —

and the s'd Christian Indians having committed their Deed of Gift from sd Sachim unto my Custody, which Deed was subscribed and sd Josias told me it was by himself; and sometime after the sd Sachim came to me & desired me to Burn sd Deed or writing, saying that if I would do it he would give me some of the land, but I refusing sayd I would not undoe those praying Indians to whom it was granted. The Sachim replyed saying it may be you think I will give you but a little piece, then

[1]The purchase made by Rogers was authorized by the town of Tisbury, when it was voted "that Will. Rogges shall purchchis therty eakers of land of (Jo)sias Sogimer for an inheritance........and what the saide rogers can purchis more it is to returne to the towne againe" (Tisbury Records, 13). The deed is recorded, Vol. III, fol. 288, Dukes County Registry.

[2]Dukes Deeds, I, 340. There is no record of the disposal of this land from Bevan and it is probable that it reverted to the Indian Town.

[3]Superior Judicial Court Mss., No. 3834.

[4]Dukes Deeds, I, 357.

[5]Ibid., III, 476.

[6]Ibid., III, 19.

[7]Ibid., I, 248.

[8]Ibid., I, 207.

I sayd how much will you give me if I burn the Deed he then answered I'lle will give you halfe, then I told him he had no love for the Christians & I will not do it if you will give me all of it.[1]

The sale to Isaac Chase, to which he refers, was made on Aug. 15, 1682, and comprised the tract between Great James pond and the Black Water brook, as far south as Old House pond, and the town of Tisbury gave authority to Chase to make the purchase less than a month before the transaction was completed.[2] Notwithstanding the premises stated, there was growing up a continued opposition to the alienation of this territory, and as Josias himself avers, "Ev(er)y(man) have made much Trouble about Land (I) have sold to the English and some men say that the Praying Indians Must have their Town I formerly gave them." Accordingly, on Aug. 26, 1699, the ancient Sachem executed a deed of confirmation, of the mile square previously granted, describing the bounds as above given. It was the last recorded act of this "bad" Indian chief, in which he left to his people the original tract, in perpetuity, as he had given it to them in his simple way, forty years before. Although not a Christianized native, his recognition of the portion of his sachemship which had embraced the new religion, was an act which measures up well with the attitude of the whites who dealt with him. He died somewhere between that date and Aug. 17, 1702, and on the highest hill of Christiantown, some monument should be erected to this historic sachem of the Takemmy tribe of the Algonquian race, as a memorial of an Indian who dealt fairly with his own people and justly with the whites. In his last words to "the great English Justices to helpe me who am an Indian," he solemnly announced in his appeal for justice, in the legal proceedings growing out of the greed of the whites for his territory: "I have don the English no hurt nor don anything out of the Indian custom." This well might be the epitaph on the place marking his memorial.[3]

On Aug. 18, 1702, Zachariah Peeskin, "son and heir to Josias Keteanummin, late deceased, sachem," executed a deed amplifying the grants of his late father of the territory of Christiantown, in the following terms, in favor of the Indians Wekommooinnin, Ashahhowanin, Isaac Ompanit, Cottoowan-

[1]Superior Judicial Court Mss., No. 3834.

[2]Dukes Deeds, I, 281; comp., Tisbury Records, 16.

[3]Superior Judicial Court Mss., No. 4974.

nawook, Stephen Nashokow and Wawapeehkin, as trustees, and to their heirs and successors: —

Upon serious reflections finding that my said father Josias as well jointly together with Wanamanhut firstly as latterly before his own decease, being sole lord and sachim of the said domionion of Takemmy, had and did not only according to the usual custom of the time in use but for better affirmance thereof, by request of my father said Josias, obtained the favor of the then English Governour, Thomas Mayhew, late deceased, of his assistance to commit the same to writing, give and convey a considerable part of said sachimship and lands to the same belonging, for and to the use of all such, within his said sachimship as did or hereafter should profess the Christian religion,......as an addition to the said grant all and every the lands, soils, waters, fishing and fowling, royalties and privileges, woods, marshes and all other rights, estate, of what nature soever,......to the use of the Christians of the Protestant religion, natural subjects of the siad sachimship.

The regulation of this grant was provided for in the person of the Governor of the Massachusetts Bay, for the time being, and exception was made in favor of the sachem's "right of drifts, wrecks on the beach or sea-shore." The deed was "approved" by the following Indians, probably to conform to the requirements of the ancient trustees, in the following manner: —

We the subscribers inhabitants of that part of Marthas Vineyard, called Takemmy, assent to the within written conveyance:

Ely Shokaw	Job Soomanau	Isaac Ompanit	Nen Amos
William Nunmin	Thomas Paul	Nen Abel	Jonathan
Francis	Ezekiel Ammuck	Hosea Manhut	Samson
Wecammoone	Japhet	Wanahut	Stephen
Wawapekin[1]			

CIVIL GOVERNMENT.

The government of Christiantown, as far as the management of the land was concerned, was vested in Governor Mayhew and five Indians as Trustees, and their heirs and successors from the year 1669, as before related. From fragmentary references it is certain that a form of civil government, like the town organization of the whites, was settled in this little Indian village. Governor Mayhew is authority for the statement that Josias and Wannamanhutt "Did Committ the Government Thereof into my hand and Posteritie forever."[2] The form of government instituted by Mayhew

[1]Dukes Deeds, I, 417. In the report of a committee on Christiantown lands, in 1762, it is stated that Zachariah gave a deed previous to this on April 6, 1702, but if so it was not recorded.

[2]Ibid., I, 378.

was probably suited to the monarchial customs of the Indians at first, rather than the democratic order. An Indian "magistrate" of this town is mentioned in 1690, and it is altogether likely that native courts were instituted here, as in the other parts of the island very early. How soon a regular town government was formed cannot be stated, but while there is no record of such before 1700, it is probable that one existed then.

The trustees of the Indian Town in 1696 were Isaac Ompanit, Stephen Nashokow and Obadiah Paul, and in a case relating to disputed land, they refer to the rights "of them selves and body politick as a town."[1] In 1703 Stephen Shokow (an abbreviation of Nashokow) was "Justice of peace for the Indians of Takymmy."

Of Isaac Ompanit, the author of "Indian Converts," says that he "was a *Magistrate* as well as a Minister among his own Countrymen, and faithfully discharged the Duties of that *Office*, according to the best of his Skill and Judgment, not being a Terror *to good Works, but to those that were Evil.*"[2]

The Indians, however, as a tribe, were under the guardianship of the Society for the Propagation of the Gospel in material as well as spiritual matters. An instance of this occurred in 1714 respecting the use of a house belonging to the town, and evidently built by the society.[3] In addition to this, agents were appointed by the provincial authorities to attend to certain defined duties regarding their legal rights. In 1731 Experience Mayhew held this office, and he presented a petition to the General Court, setting forth "the inconvenience they are under for want of the power of chusing officers among themselves" and praying that they may be constituted "a Seperate Town or Precinct or have the priviledges necessary for the Chusing & Appointing of officers among themselves for the ordering & managing of their own Affairs."[4] The latter

[1]Sup. Judicial Court files, No. 4714.

[2]Op. cit., p. 60.

[3]In answer to Thomas Paul of Christian Town, who is angered that Isaac Ompane, of the same town, lives in the Town's English House Rent free. It is directed and ordered that Isaac Ompane for the future pay twelve shillings per annum Rent for the said House so long as he dwells in it, which shall go towards reimbursing the Widow Abigails Lease. And it is very necessary that the Town speedily join together as one Man, and pay what is owing to the said Widow. And the twelve shillings per annum shall be employed in some other public use of the Town, and shall be paid accordingly to the Select-Men thereof by Isaac Ompany, who has been the principal Doer and Sufferer in Recovering the Same. Sewall, Thaxter, Thomas Mayhew, Esq. Benjamin Skiff, Esq. April 8, 1714. (Sewall, Diary, II, 432.)

[4]Acts and Resolves, XI, 639, Chapter 137.

alternative was adopted and they were given restricted civil rights of election of officers to conduct their business. There is a record of "a Legall Town Meeting held on the Fifteenth Day of March A.D. 1735 at Christian(town) whereof Amos Oyeninkesit was Moderator," and the record is attested by Zachariah Papamek as the Town Clerk. A similar record exists in 1743.[1] In 1762 a committee appointed by Governor Bernard, to correct certain abuses against the Indians, reported that they were "further of the opinion that they be no longer under Guardians," But this consummation was not reached for a century.

RELIGIOUS HISTORY.

In pursuance of the object of their existence as a religious community, a meeting house was built for them in the time of the Governor, before 1680, and this was replaced about 1695 by another. How long this building, or any of its successors, existed is not known, as no records remain to throw light on the subject. That a meeting-house was standing in 1770 appears from a contemporary document, and scattered references to "the Indian meeting" occur throughout that century. In 1732 two flagons of silver were presented to this congregation by the Old South church of Boston.

The local English ministers of Tisbury, beginning with Torrey and followed by Hancock, exercised a supervision over the native church and frequently preached to them in Algonquian and administered the sacraments. In addition to this, the Society for the Propagation of the Gospel supported a general missionary for the island until the Revolution. After this the society organized in Boston in 1787, continued the patronage of the mission for a century. Indian preachers conducted the regular services, assisted by native deacons. In 1858 it was reported that "for some years past this tribe has had no regular stated worship."

In 1870 a church of eight members was formed and services were held in a building originally built for a school. No regular minister was attached to this organization, but it had occasional services supplied by the North Tisbury Baptists. After a precarious existence for about twenty years it ceased to be used for religious services and is now unfit for occupancy as such.

[1]Acts and Resolves, Dukes Deeds, VII, 238.

NOTED "PRAYING" INDIANS.

John Amanhut. — He was son of Wannamanhut, the sachem, and was a preacher in this town. He was the father of Hosea Manhut, also a preacher, and an ordained Pastor of "the Indian Church at the West End of this Island." He died in March 1672.[1]

Joel Sims. — He was son of Pockqsimme, and being well instructed in his youth, was called upon to preach to his people in this town. He died young, about the year 1680, "much lamented."[2]

James Sepinnu. — He was a brother of Tackanash, the colleague of Hiacoomes, the first Indian convert on the island. He was one of the early preachers in this town, and died here about 1683.[3]

The foregoing persons appear among the "Godly Ministers" of Experience Mayhew's book, and those which follow are classed as "Good Men," who resided in Christiantown during his knowledge: —

Noquittompany. — Beyond the fact that he was a "praying Indian," and the father of Isaac Ompanit, nothing remains to be said further of him. He died about 1690, probably of the "distemper" which carried off so many of the Island Indians at that time. His daughter married the sachem Josias.[4]

Job Somannan. — His father was a "praying Indian" bearing the last name, and his mother was classed as a "heathen." Job was taught to read in his native tongue, and in later years could read and write in English. He was a weaver by trade and "a great Lover of good Books." While a "good" Indian, according to Mayhew, yet he "had such Apprehensions of the Holiness that was necessary to qualify Persons for the Enjoyment of Church Privileges, that he thought it not safe for him to venture to lay claim unto them." He died in 1718.[5]

Henry Ohhunnut, alias Jannoquissoo. — This native "meeting with some Trouble on Marthas Vineyard, which made his Mind uneasy," left the island and went to Natick,

[1]Indian Converts, 72.
[2]Ibid., 73.
[3]Ibid., 73.
[4]Ibid., 84, 197.
[5]Ibid., 110.

where he sat under the Apostle Eliot's preaching, and became a "Peantamaenin, i. e. a praying Man." Later he returned hither, married, and lived a "sober life" ever after. He died in 1724.[1]

Of the noted Indians who were connected with the Church in Christiantown from the earliest times, according to the author of "Indian Converts," the following named have been given special notice: —

Wunnanauhkomun. — An Indian minister, and perhaps the first who exercised that office here. His wife was called Ammapoo, and by the English, Abigail. She was a daughter of Cheshchaamog, sachem of Homes Hole and a sister of Caleb Cheshchaamog, who took a Degree at Harvard in 1665. This preacher died about the year 1676.[2]

Assaquanhut, alias John Shohkow. — He was a son of a "praying Indian" of Takemmy, called Nashohkow, being one of five sons of his parents. He was a ruling elder of the church of which Tackanash was pastor. He died in this settlement about 1690.[3]

Micah Shohkow. — He was a brother of the foregoing, and is classed with the "Godly Ministers" in Mayhew's book. He "was a lover of strong Drink the former part of his life," but he reformed, and "frequently preached to the Indians on the Island, but especially to those in that Town in which he lived and died." His death occurred in 1690.[4]

Stephen Shohkow. — He was a brother of the two previously named, and being brought up "in a pious English Family," where he received an education, he became a preacher to his people in after years. He was drowned in the year 1713, by the oveturning of a canoe.[5]

Isaac Ompanit. — He was a ruling elder of the church in this town, and the son of an Indian called Noquitompany. Isaac was a civil magistrate, as well as a leader in religious matters. Mayhew gives him a good character for piety and honesty. "He was much vexed by some controversies which arose betwixt the Indians of the Place where he lived, and some of their English Neighbours, respecting the Title of the Land which the Indians claimed, "says Mayhew, "the Trouble

[1]Indian Converts, 126.
[2]Ibid., 20, 148.
[3]Ibid., 28.
[4]Ibid., 30.
[5]Ibid., 54.

whereof fell much on him, he being a leading Man in the Place; But I believe he acted with a good Conscience in that Affair."[1]

Paul, commonly called Old Paul, who died at Christiantown about the year 1676, "was generally esteemed a godly Man," says Mayhew, "being a Serious Professor of Religion, constant in the Performance of the Duties of it, and as far as I can learn, without any Stain in his Life and Conversation."

John Howwannan.—A "praying Indian," who died about 1678.

Pattompan.—He was a brother of John, Micah, Stephen and Daniel Shokow, all preachers, "and esteemed like them for Piety." He died in 1688.

POPULATION.

The Indian population of Christiantown is first reported in 1698 as 82, and no other record is known for the next sixty years. In 1762 it was 54; in 1790 it was 40; in 1828 it was 49 and in 1858 it was 53, of which number 23 were males and 30 females.

ANCIENT LANDMARKS

ALGONQUIAN PLACE NAMES.

It is a singular fact that this Indian settlement has preserved scarcely any local names of Algonquian origin. The few that have come down to us in the records are here noted.

Waakesha.—In a deed dated 1742, transferring land in Tisbury, "a place called by the Indians Wackesha" and near to the dwelling house of John Merry, is mentioned. (Deeds, VI, 512.) In 1743 Waakesha in Christiantown is mentioned. The word is probably a boundary designation, Wequshau, "as far as it goes," and it forms the basis of several local place-names on the Vineyard.

Wahquide.—Hosea Manhut, an Indian sold to Elisha Amos, Indian, 8 acres of land at "Okokame Christiantown ....it is called Wahquide." 1726. (Deeds, VI, 39 written in the Indian language.)

[1]Indian Converts, 59.

ENGLISH PLACE NAMES.

Dancing Field.— This place, where the aborigines held their ceremonial dances, was situated on a level plateau to the northeast of the (true) Indian Hill.

Hester's Field.— This was a part of the Western portion of Christian Town, as described in a document of 1737-8. (Cong. Lib. Athearn, Mss.)

SCHOOLS.

Educational privileges for the Indians have been provided by the several societies devoted to missionary work among that race; but definite information is wanting to warrant particulars. In 1714 Job Somannan was the schoolmaster and in 1724 the "school" was mentioned. These are the earliest references to this subject. In the middle of the next century the school had an allowance of $100 from the state and in 1858 there were reported fifteen children of school age, with an average attendance of nine scholars during the five and a half months annually devoted to term work.

LATER ENCROACHMENTS OF THE ENGLISH.

The settlement of the bounds of Takemmy and Christian-town in 1709, by the survey of Otis and Bassett, kept the English in check for a number of years, but the cupidity of the white man, and the ignorance of the red man, worked out its inevitable result. Gradually in the course of time, as the decades passed and the memory of the restrictions was lost, purchases were made by the whites of the complacent native, sometimes for a valuable consideration, oftentimes for an inadequate payment. An instance of the former class is that of Deacon Stephen Luce, who paid in specie £146-13-4 for a tract in the Indian town. The Society for the Propagation of the Gospel was notified in 1760 of this condition of affairs, and immediately petitioned Governor Bernard to investigate these violations of local and province laws. A committee was appointed and made an exhaustive examination of the premises and the history of the land rights of the natives. They made a report in 1762, in which they declared all purchases made by the whites since 1699, when Josias confirmed his grant, to be illegal. This required a wholesale eviction, for between three and four hundred acres had been sliced off three sides of Christiantown, but it will be no surprise to learn that such a proceeding met with but scant consideration. The committee said:—

> if those Indians had the Right in the Land they Sold, it is plain it was against the Law of the Province for them to Sell, or the English to buy, and yet for those English late Purchasers in Christian Town, to be turned out of their Houses, which are eight in number: and their Improvements, loose all their Labour in the Stone Walls and the great Improvements they have made, and the money they paid as the purchase consideration for said Lands, seemed very hard: And on the other hand for the Indians to be deprived of their Inheritance, and not thro: any Fault of their own seemed as hard, This put your Committee to a great Plunge at last the following Expedient was thought of; namely, That the English late Purchasers at Christian Town, should return to the Indians of the Lands they purchased, more than a sufficient Quantity for the Indians comfortable support, which are but fifty four in number Men Women and Children. This proposal both English Proprietors and Indians acquiesced in, and unanimoulsy came into. The bounds were made and Agreed upon by both, as by their respective Petitions more fully will appear.

The committee "upon the whole" gave it as their final opinion that about 160 acres should be returned to the Indians by the purchasers by deed to the Society, according to metes and bounds detailed by them; and that the land remaining to the Indians be confirmed to them as in common and undivided. These recommendations were carried out.

FINAL DIVISION IN SEVERALTY.

This condition of common ownership as obtained, lasted for sixty-five years longer, when the General Court, in 1828, passed an act to parcel out the undivided lands to the existing descendants of the Praying Indians, then resident in the town. About three hundred and ninety acres were so divided into nineteen lots, of which one was left for a meeting-house, three for the support of the poor, and a "common" of about ten acres. This gave about twenty-five acres to each share.

The undivided common lands remained in this state for sixty years longer. On Dec. 1, 1878 Judge Defriez, sitting as a probate court, under the provisions of an act of the legislature ordered their division. Joseph T. Pease and Richard L. Pease were the commissioners for this purpose, and exactly one hundred persons, mostly living in other places, participated in the division of these few remaining acres of little market value.[1]

[1]Chapter 463, Acts and Resolves, 1869, p. 780.

The present representatives of the "praying indians" of Manitouwattootan are few in number, Joseph Quannowill Mingo and wife, and his son, Samuel Mingo, a widower, constituting this remnant. The former, now over four score years of age, an upright and intelligent citizen, has given the author valuable help in a clearing up many obscurities in the early annals of this place.

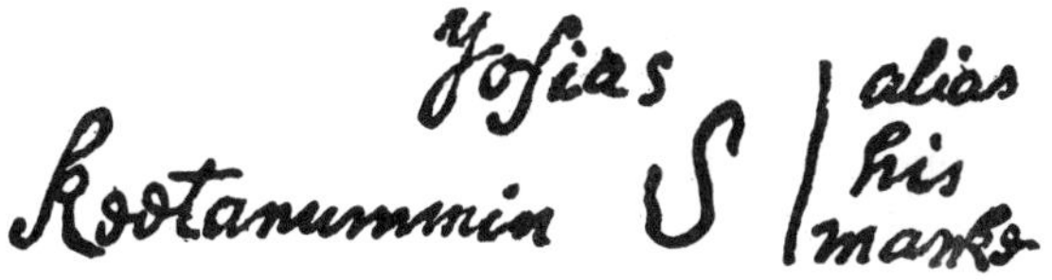

THE SIGN MANUAL OF JOSIAS, SACHEM OF TAKEMMY.

1694.

CHICKEMMOO.

PURCHASED BY THOMAS MAYHEW.

One of the earliest acquisitions of property made by the elder Thomas Mayhew, outside of his home lot at Great Harbor, was the section of land on the North Shore, then and ever since known as Chickemmoo. Although the owner of the soil by purchase, yet in accordance with his custom of honorable dealing with the native inhabitants of the districts where he obtained special titles, he bought from the sachems their rights in Chickemmoo, for which he paid them in coin or its equivalent.

In consideration of "the summe of Ten pound to my content," Cheesechamuck, the Sachem of Homes Hole executed the following deed:—[1]

This doth witness that I Cheesechamuk, the Sachim of Holmses hole doe by these presents sell and set over unto Thomas Mayhew the Elder of the Vineyard one Quarter part of all that land which is called Chickemmow for him the said Thomas Mayhew his heires and assignes to Injoy for ever: the said one quarter of the land of Chickemmow is to begin at ltchpoquaset Brook and so to run by the shore till it comes to the sea side ward and so the said quarter part of land is to runne into the Iland from the sea side to the Middle line of the said land called Chickemmow; the said Thomas Mayhew is to have four spans round in the middle of every whale that comes upon the shore of this quarter part and no more: the hunting of Deire is common, but no trappes to be set:

In witness to this Deed of sale I have set my hand unto it this tenth Day of August 1658

The Marke
X
of Cheeschamuck

Having acquired the rights of the sachem of the Homes Hole territory in this property, the elder Mayhew next bought out the rights of another sachem, Tewanquatuck, which is recorded in the following deed of sale:—

This doth witness that I, Towanquatuck, sachim, for him his heirs and assigns the one quarter part of that land called Chickemmoo, joining to that land I bought of Cheeschamuck, by the sea side, with all the priviledges thereunto belonging unto Thomas Mayhew his heirs and assigns to enjoy forever and I do acknowledge that I have had in full payment for that land aforesaid the full sum of ten pounds:

Witness hereunto my hand the eight day of october 1659

Towanquatuck, his mark[2]

[1]Dukes Deeds, I, 355.

[2]Ibid., I, 182.

By these two purchases, Mayhew had acquired half of the Chickemmoo region and it was ten years before he obtained the remainder. On Feb. 2, 1669, he bought of Maquaine, a praying Indian, one eighth part, and on April 25, 1669, Towanquatuck sold to him three eighths, thus completing the acquisition of the entire property.[1] It will be noticed that there is no description of the extent or limits of the territory involved and this very question arose later. In the charter granted to Tisbury Manor in 1671 the bounds of Chickemmoo are thus stated:—

> ......bounded on the East by a Spring called by the name of Kutta-shim-moo, on the West by a Brooke called Each-poo-quas-sit, on the North by the Sound & on the South by the Bounds of Takemmy.[2]

Chickemmoo is an Algonquian word and in the last two centuries and a half it has retained its proper spelling with but little and unimportant variation in the records. In 1684 it was written in one deed Kutchickemmo,[3] the prefix, meaning great, thus only qualifying its definition, which is "a fish weir" or "a place of the fish weir," perhaps "place of great fish weir."[4] This had reference probably to the present Herring creek on the east corner bound of Chickemmoo, where our aboriginal predecessors undoubtedly set their nets for the alewives that annually ran up into Chappaquonset pond to spawn. In local parlance it is pronounced Chekamy. This tract of land became a well defined section of two towns, widely separated from the parent settlements of both, and was always given special treatment by them. For this reason it is here treated as a distinct local entity.

Ancient Landmarks.

ALGONQUIAN PLACE NAMES.

Conaconaket.—This word is used to describe a "Line" or boundary in Chickemmoo in 1701. John Daggett sold to Thomas Butler certain land "where was a brick kill," and from thence "northerly till it meets with Conaconaket line." (Deeds, II, 44.) In a subsequent instrument John Daggett,

[1]Dukes Deeds, III, 467; V, 321.

[2]New York Archives, Patents, Vol. IV, fol. 73.

[3]Dukes Deeds, I, 273.

[4]A similar name occurs in Rhode Island on Pawcatuck river, Chickmaug and another form in the Cree dialect is Chickamauga.

in 1711, sold to James Cottle certain land near Thomas Butler's, and referred to the "Nowconaca line," which is probably one and the same with the first named reading, the letters k-e-t being omitted from the termination, and N-o being prefixed (ibid, III, 83). "Necorneca head line" is mentioned in 1734 (ibid., VI, 140). The modern spelling is Makonikey. This line bisected Chickemmoo into a northern and a southern half, running at right angles with Savage's line.

The name is the equivalent of the Massachusetts Nukkonohkee, meaning "old land" or "ancient place," and the Narragansett "Necawn-auke". Like many similar words, it came to describe a location inclosed by the line and is now applied to Makonikey Heights and Makonikey Head.

Ponkquatesse. — The spring, called by this name in 1703, was one of the sources of the Black Water brook. In Plymouth there was a name of like derivation, Ponkatesett, a marsh in that town. (Plymouth Deeds, I, 87).

Weechpoquassit (1658), or commonly written Eachpoquasitt, is a boundary designation. Eachpoquassit was the natural boundary line between the sachemships of Takemmy and Nunnepoag, at that part of the island; it also was the west bound of Chickemmoo. The meaning of the word has already been explained.

ENGLISH PLACE NAMES.

Black Water Brook. — Same as Eachpoquasitt [q.v].

Black Pond. — There were two small ponds called by this name, (1) near Lambert's Cove, as one of the chain of ponds, visible from the road, and (2) in the northeast part of Chickemmoo (1765).

Duck Pond. — A small pond in the rear of the Edward Cottle place.

Half Moon Pond. — This was alluded to in 1727, in a deed from Israel to David Butler, wherein the grantor says:— "beginning at the North East part of a pond called half moon pond, then westerly to a fence and then Northerly to Great James Pond" (Deeds, IV, 260). Samuel Lambert lived close to Half Moon pond in 1732. (Deeds, V, 279).

James Pond. — The first occurrence of this name is in 1682 and it probably was so called on account of James, Duke of York, as in 1700 it was designated as "Pond Royall." Before this it had been called Onkakemmy pond and Eachpoquassit pond. The modern name for it is Great James pond.

Muddy Pond. — A small pond near William Athearn's.

No Bottom Pond. — Another small pond next to William Athearn's, the two being of the chain of four in that locality.

Spectacle Pond. — A small pond in the central part of Chickemmoo. This is not an uncommon name for small bodies of fresh water at that period. The word is used in its ancient signification of a reflection or mirror, meaning a clear sheet of water like a mirror. There is a Spectacle pond in Falmouth, one in Sandwich and one in Wareham.

Whirlwind Neck. — This was applied to a dam on the eastern branch of the Eachpoquassit brook at the turn of the stream.

ANNEXED TO TISBURY MANOR, 1671.

When the elder Mayhew and his grandson Matthew secured the town charters for Edgartown and Tisbury in 1671, it will be recalled that a third grant was made to them personally at the same time, for the Manor of Tisbury. The particulars of this grant will be detailed elsewhere, and it will be only necessary to say that this latter manorial grant included several scattered tracts of land in Chilmark and the Elizabeth Islands, including Chickemmoo, which was within the bounds of Tisbury. Chickemmoo being administered by the Lords of the Manor of Tisbury thus became an independent parcel of territory within the chartered limits of another town, and such an anomalous situation speedily led to complications that set two towns by the ears and became the basis of legal entanglements between property owners and tax collectors. During the life of the elder Mayhew his personality prevented any difficulties arising from this situation, but after his death when the lordship passed to Matthew his grandson and later to Thomas Dongan, the dissatisfaction in Tisbury grew into open expression. As soon as Massachusetts assumed jurisdiction, in 1692, over the Island, Simon Athearn persistently complained of these incongruous subdivisions, as elsewhere related, and advocated a consolidation into two towns. In one letter to the General Court dated Oct. 20, 1694, he says:—

If major mayhew object, this I say it seems as Expedient as for Chilmark to Jump over tisbury to Chikkemoo & to Jump over the Sound to Elizabeth Ils: The end of this motion is to heal our being cut in pieces, and to reduce us all in to a competent Township to maintain the worship of God & serve the King & Cuntry.[1]

FIRST SETTLEMENT

During the lifetime of Governor Mayhew, the proprietor of the land and its manorial lord, no attempt was made to settle this region and at the time of his death not an acre of it had been sold by him. In his will, dated June 16, 1681, he disposed of it in two equal parts to his daughters, Hannah Daggett and Martha Tupper, of which the western half fell to the favorite daughter, the wife of Thomas Daggett. This became an accomplished fact when his will was admitted to probate, March 8, 1682, just after his death. Three months after this a definite step towards settling this region was taken by Isaac Chase, a recent arrival from Hampton, N. H., and he applied to the selectmen of Tisbury for permission to acquire property there. The following record shows the action taken by them:—

This: 25: of July 1682

The tounsmen of tysbury do give liberty unto Isack Chace to purtch asartain parsel of land it being forty acres lying one the east side of wechpaquaset pond upon the condison that the foresid Izack chace shall and do setel a mann well proved Among men upon the aforesaid land within fore years after the date of this record and if the fore said Izack chace Do not setel the land as is Above...... the toun shall have the land paying the charg of purchas......[2]

With this authorization Chase proceeded to negotiate with the Sachem Josias, and on August 15th following he had succeeded in securing a large tract which was thus described:—

bounded eastwardly by a river or small brook called Echpooquaset River; westerly by a pond called Echpooquasit pond by the English James his pond and the middlemost of these small runnes of water at the southern end of the said pond from the Southern end of which runne of water to goe by a straight line to the north east corner of a pond lying in the woods commonly called Mekonnichashquat; and from thence extending by a straight line to the middle of a small swamp lying near the head of the aforesaid brook caled Eachpooquasit; and from the middle of sd swamp by a straight line to the head of said river or brook called Echpooquasit which sd brook runeth through the woodes to a little pond called the black pond & from thence into the Sea or Sound which is the North boundes.[3]

[1]Mass. Arch., CVI, 96.
[2]Tisbury Records, 16.
[3]Dukes Deeds, I, 281.

Mekonnichashquat pond is now known as Old House pond and the rest of the description is so clear, an unusual merit in those days, that it scarcely requires any further statement to locate it accurately.

It is presumed that Chase fulfilled his part of the bargain made with the selectmen, and settled "a man well A proved Among men upon the aforesaid land within fore years after," but if he did so there is no record of his personality. This purchase and the Governor's death had the effect of opening up Chickemmoo for the sons of the pioneers who wished for broad acres of their own. Joshua and John Daggett (12), sons of Mrs. Hannah Daggett, had built a house there, on their mother's portion before 1688, and in order to invest them and her with the full panoply of patentees' rights, Matthew Mayhew in August, 1688, confirmed to "his loving aunt" and his two cousins a tract about a quarter of a mile wide "by the Sound from said Eachpoquassit Eastward."[1] It is not believed that Joshua lived on this land, as he was a resident of Edgartown, but the house of John Daggett is frequently mentioned in later years and it is believed that this place was his home in 1688 or earlier.[2] Three years later Mrs. Hannah sold to her son, Capt. Thomas Daggett late of Bristol, R. I., March 18, 1691, one quarter of Chickemmoo, and on Sept. 16, same year, gave her son Joshua another quarter.[3]

The other daughter of the old Governor, Mrs. Martha Tupper of Sandwich, who owned the eastern half, found a purchaser for the entire tract of twelve hundred acres [by estimation] in Isaac Chase, who on Feb. 20, 1691-2, completed this great transfer, probably the largest on record on the island between individuals.[4] Two years later Chase added to his already large holdings on Jan. 2, 1693-4, by acquiring the rights of Captain Thomas Daggett just mentioned. Chase now owned both ends of Chickemmoo and probably three quarters of the entire territory. Still he continued to purchase and on Nov. 16, 1698, he bought one hundred acres next adjoining the Tupper tract of Ephraim Savage of Boston and

[1]Deeds, II, 341.

[2]The plan of Tisbury in 1694 shown on p. 6 shows two houses in Chickemmoo. It is certain that one was John Daggett's and we may surmise that the other was on the Chase property occupied by his tenant, "a man well A proved."

[3]Dukes Deeds, III, 294; V, 84.

[4]Ibid., I, 187.

from that day to this, over two centuries, the dividing line between the two halves of Chickemmoo has been called Savage's Line.[1] Meanwhile on the other half the Daggetts were transferring to each other, until it became necessary to straighten out ownerships, and a division of their property by metes and bounds was made before 1700.

THE ANCIENT BOUNDARIES IN DISPUTE.

The question began to arise at this time concerning the limits of Chickemmoo on its western boundary. Some claimed that it extended to Great James pond, which would seem to have been the natural delimitation instead of the little Black Water brook just east, as held by others. But this did not prevent the sale of property in that region. Thomas Butler (11) of Edgartown made the first of his many purchases in Chickemmoo of Joshua Daggett in Feb. 6, 1700, a sixth of the western or Daggett half, excepting tracts disposed of to his brother, John Daggett.[2] On Dec. 27, 1700, Butler purchased another sixth of the same grantors,[3] and on March 6, 1700-1, Butler bought of Chase the tract between Great James pond and the Itchpooquassit river or brook which had been sold to Chase in 1682 by the Sachem.[3]

Meanwhile the Tisbury proprietors were agitating the boundary question and levying taxes on the strip sold by Chase to Butler, who resisted payment. On Sept. 27, 1703, the town met to consider and voted:—

> that Simon Athern Joseph daggit and John Cottle shall in the behalf of this Town forthwith go and procure three Indifferant Indians of good Report to Joyn with them to settle and Run the Lyne between Nashowkemuck and Tisbury & on the Est side Tisbury [4]

This committee took with them Sam Mackakunit, an Indian preacher, from Edgartown, Pattook an Indian magistrate and Isaac, a Christian Indian, to give evidence in person on the spot, but they were warned off by Butler as trespassers. However the Indians unanimously agreed that the bounds

[1]Ibid., I, 391. It is not known how Ephraim Savage obtained his title. He was a Boston merchant and probably got it through business dealings with one of the Daggetts, although his name does not appear as a grantee in the land records. This effectually disposes of the legend that it was called after the savages of the region who annually fought at that line.

[2]Dukes Deeds, I, 237, 156.

[3]Ibid., I, 158.

[4]Town Records, 46.

between Takemmy and Nunpoag "was so settelled many years ago......:—"

that is at the black water or weechpoquasit being the pond and Run of water: into the sound and said bounds to Run southwardly as the said Run of water Cometh from the spring, Called, ponkquatesse, and from said spring of water to the midle of watchet. on the south side of this Iland so that all the Est side of said bounds to belong unto nunpoak, and on the west side of said ponds unto Takymmy,[1]

THOMAS BUTLER'S LEGAL WAR WITH TISBURY.

Thomas Butler

But if the Indians considered it "settelled," Thomas Butler did not, and he promptly had warrants served on the committee of Tisbury townsmen for trespass and on Oct. 5, just eight days after, the case was tried and Butler won the suit.[2] It is to be supposed that such would be the result with all the family influences at work on and off the bench to uphold the Daggetts in their warranty sales to Butler. However, the case was clearly misjudged, as the evidence of the Indians was unanimous and further investigation only confirmed their contention. Accordingly the selectmen of Chilmark, as the titular proprietary of Chickemmoo, and the selectmen of Tisbury agreed to submit it to the arbitration of a committee of Indians, to be chosen by Experience Mayhew, in order that the question might be settled according to right and justice. The committee of Indians and all concerned met as agreed and their findings are thus recorded:—

whereas we Japhet hannit Isaac wannatta Jacob sokkokkono Joshua seiknout sachim samuell mackkacunit and pautoh. Late sachim of Checkemmo was notified by mr Experience Mayhew or his order that wee are Chosen by mr Nathon skiff and nathon Bassit sellect men of Chilmark: and by simon Athern and John Manter of Tisbury to be a Committy of Indians to goe on monday the seventh day of Feburary and shew the place that is Called weechpooquasset: brook of water and the bounds between the Land Called Cheeckemmo: and the sachimship of Takymmy. and we being met together at the north shore. on marthas vinyerd at the place Called weechpoquasset: with divers others of our adged and Cheif Indian men being preasent & also mr Nathon skiff and nathon basset. sellect men of Chillmark being preasent and mr Josiah Torrey and John daggit. being preasent. and Simon Athern Joseph daggit and John manter men appointed of Tisbury being preasent at weechpooqusset on the seventh

[1]Tisbury Records, 47.

[2]Dukes Court Records, Vol. I.

day of February anno domy 1703-4 we whose names are under written doe Determine that the brook of water that runneth into the sound: being to the Estward of onkkekemmo pond is the only aintient place Called weechpooquasset and the True line and bounds between Checkemmo: and Takymmy as the said brook or run of water lyeth from a sartain spring of water Called ponquatisse which spring is to the north Est of Thomas butlers now dwelling house. and the land on the Est side of the said ponquetissee run or brook of water is Checkemmo land hear to fore belonging to the sachim Towantaquit: and on the west side of the saide ponquetissee and wechpoquassit watter: is the land of Takymmy sachimship now Called Tisbury: here to fore bellonging to the sachm Josias. (signed) Joshua seiknuit Japhet hannit Jacob sokkono patoo Isaac wanata Sam mackkacunit[1]

Thus was the ancient bound of Chickemmoo finally "settelled" as it had existed to mark the dividing line between the Sachems of Nunpoag and Takemmy.

COMPROMISE REACHED.

Butler acquiesced in the decision and, as a result of a conference between him and the Tisbury people, a compromise was reached. This is best explained by quoting the agreement as it is spread out on the town records : —

For & in Consideration of an Isue of a Controversie depending Between the freeholders of Tisbury in dukes County & Thomas Butler of sd place viz: that sd Butler have and doe by these preasents release and discharge Isaac Chase Simon Athern & Joseph daggit of Tisbury from suffering any loss or damage by vertue of a Judgment of the inferiour Court held in Dukes County in october 1703 so that no Excicution of any Judgment found for sd butler against sd Chase Athern & daggit at sd court shall be taken out but for Ever bard & stayed as a thing dead in law and also the sd Isaac Chase simon Athern & Joseph daggit do by these presents release & discharge the sd Thomas butler from answering an apeal or renew about sd Judgment: moreover for peace sake the freeholders of Tisbury so far as it Concerns them do grant & it is voted by the maior of the freeholders of Tisbury preasent at a Leagoll Town meeting held there the 20th day of march 1703-4 that Thomas Butler is granted to have the feesimple right of all that land which Isaac Chase bought of the sachim Josias at wechpoquasset in Tisbury the deed bareing tate the 15th of august 1682 with his now dwelling house possesion to the southward of sd purchase to Thomas Butler to unite with town of Tisbury in peace & love; further more it is voted by the freeholders of Tisbury abovesd that if the inhabitants of chillmarke shall at any Time: destrane upon the aforesd butler on the west of wechpoquassit or ponquatesse by vertue of any rat bill that shall by them from this time forward be made or procured and also provided that sd butler do prosecute against the said In-

[1]Tisbury Records, 47, 48.

habitants of Chillmark for sd money so distraned then said inhabitants of Tisbury to stand by and defend sd Butler in sd sute or sutes so prosocuted to afect and make up to sd Butler all his damages sustained if any be in sd prosocutions by and if at any Time the sd Thomas Butler for with within the bounds of Chillmark by vertue of any lyne fairly made then we the Inhabitants of Tisbury to Reimburs all the money heretofore Taken by Distrant by any Constable belonging to Tisbury from sd Thomas Butler Consented by me THOMAS BUTLER[1]

From this interesting treaty of peace we learn the location of Butler's house among other things and can be reasonably certain in placing it not far from Old House pond, which was the limit of the Chase purchase.

AGREEMENT WITH THE PRAYING INDIANS.

Butler thereupon endeavored to satisfy the chief Indians of Christiantown, who were abuttors on the west side of Chickemmoo, and on May 15, 1705, he reached the following agreement with Isaac Ompanit, trustee, Asa Howwanan, minister, Thomas Paul and Zachariah Papameck concerning their dividing line because of the "many years of contest and discord," viz.:—

Beginning at a Swamp wood tree standing on the beach about four or five rod from the pond, being the Eastern side of sd pond called Aukekemmy pond, and from thence extending southwardly into the island to a white oak tree marked and a heap of stones laid at the root thereof for a bound mark: near the head of the pond about the middle between two springs at the head of sd pond; and from thence to a stick pitched into the ground and heap of stones laid thereto for a boundary being at the east side of the fielde commonly (called) White Pockets field; which foremen-tioned boundary said parties have set and made......and as for the western bound of sd Chickemoo; between sd Chickemoo and said lands called Christiantown

This divisional line was more definite than any of the preceding general "testimonies" of Indians and the subject may now be better understood by further reference to the accompanying map of this region.

Although Butler had legislated himself out of Chilmark and into Tisbury, yet he was between two fires and still a lawful denizen of an outlying section of Chilmark. This latter town "rated" him as did Tisbury, owing to the fact of one community holding jurisdiction over a portion within

[1]Tisbury Records, 149.

the bounds of another.[1] To add to the anomalous situation Chilmark was not an incorporated township under the Massachusetts law. It was still the Manor of Tisbury doing business as a town. Consequently Butler refused to pay taxes to Chilmark and did pay the assessments laid on his property by the Tisbury tax gatherers. In order to free himself of legal or financial consequences he made a further agreement with the townsmen of Tisbury: —

> it is voted at a Legal Town meeting held this 14th day of May 1708. that whereas Captain Thomas Butler having been Rated divers years to Two towns to witt Tisbury and Chilmark to his grate detrement & and damage and now the saide thomas butler doth freely put himself under this Town Tisbury for the futter in the payment of all publique Taxes, wherefore it is now voted that the saide Thomas butler shall sit Rate free in this Town for the space of three years and halfe after the date of these preasents provided that Chilmark doth wholly omit Rateing the said Butler till such time as the bounds be setled between Tisbury and Chilmark on the Est side of Tisbury[2]

EARLY SETTLERS.

With the advent of the century there were two known families resident in Chickemmoo, John Daggett's and Thomas Butler's, comprising twenty souls. The next person to acquire property here was Ebenezer Allen (7) of Chilmark, who bought out the entire homestead holdings of John Daggett "esteemed to be worth £300," in December, 1705, and several years later Daggett removed to Attleborough, Mass., where he thenceforth resided. It is not believed that Ebenezer Allen came here to live, as he was a land speculator in all the Vineyard towns. Isaac Chase (22) purchased in 1706 a portion of his father's tract and probably settled there, as his widow and children occupied the premises after his death. In 1711 James Cottle (10), who had lived in the Keephigon district of Chilmark, made the first of a number of purchases here including land adjoining the Black Water brook and

[1]In observance of advice from her Maiesties Court of quarter sessions held at Edgertown in March 1707 to the sellect men of Tisbury to chuse and nominat men of this Town to Joyne with men Chosen and appointed by the Town of Chilmark to setle the bounds between Tisbury and Chekemoo being part of Chilmark it is voted at a Town meeting that Joseph daggit and John Manter Junier shall serve and act in that affaire for this Town Tisbury (Tisbury Records, 55).

[2]Tisbury Records, 56. The Chilmark records contain only a brief reference ralative to this controversy, but they do not begin till 1704, and therefore subsequent to its inception. In March, 1708, Pain Mayhew and Ebenezer Allen were chosen "to run a line between Tisbury and Thomas Butler" (p. 9).

bordering on the Sound. This land has been identified with the Cottle family ever since, through its occupation by his descendants. Henry Luce (7), next in point of time, bought in 1718 one hundred acres east of Savage's line bounded south by the Homes Hole path. In 1720 Ichabod Allen (9), younger brother of Ebenezer, also of Chilmark, bought all of the John Daggett purchase made by his brother fifteen years previously, and thenceforth became a resident of this section. The same year William Swain of Nantucket acquired two hundred acres bordering on Tashmoo pond, part of the Chase

HOME OF CAPT. NATHAN SMITH (CHICKEMMOO).
IN REVOLUTIONARY DAYS.

property, but it is not known that he came here to reside. Samuel Merry (8) came next in 1723, purchasing a tract adjoining Ichabod Allen, and his descendants occupied it for several generations. In the next three years came Samuel Hatch (44) and his brother Zaccheus (47) from Falmouth, and they were owners of a large tract bounded east by Savage's line and extending from the Neconaca Head line to the Sound.

Samuel died in 1739 and his brother had removed, probably before this. Next in order of time came Joshua Weeks, a miller, who in 1726 bought sixty acres, just south of the

Hatch's tract. Whence he migrated is not known, but he had married before 1710 Abigail West (11), daughter of Dr. Thomas, of Homes Hole, and they were members of the Sabbatarian church in Newport at that time. Samuel Coffin of Nantucket bought two hundred acres of the Chases, bordering on the Sound, but he is believed to have been a non-resident owner. Joseph Parker came from Falmouth in 1730 and purchased the land previously owned by the Hatch brothers. He sold it to Thomas Smith (355) of Edgartown in 1734 and it was occupied by the descendants of the latter for several generations. It was the home of Deacon Ransford (410) and Capt. Nathan Smith (415) of the Revolutionary period. Jonathan Dunham (60) in 1735 bought thirty acres of Thomas Smith's lot and remained until 1743, when he removed to Sharon, Conn. In 1737 Bryant Cartwright, son-in-law of Joshua Weeks, bought a part of the Weeks' property and resided on it for about forty years. He was also a Sabbatarian Baptist and before 1767 removed to Hopkinton, R. I. Nathaniel Pease (140), long a resident of Edgartown, bought the Jonathan Dunham house and farm in 1743, but it is not certain that he removed to Chickemmoo to reside. In 1745 John Lewis, perhaps of Yarmouth, Cape Cod, came here and purchased a shore lot in the eastern half of the Chase property. In 1747 the brothers Eliakim (420) and Peter Norton (421) made the first of a number of purchases here and Eliakim became a resident. With his brother he owned 120 acres jointly, and 400 acres individually. John Mayhew (120) was a purchaser in 1748, but it is not believed that he removed hither from his home in Chilmark. This property was deeded in 1756 to his son Malatiah (270), who disposed of it six years later.

These were the proprietors and settlers of Chickemmoo up to 1750, and at that date, reckoning the known families resident in this district, there was a population of about 150 persons.

CHICKEMMOO ANNEXED TO TISBURY

The incongruous isolation of this section from the parent town of Chilmark became a source of great inconvenience to the people of Chickemmoo as the settlement here grew in population, and in 1736 they prepared a petition, headed by David Butler, Ichabod Allen and others, shewing that they live Eight Miles from the Meeting House in said Town, and but four from Tisbury Meeting House, which they must pass by in their Travell to Chilmark; And therefore praying That the whole Tract of Land called Checkamo with their Inhabitants and their Estates may be sett off from Chilmark and Annexed to the Town of Tisbury.

This was heard by the General Court, "together with the Answer of Payne Mayhew Esqr,"[1] and the matter being fully considered, the following law was enacted Dec. 30, 1736:

> Ordered that the prayer of the petitioners be so far granted as that the pet'rs with their Estates lying in the place Mentioned be and hereby are to all Intents and purposes Set off from the Town of Chilmark and Annexed to the Town of Tisbury for the future; provided the pet'rs be and hereby are held and subjected to the payment of all Rates & Taxes what soever which have hitherto been Assessed on them by the Town of Chilmark, or otherwise by Order of Law.[2]

The separation was probably a relief to Chilmark, and if we may judge from the town records, Chickemmoo occupied very little space in the calculations of the townsmen. The name does not occur half a dozen times up to the transfer of jurisdiction.

From this date the history of the Chickemmoo district is a part of the annals of Tisbury and it will not be further considered separately from the town at large. In the division of the old town of Tisbury in 1892 this ancient district was bisected and it has consequently come to be a part of three towns in its existence, Chilmark, Tisbury and West Tisbury.

[1]The Chilmark records have no reference to this matter.

[2]Province Laws, Chap. CXVIII (1736). As showing the slow rate of dissemination of news at that time a deed dated in Oct. 20, 1737, nearly one year after recites that the land is "in Checamoot late of Chilmark but now Supposed to be of Tisbury" (Deeds, VI, 200).

OLD CURB WELL, WEST TISBURY.

ANNALS OF CHILMARK

ANNALS OF CHILMARK.

NASHOWAKEMMUCK.

This was the Indian name for Chilmark, although the bounds of the section known to the Indians as Nashowakemmuck do not entirely correspond to the present limits of this town. This name of the greater part of Chilmark is formed of two Algonquian words, Nashowa- and kemmuck, meaning "the half way house," the significance of which is not clear. It may have referred to a school house, or an Indian house or stockade.

BOUNDARIES.

As defined in the charter of Tisbury Manor, in 1671, this region was bounded as follows: "beginning at a Place called Wakachakoyck & goeth to the River Arkspah, running from the said Wakachakoyck by a straight line to the middle of the Island, where is the middle line that divides the Land of Towtoe and others & the Land sold to the said Thomas Mayhew and from the Place that line meeteth the middle Lyne soe dividing the land as aforesaid to goe to the Harbour on the North side of the Island called Wawattick."

On May 12, 1685, Matthew Mayhew gave the following description of Nashowakemmuck: "The land called Nashowakemmuck, bounded easterly by the bounds of line between Takemmy or Tisbury and the said Nashowakemmuck; southerly by the sea; northerly by a line called the Middle Line, beginning at a rock which parteth, or is bound between the north and south partition of that part of the said Island of Martin's Vineyard, and from thence extending westardly, as the line hath been run or set until it meet with a line to be drawn from the harbour on the north side of the Island, called Waweaktick, to the westermost part of the fence, now standing on the south side of the Island, called Wesquobscutt now or late in the tenure or occupation of Nathaniel Skiff; which said line so to be drawn is the western bounds of the said lands."

Chilmark was a unique town, territorially, for many years, as it comprised three outlying tracts, widely separated, viz: Chickemmoo, which was within the corporate limits of Tisbury, Nomans Land and the Elizabeth Islands. In 1736 Chickemmoo was made a part of Tisbury, and in 1864 the town of Gosnold was formed from the Elizabeth Islands. Including Nomans Land, which still remains to her of her ancient possessions, the town boundaries on the east, adjoining Tisbury, have not changed. The western boundaries are at Menemsha creek, thence by a line drawn through the Menemsha pond to the narrowest part of Nashowaquidset neck where it joins Gay Head; thence across in a straight line to Squibnocket pond; thence southerly across to the point near the old house of Abner Mayhew; thence northerly to the northwest corner of the pond; thence across the beach to the sea in a southwest direction, as marked by stones.

CHILMARK.

This name is first given to the Manor of Tisbury in a deed from Thomas Mayhew to Daniel Stewart, March 26, 1680, where Mayhew calls himself "of the town of Chilmark in the Manor of Tysbery." It is mentioned in another deed under date of April 1, 1693, and appears on Simon Athearn's map of 1694. The reason for the bestowal of this name is found in its relation to the Mayhew family at the time Thomas Mayhew lived in the adjoining parish of Tisbury. It was undoubtedly found that confusion arose from the use of the names of Tisbury Manor and Tisbury, a condition which Mayhew remedied by reviving the old familiar title of one of the ancestral homes of his family.

THE ENGLISH CHILMARK.

The earliest record of this parish is in the Saxon Chartulary of Wilton Abbey, in which King Athelstan makes a grant of the place called "Childmearc." In the Domesday Book it is designated as Chilmerc, and is placed among the lands of the church of Wilton. It then contained fourteen ploughlands, fifteen villagers, twelve borderers and twelve freedmen, occupying twelve ploughlands. The mill paid

VILLAGE STREET, CHILMARK, ENG.

twelve shillings. "Here are," it records, "five acres of meadow and ten acres of thorns."

In "Nomina Villarum" it is mentioned as belonging to the Abbey of Wilton, until the 35th year of King Henry VIII (1545), when it, with the site of the monastery of Wilton and divers other manors, was granted to William Herbert, Earl of Pembroke, and his wife. The church living is still a gift of the Earls of Pembroke.[1]

The church is dedicated to S. Margaret, and is an interesting example of early ecclesiastical architecture. It is cruciform in shape, with a steeple, having a clock, rising from the junction of the nave and transept. The doorway is ornamented with curious effigies carved in stone, supporting the arches. The rector has as a residence a beautiful stone house of Elizabethan architecture, situated on the glebe of the parish. The village is quiet and picturesque, apparently devoted to bucolic pursuits. Its population in 1800 was 406 and in 1886 was 554, about the same general size as our own New England Chilmark. It was the birth place of Thomas Macy, the well known settler of Nantucket, and a cousin of our Thomas Mayhew. Macy stones are to be seen in the church-yard now.[2]

POPULATION.

Chilmark was the last of the three original towns to become settled, and it is not until toward the end of the 17th century that any appreciable population resided in its limits.[3] By reference to the genealogies of the families known to have been living here in 1700, a total of 73 persons can be counted at that date. This makes no account of "others" who may have been here in the capacity of teachers, servants or laborers on the farms, exclusive of Indians. Perhaps ten or a dozen more, at the outside, would cover this class of transient residents. That Chilmark increased more rapidly than the other towns in population in this century is known from taxation and valuation lists, but no definite statistics are available

[1]Hoare, History of Wiltshire, IV, 124.

[2]A will of Thomas Maycie of Chilmark, dated 1575, was found by the author during his visit to England. It mentions sons Thomas, John, Philip and William, one of whom was probably the father of the Nantucket settler.

[3]In 1692 there were about twenty families residing in Tisbury and Chilmark, the exact number in each not known. It is not far from the actual truth to divide this number in two and thus give twelve and eight respectively to these adjoining settlements. We can thus estimate about 40 persons living in Chilmark at that date.

until 1757 in an "alarm list" of males which numbers 91 able to respond. Using 5 as a multiple we have a total of 455 souls at this date. The Provincial census of 1765 is more accurate and from this we obtain the following figures:—families, 114, comprising a total of 546 souls living in 90 houses. Of these 159 were males and 179 females above sixteen years of age; 152 male and 156 female below sixteen; 17 negroes (9 male and 8 female) and 188 Indians, of whom 72 were male and 116 female.

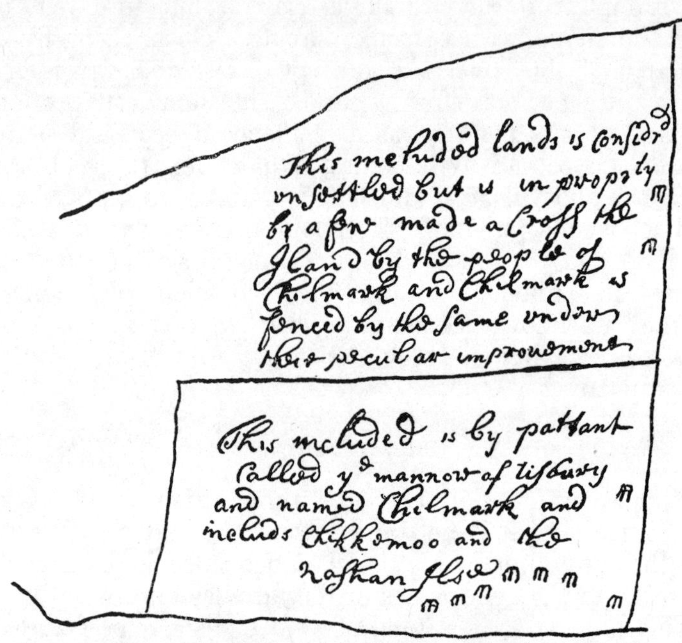

ANCIENT PLAN OF CHILMARK, 1694.

DRAWN BY SIMON ATHEARN

It was the second town in population at that date, though the large proportion of Indians living here accounts for this lead over Tisbury. Ten years later, in 1776, the population is estimated at about 700, or about one quarter of the entire enumeration of the island.

The first national census of 1790 gives us the enumeration by names, and from this the following statistics are drawn: total population 770 (whites), of which number there were 199 males above sixteen years, 157 below sixteen and 404 "free white" females. There were ten "other free persons," presumably negroes.

The following figures show the population of Chilmark as enumerated in the decennial censuses of the United States from 1800 to the present time:—

In 1800 it was 800; in 1810, 723; in 1820, 695; in 1830, 691; in 1840, 702; in 1850, 747; in 1860, 654; in 1870, 476; in 1880, 494; in 1890, 353; and in 1900, 324.

Chilmark has had an irregular but steady decrease in population since 1800, although the two towns of Gosnold and Gay Head were formed from this population, which in a large measure accounts for losses since 1860. The state census of 1905 showed a population of 322.

The crude but valuable sketch plan of Chilmark in 1694 (on the preceding page) is the earliest one of its kind known to the author, and it is a part of a rough map of the whole island. The legends on the plan are as follows:—

This included lands is considrd unsettled but is in propr(ie)ty by a fenc(e) made a Cross the Iland by the people of Chilmark and Chilmark is fenced by the same under their peculiar improvement.

This included is by pattant Called the mannor of tisbury and named Chilmark and includes Chikkemoo and the Nashan Ilse.

Seven houses are shown on the south road, one near the present Middle road, and two in the Keephiggon district, ten in all. The houses on the south road can in part be identified as the residences of James Allen, Nathaniel Skiff, Benjamin Skiff, Nathan Skiff, Rev. Rodolphus Thatcher, and probably Thomas Mayhew and Nathan Bassett. The house in the region of New Mill river is that of Richard Ellingham, and in Kephigon of Samuel Tilton.

ANCIENT LANDMARKS.

ALGONQUIAN PLACE NAMES.

Arkessah–Arkspah.—In the grant of the Manor of Tisbury, dated July 8, 1671, the "river Arkspah running from the said Wakachakoyck" is mentioned, as one of the bounds of Nashowakemmuck. As far as known this is the only occurrence of this name as applied to a place in Chilmark. As written in the patent of the manor it is probably an error for Arkessah made by the clerk or copyist who engrossed the document, due to ignorance of Indian names. In the opinion of the author it is an abbreviation of Wachap-Arkessah, the Algonquian name for Pease's brook.

Keephikkon. — This place is mentioned in 1663 (Dukes Deeds, I, 93). This word has a great variety of forms, Keephickon (1671), Keipheigon (1675), Cephecand (1678) and Ciphecan (1684). The modern spelling, Cape Higgon, is a blunder, similar to the error made in Cape Poge. It means "an artificial enclosure," and the word refers to the land purchased by Thomas Mayhew of the Indians in 1663, which was enclosed by a fence. In the Delaware dialect it is Kup-hei-gan, and in Otchipwe it is K-pah-i-kan, all meaning "something that shuts in."

In the charter of Tisbury Manor, dated July 8, 1671, the following description of the bounds of this section are given:—"Another parcell of Land called Ceep-hickon Bounded on the East by the Westermost Bounds of Takemmy from whence it extendeth about a Mile and halfe Westward along the Sound, which is the North Bounds, and to the South reaching to the middle of the Island."

It is thus described by Matthew Mayhew, May 12, 1685:—"The whole containing by estimation one English mile and a halfe by the Sound, and extending to the beforesaid rock (Waskosims) and middle Line from the Sound southerly."

Muckuckhonnike. — In a deed of land from Thomas Mayhew to Daniel Steward, dated March 24, 1680, this name is given to a tract of land in Chilmark, "being on the beach opposite against the point of a neck of Quanaimes which John Mayhews house standeth upon" (Deeds, I, 266). This word is a compound of Mukkonne- and auke, signifying "Land of the congregation or assembly," and probably refers to one of the missions for the natives conducted by one of the Mayhews in this vicinity.

Meshpootacha. — This is the cove at the division line of Quia-naimes and Quanissoowog, first mentioned in a deed dated Aug. 20, 1681, Thomas Mayhew to John Mayhew, as a "cove of watter called by the Indians Mesputache." (Deeds, I, 407.) The modern name for the point designated is Black Point, and it is also applied to the cove adjoining. The word is from Massa-pootoe-ohke, "great swelling-out land." A similar name occurs on Long Island, Masspootupaug, now known as the Great South bay, the definition being "the great spreading-out water place." (Southampton Records, II, 27.)

Mossommoo. — In a deed from some Indians to Hannah Skiffe in 1737, conveying land in Chilmark, a neck called

"Mossommoo" is mentioned (VII, 247). Massachusetts dialect, Mosommo "where shearing (of sheep) is." Probably a place where it was customary at one time to gather the sheep together for shearing. The word, like many others, is of date subsequent to settlement of the island.

Menemsha. — *Monamesha, Unanemshie and Manamshounk* are variations of this name in the records. "Westermost land of Nope (alias) Martin's Vineyard........which land is distinguished or bounded from the rest of the land of Martin's Vineyard by a certain creek called by the name of Manamshounk, which land is called by the Indians Aquinnah & by the English Gay Head" (Deeds, III, 12). The name originally did not belong to the creek or the pond, but probably indicated a standing tree or pole placed on one of the hills near the creek, or it may have been the name of the locality itself, "as seen from afar." The terminal -unk is an inseparable generic denoting a solitary standing tree, while the adjectival prefix signifies "a vision" (Massachusetts). The reading would therefore be, "the observation tree or pole," erected for the purpose of signalling, when the whales were in sight. Monamansu-auke, meaning, "place of observation," may apply to Prospect hill, the highest on the Vineyard in the region of the Menemsha pond.

Nashowaquidsee. — "Nashawaqueedse" is first mentioned in 1684, and later, in 1703, the neck is called "Nashowaquetset" "Nashaquitsa," "Nashawaqueedsee," "Nashouahquedset." This word in the full Algonquian rendering is Nasawa-aquiden-es-et from the radix, Nazhwi or Nizhwi, the numeral two, which can be translated the divided or doubled; aquiden, meaning an island, es diminuitive, rendering it islet, or a little island, and -et, the locative suffix. The rendering therefore is "at the little divided island," referring, probably to the insular formation between Menemsha and Squibnocket ponds.

Nimpanikhickanuh. — This was the name of the place where the Rev. Experience Mayhew lived in Chilmark. In 1722 he wrote that it signified in English, "the place of thunder clefts," because there was once a tree split by lightning at that spot.

Quinames. — A neck called "Quanaymes" in Nashowakemmuck, is mentioned in a deed dated May 17, 1664, and again in a deed dated 1678 (I, 265). The definition of this word is "the long fish" (eel), and refers to a locality where the Indians caught them. In the will of Thomas

WEQUOBSKET CLIFFS. NOMANS LAND IN THE DISTANCE.

Mayhew, Sr., this neck is called Quannaimes or Quannissoowauge (Deeds I, 327). Matthew Mayhew sold to his brother John, Nov. 8, 1687, certain "land called Quanso or Quanimset" (Deeds III, 174). In 1712-13 the neck was described as "called by the name of Quansow alias Nomagua" (Deeds III, 104). There was a Quansue on Nantucket, now called Consue. The modern spelling on the Vineyard is Quansoo.

Saphehogasoo. — John Pachaket, Indian of Gay Head, in a deed to Zachary Hosewit, of land in Chilmark, mentions a neck "called Pachok neck or by the Indian name of Saphehogasoo, 1738" (Deeds VI, 294). John Phillips, one of the sachems of Nashowakemuck, to John Pachaket "my kinsman," a tract of land at a place "known by the Indians Pokawamet......small neck called Sapachchogasso" (Deeds IV, 12). This name was intended for Sha-pachaug-as-ṣoo, "at the midway turning place." In 1759 it is called Pechockers neck, near Gunning point (Deeds VIII, 659).

Squeppunnocquat. — Squibnocket, modern. The definition is "A place where the red ground nut grows." M'squepun-ock-ut; it was probably the bulb of the orange red lily (Lilium Philadelphicum) which grows in great profusion around this region. In various dialects it is known as the meadow ground nut. The Indians ate the roots, which are long in boiling, and they taste like the liver of sheep.

Tiaskuhkonuh. — In a deed, dated 1719, Experience Mayhew sold land at Quansoo running due north from a cove of water called T(S)iashkuhkonuh (Deeds, III, 248). Experience Mayhew sold to Elishab Adams in 1737 a tract of land in Chilmark and mentions a "cove of water called Siashkakonsett" (VI, 236). It is difficult to say to what this name originally applied. It may have been "a path," "a bridge," "stones laid down for crossing," etc. "a place trodden down," Massachusetts Eliot Tashkuhkan-ah, "he trode down" (2 Chron., 25-8). Tashkuhkon- "Trodden" (Isaiah, 28-8). Tashkuhkon-es-et "at a place trodden down."

Wawaytick. — This was the name of the creek which empties Menemsha pond into the Bight. The first occurence of the work is in the patent of Tisbury Manor, under date of July 8, 1671: "the Harbour on the North side of the Island called Wawattick." In Kendall's "Travels" (1807) it is spoken of as "Wawaytick Creek which runs from Menemsha Pond." In all Algonquian dialects Wawi indicates "round" because it refers to the shape of an egg, called by the same word. The last syllable -tukq, tick, is defined as a tidal inlet, or creek, and the whole in its application is freely rendered as "round, or winding-about, creek; the winding creek," which is a correct description of this crooked stream (Deeds I, 384).

Wequobscut. — "Wequobsket" is first mentioned in a deed dated 1695 (I, 385). "Wequobset Cliffs" mentioned in a deed dated 1697 (I, 387). Thomas Mayhew in his will (1725) writes it Weaquabsqua (Probate I, 160). This word is probably an attempt of the Indians to describe an artificial bound-mark. It is from the words: Wequ-obsk-ut, meaning "at the ending rock," and refers to the well-known "Stone Wall" in Chilmark, at the southwestern boundary of Nashawakemmuck.

Wachapakesuh. — This was a small brook, probably the one next west of the "fulling mill brook," and is referred to in a conveyance from Matthew Mayhew to Benjamin Skiffe, July 20, 1682, viz: a neck called Nathaniel's Neck, in Nashawkemmuck, containing 18 acres, "bounded Easterly by a brook which runneth into a pond which pond is the South bound: westwardly by a small brook called by the Indians Wachapkesuh: North by the foot path or road which goeth towards the west end of the island, crossing the said brook." It is without doubt the stream known to the English as Pease's brook.

Wakachakoyck. — In the grant of the Manor of Tisbury, dated July 8, 1671, the bounds of Nashowakemmuck are described as "beginning at a place called Wakachakoyck." This word is a compound of Wek-adch-ohke (auke), the meaning of which is "land or place at the end of a hill." This is the only occurrence of the word in our records and its location is in doubt.

ENGLISH PLACE NAMES.

Beetle Bung Corner. — The junction of the Middle road and the Menemsha road has been called by this curious name for nearly two hundred years. A clump of hornbeam trees growing near this spot gave it the name of Beetle Bound Tree corner as early as 1729 (Deeds V, 67), because the trees marked a boundary. The name Beetle "Bung" corner is a clumsy and meaningless corruption of the original signification of the name. Hornbeam wood was used then in the manufacture of beetles for loosening the bungs of casks and hogsheads, and the trees were sometimes called beetlewood trees.

Fulling Mill Brook. — The Fulling Mill brook is mentioned in a deed dated 1694. It starts in a swamp near the middle road and empties into Chilmark pond.

Mile Square. — The "Mile Square" in Chilmark was a tract bought by Matthew Mayhew of Chipnock, an Indian, and his daughter, about 1703, and adjoining Menamsha pond.

Mark's Valley. — Ebenezer Allen in a deed to John Allen sold land in Chilmark, and mentioned "Markes Valley" (Deeds III, 394).

Nabs Corner. — The junction of the Chilmark-Tisbury line and the South road has borne this name for over a century. It derived its name from one Abigail Dunham, single woman, who lived near there, before 1800, and achieved considerable notoriety during her life.

New Mill River. — Matthew Mayhew conveyed to Capt. Benjamin Skiffe in 1696, the right to use "New mill river," "to improve for a mill" (Dukes Deeds I, 125). It flows along easterly, parallel to the Middle road, crosses the Tisbury line and continues its course through that town.

Pease's Brook. — Mentioned in a deed, 1697, as near the Sugar Loaf rock in Chilmark. It empties into the western end of Chilmark pond, after a long circuitous route starting beyond the Middle road. It is not known for whom it was named, as none of this island family owned land there. It may have derived its title from some incident connected with one of them.

Pamehannit's Field. — Mentioned in a deed from Matthew Mayhew to Nathan Bassett in 1705. "Pamehannits Field now the top of the Hill," east of the Fulling Mill brook (Deeds II, 25).

Roaring Brook. — This stream of water, emptying into the Sound, is first mentioned in a deed dated in 1681 (I, 263).

Sugar Loaf Rock. — This well-known landmark is first mentioned in 1677, and retains this designation to the present day (Deeds I, 387).

The Stone Wall. — "A place called the Stone Wall" is mentioned in a deed in 1732. See Wequobsket.

FIRST PURCHASES OF LAND BY THE MAYHEWS

The first attempt of the Mayhews to acquire the Indian "rights" in the present limits of the town of Chilmark, was made by the younger Mayhew, before 1657, but as the date is not of record, it may only be surmised when it was accomplished. It was the tract

> beginning at a Place called Wakachakoyck & goeth to the River (Wachap) arkessah, running from the said Wakachakoyck by a streight Line to the middle of the Island where is the middle Line that divides the land of Towtoe and others & the Land sold to the said Thomas Mayhew: and from the Place that Line meeteth the middle Line soe dividing the Land as aforesaid to goe to the Harbour on the North side of the Island called Wawattick.[1]

This tract was called by the Indians "Nashawakemmuck," and represents all the territory south of the Middle line, and between the Tisbury bounds on the east and Pease's brook and Menemsha pond on the west. It is not known for what purpose he bought this land, but his early death prevented the carrying out of any design he may have had for the settlement of this region. The next purchase was made by the elder Mayhew on Feb. 3, 1663, when he bought of Kemasaoome and Mamooampete, for the sum of five pounds, the neck called Quanames. The conveyance recites that

> the said Neck is bounded to the Westward by the Pond: to the Eastward by the midst of Ukquiessa, and so to run up in a straight line into the woods to the path that goes from the school house to Tiasquam, somewhere between the bridge and the school house and not further into the woods: and it is to goe to the sea so far as the bounds is according to the line that runs through the midst of Ukquiessa Pond aforesaid.[2]

This tract was bounded east by the Great Tisbury pond, west by Chilmark pond, and by the South road on the north. On Sept. 20th of the same year, Mayhew made another purchase comprising land on the north side of the Middle line. The grantors were three brothers of Towtowee, the sachem of that region, and the land purchased was described in the following terms:—

> which land lyeth from the midst of the Pond Kyphiggon to Koyhikkon way in the natural bounds by the seaside between Nashowakemmuck and Takemmy: and so to run into the middle of the island, and be at

[1] N. Y. Col. Mss., Patents, IV, 73.

[2] Dukes Deeds, II, 39. He sold this on July 14, 1673, to his two grand sons, Thomas and John.

the same breadth threw in the midst of the Island as it is by the sound side, for the which land We Konkoononammin, Makekonnit and Keesquish do hereby acknowledge that the said Thomas Mayhew .... shall have as much land by the sea side from the midst of the said poynt

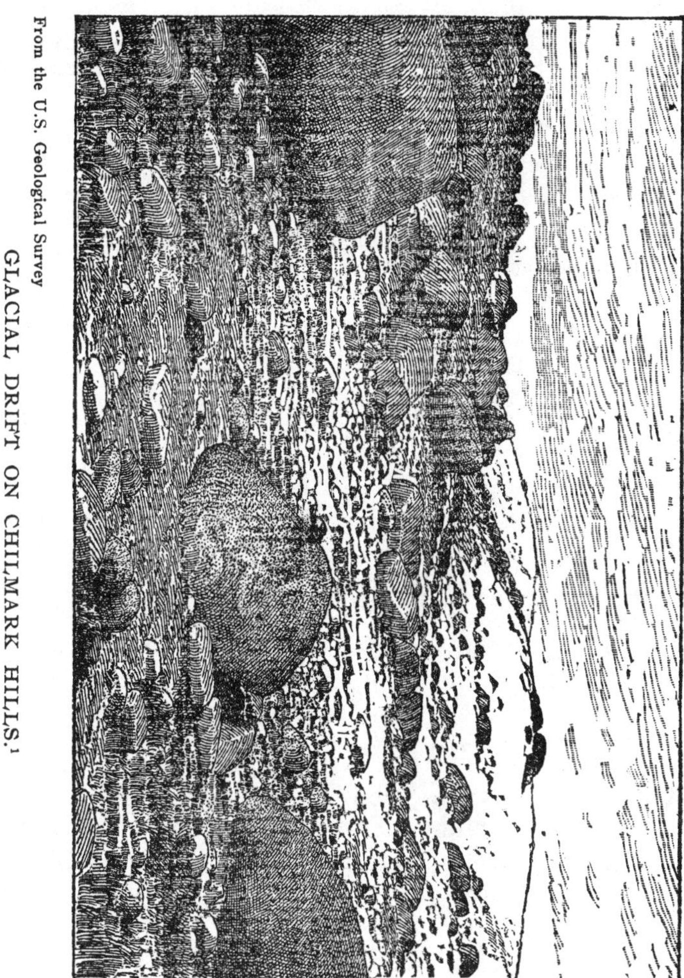

From the U.S. Geological Survey

GLACIAL DRIFT ON CHILMARK HILLS.[1]

(pond ?) Keephiggon as shall make the breadth by the sea side three quarters of an English mile Beginning at Keephiggon aforesaid, for which we do acknowledge we have rec'd four pounds in full satisfaction.[2]

[1]It is probable that Crevecoeur after viewing a scene like this at the time of his visit in 1782 reported the valuable observation that "Chilmark contains stone for fencing." (Lettres d'un Cultivateur Americain.)

[2]Dukes Deeds, I, 93-4.

On May 17, 1664 Mayhew added to this tract, by purchase from Kessukamuh, of a square mile "beginning at the middle of the pond at Keepehiggon" and running a mile by the Sound, and a mile into the "midle of the Island."[1] This overlapped the other, and increased the tract by a quarter of a mile. It is the land in the extreme northeast part of Chilmark, adjoining the Tisbury line. Likewise on the same day he obtained from Pamehannet, the sachem of Quanames, father of the celebrated Japhet Hannet, a quitclaim of all his rights in that neck.[2] Four years later he bought of Josias, the sachem of Takemmy, on June 27, 1668,

> all that land that lyeth to the Eastward of Quanaimes, which Pemehannett and Kemasoome sold to the said Thomas Mayhew........from Quansooway along by the Fresh Pond till it comes to the issuing forth of Tyasquan: and from thence up to the bridge wch is at the path that comes from the mill: and so from the bridge along the school house path till it meets with the land sold the said Mayhew by the said Pamehannett and Kemesoom: so this land is bounded to the Westward by that which was Pamehannetts: by the Sea on the South: by the Fresh Pond to the Eastward: and Northerly by Teeassquan River to the bridge: and then by the school house path till it meet with aforesaid land which was Pemehannetts.

The consideration for this was a "cow and suit of clothes from top to toe," and seventeen pounds in money.[3] This land is on the western shore of Tisbury pond and extends to the South road, and bounded on the west by an imaginary line from "Nab's Corner" to Mesapootacha cove.

THE MIDDLE LINE.

These purchases from the Indians secured to the Mayhews the fee of all of the southern and eastern portions of Chilmark, leaving a section bordering on the Sound and on Menemsha pond under the control of the natives. The reference to the "Middle Line" makes it desirable to have an authoritative definition of its relations to the lands in question, and the following quotation from an agreement concluded between Matthew Mayhew and the Indians as to this well-known bound mark shows its location:—

> a Line drawn straight from a great Rock standing by takemie bound to the middle of a line drawn across the island and so to the pond: said

[1]Dukes Deeds, I, 93.
[2]Ibid., I, 92.
[3]Ibid., I, 408.

line to be drawn across as near the said pond as may be called Monamesha pond.[1]

The rock mentioned is the present landmark, known as Waskosims rock, on the dividing line between Tisbury and Chilmark.

It is not believed that at this time there were any white settlers residing within the present limits of Chilmark.

These individual purchases of the "rights" of the Indians by Mayhew gave him undisputed control of by far the largest tract of land in severalty upon the island, and from his subsequent movements in regard to it, we are justified in concluding that he intended to retain it as a large landed estate, modeled after the medieval ownerships of the land in England and on the continent.

CREATION OF THE MANOR OF TISBURY

When Thomas Mayhew and his grandson, Matthew, went to New York in the summer of 1671 to settle the questions of jurisdiction and government of this island with Governor Lovelace, as elsewhere related, he probably had in his mind a clear outline of what he wished to secure from the representative of the Duke of York. He was now an old man, and had risen to a unique position among his colonial confreres. Doubtless his thoughts harked back to the place of his birth and the scenes of his childhood, and the recollections of Tisbury with its manor aroused in him a desire to become the head of a like social institution, the first of a line of Lords of the Manor in another Tisbury. He had recollected the Arundels of Wardour, the hereditary Lords of Tisbury Manor in Wiltshire, living but a short distance from his boyhood home, and the grandeur of their position, holding dominion over their broad acres, with tenants filling the manor barn every harvest, as acknowledgments of their fealty, in lieu of knightly service; and having already had a taste of the headship of a community for many years, upon a sort of mutual agreement, or compact plan, he now wanted the legitimate fruit of his position made distinctive. Thus, when he laid his desires before Governor Lovelace, one of them was nothing less than the creation of a manorial demesne on the Puritan Vineyard, with himself and his grandson Matthew as joint Lords of the Manor, and so in succession to their heirs male.

[1]Deeds, III, 435.

This idea did not meet with the least disfavor in the mind of the royal governor, himself son of a knight, and as there were already several manors erected in the Province of New York, a ready acceptance of it was found. Doubtless he considered it a good idea to plant before the eyes and under the noses of the Dissenters and Puritans of Massachusetts a conspicuous example of the good old customs of "Merrie England" with its armorial county families and loyal tenantry.

Accordingly on the day in which the two patents of Edgartown and Tisbury passed the seals, there was issued another, creating Tisbury Manor out of the several purchases made by Mayhew in the present territory of Chilmark, Tisbury and the Elizabeth Islands, heretofore described, the full text of which is herewith incorporated to show the terms and extent of this grant.

The following is a copy of the "Patent or Confirmacon of Tisbury Mannor unto Mr Thomas Mayhew & Mr Matthew Mayhew his Grand Childe:—"

FRANCIS LOVELACE Esq: one of the Gentlemen of his Ma'ties Hon'ble Privy Chamb'r and Governor Gen'll under his Royall Highness JAMES Duke of Yorke and Albany &c of all his Territories in America: To all to whom these Presents shall come sendeth Greeting:

WHEREAS there is a certaine Island within these his Royall Highness his Territoryes in Length over against the Maine neare East and West & being to the North West of the Island Nantuckett wch said Island was heretofore Granted unto Thomas Mayhew Sen'r & Thomas Mayhew Jun'r his Sonn by James Forrett Agent to William Earle of Sterling in whom the Government then was a considerable part or Severall parcells of wch said Island hath by the said Thomas Mayhew Sen'r & Thomas Mayhew Jun'r his Son been purchased of the Indian Proprietors & due satisfaction given for the same whereof for diverse Years past they have been & still are in quiet & Lawfull Possession the Particulars of which said Parcells of Land are as hereafter is sett forth vizt That is to say a Certaine Piece of Land called Chickemote bounded on the East by a Spring called by the Name of Kutta-shim-moo on the West by a Brooke called Each-poo-qua-sitt on the North by the Sound & on the South by the bounds of Ta-kem-my: An other Parcell of Land called Keep-hickon Bounded on the East by the Westermost Bounds of Takemmy from whence it extendeth about a Mile and halfe Westward along the Sound wch is the North Bounds, and to the South reaching to the middle of the Island. Then a piece of Land called Quia-names Bounded on the East by Takemmy Pond on the West by Nashowakemmuck Pond & a foot Path wch Goeth from the said Pond to a Brooke called by the Name of Tyas-quin wch Brooke is its North Bounds: As also the Land called Nashowa-Kemmuck Sold to Thomas Mayhew Jun'r beginning at a Place called Wakachakoyck & goeth to the River Arkessah, running from the said Wakachakoyck by a streight Line to the middle of the Island where is the middle Line that divides the Land of Towtoe and others & the Land sold to the said Thomas Mayhew and from the Place that Line meeteth the middle Lyne soe dividing the Land as aforesaid to goe to the Harbour on the North side of the Island called Wawattick: Together wth two of the Elizabeth Islands called Kataymuck & Nanname-sitt & other Severall Small & Inconsiderable Islands in Monument Bay: NOW for a Confirmacon unto the Said Thomas Mayhew Sen'r & Matthew Mayhew his Grand Childe the Son & Heyre of Thomas Mayhew Jun'r in their Possession & enjoymt of the Premisses KNOW YE that by Vertue of the Commission and Authority unto mee given by his Royall Highness upon whom (as well by the resignacon & Assignmt of the Heyres of the said Wm Earle of Sterling as also by Graunt & Patent from his Royall Majestye CHARLES the second) the Propriety & Governmt of Long Island Martins Vineyard Nantuckett & all the Islands adjacent amongst other things is settled, I have Given and Granted & by these Presents doe hereby Give Ratify Confirme & Graunt unto the said Thomas Mayhew & Matthew Mayhew his Grand Childe their Heyres & all the aforementioned Pieces & Parcells of Land Islands & Premisses to bee Erected into a Mannor & for the future to be called & knowne by the name of TYSBURY MANNOR Together wth all the Lands Islands Soyles Woods Meadowes Pastures Quarrys Mines Mineralls (Royall Mines excepted) Marshes Lakes Waters Fishing Hawking Hunting & Fowling within the Bounds & Lymitts afore described And all other Profitts Comodityes Emoluments & Hereditamts thereunto belonging or in any wise appertaining To bee holden according to the Customs of the Mannor of East Greenwch in the County of Kent in England in free & comon Soccage & by Fealty only: And the said Mannor of Tisbury shall be held Deemed reputed taken & bee an Entire Enfranchized Mannor of itselfe & shall allwayes from time to time have hold & Enjoy like & equal Priviledges wch other Mannors within the Governmt & shall in noe mannor or any wise bee under the Rule Order or Direction of any other place but in all Mattrs of Governmt shall bee Ruled Ordered & Directed according to the Instructions I have already given for that Island in Generall or hereafter shall give for the Good and Wellfare of the Inhabitants by the Advice of my Councell: To have and to hold the said Mannor with the Lands thereunto belonging with all & Singular the Appertenances & prmisses unto the said Thomas Mayhew & Matthew Mayhew their Heyres and Assignes to the Proper use and behoofe of the said Thomas Mayhew and Matthew Mayhew their Heyres & Assignes forever Yielding Rendring & Paying therefore Yearly & every Yeare unto his Royall Highness the Duke of Yorke his Heyres & Assignes or unto such Governor or Governors as from time to time shall bee by him Constituted & Appointed as an Acknowledgmt two Barrells of Good Merchantable Cod-Fish to be Delivered at the Bridge in this City.

Given under my Hand and Sealed wth my Seale & wth the Seale of the Province at Forte James in New Yorke on the Island of Manhattans this eighth day of July in the three and twentyeth yeare of the Reigne of our Sovereigne Lord CHARLES the Second by the Grace of God of England Scotland France and Ireland King Defender of the Faith &c & in the yeare of our Lord God One Thousand six hundred seaventy & one.

It will be thus seen that practically the whole of the present town of Chilmark, with the district of Chickemmoo, now in Tisbury, and the Elizabeth Islands were erected into a Manor, like unto the ancient form known in England, and the elder Mayhew and his grandson were created joint Lords of the Manor of Tisbury, by virtues of the Patent of Confirmation. This was a strange and unique proceeding for these Puritan people, and is without a parallel in the present limits

THE FISH BRIDGE, BROAD STREET, NEW YORK, WHERE THE QUIT RENT OF TISBURY MANOR WAS PAID.

of New England. The grant gave the Mayhews peculiar legal privileges, by which all persons residing within the boundaries of their manorial lands were tenants, subject to their jurisdiction, in all matters of government. To understand this it will be necessary to define what a manor was and is, in the English system.

THE ENGLISH MANOR.

In English law a Manor is an estate in land, to which is incident the right to hold certain courts, called courts baron. The legal theory of the origin of manors refers them to grants from the crown, as stated in the following extract from Perkins'

Treatise on the Laws of England: "The beginning of a manor was when the king gave a thousand acres of land, or a greater or lesser parcel of land, unto one of his subjects, and his heirs, which tenure is knight's service at the least. And the donor did perhaps build a mansion house upon a parcel of the same land." A manor, then, arises where the owner of a parcel so granted has in turn granted portions of it to others, who stand to him in the relation of tenants. The name manor is of Norman origin, and signifies the same as the word fief in France. In some of the United States formed by English colonists, a tract of land occupied or once occupied by tenants paying a fee-farm rent to the proprietor, sometimes in kind, sometimes in stipulated services, is the transplanted form of manor as seen in New England and New York. In Colonial times these resembled the old English manors, their possession being in most cases accompanied by jurisdiction.[1]

Certain domestic courts could be held by the Lord of the Manor, called Courts Leet and Courts Baron. A Court Leet was a court of record held in a particular manor before the steward of the leet, or district covered by the manor, to determine petty offences, indictments to a higher court, and having some administrative functions. A Court Baron was a small court held in the manor, consisting of the freemen or freehold tenants of the manor, presided over by the Lord of the Manor, for the redressing of misdemeanors and settling tenants' disputes.

The domain was held intact by the Lord Proprietor, and farms let to tenants who were required to pay a "quit-rent" which was due the Lord from the free-holders and copy-holders as an acquittance from other services, such as military duty, or other forms of fealty to the proprietor of the soil.[2]

QUIT-RENTS OF TISBURY MANOR.

Payment of these quit rents was to be in perpetuity, and constituted an "acknowledgment" of the continued sovereignty of the Lord of the Manor and his heirs or assigns, In the management of the Manor granted to the Mayhews, they alienated portions of the soil, but retained the "acknowledgment" of certain annual, or more frequent, payment of trifles

[1]Maine Early Laws and Customs, 302; comp., Stubbs, Constitutional History, 98

[2]It was also called the chief-rent.

to signify their manorial privileges. During the lifetime of the elder Mayhew none of the manor was alienated, except two pieces in the Quansoo region, to his grandsons John and Thomas Mayhew, and it is not known that he demanded any quit-rents from them. In a sale of a part of the Elizabeth Islands, however, he instituted the custom of requiring quit-rents, and the first case was that of John Haynes, who agreed to pay "2 good sheep at the Manor House on November 15th yearly and every year."[1] It is not known where the "Manor House" was, if it existed in anything more than name. Possibly it was the house occupied by John Mayhew at Quansoo, or Quanames. After his death, Matthew Mayhew, as surviving patentee, kept to the custom of requiring the annual payments of such "acknowledgments" in true English style. Usually in the mother country the quit-rent was "a good fat capon," to be delivered at Christmas or Whitsuntide, or oftener, but Mayhew varied his requirements to all sorts of small articles. One was obliged to bring annually to him "a good chees,"[2]; another "one nutmegg" as a tribute,[3] and he required "his beloved brother John," who was permitted to occupy certain land, "one mink skin" to be paid yearly "at my mannor house in the mannor of Tisbury," on the 15th of November each year.[4] Benjamin Skiffe was made to bring "six peckes of good wheat," annually.[5] As late as 1732, Sarah, widow of Thomas Mayhew (3), in a deed to her two daughters conveying land in Chilmark, referred to the "Quitt-rents which shall hereafter become due unto the Lord of the Manner......which is one Lamb."[6]

As may be imagined, this transplanted form of manorial government with its suggestions of "lords" and tenantry and "acknowledgments" was not favorably received by the people in the adjoining towns. It gave them an insight into what would occur if the ideas were carried out to their logical sequence. But Mayhew proceeded with his plans for an exclusive domain which should be separate from all the rest of the settlements on the Vineyard. Very early he had surrounded a part of this territory with a fence, and the name of one of

[1]Dukes Deeds, I, 45.
[2]Ibid., I, 346.
[3]Ibid., I, 265.
[4]Ibid., I, 27.
[5]Ibid., I, 110.
[6]Ibid., VI, 56.

his divisions, Kuppi-egon, or Kupegon, meaning an artificial enclosure, is a survival of this fact. Simon Athearn gives us a commentary on the situation, which doubtless voiced the sentiments of the settlers, when he said that they "have impropriated a Cuntery by a fenc to themselves" and again referring to the same subject in describing Chilmark: "This included land is considered un settled but is in propr(ie)ty by a fenc made a Cross the Iland by the people of Chilmark and Chilmark is fenced by the same under their peculiar improvement."[1]

THOMAS DONGAN, EARL OF LIMERICK, AND THE SOCIETY FOR PROPAGATING THE GOSPEL.

It has been related elsewhere (Vol. I, pp. 174-6) how Matthew Mayhew, in April, 1685, was created Lord of the Manor of Martha's Vineyard, by Governor Dongan, and after enjoying the honor for nearly three weeks, he sold the title and privileges to the creator himself. Thenceforth Dongan was Lord of the Manor, or what remained after Mayhew had excepted most of the Vineyard in the transfer of title. As portions of the land which actually passed to Dongan were situated in this town, his connection with it becomes of interest to students of its early annals. These tracts were the eastern half of the Kephigon district of Chilmark and Squibnocket, for which annual quit-rents were exacted.[2] Dongan appointed Mayhew as his steward, and this relationship was maintained for twenty-five years, until the latter's death. Most of this territory, including the Gay Head peninsula, which formed the bulk of his "manor," was inhabited by Indians, and as tenants, they were poor pay and much care. It is not to be presumed that the lambs, nutmegs, corn and mink skins which they paid ever found their way to his cupboards, though they were religiously collected by his agent. The Society for the Propagation of the Gospel, by reason of its missionary work on the island among the natives, came to feel that with an absentee land-

[1]Mass. Archives, CXIII, 94.

[2]Thomas Mayhew paid to Matthew, as agent for Colonel Dongan, who succeeded to the Lordship of the Manor, one lamb yearly "for the neck of Land called Squpnockett" (ibid., V, 89), and the Society for Propagating the Gospel in New England, which bought Dongan's rights in 1715, continued to receive the annual tribute of "one Lamb" for the same property as late as 1724 (ibid., V, 89).

lord disinclined to part with his broad acres, their efforts to uplift the Indian to the plane of civilization would be of little avail under such conditions. When Mayhew died, in 1710, the earl of Limerick was living in London, and the society determined to buy out if it could, the manorial rights of Limerick, and give the Indians the benefit of sympathetic landlordism. Accordingly, after some negotiations initiated by Jeremiah Dummer and conducted by Sir William Ashhurst, Governor of the company, and Judge Sewall, a sale was effected on May 10, 1711, and the Society in its corporate capacity

ARMS OF GOV. THOMAS DONGAN,
LORD OF THE MANOR OF MARTHA'S VINEYARD.

became Lord of the Manor.[1] Livery and seizin was not taken, however, for eighteen months after the purchase.

Three years after this Judge Sewall visited the Vineyard and saw the Chilmark portion of the property, and recorded this incident as follows:—

April 9, 1714. Go to the top of Prospect Hill, from thence to the Sound and by Mr. Thomas Mayhew's direction viewed the River falling into the Sound, [Roaring Brook], and the Shoar all along to the end of the 327 Rods which extends Southward to the middle-Line, containing about 1000 Acres which belongs to the corporation.[2]

[1]Records of the New England Co., pp. 93-96; comp., Sewall, Letter Book, I, 422, Dukes Deeds, II, 311, 327. The Governor of the Company, in a letter expressing his satisfaction with the acquisition, said: "I hope it will be the means to make the Indians live comfortably upon it and prevent their scattering abroad, which would certainly have brought their offspring back again to their old Idolatry."

[2]Sewall, Diary, II, 432.

The Society subsequently acquired other property in this region by purchase, and for many years acted in the capacity of guardian of the spiritual and material interests of the native.[1] The property was gradually sold to them individually as they obtained means to purchase.

THE FIRST SETTLER.

The peculiar relations which the Manor of Tisbury, or Chilmark, bore to the Mayhew family, being a sort of personal appanage of the successive Lords of the Manor, make it somewhat difficult to determine the conditions of early settlement in this territory. In other words, to separate tenants from land owners and actual residents, when the charter was granted in 1671, is a difficult matter. For example, the first recorded deed of sale of any part of the present territorial limits of Chilmark made by the proprietors, is under date of Feb. 26, 1677-8, when Matthew Mayhew, Lord of the Manor, sold fifty-five acres to James Allen, of Tisbury, and in this deed the "land of John Manter" and "Meadow of William Swift" are mentioned. This would indicate that Manter and Swift were then either living in or owning land there, but no deeds to them are of record, showing such ownership. It is known that Allen, one of the Tisbury proprietors, was a great land speculator, but it is reasonably certain that he, then and for some years after, resided in Tisbury. Manter also was one of the original proprietors of Tisbury, lived and died there, and his holdings in Chilmark must have been as a non-resident, merely for agricultural purposes. As to William Swift, the county records contain no records of purchase or sale by him, and yet, in addition to this "meadow" in Chilmark, he had a "lot" on Eddy's Neck in Tisbury the same year. How he came by it, or in what way it passed out of his hands, is not known. It is doubtful if he was anything more than a non-resident land owner in either town.[2] It is thus apparent that Allen, Manter and Swift can be eliminated as residents of Chilmark at that time, and we then come to the first definite evidence of an actual settler. This is shown in a deed executed by Governor Mayhew, in 1680, to Daniel Steward, in which is

[1]Deeds, III, 543. Experience Mayhew to Samuel Sewall, Treasurer of the Society in 1723.

[2]He was the son of William Swift of Sandwich, and at the date of the deed above referred to, he represented that town in the General Court of the Colony of Plymouth. Savage, Gen. Dict., IV, 242.

conveyed a parcel of land "opposite against the point of a neck of Quanaimes, which John Mayhew's house standeth upon."[1]

From this we can safely conclude that for some time prior to March 26, 1680, young John Mayhew had been living at Quanaimes, and he may he reckoned as the first actual white settler in the limits of Chilmark.[2] It is probable that his residence dated from about 1672 or '3, when he married and reached his majority, and presumably "set up his Ebenezer" as a consequence. The life work of this young man had already been chosen, and he selected Chilmark as the field for his labors among the Indians of the town. He had acquired of Toohtowee, Sachem of the north side of Martha's Vineyard, half of his rights as such, and on Feb. 4, 1673, the son, John Toohtowee, "confirmed" the purchase,[3] which gives us an indication of the time of his adoption of this town as his home. In the little house at Quanaimes, built by John Mayhew, was born in the year 1673 the famous Experience, author of "Indian Converts," and after the property had descended to him, as the "first born son," it disclosed the light of day in 1720 to his no less famous scion, the Rev. Jonathan Mayhew, the great pulpit orator. This spot, therefore, may well be regarded as the cradle of Chilmark's most distinguished sons, and is worthy of perpetual designation as the homestead of its earliest resident.

SUBSEQUENT SETTLEMENT AND THE EARLY SETTLERS BEFORE 1700.

Next in point of time, as respects the acquisition of property, is James Allen, whose earlier connection with the settlement of Tisbury has been recorded in the annals of that town. His first purchase of land in Chilmark consisted of fifty-five acres, situated near Abel's hill on the south side of the road, under date of Feb. 28, 1677-8.[4] Shortly after he bought ninety acres extending from the road southward to the pond,[5] and eight years later, May 7, 1686, twenty acres more adjoining

[1]Deeds, I, 266.

[2]He was in Tisbury in 1677, but whether as a settler or transient is not clear. (Letter to Joseph Norton, in possession of Wm. J. Rotch.)

[3]Deeds, III, 201.

[4]Deeds, I, 277. He sold this to Thomas Mayhew on March 7, 1680-81 (ibid., I, 90).

[5]Deeds, I, 265. April 2, 1678.

the last purchase.[1] When he ceased to be a resident of Tisbury, and became a citizen of this town, is not known. It was sometime after 1682 and before 1690, on which latter date he is referred to as "of Chilmark,"[2] and again in 1692 he is described as "of Chillmark."[3] From these dates, and an unknown period before, we may consider him a resident, and claim continuity therefrom till his death. It is traditional that he lived half a mile north of the old meeting-house, and this is probably correct.

Daniel Steward was the third land owner, chronologically, by his purchase of a parcel of meadow, before referred to, March 24, 1680, situated "on the beach opposite against the point of a neck of Quanaimes."[4] Whether he ever lived on this property is open to much doubt. He is called "of Tisbury" and did not retain the land long, selling it on August 14, 1684, to Simon Athearn. He resided in Edgartown till his death.

With the advent of Benjamin Skiffe, another resident of Tisbury, we are on surer footing, as he became identified with this town, and at his death was one of its best known citizens. He made his first purchase Feb. 6, 1681, consisting of land on the west side of Roaring brook.[5] The next year, July 20, 1682, he bought a neck of land called Nathaniel's neck, containing eighteen acres, "bounded Eastwardly by a brook which runneth into a pond, which pond is the South bound: westwardly by a small brook called by the Indians Wachapakesuh: North by the foot path or road which goeth towards the west end of the island, crossing the said brook."[6]

The location of this land is so carefully described that the reader can easily determine its boundaries, between the Fulling mill and Pease's brook, and south of the road.

Richard Ellingham, who came here from Barnstable, bought of Matthew Mayhew in 1683, eighty acres of land, eighty rods wide on the New Mill river and running one hundred and sixty rods northerly therefrom, being the second lot from the Tisbury-Chilmark line, on the present Middle road. He

[1]Deeds, II, 277.

[2]Court Records, Vol. I.

[3]Deeds, I, 155. His name appears in the Tisbury records as on a committee in 1692 and 1697 on land matters (Town Records, 24, 32).

[4]Deeds, I, 266.

[5]Deeds, I, 263.

[6]Deeds, I, 346. The quit rent for this land was "a good chees" annually.

was a transient and lived here less than ten years, selling out his interests in 1692 to James Allen.[1]

A younger brother of Benjamin Skiffe, also a resident of Tisbury, began to make purchases of land in this town a few years later. Nathan Skiffe was one of the early settlers in the adjoining town, where he had, as a young man, held property and acted as one of the officials, but he decided to remove, and on Aug. 16, 1686, he purchased of Matthew Mayhew fifty acres of land bounded southerly and westerly by Pease's brook, which means at the turn of this stream at the end of the South road.[2]

Samuel Tilton, who had previously owned land at Homes Hole and Tisbury, became a purchaser of property in this town March 30, 1688, when he bought of Matthew Mayhew, eighty acres described as follows:—

> .... bounded Northward from the corner of the fence in a valley or bottom of a field called Japhets, on the same line as fence to a swamp near the River called Milne in length about 80 poles: Southwardly by a fence in the valley about 80 poles westwardly: and bounded Westwardly by a parallel line drawn from the westward part or end of said Southern bounds paralel to said eastern line till it meet or cometh to the aforesaid Swamp, and Northwardly by said Swamp........[3]

This land was in the Kephigon district and adjoined the Thomas Harlock property on the east.

The next new resident was Nathaniel Skiffe, the third of the Skiffe brothers to become identified with the town. He bought, Oct. 3, 1689, one hundred acres to the south of Pease's brook, extending to the cliffs, and from time to time, as long as he resided on the island, added to his estate.[4] He removed about 1713 to Windham, Conn.

The next new land owner was Ephraim Higgins, who came here from Rhode Island, and bought a tract of land March 14, 1689-90 near the "Stone wall." It is presumed that he occupied and improved it, and it was held by him until his death, about fourteen years after.[5] He was probably a single man.

William Homes was here at this period as a transient

[1]Deeds, I, 115, 135. He was probably a carpenter, as he was employed to build the church at Edgartown in 1685.

[2]Deeds, I, 341.

[3]Deeds, 1, 84.

[4]Deeds, I, 107.

[5]Deeds, I, 68. Richard Higgins, his "brother and sole heir," disposed of this property in 1714 to Benjamin Skiffe (ibid., II, 58).

resident, in the occupation of school teacher. He did not remain as a permanent resident, although he acquired some property April 3, 1690, at Squibnocket.[1]

Reverend Rodolphus (or Ralph) Thacher, who had come to the town in a pastoral relation to the people, became a proprietor of forty-five acres on the South road, Feb. 13, 1694, and built a house thereon, which he occupied with his family.[2] This lot adjoined Benjamin Skiffe's on the east.

Nathan Bassett came from Sandwich, on the Cape, and settled in town, next in order of time. His first purchase was thirty-five acres, July 4, 1694, the land being situated near Abel's hill.[3]

In 1697 another permanent resident was added to the little settlement in the person of William Hunt from Dorchester. He bought, September 9th, in that year, a tract of land situated near the Wequobsket cliffs, and settled there with his family.[4]

There were several non-resident owners of property who bought land in town before 1700, Richard Sarson and Thomas Harlock of Edgartown and John Case of Tisbury, but they cannot be reckoned as actual settlers of Chilmark.[5]

Thus, at the close of the 17th century, about 25 years after John Mayhew first built himself a house at Quansoo, the town population comprised the following heads of families: Experience Mayhew, John Mayhew, Pain Mayhew, Thomas Mayhew, James Allen, Ebenezer Allen, Nathaniel Skiffe, Benjamin Skiffe, Nathan Skiffe, Samuel Tilton, William Tilton, John Tilton, Nathan Bassett, William Hunt, and Rodolphus Thacher, fifteen households in all.

SKETCHES OF THE EARLY SETTLERS.

NATHAN BASSETT.

Nathan Bassett

Nathan Bassett was the first of his name to come to the Vineyard. He was a native of Cape Cod, born about 1666-7, and prior to his migration hither

[1]Deeds, I, 175. He had been in Chilmark several years and returned to Ireland in 1691.

[2]Deeds, I, 365.

[3]Deeds, I, 67.

[4]Deeds, I, 387.

[5]Deeds, I, 135, 153; II, 27.

had married Mary, daughter of John and Hope (Chipman) Huckins, about 1690, at Barnstable. He came to Chilmark about 1694, bringing two children and established his residence on his purchase near Abel's hill. By occupation he was a blacksmith, and he carried on his smithing in a shop near his house. Parson Homes said of him, "he was one that feared God and was peaceable and industrious," and this character he maintained throughout his long life. His public services were of a modest nature, being chosen surveyor of highways in 1713, 1718-21, 1724-6, 1736, and fence viewer on several occasions. He was an invalid for a long time, being a sufferer from palsy before his death, which occurred Nov. 16, 1743, in the 77th year of his age. His will, dated Jan. 31, 1740, in which he styles himself "gentleman," was probated Nov. 29, 1743, and the inventory of his estate amounted to £256–18–8 as reported by appraisers. His wife, "a peaceable, industrious and pious woman," predeceased him eight days, and left a will dated Jan. 31, 1739-40, which was probated the same time with her husband's will.[1] He was a public spirited man and gave to the town, in 1724, the site for a meeting-house.

JOHN HILLMAN.

There is a tradition common to all the scattered descendants of this pioneer that he was "shanghaied" and brought to this country when 16 years of age, being taken from a fishing boat in the river Thames.

As he was born in 1651 this would make it about the year 1667 when he landed here. The intervening time (1667-1675) is a blank, for being only a youth on arrival he was probably employed as a servant or apprentice until he reached his majority. It may be surmised that he lived in the vicinity of Salisbury or Hampton, whence came so many of the earliest settlers of this island and Nantucket. Where this place was is not known, and the first definite knowledge we have of him is at Tisbury some time between 1675 and 1678, when he came into possession of the half lot and share of Samuel Tilton, on the east side of Old Mill brook. This he sold in January, 1679, to Elizabeth Norton, and the next record we have about him is at Nantucket. At that place his oldest child was born

[1]Dukes Probate, III, 154-163. In his will he bequeaths a silver tankard and a seal ring to his eldest son, Samuel.

in 1682, and there he had found his wife, Hannah, daughter of Edward Cottle. One account states that he was a Welchman and a gardener, but the others call him a worsted comber, and the records describe him as a weaver. In a legal document he is called "an Englishman," which may be taken in the restricted sense, or as an English subject.

He returned from Nantucket about 1685 and again settled in Tisbury where "he hired a farme of Simon Athearn ......for the Terme of 7 years at a place called Wampache, the which he quietly dwelt on 3 years of the time."[1] This tract of land was called the "Red Ground" and became the source of prolonged litigation between Athearn and the Praying Indians, who claimed it belonged to Christiantown. There is likewise no record to show when he removed to Chilmark unless we accept the purchase of Oct. 3, 1711, consisting of twenty acres and a quarter share of common rights, as the date of his settlement in the town.[2] This leaves thirteen years unaccounted for since the expiration of his lease from Athearn, and so far the gap cannot be bridged. In fact, his whole residence here, covering a period of perhaps forty years, till his death, has given us but few indications of his presence during that entire time.

WILLIAM HUNT.

He was the son of Ephraim and Ebbot (——) Hunt of Weymouth, born about 1655, and prior to his removal to Chilmark he had resided in Dorchester for a time. His purchase of land in 1697 is the probable date of his coming here, and that he was married, his wife's name being Jane, and brought a family with him, appears from collateral evidence. His life here was without incident as far as the records show and the only public office he held was selectman in 1705, which he kept one year. Homes, in his diary, makes the following note of his death under date of January 8, 1726-7: "Last night before sundown Old William Hunt departed this life he was a man of good age, had been long fraile. He died suddenly none of his family knowing when he died." His age was "about 73 years," according to the gravestone. He made his last will March 13, 1721-2, and it was proven April

[1]Deposition of John Hillman in 1698 aged 47 years (Sup. Jud. Court files, No. 4974). The deposition means that he resided on this farm the whole time, but that the latter part of his occupancy was in litigation.

[2]Ibid., III, 280.

5, 1727. In it he bequeathed the personal property to his grandchildren and the residue to his son William, who was appointed as executor.[1] His wife died some years before him on May 7, 1720, and some of their descendants live in Nova Scotia. The name is extinct in the town.

THOMAS LITTLE.

Early in the 18th century there came to Chilmark this young man, son of Lieut. Isaac Little of Marshfield, born Dec. 15, 1674, and graduated in the class of 1695 from Harvard College. He had married, Dec. 5, 1698, Mary Mayhew (42) of Edgartown, and in May, 1709, purchased two twenty acre lots in Chilmark, which is the presumed date of his settlement here. While a resident here he practiced law and presumably medicine, for his education warranted, in those days, the employment of his talents in all the arts and sciences.[2] He died early, however, in 1715, leaving a widow and six minor children. His estate was divided in June, 1725, at which time his eldest son Thomas was residing in the town, succeeding to his father's professional work.[3] The widow married Jonathan Bryant of Pembroke before 1719, and the younger children became residents of Plymouth and Middleborough. The family became extinct here a decade before the Revolution.

JOHN MAYHEW.

John Mayhew

He was the youngest son of Thomas and Jane (Paine) Mayhew and was born in 1652 at Edgartown. An excellent contemporary sketch of his life, written by Rev. Thomas Prince of Boston, is here quoted in full, as published. (Indian Converts, pp. 302-6).

This Gentleman being but about five Years of Age at the Loss of his Father, thereby unhappily missed the Advantage of a learned Education; for want of which, together with his full Employment at home, and his not being inclined to appear abroad, he very much confined himself to the Island, and was not so extensively known: and thence it is, there has been too little hitherto publickly said of this Gentleman, con-

[1]Dukes Probate, II, 19.

[2]He is called "Doctor" in the Probate Records.

[3]Dukes Probate, I, 3.

sidering his great Worth and Usefulness. But I can assure my Reader that he fell not short either of the eminent Genius or Piety of his excellent Progenitors.

He was early inclined to the Ministerial Work: and having the Benefit of the Grandfather's wise Instructions, and of his Father's Library; and being a Person of more than ordinary natural Parts, great Industry and sincere Piety, he made such a large Proficiency in the Study and Knowledge of divine Things, that about 1673, when he was twenty one Years of Age, he was first called to the Ministry among the English in a new and small Settlement, at a Place named Tisbury, near the middle of the Island; where he preached to great Acceptance, not only of the People under his Care, but of very able Judges that occasionally heard him.

But he also naturally cared for the Good of the Indians, and, understanding their Language well while he was a very young Man, he used frequently to give them good instructions, and even the chief Indians on the Island often resorted to him for Counsel. And being arrived at the Age above-said, they would not be contented till he became a publick Preacher to them likewise: so ardent and urgent were their Desires, that he could not deny them, even tho his thrice honoured Grandfather was then a laborious and acceptable Preacher among them.

He taught alternately in all their Assemblies a Lecture every Week, and assisted them in the Management of all their Ecclesiastical Affairs. And tho what was allowed him was very inconsiderable indeed, yet he went steadily on in this pious Work, and would not suffer any Affairs of his own to divert him from it, nor was there scarce any Weather so bad as to hinder him.

And having both the English and Indians under his Care, his Diligence was now to be doubled, especially after his Grandfather's Death in 1681; and this much the more, by reason of certain erroneous Opinions in danger of taking Root in the Island. Mr. Mayhew was rightly for repelling them with spiritual Weapons: and being a Person of very superior Abilities, and Acquaintance with the Scriptures, he used to desire such as began to imbibe those Principles, to produce their Reasons; and those who wanted to be resolved in their Difficulties, to give him the advantage to resolve them in publick, that others might also receive Light and Satisfaction; whereby they came to be more clearly instructed, and more fully convinced and satisfy'd, than in the ordinary Way of Preaching, which yet always preceded the other. In short, he had such an excellent Talent for the Defence of the Truth against Gainsayers, that those who would have spread their Errors, found themselves so effectually opposed by the Brightness of his Knowledge and Piety, and the Strength of his argumentative Genius, that they could make no Progres in their Designs on the Island: and the churches and People, and in them their Posterity were happily saved from the spreading of those erroneous Opinions, and the Disturbance and Troubles they would have produced among them.

And as for the Indians, his Custom was to tarry some time with them after the publick Exercise was over, allowing them to put Questions to him for their own Instruction, and also trying their Knowledge, by putting Questions to them. And he was so well skilled in their Language, as to be able to discourse freely with them upon any kind of Subject, and to preach and pray in their Tongue with the greatest Readiness.

He was a person of clear Judgement, great Prudence, and of an excellent Spirit; and the Indians very much repaired to his House for Advice and Instruction, and also for Relief in their Wants. And as he was fully persuaded, that many of them were truly religious he would sometimes say, "that tho he had but little Reward from Men, (having but about five Pounds a year for his Labours among them) yet if he might be instrumental in saving any, he should be fully satisfy'd, and think himself to be sufficiently recompensed." But after the honourable Commissioners came to be acquainted with him, and the eminent Service he did, they raised his Salary to thirty Pounds, which was about two years before his Death.

He walked in his House with a perfect Heart; having his Children and Servants in all Subjection, they both loving and fearing him, and being frequently and seriously instructed and counselled by him.

He lived and dy'd within the Bounds of Chilmark, but constantly preached to the English at Tisbury, for the space of fifteen Years to his Death, and about as long once every Week to one or other of the Indian Assemblies on the Island; besides abundance of Pains he took more privately with them. He rather made it his aim to serve his Generation by the Will of GOD, than to be known or observed in the World; and therefore went but little abroad. The whole of what was allowed him, for his incessant Labours both among the English and Indians, put together, would scarce amount to ten Pounds per Annum, except the two last years of his Life as aforesaid; and yet he went on chearfully, in Hopes of a rich and joyful Harvest in Heaven.

And having finished what GOD in his all-wise and perfect Providence saw meet to imploy him in, he deceased on February 3, 1688-9, about two in the Morning, in the 37th Year of his Age, and the 16th of his Ministry; leaving the Indians in a very orderly Way of assembling on the Lord's Day for publick Worship in four or five several Places, and of hearing their several well instructed Teachers, who usually began with Prayer, and then after singing of a Psalm, from some Portion of Scripture spake to the Auditors: as also an Indian Church, of one hundred Communicants, walking according to the Rule of the Scriptures.

In his last Sickness he expressed a Desire "if it were the Divine Will, that he might live a while longer, to have seen his Children a little grown up before he died, and to have done more Service for CHRIST on the Earth." But with respect to his own State before GOD, he enjoyed a great Serenity and Calmness of Mind, having a lively Apprehension of the Mercy of GOD, thro' the merits of CHRIST; Far from being afraid to die, having Hopes, thro' Grace, of obtaining eternal Life by JESUS CHRIST our Lord. He counselled, exhorted and incouraged his Relatives and others who came to visit him: And with respect to himself, among other things, said, "He was persuaded that GOD would not place him with those after his Death, in whose Company he could take no Delight in his Life-time."

His Distemper was an heavy Pain in his Stomach, Shortness of Breath, Faintness, etc. and continued from the End of September to the time of his Death. And thus expired this third Successive Indian Preacher of this worthy Family; after he had set another bright Example of disinterested Zeal for the Glory of GOD, a lively Faith of the invisible and eternal World, and a generous and great Concern for the Salvation of all about him.

And now I need not say, that his loss in the Flower of his Age, and especially so soon after his Grandfather, was much lamented by both English and Indians; and many good People yet living express a very grateful Remembrance of him.

He left eight children, the eldest of which was but sixteen Years of Age, and soon succeeded him in the Indian Service.

THOMAS MAYHEW, 3d.

The second son of Rev. Thomas Mayhew, Jr., born in 1650 chose this town as his home, although he resided for a while in Tisbury, where from 1674 to 1679 he was town clerk. In 1680 he purchased sixty acres of land in the new settlement at Chilmark, and thenceforth spent his life here as a resident. His birth gave him prominence through family influences and during all of his adult life he was an office holder. He was an associate justice of the King's Bench from 1692 to 1699 and chief justice 1699 to 1713 of the same court. Parson Homes, in his diary, gives us this account of his last days: —

> On the twenty first of July Anno 1715 being Thursday about two of the clock in the morning Thomas Mayhew Esqu'r of Chilmarke departed this life he had been for several yeares troubled with the distemper called the kings evil by which he was brought neere the gates of Death but by some applications made to him by an Indian doctor he recovered so far that he was able to rid about and look after his affairs, but in the latter end of the spring or begining of summer this year he was suddenly taken with a stopag of his urine and a violent pain in his right leg, after some time his left leg swelled pretty much yet the paine continued in the other leg, by the use of means the stopag of his urine was removed, yet the other symptoms continued. After some time there came a doctor to the Island that thought the swelling and pain in his legs might be removed by bathing and sweathing, which preceded accordingly in some measure, but after some time the swelling proceeded upwardly and he was siesed with an inwerd fever and shortness of breth which prevaild upon him till it carried him off. His nostril and throat grew so sore some days before he died that he could not speak so as to be understood, he was a man of good sense considering his education and seemed to be piously inclined tho he did entertain some singular opinions in religion.

The nephew, Experience, has also left this brief notice of his uncle: —

He was long impowered in the Government of the Indians there, and was both singularly spirited & accomplished for that service: as he was on divers other accounts a very excellent Person.[1]

He married Sarah Skiffe (5), who was born Oct. 12, 1646, and survived her husband until Dec. 30, 1740, when she passed away in the 95th year of her age.

BENJAMIN SKIFFE.

Benia skiffe justice of peace

In his day and generation Benjamin Skiffe was the most prominent man in Chilmark, and held a commanding position in civil and military affairs throughout the county. Indeed, he was the leading citizen of the Vineyard, after the death of Matthew Mayhew. Benjamin was next to the youngest of the four sons of James Skiffe, Senior, who came to the Vineyard. He was born Nov. 5, 1655, probably in Sandwich, where his father resided and had been a prominent citizen for many years. He was a witness to a deed in Tisbury on Dec. 24, 1677,[2] and it is probable that he had gone to Tisbury before that with one of his brothers, either James or Nathaniel, as an inmate of their homes.[3] There he first saw the young girl who had lately moved there from Hampton, and who first attracted his admiration.

The girl, Hannah, daughter of Joseph Merry, was five years his junior, and on Feb. 20, 1679-80 they were married. Where they set up housekeeping is not known, but the next record we find of him is a purchase of land in this town on Feb. 6, 1681, consisting of a tract on the west side of Roaring brook.[4] The next year on July 20, 1682, he bought the land called "Nathaniel's Neck," but it cannot be determined whether either of these were used by him as a place of residence.[5] From all evidences he still remained in Tisbury and is called of that town in 1681, 1682 and 1688, and on March 17, 1687, was chosen town clerk there.[6] He was elected county com-

[1]Brief account of the State of the Indians (1720).

[2]Dukes Deeds, I, 267.

[3]James came to Tisbury in 1671 and Nathaniel before 1674. The younger brother Nathan does not appear on record till 1675.

[4]Dukes Deeds, I, 233.

[5]Ibid., I, 346.

[6]Tisbury Records, 18.

missioner in 1686, apparently to represent Chilmark, as the other two were citizens of the sister townships. He continued to act as town clerk of Tisbury from his first election in 1687 to 1693 inclusive, and not until 1695 is he called "of Chilmark." He was a proprietor of one share in the town, however, in 1692.[1] His residence was on the east side of the Fulling Mill brook, not far from the site of the mill which stood on its banks, in sight of the South road. He bought one hundred acres on Feb. 13, 1694, jointly with Pain Mayhew, and it is supposed that it was for the purpose of carrying on the mill which he had erected there for fulling cloth.[2] Two years later he bought the mill privileges of New Mill river "to improve for a mill," but it is not known whether another one was built there by him.[3]

When the great political change of jurisdiction over the Vineyard took place in 1692, it appears that Skiffe was one of those who did not like the transfer, and he took sides with the Mayhews in the policy of passive opposition. "Capt'n ben Skiffe," wrote Simon Athearn in October of that year, "have bene very bussie against the government from this place," and as a consequence he recommended that Skiffe be superseded as Captain of the military company as "the most likely way to bring the company to obediance."[4]

But Athearn was not able to carry his point in this matter, and Skiffe continued to be a leader in military affairs as well as in civil life. He was for some time prior to 1692 Captain of the Foot Company of Militia of Tisbury and Chilmark combined, and is referred to as Captain Skiffe in 1693 and 1695. In 1703 he appears as Major Skiffe and thereafter is known by that title, and late as 1709 he was in command of this body of troopers.[5]

The town availed itself little of his services in an official capacity. For three years only, 1706-7-8, he served it as selectman, but his time was in requisition for more important duties to which the whole island unanimously called him. In those days the three towns, as at present, sent but one repre-

[1]Court Records, Vol. I. It is difficult to separate the relations of proprietors and residents, as there were non-resident proprietors who were entitled to hold office and draw lots.

[2]Dukes Deeds, I, 233.

[3]Ibid., I, 125.

[4]Mass. Archives, CXII, 424.

[5]Savage says he was employed "in an important trust" by Governor Dudley in 1704, but the author has no data in confirmation of it (Gen. Dict., IV, 706).

sentative to the General Court, and for five years, 1707-1711, 1715, and 1717, he was the "member from the Vineyard."[1] In 1716 Edgartown voted to send him again if Chilmark would join, but it does not appear that this was done.[2] In 1700 he was one of the judges of the Court of Common Pleas for this county, and on the death of Matthew Mayhew in 1710, Major Skiffe was appointed Judge of Probate for this county in succession and held the office until his own decease eight years later. It will thus be seen that this man was one of the foremost men of his time, whom all were ready to honor with such marks of confidence and respect as was in their power to bestow. He seemed to have stood well with the influential Mayhews and thus steered clear of the difficulties into which his brother fell by antagonizing them. There is an entry in the town records of Edgartown significant of the esteem in which he was held by other communities. On Jan. 22, 1707-8, the town voted that "Major Benjamin Skiffe, Esqr. shall be requested by their Clerk, Thomas Trapp, to be at their next meeting at Edgertown to assist them in their public or common affairs as moderator; and do order their said clerk to request the same in their behalf."[3] This appears to be an unusual and unique compliment.

Major Skiffe, in his last illness, made his will on Feb. 15, 1717-18, and died two days later. He left a large property which was inventoried by the appraisers on Feb. 23, 1719, and returned as amounting to £2748–10–5, probably being the richest man in the town.[4] He was childless, but had adopted young Beriah Tilton (23), born in 1703, and to him he bequeathed, subject to Mrs. Skiffe's contingent interest, the homestead and mill adjoining. He also gave bequests in his will to his niece, Sarah Athearn, daughter of his brother Nathan, and to his brother-in-law, Thomas Pease. The following is an abstract of his will:—

To Hannah my dear and loving wife......my sole executrix...... all my estate....to dispose of as she sees fit....if she dont dispose of the same in her life time then my will farther is that Beriah Tilton, a lad that now dwells with me, shall have my housing, mill and lands adjoining ......to Sarah, wife of Solomon Athearn of Tisbury, a certain tract of land lying in the Town of Chilmark, near the Stone Wall pond, being

[1]Chilmark Town Records, 6, 7, 8; Tisbury Records, 62.

[2]Edgartown Records, II, 79.

[3]Ibid., II, 90.

[4]Dukes Probate, I, 65-7.

THE OLD SKIFF HOUSE, CHILMARK.
NEAR THE PAINT MILL.

partly purchased of the Indians & part not purchased—the lands intended being held by me under Col. Thomas Dongan. I give her the whole of said tract as well the right to purchase as the already purchased.

I give to my brother Nathan Skiffe the right of purchase or patent right in a certain tract of land lying at Monamesha in the town of Chilmark, which patent or right of purchase I had of Major Matthew Mayhew, deceased.

I give to Thomas Pease of Edgartown all the right title and interest which I have to any lands in Sanchacantucket Neck.[1]

His widow survived him many years and died Feb. 27, 1758, at the great age of 98 years. They lie buried in the Chilmark burying ground on Abel's hill. She was a woman who partook of the distinctions accorded to her honored husband, and was called and known as Madame Skiffe. At her death she bequeathed to Beriah Tilton her "whole and sole personal estate" and made him executor. She had disposed of her real estate by deeds of gift and otherwise, but the homestead and mill remained in his possession as designed by her husband.[2] This property descended to Beriah's son William and thence to his children, and was held by descendants till about 1897, when it was sold to George W. Blackwell.

SAMUEL TILTON.

This progenitor of a family, prominent in the annals of Chilmark for two and a half centuries, was the son of William Tilton of Lynn, Mass., by his second wife, Susanna. He was born in 1637-8, probably in that town, and at the age of sixteen was orphaned by the death of his father. The widow remarried shortly after, Roger Shaw of Hampton, N.H., whither the young family of Tiltons moved and resided with their step-father. His mother died before 1660, and the young man, left without either parent, learned the trade of carpenter, and on Dec. 17, 1662, married Hannah Moulton of that town.[3] About 1673 he came to the Vineyard with his wife and three children, probably in company with Isaac Chase and Jacob Perkins, his Hampton neighbors. He was granted a lot of land in Tisbury, Feb. 5, 1674, on the east side of Old Mill Brook, and two years later in partnership with

[1]Dukes Probate, I, 63.

[2]Ibid., IV, 53.

[3]Hampton Town Records. It is not known who her parents were. Two families of Moultons lived in Hampton at this time, headed by Robert and William, both from Ormsby, County Norfolk, England.

Chase and Perkins, bought one-sixth of Homes Hole neck.[1] He sold out his home lot in Tisbury before 1678, and took up his residence in this town about that date. By various purchases he acquired a large tract in the Kephigon district, bordering on the Sound and extending to the Middle line. Here he lived an uneventful life, without known public service for nearly sixty years. His wife died April 11, 1720, and he survived her eleven years. He died Nov. 29, 1731, "in the 94th year of his age" and Parson Homes thus characterizes him: "He was a man of good understanding, was an anti-pedobaptist in his judgment, but pious and regular in his conversation. He was against swearin and usery." His will dated June 15, 1718, and probated March 7, 1732, disposes of his property, including carpenter's tools, to his sons, and the daughters received shares of personal and real estate.[2]

EARLY TRANSIENT RESIDENTS.

JOHN CHIPMAN.

This transient resident came in the early part of the 18th century from Sandwich. He was related by marriage to Nathan Bassett, being a native of Barnstable, the son of Elder John and Hope (Howland) Chipman. He was born March 3, 1669-70, and resided in Sandwich from 1691 to 1712, when he removed to Chilmark and staid a couple of years. Returning to Sandwich, he lived there from 1714 to 1720 and again settled here. He was a man of distinction, versed in legal knowledge which he exercised in a professional way, though calling himself a "cordwainer."[3] While here he was local agent for the Society for Propagating the Gospel. He removed to Newport, R. I., about 1727, soon acquired political prominence and became one of the Governor's assistants. He died in 1756, aged 86 years. He was thrice married, (1) to Mary Skiffe, (2) widow Elizabeth Russell and (3) to a Miss Hookey of Rhode Island.

RICHARD ELLINGHAM.

This early settler came from Barnstable to the Vineyard about 1683. It is probable that he was a carpenter and

[1]Tisbury Records, 7; comp., Deeds, I, 283. He was called "of Homes Hole" in this deed and this section was probably his actual residence from the time of his settlement on the Vineyard until removal to Chilmark.

[2]Dukes Probate, II, 69.

[3]Dukes Deeds, III, 93.

builder, as in 1685 a committee of Edgartown were empowered "to treat with Richard Ellingham about finishing the Meeting house" in that town. His residence here extended over a period of nine years, until 1692, when, with his wife Hannah, he sold his property on the Middle road and returned to the Cape. It is not known whether he left any descendants here in the female line, there being none of his own name after his departure.

DIVISIONS OF LAND.

There were no proprietors, nor "home lots" as in the other towns for the reasons already explained. Consequently there was no formal division of the original territory of Chilmark, as occurred in Edgartown and Tisbury. The disappearance of the early proprietory records compels us to resort to collateral sources for information as to what was done in the matter of establishing a system of proprietorship. The land owners were actually tenants of the Lord of the Manor with right of purchase, not possessors in fee simple. In 1695, Matthew Mayhew executed a document, which is quoted below in part, to adjust the conditions of ownership in Chilmark to like circumstances in other towns on the island. By this document he created a proprietary of thirty shareholders, or owners of common land, of which number he retained eighteen in his own hands, or a majority of the shares, so that he still controlled the material interests of the new corporation. The deed of gift is as follows:—[1]

Whereas Matthew Mayhew of Edgartown hath late stodd ceased of an estate in lands on Martha's Vineyard commonly called Nashowakemmuck or town of Chilmark, bounded on the east by a line crossing sd Island . . . . between the said Nashowakemmuck and Takenny, on the west by a line drawn from the westermost part of the lands of Wequobscutt now or late in the tenure and occupation of Nathaniel skiffe directly to the mouth of the harbor on the north side of sd Island called Wa-we-attake or menamesha harbor: northward by a line drawn from the great rock lying in sd east line and southerly by an highway between sd Tysbuarie and Chilmark a pond caled Nashowakemmuck pond and the sea or ocean; and whereas the sd Mayhew intending the settlement of sd land and premises & granting the same unto such parts & proportions as might entertain inhabitance sufficient for a town of at least thirty families. Hath at several times under his hand & seal given and granted several parts or allotments or portions or sd tract of land with

[1]Dukes Deeds, Vol. 1, 384.

right in common within the commons of the same, viz. land now or late in the tenure of Thomas Mayhew, Esq., one right,; land &c of James Allen Esq. three & ½ rights; land &c of Samuel Tilton, one right,; land &C of Pain Mayhew; son of sd Matthew Mayhew one right; Capt Benjamin Skiffe one right; land &c of Nathanel Skiffe one right, land &c of Nathan Skiffe one right; land &c of Nathan Bassett one half common or right; and to Thomas son of sd Matthew one right; Mr. Ralph Thacther one right; And whereas it may happen that question and debate might hereafter arise of the true intent and meaning of libertie in common to be holden by the several grants by him the sd Matthew Mayhew granted and made.

Know ye that Hee the sd Matthew Mayhew doth by these presents declare grant and promise that every right in common by the sd Matthew Mayhew granted doth and shall be construed, deemed and taken to intend to contain one thirtyieth part in common of and in all and evrie the lands within the afore mentioned bounds and limits of Nashowakemmuck or town of Chilmark.

The number of shares was thirty, and as far as information is available on this point, there was no change in this common denominator.[1] The lots in this division were about thirteen acres each.

Some time before 1704 a division known as "Woodland Lots," of about fifteen acres each, situated along the Middle line, were divided to the proprietors.

About 1714 the "Second Division" of common land was made and before 1717 another division, designated as "Hill Lots" on the west side of New Mill river.[2]

INCORPORATION OF THE TOWN.

Owing to its peculiar legal status Chilmark had no corporate existence as a township for many years. In a law of 1697 it is called the "Town of Chilmark," but this was an error, due to lack of information on the subject on the part of the General Court.[3] Still the inhabitants, as early as 1696, were organized into a body politic and had chosen selectmen for that year.[4] This situation lasted until 1714, when a petition was presented to the General Court for incorporation. The town records of Chilmark have no reference to the subject, and the following entry from the state archives is our only knowledge of the fact:—

[1]Dukes Deeds, III, 64, but compare III, 320, where a "five and twentieth" share was sold in 1717.

[2]Ibid., III, 319.

[3]Acts and Resolves of Mass., VII, 118.

[4]Edgartown Records, I, 38. The Chilmark Town Records record the acts of the inhabitants as of a "town meeting."

30 October 1714

Upon Reading a Petition of Experience Mayhew, Agent for the Manour of Tisbury, otherwise called Chilmark, Praying that the said Manour of Tisbury, alias Chilmark, and all the Lands belonging thereto in Marthas Vineyard, and all other Lands Westward of the Township of Tisbury on said Island (Gay Head excepted), with an Island called No Mans Land, may be made a Town or Township, by the name of Chilmark with the Powers and Privileges to a Town or Right appertaining and belonging:

ORDERED that the Mannor of Tisbury, commonly called Chilmark, have all the Powers of a Town given and granted them, for the better Management of their publick affairs, Laying and Collecting of Taxes granted to his Majesty for the Support of the Government, Town charges and other affairs whatsoever, as other Towns in the Province do by Law enjoy.[1]

At the town meeting held Oct. 25, 1716, Captain Zachariah Mayhew was chosen as agent of Chilmark "to present petision to the general Court for the inlargment of sd town," but it does not appear what extension of powers or limits was desired, unless it related to the addition of Nomans Land to the jurisdiction of Chilmark, as seems probable. It will be explained in the section which deals with that island.

TOWN ANNALS, 1717–1742.

A chronicle of the happenings in this small community for a quarter of a century in provincial times, may afford us an insight into the life of the people at that period. Such a glimpse is obtained in the diary of the Rev. William Homes, and the following extracts from it cover the twenty-five years, 1717 to 1742, and include the things good and bad that befell them: —

February the 18 (1716-17). A violent storm of snow and Sleet is described, lasting several days, during which "many sheep were burryed under the snow."

March 22, 1716-17. I found some sheep that had been burried under the snow that fell Feb 21 one of wch was still alive. She was taken out the 23d of March alive and continued to live for several days; she had continued under the snow without any food about 31 days.

August 15. 1718. * * * This day about two of the clock after noon several children particularly Ben: Ward and Thomas Allen having got a shot gun and some powder were diverting themselves near John

[1]Records, General Court, IX, 428. It will thus be apparent that the date of incorporation shown on the town seal as Sept. 14, 1694 is an obvious error. The "Vital Records of Chilmark," published 1904 by the N. E. Historic Genealogical Society, contain the statement that Chilmark "was established September 14, 1694, from common land." The source of this statement is not known, but it is incorrect.

Allen's barn, where were a considerable quantity of English grain and hay, some in the barn, and some near it in stacks. Ben: Ward having a brand of fire in his hand, seeing his uncle Captn Mayhew riding by to sermon, threw the brand out of his hands, that his uncle might not see it. It chanced to fall near some English grain, which presently took fire, and consumed the barn and all the English grain to ashes in a very short time. All or most of the men in town presently came with an intent to extinguish the flames, but they did not effect anything.

8ber 19. 1718. On Monday last the house of Mr Zephaniah Mayhew was burnt to the ground by an accidental fire and much of his household stuff and wearing clothes were consumed in the flames. On Thursday James McLelland came here to look after his sons effects and went last week to Nantucket on that designe

Dec. 16. 1718. This evening about 8 of the clock. Capt Zaccheus Mayhew his barn catched fire. How is not certainly known, and burned down to the ground, together with all his hay, except one load.

Jany. 10 1719-20. The week past hath been very cold especially Thursday last. Mr Bryce Blair by a fall yesterday in the evening broke his left arm above the elbow.

7ber 4. 1720. * * * Our house was raised on Tuesday of this week being the 6th day.

Xber 25. 1720. * * Our people here. some of them, brought a drift whale ashore at Sqiubnocket on friday and cut her up on Saturday.

July 12. 1724. * * * On friday last we raised our new meeting house. Gershom Cathcart, a young man belonging to New town fell from the third story, and was very much bruised. His recovery is uncertain [his] reason seems not to be impaired by his fall. Lord make the providence a wakening to others!

August 23. 1724. * * * I took occasion to reprove some young folk publickly for their irreverent and profane deportment in the time of Gods publick worship

8ber 25. 1724. * * * I am informed that 7 Indians belonging to Gay Head coming from Rhod Island home in a whale boat were all lost, as is generally thought. It is said they were in drink when they went on board.

Jan: 10. 1724-25. * * * Last Monday son Allen carryed two men prisoners to Boston, viz: Capt Lane and Mr McGowan:

Xber 5. 1725. * * * Last week a sloop came ashore on the south side of the island, the men and cargo were saved, the master having been long sick died Friday night last and was buryed this day. His name was Cash. the sloop belonged to Rhod Island.

March 13. 1725-26. * * * The snow which has continued for most part since some time in November is now almost gone.

August 27. 1727. We had an account last week that King George died June 11th last past in Germany on his journey to Hanover, and that his son the prince of Wales was proclaimed King under the title of George 2.

9ber 5. 1727. Last Lords day, in the afternoon, about 11 of the clock we had a shock of an earthquake, that continued above a minute: it was considerably great, but seemed to be greater in some places than others, whether it hath been felt all the country over or not I have not yet heard.

9ber 12. 1727. I understand that the earthquake was much more severe easterly than in these parts.

Xber 31. 1727. We had a public fast on Wednesday last on account of the earthquake.

July 7. 1728. We appointed Wednesday last to be observed as a publick fast, but we had a plentiful rain on Tuesday which occasioned our changing the fast into a thanksgiving.

June 8. 1729. I baptized a negro of Captn Mayhew called Ceasar this day.

July 9 [1737] and the night after it, we had excessive rains which raised the rivers upon this island to such a degree that the dams of the water mills were carryed away by them, and the mowing ground near the rivers was very much damnified, to the great loss of several of the inhabitants.

August 11, 1737. The sky towards the N. and N.W. appeared with an unusual redness, which continued for some time extending itself more and more easterly. About 11 the red was mixed with white streaks that were very luminous, being broad below and gradual growing narrower till they ended in a point. About midnight there appeared a bow reaching from east to west in the form of a rainbow, only there was no diversity of colors, the whole bow was luminous so that the air was lighter than it is at full moon, tho, it was 2 or 3 days before the change [of] the moon. It did rather resemble day light before the sun rises than moonlight.

Xber 7, 1737. About 10 at night there was felt by several persons on the island, Martha's Vineyard, the shock of an earthquake.

November 21. 1738. There came a ship ashore on the South side of this island, belonging to New York. She came last from Jamaica: the lading and mens lives were saved, but it is supposed the ship cannot be got off again.

The first that was seized with that called the throat distemper in this town was Susan Allen; the next was Abigail Hillman, both these died. The next Katharine Smith, she also died. Next Mrs Little, she is in a fair way of recovery. Next Sam: Bassett's daughter, she also is in a hopeful way: next Bethia Clark and my grand daughter Mary Allen

7ber 17. 1740. Was observed through the island as a day of fasting and prayer to beg mercy of God that the distemper that has prevailed among us for some time might be removed and health restored ....A child of Zach: Hatch died of the throat distemper this night.

7ber 6, 1741. We had this summer a drought that hurt both the grass and the Indian corn very much. This was accompanied with an unusual number of grasshoppers that devoured both grass and corn.

9ber 12. 1741. We had a general Thanksgiving appointed by our Governour, William Shirley Esqr.

Oct. 19. 1724. About three afternoon the chimney in the room where I commonly stay catched fire, and being very foul, burned very fiercely, which put the whole house in no small danger. It continued to burn till within the night. It was a day time and the wind very high, yet through the mercy of God we received no great damage, only the mantle tree catched fire and is part damnified. Several of our neighbors came to our assistance seasonably. I desire to bless God for our preservation.

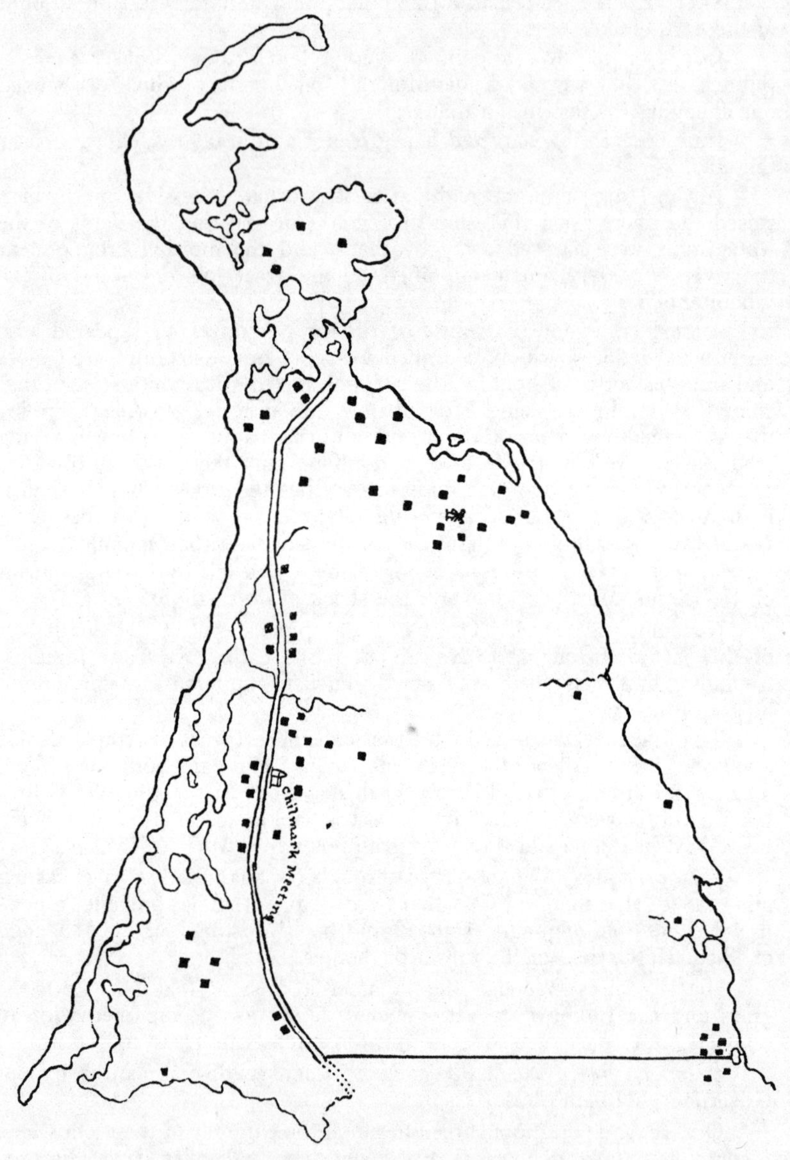

CHILMARK IN 1780
FROM DES BARRES "ATLANTIC NEPTUNE"

ECCLESIASTICAL AFFAIRS.

MINISTRY OF JOHN MAYHEW.

The beginnings of the church history in this town date from the coming of John Mayhew, who settled here about 1673 and established himself in the work of a missionary to the English and natives. His connection with this special field of labor has already been detailed (I, 247-9) and it will only be necessary to say that the people in this town, because of the fewness in numbers, formed a union with those of Tisbury under the pastorship of John Mayhew. This combination existed until his death in 1689 when, as his gravestone states, he was "Minister of the Gospell to the Inhabitants of Tisbury & Chilmark united." The language makes it clear that there was no organized church at that date, although it is quite certain that a meeting house had been built for their accommodation in this town.[1] When it was erected cannot now be determined, though we know that it was located on Abel's hill, probably in or adjoining the old cemetery inclosure.

MINISTRY OF RALPH THACHER.

When the successor of Mayhew came is not known. The loss of the church records, prior to 1787, makes much of our present knowledge fragmentary, as obtained from many scattered sources. In a document dated Feb. 13, 1694, Mr. Ralph or Rodolphus Thacher was spoken of as "now minister of the Gospell at the Town of Chilmark," and this probably affords us a close intimation of the time of his coming hither. He was a native of Duxbury, born about 1647, the son of Thomas and Elizabeth (Partridge) Thacher, and named for his maternal grandfather, the Rev. Ralph Partridge of Duxbury. He was not a college graduate, and prior to his pastorate here had lived in his native town, where he served as constable and town clerk. He had married Ruth Partridge of Duxbury in 1669 and was the father of nine children, all of whom, with the possible exception of the oldest son, who was of age, he brought with him to Chilmark.[2] There is no record of his ordination, and as he was not bred to the ministry, his work here partook of an irregular mission-

[1]This is proven by a reference in Tisbury Records, June 12, 1701, to "the meeting house in Chilmark" then existing. (I, 40)

[2]Savage, Gen. Dictionary, IV, 272; Mather, "Hecatompolis (Magnalia)," I, 27; Gen. Reg., XI, 242; Winsor, Duxbury, 178, 325.

ary character. He lived on the South road, and both he and his son of the same name acquired considerable property here.[1] In 1714, when Judge Sewall visited Chilmark, Parson Thacher and his son called to "Welcom me to the Island," as the diarist records it.[2] At this time he had been in continuous pastoral work here for over twenty years, of which no memorials remain. He was then nearly three score and ten and early in the year he had severed his connection with the church and removed to Lebanon, Conn., whither some of his children had already gone.[3] During the last years of his pastorate a middle-aged Scotch-Irish clergyman had come to Chilmark and was engaged in teaching the town school, and when the aged minister departed this younger man was selected to take the vacant pulpit.

MINISTRY OF WILLIAM HOMES.

Will· Homes

William Homes was born, probably in Ireland, in the year 1663. He first came to America in the year 1686, when he was twenty-two years old. There is no known record of the fact, whether he came from Ireland at that time, or from Scotland, though the former has usually been assumed. It was about the period of his first coming over that both Scotch and Scotch-Irish commenced emigrating to America to escape the persecution of the Stuarts and the Prelacy. After his arrival he was engaged as a teacher at Chilmark, and the people continued to employ him as a teacher to their children for several years, when he returned again to Ireland in July, 1691. He presented "satisfactory testimonials" to the Presbytery of Laggan, and after preaching a "tryall" sermon was given a temporary license to supply vacant pulpits. He was ordained Dec. 21, 1692, at Strabane, a borough town twelve miles southwest of Londonderry, Ireland, by the Presbytery of Laggan, and was settled as pastor of the Scotch Presbyterian parish there. He was often chosen moderator of the Provincial Synod. While there he married, Sept. 26, 1693, Katharine, daughter of Rev. Robert Craighead, who had been minister

[1]Dukes Deeds, I, 365. He sold his residence to his successor, Rev. William Homes, (ibid., III, 102).

[2]Diary, II, 432.

[3]He witnessed a deed here in September, 1714, and in April, 1715, he calls himself of Lebanon.

of Donoughmore in Donegal, and who was translated to Derry in the beginning of the year 1690, and continued there until his death, Aug. 22, 1711. In the adjoining parish of Urney another William Holmes was ordained in 1696, and this led to a confusion of identity. To distinguish him from his namesake, our subject was called "William Homes, the Meek.[1]

In 1714 he came again to America and revisited Martha's Vineyard, at the age of 50.[2] The people of Chilmark remembered the young man who had previously taught among them, with satisfaction, and invited him to become their pastor. There remains no record in possession of the church or town to give us any details of his agreement with the people. A note in his diary is our only knowledge of the beginning of his pastorate. He wrote: —

> On the fifteenth of 7ber [1715] I was installed in the pastorate office in the congregation of Chilmark there were then but two members of that church that wer men, viz Nathan Skiffe and Benjamin Mayhew that day Mr Experience Mayhew who was formerly a member of the Indian church upon this Island having obtained his dismission from thence was joyned to this church. On the second of October Mr Nathan Basset & Mr Ja: Allen were added to the church here and were both baptized that day.[3]

It is not known whether there was a formal service of laying on of hands with other symbolic ritual of the Puritan church, but it seems from all circumstances that such was not the case. Mr Homes was a Presbyterian by birth and education. His salary was £60 at first, and in 1723 the sum of £80 was raised for the ministry.

SECOND MEETING-HOUSE.

In September, 1723, a town meeting was called "for the ordering the building of a publique meeting house" and as a result of their deliberations the following vote was passed:—

> Voted by the major part of the meetors present that their be a house built att the charge of s'd town for the End and use afores'd and that the s'd house be of the Dementions following (viz) forty feet in Length and 35 feet in breadth and 20 feet between Joynts, or any other Dementions

[1]Our William Homes has been credited with graduation from Edinburgh University in 1693, but the author is of the opinion that the degree belongs to the other William Holmes. It is unlikely that our subject was a student at Edinburgh after he had been ordained as a minister.

[2]When Judge Sewall visited the island in April, 1714 he notes in his diary that "Mr. Homes who boards at Mr. Allen's to teach school" dined with him.

[3]The use of the term "installed" indicates that having been previously ordained in Ireland, a settlement as pastor only was necessary.

that may be thought more Convenant by such agents as Shall be Chosen by the town to manage the affaires; provided it amounts to so much and no more Square roome in the whole as above expressed: and that the s'd house be finished att or before the first Day of November in the year 1724: and that the agents to manage the afair to procure the s'd house to be built be Pain Mayhew and Zacheus Mayhew Esqrs and Shubal Smith To hire a carpenter and other workmen to build the above house, and that the method of finishing the s'd house be whooly Left to the Decretion of the s'd agents........
Voted att the meeting above that the meeting house Shall set on the hill neare the old or present meeting house in s'd town by the County Roade.[1]

The site for this new building was given July 10, 1724, by Nathan Bassett "for the Incouragement of the Publick Worship of God."[2]

The frame was raised in July, 1724, and the senior member of the building committee makes the following entries in his account book of his expenditures at this function:—

To wheate	0–12–0
to flower	1– 1–0
to buter	1– 0–6
to shuger	1–13–0
Spice	0– 2–0
Nutmegs	0– 2–6
Bear	1–15–0
Rum gall'ns 10½	6–06–0
Bred	0–06–0 [3]

The ingredients provided by the committee indicate that they had an ample quantity of rum punch, beer and cakes, with an unnecessary amount of bread.

The building was completed in the fall of that year, and a committee of Edgartown and Tisbury men were chosen to attend to the troublesome question of allotting pews and pew room to the worshippers.[4] The three arbitrators or "any two of them agreeing" were empowered to "Determine who of sd Inhabitance shall have Roome in sd house for the buld-

[1]Town Records, I, 32. The old meeting-house was sold after the completion of the new building.

[2]Dukes Deeds, V, 22.

[3]Pain Mayhew's Commonplace Book (1724). Parson Homes also makes the following reference to the raising in his Diary: "July 12. 1724. * * * On friday last we raised our new meeting house. Gershom Cathcart, a young man belonging to New town fell from the third story, and was very much bruised. His recovery is uncertain [his] reason seems not to be impaired by his fall. Lord make the providence a wakening to others!" It may be stated that young Cathcart recovered and survived to a ripe old age.

[4]The committee consisted of Enoch Coffin and John Norton of Edgartown and Experience Luce of Tisbury (Town Records, I, 40).

ing of pews, who the first Choice and so on to the Last." The number of pews on the main floor was twelve, and four in the front gallery, and the persons given permission to build were required to have them "bult Workman Like," within a year or "Loose his privilege." The entire cost of the new meeting-house was £448, exclusive of the pews.

Following the completion of the church the town made in 1728 a permanent increase in the salary of Mr. Homes to £80 yearly, and for the next eighteen years the story of his pastorate is without special interest. He discharged the duties of a village parson faithfully altogether for thirty-one years, and acquired here and elsewhere a high repute for his piety, humility and learning. He was the author of five printed volumes, dealing with theological subjects, three of them published during his life. The earliest, "A Discourse concerning the Public Reading of the Scriptures by the Lord's People in their Religious Assemblies" (1720), had an extensive circulation. His sectarian affiliations with the Presbyterian order prevented his recognition by the Congregational body by which he was surrounded, and having no college associations here, his isolation was further increased beyond what would naturally follow work on a secluded island.

He became too feeble to preach regularly in 1744, and died June 17, 1746, at the age of 83, and lies buried in the cemetery on Abel's hill.

In the library of the Maine Historical Society there is a manuscript volume of 96 pp., of the size known as quarto, bound in contemporary leather and containing the notes of births, marriages, deaths, and important events occurring within the personal knowledge of the diarist. It is closely written from cover to cover, even the fly leaves and insides of the covers being utilized by the original owner or its subsequent possessors. It is the diary or note book of the Chilmark pastor, begun in 1689 and continued to 1746. The author of this history copied the historical and genealogical entries found therein and published them in 1895-6.[1]

The greater portion of the diary is made up of weekly entries dated "Lord's day," detailing his texts and sermon, of which the following is a sample of the whole:—

> xber 7 1718 being Lords day I preached before noon from 1 pet 24 to whom coming as unto a living stone and after sermon administered

[1]See N. E. Genealogical Register, Vols. XLVIII and XLIX.

the sacrament of the Lords supper afternoon I preached from Col: 1. 13. Who hath delivered us from the power of darkness in all which I hope I was assisted the Lord follow my poor labours with a rich blessing to edification and salvation of souls.

These weekly entries are usually followed by some note of a death, "remarkable providence," birth, baptism, admission to church membership, state of weather or such kindred items. The first few leaves of the book contain his family record, sons, daughters and grandchildren, with a list of marriages and deaths in the town of Chilmark during his residence.[1]

Mrs. Katherine Homes survived her husband several years and died in 1754, aged 82 years. She is buried by his side.

MINISTRY OF ANDREW BOARDMAN.

During the last month of the incapacity of Mr. Homes his pulpit was occupied by temporary supplies, Bellamy Bosworth, Richard Pateshall and Andrew Boardman. The church and town extended a call to the last named to become their pastor, at a salary of £200 old tenor. He accepted in April, 1746, and was ordained in September following. Andrew Boardman was born in Cambridge, Mass., Feb. 20, 1720-1, the son of Moses and Abigail (Hastings) Boardman of that town, and was graduated in the class of 1737 from Harvard College. He was unmarried when he came, but a year after he took to himself Catherine Allen (41) of Chilmark, to wife, and thus identified himself with the people among whom he ministered. His pastorate was uneventful as far as we can gather from the records of the town, although he suffered the usual difficulties of his colleagues at that period, from the fluctuations of value in the currencies of the Province, and a final settlement with his heirs was not effected till ten years after his death. He had served the town over thirty years when he was stricken with small pox and died therefrom Nov. 19, 1776, in the 57th year of his age. He left a widow and nine children. She married a second husband, in 1780, Shubael Cottle (53), and died in 1802, aged 75 years.

[1]This diary became the inheritance of his daughter Hannah, who never married, and in her old age she went to live with Deacon James Allen, her nephew. She died in 1790, aged 94 years. Zebulon Allen; son of James, carried the diary to Maine in 1818 and dying in 1837, it was presented to the Historical Society by his heirs. It should be placed in some suitable depositary on the Vineyard, as it relates wholly to Island matters for a period exceeding half a century.

MINISTRY OF TIMOTHY FULLER.

The successor to the deceased minister was not found for several years. Rev. Timothy Fuller began to preach in March, 1778, and under a temporary arrangement continued to fill the pulpit for over three years, but notwithstanding several committees were chosen to "treat" with him, nothing was accomplished. It was a time of unrest, socially and financially, and doubtless the town was unable to meet his requirements and settle the unpaid salary of their late minister.[1] Timothy Fuller was born May 30, 1739, the son of Jacob Fuller of Middleton, Mass., and was graduated in the class of 1760 from Harvard College. Before preaching here he was settled in Princeton, Mass., 1760-1776, and came here as a married man with a family. He left Chilmark about 1782 and finally settled in Merrimac, N. H., where he died in 1805, aged 69 years. After his departure the church and town extended a call, in 1783, to Rev. Asa Piper, but he did not accept.[2]

THIRD MEETING-HOUSE.

The meeting-house built in 1724 was now about sixty years old, undoubtedly out of repair, and owing to the growth of the town, somewhat inconveniently located. In April, 1782, it was voted to remove the old building to a place which would better accommodate the people, and a committee of nine were selected to accomplish this delicate task.[3] It is evident that they failed, for in March, 1783, the town selected Stephen Luce and Ezra Athearn of Tisbury and Malatiah Davis of Edgartown "to view the town and Pick upon some convenient spot or place to set the meeting house upon."[4] This committee promptly reported a site, but when the town voted on the report. "it went in the negative."[5] For a year and a half the matter rested, until on Sept. 21, 1784, the town voted to move the meeting-house "to a knole in Prince Look's land," and appointed a committee to buy the necessary land.[6] Again nothing was done for another year, when in November,

[1]In 1781 the town appointed a committee to "set Price on the Pork & Corn that was paid the Rev. Timothy Fuller Last year."

[2]Town Records, I, 199.

[3]Ibid., I, 188.

[4]Ibid., I, 192.

[5]Ibid., I, 192.

[6]Ibid., I, 197.

1785, the town voted to build a new meeting-house "on Abels hill near Abel Abels house where the commity here to fore Pointed out as the most convenient spot."[1] The usual committees were appointed to carry out this design, but in the next month another town meeting upset this arrangement and voted that "the meeting house be Repared as it now stands."[2] This comedy of cross purposes, which had been enacted for nearly four years, was continued for a while longer. In January, 1786, a committee was chosen to find the center of the town, and they reported that it was "forty Rods east from a stile in William Stewarts fence in the division between his two east Plases and 20 Rods southly."[3] The townsmen then voted to "remove the old meeting house to the hill near Abels here to fore chosen and Rebuild the same;" to purchase "half one acre of land of William Stewart about twelve Rods North from the Gate near Abel Abels" and selected a committee "to Draw a Plan of the new meeting house and a Plan how to Proceed in building the same." The committee advised the expenditure of £300 in tearing down the old structure and utilizing the available material in rebuilding on the new site. This was the final settlement of the question of a site, which was on the cross road that leads from the old Warren Tilton house on the South road to the Middle road, on a hill near the latter highway. The work of construction was similarly juggled at various town meetings during the building operation, and it is impossible to tell anything positive about its dimensions or architecture. A traveler in 1807 says of it: "Chilmark meeting house is without spire and in all respects humble in exterior appearance."[4] It had a porch entrance carrying stairs to the gallery, and interiorly the gallery extended on three sides. The congregation, in high back box pews, received the solemn warnings of the preachers perched in a lofty pulpit, surmounted by a great sounding board. It was austere in appearance both inside and outside.

MINISTRY OF JONATHAN SMITH.

During the four or five years of wrangling about rebuilding the meeting-house the town was without any regular ministrations. The old building was in a discreditable con-

[1]Town Records, I, 205.
[2]Ibid.
[3]Ibid., I, 206.
[4]Kendall, Travels, II, 184.

dition. In 1785 the town voted "to Board up the windows ......and other Parts of the House that is necessary," and we may conclude that the cause of religion was at low ebb. In 1787 the town finally secured a candidate for the vacant pulpit in the person of Jonathan Smith. He was a native of Hadley, Mass., born Jan. 28, 1748, and was graduated in the class of 1768 from Harvard College. It is presumed that he was a bachelor of about forty when he came here, as he married two years later, in 1789, Anna Williams of Sandwich, Mass. In August, 1787, the church extended a call to him to become the pastor, and the town at once concurred, offering him £110 as an annual stipend. He accepted under date of Dec. 1st following, and the town voted at once "to support and strengthen the Gallerys for the ordination" and to reserve the "two front gallerys and the womens four long Gallerys for the Singers" at the ordination services."[1] Committees were appointed to entertain "the councell" and the long religious drouth was to be broken in a series of ecclesiastical festivities, with a new minister in a new meeting house.

Rev. Jonathan Smith was ordained to the pastoral care of the church of Christ in Chilmark, on the twenty-third day of January, one thousand seven hundred and eighty-eight.

The following named persons belonged to the church at the time of the ordination:—[2]

Mr. Zachariah Mayhew & Elizabeth his wife
Matthew Mayhew Esq.
Dea. James Allen & Martha his wife
John Bassett & Jane his wife
John Cottle & Zerviah his wife
John Mayhew
Jeremiah Mayhew & Fear his wife
Robert Allen & Desire his wife
William Steward & Deborah his wife
Nathan Mayhew & Abigail his wife
Hannah Homes
Widow Anna Allen
Widow Deborah Allen
Widow Remember Skiff
Widow Mary Tilton
Mercy, wife to Seth Mayhew
Hannah, wife to Elijah Smith
Mary, wife to John Allen, Esq.
Zerviah, wife to Ezra Hilman
Ruth, wife to Timothy Mayhew
Elizabeth, wife to Josiah Tilton
Widow Rebecca Norton
Widow Elizabeth Butler
Widow Peggy Mayhew
Mehitable Mayhew
Mary Hunt
Margaret Allen
Hannah Wyer
Catherine Boardman
Eleanor Mayhew

[1]His acceptance is spread upon the town records (I, 218). In it he says: "As my Residence with you will separate me at a great Distance from many of my acquaintance you will cheerfully from time to time indulge sufficient opportunity to visit my friends & near connections."

[2]Chilmark Church Records. The entry above quoted begun the present oldest book of records of the Congregational church.

Widow Mary Tilton
Zilphah, wife to Joseph Tilton
Beulah, wife to Samuel Tilton
Abigail, wife to Reuben Tilton
Rebecca, wife to Stephen Tilton
Jerusha Mayhew
Bethia Mayhew
Ruhamah Tilton
Widow Thankful Pitts

The pastorate begun so auspiciously, became the longest in the history of the church. He survived the widespread controversy over the ministerial taxes, which caused so much trouble in other towns,[1] and passed safely through the early opposition of the newly imported religions, the Methodist and Baptist. For forty years he remained as the beloved pastor of this flock, until Sept. 4, 1827, when fourscore years of age, he "was dismissed by his desire on account of ill health." His wife had died in 1807, and lies buried in the old cemetery, and after his work was ended here, he returned to his native place in 1827 to spend the few declining days left to him. He died April 14, 1829, aged 81 years.

FOURTH MEETING-HOUSE.

With the advent of a new pastor in 1841 the usual zeal to build a new house of worship, or repair the old, overtook the members of this parish. The existing building was about fifty-four years old, had suffered much from disuse and lack of care, and it was considered wiser to erect a new meeting-house rather than patch the old timbers. Accordingly a new building was erected about twenty rods to the southward of the old house, and was completed early in 1842 and dedicated February 2nd that year with appropriate ceremonies. The old structure was torn down, the lumber parcelled out in lots and sold at public auction. This was the last meeting-house erected by this denomination, and served the gradually decreasing remnant of its former numerical strength until about 1875 when it was torn down, and the last relic of the historic church of Chilmark went down into oblivion.

SUCCESSION OF PASTORS.

The loss or destruction of the records of this church has rendered an accurate and complete account of it a matter of difficulty, and much that might be definitely stated can only

[1]In 1801 the town chose an agent to represent it at the Court of Sessions, "with regard to Benjamin Bassett Esquires Ministerial tax" (I, 256). In 1805 this tax for 1801 and 1802 was remitted to him (I, 308).

be given approximately now.[1] The church organization was officially known as the Congregational Union Society and was in affiliation with that religious body which had a general or parent association in New England.[2] This general association has no records of the Chilmark church in its published reports until 1837, when it is marked "Vacant." It may be fair to conclude that it had remained so since the death of Rev. Jonathan Smith. It was without a pastor until 1841, when Rev. Luke A. Spofford was employed as "stated supply." In the year following, on Feb. 2, 1842, he was regularly installed as pastor. The installation sermon was preached by Rev. Mr. Hooker of Falmouth; the charge was given by Rev. Ebenezer Chase of West Tisbury, and the right hand of fellowship by Rev. Allen Gannett of Edgartown.[3] Mr. Spofford remained five years (1841-1845) and from his departure until 1850 the pulpit was vacant, except for temporary services held as clergymen could be obtained.[4] Silas S. Hyde was "stated supply" in 1846, and in 1850-1 Elijah Demond held the same status. Nathaniel Cobb, an eccentric individual, preached here regularly in 1852 and 1853 and occasionally in the next year. Thomas W. Duncan followed as "stated supply" in 1856-9, and after his departure the pulpit was vacant for the next ten years (1860-9). Elijah Demond returned as acting pastor for two years following (1870-1) when it again became vacant. William H. Sturtevant was acting pastor 1875-6-7; the last of the clergymen who had official connection with this religious society.

The Congregational church died a natural death about this date — perhaps it was really defunct before the official records indicate. The old building was difficult of access and the younger element were attracted to the newer religious doctrines taught by the Methodists. In its latter days the attendance on the Sunday services was principally of the aged, and when they died there was none left to sustain a regular ministry.

[1] The late William Norton of Menemsha was the last clerk and custodian of the Church records. After his death no further trace of the books can be found and from all circumstances it is believed they were destroyed.

[2] Tisbury Town Records, 367-8, 373. A number of residents of Tisbury were members of this Society in 1815.

[3] Autobiography of John Adams, 404.

[4] Rev. Richard Cecil Spofford, his son, died in this town May 25, 1843, of consumption and is buried at Abel's Hill. A daughter also died in the following July and these sad events doubtless caused his departure from the town.

THE BAPTIST DENOMINATION.

The act incorporating the First Baptist Society of Tisbury in 1803 specifies a number of the incorporators as residents of Chilmark, and it is possible to enumerate from the list those persons who belonged in this town. From it the following names are taken: Ezra Allen, Joseph Allen, Lot Cottle, Theophilus Mayhew, Jonathan Tilton. There may have been others who identified themselves with the Tisbury church in later years, but there are no records to throw light on the matter. It is not believed that any independent organization was ever formed in this town.

THE METHODIST CHURCH.

The first itinerant preacher of this sect to penetrate the Vineyard as far as Chilmark, was the Rev. Joshua Hall, in 1797-8, when he was stationed at Homes Hole, to which this town was connected under the existing system of supervision. He organized a small "class" at that time, but ten years later (1807) there were reported to be only four Methodists in the town.[1] In 1810 the "class" was revived, being reinforced by Shadrach Robinson, who had removed hither from Naushon and whose house became a home for the preachers and a place for their meetings. Another of the early and prominent Methodists in this town was Captain Francis Tilton (296), and after his sudden death, following a return from a long voyage in 1828, his widow continued to receive in her house the faithful of this small flock for "class" and prayer meetings.[2] In 1827 the old Methodist meeting-house in Edgartown was purchased, moved up here in sections and reconstructed on a site on the Middle road, opposite to the present meeting-house. The growth of the congregation was now steady and increasing, until in 1833 it was separated from the parent organization at Homes Hole and set out upon an independent career. Philip Crandon was the first preacher assigned to the new station, and following him in order came James Bicknell, 1835; Elijah Willard, 1836; Joseph Brown, 1837; (none in 1838); Otis Wilder, 1839; Thomas D. Blake, 1840; Charles D. Cushman, 1841; Ebenezer Ewins, 1842; and in 1843, William Nanscoin.

[1] 2 Mass. Hist. Coll., III, 63.

[2] During all these years the preachers of this sect on duty at Homes Hole or Edgartown came regularly to Chilmark as a part of their missionary work.

During the ministry of the last named a new house of worship was finished, the one in present use, and in January 1843 it was dedicated with appropriate ceremonies. It cost about $2,000, and had a seating capacity for 300 persons. The succession of ministers since that time has been as follows: George W. Wooding, 1844; Nahum Taintor, 1845-6; O. P. Farrington, 1847; Henry Mayo, 1848; Lewis Bates, 1849;

CHILMARK METHODIST CHURCH.

Thomas Slater, 1850-1; Robert C. Gonegal, 1852-3; John Tasker, 1854-5; William Sheldon, 1856; John F. Fogg, 1857; Franklin Sears, 1858-9; James H. Cooley, 1860; George D. Boynton, 1861-2; Abel Alton, 1863-5; Josiah C. Allen, 1866-8; Seth B. Chase, 1869-70; D. J. Griffin, 1871-3; B. K. Bosworth, 1874; E. S. Fletcher, 1875-7; H. S. Smith, 1878-80; Isaac C. Sherman, 1881-3; John N. Patterson, 1884-6; Winfield Hall, 1887-8; C. T. Hatch, 1889-91; C. S. Thurber, 1892-4; B. K. Bosworth, 1895; J. S. Bell, 1896-8; C. W. Ruoff, 1899-1901; B. F. Raynor, 1902-4, and A. Stanley Muirhead, 1905-7.

SCHOOLS AND EDUCATION.

The earliest references in the records of the Vineyard in connection with this section are to a "school house." The allusions to this "school house" are not yet clear, unless we assume a native mission school taught by one of the young sons of the deceased Thomas Mayhew, Junior, either Matthew or Thomas, or possibly John, for it will be remembered that Matthew was brought up to teach the Indians, and was given an education for that purpose. There was an Indian meeting "about eight miles off my house," wrote the Junior Mayhew in 1651, and this distance would bring us to the present village of West Tisbury, and the writer announced his intention of setting up a school for the natives during that winter. It is probable that such an one was established somewhere to the westward of the Tiasquan river on the South road, not far from the dividing line between the two towns, before he died, but whether it was in Tisbury or Chilmark is not understood from the scant description.

There are no references to a school in this town prior to 1729, at which time the town voted that sessions be held in the spring "att the place where it now is," and further provision was made for the several sections of the town as follows:—

> July and August & September near Willm Hunts provided the people westward of the fulling mill River provide a Suitable house there for that purpose: and att Kephickon October and November (if) the people in that part of the town provide a house as aforesd.[1]

The sum of £50 was appropriated to carry into effect this vote of the town. The peculiar territorial situation of Chilmark, with its scattered segments, Elizabeth Islands, Chickemmoo and Nomans Land, rendered the administration of school affairs not only difficult, but expensive. The several sections demanded facilities equivalent to those arranged for the central settlement, and as a result there was constant

[1]Town Records, 48; Feb. 14, 1728-9.

bickering in town meetings whether there should be a "fixed" or a "moving" school from year to year.[1] In 1731 the townsmen could not settle this question among themselves and called in outside advisors. Samuel Cobb, Jabez Athearn and Abner West of Tisbury were requested to act as referees on this disputed problem. They rendered the following decision: —

We the Subscribers as a Comittee within Spesifyed being mett togather and haveing heard the Lauvall Information of the within mentioned agents as also Considered the particulars of the within note & upon the whole Determin that the within mentioned School be kept for the Space of ten months in Each of the two years at the foot of the bureing hill between the bureing hill and the meeting house in Chilmark & the Space of two months (in) october and november at the house of David Butler at Cheekommo in sd Chilmark and that the Cost and Charge for School Rooms be Defrayed by the whole town.[2]

As a result of this report the town voted that Pain Mayhew

Do procure a Suteable house for the use of sd town and att their Charge for the keeping the towns Scool in the Same to be twenty feet Long Sixteen wide and Six in the upright and to Chose the Same to be Sett att the place ordered by the Com'tee appointed for that end to sit near the meeting house in sd town and to be finished as the sd mayhew Shall think best and most Convenant for that use.[3]

The location of what is probably the first town schoolhouse built for the purpose, is sufficiently clear to all residents and does not need further explanation. The sum of £50 was voted, later in the year, "to pay the present school master for his service," but it is not known who he was. It is probable that it was Francis Bryan, who occupied that position the two following years, and whose services were the cause of litigation. In 1732 Zephaniah Mayhew, one of the selectmen, entered complaint against Bryan before the court because he refused "to teach Sundry children belonging to sd Town & perticularly a servant Girl of the Plaintiffs."[4] The next year John Allen sued

[1]Recently a suit was tried involving this same trouble, a lack of school privileges at Nomans Land. A resident of that island sued to compel the town to provide school facilities at that place, and being defeated appealed to the Supreme Court. The final decision (1908) was against the contention of the plaintiff.

[2]Chilmark Records, May 18, 1731.

[3]Ibid., June 22, 1731. Mayhew was also ordered to make arrangements with David Butler for school rooms in the Chickemmoo district, "until the school house can be built."

[4]Athearn Mss., Congressional Library.

Bryan for punishing his son, William Allen, "with a Large Cane or Walking Staff." The schoolmaster won the case, but the experiences were such that he decided to labor in other fields, and as a result the town was "presented" in Court in 1737, by the Grand Jury for "not haveing a skole Master."[1] Not only did it have no schoolmaster, but no school-house, for Pain Mayhew had evidently neglected to carry out the wishes of the town as above expressed, for in 1733 the following vote was passed: —

voted that there be a Small house bult att the Charg of & for the use of sd town to be Sett near the meeting house the sd house to be 17 feet Long 14 wide & Six in the upright to be Covered Either with Clabord or Shingles on the wall the wall to be plastered with Lime and the Chimney to be brick and that Willm and Josiah tilton be the towns agents to procure the Same to be Done as Soon as may be.[2]

In 1742 this diminutive building needed some repairs, but the motion to accomplish it "past in the negitive" at one meeting, and at an adjournment the following vote was recorded on the subject: —

voted that the voate past att a meeting in July Last respecting the School be reconsidered and after a considerable Silance it was proposed to reconsider the Last vote and voted accordingly and then that the vote past in July as above be reconsidered So far as the time remaned of the three years as Shoild be remaining after the time expired that the School master was hired for and then brake up the meeting.[3]

Spelling and confusion of expression like that might break up any meeting, and the reader is left to decide what the town really decided to do in the premises. In 1743 the town voted "the school house be removed and set near the tan fats by the house of Noah Abel,"[4] and in a burst of fortitude further decreed that it should be kept there "for the space of ten years next coming." Meanwhile the Chickemmoo

[1]Athearn Mss. The Grand Jury, in view of its own spelling, might have been indicted for the same offence.

[2]Town Records, Jan. 26, 1733. This reduced the dimensions by several feet each way, and "Six feet in the upright" indicates the need of a short teacher. It was finished in December following.

[3]Town Records, Nov. 1, 1742.

[4]Several references to this locality require that its exact situation be indicated. There is a place still known as the "Tan Yard," on the easterly side of the brook which flows across the Middle road, a little to the eastward of the house of the late Capt. Horatio W. Tilton, and thence down past the house formerly occupied by Beriah T. Hillman, Esq., finally discharging into the cove. This brook has its source in the "Peaked Hill Place" in swampy ground, and the "tan fats" or yard was near the source of this brook.

district had been eliminated as a factor in this burdensome problem, but the several communities at Keephigon, Elizabeth Islands, Menemsha and the other outlying precincts kept the question always a source of contention at the yearly meetings. In 1758 it was voted that there be a "fixed school," for the ten years ensuing, "to be kept on the land of Zachariah Mayhew near Wm. Stewards," and a committee was appointed to provide suitable accommodations. Five years later, there being some uncertainty about the regularity of service, an inspector was appointed to "see if the Town School be Regerly Kept," and also to see "if Mr. Steaven Skiff will go and keep a Regular School the year out according to agreement and to make good the lost time."[1]

The ten years having elapsed, the town renewed the vote, establishing it for another decade near the "tan fats." In 1777 the sum of £250 was raised "for a school or schools" and a committee was appointed "to divide the town into districts as will be most for the advantage to the inhabitants."[2] In 1789 a similar vote was passed, and the school-house at that time was situated "on the land of Robert Allen & near the place where the house of Capt. James Allen deceased lately stood."[3] The money was to be divided according to the number of children in each division. Owing to the large area and the scattered settlements, this involved further friction and families were changed from one district to another to obviate the hardships of arbitrary divisional lines. A school census, "from twenty one years old and under" was ordered in 1790 to aid the selectmen in apportioning the school funds. This plan was followed until the close of that century. In the beginning of the next century the school districts were divided by a north and south line, drawn from "the roreing brook leveing Pain Tilltons and Prince Look to the Westward said line running thence to the meeting house thence south easterly untill it comes to the sea."[4] The sum of two hundred dollars was raised in 1801 for educational purposes.

In 1850 there were three public schools in the town, with an attendance of 133 scholars, for the support of which $333 was raised by taxation. The teachers in this period

[1]Town Records, July 8, 1763.

[2]Ibid., I, 163.

[3]This was the school for the southern division of the town. May 1st was set as the time for opening schools.

[4]Town Records, I, 259.

for the following decade were A. J. Blake, Rev. Elijah Demond, (the Congregationalist Minister), Quincy E. Dickerman, subsequently master of a Boston school, Charles E. Alden, Bartlett Mayhew and J. Dana Bullen. In 1863 there were 182 scholars enrolled and $451.50 was the expenditure for that year. The school-houses were situated then as follows: (1) Western District, near Beetle Bound corner (the present site), and the teachers were Ruth H. Nickerson, principal, and Charlotte J. Hillman, assistant; for the winter term, I. N. Kidder, principal and Ada S. Luce, assistant. (2) North East District, in Keephigon, near the Tisbury line, and the teachers were Cyrus M. Lovell (summer) and Henry H. Luce (winter). (3) South East District, on South road, near Nabs corner, and the teachers were Josephine R. Cottle (summer) and Cyrus M. Lovell (winter).

MILITIA.

As elsewhere related, the military affairs of this town were merged with Tisbury, and the combined company was under command of Benjamin Skiffe for many years, until he was promoted to be major of the County Regiment. Zachariah Mayhew became identified with the militia, and is given the title of Captain immediately following the death of Skiffe, and it is presumed he commanded the local company.[1] His brother Zaccheus, however, had a longer record in connection with the town militia, and became its captain some time before 1718. In the French and Indian wars this combination with Tisbury terminated, and in 1757 the company, still under command of Zaccheus Mayhew, had the following additional officers: Fortunatus Mayhew, Lieutenant; Eliashib Adams, John Basset, Uriah Tilton and Josiah Tilton as Sergeants, and Zaccheus Mayhew, Jr. as Ensign.[2] In 1761 there were two companies of foot in Chilmark, of which the first was under command of Cornelius Bassett as Captain;[3] Samuel Mayhew, First Lieutenant;

[1]Town Records, under date of Oct. 25, 1716, page 11, Zachariah Mayhew devoted his time for most of his life to missionary work among the Indians.

[2]Mass. Arch., XCIX, 24.

[3]Ibid., XCIX, 24. Captain Bassett was also Lieutenant Colonel of the County Regiment of Militia.

Uriah Tilton, Second Lieutenant, and Mayhew Adams as Ensign. The second company was under command of Robert Hatch as Captain, Lemuel Weeks as Lieutenant, and Zephaniah Robinson as Ensign. There was also an Indian company in the town at this time under the command of the following officers: Adonijah Mayhew, Captain; Lemuel Butler, Lieutenant, and Thomas Daggett, Ensign. Neither the town records nor other sources of information furnish evidence of activity in local military affairs subsequent to the Revolution. In 1794, when the Major General of the state militia issued orders to those towns which had no organized companies to supply the deficiency, Chilmark directed the selectmen to "write to Major General Goodwin themselves or by joining with the other towns in Dukes County requesting a suspension of his orders to organize militia" and further desiring Beriah Norton of Edgartown to assist said town in making said request."[1]

TAVERNS.

Chilmark has never been a tavern town, and no record has been found by the author showing that a license was granted for the express purpose of "keeping a publicke house," except in one year. Undoubtedly Chilmark was one of the towns referred to in 1694, which "thinck it inconvenient to have such houses." In 1715, however, Ebenezer Allen, and in 1722 William Clark and Lemuel Little were licensed as "innholders in Chilmark," and obtained a license as such. It is believed that these licenses cover rather the retailing of "strong drink," as three taverns in the town were not required for the convenience of wayfarers at that period. Situated as it was and is, the need of such houses occurred so infrequently, that private homes have always been ample, and at the service of the "stranger within its gates" temporarily.

The following named persons were licensed innholders in the town of Chilmark by the County Court for the years specified: Ebenezer Allen, 1715-16; William Clark, 1722-32; Zaccheus Mayhew, 1735-8; Bethiah Mayhew, 1738; Thomas Mayhew, 1761; Zephaniah Mayhew, 1746-7; Josiah Tilton, 1748; William Hunt, 1749-52; Uriah Tilton, 1749-51; John Allen, Jr., 1752-3; John Cottle, 1741-65; Cornelius Bassett

[1]Town Records, I, 240.

1761-73; Salathiel Tilton, 1769; Abisha Cottle, 1772-7; Beriah Luce, 1781-2; Ebenezer Bassett, 1782, William Stewart, 1782-4; Benjamin Bassett, 1786-7; John Allen, 1786-7.

PATHS, HIGHWAYS AND BRIDGES.

The South Road. — This was the first "hie way" in the town and probably existed as a foot or cart path from the earliest occupation by the English. Undoubtedly it followed the old trail used by the Indians in their intercourse between Takemmy and Nashowakemmuck. It was a continuation of the "Mill path" or "school house path" from Tisbury, and was gradually extended as the settlement grew. In 1704 the selectmen, upon petition, laid it out as appears by the following record: —

> beginning att the road on the top of the hill near the meeting hous runing to a heap of stones near the house of Nathan Basset and from thence running to a stake and a heap of stones, being in an old field sometime within the Inclosour of nathan basset: and from thence to the northerly Corner of the land of Ebenezer Allen and so where the way now runs that is on the south side of the Land of Willm. Tilton. Dated Sept. the 14th, 1704.[1]

In 1786 this road extended a distance of $3\frac{3}{4}$ miles from the Tisbury bounds, or to the turn at Ephraim Mayhew's corner. It was the only open town road in the existence of the town until the following century, excepting of course cart paths and other indefinite ways of communication.

Menemsha Road. — In January, 1738-9, the inhabitants petitioned the county Court for a road from Menemsha pond to the common (south) road, but it was not laid out till 1748, when damages to the amount of £55 were assessed and allowed to abutting owners. It is the road which leads from North Shore past Beetle Bound corner to the South road at the Ephraim Mayhew place.

Tea Lane. — According to tradition this road derived its name from an incident that occurred during the embargo on tea, in the days prior to the Revolution. Captain Robert Hillman (146), returning from a voyage to England, brought some of the "forbidden fruit" for the use of an invalid aunt, the wife of his uncle Silas (45). The patriotic authorities learning of it, endeavored its seizure, but were unable after

[1] Town Records. I, 15.

several searchings to locate the depositary, which was the barn, and Aunt Eunice had her cheering cups in spite of the officials whose duty it was to confiscate this contraband article that became the exciting cause of the great struggle.

Middle Road.— Upon petition of Samuel Tilton, 2nd, and 150 others this road was laid out by the County Commissioners, Dec. 30, 1845, from Baxter's Corner, West Tisbury, to the Gay Head line, including a bridge over Harry's creek. The length as surveyed was six miles, 290 rods, having a width of two rods.

North Road.— The County Commissioners, upon a petition of John Hammett and 216 others, accepted the layout of this road, Sept. 17, 1849, and it was finished two years later. It extended a distance of 6 miles, 74 rods, from the village of North Tisbury to Menemsha creek.

THE U. S. GOVERNMENT SERVICES.

The general government is not represented in this town by any of its departments except the postal service. An office was established in 1822, and Matthew Mayhew was commissioned, Dec. 25, 1822, as the first postmaster. The office was, and is now, located at the house or store of the incumbent for the time being. The successors in the postmastership have been as follows: Ephraim Mayhew, commissioned Oct. 13, 1836; Tristram Allen, Jr., March 30, 1842; Mrs. Tamson Allen, July 13, 1864; John Dunham, Sept. 7, 1865; James T. Mosher, April 20, 1883; George West, Jan. 27, 1886, and E. Elliot Mayhew, May 18, 1897 (present incumbent). The name of this office was changed from Chilmark to Squibnocket in 1883, and remained so till 1898, when the original town name was resumed as its official designation.

INDUSTRIES.

MILLS.

Three brooks, the New Mill river, Roaring brook and Fulling Mill brook, having their sources in the high hills of Chilmark, afforded sufficient water power to run several mills.

Fulling Mill. — The earliest one established was the fulling mill, some years prior to 1694, of which Benjamin Skiffe was owner and manager. It was situated several rods to the north of the South road and the old dam site is still visible to the traveler crossing the bridge that spans the brook. How long it was in operation as a fulling mill is not known, but the map of 1795 shows it in existence at that date.

Grist Mills. — There was a grist mill on New Mill river, probably before 1700, as Benjamin Skiffe was granted the privilege to establish one in 1696 (Deeds, I, 125) and the map of 1795 shows one at that date near the Tisbury line.

A grist mill was built on the Roaring brook, probably by John Hillman (12), before 1728, and it was operated after his death by the widow and her brother-in-law, Benjamin Hillman (13) (Deeds, VII, 224). A new one was erected on this site in 1849 by Francis W. Nye, and the mill is still standing, though not in operation.

A grist mill was established about 1850 on the Fulling Mill brook by Samuel Tilton, and was in operation for about ten years. The buildings have since then been devoted to other uses.

WOOL.

Sheep raising has been one of the principal industries from the earliest times in Chilmark. At the time of Grey's raid, when the ten thousand sheep were commandeered, this town lost nearly one half of the entire number. In 1837 the farmers had a total of 6470, of which 1600 were merinos, and the average weight of each fleece was two pounds. The production of wool in that year was $5,180.

In 1850 the farmers owned 5,568 sheep, of which 1,400 were in one flock (William W. Swain's). The production of wool was 13,195 pounds in that year.

IRON ORE.

Long before the Revolution bog iron was taken from the swamps on the estate once owned by John Hillman and in the possession of his heirs.[1] It is stated that during the war of Independence the product of this mine, if it may be so called, was smuggled across the Sound to the forges of Taunton and converted into ammunition when the supply of lead became diminished. Crevecoeur's map of 1782 notes the location of this mine as one of the principal points of

[1]Dukes Probate, III, 153. Division of estate in 1743 refers to the "iron ore swamp."

interest on the island. Dr. James Thacher, in his "Observations upon Iron Ores," makes the following reference to it:

> There is on the island of Martha's Vineyard a mine of iron ore of considerable extent and value. It is brought to our works in large lumps of a reddish brown colour, affording about 25 per cent. and it is worth six dollars per ton. Iron from this ore exhibits a peculiar degree of smoothness and lustre.[1]

During the war of 1812 this mine furnished the ore that was cast into balls for the guns of the "Constitution," if we may rely on legend, and it is not difficult to give this tale some credit.[2]

TANNERY.

There were tan pits in operation as early as 1726,[3] situated on the east side of Peaked hill, near the middle road; not far from the town hall.

PAINT MILL.

Hiram and Francis Nye, who had come here from Falmouth, established a paint mill about 1850, for grinding colors out of the clayey deposits found near the shore. The highest annual production while it was in operation was about 46,000 pounds, valued at $5,000, and the mill was situated on a brook now called Paint Mill brook.

BRICK KILNS.

About sixty years ago Messrs. Smith and Barrows established a plant for the manufacture of pressed brick near the outlet of Roaring brook. It was a large industry for the town at first, employing a dozen laborers, and the production was about 600,000 bricks of the value of $2,400 annually. While there was wood enough to burn the bricks the manufacture continued, but after twenty years the fuel was exhausted and the works had to be abandoned. Nothing remains but an old water wheel, a wooden flume to supply it with water, a smoke stack and ruined walls. The clay beds are not yet exhausted.

[1] 1 Mass. Hist. Coll., IX, 257.

[2] Hines, "Story of Martha's Vineyard," 161.

[3] Homes, Diary. It may have been operated by Thomas Blair, a Scotchman who lived next the pits at that date.

CHILMARK IN 1908

This town is nearly two centuries old since the date of its incorporation as such by its present name, and two hundred and thirty-seven years old reckoning from its establishment as Tisbury Manor. It has been segmented more than the other two original towns, losing the Elizabeth Islands and Chickemmoo from its material assets. Its condition at this time as shown by the assessor's books May 1, 1908 is as follows:— Personal estate assessed, $57,225; real estate assessed, $232,708; total $289,933. Acres of land assessed, 10,436; number of dwelling houses, 171; horses 111; cows, 115; other cattle, 93; sheep, 2145.

ANCIENT STONE CORBEL
(DOORWAY ARCH),
S. MARGARET'S CHURCH,
CHILMARK, ENG.

NOMANS LAND.

DISCOVERY BY GOSNOLD, 1602.

This island, situated two and three-quarters miles to the southward of Gay Head, enjoys the distinction of being the first land touched by Gosnold in 1602 and receiving from the explorers the name of "Marthaes Vineyard." This title, as we know, became attached to the present island bearing the name, although the reasons for the transfer of nomenclature are not understood. When Gosnold and his companions landed here it was "a disinhabited island," but the two journalists of the voyage give detailed accounts of their investigations of its natural features. They found it "full of wood-vines, gooseberry bushes, whortleberries, raspberries, eglantines, etc. Here we had cranes, steames, shoulers geese

FIRST REPRESENTATION OF NOMANS LAND.
FROM THE SIMANCAS MAP, 1610.

and divers other birds which there at that time upon the cliffs being sandy with some rocky stones, did breed and had young. In this place we saw deer; here we rode in eight fathoms near the shore where we took great store of cod,—as before at Cape Cod, but much better."[1]

The subsequent history of the island, after this elaborate introduction to the world, is practically a blank for over half a century, and but for its appearance on the maps of this period nothing is known of it.

SUCCESSIVE CHANGES OF NAME.

The christening of Gosnold did not stick to this lonely isle of the sea, and it came to have a variety of titles in the maps of the seventeenth century. The second name it bore

[1]Archer, Relation of Captain Gosnold's Voyage, 4.

was "Hendrick Christiaensen's Eylant" in 1616 and "Ile de Hendrick" in 1646, both having reference to the Dutch explorer of that name who probably visited it. The curious name of "Dock Island" appears on a map of 1675, but it was not repeated in later charts.

After its inclusion in the jurisdiction of New York it came under other influences, and in 1666 was first called "Nomans Land," also the Isle of Man. The origin of the name "Nomans" is not known. It is usual to attribute it to a combination of two words, No Man's Land, as descriptive of its ownerless condition, but while this is the easiest conclusion it does not seem to be the correct one. The word is scarcely ever divided and its almost universal spelling is Nomans Land from the earliest times. There was a great Powwaw on the Vineyard called Tequenoman residing here when the English came and it is possible that he had jurisdiction over, or ownership of, this small island which came to bear the last half of his name, (Teque)nomans Land. This name became attached to it at the time above noted and has been its sole title ever since. The Indian name (1666) was Cappoaquit.[1]

EARLY OWNERSHIP.

Nomans Land was not included by name in the original sales of Gorges and Sterling to Mayhew in 1642, and it does not appear that the Governor or his family ever assumed jurisdiction over it or disposed of it by sale. Immediately after the Duke of York obtained his charter for New York, in 1664, his representative proclaimed the authority of the Duke's patent over this island, and on Aug. 3, 1666, granted it to William Reeves, Tristram Dodge, John Williams and William Nightingale, conditional upon the establishment of a fishing trade, construction of a harbor within three years, and the annual payment of one barrel of cod fish as a quit-rent.[2] It was further stipulated that when a certain number of families settled on it the privileges of a township would be granted and a justice of the peace appointed. These conditions were not fulfilled within the three years and the grant was forfeited. This failure, according to the statement of John Williams, was due to "the default of his Partners," and upon his petition the grant was renewed to him June

[1]Dukes Deeds, I, 70.

[2]New York Col. Mss., Patents, I, 50.

28, 1670; "to settle a fishing trade there," and again, on Feb. 23, 1674, he obtained a second renewal.[1] It is not believed that anything was ever done under these patents and it remained in the gift of the Duke for ten years longer. When Governor Dongan invested Matthew Mayhew in 1685 with the Lordship of Martha's Vineyard, he included Nomans Land by name in the patent and a few days afterwards Mayhew sold it to Dongan, who thus came into possession of the island by purchase.[2] Dongan sold it on August 3, 1689, to William Nichols of Islip, Long Island, for a money consideration and a "good fat lamb" annually.[3] The island was held by Nichols for twenty-five years, probably without occupation, until Oct. 17, 1715, when he sold it to Jacob Norton (32) then of Newport, R. I., in whose possession and that of his heirs it remained for over half a century.[4] Jacob Norton gave one quarter of the island in 1742 to his daughter Abigail (77), wife of Peter Simon of Newport, and she sold this share in 1772 to John Banister of the same place. The remainder, after his death (1743), descended to his sons, Shubael (69) of Bristol, R. I. and Jacob (73) of Chilmark and their heirs. Shubael had died before his father (1737) and Jacob shortly after (1750), and the island came into frequent litigation between the various claimants.

EARLY OCCUPANCY.

The first record of any settlement here is in the early part of the 18th century. Judge Sewall in 1702 says of Nomans Land, that the "Inhabitants (are) mostly of the 7th day Indians," i. e., Sabbatarian Baptists. It is probable that with the purchase by Norton in 1715 the first Englishmen came here to live. His son Jacob came here to reside soon after and in 1722 was granted a license as innholder of Nomans Land. Doubtless he continued a resident with his family till his death, and Samuel Norton (413) who married his sister, Mary (71) is called in 1740 "of Nomans Land." These two families numbered twenty souls in 1750, and there may have

[1] N. Y. Col. Mss., Court of Assizes, II, 538; Patents, IV, 91.

[2] The aboriginal ownership at this time, the first on record, was vested in the Sachem Cascanabin, who sold the western half May 1, 1686, to his brother Tackquabin (Dukes Deeds, I, 70).

[3] John Philip, sachem, sold the island in 1692 to Matthew Mayhew as steward for £50 and Mayhew sold his "rights" to Nichols the next year (Dukes Deeds, I, 137-138).

[4] Dukes Deeds, III, 395.

been others living there besides. They were probably engaged in fishing, as at that time the surrounding waters were considered "the only certain places for Fishing for Cod."[1] It is not supposed the place was valuable from an agricultural point of view, though in 1745 it was testified that the island was valued at £10,000, old tenor.[2] Another early settler was Israel Luce (67), [b. 1723, d. 1797], who removed to Nomans Land as a young man and spent the rest of his life there as a resident and was buried there. His sons Daniel (290), Thomas (292), and Ebenezer (294) remained on the island with their families until their deaths. George H. Butler was a resident about forty years (1860 to 1898), and Henry B. Davis with his family are the only inhabitants of the island at the present time.

ANNEXED TO CHILMARK.

The status of this island up to 1714 was an anomalous one, though being practically unoccupied except by Indians, it gave little concern to the people of the Vineyard. In the act of Oct. 30, 1714, when Chilmark was made a township, "an Island called No Mans Land" was included in its corporate limits.[3] Two years later, for some reason, not now understood, the new town petitioned to have "an Island call'd No Mans Land" added to it and the General Court, on Nov. 30, 1716, passed the necessary resolve.[4] Since this time the island has remained a part of Chilmark, though it has always occupied, until recently, a negligible share in the concerns of the town. It is scarcely mentioned in the proceedings of the annual meetings for years at a time.

[1]Sewall, Diary, III, 397.

[2]Evidence given by Jeremiah Mayhew, husbandman, and Elishab Adams, cordwainer (Sup. Jud. Court Mss., 61016).

[3]Records General Court, IX, 428.

[4]Acts and Resolves, IX, 508, ch. 140.

ANNALS OF TISBURY.

ANNALS OF TISBURY.

TISBURY.

The town of Tisbury, incorporated July 8, 1671, included the present town of West Tisbury, the region originally settled by the early proprietors, — and the limits of the town remained intact, territorially, until May 1, 1892, when as a result of a long continued agitation, the old town was divided. The portion formerly known as Homes Hole Neck retained the corporate name and ancient records of Tisbury, and the settlement at West Tisbury, where the town had its first beginnings, took the latter name.

BOUNDARIES.

The present town of Tisbury, in consequence of this division, represents but a moiety of the original limits of the old town. Its boundaries are as follows: —

1. Stone monument at Makonikey near the Sound shore.
2. Same on top of the hill at Makonikey.
3. Same on North Shore road, near site of old school-house.
4. Same, top of hill in D. D. Norton's pasture.
5. Same, in woods, westerly from gate of Shubael Weeks.
6. Same on South side of State Highway.
7. Same S. W. from M. M. Smith's, edge of woods.
8. Same, easterly side of Chickemmoo path.
9. The Four Town Bound.
10. Thence on straight line to head of Tashmoo pond.
11. Thence on straight line to Stepping Stones, head of Lagoon.
12. Line dividing Lagoon through outlet at bridge, Beach road.

The boundaries on all other parts are water; included within these limits is the village of Vineyard Haven, which contains the greatest portion of the population of Tisbury.

NOBNOCKET.

This was the ancient name bestowed by the natives on all the territory covered by the village of Vineyard Haven, in the present town of Tisbury. The Sachem Ponit, in 1682, calls himself "of Nobnocket alias holmes his hole," and his jurisdiction extended north of a line drawn from the stepping stones to the head of Tashmoo, to include the entire neck. Eliot uses an adjectival prefix in various forms to indicate "dry," one of which forms is Nunnob, which he abbreviates to Nob (Isaiah, XI, 15; XLIV, 3). In the Narragansett dialect the nasal sound of N is heard before the vowel, which accounts for the intrusion of the N in Nobnocket, giving us an etymology of Nob(n)ocket, meaning at the dry land or place. This may indicate that the original Nobnocket was a place where the Indians settled on the shore, an enclosed place, a designation which afterwards was extended to include the whole region above described as Ponit's Sachemship.[1]

HOMES HOLE.

This is the oldest place name on the Vineyard, dating from 1646, when "the eastermost chop of homses hole" is first mentioned, only a quarter of a century after the settlement of Plymouth. The word "hole," as given to a small inlet of water affording shelter to boats, is of common occurrence in this region. Familiar instances are Woods' Hole, Robinson's Hole, and Quick's Hole, and the prefix in each instance is probably derived from personal names. In our case, however, it has another origin, which is doubtless aboriginal, as it is probably derived from "Homes," meaning an old man (Roger Williams, Key.), and the entire name signifies "old man's hole." A similar place name, with identical variations in orthography, is found on Long Island at North Sea — Holmes Hill, which in early records was called "Homses" and "Homses Hill."[2] The word "homes" indicates decrepitude as applied to an aged person, and probably was applied to an old chief who made this place his abode when the first settlers, in 1642, came to the island. This name was retained for nearly two hundred years, when it came to be changed to Holmes Hole, after the spelling of the family of Holmes who had settled here in the previous century.[3]

[1]This name appears but once in the records, which is rather unusual for a territorial name.

[2]Southampton, L. I. Records, II, 310. In a note to an Indian deed of 1663 there is found this: "and there lived an old Homes and his sonne, &c." (Smithtown p. 1)

[3]Dukes Deeds, VIII, 53. The Holmes family of Vineyard Haven are descended from John Holmes, first of the name, who in 1760 became a land owner on the Vineyard.

VINEYARD HAVEN.

The name of Holmes Hole became officially eclipsed in 1871, as a result of persistent agitation on the part of a number of residents. The original name had in it but a faint suggestion of dignity or character, and to hail from a "Hole" was a source of chagrin to many of its inhabitants when traveling abroad. A number of substitutes were suggested, including Tisbury Harbor and Vineyard Haven, and the latter finding the most favor with the majority, it received its confirmation on Feb. 21, 1871, by the general government, when the Post Office Department officially adopted the name for the office. This new title is a more euphonious and appropriate name than its predecessor, as the harbor has been the great haven of the Vineyard from time immemorial, and doubtless this last christening will survive for many generations.

POPULATION.

There being no separate enumerations of the residents of the present town of Tisbury prior to the division in 1892, only fragmentary evidences are available to enable us to form an estimate of the population at long intervals, before that date. In 1700 the families of Thomas West, Isaac Chase, and Edward Cottle comprised all the known residents in the present town limits, and the three households numbered 27 persons of all ages and sexes. In 1750, by a computation of the families known to have lived here at that date, West, Chase, Wheldon, Daggett and Norton, a total of about 100 souls can be placed, of which the Chases furnish 40, Wests 30 and the rest is divided between the others. It makes no account of transient residents, of which there were doubtless a goodly number, as happens in every seaport.

In 1775 a map of Homes Hole and the present town limits, including the eastern part of Chickemmoo, shows forty-one houses, which can be estimated as containing forty-five families of five each, comprising a total of 225 persons. An examination of the national census of 1790 enables the author to locate about 350 persons in the town limits on that date. In 1807 a writer who investigated conditions in the county stated "there were about 70 houses in Homes Hole."[1] Adding fifteen for Chickemmo, and estimating that they housed one

2 Mass. Hist. Soc. Coll. III.

hundred families, we can use the accepted multiple and obtain a total of 500 souls at that date.

In 1838 another writer stated that there were about 100 dwelling houses in Homes Hole, and from a similar calculation, allowing for an increase in Chickemmo, we can estimate about 700 persons residing here.[1] In 1850 the number of inhabitants in Homes Hole, "extending to the head of Pond and Sylvanus Luces" was 1074,[2] showing for the first time an increase over the western half of the original town. Nothing further is available in subsequent enumerations until the census of 1890, when this town had, in round numbers, about 1050 persons. The census of 1900 showed 1149 inhabitants residing in our present town limits, and the state census of 1905 showed a population of 1120.

ANCIENT LANDMARKS.

ALGONQUIAN PLACE NAMES.

Ashappaquonsett, (1671). — The modern form is Chappaquonsett. It is probably from the Algonquian words, Ashappaqu'un-es-et, meaning "where the nets are spread," that is, to dry. The name seems to belong to the creek which forms the outlet of Tashmoo Lake, and the definition applies perfectly to the low sandy formation of that region, where the Indians had one of their chief fishing stations.

Kuttashimmoo, (1671). — All the early deeds refer to a spring called Kuttashimmoo, the etymology of which is represented by the Algonquian Keht-ashim-ut, meaning "at the great spring." It is variously spelled, Ketesshumue, Catashmoo, and is now shortened to Tashmoo. The name belongs to the spring, but it was early (1682) applied to the pond into which it flows.

Komoquisset. — This name, with a variation of Cumaqueast, occurs in 1691 in a deed to Thomas West, and relates to a place included in his purchases in this region. From analogy it is probable that it means the "place of the house," perhaps that of the Sachem of the locality.

Maneh-chahhank-kanah. — This name was applied to the deep valley, now called "Chunk's Swamp," a corruption of the middle portion of the Algonquian word, a result that

[1] Barker, Hist. Coll. of Massachusetts.

[2] Mss. notes of R. L. Pease, who took this decennial census.

usually happened in similar cases. The meaning of it is "the fenced planting field," a place probably set off by the Indians for their cultivation.

Machequeset. — This was a swamp on the east side of Tashmoo, so called in 1729 (Deeds, IV, 342, 347). It is probable that the same word appears in another form, Chaqusitel, a corruption of (Ma)chaqu(e)sitel, as "caled by the Indian Sachem and Indians" (ibid., IV, 26). It means the "poor or miry place."

Qussuck-quea-queatess (1684). — This was a spring in the Kuttashimmoo region, and may be another designation for the "great" spring itself.

Uquiessah. — This was the name given to Little Neck. It occurs in other places on the Vineyard, and has the significance of a boundary term, "as far as" or the "ending," or terminations of some land or property.

Weaquatickquayage (1673). — This name, denoting the land at the head of Lagoon pond, is spelled in a variety of ways, owing to its complicated formation. The more modern form is an abbreviated one, Weahtaqua, and it is sometimes spelled Webbataqua, which is fanciful as well as incorrect. It occurs frequently through New England, and an early instance of it is on the neighbouring island of Nantucket. It is a compound of We-a-qua-tukq-auke, which is a word meaning "land at the head of the tidal cove." In the Court records of 1685 the bounds of "homses hole neck" were adjudged by Samuel Tilton and Thomas Mayhew as arbitrators "to have bin set by towonticut by a fut path which gose from weakuttockquayah unto cuttashimmoo on the other side of the neck." Matthew Mayhew wrote it Waquittuckquoiake (Deeds, I, 69). "at holms his hole or the Springs at the head of that Cove called Weahtaqua" (Mass. Arch., CXII, 422; dated June, 1692) shows the gradual elision.

ENGLISH PLACE NAMES.

Bass Creek. — A salt-water creek which emptied the Lagoon. Its original course may have been midway of the beach which separates the harbor, but before 1781 it had cut a channel along the line of Water street, and was six or seven feet deep a century ago. Small draft vessels entered this creek and discharged cargoes on the shore adjoining the "Great House" and other inns in that vicinity. It derived its name, probably, from an incident occurring in the winter of 1778 following Grey's Raid, when a large number of bass were frozen in the creek and furnished food to the impoverished inhabitants.

Ferry Boat Island. — The larger of two grassy islands in front of the Marine Hospital is called Ferry Boat, because it was the landing stage of Isaac Chase's ferry in colonial days.

Lagoon. — This body of salt water was originally called the harbor of Homes Hole, and later, until about 1740, Waketaquay pond or some form of that Algonquian place name. It is first of record as the "lagoon of salt water" about 1743, as far as known, being then so called in a deed.[1] From that time forward, this name was applied to it with increasing frequency, until it had supplanted all other names. It is an English derivative from the Spanish and Italian words *laguna* (Latin *lacuna*), meaning a lake in general terms. In the restricted sense it is applied to a lake or body of water on a coast, formed by a belt or reef of sand thrown up by sea action. This is the actual topography of our Lagoon, but by whom it was so called at first is not known. The word may have been applied by a Spanish or Italian salior who happened in the harbor, or by a resident who had sailed the Spanish Main and learned the significance of the word.

Manter's Hill. — The high land on Main street which has its summit near the present Sanitarium. It derived its name from Jonathan Manter (62) who married Sarah Chase (102) in 1755, and began a series of purchases of land in Homes Hole neck two years later, through which he became one of the largest land owners of his day. His property extended from the harbor to Tashmoo, and in the house which he built on this estate, probably about 1755-6, was born, in 1757, his daughter Parnell, one of the "Liberty Pole" heroines.

Mount Aldworth. — A name recently applied to the high land on the Edgartown road, overlooking the harbor. It was erroneously bestowed under the supposition that Martin Pring landed here in 1603, but reference to Vol. I, p. 78, disposes of that theory.

Rand's Hill.— The first high land on the State highway to West Tisbury, after leaving Vineyard Haven village, was called Rand's hill a century ago. It derived this name from

[1]Dukes Deeds VI, 530, Westt o Melville (entered August 22, 1743). It was called Wakataqua pond in 1739 (Probate, III, 111).

VIEW OF HOMES' HOLE IN 1838

SALT WORKS ON THE SHORE

Caleb Rand, who purchased a tract there in 1755 of Thomas West.

Red Coat Hill. — A name sometimes applied to the first high land on the State highway after passing Tashmoo, on the way to West Tisbury. It is said some accoutrements of a British soldier were found there, probably the relics of Grey's Raid.

Slough. — A small marshy pond near the Arnoux estate on the West Chop road. It was in existence in 1725, but has recently been obliterated by improvements to the property in that vicinity.

SALE OF WEST CHOP BY INDIANS, ABOUT 1663-4.

It is probable that for many years subsequent to the settlement at Edgartown, West Chop, like its opposite neighbor, East Chop, remained uninhabited by whites. The first intimation which we find of the settlement of English on this territory, which was uniformly called Homes Hole neck, is undoubtedly found in the following letter from Thomas Mayhew, Sr., to Gov. John Winthrop, Jr., of Connecticut, regarding a purchase made of the Indian sachems, Poketapace and Pesoonquan, by Thomas Layton and Peter Tallman, two land owners, and possibly residents of Edgartown.

5-1-64 Uppon the Vyneyard

Right Worshipfull Mr John Wynthrop

Sir:-

I desire youe to resolve me if any man can possesse that he doth purchase of the heathen, without the leave of the pattentees. Under correction I thinke not: because the land is absolutely conferred on the pattentees & successours as firm as possible can be, by the state of England & all the pattentees graunt to such ass in freinshipp with them are assured to holld it: so it is in this pattent & in your pattent, as I take it, a coppy whereof I have seene. I suppose your sellfe can tell if any such liberty to be taken or not, in a word or two by any leave from his Majestie: to me it annyhilates pattents. Tis my case: I hope to receive a word about it. Thus with my service to your kind and deservedly honored sellfe I rest

Your servant to command

Thomas Mayhew.[1]

What reply Winthrop made to this communication is not known, but the position stated by Mayhew was unquestionably the proper and legal one. The exigency caused

[1] 4 Mass. Hist. Coll. VII.

Mayhew to act for the protection of his vested interests on the Vineyard, and he called together the principal Indians of Taakemmy for a council about the sale of lands within their territory, and on Aug. 24, 1664, Papamek and twenty-nine other "gentlemen and common Indians" agreed with Mayhew that there "shall be noe land sold within the bounds of Takemme without the consent of the two sachims . . . . that is Wanamanhut (and) Keteanum." And they further declared "that John Poketapace (and) Mr. Pesoonquam weer never owners of the land sold to Peter Tallman: and we all agree as one man to withstand and reject that bargain."[1]

It appears that when Thomas Layton and Peter Tallman, who had been residents of Rhode Island, living in Portsmouth and Newport respectively, made a purchase of Homes Hole neck of those two Indians, they did so without the consent, and possibly without the knowledge, of the patentee. When this purchase occurred is not known, as no record of it appears, but it was prior to 1664, when the above letter was written and the council of Indians held. Whether Layton and Tallman purchased it for occupancy or as a speculation is also equally indeterminate, but it appears that about 1667 the two purchasers authorized Francis Usselton, also a resident of Edgartown, to take possession of the Neck in their name and behalf, and that acting upon this authority he did so, remaining for some months in occupancy as their agent.

FRANCIS USSELTON—SQUATTER.

Usselton is therefore to be reckoned as the first white man to establish a residence in the present limits of Vineyard Haven. Where his house was cannot be determined, but he has left his name upon the fine headland down the neck, known as Husselton's Head, a corruption of the settler's surname. In the division of the Chase property in 1726, the sixth lot was bounded by a "stake standing on the south side of a hollow called Usingtols hollow," which is the ravine just south of the Head, represented by the lane leading to Edward C. Lord's store. It may be surmised that here was the temporary abiding place of Francis Usselton, which gave it the name. This man first appears in New England at Wenham, Mass., where he married Sarah Barnes, Nov. 25, 1655, our first record of him, and there two children of this marriage

[1]Dukes Deeds, I.

are entered, viz: Mary, born Aug. 17, 1656, and John, born Sept. 20, 1657.[1] The Essex County Court files furnish considerable evidence that Francis was a litigious man, as he is either plaintiff or defendant in civil and criminal suits in 1659 and 1660, a number of times; in the latter year he is called of Topsfield, the town adjoining Wenham. When he came to the Vineyard can not be accurately determined, but the first recorded date is Dec. 2, 1659, which overlaps that of record in Topsfield.

He must have come here about 1661, as the last date of his appearance in Essex County is Oct. 8, 1660, and we can rely on the correctness of those, as they are original records, while Edgartown has only an abstract of her first books. His first appearance here is in the Courts, in which he sued Thomas Jones for defamation, and James Pease sued Usselton for "Belying his wife." Both these cases, which are entered at one session of the court, may be related to one matter. It appears that Usselton bought at one time forty acres at the Elizabeth Islands of Thomas Mayhew, Sr., but the exact date is not known, and his earliest change of abode might have been to that region. Whatever the facts, he soon disappears from view after his eviction from the squatter rights he assumed in behalf of Layton and Tallman. As our first resident, however, his name should be perpetuated where it has had a standing for over two centuries.

EVICTION OF USSELTON.

Mayhew brought suit against Layton and Tallman for trespass on the part of their agent and recovered judgment. Armed with this authority he delegated Richard Sarson, John Eddy, John Gee, and James and John Pease of Edgartown to go to the Neck and dispossess, forcibly or otherwise, Tallman's and Layton's representative. Whether this was accomplished forcibly or peaceably does not appear, but that it was effectual is of record. On the 18th of June, 1667, as a reward for their services, Mayhew deeded Homes Hole neck to these five persons, Sarson, Eddy, Gee, and John and James Pease, which he divided into six parts, reserving one-sixth for himself "in consideration of their reall indeavour to dispossess and keep out intruders from the same land presumptuously without

[1]Contemporaneously with Francis there lived in Wenham a Charles Usselton, who may have been a brother, or a son by a former marriage.

permission."[1] Only one of the five grantors utilized his grant for the purposes of settlement.

After leaving the Vineyard, Usselton went to Newport, R. I., where he got into difficulties of a similar character. He was banished from that Colony about 1670 or 1671, but undertook to defy the authorities, as appears by the following record relating to the affair:—

Whereas, ffrancis Uselton was by the last Generall Court of Tryalls sentenced to depart this Island, and not to return without leave of two Magistrates; and he the said Uselton; contrary to the said Court of Tryall's sentence, comeinge into the towne of Newport and publickly walkeinge the streetes in the time of the Assemblys sittinge, which being taken notice off, and he sent for into the court, to answer for his contempt, instead of giveing the Assembly satisfaction; he the said Uselton, upon orders to the court to depart, as he was goeinge out of the Court turned back and did publickly in the Court Jeere the authority in a scornfull manner, saying to the Governor, "Your honorable wife," and "I thanke your justice," with many other scornefull contemptuous carriages; for which misdemeanure and contempt, the Court doe sentence the said Uselton to be forthwith whipt, with fifteene stripes.

And alsoe it is ordered that the said ffrancis Uselton shall forthwith depart the Colloney; and if he shall come to abide in any towne of this Colloney hereafter it shall be in the power of any two magistrates to cause the said Uselton to be sevearly whipt and sent away.[2] (Dated June 6, 1671.)

His further history is unknown to the author.

SUBSEQUENT SALES BY THE SIX SHAREHOLDERS.

As previously stated, none of the six shareholders remained here for settlement. All of them disposed of their rights in the following manner: First, Richard Sarson sold his sixth to Thomas Trapp, Feb. 12, 1669. Second, John Eddy exchanged his sixth with the proprietors of Tisbury for a proprietor's share in the town of Tisbury. Third, the share of John Gee became a source of subsequent litigation because of his death in 1669, and the removal of his heirs to the mainland. Fourth, James Pease sold his share to Thomas Trapp Jan. 31, 1669. Fifth, John Pease conveyed his sixth Aug. 26, 1669, to Thomas Lawton. Sixth, the sixth remaining vested in Thomas Mayhew passed by inheritance to Matthew Mayhew.

[1]Dukes Deeds I, 239. He sold "so much right in all that land that is claymed by Thomas Layton and peeter Talman of Road Island, ner holm's his hole uppon the Vineyard."

[2]Colonial Records of Rhode Island.

The sixth belonging to John Gee, as before stated, remained in abeyance for many years and requires particular examination. It appears that his widow, Hazalelponah (a name, the like of which has never before come to the author's knowledge), removed to Boston with her three daughters, Mary, Martha, and Anne. The widow married Obadiah Woods of Ipswich, as his second wife; and according to contemporary testimony, when he brought his new wife to Ipswich from Boston it was "the talk of the times," whether because of her name or his second venture does not appear. Of the daughters, Mary married Thomas Pickering of Greenland, N. H., Anne married Samuel Hodgkins of Gloucester, and Martha married Thomas Cotes.

Mary Pickering, in 1730, laid the foundations for her claim to the property rights of her father in Homes Hole neck by a deposition showing her parentage, and further depositions are on record establishing the marriage of the widow Gee and her daughters. Mary (Gee) Pickering sold her rights to her kinsman, Amos Merrell of Boston, in 1730, who in turn disposed of the share to Joseph Callender of Boston. The rights possessed by the other heirs do not seem to have been asserted.

The ownership was now vested in Thomas Trapp, two-sixths; Thomas Lawton, one-sixth; Proprietors of Tisbury, one-sixth;[1] John Gee's heirs, one-sixth, and the Mayhew estate, one-sixth. Isaac Chase began to buy these shares in 1676, and by subsequent purchases in 1682, 1683 and 1699 had acquired all but the share belonging to John Gee, and a fractional portion held by William Rogers.

Joseph Callender, who had acquired the Gee interest by purchase, as above stated, entered suit against Abraham Chase, one of the heirs of Isaac, in an action of ejectment, at the November term of court, 1733, claiming one-sixth of Homes Hole neck. The jury returned a verdict in favor of Callender, and Chase appealed. The claim of Callender was finally sustained, and Chase quieted this obstacle to his complete ownership of the Neck by purchasing from Callender for £185, July 19, 1734 (Deeds, VI, 44). Mary Pickering, the surviving daughter of Gee, living at Greenland, N. H., gave a quitclaim to Chase also, and his title was finally satis-

[1]The proprietors of Tisbury sold the Eddy sixth to Samuel Tilton, Isaac Chase and Jacob Perkins. Jacob Perkins and Isaac Chase sold to Samuel Tilton 1/3 of Homes Hole Neck, Oct. 11, 1676 (Dukes Deeds I, 283). Samuel Tilton sold his $\frac{1}{3}$ of $\frac{1}{6}$ to William Rogers in October, 1699 (Nantucket Records III, 17).

factory. As late as 1773 some of the descendants of Gee gave a surrender of their rights to the then owners of land on this neck.[1]

THE NECK JOINED TO TISBURY.

In order to place this outlying territory under a settled jurisdiction, Governor Mayhew decided to join it to the town of Tisbury, recently incorporated, and in 1673 he made the following assignment of his rights in the soil to the new township:—

ffor as much as I Thomas Mayhew have received some instructions from the governor generall Lovelace of the Province and for the peaceable goverment and wele ordering of this Island called Marthas Vineyeard and a certain necke of Land on the west sid of holmes harbour being purchased and like to be Inhabited by English men where for be it known unto all men by these presents that I do for myself heires and assignes grant & assigne the s'd necke of Land to belong unto the s'd town Tisbury on the Vineyeard that the said necke and Inhabitants and estats theire being to be lyable owe and to pay all publike charge with the town of Tisbury as they may be justly rated upon their Lands persons or estats and they to remain and continue untill the sd necke of Land be a particullare township of itselfe or with other lands adjacent Wittness hereunto my hand this 2 day of August 1673

per me THOMAS MAYHEW
Governour[2]

EARLY SETTLEMENT.

In the following year Isaac Chase, probably in company with Samuel Tilton and Jacob Perkins, all of Hampton, N. H., and related by marriage, came to the new town of (West) Tisbury with a view to a permanent settlement. All were young men, Chase recently a widower of 24, Perkins 34 and Tilton 37 years, and they decided upon Homes Hole neck as the place where they would build their new homes. Chase was refused permission to settle, but later the town allowed him the privilege.

They first acquired the two sixths interest in the Neck belonging to the town (the Mayhew and Eddy shares), but the partners of Chase decided shortly after to leave for other places. Tilton had been granted a home lot in West Tisbury, and later he removed to Chilmark.

Perkins was first mentioned in the records in 1674 as "of Homes Hole." He was a married man, and it is to be

[1]Deeds, X, 257, Hodgkins et als to Norton.
[2]Tisbury Records, 6.

supposed he brought his wife and family with him to the Vineyard. His residence here was of short duration, as he incurred the enmity of the Mayhews by testifying against Thomas Daggett in the suit against James Skiffe, 1673, and from that time on his lot was not a happy one. Little persecutions followed on each other, until he sold out his interests here in 1676, and settled at Succanesset (Falmouth).

In 1682, Thomas West, who had been a resident of Tisbury, living on the west side of Mill river, sold his property at that place to Arthur Biven and chose his new home at Nobnocket, adding himself and family to the Chases, already at Homes Hole. He bought of Ponit, the Sachem, son and heir of Cheesechamuk, the old Sagamore of that region, thirty acres of land Feb. 8, 1681-2, "with liberty to build a house." This tract was on the site of the U. S. Marine Hospital, and was the first of many purchases made by Doctor West of land adjoining this homestead, until he had acquired several hundred acres on the west side of the Lagoon, as far south as the head of that inlet and towards Kuttashimmoo beyond the state highway.

Another resident of West Tisbury followed Dr. West to this new territory, in the person of Edward Cottle, who in 1695 made his first purchase of land bordering on the Lagoon, and extending half way towards Kuttashimmoo. It is not known when he came here to reside, but as he sold his home lot in West Tisbury in 1700, the presumption is that he had before that latter date built his new house at Manehchah-hankkanah, the name given by the Indians to the locality where his purchase was made.

For thirty years these three families were the only known residents of this region, and in this time the children of the Wests, Chases and Cottles had grown to manhood, married, and most of the girls removed to homes of their own.

DIVISIONS OF LAND.

There were no proprietor's divisions of lots in Homes Hole that are of record, but the six shareholders must have made some allotments in severalty, as appears by scattering references to such a division. In 1674 Matthew Mayhew sold to Perkins four acres of upland "containing the bredth ½ of the Southermost lott layed out at sayd Homes Hole."[1] William Weeks,

[1]Dukes Deeds, I, 336.

in 1683, sold one-sixth part of the "two Southermost lots of land: 42 poles by the harbor extending to the fresh pond."[1] Again in 1685 Weeks sold "one compleat half of one third part of the two southmost lots of land upon the Neck."[2] It is not recorded how Weeks came into possession of these lots, as the six shares granted by Governor Mayhew are all accounted for by continuous transfer of titles. It may be that some additional land was acquired by them of the Indians and subdivided, of which Weeks acquired a part. This would seem probable, as in 1681 "the English lyne" is first referred to, and again in 1685 it is spoken of as "the line which parts the English land from the Indian land."[3] This line probably ran from Bass creek to the head of Tashmoo pond, and marked proximately the southern boundary of the grant of 1668 to the six shareholders.

As all of this land passed into the possession and occupation of Isaac Chase before 1685, and was held by him throughout his life as the sole proprietor, but one allotment or division was made by him as successor to the shareholders, until 1725 and 1726, when the entire neck was surveyed and allotted in nine parts by metes and bounds to his heirs.[4] The results of this division into lots are shown in the accompanying map of Homes Hole neck.

SETTLERS BEFORE THE REVOLUTION.

In the southern extremity of the town, at the head of the Lagoon, the two daughters of Edward Cottle, Esther and Abigail, married, the first a Harding about 1721, and the second John Presbury about 1725, and these two new comers resided on the Cottle property for a few years, for both died early. The widow, Esther Harding, remarried as also did the widow Presbury, but neither marriage resulted in a material increase of the settlement. In the outskirts of the town, owning property here and in Edgartown, but having his house in the latter, lived Henry Luce, who may be reckoned as part of the community within our limits. About 1734 John Crosby

[1]Dukes Deeds, I, 78.

[2]Ibid, I, 73.

[3]Ibid, III, 314; comp. I, 73.

[4]In 1712 on the same day, Isaac gave to his sons, Abraham and James, one sixth each of his land on the Neck (III, 17, 81) and in 1714 the latter sold his share to Abraham (III, 82) and thus one third of the neck became vested in the older brother.

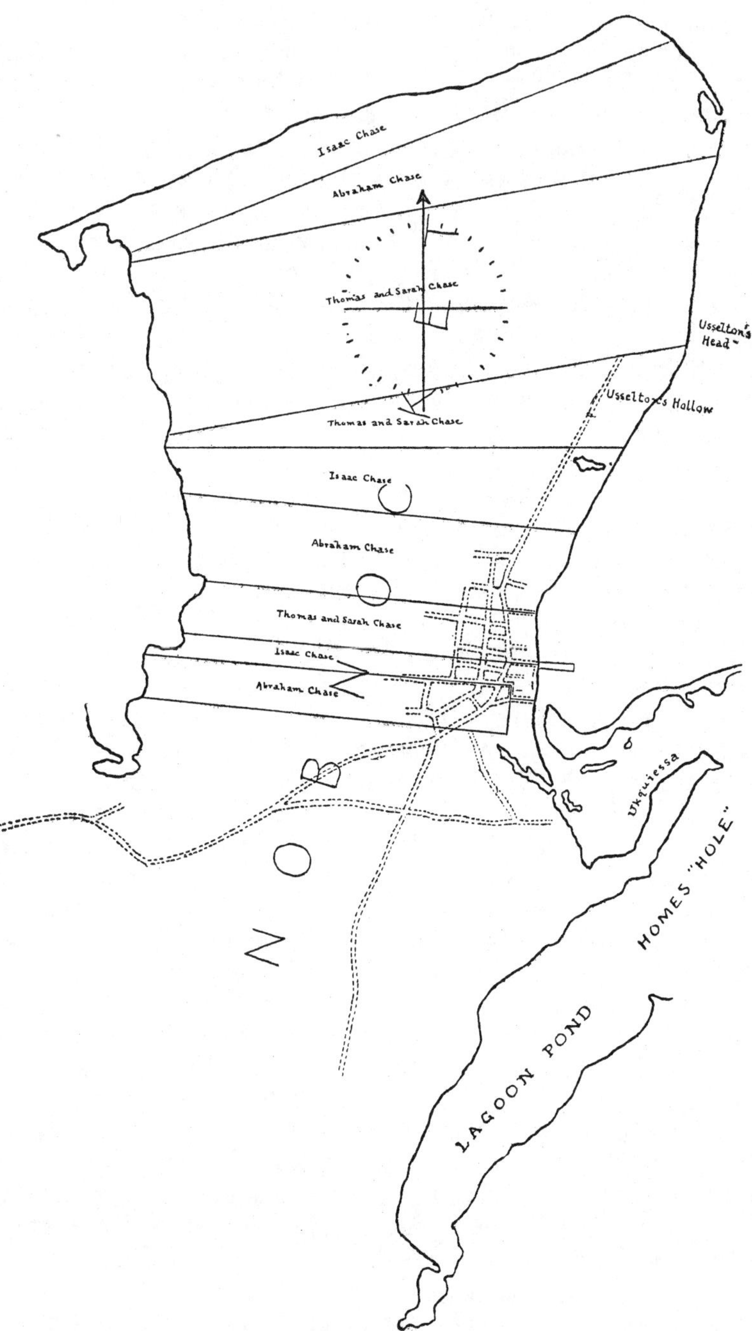

DIVISION OF CHASE PROPERTY, HOMES HOLE NECK, 1725.

from the Cape, married a daughter of Henry Luce and became a settler in the Lagoon region on lands given by her father, and from him descended a family which resided here until the second quarter of the last century.

The marriages of the two brothers, Samuel and Seth Daggett of Edgartown, in 1733 and 1734, to Sarah Chase and Elizabeth West, respectively, brought into the town at that time the first members of that family, and added their names to its annals for the succeeding century. About the same time John Whelden, from the Cape, married a daughter of Abraham Chase and became identified with the small settlement, and in 1745 John Ferguson from Kittery, Me., married another daughter and made his home here. Ebenezer Allen of Chickemmoo, about 1743, married the widow of Samuel Daggett and settled here on the property owned by his wife, and set up housekeeping and innkeeping. In 1748 Bayes Newcomb of Edgartown brought his large family and became a resident. Jonathan Manter of Tisbury married Sarah Chase, one of the co-heirs of Thomas, in 1755, and came here to live on her large landed estate, known since as Manter's hill. At the same time Caleb Rand from Charlestown, a mason by trade, and Shubael Butler of Edgartown, a weaver, were added to the town's population. In 1757 James Winslow, a pilot, came here and married a daughter of Isaac Chase, and in 1759 John Baxter came from the Cape to keep a tavern. Thomas Winston became a resident about this time, and in after years married the widow, Mercy Chase, and succeeded to the business of innkeeping. He left no descendants. In 1761 Shubael Dunham of Edgartown settled in the Tashmoo region of Chickemmoo with a large family of children, the first of the name in this town. John Holmes, a blacksmith, who had been living in Eastville for a few years, made his first purchase of land here in 1765, and became a permanent settler. In 1767 Thomas Manchester of Rhode Island, and in the next year Jabez Downs, from the Cape, were added to the growing town. Some time after, the exact date being unknown, the earliest of our Portuguese settlers, Joseph Dias, came to this place and his descendants remain here at the present time. These names represent the new element which became identified with Tisbury in the first century of its annals, no account being made of the multiplication of the pioneer families, who had by the opening of the Revolution increased and multiplied rapidly.

SKETCHES OF THE EARLY SETTLERS.

ISAAC CHASE.

Isaac Chase

The progenitor of the Chase family of Martha's Vineyard, was born in Hampton, N. H., April 1, 1650, the third son of Thomas and Elizabeth (Philbrick) Chase. The family genealogies state that Thomas came from County Cornwall, England, to New England, and was the son of Aquila Chase of the Chesham, County Bucks family, whose pedigree extends back several generations. In what way Isaac Chase came to be interested in this distant island is not known, but the neighboring town of Salisbury, Mass., had already furnished many settlers for Nantucket, men of Quaker faith, and through this source it is probable that his knowledge of the Vineyard was acquired. At the age of 24 he came to Tisbury to settle (1674), but the townsmen refused the privilege to him for some reason at that time. Possibly it was because of his religious beliefs, which were of the Quaker doctrinal variety. "The townsmen of Tysbury," so reads the record, "do not give unto Isack Chace of Hampton liberty to settle in the town."[1] However he must have overcome this refusal before long, as we find him in less than two years making purchases of land in the town limits.

He must have been possessed of more than the average wealth at that time as he became, before 1700, one of the largest landholders on the Vineyard. He began his purchases of Homes Hole neck in 1676, as elsewhere related, and finally became its sole proprietor. His property in the Chickemmoo region was second in extent of acreage. His initial purchase in 1682 became a subject of dispute with the Sachem and the town, and was relinquished; but in 1692 he bought the entire eastern half of Chickemoo of Thomas Tupper, consisting of 1200 acres, and was continually adding to his domain in that region.[2] He rarely sold any portion of these acquisitions and all of it, practically, became the heritage of his heirs.

[1]Tisbury Records, 8. We may surmise that they finally gave him permission to inhabit at Homes Hole, in the uttermost part of the town, many miles from the dwellings of any settlers. He was of Hampton in October 1673 (Norfolk Co. Deeds).

[2]Deeds, I, 130, 187, 281, 391.

His occupation, as elsewhere detailed, was that of blacksmith, inn-holder, and ferryman, and these he followed until his death. Although by religion a Quaker, yet he does not seem to have been ultra orthodox in the faith, for he took military office as Lieutenant in the Company of Foot in Tisbury before 1692, and thus broke one of the principal tenets of that sect. In the political upheavals of that time Simon Athearn thus refers to him: "Mr. Isaac Chase the Leueten't without oath he pleading for the quakers."[1] During the remainder of his life he was generally called Lieutenant in the records of that period.

He died May 19, 1727, and his will, dated Feb. 12, 1721-2, was proven in July, 1727. By it he bequeathed what lands he had not given away in his lifetime to his widow and surviving children and grandchildren. The Chickemmoo property was mostly deeded to his several sons, 1706–1718, and the Homes Hole neck was to a large extent, 1705–1717, similarly disposed of to Thomas, Isaac and Abraham. In 1725 this remained undivided and Lieut. Isaac and his son Abraham entered suit against the heirs of Thomas and Ebenezer Rogers for a partition. This was done, and the division then made by the jury is the basis of all land titles in Vineyard Haven north of the creek in front of the hospital.

Isaac Chase was twice married; first to Mary, daughter of Isaac Perkins of Hampton, Feb. 20, 1673, by whom he had no issue; second to Mary Tilton, probably sister of Samuel of Hampton and Chilmark, Oct. 5, 1675, by Rev. John Mayhew. By his second marriage he had six sons and six daughters, who left a large progeny here and in Nantucket. He was a man of sterling worth and scrupulous honesty, and his life was singularly free from contentions and litigations with his neighbors.

EDWARD COTTLE, JR.

The eldest son of Edward Cottle of Salisbury, named for his father, was born in that town Sept. 28, 1666, and followed his father in his various wanderings until he came to the Vineyard. He bought land in this town on the west side of the Lagoon, in 1695, of Ponit the Sachem of Homes Hole, and thereafter added to this until he owned a considerable

[1]Mass. Arch., CXII, 424. This is the only reference to the Quaker proclivities of Chase to be found in the record. The allusion to the oath relates to their objection to swearing, although willing to affirm to an act or statement.

tract adjoining the Presbury and West lands.[1] There he lived with his half-breed wife, Esther Daggett (22) of the "Bow and Arrow" family, daughter of Joseph and Alice (Sissetom) Daggett. He had wedded her between 1690 and 1698, and one child was born to them, a daughter named Esther, about 1700, who married first a Harding (after 1718), and second (about 1725) Manasseh Kempton. This half-breed wife died before 1702 certainly, and probably sometime earlier.[2] He remained a widower until about 1701, when he took as a second wife Abigail, daughter of Joseph and Sarah (Holley) Allen of Dartmouth, Mass.[3] By this union another daughter was born, June 6, 1702, and she was called Abigail. This girl married three times, (1) John Presbury, (2) Benjamin Luce, and (3) Samuel Lambert. Besides these matrimonial ventures his career was an uneventful one. He appears in court but once as a plaintiff (1736) and in 1733 he was a juror, and this constitutes his sole record.[4] He made his will Nov. 2, 1748, "being grown old & stricken in years," and it was probated Nov. 2, 1751, the proximate time of his decease, when he was about eighty-five years old.[5] He bequeaths all his property to his daughter Abigail and her second husband. His wife, who was born April 1, 1663, had predeceased him Dec. 25, 1733, aged seventy years.[6]

JOHN CROSBY.

This settler was probably the son of Simon and Mary (Nickerson) Crosby of Harwich, Cape Cod, baptized April 13, 1701, in that town, He came here about 1732 and married, before 1734, Sarah Luce (53), probably through the family relations between the two families established in 1704 by the marriage of his aunt Ann to William Luce (9). His father-in-law gave his wife a farm of twenty acres near Tashmoo in Chickemmoo, and they resided there for the remainder of the time covered by our present knowledge of his life. It would seem that his wife died at some time unknown, and

[1]Dukes Deeds, II, 65. His house was in the Edgartown limits.

[2]Descent from the "Vineyard Pocahontas" may be traced through the Hardings.

[3]For proof of this see Bristol Deeds, XIII, 41 and Sup. Jud. Court Mss. No. 29518. Nathaniel Pease testified that he was present at the wedding.

[4]He was an illiterate man evidently, as all documents bearing his name as grantor or deponent are signed with "his mark."

[5]Dukes Probate, III, 274.

[6]Holmes' Diary.

he remarried in 1752 a Mrs. Sarah Tisk[1] and that he was living here in 1758, signing as a witness on that date.

JOSÉ DIAZ *alias* JOSEPH DIAS.

It is believed that he was the first immigrant of the Portuguese nationality to come to the Vineyard, and one of the Western Islands was probably the place of his birth.

He was a young man when he arrived in this country, and soon had attracted the attention and won the heart of Sarah Manter (110) of this town. They were married, Jan. 4, 1780, and he soon joined the cause of his adopted country in the struggle against England. He was captured and sent a prisoner to that country, but secured a release after "a distressing captivity." Upon his return home he became a convert to the newly-expounded Baptist teachings, in December, 1780, and the incident is thus related by an eye witness:—

> By seeing and hearing of these wonders of divine grace his vows in trouble were brought with authority upon his mind; and though the temper set in violently with his suggestions, that there was no mercy for him, and that he had better go and drown himself, in the evening after the communion (December 21st) yet sovereign grace prevented it, and set his soul at liberty so that he was soon after baptized and joined to that church.[2]

The rest of his brief experience in a land of strangers was tragic, and the whole borders on the romantic. He went forth once again to do battle for his adopted country, and for the second time fell into the hands of the British as a prisoner of war, and was consigned to a living death on the hulk "Jersey," of infamous memory. There he died in 1781 as a patriot and martyr, leaving a widow and an infant son, born the year of his decease.

JOHN FERGUSON.

He was a master mariner engaged in the West India trade, and frequently made this haven on voyages from his home in Kittery, Maine, to southern waters. As a guest at Abraham Chase's Inn he met Hannah (55), the young daughter of "mine host." Captain Ferguson was the son of Alexander and Elizabeth (Frost) Ferguson, born Aug. 8, 1710, and she

[1]This name is as written in the Tisbury vital records. It is probably an error for Fisk.

[2]Backus, Church History, II, 375.

was fifteen years his junior. Difference in ages made no difference in their sentiments however, as their banns were published Nov. 2, 1745, and they were married soon after. Nothing further is known of him, except that a family of seven children were born to them and baptized here. He was probably occupied in coastwise traffic, and had died before 1769, but the date and place of his death is unknown, probably in the West Indies of some tropical fever, which took the lives of so many of our people in those days. The toll from this cause was a constant drain on the male population.

JOHN HOLMES.

The family tradition that this settler came from Plymouth seems the probable truth, though extended search among the records of that county fails to find confirmation.[1] The age given on his gravestone practically tallies with the birth record of John, son of John and Mercy (Ford) Holmes, born June 22, 1730, in Plymouth. If this be the solution of the problem his father was later of Kingston, died there in 1746, and in his will mentions his minor son John.[2] Our John first appears in the Vineyard ten years after this, and is enrolled in 1757 as a private in the militia company of Edgartown. He was a blacksmith by trade, and made his first purchase of land Jan. 8, 1760, in the village of Eastville, at Quaise neck.[3] He resided there about five years, and on Oct. 30, 1765, bought half an acre of land in Holmes Hole neck, where the Thomas Dunham tavern formerly stood.[4] Thenceforth he was identified with this town, and his descendants continued to reside here until the present day. He was chosen constable in 1776 and 1791, the only town offices held by him. Here he became a sound pilot, an occupation which he followed to the end of his active life, and for which he was commissioned in 1783 by Governor Hancock. He died Oct. 29, 1812, in the 84th year of his age, leaving a widow and two married daughters. His son John, also a pilot, had predeceased in 1795, and through him the present family descends.

[1]The author has examined all the wills and administrations of Holmes decedents in Plymouth County, and abstracts of each are in his possession.

[2]Plymouth Probate, XI, 141. This would account for lack of evidence to connect him with the Vineyard, as he was not of age.

[3]Dukes Deeds, IX, 17.

[4]Ibid, IX, 485; XX, 13.

THOMAS MANCHESTER.

This settler came here from Rhode Island, and probably was a relative, if not a son, of the Nathaniel Manchester of Portsmouth, R. I., who married Elizabeth Norton (56) of Edgartown in 1716, or of William Manchester, who married Bethiah Norton (55) the year previous.

He married Eunice Norton about 1757, and made his first purchase of land July 25, 1767, from the widow Mercy Chase.[1]

STEPHEN PRESBURY.

He was probably the son of John Presbury, a shoemaker, sometime of Salisbury and later of Saco, Maine, where in 1670 he had bought a tract of land.[2] This John died in that Province before Nov. 3, 1684, leaving three sons, of whom one was Stephen, and the name is so unusual and without recurrence at that period, that we can assume the relationship fairly established.[3] This Stephen was a witness to a deed in Kittery, Maine, in 1686, and the next we learn of him is in 1704 when he was called "of Chilmark," meaning that part of it known as Chickemmoo.[4] It is not known where he had resided in the eighteen years intervening, but it can be surmised that he may have gone to Sandwich, Cape Cod, where he married, about 1693, Deborah, daughter of Stephen and Lydia (Snow) Skiffe of that town. His homestead was at the head of the Lagoon within the boundary line of Edgartown, but his closer proximity to the settlement at Homes Hole, where he lies buried, makes his classification as an early settler of this region the natural one.[5] His residence here was absolutely without incident of any kind, as he held no offices, appeared in court once as a plaintiff (1729) and in all the twenty-five years of his life on the Vineyard he did not so much as witness a deed or document of any kind, an unusual fact, His will, dated April 6, 1730, was proved June 30, 1730, and disposes of his property to "my seven daughters" and the children of his only son John, deceased.[6] He had died May 17, 1730 in his 58th

[1]Dukes Deeds, IX, 668.

[2]York Deeds, III, 42. John of Saco was probably the son of that John of Sandwich, Cape Cod, whose death in May, 1648, is recorded.

[3]Ibid, V(I), 35.

[4]Dukes Deeds, III, 77; comp. York Deeds, IV, 134.

[5]He was a land owner in the three towns. (Deeds, III, 114, 504; IV, 108, 217).

[6]Dukes Probate, II, 56.

year, and his widow Deborah survived, dying March 11, 1743, in the 73d year of her age.[1]

DR. THOMAS WEST.

The first of the name of West to come to the Vineyard was Thomas, a son of Francis West of Duxbury, and from him have descended many of his name who became noted in succeeding generations in the ministry and learned professions, and distinguished in colonial military affairs. Francis West, his father, was born about 1606 and lived in Salisbury, Wiltshire, England. He was a carpenter by trade, and is said to have come to Duxbury as a single man, upon the invitation of Nathaniel Thomas of Marshfield, and after his arrival in his new home, married Margaret Reeves, Feb. 27, 1639, by whom he had five children, Mary (1640), Samuel (1643), Thomas (1646), Peter (1648), and Ruth (1651). He died Jan. 2, 1692, aged 86 years. The descendants of Samuel are mostly found in Connecticut, and those of Peter in Plymouth Colony.[2] Few traces of Thomas are found in the Massachusetts records prior to his emigration to the Vineyard. He witnessed a deed in 1667,[3] and is mentioned in the county Treasurer's accounts of June, 1671.[4] Between that date and Sept. 30, 1673, he came to this island, probably through his association with the Skiffes, as his sister Ruth became the wife of Nathaniel in later years. It is possible that West resided in Newport, R. I., prior to his removal hither. On Sept. 30, 1673, he entered suit against the townsmen of Tisbury respecting his property rights, and his lot, mentioned the following year, was situated on the west side of Old Mill river to the north of the old cemetery, next that of James Skiffe, Sr.[5] Thomas West was evidently a man of education and superior ability, and the first known practitioner of medicine and surgery on the Vineyard. In addition to this qualification

[1]These are the gravestone records, but both seem to be incorrect. The birth of Deborah Skiffe is recorded in Sandwich on July 14, 1668, and thus she was in her 74th year. The age given on his stone would make his birth year 1672-3, but in 1686 he was a witness in Maine. He was probably older than his wife.

[2]See N. E. Gen. Reg., LX, 142. The claims made in print and private that Thomas West was the son of Admiral Francis West of the well known English family have no bases in fact.

[3]Plymouth Deeds, III, 101.

[4]Plymouth Col. Rec. VIII, 133.

[5]Tisbury Records, 8.

he must have been learned in the law, for he was the "Kings Attorney" in June, 1681, and is mentioned in 1687 and the three following years as the King's Solicitor and "Their Majesties Attorney." It is probable he held this office continuously from the first recorded date. He prosecuted the first trials for murder held on the island in the years mentioned.[1] Thomas West also has some further distinction in his religious affiliations. With his wife he became a member of the Third Sabbatarian (Seventh Day) Baptist Church of Newport, R. I., at some time prior to 1692, and various West descendants were attached to that communion for many years after.[2] His daughter and their children in other names are to be found among the members of this church. In 1702, however, he was excommunicated for disobeying the tenets of the communion, but his wife and other members of his family continued in good standing.[3]

In the spring of 1682 he sold his lot in West Tisbury and made the first of a series of land purchases at Homes Hole, which from that time to his death became his residence.[4] This property, by continued acquisition extended from the Lagoon on the north to the Cottle property (head of Lagoon) on the south, and his house was situated near the site of the U. S. Marine Hospital. After his death it descended to his sons in shares and "set offs," but in time his eldest son, Abner, acquired the most of it by purchase from the other heirs.

During his life he had the usual experiences observed among his neighbors as respects his business and social relations. He was indicted and fined in 1678 for "unsavourie speeches" and sued for defamation in 1687 by Simon Athearn.[5] He was elected "townsman" of Tisbury in 1678, and in 1679 was on a committee to "make rates."[6] Beyond these references other mention of him in the records is incidental. He

[1]Dukes County Court Records.

[2]Records Sabbatarian Baptist Church. At the same time Peter and Ruth West are found in the list of members 1692, and it is probable they were his brother and sister of these names.

[3]The order is as follows: "At a General meeting of the Church at Westerly Sept. 19, 1702, at Thomas Burdicks house, upon debate of the case of Thomas West of Martha's Vineyard, who having been several times admonished for his breach of the Sabbath, the church did proceed to a rejection of said West and appointed Bro. Wm. Gibson to draw up sentence of the congregation relating thereunto in writing to be sent to said West."

[4]He bought land at Homes Hole on February 8, 1681-2, and sold his lot on Old Mill river, April 10, 1682. (Dukes Deeds, I, 31, 375)

[5]Dukes Co. Court Records.

[6]Tisbury Records, 12, 13.

made his will on Jan. 15, 1698, and died Sept. 6, 1706, in the sixtieth year of his age. In this document he bequeaths to his "eldest son" Abner the estate as far south as "Chunckes" swamp. To son Thomas certain land next southerly, and to son Peter a tract adjoining the previous bequest; to son William "all that creek stuff or meadow land which I bought of Mr Sam" (Indian). "Nextly" it continues, "I will and bequeath all my books and surgery instruments unto my son Thomas, a gun to my son Sackfield and a sword to my son Judah." His movable estate was left to the widow Elizabeth, "for bringing up the children," and he mentions his "four" daughters in this connection. "My will is," he directs in conclusion, "that none of my children be disposed of without the advice of Brother Nathaniel Skiffe and my son Abner, whom I do make overseers to this my will."[1]

The name of one of his younger sons, Sackfield, is of curious coincidence, as Sackville is one of the family names of the noble West family, Lords De la Warr of the peerage of England.[2] It is not to be supposed, however, that the Duxbury carpenter had any connection whatever with this armigerous family. Diligents earch has failed to disclose the maiden name of his wife, Elizabeth, who was born in 1653 or '4, and survived her husband many years. She died Feb. 16, 1728, "in the 75th year of her age," and the gravestones of both the Doctor and his wife are in good preservation at West Tisbury. At least six of their descendants were graduates of Harvard College before 1800, and were men distinguished in the annals of the New England pulpit.

JOHN WHELDON.

Marriage with one of Abraham Chase's daughters, Abigail, brought John Wheldon to Homes Hole. He was probably the son of Thomas and Elizabeth (Marchant) Wheldon of Yarmouth, Cape Cod, born July 21, 1707, in that town. He was a seafaring man and followed the particular occupation of a Sound pilot in these waters. He came here about 1730-40,

[1]Dukes Co. Probate, I, 8. The property was not finally divided until April 3, 1722, when the children who did not receive landed bequests by will were given their shares (ibid. I, 125).

[2]No emigrant to New England of the name of Sackfield or Sackville in the 17th century has come to the notice of the author, and it does not seem, therefore, to be the name of the wife of Thomas West whose name was thus perpetuated. It should be said that the Sackville connection with the Wests is of comparatively recent date, and no importance can be attached to it as relates to our Sackfield West.

and he and his wife received from her father, May 29, 1741, a large tract of land extending from the harbor to Tashmoo.[1] His death occurred about 1755, as administration of his estate was granted to the widow December 18 that year. Three sons, John, Joseph, and Timothy were lost at sea in 1769 in one vessel.

JAMES WINSLOW.

He was born about 1732-3, and came to Homes Hole some time before Oct. 30, 1765, the date of his first purchase of land in the town.[2] He was married here to Rhoda Chase (131), Nov. 3, 1757, which may be taken as the probable time of his settlement. His occupation was that of a Sound pilot as early as 1769, and he followed this throughout his active life.[3] He was twice married, his second wife being Elizabeth, daughter of John Holmes, and two sets of children were born to him. His death occurred Aug. 26, 1805, in the 73d year of his age. Nothing certain is known of his former residence or parentage. There were Winslows in Rochester and Freetown who had business dealings with the Vineyard before 1750, and it is probable that he came from that section.

EARLY TRANSIENT RESIDENTS.

JOHN BAXTER.

In 1759 this person was licensed as a tavern keeper. He was probably an uncle or near relative of the Malachi Baxter of Yarmouth, Cape Cod, who settled here after the Revolution.[4] He does not appear as a grantor or grantee of property, and doubtless was a tenant only during his stay here. His inn was destroyed by fire in 1762, and after that no more is heard of him in town.

MANASSEH KEMPTON.

The identity of this transient is not satisfactorily established. He appears here in 1725 as the husband of widow Esther (Cottle) Harding, whom he had married in that year

[1]Dukes Deeds, VI, 452, 454, 458.

[2]Ibid, X, 288.

[3]Ibid, X, 187.

[4]There were Baxters here before that date. In the muster roll of a New York company of troops, French and Indian war, 1762, appears the name of Simon Baxter, carpenter, aged 46, whose birthplace is given as Martha's Vineyard. (Rep't N. Y. State Historian, Colonial Series, II, 726-7.)

probably (Court Records). He remained here perhaps four or five years, as traces of him are found in 1726, 1728 and 1729, his wife having died before the latter date, but whence he came or whither he went resolves itself into guessing, after much search.[1] It is probable that he is Manasseh Kempton of Plymouth, who had married Mehitable Holmes of that town about 1715 and bought land same year. Two children were born to him, and he sold his property in 1721 and apparently removed elsewhere.[2] The dates permit migration to the Vineyard, where he married a second time and, after a short stay, again changed residence to Southampton, L. I. In 1733, in a deed, he calls himself a "gunsmith" of the last named place, "formerly of Plymouth" and refers to his uncle Manasseh Kempton of Dartmouth, and his cousin Ephraim of Plymouth.[3] As no wife signs with him these conditions fit the conclusion that he was the above described Manasseh, son of Ephraim of Plymouth. Our court records indicate that a child was born to him here, but its sex or survival is not known. He was neither grantor nor grantee while resident in town.

JACOB PERKINS.

He was the son of Isaac and Susanna Perkins of Hampton, N. H., baptized May 24, 1640, in that town and his younger sister, Mary, was the wife of our Isaac Chase. He came to the Vineyard about 1674, with his brother-in-law probably, and perhaps also in company with Samuel Tilton, bringing a wife and one child. While here a second child was born to them.[4] By occupation he was a tailor, though it would seem that little of this class of work would occupy his time here with so few settlers. His stay here was brief and troublesome, because of the enmity of the official ruling family, arising from his testimony against one of its members in the slander suit of Daggett *vs.* Skiffe, as related elsewhere.[5] Like a considerable number, who at this time were leaving the Vineyard on account of the petty persecutions following the "Dutch Rebel-

[1]He was sued in 1726 (Dukes Co. Court Records); gave evidence in 1728 (Sup. Jud. Court Mss. 21403), and was sued in March, 1729, in our local court.

[2]This may be the date of his removal to the Vineyard. (Davis, "Landmarks of Plymouth," 207).

[3]Bristol Deeds, XXI, 466.

[4]His first purchase here was February 10, 1674. (Dukes Deeds, I, 336). He was called "Jacob Perkins (late of Hampton) now of Holmeshole on the Iland of Martyr's Vineyard." 24-12 mo. 1674 (Norfolk Co. Deeds, III, 20).

[5]Vol. I, 167 (note).

lion," he concluded to remove to a more congenial location, and removed across the Sound to Falmouth, where on Oct. 31, 1677, he bought a homestead of William Weeks, Senior.[1] His stay in Succanessit was also brief, for on Feb. 8, 1678, he sold this property, and on May 8, 1679, he repurchased an estate in Hampton, and ever after resided there. He was living in 1693 with his wife in that town.[2]

CALEB RAND.

This transient came here in 1755 from Nantucket, and lived on the West Tisbury road, just outside the present village of Vineyard Haven. He was the son of John and Mehitable (Call) Rand of Charlestown, born Dec. 6, 1703, and had married, Aug. 4, 1726, in that place, Katherine Kettell, by whom he had eleven children. The five eldest were of age and unmarried when he came here, and they all married here. He remained until about 1761, and returned to Nantucket, where he died in 1768, aged 65 years. The sons and daughters removed to Cornwallis, Nova Scotia, about 1760, and their descendants still reside in that province.

SAMUEL TILTON.

He was a transient resident here before 1676, and removed to West Tisbury and later to Chilmark, where he ended his days. A sketch of him appears in the annals of the latter town.

THE CONSTABLEWICK OF HOMES HOLE.

Although a part of old Tisbury for purposes of taxation, yet the people of Homes Hole and the place itself occupied very little time and space in the consideration of the freemen of West Tisbury. The name of Homes Hole is not mentioned in the town records from 1673 to 1737, nor is there any reference to it indirectly. From the latter date it occurs irregularly every few years to 1780, when it begins to be recognized in the bestowal of some of the minor offices, such as tithingman, surveyor of highways or warden. In 1783 it is spoken of in the records of Tisbury as "that tract of Land Called Homeshole." Not until 1788 was a selectman chosen from this section

[1] Barnstable Town Records, I, 36.

[2] Norfolk County Deeds, X, 44.

[Samuel Look] but from that date it had a representative annually. In 1804-5-6 two residents of Homes Hole were on the board of selectmen. The first town meeting was held in Holmes Hole in March, 1807, at the Proprietors' meeting-house, and thenceforth the annual meetings were holden in West Tisbury and Homes Hole alternately.[1]

For the first time in the records, in 1763, it was called the Constablewick of Homes Hole, a title signifying a district within the jurisdiction of a constable, similar to a parish in ecclesiastical law.[2] It was treated as a separate community and place by the rest of the inhabitants of Tisbury, and beyond according it certain school privileges required by law, it was left to shift for itself in all other things. This reached a formal culmination in 1782, when the townsmen voted that all persons and estates

> to the Eastward of a Line Drawn from the Stepping Stone (A Place known by that Name at the head of the Lagoon or Cove of Water Dividing Said Homseshole from the Town of Edgartown) To Cuteshmoo Spring [be exempt] from paying any Taxes in the Town of Tisbuary for the future Except Common Wealth Taxes, As also that Said Inhabitants Recieve no benefit or Assistance from the Town of Tisbuary for any charges that may Arise on Said Inhabitants for the future, Said Vote Passed in the Affirmative without one Dissenting Vote.[3]

This practically left Homes Hole without obligation to pay any rates except state levies. The interests of the two places were antipodal, not only in ecclesiastical affairs, which we shall learn, but in secular matters as well. The "Hole" was given over to maritime business, the outfitting of ships, the haven of weather-bound craft, and the home of Sound pilots. The west parish was occupied solely in agricultural pursuits.

ECCLESIASTICAL AFFAIRS.

The church affiliations of the first settlers were so diversified that it might be said each one had a different religion from his neighbor. Isaac Chase was a Quaker, Thomas West

[1]In 1838-9 and 1841 the town meetings were held at the taverns kept by Thomas Dunham. In 1843 and 1845, at the Union Wharf store, 1847 to 1852 at the school house, South District, 1852 to 1864 at Capawoc hall. The office of selectmen was removed to Homes Hole before 1852, and in 1857 an effort was made to bring the office of town clerk from West Tisbury, but it failed at that time.

[2]Tisbury Records, 183. The "Liberty of Tisbury" occurs in a document of 1730, signifying a place having special privileges. (Athearn Mss. Cong. Library).

[3]Tisbury Records, 246.

a Sabbatarian Baptist, Edward Cottle a Congregationalist probably, Samuel Tilton an Antipedobaptist and so on. It is evident that there could not be any important events relating to ecclesiastical affairs under such conditions, and it is probable that in the absence of a minister and meeting-house, each one acted as priest in his own household for the first half century after the settlement. Thomas West, who was a member of a congregation of his faith in Newport, may have acted as a lay preacher or missionary in this vicinity during his life. A Quaker traveler on a visit to Nantucket in 1704 had a dispute with one Thomas West on religious subjects and he records in his journal a "paper" written by West in their controversy.[1]

This faith was held by some of the Wests for two or three generations and was adopted by persons intermarrying with them. His grandson, Thomas West (20), a graduate of Harvard, 1730, was "statedly employed to preach the Gospel to the Indians" here before 1745, and in contemporaneous documents is called a "Preacher of the Gospel."[2] It is not to be supposed that he exercised ministerial functions here solely for the Indians, and left a large body of English people without the "benefit of clergy." There is no violation of probabilities in assuming that a small meeting-house was built here by the contributions of the settlers of Homes Hole at this early date, or that services were held in a school-house. Nothing definite is known, however, on this subject, and we can only infer that traveling missionaries of various denominations came here from time to time, by chance or design, and supplied an irregular form of religious "exercise" to them.[3]

PAYMENT OF MINISTERIAL TAX REFUSED.

Under the laws and customs of the times they were taxed for the support of the "orthodox" ministry, and the meeting-house at West Tisbury, which they could not attend because of the great distance and difficulties of traveling. This was borne by them for many years without protest, though the

[1]Journal of Thomas Story, p. 350-359. It is only surmise that this is our Thomas West.

[2]Acts and Resolves of General Court, XIII, 508; Dukes Deeds, VII, 157.

[3]In 1779 Mr. Damon, the pastor at West Tisbury, was granted liberty to preach one-fourth part of the year at some part of the Northward & Eastward part of this Town" (Tisbury Records, 231).

burden was growing more obnoxious to them at every assessment. Accordingly, after much consideration, they agreed, in 1780, to resist further collection of such taxes, and the townsmen of West Tisbury assembled in special session to deal with the crisis, on June 6, 1780, passed the following vote: —

Tisbuary ss: At A Town meeting Legally warn'd & held at the Townhouse in Tisbuary on Tuesday the 6th of June A D 1780 Deacon Stephen Luce being Moderator, and then it was put to Vote to See whether Said Town of Tisb'r would Chuse a Committee to Treat with the People of Homseshole to know what the Cause is that they Refuse Paying Taxes to the Ministree, and what would be Satisfactory to them and the Vote passed in the Affirmative and then it was put to Vote to See whether Mr Benjamin Burges & Ezra Athearn Should be Sd Committee and the Vote passed in the Afirmative, and Also it was Voted they Should Make report of their doeings at the next Town-meeting[1]

Whatever came of this found no record in the town books, and it evidently was an unsuccessful effort at a compromise. The reason for this situation is to be found in the establishment that year of a new sect here, the Calvinistic Baptist, and its adoption by a large proportion of the residents of Homes Hole. The question at issue was not a theological one, but related to the more important one of church and state, the settlement of which involved the whole policy of public support for the clergy.

TISBURY AGREES TO RELEASE HOMES HOLE.

In the fall of 1782 they presented a verbal request to the town as follows: "Requesting that they may be Exempted from Paying any Tax for the Support of the Presbeterian Ministers for the future in the Town of Tisbuary by Reason they are of the Baptist Perswasion."[2]

A town meeting was called for Sept. 25, 1782,

and at Said Meeting James Athearn Esqr was chosen Moderator And then A Vote was Call'd to See Wheather Shobal Cottle Esqr Deacon Stephen Luce & Mr Ransford Smith Should be a committee to hold A Conferance with the Inhabitants of Homseshole and Some Persons Adjacant Relative to the Above Request or Pettion and to make Report of their doeings at the Adjornment of this Meeting, and the Vote passed in the Affirmative and then Sd Town Meeting was Adjorn'd.[3]

[1]Tisbury Records, 236.
[2]Ibid., 245.
[3]Ibid.

As a result of this conference the town at the adjourned meeting directed the Moderator to "aquaint the Said Inhabitants of Homseshole that they Pettition this Town for their being Dismissed from Paying Ministeral Taxes (if they see cause)." The following petition was then prepared: —

To the Inhabitants of the Town of Tisbuary in the County of Dukes County in Legal Town-meeting to be assemble'd on Tuesday the 19th Day of October 1782.

The Memorial of us whose Names are under writen being Inhabitants of that Part of Said Town Commonly Call'd Homseshole beg Leave to Represent that Notwithstanding our great Desire to Promote Religion and attend the Publick Worship of God at all Times must needs say that Considering our remote Scituation from the Meeting-house or Place of Worship in Said Town and being Attended with Such Conspiscious Inconveniencies that need not be Enumerated, Desire that wee may be Released from paying any Part towards the support of the Gospel in Said Town Except among our Selves in Such a A Manner as will be most for our Religious profit Or otherwise releas us Agreeable to Justice & Equity as to you may Seem fit all which is Humbly Subitted[1]

Isaac Daggett	Nathaniel Skiffe	William Smith
Levi Young	Elizabeth West	Jonathan Raymond
George West	Jesse Luce	Charles Edmondson
Jeruel West	Peter West	

HOMES HOLE SET OFF AS A PARISH.

On Nov. 25, 1782, the town voted unanimously to release them in accordance with this petition, but it is evident that such an action was beyond the power of the town, and the good intentions were frustrated.[2] The collection of this tax went on for several more years. In July, 1790, the people of this settlement again started a movement to be made independent of Tisbury. They made the following request to accomplish this: —

That the Said Homseshole Should be Sett off as a Precinct, and after Due Consideration it was Movd and Seconded and put to Vote and passed in the Affirmative that it Should be Sett off for a Precinct as far to the Westward as the Line Called Savages Line and So continu'd the Same Course from the Sound to the Line of Edgartown to be Sett off from Said Tisbuary as a Seperate District, Provided they Support their own School and the Poor within the Same District and all other charges arising within the Same District, Except the Taxes due to the Commonwealth[3]

[1]Tisbury Records, 245.

[2]At a town meeting held November 25, 1792, this was reconsidered and it was voted "that the former Vote be nul and Void and of no effect any more" (ibid. 288).

[3]Tisbury Records, 276-7.

In the following May the town met and passed this vote on the subject: —

That the Select Men of Tisbuary be Impowr'd to give an Order on the Treasurer of Tisbuary to Pay the Several Persons Taxed to the Ministers Tax in Tisbuary Living to the Eastward of Teshmoo Spring So Called that are Inhabitants in Said Districts of homseshole Taxed in the Rate bills David Look Constable of Tisbuary for the year 1790 has to Colect, May the 18th AD 1791[1]

But this did not meet the desires of the people here, the repayment of taxes, as they wished for separation, and having failed to obtain satisfaction at home, they preferred a petition, in 1793, to the General Court asking for the establishment of Homes Hole as the East Parish of Tisbury.[2] James Athearn, Joseph Athearn and William Case were chosen as "Sutable Persons as a Comitte to Respond to the Pettition of the Inhabatants of Homes hole."[3] Nothing came of their request at this time and the residents of Tisbury made them the following offer: "That the Inhabitants of Homeshole . . . . . have for the future Such part of the preaching by the Settled minester in Tisbury, Carried on in homes hole in proportion to the taxes they may pay towards the minesters Sallery in S'd Town."

Samuel Look and Thomas Cottle, who were the leaders of this movement, joined in a petition to the County Court for relief from the ministerial tax. The petition is dated Oct. 28, 1794, and recites that they "have been Induced to join with the Inhabitants of homses hole to build a meeting house where we can attend with our families," and that they paid more at Homes Hole than they are taxed for in Tisbury for the support of Mr. Asarelah Morse, the minister. Having petitioned the selectmen without result, they now pray the Court for relief.[4] Ezekiel Luce was appointed to answer this before the Court. Further consultations and efforts at a peaceful conclusion of the controversey were in order, and the following record of a meeting held on Dec. 22, 1794, brings the issue forward: —

Voted by the Voters then present that Ezekiel Luce Benjamin allen Cornelus Dunham on the part of the town of Tisbury westward of Savages line and Samuel Look Thomas Cottle John Homes on the part of Said town Eastward of Said line be a Committe to meet at Some time and place by them to be agreead upon in order to Settle any disputes

[1]Tisbury Records, 282.

[2]This petition cannot be found in the Massachusetts archives.

[3]Town Records, 290. The answer of this committee cannot be found.

[4]Dukes County Court Files.

Subsisting or that may arise with regard to Minestearil Taxes in Said town and in Case the Said Committe Should not agree they are to Call in the assistance of Mr Matthew Mayhew J'unr of Chillmark the Determination of them or the major part of them to be for the future regulation of minesteril Taxes upon both Sides of the before discribed line as well as any other disputes with regard to back taxes.[1]

This committee, or a majority of them, for Cornelius Dunham and John Holmes did not sign it, made a report to the town on Jan. 12, 1795, and after reciting a preamble respecting the general character of the dispute, make the following recommendations: —

haveing a real desier that peace truth & Equity may at this and all times take place. We hereby agree to the following articuals hereafter named Viz that the taxes of all those persons to the East of the aforsaid Saveges line have there taxes remitted in the bills in which they have been taxed to pay to the Rev'd Mr Morses Sallery as far back as the year of our Lord 1787 this intends no more then those persons who are now living between the aforsaid Saveges line and Cuteshmoo Spring and So on the west Side of the pond to the Sound and no more.

And we further agree that the people on the East Side of the aforsaid Saveges line forthwith petition the general Court that they may be Sett off as a precinct or parish and that the town Join with them in this petition.[2]

Nothing was done about the petition for a year, and on Jan. 6, 1796, Nathan Smith, Benjamin Allen and Elijah Look, Jr., were appointed a committee to "Join a Committe of the inhabatants of homes hole . . . . . in prefering a petition to the General Court that said Inhabitants might be incorporated into precinct or parish." This was done, and the law creating the East Parish of Tisbury, from the inhabitants living east of Savage's Line, was passed that year by the General Court.

THE PROPRIETORS' MEETING-HOUSE.

The need of a house of worship for this settlement became urgent after the organization of the Baptist society in 1780, but there was nearly an equal number of adherents of the ancient Congregational society established in West Tisbury, and it was impracticable to build a meeting-house for the use of any particular denomination by general taxation. Therefore the expedient was devised of erecting one by voluntary contributions from members of all varieties of belief, which

[1]Tisbury Records, 294.

[2]Ibid., 296.

should be open to all ministers and sects in an equitable division of time. Those who gave towards its construction became thereby shareholders in its management, and the building came to be known as the "Proprietors' Meeting House." It was probably erected in 1788, as on Jan. 3 of that year, Peter West for the sum of £9 sold a tract of land to John Holmes, Jonathan Manter, Isaac Daggett, Samuel Look, and Abraham Chase, "as a committee for the proprietors of a meeting house to be built at Holmes Hole." This committee represented the Baptists and Congregationalists, and the proportion of proprietors was about two thirds of the first-named sect and the rest of the orthodox church, or those without religious preference. The occupancy of the building was divided in that proportion. The clergyman at West Tisbury held services for his third of the time in consideration of the payment of the ministerial tax, but after its abolition this incentive was lost, and the "orthodox" element gradually dwindled to the vanishing point. Parson Thaxter of Edgartown also held services here after this time, giving regular "lectures."

This Proprietors' meeting-house was located on the highway, on what is now the northwest corner of Main and Spring streets. The architectural features comprised a simple building with four straight walls, unpainted, and a pitched roof, without steeple, belfry or blinds. Three doors opened on Main street and within could be seen a gallery above, high-back box pews below, over which the tithing man would prod his long stick to curb the mischievous pranks of youth or arouse the aged from their slumbers. A sounding board formed a resonant background for the preacher in the tall pulpit.[1] A traveler who visited this place in 1807 called it " a small neat church."[2]

For about half a century this meeting-house served its purpose as a shelter for all kinds of theology and its expounders. In 1832 the Methodists withdrew and built their own meeting-house and the control of this one fell into the hands of the Baptists by heritage and possession. It lasted until 1837, when it was no longer fit for occupancy and was taken down to make way for another.[3]

[1]In 1819 a wood stove was installed, and the pipe led out through one of the side windows.

[2]Kendall "Travels," II, 201.

[3]The last town meeting was held in it in May, 1837, and in November of that year the school-house was used for that purpose.

THE BAPTIST CHURCH.

The earliest schism from the orthodox body on the Vineyard comprised persons who had adopted the doctrines of the Baptist religion, or, as it was then called, the Anabaptist. Peter Folger is supposed to have held this belief, and about 1675 he joined the Baptist church in Newport, though this was after he had become a resident of Nantucket.[1] It is stated by a religious historian "that Baptist ministers had preached among the English on the Vineyard at times ever since 1753," but there is no record of these persons, times nor places.[2] The beginning of this denomination as an organized religious association, in definite numbers, is thus described by the same writer: —

> By afflictive providence and private means of grace four persons near Holmes' Hole were awakened to a sense of their sin and danger, and in the Spring of 1780 they experienced a happy deliverance of soul. And no sooner was light granted to them than they endeavored to hold the same forth to others, which brought them to set up religious meetings and a number were hopefully converted by these means.[3] And about the last of June they sent for Elder Lewis of Freetown, who went over in July, and preached and baptized a number of them. He did the like in August and October, as Elder Hunt also did in November, and by particular request I [Isaac Backus] met them there in December when a careful inquiry was made into their sentiments and views and the order of the gospel, with the solemn nature of the Christian profession was publicly laid open and inculcated. After which on December 21, 1780 we saw fifty persons solemnly sign covenant together, to whom six more were added on the 24th, and all of them sweetly communed together at the Lord's table. The high sheriff of the county[4] was a leading member of this church which contained some persons of every rank among them.[5]

The new religion prospered rapidly, and soon had increased to about eighty members. No regular preacher was

[1]Backus Church History of New England, III, 167. It is said by the same authority that the Indians became converted to this creed by Folger's preaching.

[2]Ibid, III, 167. They were probably itinerant missionaries.

[3]A document dated June 10, 1780, certifies that the subscribers "are of the minds to have a Baptist minister to preach the Gospel to us," and it is signed by Jonathan Manter, Zephaniah Chase, Abraham Chase, Levi Young, Timothy Chase, Ephraim Norton, George Hillman, James Winslow, David Merry, Andrew Newcomb, Shubael Butler, Benjamin Benson and Malachi Baxter. These may be reckoned as the earliest Baptists in this town.

[4]Major Peter Norton [421] 1718-1792.

[5]Backus Church History, II, 375. He adds: "The husband of one of them was born among the Portuguese and was now newly returned from a distressing captivity in England." This probably refers to Joseph Dias, who married Sarah Manter [110].

employed, although an effort was made to hire one.[1] Elders Hunt and Burroughs and other missionaries continued to make periodical visits during the first years of the establishment of the sect, and efforts to secure a settled minister were renewed whenever an opportunity seemed to offer. "When we have no preacher" say these zealous adherents of the new creed in 1791, "and the weather permits, we still assemble and worship God by singing reading and praying."[2] This situation continued for the ensuing decade, and notwithstanding these discouragements the society grew and flourished. Incorporation was determined upon by those of the Baptist faith from all parts of the Vineyard, to settle the question of taxes for ministerial support.

In 1803, John Davis and seventy-five others addressed a petition to the General Court, praying for incorporation as the Baptist Society of Tisbury. The town of Tisbury at its April meeting instructed the selectmen [Ezekiel Luce, William Athearn and Rufus Spalding] and Benjamin Allen "to consult and draw a remonstrance to a petition Sent by a number of the Inhabatants of Tisbury, Chillmark & Edgartown praying to be incorporated into a religious baptiss Society," but a year after (1804) the town reversed itself and instructed its representative to the General Court to "aid and assist to have the Said incorporation established and enacted into a law."[3] This was accomplished June 28th that same year.[4]

Ezra Allen	Eleazer Dunham	Jonathan Manter
Joseph Allen	Shubael Dunham	Jonathan Manter, Jr.
Joseph Athearn	Cornelius Dunham	Theophilus Mayhew
Jonathan Athearn	Abijah Gray	Jonathan Merry
Belcher Athearn	Freeman Gray	William Merry
Francis Chase	John Gray	William Merry, Jr.
Hugh Cathcart	Abijah Hammett	Stephen New
Jonathan Cathcart	John Hancock	Samuel Norris
Abraham Chase	Ephraim Harding	Darius Norton
Joseph Chase	Elijah Hillman	Samuel Norton
Nicholas Chase	Jethro Hillman	Isaac Norton
Joseph Chase, Jr.	John Holmes	Base Norton
Lot Cottle	Benjamin Luce	Obed Norton
Samuel Daggett	Matthew Luce	Peter Norton
Silas Daggett	Isaac Luce	Henry Norton
John Davis	Silas Luce	Henry C. Norton

[1]A minister named Dodge was called in 1781, but declined "as he is not willing to settle over any church for the present."

[2]Address to the selectmen of Tisbury signed by John Manchester and thirty-three others.

[3]Tisbury Records, 318, 322.

[4]An act to incorporate a number of persons in the towns of Edgartown, Chilmark and Tisbury, into a religious society by the name of the First Baptist Society in Tisbury.

Benjamin Davis
Rufus Davis
William Davis
Meletiah Davis
Dennis Davis
Henry Davis
Zadock Davis
Cornelius Davis
William Downes
Paul Luce
Bernard Luce
David Luce
Elisha Luce
Warren Luce
Jesse Luce
Jesse Luce, Jr.
Thomas Manter
Peter Manter
Archelaus Pease
David Reynolds
Prince Rogers
Silas Rogers
William Rotch
David Smith
Mathew Smith
Jonathan Tilton
Benjamin Trask
Beriah Weeks

Of these about thirty resided in the present limits of Tisbury, and the entire list shows what an extensive schism had been made in the Congregational society.

On Feb. 20, 1804, Ezra Kendall was called to the pastorate and accepted, and the society at last secured their first settled minister. He was characterized by Parson Thaxter as "a man of small education, warm temperament and great zeal," but he lasted only a short five months. He was succeeded, after an intermission of two years, by Abisha Samson of Providence, who was ordained in June, 1806, and his term of service was very successful. During this term he received permission to engage in business to eke out his scanty income, and in 1811 resigned because "his preaching was not profitable," according to his letter requesting dismissal. For the next ten years a succession of Elders, Bartlett Pease (398), Samuel Nelson, Simeon Coombs, Samuel Abbott, and Simeon Crowell supplied the pulpit without formal settlement. In 1820 Rev. William Hubbard became pastor and remained five years, serving both the newly organized independent branches at Edgartown and West Tisbury It is probable that the pastors at Edgartown, Henry Marchant (1826-7) and William Bowen (1828-9), with the assistance of Jesse Pease (397) supplied this pulpit until 1830, when Rev. Seth M. Ewer was settled as fourth pastor.[1] He remained three years and was followed by Rev. Flavel Shurtleff (1833-4) for five months, and David Pease (1836-7) for ten months.

[1]A townsman living contemporaneously thus characterizes this clergyman:-"The Baptist minister employed here is Mr. Seth Ewer, a man of about 50 years of age. Very resolute and determined in whatever he undertakes, but is not generally well received by the people. Should not think him to be a man of very extensive information, or much of a scholar, but has a great degree of confidence and a faculty of showing what he has to the best advantage. His sermons, though usually long, are for the most part meagre and uninstructive and often quite irksome to hear on account of the emphasis put upon almost every word, which is altogether misplaced. He has now been here almost two years, and on the whole should fear that little good had been effected by him, as that society has appeared to be on the wane ever since he came among us, besides some members of the church are so much disaffected toward him that they will not hear or support him." (Diary Dr. L. M Yale, January 6, 1833)

NEW MEETING-HOUSE BUILT.

The old "Proprietors'" house of worship had passed into the hands of this denomination, and for about fifty-two years altogether, as previously related, had served its purpose, until beyond repair. In 1837, at a cost of about $4,500, the first Baptist meeting-house intended for that use was built on the site occupied by the older structure. It was a building somewhat different in style from those heretofore constructed on the Vineyard for religious worship, and a view of it, drawn from contemporary sketches and descriptions, is here shown.

This building underwent considerable remodeling, stores were constructed underneath, the auditorium and a vestry were added.

It survived for forty-three years, and was destroyed in the great fire of Aug. 11, 1883, the only denomination in town to suffer in that conflagration.

SUCCESSION OF PASTORS, 1838–1908.

Rev. James C. Boomer was ordained and settled on April 13, 1838, and was the first pastor who gave all his time and service to this parish, as the other towns were all independently organized at this date. He remained five years, and his successors since then have been as follows: B. F. Hedden, 1843-9; J. C. Kenney, 1849-50; Wm. Stowe, 1850-4; Stephen A. Thomas, 1854-9; Justus Aldrich, 1860; Wm. Leach, Wm. Fray, J. L. A. Fish (records imperfect); J. W. Savage, 1866-8; H. B. Marshall, 1868-70; Geo. L. Lewis, 1870-1; Chas. A. Cook, 1872-4; J. W. Fuhrmann, 1874-6; Geo. L. Lewis, 1876-9; J. Coker, 1879-82;[1] J. P. Farrar, 1883-7; J. E. Hamilton, 1888-92; J. E. Locke, 1892-3; Alfred Fairbrother, 1893-1901; M. E. Fish, 1901-3; Albert E. Hylan, 1903 (present incumbent).

SECOND BAPTIST MEETING-HOUSE.

Following the loss of the old house of worship, the Society occupied Association hall until another church home should be prepared for them. On May 30, 1884, a building com-

[1]The one hundredth anniversary of this church was celebrated during Rev. Mr. Coker's pastorate, December 15, 1882, and he delivered an historical address which was published as "Historical address delivered on the one hundredeth anniversary of the Baptist Church, Vineyard Haven, Mass., by Rev. J. Coker, pastor" 8vo paper cover, pp. 14, Press of E. H. Manter, Vineyard Haven, Mass., 1882.

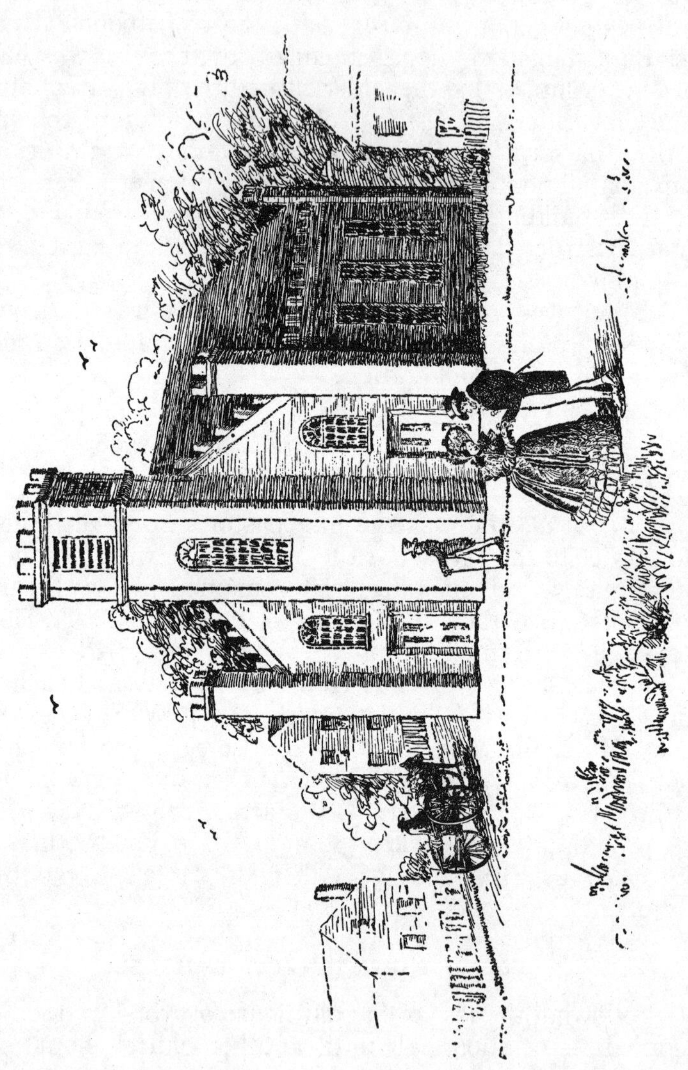

BAPTIST CHURCH, HOMES HOLE, 1837-1883.

mittee consisting of Lorenzo D. Smith, John F. Robinson, Bayes F. Norton, Mrs. Myra W. Wade, and the pastor, was chosen, and funds solicited and collected for the purpose. A new site was purchased on the corner of William and Spring streets, on which were erected a handsome church building and parsonage. They were completed in 1885 at the cost of $6,500, and dedicated the same year.

THE METHODIST CHURCH.

The story of the foundation of Methodism in this town is a part of the annals of its beginning upon the Vineyard, for the pioneers of this new sect did not confine their labors to any one locality. This town, however, has the distinction of being the place where the doctrines of Wesley were first expounded. Rev. Jesse Lee, the founder of Methodism in New England, preached his first sermon on the Vineyard in 1795 in the Proprietors' meeting-house on Main street. His journal makes this reference to the event:—

> Tuesday February 3. 1795. I prevailed with them [the captain and crew of the packet] to land me on the Vineyard. . . . .I then walked to Mr. I. Daggett's tavern at the head of the harbor at Holmes' Hole. I was kindly received and gladly entertained. The next day I gave them a sermon in the meeting house. We had a small congregation and not much life. At night I preached again with more freedom and faith than in the morning, and the word seemed to make some impression on the minds of the hearers; perhaps I am the first Methodist preacher who has visited this place for the express purpose of preaching, and even now I have visited the place sooner than I intended.[1]

Two years later, 1797-8, Joshua Hall came as the first stationed missionary.[2] He had previously been engaged in this work at Sandwich, Mass., with great success, and at the close of his term here he was able to report as the result of turning over this virgin soil on the Vineyard, hitherto unbroken, thirteen members of his "class."[3] The next was Joseph Snelling, 1798-9, also from Sandwich in turn, and he adopted the nautical style of preaching to the people, which was so successfully followed in later years by "Father" Taylor. One of his hearers said to him: "If you had been preaching in Vermont perhaps they would not have understood you; but

[1]Stevens, Memorials of Methodism, I, 328.

[2]The conference year began at that time in June or July, and the pastorates are to be reckoned on that basis.

[3]Rev. George Pickering, the presiding elder of this district, visited Homes Hole in his official capacity during Hall's pastorate.

this is the preaching we can understand." He reported twenty-four members at the close of this conference year.[1] His successor was Epaphras Kibby, who came from New Rochelle, New York, but he did not long remain, as the presiding elder transferred him before the close of the year. He was the last assignment for a decade.

The "converts" were either unconverted or had gradually drifted back to older moorings, and by 1810 the sect was almost extinct. Two women only remained as evidence of the faith at that date. Erastus Otis, stationed at Falmouth, made frequent visits here and kept the dying embers from total extinguishment. William Hinman, 1811-12; Edward Hyde, 1812-13; Wlliam Frost, 1813-14; John W. Hardy, 1814-15, Benjamin Hazelton, 1815-16, followed as general missionaries, but records are wanting to show the nature or results of their labors. Evidently it was all foundation work, as it was not till 1816-17, during the assignment of Shipley W. Wilson, that the first "class" was organized in this town.[2] The members of it were Edmund Crowell and wife, Mrs. Sarah Parsons, Mrs. Polly Hillman, Mrs. Annie Claghorn, Hannah Hammett, and two sisters, Betsey and Cynthia Grinnell. The "class leader" was Hiram Chase, a hatter, who had come from Sandwich to follow his trade. Thomas M. Tucker followed, 1817-18, and Mr. Wilson had a second pastorate immediately after. Eleazer Steele served here with considerable success, 1819-20-21, and then came "Reformation [John] Adams," famous for his revival work. His two years' labor, 1821-2-3, was a continuous round of personal pleadings week days and collective exhortations on Sundays. The results were a great numerical increase of converts, and a tribute to his zealous methods.[3] When he left the Vineyard, a farewell ode composed by him expressing his sentiments of regret at parting, contained this verse:—

At Holmes' Hole theres some grown cold
Oh Lord revive them down the Neck;
The harbour round with blessings crown
With power the devil's kingdom shake!

[1]This number probably includes all the Methodists in his jurisdiction on the Vineyard. It is not possible to say how many are to be credited to this town.

[2]During his stay here Wilson wooed and won Miss Rebecca Mayhew (665) daughter of Deacon William Mayhew, against the strenuous opposition of her parents. Religious sentiment in those days was militant.

[3]His Autobiography, edited by his son, published in 1847, gives minute details of his life here during this first pastorate, and the second five years later, pp. 92-164 and 202-284. It is a picture of conditions on the Vineyard eighy-five years ago.

"REFORMATION" JOHN ADAMS

REV. JOSEPH SNELLING

TWO EARLY METHODIST PREACHERS AT HOMES HOLE

Frederick Upham succeeded this flaming sword, 1823-4, and after him came the world-famous Edward T. Taylor, known in the annals of this denomination and in Boston, where he ended his unique career, as "Father" Taylor. His pastorate, 1824-5, left its deep impression upon the people of the town and island, as it did elsewhere in the later stages of his noted career. He was then about thirty years old and the atmosphere of the place well suited his idealism, and he readily adapted his preaching to this environment. The sea and its language, the deck and its manners, the forecastle and its sentiment, gave him constant inspiration, and he became the "sailors' preacher"[1] on this sea girt isle. He held services on vessels in the harbor, and on one of these occasions uttered the oft-quoted aspiration which has been paraphrased in verse, expressive of his love of the ocean: —

I do not want to be buried in the ground when I die. But bury me rather in the deep blue sea where the coral rocks shall be my pillow, and the seaweeds shall be my winding sheet, and where the waves of the ocean shall sing my requiem for ever and ever.

FIRST VINEYARD CAMP-MEETING.

David Culver, 1825-6, and John Adams, 1826-7, followed in succession. In this second pastorate of "Reformation Adams" the first known camp-meeting held on the Vineyard occurred in July and August, 1827, in a grove near the West Chop lighthouse. Of this event the preacher speaks as follows: —

To prepare the ground for camp meeting has required labor and fatigue. July 28, 1827 I preached on the camp ground. About 150 were present, and we had the shout of a King in the Camp. August 1, 1827 our camp meeting commenced and more than twenty preachers were present, and not far from thirty tents were on the ground. The people came from different islands, and many from the Cape, New Bedford and Boston. All parts of the Vineyard were represented. Good order was generally observed. In the first part of the meeting but few were converted, but the meeting grew more powerful and interesting, and it was hoped that more than forty experienced religion, while many backsliders were reclaimed, old professors quickened young converts strengthened and imperfect believers sanctified to God. Our meetings continued a week and we had a solemn parting. We think the meeting will prove a blessing for years to come.[2]

[1]See Life of Father Taylor by Gilbert Haven, pp. 96-100.

[2]Life of Rev. John Adams, 280.

Following Adams came William Barstow, 1828-9, who was assisted by Caleb Lamb; Hezekiah Thatcher, 1829-30; Thomas G. Brown, 1830-2. During Mr. Brown's pastorate a Sunday school was organized, and the church, in 1830, numbered thirty-five members.

FIRST METHODIST MEETING-HOUSE.

As already stated, the services of this denomination had been held hitherto in the Proprietors' meeting-house in rotation with the Baptist and others, but during the succeeding pastorate of Louis Janson (1832-3), a movement for a separate house of worship was consummated.[1] It had been talked about for some time, but an incident associated with the joint occupancy of the Union meeting-house precipitated the result. Members of all creeds were accustomed to attend services conducted by the others, if they desired. On one Sunday, at a Baptist service, when the communion was to be celebrated, the invitation to partake of the Lord's Supper was given in such a manner as to leave no doubt that none but Baptists would be welcome. This was the cause, according to tradition, of the efforts immediately begun to build a Methodist meeting-house where they would be independent. In the movement Capt. William Daggett was a leading spirit and liberal contributor, and others lent services, if they were unable to give funds. As a preliminary to perfecting their independency and the right to hold property for religious uses, the members were incorporated March 7, 1833, as the "First Methodist Episcopal Society in Tisbury." The building was completed at a cost of nearly $2,000 in July following, and dedicated July 11, that year. It is still standing on Church street, known for years as Capawock hall, and now occupied as a Masonic Temple, the property of that order.

[1]A contemporary thus characterizes the preacher:-"The Methodist Minister that is now occupied here is Mr. Louis Janson, an Englishman by birth, young, say 27 or 28, active, possessed of some natural talent, but not a very thorough education and his sermons are mostly addressed to the passions of his hearers, without being very instructive and this is true of most of the preachers of that denomination, that I have heard. There has been, however, a good deal of religious excitement under his preaching and a number give good evidence of having met with a saving change and have united with the class, which I understand to be a state of probation for six months previous to joining the church, during which time if they walk orderly, they are afterward admitted, but if not, rejected." (Diary of Leroy M. Yale, M. D., January 6, 1833.) During Mr. Janson's term the Seamen's Prayermeeting was inaugurated, and for twenty-five years it continued its meetings on the first Thursday of every month. They were non-sectarian, and sailors at sea who had attended it were expected to remember the time and hold like services wherever they might be. Mr. Janson in 1836 became an Episcopal clergyman.

SUCCESSION OF PASTORS.

Mark Staple, 1833-5; Aaron Josselyn, 1835-6; Joseph B. Brown, 1836-7;[1] Abram Holloway, 1837-8; Mark Staple (second time), 1838-9; Onesiphorous Robbins, 1839-41;[2] Henry H. Smith, 1841-2;[3] J. G. Goodrich, 1842-4; Nathan Paine, 1844-5; and A. B. Wheeler, 1845-7. During the terms of these ministers the society prospered greatly in numbers, and increased its influence in the community.

SECOND METHODIST MEETING–HOUSE.

As a result of the growth of the membership, the old building which had been in use but twelve years was found to be too small to accommodate the congregation, and the building of a new house of worship was determined upon by the society. A lot of land opposite the existing meeting-house, on the northeast corner of William and Church streets was donated by Captain William Daggett, and a larger and more pretentious structure built thereon and dedicated Nov. 13, 1845, with appropriate ceremonies. This new house had cost $6,500, and was surmounted by a tower which now carries a clock. A pipe organ, costing $1,200, was installed in 1865, to replace a small instrument worked by hand. The building has had a few additions and trivial changes inside and out and remains today substantially as originally designed.

SUCCESSION OF PASTORS.

Samuel W. Coggeshall, 1847-9; Micah J. Talbot, 1849-51; George W. Stearns, 1851-3; William H. Stetson, 1853-4; Franklin Gavitt, 1854-6; William Leonard, 1856-8; Alonzo Latham, 1858-60; Francis A. Loomis, 1860-2; M. P. Alderman, 1862-4; William V. Morrison, 1864-5; John N. Collier, 1865-6; John F. Sheffield, 1866-7; Edward Edson, 1867-70; Philo Hawkes, 1870-2; James O. Thompson, 1872-4; J. D. King, 1874-5; Eben Tirrell, Jr., 1875-7; A. L. Dearing, 1877-8; George H. Butler, 1878-80; W. F. Steele, 1880-2; W. I. Ward, 1882-5; Shepherd F. Harriman, 1885-7; George A Grant, 1887-9; Samuel L. Beale, 1890; Richard E. Schuh, 1891-2;

[1]During Mr. Brown's pastorate Charles Weeks was licensed as "exhorter," a position he occupied in this society for half a century.

[2]A parsonage costing about $900 was built during Mr. Robbins' term.

[3]45 were baptized and 43 "probationers" received in this year.

Samuel F. Johnson, 1893-6; John E. Duxbury, 1897; William D. Wilkinson, 1898-1900; William H. Butler, 1901-2; John Bearse, 1903-4; Samuel J. Rook, 1905-7.

THE CONGREGATIONAL CHURCH.

The first meetings of a religious society organized under the Congregationalist denomination were held about 1825, in the small one story building, occupied for a long time after as an undertaker's establishment, and since 1903 by Sea Coast Defence Chapter, Daughters of the American Revolution. The building was then used as a school during week days, and on Sunday for religious purposes. This school-house for years after was known as the "Chapel." It had a small cupola, within which was suspended a triangle that called the people to worship, and the scholars to struggle with the rudimentary R's. It continued to do this double duty until 1844, when members of the society felt that they should outgrow its temporary shell, and build a larger edifice devoted exclusively to their uses.

Nathan Mayhew, the school-teacher, was one of the prime movers in the establishment of the Congregational church, and became one of its Deacons.[1]

Another associate with the late Deacon Mayhew was Dr. Leroy M. Yale, and from his diary the following notes of the beginning of this society are taken:—

> In 1844, after much deliberation, Mr. James L. Barrows, Nathan Mayhew and myself formed the design of organizing a Congregational Church in this place and we obtained the services of Rev. Wm. Gould of Fairhaven who commenced preaching in a small school house and after a few weeks, a small church of ten members was organized, which was soon increased by the addition of five or six more.
>
> Having thus made a beginning and not having a suitable house for worship, we determined on building a meeting house and in the course of that season erected one at a cost of nearly five thousand dollars, in which we have since held our meetings having settled as our first minister Rev. Samuel S. Tappan, who is still with us. This step, viz, the organization of the church and building of the meeting house has called out the most violent opposition by the Baptists and Methodists, so much so that they, or individuals of the Baptist society have advanced money to the amount of 3 or 4 hundred dollars to set up a physician in opposition to me and the Methodists have built them a new house, which they did not previously design.[2]

[1]He lived in the house owned and occupied by the late Capt. James L. Smith on Main street.

[2]Kindly furnished to the author by Dr. Leroy Milton Yale of New York city, son of the elder Dr. Yale, and a native of Vineyard Haven.

Rev. Mr. Tappan remained until 1849, and was succeeded by William Fyvie, who remained one year (1850) only. The next and last settled minister was William H. Sturtevant, who held the pastorate until 1859, when he accepted a call to the West Tisbury church and the society gradually dissolved. The church building was occupied by the Universalists, and they were in turn followed by the Unitarians, but it was abandoned for church worship about 1866, and used for secular purposes as a public hall, and by the town for a town hall. It is now known as Association hall, from its former ownership by a number of shareholders. It now contains the town offices and fire apparatus.

UNITARIAN CHURCH.

Seamen's Chapel. — In 1867 Rev. Daniel Waldo Stevens was sent to Homes Hole by the American Unitarian Association as a missionary. He was a Harvard graduate, class of 1846, of the Divinity school in 1848, and from 1850 to 1862 was settled in Mansfield, Mass. For a number of years he had been doing unattached mission work for the association, and when he came to Homes Hole he saw an opportunity to serve the multitudes of seafaring men who came annually into the harbor as a port of call. A man of strong intellect, unconventional in his methods, and full of enthusiasm, he soon had established a chapel and reading room for sailors, on a commanding bluff midway to the head of the harbor. Through the aid of friends and the support of this denomination, he maintained a unique establishment where he dwelt and ministered to "Jack" at all times for nearly twenty-four years. In this way he was quite as well known to mariners on the coast as the famous "Father" Taylor, who had in earlier years carried on the same work at this place. His rooms were a veritable museum of curios, interesting and valuable, for he was a collector of historical and natural relics and knew their worth, and a splendid collection of stone implements made by the aborigines, was one of the important portions of this treasure house.[1] The author recalls this venerable man in the last years of his ministry, when after acting as sexton and ringing his own bell on Sunday morning he would continue

[1]This collection of Indian implements was removed from the Vineyard by his son after the death of Dr. Stevens, and was placed on deposit with the Bristol, R. I. Historical Society. It is a matter of great regret that this unique collection was not donated to a local museum.

the service, somewhat short of breath from his exertion. He was at his beloved chapel until his last sickness put an end to his labors. He died Oct. 1, 1891, aged 71 years, having been born Jan. 18, 1820, at Marlboro, Mass.[1] After his death the building passed into private hands, and has been remodeled into a summer residence.

Church of the Unity. — The residents who had attended Dr. Stevens' services for a considerable time desired to continue the skeleton organization that had existed in his day, but for a number of years the project of reviving his work languished. The matter was finally taken up by an association of Unitarians, called the Channing Conference. A neat building was erected by it on the West Chop road, on a picturesque knoll in the grove, in 1896, and in 1898 the "Vineyard Haven Unitarian Society" was organized to maintain services therein. Since that date a regular ministerial supply has been had, beginning with W. C. Litchfield, 1898-1903; W. H. Johnson, 1905-07; I. P. Quimby, 1907 (present incumbent). The meeting-house is generally known as the Stevens Memorial Chapel.

THE EPISCOPAL CHURCH.

On Dec. 25, 1862, the first public service of this church was held at Capawock Hall by the Rev. John West of New York, and as a result of the interest manifested, that clergyman was appointed missionary for Martha's Vineyard. Services were held for several years, but were discontinued owing to the ill health of Mr. West.

In the summer of 1866 services were held by the Rev. Benjamin Gifford, who baptized five persons. During the following winter services were held monthly by the Rev. Hiram Carleton of the Church of the Messiah at Woods Hole, with which parish this Mission had been incorporated. The removal or death of many of the communicants caused the services to be discontinued, except such as were held in private houses, as the membership was not large at this time. In this pioneer work the late Mrs. Ellen Louisa Richardson, who was one of the earliest members of the "Summer colony," was a conspicuous leader. She was a devout and devoted member of the church in another part of the state, and brought with her the zeal to carry on the mission work for her church

[1]An excellent account of his life and work appeared in the Christian Register Oct. 15, 1898.

GRACE (EPISCOPAL) CHURCH

VINEYARD HAVEN

in her adopted home. Services were again held in Association hall in the summer of 1881, by the Rev. Benjamin Gifford, the Rev. John J. Roberts, D.D. and the Rev. Arthur B. Conger. During the summer of 1882 services were held in Association hall by the Rev. Thos. G. Addison, D.D., the Rev. F. S. Harraden, the Rev. Samuel Edwards and the Rev. J. S. Beers. As a result of this renewed interest in the church a meeting was held July 17, 1882, and an Association formed for the purpose of raising money to build a chapel. Gen. Benjamin Alvord, U.S.A., was chosen Chairman; Col. Asa B. Carey U.S.A. and Laura, his wife, gave a lot of land, 50 x 100 feet, on Main street, opposite the Grove Hall house, on which to build the edifice. On Sept. 25, 1882, another meeting was held, at which articles of association and by-laws recommended by the Diocesan Convention of Massachusetts were adopted, and a permanent organization known as Grace Episcopal Church Congregation was formed. Dr. W. D. Stewart, U.S. Marine Hospital Service, was elected warden, Mr. Thos. H. Tuckerman was elected treasurer, and Miss Martha W. Daggett, secretary. It was announced by the treasurer that the sum of $1,000 had been subscribed. A building committee consisting of Dr. W. D. Stewart, Mr. T. H. Tuckerman, and Mr. H. W. McLellan was appointed.

On Tuesday, Sept. 26, 1882, the corner-stone of Grace Church was laid by the Rev. John J. Roberts, D.D., of New York. During its construction cottage services were held at the residence of Mr. Thos. Tuckerman, from Oct. 1, 1882, to June 3, 1883, by Dr. R. A. Ottiwell, lay reader. The Church was opened for divine service June 3, 1883, and on Friday, June 15, the building was duly consecrated by the Rt. Rev. Benjamin H. Paddock, D.D., Bishop of Massachusetts, assisted by the Revs. E. M. Gushee, B. R. Gifford, and John S. Beers. At this service a class of four persons was confirmed, and Holy Communion administered to fifty persons.

The records show that after this the following clergymen conducted the services in the next few years; the Rev. John J. Roberts, D.D., the Rev. H. H. Neales, the Rev. Jno. S. Beers, the Rev. Wm. S. Chase, the Rev. Jos. Dinsey, and in October, 1894, the Rev. Wm. Cleveland Hicks was appointed the first permanent resident clergyman in charge of the church. The Rev. Mr. Hicks resigned in September, 1898, to accept a call to St. Agnes' Church, New York. During the rectorate of Rev. Mr. Hicks the church building was moved from its original site on Main street to the corner of William and Woodlawn streets. The Rev. H. S. Habersham succeeded to the charge March, 1899, and served until September, 1900. The Rev. Harland H. Ryder was appointed to the charge in May, 1902, and resigned in January, 1904. Various clergymen and lay readers continued the services until Oct. 1, 1906, when the Rev. Wm. Doane Manross was appointed to the

GRACE CHURCH, VINEYARD HAVEN.

(INTERIOR VIEW.)

SHOWING CHANCEL WINDOW AND OTHER MEMORIALS.

charge, and is the present Rector. The whole island of Martha's Vineyard is now incorporated into one parish, and the rector of Grace Church, Vineyard Haven, has charge of all matters within the jurisdiction of the Episcopal church.

The church building was remodeled in 1901 by the addition of transepts and lengthening the chancel end of the nave, making the whole of cruciform shape. The enlarged church was dedicated on the tenth Sunday after Trinity of that year by the Arch-Deacon of New Bedford, the Rev. Samuel G. Babcock, assisted by a former rector, Rev. William C. Hicks. There were seven memorial gifts, one of which, a beautiful chancel window by Tiffany, was the gift of the family of Ellen Louisa Richardson and George Morey Richardson. It is the finest piece of stained glass work on the Vineyard, and represents, in life size, the risen Christ, in white vestments, coming forth from a garden of green and tinted foliage, with raised hand and finger pointing upward, as bearing an Easter message to his flock. Soft blue sky and distant hills in faint atmospheric haze complete a picture of singular impressiveness. The bell, prayer desk and chancel chairs were presented by Judge and Mrs. William H. Arnoux, in memory of their deceased children. The altar cross of polished and ornamented brass is a memorial to Rev. Henry Huntley Neales. An oaken font, a replica of the ancient stone font in the church of St. John the Baptist, Tisbury, England, in which was baptized (1593) Governor Thomas Mayhew, was presented by the family of the author of this history as a memorial to a deceased relative, Mrs. Hester Nash Myers, a devoted communicant of the church. A representation of it may be seen in Vol. I, p. 116, of this work. The communion rail, of moulded oak and ornamental brass standards, is a memorial to Emily Norwood de Forest Hicks and Lucy Cleveland Hicks, and the altar, of beautiful Gothic construction with carved columns and traceried panels, is a memorial to Emma Sheldon Strahan. In addition to these memorials, two mural tablets adorn the walls, one to Gen. Benjamin Alvord, U.S.A., and the other to Surgeon W. D. Stewart, both identified with the early foundations of this parish.

TAVERNS.

The first record of the granting of a license for a tavern on the Vineyard is found under date of March 26, 1677-8, when Lieut. Isaac Chase of Homes Hole was granted a license to keep "A Publike house." The following is the full record:

> Isaack Chase of Holmses hole is admitted to keep a publike house of Entertainment & to sell liquor &c by Retail except to the Indians and this to continue for two years at ten shillings per annum.

This house, situated in Vineyard Haven, then Homes Hole, was the residence of the progenitor of the Chase family on the Vineyard. The location of it is not accurately known, but it was about fifty yards north of the old Company Place barn, near which, in early days was the ferry stage for the boats that plied between Falmouth and Tisbury. Following the custom of so many elsewhere, Landlord Chase combined the calling of an inn-keeper with that of a ferryman.

Thomas Chase, who succeeded his father, as eldest son, and in the course of time, Abraham Chase, who probably built the "Great House," were inn-keepers at Homes Hole. Thomas was the ferryman, following in his father's wake, and with his sloop "Vineyard" piloted travelers to his inn by the beach. At the same time, Thomas West was granted a license in 1722 to be an innholder at Homes Hole; his tavern was the house in which he lived near the Marine Hospital.

In 1722, Thomas Chase having deceased, his widow Jane was licensed the next year in succession to her deceased husband, and the energetic widow maintained the inn until her second marriage in 1724, to Thomas Cathcart. Thomas Cathcart died in 1732, and in his will calls himself an "innholder," which indicates that he continued the business until his decease. The widow Jane survived till 1750, and presumably maintained the inn, where we may surmise that the dispenser of spiritual comfort to her guests and general factotum was her mulatto servant, Ishmael.

The "Great House" was doubtless the tavern kept by Abraham Chase. Among the patrons of the house were the sailors who came into Homes Hole, storm-bound, to find good cheer while waiting for fair weather. One of this class found here a bride, the inn-keeper's daughter, Hannah. The happy "Jack Tar" was Captain John Ferguson of Kittery, Maine, and probably they were married in that house in 1742. Their son John became a captain when he came to manhood. The "Great House," remaining in the hands of Abraham Chase, passed to his widow, who, marrying again, with her husband, Thomas Winston, transferred it in 1777 to Elijah Smith, Senior, and the latter sold it in 1796 to his son, Elijah. It remained a public house, it is believed, under the last named owner.

Thus it will be seen that the business of tavern keeping on the Vineyard in early days descended in family succession. The former generations of travelers to the Vineyard were thus able to return to familiar hearths and the convenient taprooms of Chase's at Homes Hole and Sarson's (later Worth's) at Edgartown, with a feeling of homecoming.

It may be safely believed that' 'Chase's" was not the only tavern, for the business of tavern-keeping was not confined to one or two persons. Very few of the old houses in our village have not been at one time or another a "licensed inn," and the occupation of bum-boating, fishing, and keeping tavern were combined by many. It will only be feasible to speak of the more prominent.

Another "innholder" of Homes Hole was Ebenezer Allen, son of Ichabod of Chilmark, who had married Sarah Chase. In 1745 he was first licensed as "innholder" of the constablewick of Homes Hole, and this fact should be interesting, because Maria Allen, one of the three "liberty pole" heroines, was his daughter, and we may easily suppose that this dashing young girl was the moving spirit in the life of the tavern kept by her father. Its location is not definitely known, but it was undoubtedly on the land set off to his wife in the division of the Chase property.

In 1759 John Baxter kept an ordinary in this town. Its location is not known, and as he was not a property owner, he presumably hired a house of Jonathan Manter for the carrying on of his business. The only reference to it is found in the Boston News Letter, issue of May 5, 1762. It says: —

> We hear from Marthas Vineyard that on the 29th of last month the house of Mr John Baxter, Tavern keeper at Holmes' Hole, was consumed by fire with most of the household furniture and goods that was therein. It was occasioned by a defect in the Chimney. The whole was consumed in eight minutes.

The tavern kept by Joseph Claghorn (b. 1753, d. 1805), in the house now owned by Deacon Holmes Athearn, was a famous one in its day, and the sign of it is still in existence, covered with paintings of various sizes of receptacles for liquids. After viewing the wide choice of measures, the traveler would hardly need the invitation of "Walk In," which accompanied these pictorial representations of the kind of cheer dispensed there. The only problem that might arise in his mind, after investigating these generous tankards, would be whether he could walk out.[1]

This Claghorn Tavern is also interesting because at one time Polly Daggett Hillman, another of the "liberty pole" heroines, lived there. Joseph Claghorn followed in the foot-

[1]The author has been told that this sign was suspended from an iron arm swung from a tall pole, after the manner of tavern signs, and not from the house.

steps of his grandfather, Thomas, who was an innkeeper at Eastville. The Branscomb house on Beach street was an inn before 1800 to about 1812, being the residence of a village factotum, Dr. Rufus Spaulding, who was doctor, postmaster, justice, village librarian, inn-keeper, and Master of the lodge of Masons. The adjoining lot was occupied by Jane, wife of Timothy Luce (1016), who also kept open house for wayfarers, a business that has been maintained for a century at the same place; the present Mansion house, our most pretentious modern hotel, rises over the cellar hole of the modest

SIGNBOARD OF THE JOSEPH CLAGHORN TAVERN.

inn of Mistress Luce. It was later kept by Matthew Butler. Forty years ago "Porte Crayon," the famous artist of Harper's Magazine at that period, visited our island and thus speaks of the Mansion house, then kept by the late Mrs. Nickerson: "A civil porter" he says "takes charge of our baggage and conducts us to the house of entertainment, kept by Mrs. Captain Leander West, an old-fashioned country inn, and as full of comfort, tidiness and snugness as all the old fashioned places are supposed to be.".

In the olden times it was customary for captains, supercargoes and passengers to come ashore and put up at the taverns, sometimes for weeks, while their vessels rode at anchor, wind-bound, in Homes Hole. Frequently these vessels carried persons who in later years became prominent, and it has been stated that Commodore John Paul Jones was a visitor to our haven under the above conditions, and was well remembered by "Aunt Sally" Claghorn.

"Smith's Tavern" was first kept by Silas Daggett (1757-1825), and afterwards by Captain David Smith (1757-1818). The house lately owned by Dr. William Leach was a tavern

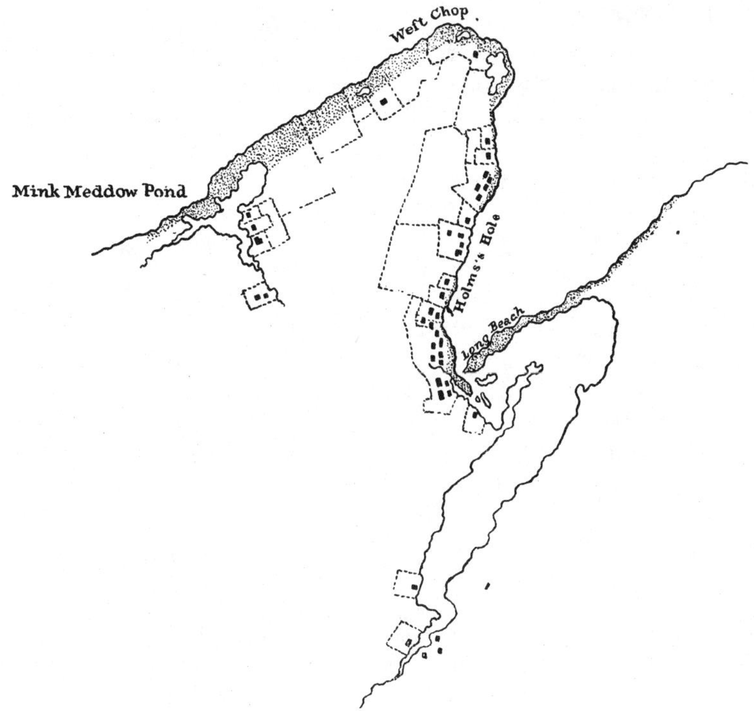

MAP OF HOMES HOLE, 1775.
FROM THE DES BARRES CHART.

of more modern times, known first as the Berkshire House, kept by Capt. Wm. Downs, and later as the County House, kept by James Shaw West.

Space will not allow of the particular enumeration of other and later taverns, the Dexter House on the beach, the Thomas Dunham house (where Joseph Chase follows the occupation of his ancestor as "mine host," nor of our latest creations, the Tashmoo Inn and The Cedars). The historian of the future must preserve their traditions.

The following named persons were licensed inn-holders in the precinct of Homes Hole by the County Court for the years specified:—

Isaac Chase, 1716-26; Jane Chase, widow, 1722-3; Thomas Cathcart, 1726-30; Jane Cathcart, his widow and successor, 1732; Thomas West, 1722-42; Abraham Chase, 1728-63; Thomas Chase, 1733; Samuel Daggett, 1736-7; Elisha West, 1741-64; Peter West, 1741; John Whelden, 1742; Thomas Claghorn, 1742-3; Ebenezer Allen, 1745-63; Shubael Butler, 1747-59; Joseph Allen, 1750; John Baxter, 1759-61; Jonathan Manter, 1761; Zaccheus Chase, 1764; John Holmes, 1765-71; Isaac Daggett, 1766-1804; Cornelius Norton, 1776-87; William Worth, 1798; Silas Daggett, 1798-1804; Thomas Dunham, 1799-1806; Rufus Spalding, 1802-6; David Smith, 1805-6.

PATHS, HIGHWAYS AND BRIDGES.

Beach Street.—This highway, usually called the ferry road, was the first to be officially laid out in February, 1763, and again in May, 1776, though it had been a town way since the beginning of that century. The ferry landing on Bass creek was at the foot of Beach street, and probably it was the first and only public street into the settlement at that time. The following record describes the way as laid out on the last named date:—

> . . . . .Beginning at the Great Gate afores'd and to run Easterly in The Southmost Cart Way that runs from sd Gate to the Harbour: said way to be Forty feet from the Furthermost Rut of sd Cart Way untill it comes to a heap of Stones near the Cherry Trees that stand to the Eastward of Mr. Abraham Chases Barn, and from that to the Harbour or water, as the Road or way now Runs: and from that to the Crick where the ferry boat now Lyes at the Stage Forty feet wide from high water mark.[1] . . . . .

In 1801 this street was resurveyed, and it was determined at that time where the landing stage of the ferry was formerly situated. "Which place," the committee stated, "is North 54° East from the top of the Chimney of Jedidah Coffin's dwelling House, and N. seventy degrees East from the Top of the Chimney of Robert Cottle's dwelling house."[2]

[1]Abraham Chase was given liberty to set up a gate across said way, "near where the Try House stood formerly, if he see cause." He was awarded two pounds damages. (Dukes Co. Court Records, May term, 1776.)

[2]Ibid., April term, 1801. These chimneys are yet standing, the Coffin house being now known as the Cromwell house, and the one next west (Crowell) was the West-Cottle house.

Main Street. — As the settlement grew northward a way was made by carts parallel to the shore. It was the usual "path" blocked by gates and bars at each cross fence, while at the junction with Beach street the Great Gate, so called, was erected, which shut off the entire Neck. This way was laid out in October, 1798, and the official record of its course is as follows: —

Beginning at North side of the Old Highway that leads from the Head of Homes Hole Harbor to the town of Tisbury the East Corner Post of Peter Butlers frunt Inclosure and from thence North 25 Degrees East till it comes to the Divisional Line between the Meeting House Lot on the North side thereof and Land of Wm. Smith to a stake. . . . . thence North 10 Degrees East to the East corner of Silas Daggett's frunt yard and to continue northerly by said Daggett yard to the North Corner thereof, thence North 2 Degrees East to a stone . . . . . between the Land of Isaac Daggett and the Land of Jonathan Manter thence North 2 Degrees west to a stone . . . . . two foot to the Westward of a black cherry tree standing opposite to the said Manter's House; thence North 10 Degrees West to a stone . . . . . on the north side of Manter's Land and to continue in the same direction across the Land of Thomas Wheldon to a stone . . . . . on the North side thereof. Thence North twelve degrees West to a stake . . . . . twenty-seven foot Westward from the Westernmost bound of Timothy Chases Fence as it now stands.

The above described line thus far to be the Westerly Bounds of said Road, and from said Line to take its breadth Easterly full twenty-seven feet in all its parts and windings.

And from the last described stake and stones to pass over said road Eastward to another stake and stones standing at Right Angles and twenty-seven feet Distant which is the easterly bounds of said Road, and from thence to continue Northerly as the Old Cart Way now goes, and parallel thereto, and three feet to the Eastward of the Eastermost Cart Rut, until it comes upon the land of John Holmes to a large crotched black oak tree . . . . . standing on the East side of said Cartway and something to the Northward of where the Path that leads to the house of the sd Holmes turns out of the sd Cart way and then from said black oak tree to continue on the same course on a straight line to a stake standing on the Beach at the Hollow (so called) and so to the Water or Harbor and to continue Northerly by the Harbor till it meets with the Head of the Point Pond (so called) and southerly till it comes to the foot of the Upland and to be in Breadth forty foot in all parts.[1]

It was ordered that it continue an open highway and no damages were assessed on the property improved by the survey.

No changes have been made in this layout since that date, but in 1818 there was a petition to the Court from the property holders for permission "to maintain a Gate across

[1]Dukes County Court Records, October term, 1798.

the County highway that leads from the head of Homes Hole harbour towards the West Chop . . . . . in the lands of the late Timothy Chase at or near the house of John Cleveland." This was granted and maintained for many years. It was not till 1889 that the road from the Slough to the Lighthouse was cleared and graded, its width marked and the surface dressed with shells. It is now a splendid highway its entire length.

Wharf Street. — Some time prior to 1834 the way leading from Main street to Union wharf was laid out. It began according to the record, "at the South westerley corner of Capt Charles Smiths lot and runing by said Smiths and Jonathan Luce Jr Land to high water mark the course to be S 89° E distance twenty three rods & Eight feet to a bound there Sett Making said road forty feet wide at the High water line and thirty feet wide at the head."[1]

High Street. — This street was laid out, and connection established with County road, in 1845, by the lane near the Methodist parsonage.

Centre Street. — Laid out in 1854 to Franklin street.

Franklin Street. — Laid out from Spring to Church streets 1854 and continued in 1891 to Woodlawn avenue.

Church Street. — Laid out in 1854 to Franklin Street.

Spring Street. — Laid out in 1854 to Franklin Street.

Water Street. — Laid out in 1855 from Beach to Wharf.

William Street. — This street received its name as a compliment to Captain William Daggett, prominent in town and church affairs. It was officially laid out in 1864, as far north as the lane leading by the old "Chapel" school house.

THE U. S. GOVERNMENT SERVICES.

THE POST OFFICE.

The first representative of the general government to be established here was the Post Office department, which appointed Isaac Daggett, on Jan. 1, 1795, as postmaster of Homes Hole. At that early time the office was in the residence or store of the occupant of the position, and it is probable that it was then in his store and tavern on Wharf street. He held this appointment only a brief time, and was succeeded

[1]Tisbury Records, 512.

CAPT. WILLIAM DAGGETT
1773–1858

Apirl 1, 1796, by Joseph Claghorn, who then lived in the Hillman house on Water street, where the office was probably carried. The position was held by Claghorn for exactly two years, and he was succeeded by Silas Daggett (115), who kept the tavern on the corner of Main and Centre streets. After him came Dr. Rufus Spalding, who was appointed Jan. 1, 1803, and took the office to his residence on Beach street. His successor was Theodosius Parsons, appointed March 23, 1812, and he held the office for sixteen years, keeping it in his house on Main street, opposite Spring street.[1] Capt. William Cottle (105) was the next postmaster, commissioned Jan. 28, 1828, and the office was located in his store adjoining his house on Main street, opposite Centre street. He died 1830, and it appears that the Postmaster General wrote to the people here to select a successor. The town records contain the following entry:—

> Voted by ballot for a suitable man to keep the post office in holmes hole in answer to a Request from the Postmaster General. Votes being brought in & counted for Charles West seven for William Downs one[2] [November 24, 1830].

This town meeting of eight voters had no effect upon the matter, for before they had solemnly met to vote, a successor was already appointed, Nov. 11, 1830, in the person of Capt. Shubael Dunham (257), who lived on the spot now occupied by the present post office, corner of Church and Main streets. He held the office till his death, in 1835, when he was followed by his son George Dunham (425), who was commissioned March 2, 1835, and held the office for over twenty-three years, the longest tenure of any of our postmasters. His successors have been as follows: Eliakim Norton, appointed Sept. 15, 1858; James Norton, Feb. 14, 1861; James D. Peakes, July 25, 1861; George N. Peakes, Nov. 7, 1881; John F. Robinson, Sept. 18, 1885; Horton Johnson, 1900-1902; Stephen Cary Luce, 1902 (present incumbent). After the fire of 1883 the office was located in Lane's block till the appointment of Mr. Luce, who removed it to the corner of Main and Church streets, where it now is.

In February, 1871, the Department sanctioned the change of the name of the office from Holmes Hole to Vineyard Haven.

[1]He was from Greenwich, Conn., and had served as a soldier in the Connecticut troops. He was in the Lexington alarm list, 1775, and served as a gunner in Col. Lamb's regiment of artillery. His enlistments covered the war from start to finish.

[2]Tisbury Records. 479.

CUSTOMS SERVICE.

In 1817 Homes Hole was made a sub-port of entry for Edgartown, in consequence of the growth of this place as a maritime centre. Prior to that, Capt. William Worth (65), was acting as customs officer here, until his removal in 1814 to Charlton, Mass. His nephew, Henry Pease Worth (72), was the first Deputy Collector, under appointment dated Nov. 29, 1817, and he held this position nearly fifty years. His office was in a building where the Public Library is now located, on Main street. He was succeeded, June 17, 1861, by Capt. Henry W. Beetle, a native of New Bedford, who held the office for nearly thirty years, until his death. The present incumbent, Lorenzo F. Luce, was appointed Aug. 16, 1890, and it will be noted as an unusual circumstance that for a period of over ninety years (1817-1908) there have been but three persons to occupy this office in succession.

MARINE HOSPITAL SERVICE.

This town was the first on the Vineyard to have a public hospital. The harbor of Homes Hole was much frequented in colonial days by sailing craft from all ports on the north and south Atlantic coasts, and diseases of a contagious character, like small pox, were frequently spread by the crews of vessels riding at anchor here, while weather-bound. In August, 1763, the town gave Dr. Samuel Gelston of Nantucket permission to "Cary on and Practice Inoculation of the Small Pox in Soume Suitable Place at Homeses hole" under certain provisions and restrictions. He was obliged to treat all cases of small pox landed here, "without any Demands from the Town their for," and further required to pay six shillings for every person inoculated "While he Practices in that Distemper." How long he carried this on is not known, but this arrangement was renewed the next year.[1] The location of the hospital is not of record, as it was only a temporary structure in all probability. In 1798 the Justices of the County Court petitioned the General Court of Massachusetts to erect a hospital for contagious diseases on the Vineyard, and suggested "that the West side of Homeshole Harbour would be much the most Convenient place for such a Building." But after securing an appropriation the committee located it at

[1]Tisbury Records, 183-5.

Eastville. Nothing further was done until 1822, when the town

Voted to Petition Congress to erect a Hospital in this Town for the reception of Distressed Seamen or make Some Provision for Seamen that may be landed here destitute of the means of Support.[1]

This failed to accomplish any result, and another was sent, April, 1826, to Congress, "praying that some provision might be made for the relief of the sick and disabled seamen arriving at this port."[2] The Secretary of the Treasury, who had charge of such matters under the law, directed the Collector of Customs at Edgartown to make some suitable arrangements. This was done immediately, and Dr. Daniel Fisher contracted to furnish subsistence, lodging, medical attendance and nursing for all cases that might be brought into port for the sum of $300 per annum. This arrangement apparently lapsed or was not properly carried out, as on Dec. 24, 1836, the Secretary wrote the Collector that "Complaints are made to the Department that no provision is made for the relief of sick and disabled seamen in that part of your District in which the harbor of Holmes Hole is situate."[3] He ordered the Collector to make the necessary arrangements, but it not known how the directions were carried out.

The Secretary of the Treasury, Hon. Levi Woodbury, on Dec. 11, 1837, in a report to the Senate on the subject, recommended that "a Marine Hospital be located at Holmes Hole or Edgartown or some other convenient point in the neighborhood of Marthas Vineyard." From 1853 to 1861 Dr. John Pierce had the contract for medical services, but his appointment caused dissatisfaction because of his residence in Edgartown. Numerous petitions were sent to the Department in 1854, asking for his removal and the appointment of Dr. Moses Brown, who resided here.[4] In 1856 Dr. Ralph K. Jones was an applicant for the appointment, but Dr. Pierce survived the campaign against him until 1862, when Dr. D. A. Cleveland obtained the office.[5] He was followed by Dr. William Leach, who erected a small hospital on the Edgartown road in 1866, especially for the treatment of sick seamen. This was an improvement over the old method of "farming

[1]Tisbury Records, 417. William Cottle and Captain Seth Daggett prepared the petition.

[2]Custom House Records, Edgartown.

[3]Records Treasury Department (M. H. S.) I, 92.

[4]Ibid., III, 235.

[5]Ibid., III, 500.

out" these cases, but it was still unsatisfactory, from an administrative standpoint, to the Department. Accordingly, in 1879, the late Surgeon General Hamilton, in charge of the Marine Hospital Service, made a personal visit to Vineyard Haven to inspect the situation. He secured as temporary quarters for sick seamen the abandoned lighthouse building at the head of the harbor, and converted it into a hospital.[1] It was opened on Nov. 28, 1879, under the charge of Acting Assistant Surgeon W. D. Stewart of the general service, and became a marine hospital and a station of the first class officially. This officer, who had greatly endeared himself to the community through a period of seven years, died October 30, 1886, and was succeeded temporarily by Assistant Surgeon Seaton Norman, and later as a regular detail by Passed Assistant Surgeon R. P. M. Ames (1886-1889). From this time forward the hospital has been under command of regularly commissioned officers as follows: Surgeon Charles E. Banks, 1889-92; Passed Assistant Surgeon Elisha R. Houghton, 1892-6; Passed Assistant Surgeon J. C. Perry, 1895 (temporary); Passed Assistant Surgeon Duncan A. Carmichael, 1896-7; Passed Assistant Surgeon Wm. J. S. Stewart, 1897-8; Assistant Surgeon Sherrard Tabb, 1898-9; (temporary)[2] Surgeon Frank W. Mead, 1899-1901; Surgeon Duncan A. Carmichael, 1901-5; Assistant Surgeon William C. Rucker, 1905-7; Acting Assistant Surgeon E. P. Worth, 1907 (temporary).

The present hospital building is of modern construction and recently built on additional land adjacent to the old lighthouse grounds. The following extract from the report of the Surgeon-General conveys particular information as to the new structure:—

> Through the assiduous efforts of Surgeon Charles E. Banks, then on duty at this station, Hon. Charles S. Randall, member of Congress from this district, and the Surgeon General, an item of $20,000 was included in the Sundry civil bill for the erection of a new hospital at this station, which bill became a law on March 4, 1891.
>
> Plans were prepared by the supervising architect, and the construction of the new hospital was begun on December 16, 1894. It was completed

[1]The building and grounds (50 x 380) were transferred by the Lighthouse establishment.

[2]This officer will be kindly remembered by the residents of Vineyard Haven for his bravery and untiring efforts in the dangerous work of rescuing shipwrecked sailors in the terrible storm of November, 1898, when 26 vessels were driven ashore and a number of the crew perished from cold and exhaustion in sight of the beach, almost beyond human help.

UNITED STATES MARINE HOSPITAL, VINEYARD HAVEN

COMPLETED IN 1895

in October, 1895, and furnished and opened for the reception of patients on December 30, 1895.[1]

The hospital station now incorporates the old lighthouse building and ward as a part of the establishment, these original buildings serving as apartments in the rear for employees, storerooms and other adjuncts of a hospital.

In the twenty-five years since its establishment, this hospital has treated about 6,500 sick and disabled seamen, an average of about 250 cases annually.

U. S. WEATHER BUREAU.

A station of this service was opened here in November, 1886, and the office established in the Mansion House by H. H. Curley as Observer. The headquarters for this meteorological district were at Nantucket. The late Lieut. Max Wagner, U.S.V., then in the Weather Bureau, succeeded as officer in charge, and he was followed by William W. Neifert (1890), Harvey B. Dick (1893), and Cornelius J. Doherty (1900), all of the general service. In 1895 the telegraphic business was sold to the Martha's Vineyard Telegraph Co., and the meteorological work discontinued, June 18, 1900, after being in existence fourteen years. The records of the station were sent to the Bureau in Washington, and an abstract copy deposited with the late Thurston W. Tilton for convenience of reference locally.

LIGHTHOUSE ESTABLISHMENT.

West Chop. — Under provision of an act approved March 3, 1817, by which the sum of $5,000 was appropriated therefor, a lighthouse was built on the point of West Chop, on the bluff.[2] Constant erosions of the shore by the swift tidal action at this exposed locality caused the government to remove it further back in 1830, and again in 1846 to its present position, for similar reasons.[3] Since the latter date the tower has been increased in height. It is a fixed white light, with a red sector, and a steam fog whistle is an auxiliary part of this important aid in the navigation of the Vineyard Sound.

[1]Annual Report Marine Hospital Service, 1896.

[2]U. S. Statutes, III, 360; VI, 192.

[3]Jurisdiction was ceded by the state in 1817 and 1830. (Acts and Resolves ann. cit. II and III.)

The keepers have been three in the past ninety years: James West, 1818-48; Charles West, 1849-68; Charles P. West, 1869 to present time.

Harbor Light. — In the appropriation act of March 3, 1851, the establishment of a harbor or range light at the head of Homes Hole was authorized, and $3,500 made available therefor.[1] Jurisdiction was not ceded for two years by the state, and then a two-story house with a small lantern tower[2] was built in 1854 on the edge of the bluff, in front of the U. S. Marine Hospital. Originally there were three range lights connected with the house, but they were abandoned for one in the cupola. Matthew P. Butler was the first light keeper, and he was succeeded by Moses T. Cromwell. It was abandoned about 1875, and in 1879 was transferred to the Marine Hospital service. In recent years a red lantern, suspended nightly from a flag staff of the hospital, acts as a substitute range light for entering the harbor.

INDUSTRIES.

Salt Works. — At the time of the Revolution there were large pans on the shores of Bass creek, where salt was manufactured by the ancient method of evaporation of sea water. They were in existence in 1840, and others at or near the herring creek, owned by Isaac Luce, were erected at least twenty years previously.

Whale Fishery. — This town had an indirect connection with this business through its seafaring men, who went out as masters or sailors of vessels outfitted elsewhere, but there was no local establishment for the accommodation of whalers.[3] In 1850 three vessels engaged in this industry were owned here, the ships *Ocmulgee* and *Pocahontas* and the bark *Malta*, representing an investment of $68,000, which had brought a return of $125,378 that year. This industry has today its representatives resident in Vineyard Haven, Captain Leander Owen, a whaler of the old sailing craft days, survivor of the great Arctic disaster of 1871, whose eyesight was permanently injured by Arctic "ice blindness," and Captain Hartson H.

[1] U. S. Statutes, IX, 627.

[2] Acts and Resolves, 1853, p. 72. The building was used as a residence by the keeper and his family.

[3] There was a Try house near Beach street before 1800, but it had become disused by that date. It was probably erected for trying out the oil from whales.

Bodfish, now a successful leader in the steam whaling business of the present-century methods.

The merchant service, however, has been the principal field of activity for this community from the earliest times. The men of Homes Hole, young and old, have ventured afar on the seven seas for generations, have carried our flag to the most distant parts of the navigable globe. To name them would be almost a census of its male inhabitants in every decade.

Herring Fishery. — The fine herring run and fishery at Ashappaquonsett has been a famous and prolific domestic industry from time immemorial, and it is a common heritage of the townsmen unto this day. But it represents a century of wasted opportunity for the development of an industry productive of revenue for the town. As an annual free-for-all spoliation it neither benefits the few nor profits the town as a whole, as managed in the past.

Harness Factory. — In 1872 a harness factory was established by R. W. Crocker and from small beginnings, grew to be a large and valuable industry. At times nearly a hundred people found employment through its operations, directly or indirectly. It was incorporated in 1892 as the Crocker Harness Company, under new management, but after a short career suspended operations and finally went out of business. The building remained unoccupied for a number of years, and was finally destroyed by fire.

Corn Mill. — A steam grist mill was established on Water street in 1881 by William J. Rotch and is yet in operation, under the management of William P. Bodfish.

Leather Embossing. — A factory for the embossing of leather in artistic designs for ornamental purposes was established by the Luxemoor Co., operating under letters patent. The head of this enterprise was William Barry Owen as financial backer. It closed down in 1908, and is now a thing of the past.

EDUCATIONAL MATTERS.

There is nothing in the town records, or other documents to show that the schools had any place in the thoughts of the town before 1737, though we may surely suppose that something had been done in this line which is not of record. One of the West family, Thomas (20), had been graduated from

Harvard in 1730, and he must have received his preliminary education here. The first town record, under date of Feb. 14, 1736-7, provides a school "the Remaining part to Compleat a year (two months) to be keept at some Convenient place at Homeses Hole," and Abner West was the committeeman for that year.[1] No further reference occurs till 1749, when a similar provision was made,[2] and again in 1752 the school was "to be keept at Homeses hole two Months."[3] A quarter of a century elapses before another allusion is made to schools, in December, 1776:—

> Thirdly it was Likewise Voted at Said meeting that the People of Homseshole in the Districts of Tisbuary are to be provide a School for themselves to Extend Westward as far as Thomas Smiths sam'l Looks Silvanus Luces and to Draw their proportion of Monney Out of the Treasury for Said School for Three Years Ensuing the Date hereof[4]

In 1792, the next record, this village was made the 4th School District of Tisbury, and the ensuing year Samuel Look, Timothy Chase and Abraham Chase were appointed the school committee.[5] These infrequent references, half a dozen in a century of existence, give meagre details on this topic, but the context implies continuity.

In the first year of the 19th century the town raised $250 for schools, but the proportion for this precinct was not calculated; probably about $100 would closely proximate the allotment. In 1821 it was $112.67; in 1830 it was $215.54; in 1840 it was $313.17; in 1850 it was $600 (estimated); in 1860 it was $800 (estimated); in 1871 it was $2,404.95; in 1901 it was $3,603.50; an increase of thirty fold in the century with half as many scholars. The attendance has ranged from 329 in 1821 to 298 in 1830; 152 in 1872 and 160 in 1900, a reduction of over fifty per cent. in that period.

The location of school-houses, like all matters pertaining to the early annals of education in the town, is lost in the obscurity of the past. Probably the first school-house was erected at the junction of Beach street and the County highway, but when it was built is not of record. It was called the South school after 1829, when the town was divided into two districts, and the second school-house was built, probably in

[1]Tisbury Records, 102.
[2]Ibid., 130.
[3]Ibid., 144.
[4]Ibid., 218.
[5]Ibid., 286.

that year or the next.[1] This new school building was the "Chapel" so called, now the home of the Sea Coast Defence Chapter, D.A.R. In 1850 there was a third school-house built on the West Chop road, opposite the Slough. The present commodious building on Church street accommodates the primary, intermediate, grammar, and high school grades. It was enlarged in 1900, fitted with modern sanitary and hygienic furnishings, and is a model suburban school, houses all the scholars in town and furnishes instruction in the highest grade for pupils from other towns.

The names of teachers employed in the early times are not recorded. Joseph Claghorn (162) was the first known "Schoolmaster" in the town, probably from his coming here (about 1788) to his death (1805), and he taught in the old South school. Nathan Mayhew (801), a native of Chilmark, born 1798, was the next school-teacher of note. He had removed with his father to Farmington, Me., about 1808, but returned about 1825, and settled in this town as a teacher in the public school. He owned and occupied the house recently in the possession of Captain James Lawrence Smith, and the new school-house across the lane was the scene of his labors as a pedagogue for a quarter of a century. He removed to Norton, Mass., about 1853, and later lived in Boston. He died in 1865 at Milton, Mass. at the residence of his son, Rev. Wm. H. Mayhew (now of Yarmouth Port), and his body was buried in Milton cemetery.

Contemporaneously, the Rev. Seth Ewer, the Baptist preacher, taught the South school and subsequent to them came J. Dana Bullen, John Gower, Rev. J. C. Boomer, George B. Muzzey, S. W. Hathaway, E. K. Parker, Charles E. Mosher, Judge Hammond, now of the Superior Court of Massachusetts, Thurston W. Tilton (1874 to 1898 at intervals), H. H. Lovell, Timothy P. Weeks, Louis A. Fales and Arthur C. Clarke.

As in the other towns, there were many teachers of private schools in the course of the past century. Chief of these must be mentioned the late Abigail W. Daggett (b. 1798), who taught in the forties and fifties.

GROVE HILL SEMINARY.

A private school for girls was established in 1870 by Rev. Horace B. Marshall, at that time in pastoral charge of the

[1]An extra sum was raised for schools in 1829 and 1830, probably for this new house, though not so specified.

Baptist church in this village. The venture was only partially successful after several years' trial, and the building passed into the possession of the late Joseph Nickerson and his wife, Love (Robinson) Nickerson, who used it as a hotel. It was called the Grove Hill house during this period, and after the death of the proprietors became the property of the late Major C. R. Barnett, U.S.A. It was then remodeled for a private residence, and is now a part of the Barnett estate.

MISCELLANEOUS ANNALS.

PHYSICIANS.

The first practitioner of medicine on the Vineyard, Dr. Thomas West, was a resident of this town, and three of his descendents in the male line have followed in his professional footsteps here, Elisha West, Elisha West, Jr., and Silas West. Dr. Benjamin Trask came here from Sandwich before 1800, and practised until his death (1821). He resided on Main street, on the site of Eagleston Block. Dr. Rufus Spalding (1800-1812) was his contemporary and rival in medicine, politics and religion. Dr. Forsyth was settled here before 1832, and about the same date Dr. Leroy Milton Yale, father of the late distinguished New York physician of the same name, came to practise here. In the next decade came David Crossthwaite, a native of England, who died (1849) early in life. In 1850 there were five physicians resident in town, George N. Hall from Baltimore, Md., Moses Brown from Kensington, N.H., Nathaniel Ruggles from Rochester, Mass., and his son, Charles A. Ruggles, and Ralph K. Jones, a young graduate from Stockbridge, Mass. Ten years later George T. Hough was the leading physician. Following him came William Leach (1863) and Winthrop Butler (1868), the latter a native of the village and fresh from arduous duties in the Civil war. Of him it is a duty and a pleasure for the author to record a brief narration of his life and labors in this community. He was born June 25, 1838, the son of Matthew P. and Martha Allen (Robinson) Butler, and received his preliminary education here in the public schools. One year was spent at Cushing's Family school in Middleboro, Mass. (1858), and another (1859) at the Dukes County Academy in the completion of his education in the higher branches. He chose the medical profession for his life work, but his

DR. WINTHROP BUTLER

1838–1907

studies were interrupted by the Civil war, and he entered the Navy for service in the medical department, ranking as an Assistant Surgeon. He served three years in the Gulf Squadron, until the close of the war. Then he resumed his course, and was graduated March 6, 1866, from Harvard Medical school. After practising for one year in Groveland, Mass. (1867), he returned to his native town, and thenceforth devoted himself to a practice which covered the western half of the Vineyard.

In 1903 he suffered a paralytic stroke, and it was the warning signal to him to lay down the exhaustive work of a widespread country practice, and do for himself what he had for thirty-five years so ungrudgingly done for others. Thenceforth he lived in quiet retirement, greeted daily, as he was able to go about, by the affectionate salutations of all who knew him, until on April 22, 1907, a career narrowed only by the natural opportunities of its insular limits, but none the less noble by its perfection of achievements and ideals, passed into the memory of his friends and became a splendid heritage for this community. He was the typical physician of the. "old school" of gentlemen, courteous in every relation of life, generous to a fault, charitable in his estimates and splendid in his standards of action. His portrait opposite this, gives an index of the handsome head, which was well carried by his tall graceful figure, and it will serve to us of his day and generation as a reminder of this fine, gentle, manly spirit, this skilful, loyal, well beloved physician.[1]

Dr. Charles F. Lane and Orlando S. Mayhew are the present representatives of this profession in Vineyard Haven.[2]

CEMETERIES.

Crossways. — This "acre" contains the oldest interments in the town, beginning with the year 1717, the date of the earliest remaining stone, but it is probable that it was in use some years before that, although Dr. Thomas West, who died here in 1706, and his wife (d. 1724) are buried in West Tisbury. It was located on the West property, and probably was given to the town for a public burial place. In 1756

[1]The Duodecimo Club of Vineyard Haven, of which he was the president, contributes this portrait to the Annals of Tisbury as a tribute to his memory.

[2]Dr. Frank B. Look (1858-1908), a native of West Tisbury, established a sanitarium in this town in 1905, remodeling the Owen house for the purpose, but his death in 1908 terminated his career after three years of labor in founding the institution.

Abner West donated an acre to the "People of Homes Hole" on the Edgartown road, "to build a meeting house upon, or Scoule house or to bury our dead in."[1] It is not known whether this gift was accepted for the purposes specified.

Franklin Street. — In the rear of Association hall is a burying ground on the corner of Centre and Franklin streets, occupied as such before 1800, and increased in size in 1803 by a gift from Abraham Chase.[2] The oldest stone in this ground is that of Abigail, wife of Isaac Daggett, who died in 1770, but the inscription states that the body was removed, in 1805, from the family burying ground. The oldest stone, after this, is dated February, 1803, and most of the older stones range from 1805 to 1817.

Oak Grove. — This latest addition to the town's cemeteries is on the old highway from the village to West Tisbury, and was first acquired in 1863 and plotted for use. The original owner, Edward T. T. Smith, engaged in this as a private venture, and in 1869 he sold his interests to James Lyon Luce. In 1886, the heirs of the late James Lyon Luce sold it to Stephen Carey Luce and Henry H. Smith, and acquiring adjacent property laid out additional lots according to plans drawn by John H. Crowell.[3] On May 2, 1900, this was conveyed by the owners to the Town of Tisbury, and the ground is now under the care of commissioners elected by the town. Since then additional land has been acquired, the ground suitably fenced, and an ornamental stone gateway completes the attractiveness of this resting place for the town's dead. The cemetery now contains about twenty-four acres.

Private Grounds. — The Holmes–Dunham plot on the West Chop road, has been occupied since 1791. The famous John and Lydia Claghorn stone is in a separate enclosure on the heights back of the hospital, and a stone to Seth Daggett, who died of small pox in 1779, is on the Tashmoo farm.

FORTIFICATIONS.

There are no annals of a military nature in connection with this town that are worthy of record, except some earthworks constructed during the Revolution. They were situated

[1]Dukes Deeds, VIII, 437.

[2]Ibid, XV, 27. The deed of 133 rods began at the "corner of the Land now and formerly occupied as a Burying Ground."

[3]Dukes Deeds, LXXVI, 572.

just north of the Seamen's chapel (Stevens) on the harbor side, and a similar breastwork was thrown up on the Sound shore. It is probable that they were nothing more than trenches for the protection of musketeers.[1]

THE MASONIC LODGES.

King Solomon's Lodge in Perfection 1783. — The first lodge of Free and Accepted Masons to be organized on the Vineyard was chartered in this town under the title of "King Solomon's Lodge in Perfection" in 1783, by the thrice illustrious Bro. Moses Michael Hayes, Deputy Inspector General, S. R., for North America.[2] It was authorized to confer fourteen degrees through the Royal Arch, in addition to its functions as a lodge of Master Masons.

The Scottish Rite Masons in America derived their authority from the order in France, established in Paris, under the title of The Sovereign Lodge of St. John of Jerusalem. The Grand Lodge of Free Masons of France, in conjunction with this Scottish Rite body, issued to Stephen Morin, in 1761, a joint warrant to establish symbolic and Scottish Rite lodges in America. Morin first went to the West Indies, where he instituted lodges and granted charters in several of the colonies belonging to this archipelago. In Jamaica he met Moses Michael Hayes, a Portuguese Jew, and Morin conferred upon him the title and powers of Deputy Inspector General of the Scottish Rite for North America. Hayes first went to New York and later to Newport, R. I., where he instituted a symbolic lodge called King David. Little was known then about Free Masonry, and the higher degrees were looked upon with suspicion, even by the Blue Lodge Masons. Hayes finally removed to Boston, where he soon became identified with the existing order, working under the Grand Lodge of England, and through the influence of John Warren (brother of Gen. Joseph) he dropped the new-fangled Scottish Rite work and was made Grand Master of Massachusetts in recognition of his labors for the craft.

[1]In a remarkable document prepared for English reading by Col. Beriah Norton when he was prosecuting the claim for repayment of the value of cattle, &c., taken by General Grey, and trying to impress the British authorities with the loyalty of the people of Martha's Vineyard, he stated that these works were constructed by soldiers from the mainland, to keep the people of the Vineyard under subjection to the rebel government!!

[2]This curious name was bestowed to distinguish it from a lodge elsewhere having the name of King Solomon.

The earliest documentary evidence of the life of this Royal Arch lodge has recently been found, dated May 16, 1787, and is a certificate of membership, engrossed, and signed by the Master and Wardens. It is worth printing verbatim because of its prime importance as establishing the status of the lodge so early.

> And the darkness Comprehended it not.
>
> In the East a place of Light where Reigns Silence and Peace.
>
> Wee the Master, Wardens, and Secretary of the Royal Arch King Solomon's Lodge held at Edgartown in the Commonwealth of Massachusetts do certifie that the bearer hereof our worthy Brother Arthur Fenner has been Regularly Initiated into the third Degree of Masonry.
>
> As such he has been Received by us; and being a True and faithful Brother, he is hereby recommended to the faver and prote'n of all free and accepted Masons wheresoever Dispersed.
>
> In witness whereof we have Caused the Seal of our said Lodge to be afixed this sixteenth day of May in the year of our Lord 1787 and of Masonry 5787.
>
> John Cooke, Mr.
> John Peas, S. W.
> Daniel Read, J. W.
> Arthur Fenner. Benj. Smith, Sec'y.

While it is believed that this lodge was instituted in 1783, yet the actual proof is not available.

The language of the certificate raises some interesting questions. It will be noticed that the location of the lodge is omitted, while the meeting was "held at Edgartown," and that all the officers are residents of that town. It is not supposed that there was a lodge room or building used exclusively by Masons for their meetings at this time. It was customary elsewhere to hold these communications in taverns or private houses, and doubtless this was the situation here, and we may suppose the lodge met both at Edgartown and Homes Hole to accommodate the brethren. The lodge is specifically called "of Homes Hole," in 1797, and for that reason it may be assumed to have always belonged here by its official location, and that the brethren met in Eastville and Tisbury at the taverns of these localities. Both towns bordered on Homes Hole, but the settlement on the west side was always known as the precinct or village of Homes Hole.[1]

No records of this lodge are known to be in existence, and but fragmentary references to it remain. In 1797 a new charter was granted by the Grand Lodge of Massachusetts, and in 1799 a complaint was filed against it with the supreme officers, but nothing is known of its character and nothing appears to have been done.

In 1798 Abijah Luce was W. M. and in 1802 the following officers are of record: W. M., Dr. Rufus Spalding; S. W., Elijah Hillman; J. W., Jonathan Luce; Sec., Benjamin Smith; Treas., Jesse Luce; Tiler, Jesse Luce, Jr. Other known members at this period were David Pease, Levi Pease, Thomas Cooke, Paul Dunham, Lot Luce, Samuel Luce, Silas Daggett and John Pease. These names include residents of Edgartown as well as Tisbury. Dr. Spalding was the Master in 1807, and it is probable he continued as such until his departure from Holmes Hole five years later.[1]

The lodge was represented in the Grand Lodge each year, at the annual communications, usually by a proxy, but after 1812 it ceased to send anybody regularly and fell into arrears. This condition lasted until 1820, when the report of the District Deputy of the 12th Masonic district states: "King Solomon's Lodge in Perfection at Holmes Hole is 8 years in arrears and has manifested a spirit of insubordination inconsistent with their obligations and the known and acknowledged principles of Masonry." A committee was appointed to investigate the status of the lodge and they reported that it had held no meetings for about eight years. Elijah Hillman, who was probably the W. M. in succession to Dr. Spalding, in a letter to the D. D. G. M. for the 12th District, admitted the conditions reported, but threatened, by implication, if the Grand Lodge

[1]Masonic Observer, March 7, 1910. The original certificate is in the possession of the Masonic Library Association, of Minneapolis, Minn. The name of the Master, John Cooke, is believed to be an error for Thomas Cooke, who is known to have been a member of the lodge in later years. There was no John Cooke then residing in Edgartown. The size of the document is about six by eight inches, and the seal referred to is a square piece of paper, affixed diagonally to the upper left corner by a wafer. The text is enclosed in a border of double lines. It is not known to whom the certificate is made, as no person of that name resided here as far as can be learned. There were several Arthur Fenners living in Rhode Island in 1790, but why the person came to the Vineyard to join a lodge when one existed in Newport, is not understood.

[1]Kendall Travels, II, 183.

revoked their charter, to continue to work the degrees under the original charter granted by Hayes.

At the quarterly communication of the Grand Lodge held December 27, 1822, it was reported that this lodge, after being many years in arrears, had finally surrendered its charter and gone out of existence. The records and jewels of the lodge were surrendered to the Grand Lodge, and were destroyed at the burning of the Masonic Temple in Boston.

Martha's Vineyard Lodge, 1859.—Twenty-five years elapsed before the interest in the craft was revived. At that date (1852) but three members of the old King Solomon's Lodge survived, and when approached by a recent arrival in the town, a Mason, Mr. Joseph T. James, with a proposition to reorganize, they could not be persuaded to join the movement. After some time this zealous brother interested Captain Benjamin Clough, Henry Bradley, Alexander W. Smith, Dr. William Leach, Daniel F. Worth and Alexander Newcomb to apply to Marine Lodge, Falmouth, for the necessary degrees. After these men were made Master Masons in that Lodge, application for a dispensation to work was presented to the Grand Lodge and granted.[1] A lodge-room was fitted up in Hiram Nye's paint shop (near the Martha's Vineyard Bank building) at a cost of $1000, and in September, 1859, these seven brothers, with James as Worshipful Master, Clough as Senior Warden, and Bradley as Junior Warden restored speculative Masonry to its respected place in the community. A charter was granted Sept. 12, 1860, and from that time the growth of the lodge was rapid, until at the close of the term of Mr. James as Master in 1863 it had about seventy members. In the half century of its life the lodge has prospered through much adversity and many discouragements. In 1883 a new lodgeroom was just completed at large outlay, when the great fire of that year swept it out of existence after one meeting had been held in it. With it went the records and jewels. After recovering from the disaster a room was fitted up over Swift Brothers' store on Main street, and there the regular meetings were held for twelve years. In 1895 a charter member, Capt. Daniel F. Worth, who had returned to his old home after an absence of thirty-five years, urged the acquisition of a building which should be owned exclusively by the lodge, and as a result of his efforts the old Capawock hall was pur-

[1]Mr. James states that he "labored hard to have the old records and jewels of King Solomon's lodge restored, but the Grand Lodge would not give them up."

chased and remodeled interiorly to meet the special needs of the order, at considerable added cost.[1] It was dedicated Oct. 25, 1895, with the elaborate ritual of the order by the Grand Master of Massachusetts, assisted by other Grand officers.

The Masters of the lodge since the charter have been: Joseph T. James, 1859-63; Benjamin Clough, 1863-4; Henry Bradley, 1865-6; William Leach, 1867; J. Wheldon Holmes, 1868; William Leach, 1869; S. A. Thomas, 1870-2; Henry W. Beetle, 1873-5; William Leach, 1876; Andrew Hillman, 1877-8; Matthew L. Smith, 1879-80; Gilbert L. Smith, 1881-90; John H. Crowell, 1891; Charles F. Chadwick, 1892; Gilbert L. Smith, 1893; William W. Neifert, 1894-6; William D. Harding, 1897; Herbert N. Hinckley, 1899; Henry W. McLellan, 1901; William J. Look, 1905; and Alvin H. Cleveland, 1906.

SUBMARINE TELEGRAPH, 1856.

The first cable to be laid between this island and the main land had its shore connection at West Chop, and it was constructed by the Cape Cod Telegraph Co. as a part of their existing system.[2] This was in 1856, and the particulars of this important event are here detailed.

The steamer *Neptune* with a party of invited guests sailed from Boston, and on the following morning, July 16, 1856, took in tow, in Homes Hole harbor, the schooner Wm. T. Conquest of New York. The schooner was placed in position at Woods Hole and commenced paying out cable, which in two and a half hours was satisfactorily laid from Woods Hole to the West Chop, a distance of five miles.

Upon its arrival the village presented a scene of unwonted animation and excitement. The connection of the island with the main was celebrated with various festivities, and more than a thousand persons were gathered to participate in the enjoyment of the occasion. At two o'clock a procession was formed under the direction of Mr. Thomas Barrows, marshal of the day, which, escorted by the New Bedford Brass Band,

[1]The lodgeroom on the second floor is 34 x 48 feet, with the usual anterooms. On the ground floor there is a banquet hall 25 x 34 feet with kitchen, toilet, coat room and smoking room. The interior is finished throughout with southern pine, and ample heating arrangements make this one of the best suburban lodge buildings in the State. The name of Capt. Gilbert L. Smith should be associated with that of Capt. Worth in the project of acquiring and improving the property.

[2]See Vol. I, 466.

marched through the principal streets of the town to the grove where the tables were laid for the dinner. About four hundred ladies and gentlemen sat down to the tables, more than twice that number being assembled in the grove. After the viands had been fully discussed, the president of the day, Capt. Thomas Bradley, briefly addressed the assembly, tendering those who were strangers a hearty welcome to the Vineyard, and congratulating all upon the successful completion of the union of the island and the main. He then introduced the toast master, Capt. Enoch Cook, Jr., who read the first regular toast, as follows:—

"Our Prodigal Sons, we hail their return from much wandering with joy and to-day greet them with the best the house affords." This toast was responded to by Chas. A. Luce, Esq., of New York, a native of the Vineyard.

The next toast was: "The memory of Franklin. He aided in our political separation from our Mother country, may his more modern successor in electric science soon unite America, not only with England, but with all the world." This toast was eloquently responded to by James B. Congdon, Esq., of New Bedford. Mr. Congdon alluded to the fact that Franklin was connected with the Vineyard through his grandfather, Peter Folger, who was the first schoolmaster on the Island.

The third toast: "To the inventor of the system of electro-telegraphic communication," called up Dr. Chas. T. Jackson of Boston, who gave a succinct and lucid history of the electric telegraph.

Toasts were given also to the "Cape Cod Telegraph Co.," to the "Press," the "Union," "Massachusetts" and "New York," all of which were fittingly responded to, the last two by Mr. Bates of Plymouth Rock, and Mr. W. L. Burroughs of New York, vice-president of the New York and Washington Printing Telegraph Company, "a man of infinite jest and most excellent fancy," well known upon the Vineyard, "where he has troops of friends," as appears by the contemporary account of the celebration.

Numerous volunteer toasts were made and responded to. The last sentiment was given by Mr. J. T. Allen of Dorchester, who, with characteristic gallantry, gave "The Marthas of the Vineyard, the true galvanic power that moves the world."

In the evening Messrs. Edge of Jersey City made a grand display of fireworks upon a hill just outside the town. The display was beautiful and brilliant and won loud plaudits from the spectators.[1]

The cable was in use about five years.

THE GREAT FIRE.

On Saturday night, Aug. 11, 1883, occurred the greatest disaster in the history of the town. A fire started in the harness factory, and before it could be smothered the whole building was ablaze. Quickly the adjoining structures caught fire, and before an hour had elapsed it was seen that a disastrous conflagration was in full sweep. The destroying flames took a southerly direction, burning many buildings on Main street on both sides its entire length. A property loss of more than $100,000 was involved in this conflagration, a terrible blow to the small village. It was the greatest disaster in the annals of the island.

When the last embers had died out it was found that the Baptist meeting-house, 32 dwelling houses, 26 stores, 12 barns, and 2 stables had been burned to the ground. A damage more irreparable was done to the beautiful shade trees on the Main street and others covered by the burnt district, as these noble trees were all killed by the flames. Such a blow might well have staggered and discouraged any community, but the present beautiful village arisen from the ashes is an evidence of the bravery of its people. Having little outside assistance except for temporary necessities, the residents got together to restore their destroyed buildings. With characteristic energy Mr. R. W. Crocker, the proprietor of the harness factory, began work on a new structure while the unburnt timbers were yet smouldering, and others followed in quick order. The quaint street had vanished, but a new line of buildings soon arose on the old thoroughfare.

SOCIAL AND LITERARY ORGANIZATIONS.

A number of organizations in this town, having for their object the direct personal benefit of the members and the general welfare of the community indirectly, merit brief mention in its annals.

The Public Library. — There was one library of 200 volumes in 1850 connected with the school system, probably

[1]Boston Traveller of July 17, 1856, abstracted from a letter giving an account of the celebration of the laying of the Submarine Telegraph to Martha's Vineyard, dated at Homes Hole, July 16, 1856.

the first public collection of books in the town. In the autumn of 1878 Miss Hannah T. Bradley organized a number of young ladies into a society called the Ladies' Library League, and in March, 1879, their books (71 volumes) were first made available for public use upon payment of a weekly charge for each loan.[1] Four years later, at the date of the great fire, they had accumulated 483 volumes, with necessary library furniture and equipment, and these were all lost in the night of that disaster. The members took immediate measures to replace their loss, with the aid of a small insurance, and in May, 1884, new rooms were opened, specially fitted for their use by the late Dr. Winthrop Butler, over his office and drug store. In the spring of 1895 steps were taken to dissolve the League and turn over the collection to the town as a public library, under the provision of the statutes governing such matters. The library numbered at this time about 2500 volumes, the accretions of the past eleven years.[2] With appropriate exercises, participated in by some of the original founders of the League, the Public Library of Tisbury was formally opened, July 31, 1895, and since that date it has grown in usefulness and strength. It now numbers 3000 volumes on its shelves.

Mrs. John R. McArthur, a daughter of the late Judge Arnoux has announced her intention this year (1909) of donating land on Main street for the uses of a public library.

Duodecimo Club.— This organization, composed of twelve gentlemen, as its name indicates, was launched in the spring of 1891, through the efforts of Dr. Charles E. Banks, to bring together the leading men of the community for mutual improvement. The club meets monthly, usually at the residences of the members in rotation, and the members present papers on subjects selected by themselves, and the meeting is then open for general discussion. This is followed by a light lunch and social intercourse. The club has been in existence for eighteen years, maintaining with continued vigor and activity a high standard in the literary life of the town.

Sea Coast Defence Chapter, D.A.R. — This flourishing chapter of the Daughters of the American Revolution was organized in 1896, after preliminary interest in the movement

[1]The first officers were: President, Miss Hannah T. Bradley; Vice President, Miss Annie Daggett; Secretary, Mrs. Mary Morgan.

[2]Of this number about half came to it as a gift, the books from the library of the late Rev. D. W. Stevens.

had been aroused by Mrs. Florence M. Banks, a member of the organization in another state. It was chartered Oct. 30, 1896, and now numbers 62 members. In 1904 the Chapter acquired the old Mayhew school-house, the "Chapel" of 1830, and converted it into headquarters for the organization, and a museum of historic and local relics. It has now a large and valuable collection of such articles, which is constantly increasing in interest by the donations of members and friends. In 1898 the Chapter erected a flag staff in front of this building, on which a bronze tablet was placed, commemorative of the Liberty Pole incident of Revolutionary days. This tablet bears the following inscription: —

TO COMMEMORATE THE PATRIOTISM
OF THREE GIRLS OF THIS VILLAGE
POLLY DAGGETT
PARNELL MANTER
MARIA ALLEN
WHO DESTROYED WITH POWDER A
LIBERTY POLE, ERECTED NEAR THIS SPOT
TO PREVENT ITS CAPTURE BY THE
BRITISH IN 1776,
THIS POLE, REPLACING THE OTHER
IS ERECTED BY THE
SEA COAST DEFENCE CHAPTER, D. A. R.
1898.

Nobnocket Club. — A social club for gentlemen was organized Oct. 4, 1902, under the name of Nobnocket Club. It has a commodious house fitted for this special purpose on the harbor front, containing billard room, card room, reading room and sleeping chambers for guests.

TISBURY IN 1908.

This town is now two hundred and thirty-seven years old, and although but a moiety of the original territory is now comprised in it, yet it has prospered and developed wonderfully in that period. The following statistics show the material condition of the town as it exists at this time: personal estate assessed, $154,475.00; real estate assessed, $1,178,667.00; total, $1,333,142.00. The total tax assessed May 1, 1908, was

$14,476.37; acres of land, 3,878; number of dwelling houses, 420; horses, 152; cows, 62; taxpayers, 647, of whom 95 are polls only.

The town has real and movable property to the value of $11,900.00, including schools, fire apparatus, etc. In addition to this the town owns, by purchase in 1907 at a cost of $95,000.00, the public water works, the Tashmoo Spring, the purest water supply in the state, which is one of the town's most valuable assets.

THE OLD MILL,
1795.
MILL HILL, VINEYARD HAVEN.

ANNALS OF OAK BLUFFS

ANNALS OF OAK BLUFFS

OGKESHKUPPE

The Algonquian name for this tract, above described, was Ogkeshkuppe (Agescape, 1660, Aukeshkeppe, Ogkeshkupbeh, etc.), the definition of which is "the wet or damp thicket, or woods," probably referring to the swampy grounds bordering on Squash meadow and Farm ponds, in the eastern part of the town. The equivalent name is found in the Massachusetts dialect, Ogqush-kuppi (Eliot), Agkess-cuppi (Cotton).[1] It was later called Sanchacantacket neck, but this appellation was evidently given to it by the English settlers, from the pond on the southern border.

The meaning of Sanchakantacket is believed to be "at the bursting forth of the tidal stream," having reference to the opening of this pond at the bridge, where the tides are so strong. In the Abnaki, a dialectal form of the Algonquian tongue, the form Sanghe dentegge is found, meaning l'embouchere, sortie (of a river), which is probably parallel to our Sanchakantacket. The word first occurs in the records as relating to the region about the pond (Edg. Rec., p. 1), and by the settlers was applied to the land adjacent as well as to the pond itself. In 1663 Sanchacantacket pond is first mentioned (ibid., 1), and in a deed dated 1660, "Wabamuck alias Samuel, son of Autumsquum, sachem of Sanchacantacket, alias Akeshkeppe neck," shows its use as applied to the region bordering upon the pond (Deeds, I, 289). Other deeds refer to the "place" called Sanchacantacket, and farm or Sanchacantacket neck (ibid., I, 89; III, 111; IV, 94).

Another name, Quasquannes, was once used, in 1660, to designate this region (Deeds, II, 253), but it probably referred to Squash meadow only, or the territory which comprised the "farm" purchased by John Daggett.

[1]The town clerk of Edgartown, in his copy of the old records, about 1720, made one of his usual blunders, and wrote it Ogisket (Records, I, 131).

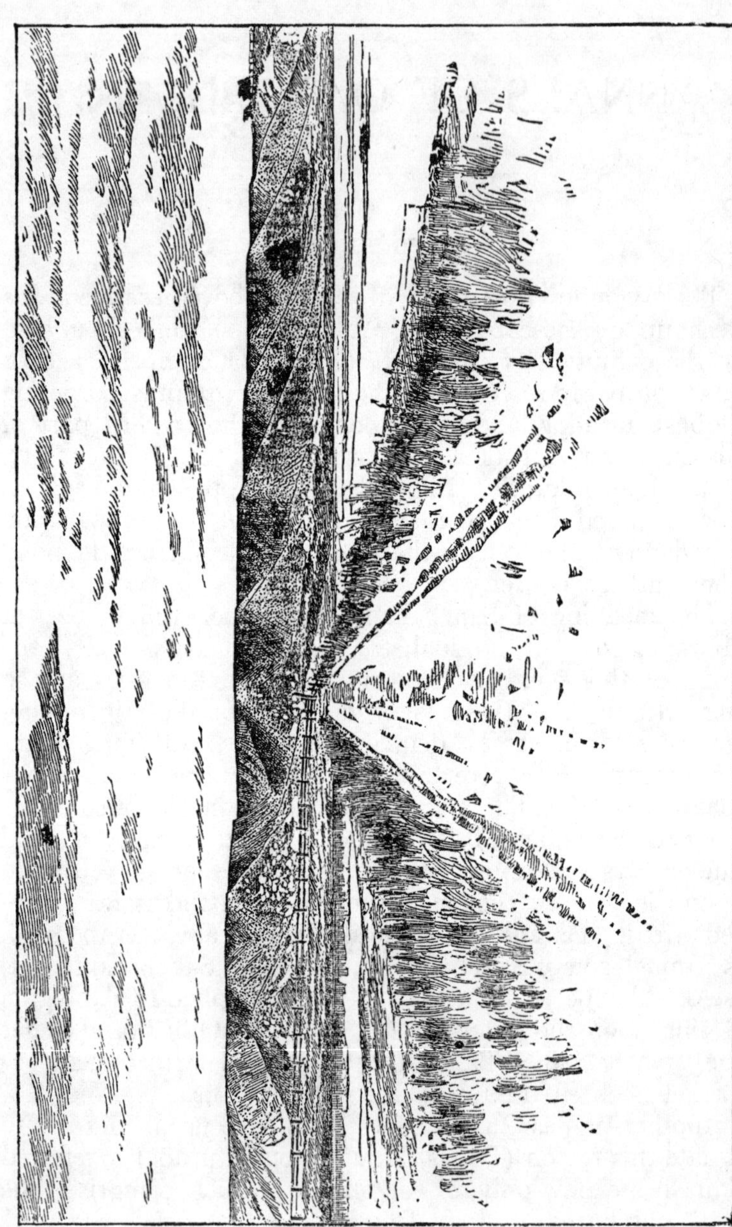

From the U. S. Geological Survey.

GLACIAL KAMES, LAGOON SHORE.

Annals of Oak Bluffs

EAST CHOP AND FARM NECK

The earliest English name for this territory was given in 1646 by Thomas Mayhew, when he called it the "Eastermost Chop of Homses Hole," as distinguished from its fellow Chop on the west side. The word is a variation of *chap*, the jaw of a vise or clamp. In the plural, it signifies the mouth or entrance of a channel, as the chops of the English Channel. It was called "Farm Neck" for the first time in the records, February 2, 1703-4, and this name has clung to it with a tenacity which time and a newer and more fancy name cannot sever.[1] This name was derived from the first grant of five hundred acres, made in 1642 to John Daggett "for a farm," which covers the present settlement of Oak Bluffs.

BOUNDARIES

The division lines of this town are those set off to it Feb. 17, 1880, when it was incorporated as Cottage City, and they are as follows:

> Beginning at the middle of the bridge over Sengekontacket, opening and running by the centre of Sengekontacket pond and Major's cove to Miobers bridge, so called; thence due west to the Four Town bound; thence to the Stepping Stones at the head of the Lagoon; thence through the middle of the Lagoon and middle of the Lagoon bridge; thence by the harbor of Vineyard Haven and the Vineyard Sound to the first mentioned bound.[2]

POPULATION

There are no records of enumeration for a census of this region prior to 1880, but a few scattering data will enable us to estimate the population. The map of Des Barres (1781) shows thirty-two houses, probably containing thirty-five families, or about 180 souls, at that date. The majority of these were located in Eastville. In 1850 a map shows twenty-six houses, or thirty families (estimated), with a probable total of 180 souls, most of whom were still located in Eastville. The first census (U. S., 1880) showed a population of 672, at which time Cottage City was then the largest settlement. In 1890 it was 1,080; in 1900 it was 1,100 and the state census of 1905 showed 1,138 souls resident in the town. Probably ninety per cent. resided in Cottage City.

[1]Edgartown Records, I, 88.

[2]Acts and Resolves of Mass., 1880 and 1907.

ANCIENT LANDMARKS

ALGONQUIAN PLACE NAMES

Anassanimsuh. — This was referred to in a deed of land dated 1691, and is in the Sanchacantacket region. Ezekiel to Isaac and Joseph Norton (Deeds, I, 88; IV, 119). It was on some portion of the earliest Norton purchases.

Assanootacket Pond. — It is recorded (1685) that Puttuspaqun, of Sanchacantacket, sold to his "cousins Hester and Ellis Daggett" a certain meadow . . . on the north side of Ohkeshkepe Neck lying between Quaniamo and the western end of Asanootackett Pond" (Deeds, I, 251), and on June 11, 1703, Ellis Daggett sold to Samuel Sarson "a certain parcel of meadow being about two acres . . . . bounded north westerly by the beach by holmses hole harbor: Southeasterly by the westward end of Asanootakut pond" (ibid., I, 89). This describes the small salt pond emptying into the Lagoon at Eastville. There was in the early days "a bridge to pass from the upland to the beach." The definition is "at the alienated tidal stream" alluding to the sale of some property, of which this was a boundary, probably the sale by Wampamog to Alice Sissetom, the mother of Ellis (Alice) Daggett.

Chqudeetussos. — Two Indians in 1717 concluded a land transaction covering a tract on the west side of Farm neck, called by the name just quoted.

Onkaw—Unkaw. — Under the above variations, as well as Ankaw, a "place" of this name on East Chop is referred to in several deeds, as Cathcart to Norton, 1699, Joseph Daggett to his daughter Alice, 1698, and same to his granddaughter, Esther Cottle, 1715 (I, 26; III, 111, 112). It is described as between a place called "Quanyamoo" and a small neck called "Oohquees," or "Ukquiessa." This name is the same as Onkokemmy, in Tisbury, and probably has the same significance. Esther Cottle, daughter of Edward, above mentioned, sold the tract given to her by the grandfather Daggett to Thomas West, Jr., innholder of Edgartown, in 1724, and it was then described as in the possession of John Talman, an "indian man of Edgartown, but formerly belonging to Allis Daggett" (ibid., IV, 107). This passed to the heirs of West, after his death in 1728, and was by them sold to various purchasers (ibid., VII, 500, 502), the name "Unkaw" being retained then (1747) as belonging to the land.

Oohquaess. — First mentioned in 1715 in a deed from Joseph Daggett to his granddaughter, Esther Cottle, conveying land at Onkaw, and "a small neck called Oohquaess being the southermost part of the meadow divided between my 2 daughters Esther Cottle and Ellis Daggitt" (Deeds, III, 111). This word has many variations, Ohqueehesoo, Ocquays, and finally Quays, which is the modern form (ibid., V, 31; VII, 4, 294). There was a Quaise in Nantucket, with an alias of Masquatuck. It is probably the same word as Ukquiessa, the name of Tisbury Great pond and denotes, "as far as," or "the end," a boundary term. In full it would be Uk-qui-es-et, "at the ending place," the last or terminal point of Ogkeshkippe neck.

Ohhomeck. — In a deed from the Indian Wabamuck to Joseph Daggett, of Tisbury, dated June 18, 1689, a certain neck, "neer Sanchakantacket harbor," called "Ohhomeck," is mentioned (Deeds, I, 16). A place called Ahomma on Dagget's farm is mentioned, probably a variation of Ohomeck (ibid., VI, 495). John Daggett of Edgartown sold, in 1734, to John Talman, Indian, a point called "the hommok" bounded northeast and west by "the Pond," southerly by a pole fence adjoining to "an island commonly called and known by the name Watchee, the olde Indian name" (ibid., V, 405). Joseph and David Potumpin sold to Elijah Butler a small island called "the Hummock" at Farm neck, Feb. 6, 1743-4 (ibid., VII, 37). The modern designation of "Hummock" is undoubtedly derived from this Indian word.

Pecoye. — This was the name of a small neck in the bounds of Farm neck, and the name survives to the present time (Deeds, IV, 114). It is derived from Pohqu-auk, meaning "open land," or land naturally fit and clear for cultivation. This is a common Indian place name throughout New England. In a deed from the Indian Ezekiel it is written Pokoiauk (I, 88).

Pateche. — In a deed, dated June 28, 1683, Thomas Sussetum, an Indian, sold certain land to Joseph Daggett, and describes it as bounded on the southeast by "Pateche pond" (Deeds, I, 15). The name is now extinct, as it is believed the pond has been filled up in cultivation of the region.

Quinnaamuk. — This name occurs in an Indian deed dated March 14, 1669, and appears later also as Quinniummuh. (It designated a beach "commonly called the long beach" and may refer to the long strip of sandy beach separating the Lagoon and harbor at that time. Deeds, II, 51; VI, 412.) Quinniaamuk was one of the Indian fishing stations. The meaning of the word is "place where the long fish (lamprey eel) is taken. At certain seasons of the year, when an inlet is cut through some of these beaches, there is a rush of these eels for the salt water.

Quanames. — This was described in a deed (I, 251), dated March 25, 1685, and also again in 1693 (III, 23); in the latter document the text is as follows: "all that upland which from the other lands lyeth and leadeth as a way to the Iland quanaimes." It is the small island off Pecoy point, on the west side of Sanchacantacket pond, northward of Major's cove, as indicated on a map of Edgartown, 1830 (Mass. Arch., vol. VII). This name occurs in a deed, dated 1759, when Isaac Norton sold one half "a certain island called Quanaimes."

Quasaquannes. — In a deed from Wampamag to John Daggett, dated March 3, 1660, he conveys a tract of land "upon the East side of the Eastermost Chop of homes hole called by the English Quasaquannes" (Deeds, II, 253). This was the tract granted by Thomas Mayhew, Senior, and Thomas Mayhew, Junior, to John Daggett, "for a farm," and probably referred to Squash meadow in its limits. This is possibly an Indian personal name, because the place was so "called by the English."

Quatapog. — This is a small pond on Farm neck. It is a derivative of the Algonquian word Wquahti-pog, meaning "the end of the pond, or water place," and probably refers to some boundary point, known to the Indians. Eliot in his Indian Bible, Genesis, XXIII, 9, uses Wquahti-konit, "end of the field," the character *W* is used by him as the prefix of the third person singular, and also for the whistled sound of W, as in "with."

Sepooisset. — Thomas Sussetum, an Indian, sold to Joseph Daggett of Tisbury, June 28, 1683, twenty acres of Farm neck, and refers to "his meadow lying at Sepooisset," on the northwest corner of Daggett's land (Deeds, I, 15). Isaac Norton, in a deed dated 1759, sold "one half a certain island called Quanaimes, and the islands hard by, also a tract of land and meadow called Seaquaneck and Sepueset." The meaning of the word is "at the little river or brook," a compound of Sepoe-es-et.

Sequaneck. — This word is referred to in the preceding paragraph, and belonged to a tract of land at the head of Sanchacantacket pond. It may be derived from Sequnan, remnant, what is left and auk (ack, eck) the generic term for land, meaning a portion remaining after some previous sale. It is also possible that it may be a personal name.

Tikhomah. — This was the name of a place near the head of the Lagoon, and is referred to in a deed, or Indian writing, conveying certain property at Weaquitaquayage (Deeds, IV, 348).

Waptesun Pond. — In 1686 this is first mentioned in a deed from Wabamuck, the sachem, to Richard Sarson, when he sold a tract of land "adjoyning near the Eastermost end of that Pond called Waptesun Pond, It being that salt Pond next ajoyning at the East side of the said [Homes Hole] harbor and att the place called onkaw" (Deeds, V, 413). It is probably the pond later known as Rufus' pond (q. v.).

ENGLISH PLACE NAMES

Boult's Farm. — This is one of those curious survivals of place names derived from transient settlers, who owned this land in 1686, "lying on the North side of Edgartown, at a place called Sanchacantacket," and known by the name of Boult's farm, containing about 100 acres, bounded as follows:

> Beginning at a small black oak tree by Myober's Bridge; thence about Northwest 215 rods to a small white oak bush or sapling, marked; thence Northeast about 80 rods to a rough oak tree formerly marked and now marked, and for a corner bound; thence Southeast 80 rods partly by the old ditch to the pond or water; thence crossing s'd water about Southeast and by South to a white oak tree marked; thence Southeast and by South 61 rods to the Old Mill dam; thence South and by East 41 rods to the gate post; and from thence from said gate post to the Horse Pond; thence to a black oak stump newly cut down; thence to the river; thence Westerly by said river to the fence of said Norton that runneth into said river; and from and by said fences to the first mentioned black oak tree by the said Myober's Bridge.

It became part of the Norton property and remains so to the present time.

Burial Hill. — First mentioned in 1713 as part of the Isaac Norton property on the northwest shore of Sanchacantacket, and again in 1723 (Deeds, III, 197; IV, 149). The ground is on the knoll (66 feet high) near by.

The Gore. — A tract of land lying to the northwest of Boult's farm (now belonging to Henry Constant Norton) and west of the road to Eastville.

Great Woods. — The tract of about two or three hundred acres extending from the Gore to the old Homes Hole road, formerly belonging to Bayes Newcomb, and later to Peter and Ichabod Norton.

Isaac's Neck. — First mentioned in 1752 as a "little neck," in the Onkaw tract, and as late as 1810 (Deeds, VIII, 307; XVII, 463). It may have received its name from Isaac Norton, who had property in that vicinity quite early.

Middle Line. — Marked the division between the "Daggett Farm" and the lots which extended to the Lagoon. The southerly end of it is indicated now by a ditch for about half a mile.

Major's Cove. — The inlet north of Felix neck, so-called in allusion to Major Peter Norton (1718-92), one of the early settlers on its shore.

Myober's Bridge. — On the boundary line between Oak Bluffs and Edgartown, near Major's Cove, so-called from an Indian in the early days.

Rufus' Pond. — This is a little pond just north of the Rufus Davis place, and has been so called since the first of that name lived in Eastville. Its Indian name was Waptesun (q. v.).

Tackenash's Field. — An Indian, named John Tackenash, living about 1680, probably gave his name to a tract cultivated by him on the northwest side of Sanchacantacket pond. (Deeds, I, 88; II, 119: Comp., Edg. Rec. 34). Also a second field, a tract of about fifteen acres on the east side of the Lagoon, midway its length, deriving its name from a squaw called Tockinosh, who lived there early in the 18th century.

Tyler's Creek. — A small brook, which runs out of a swamp between the Benjamin Davis and Christopher Beetle farms into Sanchacantacket pond. Tyler's Field bordered on this creek, and both derived titles from Tom Tyler, the Indian.

Wading Place, (1676). — The shallow water connecting a small salt pond with Major's Cove (southern shore) west of the inter-town bounds. (Edg. Rec., 21).

Annals of Oak Bluffs

FIRST SETTLEMENT

It is easier to designate the first land holders than the first settlers, because the territory was owned by men who also had lots of land in the village at Great Harbor at the same time, and it cannot be said with surety in which place some of them actually resided. The first record relating to Ogkeshkuppe occurs under date of May 16, 1653, when it was ordered that "Mr. Mayhew is to Purchase part of Ogisske (ppe) neck of the Indians for the town."[1] This was in line with Mayhew's policy of satisfying the native owners of the soil whenever the whites enlarged their sphere of improvement beyond former acquisitions, and it is presumed that Mayhew carried out the town directions. It is not known what "part" of the neck was secured in this way.

On Dec. 1, 1642, probably after their first visit to their island domain, Thomas Mayhew, Senior, Thomas Mayhew, Junior, and John Smith, granted to John Daggett, a neighbor of theirs in Watertown, the following lands on the Vineyard:

> . . . . twenty acres of land upon the point beginning at the great stone next to my lot, and twenty acres of meadow: and also five hundred acres of land for a farm: he have liberty to take up wherever he the said John Doggett wishes, only provided he take not up his farm within three miles of the spring that is by the harbor in my lot aforesaid, before I that is Thomas Mayhew the elder have made choice of twenty acres of meadow and a farm of five hundred acres for myself, the which choice not being made within one year insueing the date hereof, then the said John Doggett have liberty to chuse for himself.[2]

This was a grant both liberal in terms and in the amount alienated by them.

THE "FARM"

When John Daggett came to the Vineyard cannot be accurately stated, but the first time his name appears of record is in 1651, though it is to be supposed that he had been here for some time previous.[3] He had a home lot in the village of Great Harbour, and there is nothing to indicate that he did not reside there, as the most desirable place for residential purposes at that time. With his early grant, just referred to, he followed the custom of the patentee, and after locating to

[1]Edgartown Records, I, 131.
[2]Dukes Deeds, I, 189.
[3]Edgartown Records, I, 122.

his satisfaction, the tract of five hundred acres, three miles from a spring near Mayhew's house, he proceeded, in 1660, to buy the sachem's "rights" to the soil. On March 3rd of that year Wampamag, the chief of the Sanchacantacket tribe, sold to Daggett, "a certain tract of land which was granted by Mr Thomas Mayhew Sen, and Mr Thomas Mayhew Jr, for a farm, I say a tract of land lying upon the east side of the eastermost Chap of Homes Hole, called by the English Quasquannes, butting down to the sea on the east, being bounded on the east side by the sea, and on the north side with marked trees, running into the woods three hundred and twenty rods, and on the north side from the sea three hundred and twenty rods and on the west side three hundred and twenty rods."[1]

DAGGETT'S SUIT FOR "THE FARM"

For reasons not now known, Governor Mayhew refused to fulfill his early grant, and Daggett thereupon purchased the "rights" of the Indian sachem to the soil on the date above mentioned. Acting under the influence of Mayhew the town voted, Oct. 3, 1660, "that John Daggett, the elder, hath broken the order of ten pounds upon every acer In purchasing a farm at Sanchacontackett at the hands of the Indians without the towns consent."[2] On December 17, following, the townsmen proceeded to collect the fine by the passage of the order here quoted:

To William Weekes, Constable:

These are to warne you by the authority of this town to levie upon the estate of John Doggett, the elder, upon Martins Vineyard the sum of five thousand (pounds) upon the breach of order in purchasing lands.[3]

A penalty of five thousand pounds was a little too much for John Daggett to pay for obtaining a title to a farm which had been granted to him in due and legal form, and he resisted this absurd levy. It was not only confiscation, but it meant banishment, the favorite method of Mayhew in dealing with his enemies. As the case could not be adjudicated in the local court, because of the interest of Mayhew in the result, the parties agreed to refer it to the Plymouth Colony court for arbitration. The records of the town state "the names of those that Doth try for the farme with John Daggett:"

[1]Dukes Deeds, II, 253. Quasquannes is probably an Indian personal name.

[2]Edgartown Records, I, 133. A town order dated Jan. 4, 1652.

[3]Ibid., 130.

Thomas Mayhew for My self and all Relations in the town that is eight lotts; Mr. Butler 2 lots; William Vinson his lot & his mothers; Thomas Trapp 1 lot; Robert Codman, 1; Nicholas Norton & 2 sons; Thomas Bayes 2 lots; Thomas Burchard; Nicholas Butler; William Weeks; Goodman Jones; James Covel one half lot.[1]

This list comprises most of the resident land owners, though the names of Arey, Bland, John Burchard, Eddy, Folger, Lay and some others are not included. Of course his son, Thomas Daggett, could not be identified with the case, on either side. The town appointed Nicholas Norton and John Pease to conduct the case in its behalf, and on Oct. 2, 1662, the trial was held in Plymouth. The following is the record in the archives of that colony:

Att the Court John Doged of the Iland called Martins Vineyard complained against the towne of the said Vineyard in an action of the case for the title of a certaine prcell of land graunted unto the said John by Mr. Thomas Mayhew &c, which the said inhabitants doe unjustly and illegally disturbe him in his quiett injoyment of the same, which said case is by joynt consent of both prtyes refered to the determination of this Court.[2]

It is not known whether John Daggett had any legal counsel to assist him, but his cause was so clear that it did not require any, and the verdict was as follows:

The jury find for the plaintiffe the full title graunted to him by Mr. Thomas Mayhew Senr.[3]

EARLY TRANSIENT RESIDENTS

JOHN BOULT

With that paradoxical tendency in the perpetuation of names of persons whose stay here was the briefest, the subject of this sketch will always be associated with a farm he bought over two centuries ago, and doubtless a century hence, as at this day, the name of "Boult's Farm" will be a local place name. He came here from Boston, where he had been received into the Old South church, March 14, 1686,[4] but as he had

[1]Edgartown Records, I, 145.

[2]Plymouth Colony Records, VII, 104.

[3]Ibid. The Mayhews never became reconciled to this defeat. When John Daggett's will was offered for probate in 1673 it was accepted, "with this proviso only: that the farm is to contain 500 akers of upland and 20 akers of meadoe and no more." It was Mayhew's last thrust at Daggett.

[4]Sewall's diary, I, 127. "Mr. Bolt mentioned profane courses he had been entangled in after Conviction." In a later entry Sewall records the following notes of a conversation with Boult: "I mentioned the problem whether should be white after the Resurrection: Mr. Bolt took it up as absurd, because the body should be void of all Colour (ibid, II, 305).

taken the oath of allegiance in November, 1678, he must have been a resident in that place for some years before that date. He was, probably, a Cheshire man, as he had relatives in that county. His first purchase of land was Sept. 20, 1686, when he bought a hundred acres at Sanchacantacket, in the region now covered by the farm of Henry Constant Norton, of which it is a part. His occupation of it is somewhat uncertain, as he appears to have retained a residence in Boston, and while he was constructively here in 1688 (witness) and 1691 (ensign of the Edgartown militia), yet in 1693 he is called "merchant of Boston,"[1] and in 1694 was chosen constable of that town.[2] In 1696 he appears here as a witness to a will, in 1698 as a juror, and in 1702 as plaintiff in an action of trespass, but further doubt would seem to be removed on Oct. 29, 1703, when he sold his farm to Israel Daggett and all his rights in commons.[3] He was a plaintiff, however, in 1706, in an action for debt and is called "of Edgartown."[4] On March 10, 1706-7, he was elected overseer of the poor in Boston, and reelected the three following years, which definitely places him there.[5] His will was made June 9, 1710, and he died Jan. 29, 1711, in Boston. He was either a widower without issue, or a bachelor, as all the bequests are made to other kinsmen and friends. He mentions his sister, Rebecca, wife of John Bruen of Chester, England, chirurgeon, and their three sons; his nephew, Andrew Boult, merchant of London; and his niece, Elizabeth Sharp, widow, daughter of his deceased brother, Joshua Boult, druggist of London. To the pastors and teachers of the South and North churches, Boston, and the poor communicants of both he leaves various sums, and to his friend, Jonathan Mountfort of Boston he bequeaths his gun, silver hilted sword and silver tobacco box. The money bequests amounted in all to £160, and no real estate was mentioned.[6] He called himself a "merchant." The local tradition here is that he was a tanner of moleskins, and returned to England after he left the Vineyard, but both of these tales may be safely ignored in view of the facts shown by the records.

[1]Supreme Judicial Court Mss., No. 2751.

[2]Boston Town Records, II, 209. He was present to decline the choice.

[3]Dukes Deeds, II, 3.

[4]Dukes Court Records.

[5]Boston Town Records, II, 285, 289, 302, 312.

[6]Suffolk Probate Record.

JOHN TRUMBLE

This person was one of those early residents or lot owners whose coming and going left only a trace on the town records. Whether he lived here or was simply a transient proprietor is not known. The occurrence of his name in a deposition of John Daggett, in 1659, just discloses the fact that at some time before February 15th of that year he had a lot in this town. Daggett testifies that "Mr. Mayhew did Reserve the Land Between his Lott at the ffarm and that which was John Trumbles" and this is the first as well as the last we hear of him.[1] Who he was is not certain as there were two of his name in New England, both of whom on May 13, 1640, became freemen of Massachusetts. One lived at Roxbury, 1639, and later removed to Rowley, almost in the immediate neighborhood of Salisbury, where Robert Codman and Richard Arey resided, and it is of record that Trumble and Arey were in court together at Salem in 1646 and personal acquaintance may be presumed.[2] The other John Trumble lived at Cambridge, 1636, and later at Charlestown, where he was engaged in coastwise trading. For this reason the author feels inclined to place the identification on him, as one whose seafaring occupation would bring him to the island for a harbor, and probably in one of his trading trips he became interested in the new island colony.[3]

DIVISION OF SANCHACANTACKET NECK

Up to 1664 the most northern section which had been divided for the use of the settlers in this region was at Weenomeset, or Felix neck, but ten years later another move northward was made. The following votes of the town show what action was then taken to develop the new tract:

February 15, 1673-4.

Voted the Day and Year above writen that the freeholders have made choice of Joseph Norton, Capt. (Thomas) Daggett, Isaac Norton, Mr Benjamin Smith and Thomas Pease according to their best Judgment. for to divide the Neck called Sanchacantackett Neck.

[1]Edgartown Records, I, 110.

[2]Savage Gen. Dict., IV, 336. Essex Antiquarian, V., 169. This John Trumble is the ancestor of the famous Connecticut family of Trumbulls. The name is often spelled Thromble.

[3]Conn. Col. Rec., I, 162; comp. 3 Mass. Hist., Coll., X, 7. In 1650 John Trumble, of Charlestown, called himself "seaman in the good ship called the Wm. & George" (Aspinwall, Notarial Record, 363).

Granted unto Joseph Daggett, of Tisbury, By the Proprietors of the town of Edgartown that when the neck of Sanchacantackett Comes to be Divided that Joseph Daggett shall have his Part in the place he formerly purchased, so far as his part Comes to in the Place as he shall Chose, he allowing for the goodness of it.[1]

Granted the Day and Year above writen unto John Daggett that when the New Purchase is lay'd out that John Daggett shall have his half share Joyning to his land there, that is to say att Waketequa.[2]

The limits of this sub-division were afterwards described as "bounded by the road that now goes from the head of Wakequataqua (Lagoon Pond) to John Bolte's, including all the land to the Northeast of said road,"[3] which is practically the line now dividing Oak Bluffs from Edgartown. Some years later there was a "misapprehension" of the exact bounds of Sanchacantackett neck as "bounded by a certain path which was then lately made and used, when indeed the said path was new and not the true boundaries which was an ancient foot-path by which the Sachem bounded Sanchacantacket by his gift to the Indians," and a committee was sent to settle the matter. Joseph Norton, who lived on the southermost lot next this path, may have had the original "misapprehension," for he entertained the committee, according to neighborhood tradition, fed them well, gave them plentifully of good old New England rum, and when they had viewed paths, devious and otherwise, they came to the following conclusion: "that the said words — as the road now goes — shall intend the old path, not then wholly disused, and partly still known, especially at both ends, and not the new one."[4] This was a little mixed and might mean anything, but it went the way Norton intended. Thus this territory finally came into the hands of the settlers, the freeholders of Edgartown agreeing, in 1673, to divide all of Ogkeshkuppe neck, except the "Farm," which they had endeavored to keep from Daggett.[5] This was the beginning of the development of this town as a separate settlement.

[1]This probably refers to some unrecorded purchase from the Indians.

[2]Edgartown Records, I, 99. This vote recognized the Daggett "Farm" as excluded.

[3]Ibid., I, 88. Feb. 2, 1703-4.

[4]Ibid. June 24, 1707.

[5]It is difficult, at this distance, to know the motives of Mayhew in resisting this grant to his old neighbor, and until some musty document of the past turns up with the necessary evidence, we can only surmise the cause of his obstinacy when such a clear title rested in Daggett.

In 1707 the subject of a division of this neck received further attention, and the following action was taken:

> Voted that Benjamin Smith, Samuel Athearn and Samuel Smith are chosen to divide Sanchacantackett Neck, purchased and unpurchased, esteeming the land as if lying vacant and unpurchased; and where no grant of the proprietors hath been made shall come into a common division, the whole being twenty-six shares, saving always to such as have purchased so far as their rights are to the lands in general on said Neck.[1]

These were known as the "Sanchacantackett Shares," and comprised the land west of the Middle line the entire length of the neck from the Gore to the county road leading to Eastville. They were about forty rods wide and extended east and west from the "farm" to the Lagoon.

THE FIRST SETTLER

It is doubted whether the owner ever resided on his "farm." He had a home lot, as previously stated, in the village, and his son Thomas also resided near by, but the son's relations with Mayhew did not permit him to be independent. It is the author's belief that the youngest son, Joseph, was placed upon the farm as soon as he became old enough to attend to business affairs, probably about 1667, when he was twenty years of age, and that he made it his home, and here married his Indian wife. The litigation had driven the father away from the island, and in that year he had taken a second wife at Plymouth, and ever after that resided there, and died in that town. In so far as a guess is of value, Joseph Daggett was the first white man to reside in the present limits of Oak Bluffs, and here, in all probability, his half breed children were born, Alice, Hester and Joseph. He remained here until about 1673, when he removed to the new settlement at Takemmy (West Tisbury).

DIVISION OF THE "FARM"

In this year the father died, and bequeathed the "Farm" in equal shares, to his sons John (of Rehoboth), Thomas and Joseph of the Vineyard. Nothing was done by them, as far as known, to improve this property until 1677, when the three brothers agreed to divide it, on September 6th of that year. The instrument of division is as follows:

[1]Edgartown Records I, 89. April 14, 1707. The town had confirmed, March 31st, previously, "several tracts" of land purchased by Joseph Norton, Thomas Daggett, Matthew Mayhew, Thomas Harlock, Benjamin Smith, and James Pease of "divers Indians."

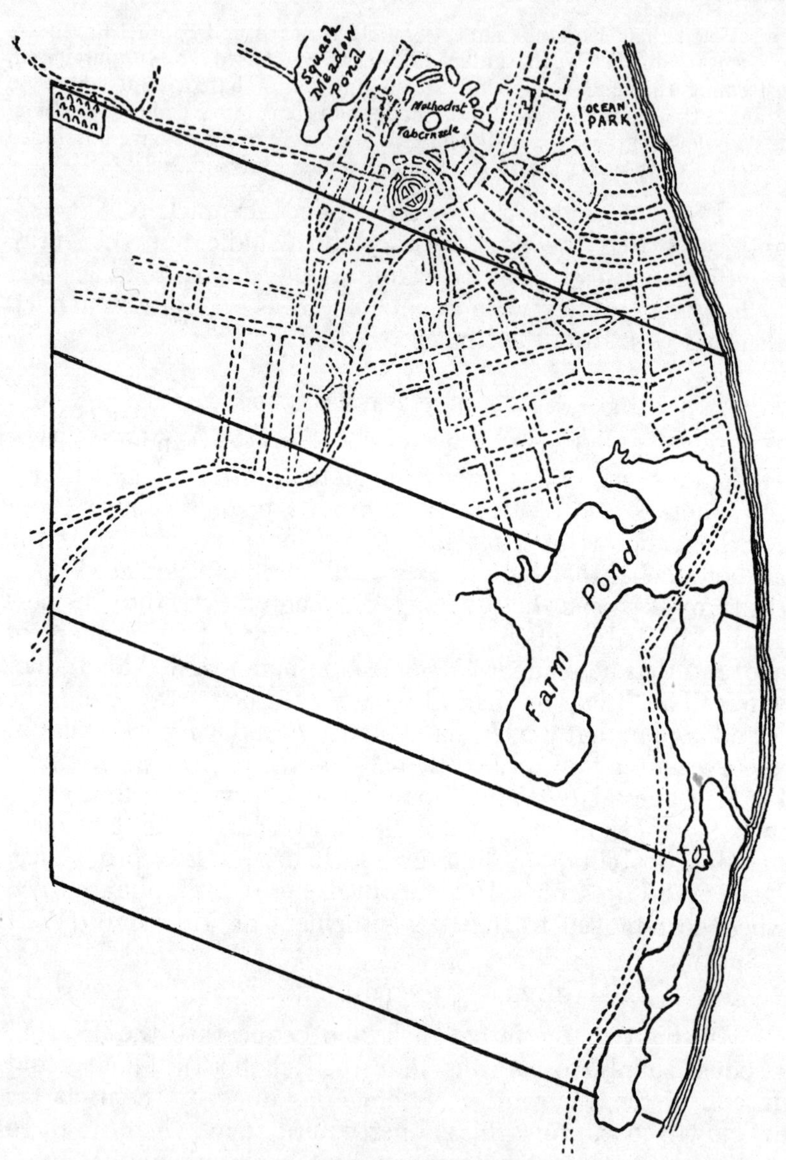

LOCATION OF
THE DAGGETT FARM,
OAK BLUFFS, MARTHA'S VINEYARD.

Know all men whom it may concern that we, whose names are underwritten, have jointly agreed to divide the farm that our father gave to us, lying upon the eastermost Chap of Homes Hole, which farm we, that is John Dogget, Thomas Daggett and Joseph Dogget, have divided, both upland and meadow. The first lott came to John Daggett of upland and meadoe, uppon the northeast, or north northeast: the second division fell to Thomas Daggett, bounded by a marked tree, standing near the head of a meadoe, commonly called the fresh meadoe: and from that tree bounded by marked trees running nearest a north west and by west course, from the aforesaid marked tree the meadoe is bounded by marked trees between the meadow and the foresaid John Daggett's upland, and so to a stake near the pond uppon the meadow, which line runs towards the northeast; and on the southwest bounded by Joseph Daggett's land and meadow, which bound runs from the westermost side of the cove commonly called the Muddy Cove, where the fence stands at the day of this writing, which fence is the southermost bounds of Thomas Daggett's meadoe: and from the aforesaid fence runs upon the upland, with a straight line towards the southwest, by marked trees, about fifty or sixty poles to a stake or post that is there set down: and from that post upon a northwest and by west line to the uttermost bounds of the farm: which northwest and by west line is the bounds between Thomas and Joseph Daggett: and from the foresaid fence upon the meadoe southerly, with the lands and meadoe upon and about the hummocks, southerly, belongs to Joseph Daggett, with all the upland southerly from the line that runs northwest and by west, as aforesaid, so far as the bounds of the farm southerly.[1]

SUBSEQUENT OWNERS OF THE FARM BEFORE 1800

This tract of land which was thus divided was situated, roughly speaking, between the head of Squash meadow and the lower part of Farm pond, extending a mile in a north and south line, and a mile into the middle of the neck, forming a square, as near as it could be surveyed and measured in those days. The accompanying map will show the location accurately, and it will be seen that it covers half of the present site of the village of Oak Bluffs. Thomas Daggett, a month later, sold his part to his brother John, of Rehoboth, Oct. 9, 1677,[2] and on July 20, 1686, the two joint owners procured from Wampamag the sachem, a confirmation of the original sale.[3] He describes the tract as "by the sea, in length, one English mile," and extending three hundred rods from the beach "into the island." This is a reduction, probably by agreement, of twenty rods in width from the first grant, probably to comprise five hundred acres, as the mile square would

[1]Dukes Deeds, I, 115.
[2]Ibid., I, 323.
[3]Ibid., I, 289.

make 640 acres. Meanwhile Joseph Daggett was adding to his portion by successive purchases of the Indians, by permission of the town,[1] but whether the land was occupied by any resident at this period is not known. It would not seem that the land was allowed to go to waste, and it is possible that there were Indian tenants who cultivated it for the owners. On Aug. 5, 1692, John ofl Rehoboth sold his two-thirds to James Allen of Chilmark, estimated at three hundred and thirty acres,[2] and Allen in turn, on March 31, 1703, sold this portion to his son Ebenezer Allen.[3] Neither of the two last named were occupants, as they were land speculators. On Dec. 5, 1707, Ebenezer Allen sold one-third of his tract, or one hundred and ten acres, being the western part, to Joseph and Isaac Norton, who had already become identified with Sanchacantacket property about the Major's cove, and were living there.[4] Isaac Norton sold the south half of this purchase to his son Isaac, Junior, July 8, 1713,[5] and Joseph sold the north half to his son Ebenezer, Feb. 28, 1734, with reversion to his grandsons, Eliakim and Peter, sons of Ebenezer.[6] On Nov. 16, 1727, Ebenezer Allen disposed of the eastern part of the two-thirds which he once owned, to John Butler, Jr.,[7] and this last owner, on Nov. 26, 1733, sold this to Simeon Butler, his brother.[8] Here Simeon Butler carried on a tannery for a number of years, until 1750, when he disposed of it all to his two sons Ebenezer and Thomas Butler, the former acquiring the northern moiety.[9] The northwestern section, which fell by reversion to Eliakim and Peter Norton, was sold by them to Matthew Norton on Dec. 11, 1747,[10] and a year later, on Dec. 3, 1748, the last named owner sold this part to Malatiah Davis (one-half), Thomas Claghorn (one-quarter), and Benjamin Claghorn (one-quarter).[11] By successive purchases of the first two, Benjamin Claghorn became full owner of this parcel, estimated to contain sixty-five acres,

[1]Edgartown Records, I, 29.
[2]Dukes Deeds, I, 151.
[3]Ibid., II, 40.
[4]Ibid., II, 200.
[5]Ibid., III, 197.
[6]Ibid., V, 381.
[7]Ibid., IV, 330.
[8]Ibid., V, 351.
[9]Ibid., VIII, 167, 263.
[10]Ibid., VII, 469.
[11]Ibid., VIII, 58

in 1750 and 1758.[1] Isaac Norton at that time still held the southwest section, which had been in his possession since 1713. Thomas Butler by his will of 1780 bequeathed his share in equal parts to his sons, William and Levi,[2] and the latter, in 1795, sold his share to William.[3]

Meanwhile, by the will of Joseph Daggett, who retained his original southern third till his death, this division fell to his son, John Daggett, of Edgartown, in 1718.[4] This portion of the farm remained undivided until after the death of John, when his heirs sold at various times (1767-1782) their shares (in sevenths) to Malatiah Davis, and it later descended to his son Benjamin and became known as the "Ben Davis Place."[5]

QUASQUANNES — SQUASH MEADOW

The oldest known name for the region which became the site of the camp meeting, and later the settlement of Cottage City, was of record, in 1660, as Quasquannes. This is probably an Indian's personal name, because the place was so "called by the English," for it is well understood that the native never bestowed personal names on places. It covered the region comprised in the "farm" of John Daggett, while just north of it was the body of water which was designated by the whites, as early as 1684, the "Squash Meadow" pond and swamp. On the fertile ground surrounding this pond the Indians doubtless had fields of squash growing here when the whites came. The word squash is derived from the Algonquian noun *askutasquash*, which was the name for this vegetable cultivated by them. The English adopted the plural *asquash* as a singular noun and formed a new plural, squashes. The portion covered by "the farm" was in the dominion of Wampamog, the sachem, in 1660, who sold it to Daggett, and in 1682 the "Squash Meadow" was the individual property of that Indian from Ipswich, son of the Sagamore Masconomet, known here by his English name of Tom Tyler. Liberty to purchase this from him about that date (April, 1682) was granted to Andrew Newcomb and John Coffin, one-half, and James Covel, James Pease, Isaac Norton, William Vinson and Joseph Norton, the other half. The

[1]Dukes Deeds, VIII, 254, 568.
[2]Dukes Probate, VI, 244.
[3]Dukes Deeds, XIII, 449.
[4]Dukes Probate, I, 24.
[5]Ibid., IX, 252, 590, 591, 667; X, 107; XI, 252

records indicate that this purchase was made, but documentary evidence is lacking to determine the descent of title from these grantees.[1]

The successive chain of ownership of the "farm" down to 1800 has been shown. The possession of the northern part devolved upon William Butler, and he also inherited the Squash meadow tract through purchases by his father and grandfather. He was therefore at the beginning of the nineteenth century the sole owner, and almost the sole occupant, of the territory now covered by the village settlement of Oak Bluffs. His next neighbor to the south was Benjamin Butler (282), who lived at the lower end of Farm pond, and still farther south near the head of Sanchacantacket pond, Benjamin Davis (34) shared with them the solitude of these vast acres of uncleared land. To the northward of him lived Ebenezer Smith on the highland of East chop, while westward on the shores of the Lagoon were the dingy wigwams of the remnants of the Indian race. Over all this section great groves of tall pine and spreading oaks furnished welcome shade to the herds of cattle that browsed in the "Great Pasture" on the borders of Squash meadow, and the only sounds that echoed through these woods were the calls of lowing kine, the bleating of a stray sheep, and the occasional crack of a woodman's axe. This condition lasted for a generation in the first third of the nineteenth century, before its primeval stillness was invaded by a throng of people who were destined to turn it into a "city" of paved streets and electric lights.

ECCLESIASTICAL AFFAIRS.

THE FIRST CAMP MEETING

The origin of the town of Oak Bluffs dates from the establishment of the annual "camp meetings" held in an oak grove on the shores of Squash Meadow pond. This location was discovered and recommended to those who had been previously attending similar meetings at Falmouth, Sandwich and Monument, by Jeremiah Pease (776), an enthusiastic Methodist "brother" and local exhorter, and by him it was surveyed and laid out. This grove was on the south side of the pond, and open fields bordered it on all other

[1]William Vinson sold one-tenth of Squash meadow in 1684, a division consistent with the number of grantees, Newcomb and Coffin owning five-tenths.

sides. It was a part of the Butler estate, heretofore described, and at this period in the possession of William Butler, from whom it was leased for this temporary occupancy.

The first camp meeting held in this beautiful grove was in 1835, and began on Monday, Aug. 24th. The area cleared for this purpose was quite limited in extent, about half an acre. A small rough board structure had been erected with an elevated seat and stand in front to serve as a pulpit. This was called the "Preacher's Tent." In front of this was a temporary altar, consisting of a railing, enclosing a space about twelve by twenty-five feet, with seats to be used mainly by the singers in time of public worship, and as a place for penitent "sinners" to come into from the congregation for prayers, following the afternoon and evening meetings. Beyond the altar were some plain board benches for the seating of the congregation. Nine tents were pitched in a semi-circle around this amphitheatre, together with some canvas shelters for cooking and dining purposes. This was the physical aspect of the first camp meeting at Oak Bluffs.

The Rev. Thomas C. Pierce, a Methodist clergyman was elected superintendent of the meeting, in the absence of the presiding elder of the district, and with a secretary to record its doings the session was opened by Mr. Pierce on Monday evening with an address. Meetings were held daily, morning, afternoon and evening, at which preachers of the Methodist denomination held forth, and the contemporary accounts in *Zion's Herald*, the organ of that sect, testify to the success of the encampment from the standpoint of public "conversions" and reclamation of "backsliders." The report of the meeting concludes with a survey of the event in the following words:

> We think the number converted during the meeting is very safely computed at sixty-five. The work is spreading on the island. Among those converted during the encampment were men of high respectability. On the morning of the close, when assembled near the stand, some two or three hundred brethren and sisters in the Lord arose from their seats and stood awhile in testimony that God had deepened the work of grace in their hearts during the meeting. Six souls were reclaimed.

The meeting lasted through that week, closing Saturday morning. By a unanimous vote it was decided to purchase the lumber which had been used in the construction of the camp, in order that it might remain on the ground for permanent use. Collections for this object secured the necessary funds and the owner freely gave his consent to the continuance of the meetings in this grove.

SUBSEQUENT CAMP MEETINGS AT WESLEYAN GROVE

Annually for ten years, in the last week of each recurring August, these meetings were held in this grove (1835-1844), of which it will not be necessary to relate the details of each encampment. The general schedule of services was the same every year, in which there were two particular ceremonies, known as the "love feast" and the "parting." At the former all the campers assembled at the preacher's tent and "testimonies" of personal experiences in the religious life were spoken by as many as could be heard in time. The "parting" ceremony was thus described: "It consists of walking in procession, two and two, around the area within the circle of tents, singing at the same time some appropriate hymn, and finally all halting, and then each passing by every other one, taking them by the hand and bidding them 'farewell'." This ceremony was most impressive and one which was always attended by a crowd of spectators, who looked on with the deepest interest and emotion.[1]

Indeed the whole series of meetings was calculated to play upon the sentiment and excite the sympathy of the participants, and often the entire assembly would sit out the night, singing and praying. On one occasion in the early morning during one of these nocturnal "revivals" it is recorded that "several of the companies left the ground in marshalled procession, and moved to the shore singing the songs of Zion." These spiritual exaltations were productive of strange exhibits of religious manifestations. A veteran "brother" solemnly announced that he had seen Wesley in a vision and conversed with him, and in the official report of one meeting we read: "Numbers who are not easily excited were shorn of their strength, and lay for hours without the power either to speak or move. Some who had doubted the reality of such exercises looked on in amazement and exclaimed with the psalmist, 'This is the Lord's doing; it is marvellous in our eyes'."

These meetings grew in attendance both of the campers and spectators in this period. The greatest number of tents was forty, accommodating 1,189 persons, and the greatest

[1]This ceremony was abandoned in 1848 for a more formal meeting at the stand.

attendance of visitors at one service was estimated at three thousand. The management of these immense crowds called for a firm executive hand and an organization to carry out the orders. Rules for the camp were rigorously enforced, and to aid in the protection of the worshippers a state law, approved April 17, 1838, making it a misdemeanor to carry on peddling, gaming or horse racing within a mile limit, punishable by fine or imprisonment, was secured by its friends. In 1838 a lease for five years, beginning Nov. 16th, was signed which secured additional ground embracing the "Great Pasture" on the Butler estate. A name for the camp ground was also selected in 1840, when the campers voted "that the grove be called Wesleyan Grove" and the secretary was authorized to procure and keep a record book for the permanent minutes of this camp meeting. The presiding elder of the district was the superintendent of each meeting each year.

SUCCEEDING ANNALS, 1848–1858

The meeting for 1845 was held near Westport, Mass., because many thought this island grove had become "an old story" and that amid new scenes the interest and enthusiasm might be increased among the campers. It was felt that the experiment of a change would test this idea and that if it proved a false notion the return could easily be made the following summer. This change of location was also consequent upon the expiration of the lease of the ground in this year. In 1846 the meeting was to be held in East Greenwich, R. I., by vote passed, but enough were wedded to the original location at Wesleyan grove to determine upon a return hither, despite the decision of those assembled at Westport. A new lease was obtained from Stephen H. and Harriet Bradley, the successors of William Butler as proprietors of the land, and the annual pilgrimage hither was resumed.

The annals of this decade are a repetition of the preceding years, with some additional developments and changes. The times of meeting varied from between Sabbaths to a period including that day, and during such times the steamboats would bring large parties for a Sunday "excursion" from New Bedford and the surrounding towns. At first this was objected to by the promoters of the meetings (1847) and the transportation company was requested not to run their boats to the island during the time of the encampment, but this came to be ignored as time went on, and the Sunday services grew to be a feature of the affair. The crowds of spectators increased yearly from about three to twelve thousand on that day, and as a rule excellent order and respectful attention was observed.[1] In this period the number of tents in the encampment gradually increased from fifty in 1848 to 320 in 1858,[2] the number of occupants correspondingly multiplied and an increase from fifty to a hundred ministers of the gospel. Distinguished visitors also came to see this unique spectacle. In 1858 Governor Banks of this state and Governor Harris of Rhode Island honored the meeting with their presence at different times accompanied by many prominent officials of both states. This same year the famous negro Henson, said to be the original "Uncle Tom" of Harriet Beecher Stowe's well known romance, visited the meeting and "exhorted." It was estimated that there had been up to 1859 over eleven hundred "conversions."[3]

This settlement of white canvas, laid out in regular form and policed, came to be spoken of as the White City, Canvas City, and similar appellations, and the communicating streets to have fancy or biblical names, much to the disapproval of the elders who saw in these signs the growth of a social and "picnic" spirit that was to be deplored.[4] This spirit increased despite the frowns of the elders, and in the crowds which came here yearly many converts were made not to the religious features of the meeting but to the beauty of the grounds, and the general attractiveness of the island as a resort for rest and recreation. The temporary tents began to be replaced by small board structures, a combination of wood and cloth on the sides or top, and permanent locations were asked for in the camp ground each recurring year, until the campers finally felt a degree of proprietorship in the spot which they had occupied continuously for a number of seasons.[5]

In 1850 a new lease was executed for eleven years at a rental of $30 per annum, with some adjoining land owned

[1]Vincent, History of Wesleyan Grove Camp Meeting, p. 185.

[2]This great increase was due principally to the segregation of families in smaller tents. These "family" tents gave rise to some trouble for the management, and none was allowed to be set up without a letter from the pastor of the church whence the family came.

[3]Among them was a "papist" and a Jew, according to the reports of the Secretary.

[4]The report for the year in speaking of the great increase of the encampment said "Quite a city, truly, and an exceedingly pleasant one."

[5]Pardon M. Stone of Providence, R. I., spent sixty consecutive summers at the camp meetings, beginning in 1846, a record which is probably without parallel.

by other parties for $6 per annum. This long lease prompted the idea of permanent improvements, and a committee was appointed to arrange a new plan for the encampment, new seating for the worshippers and other necessary fixtures.[1] The management varied somewhat, but an "agent" chosen yearly was the executive head, and as the crowds grew, committees on finance, order and similar apportionment of duty were formed to aid him. In 1856 the ownership of the grounds changed hands and the new proprietor began the demand for a higher rental.[2] In 1857 this situation became more acute and a committee was appointed to secure another site for the following year, and purchase it for permanent occupancy. This had the effect of bringing about a compromise. The property was reconveyed to the original owners, Stephen H. Bradley and wife, and a new lease for a term of ten years, beginning at the termination of the current lease (1861), with privilege of renewal or purchase at market value, was secured by the committee of campers. Thus protected the meeting in 1858 authorized the borrowing of a thousand dollars for use in permanent improvements on the grounds, and incorporation was agitated by a considerable number. This was the inception of the settlement which afterwards became Oak Bluffs.

THE BIRTH OF "COTTAGE CITY"

The succeeding decade, 1859–1869, is merely a continued story of the marvellous growth and enduring features of this famous camp ground. The attraction of this beautiful oak grove had left its impress on the memory of all who had ever visited it, and as their number yearly increased the loveliness of the location and the possibilities of the island as a summer home became more generally known to thousands of people from all parts of New England. The original religious purpose of the meeting gradually found a strong competitor in the desire and custom of many of the campers to make a prolonged stay before and after the meeting for social and personal enjoyment. The grove, which seemed a hallowed fane to many, soon began

[1]This committee consisted of Preston Bennett of Providence, Henry Tobey of Falmouth, Isaiah D. Pease of Edgartown and five clergymen, including the Presiding Elder of the district. This meeting still remained distinctively a Methodist affair.

[2]In 1855 the officers had begun negotiations looking to the purchase of the camp ground, but "such were the terms named by the proprietors that the committee recommended not to purchase." As aptly said in another place, it was "an institution," the like of which was not in all New England.

to ring with the laughter of happy children and resound to the shouts of exuberant youth spending their vacation days here.

Permanent cottages began to be built about 1859, the first one of which was erected by Perez Mason of Fall River in that year. From that time on these buildings increased with each recurring meeting, and the grove began to take on the semblance of a settlement in the wilderness. About 1865 the noble oaks which had afforded shade for the campers began to succumb to the effect of this kind of occupancy of the soil from whence they derived nourishment, and one by one they slowly died. The crowds became enormous as the years passed, reaching twenty thousand on Sundays, and much injury was inflicted on the trees under those conditions. A number were cut down in a decayed condition at the amphitheatre, and the seats beneath were shaded by an awning of sail cloth containing over three thousand yards of canvas. In the outskirts of the camp ground boarding houses and restaurants sprang up like weeds, while now and then peddlers, hawkers and street fakirs would attempt to ply their trade from tents or booths erected outside the lines of the sacred territory. As time went on the original character of the meeting was lost in the hurly burly of such thronging thousands, most of whom came for a "day off" and were prepared to have it in one way or another. The days of prayer and meditation had passed away and the season of elaboration and bustle had superseded. Nor was this the only change in the character of the "institution." Heretofore it had been exclusively a Methodistic concern, but one by one preachers of other orthodox denominations would be heard from the pulpit. The first of these was a Presbyterian clergyman in 1858, but the principal faith of these outsiders was Baptist, of whom we shall hear more in later years.

LAND COMPANIES AND REAL ESTATE "BOOMS"

This situation had its logical sequence. The demand for land for building purposes followed, and the organization of promoters of real estate interests came as a necessity. The first of these companies was composed of the leaders of these meetings, the "Martha's Vineyard Methodist Camp Meeting Association," so called, which received its charter from the Massachusetts legislature in 1860. The incorporators were twenty-four in number: Jeremiah Pease, Henry Bradley,

Caleb L. Ellis, A. D. Hatch, Joshua Remington, Iram Smith, Pardon M. Stone, William A. Wardwell, John C. Scott, Cyrus Washburn, Elisha Harris, William B. Mitchell, James Davis, William Hutchinson, Lot Phinney, H. Vincent, Sirson P. Coffin, George M. Carpenter, C. H. Titus, ——— Philbrook, J. W. Willet, James D. Butler, H. S. White, and William B. Lawton. The property which they controlled was that known as the "Camp Ground" south of Squash Meadow pond, bounded easterly by Circuit avenue and westerly by a line drawn southerly through Sunset lake.

In 1866 a number of gentlemen, with the intent of making a summer home for their families and developing the place as a resort, purchased the territory lying between the land of the Martha's Vineyard Camp Meeting Association and the sea. These persons became incorporated in 1868 under the name of the "Oak Bluffs Land and Wharf Co." Their grounds were laid out in lots and avenues, reserving many acres for public parks. Restrictions as to the sale and use of these lots protected the residents from disreputable surroundings. This property began at the present harbor jetty, thence along the beach to a point opposite the head of Farm pond; thence crossing the head of Farm pond to Sea View avenue, and along this thoroughfare to the first named point.

In 1868 the Martha's Vineyard Camp Meeting Association, finding itself precluded from the extension of its grounds in an easterly direction, and feeling the necessity of securing room for future growth before it should be surrounded by private corporations, over which it could exercise no control, purchased a tract across the pond. There was considerable opposition to this as a financial speculation and a prospective burden for the association, and after consideration this tract was transferred to private parties who had consented to assume the purchase. These gentlemen having been joined by several laymen and clergymen of the Methodist church, perfected an organization called "The Vineyard Grove Company" and in 1870 it was incorporated. Capt. William H. Phillips of Taunton was its first president, and Rev. J. D. King the agent. Additional land was purchased until more than two hundred acres were held by it from the pond to the lighthouse on East Chop, and all east of Kedron avenue. Roads, parks, circles, drives and plank walks were laid out and a wharf constructed for the convenience of landing by large steamboats or smaller craft. It was adopted by the Camp Meeting Association as its official landing. A hotel was soon erected and this section of the town began to grow rapidly. The board walk skirting the pond, 3,500 feet in length, fifteen feet wide, containing nearly 200,000 feet of plank, was lined each summer with booths and "bazaars" and became for a while the central promenade for the throngs of visitors every afternoon and evening.

Various other tracts to the northwest of this property were exploited in the following years: Belleview Heights and Sunset Heights and bordering on the Lagoon came Bay View and Lagoon Heights. Other sections felt the stimulating effect of this feverish growth, and plots of land called by the fanciful names of Green Meadow, Forest Hill, Oak Grove, Harbor Heights, Prospect Heights, Sea View Hill, Grove Dale and Ocean View found ready purchasers at equally fancy prices. Up to 1872 the "boom" was continuous and genuine, and upwards of a million dollars must have been expended in improvements made by the various companies and promoters. The panic of 1872-3, however, put a stop to this excitement, and property values fell and real estate lanquished. In time this condition righted itself and since then the growth has been steady and normal.

THE BAPTIST CHURCH

Almost on identical dates with the formation of the Methodist Society here the local Baptists organized the Oak Bluffs' Baptist Church, April 13, 1877, at a meeting held in the Worth Building (so called) on Circuit avenue. Irregular meetings had been held in this place for a number of months previous to this date under the spiritual guidance of Rev. George F. Lewis of the Vineyard Haven society. Fourteen members presented letters of recommendation from various churches and became the founders of this society, viz: Zebina E. Berry and wife, Worcester, Mass.; Samuel N. Davis and wife, Rhoda N. Linton and Electa Wadsworth, Vineyard Haven; Job H. Gorham, North Tisbury; Tristram Cleveland and wife, Lucy P. Smith and Thomas H. Norton, Edgartown; and Mrs. Henry T. Luce from a defunct church. Zebina Berry was chosen deacon, and Job H. Gorham, clerk of the new society. Ten additional persons were baptized on the first Sunday following, and the society has been in a prosperous condition ever since, a period of thirty-three years. Services were held in various places during the early days, houses, halls, etc., until July of the following year (1878), when the present house of worship, situated on the corner of Pequot avenue and Grove street, was completed at a cost of about $3,000, exclusive of labor donated by the members. It was dedicated the following month during the sessions of the Baptist camp meeting that year, and through the efforts of the Camp Meeting Association and the summer residents the balance of the debt on the structure was cancelled and the church was made free of incumbrance prior to its consecration. This support has been continued annually in the same generous way to meet the current expenses. Mr. C. B. Erwin, of New Britain, donated the bell, and later, by will, left a legacy to the society to enable it to maintain services. Six deacons have served since the establishment of the organization: Tristram Cleveland, Samuel N. Davis, Shubael L. Norton, Alonzo Pike, William H. Davis and Job H. Gorham.

Since the formation of the society 151 persons have been enrolled, of whom 41 have died, 29 transferred, and 13 dropped, leaving 68 as the present membership. In 1905 the church building was enlarged and improved at a cost of over $1,000. The present deacon, and clerk (Lucy P. Smith) are the only survivors of the constituent membership gathered in 1877 under the ministrations of Rev. Mr. Lewis. The succession in the pastorate has been as follows: Geo. F. Reid, of Edgartown, supply, 1879-80; Jesse Coker, of Vineyard Haven, supply, 1880-1; Thomas W. Crudgintor, 1882-4; O. W. Kimball, 1884-9; Alfred Fairbrother, 1889-91; J. E. Dinsmore, 1892; E. D. Mason, 1892-4; George W. Fuller, 1895-7; Ernest W. Dow, 1897-9; F. F. Thayer, 1899-1900; George W. Fuller, 1900-02; S. A. Dyke, 1902-07; George F. Newhall, 1908 (present incumbent).

THE METHODIST CHURCH

The local society of this denomination is the outgrowth of the general camp-meeting spirit in which the Methodists have been such a prominent factor. On April 15, 1877, the Rev. J. D. King organized a "class" with about forty members at a meeting held at the residence of Capt. Joseph Dias. This was the beginning of the present society, but as there was no meeting-house available for them, Sunday and other weekly services were held in a small public hall over the offices of the

Cottage City Star. On June 3, 1877, the members entered into a formal organization, and the Rev. G. M. Hamlen was appointed first pastor and held the office for three years. It was a period of activity and enthusiasm, and during his pastorate Trinity M. E. church was erected at a cost of about $10,000, located on Trinity circle. Since that date Grace chapel, adjoining the church, and a parsonage have been added to the facilities for denominational work. The society numbers 73 members at the present time. The succession in the pastorate has been as follows

F. P. Parkin, 1880-1; F. O. Holman, G. G. Switzer, L. B. Codding, 1882; F. P. Parkin, 1883-4; J. F. Cooper, 1885-7; W. E. Kingler, 1888-9; G. W. Elmer, 1890; W. L. Hood, 1891-3; R. E. Schuh, 1894-5; N. C. Alger, W. F. Taylor, 1896; W. F. Taylor, 1897-8; R. M. Wilkins, 1899-1900; R. S. Moore, 1901-4; C. E. Delemater, 1905-6; J. S. Bridgford, 1907-8; G. M. Hamlen, 1909; W. E. Handy, 1910 (present incumbent).

THE ROMAN CATHOLIC CHURCH

Between the years 1872 and 1880 a large number of the Catholic denomination were found in this vicinity during the summer months without any chance of attending service. A few of these persons, seeing the need, and desiring to keep in touch with their church, took steps which led to services being held from time to time at a private residence. Among this number was a Mr. Henry Magetts, a poor man, who lived as a butler in the family of a lady who spent her summers here. Mr. Magetts, seeing the need of a suitable place of worship, decided to purchase a lot of land and give it for the benefit of the Catholics of Martha's Vineyard, and the lot now occupied by the little Church of the Sacred Heart was purchased.

At that time the Rev. Fr. McMahon was the parish priest of St. Lawrence Church, New Bedford. It was to him, it is understood, that Henry Magetts gave the deed of land, as well as a sum of money to begin the building of the church. When Fr. McMahon was made bishop of Hartford he was succeeded by the Rev. H. J. Smith, the present pastor of that church, in whose parish this Vineyard mission belongs.

With contributions from summer visitors and resident Catholics, a frame structure was erected. From 1880 until

TRINITY (EPISCOPAL) CHURCH

1896 mass was said here only during the two months, July and August. During the time of Fr. Smith's charge, the interior was plastered, the building was clapboarded, a new gallery erected and a new platform for the altar, as well as carpets and dressing table, were supplied. In 1896 the church came under the direction of the Rev. Fr. Neares of St. John the Baptist parish, and his assistants.

Fr. Martius, one of the assistants, did much to beautify the church. During his administration a tower was erected and a fine bell placed there. Mr. John Murphy of Roxbury at this time presented the church with the stations of the cross, a set of white vestments and an altar lamp, Miss Dolan of New York giving the statue of the Blessed Virgin Mary. Fr. Neares had built a new altar and put in new pews and a furnace.

In 1901 Fr. Rosa gave a new organ duringt he summer. Mrs. H. Llewellyn of New Bedford presented the church a fine collection of books.

It has been customary in the winter to have mass on the third Sunday of each month, and the children have attended a Sunday school under the superintendency of Miss Maria J. Golding and her assistants. Mass is now said each Sunday, which is attended by the church members from all parts of the island. The resident pastor now (1906) is the Rev. Patrick E. McGee, a native of New Bedford and a graduate of Holy Cross, Worcester, and of the American College at Rome. He assumed charge of this parish mission in February, 1903.

TRINITY (EPISCOPAL) CHURCH

In 1882 the leading spirits in the Summer Colony, desirous of maintaining religious services under the ritual of the Protestant Episcopal church, organized a society for this purpose and adopted the name of Trinity Episcopal Church. While it was nominally of this sect, yet it had no official relations with the Massachusetts diocese, to which it should belong, and it is, to all intents and purposes, an independent society using the name of Episcopal because the services conform to the ritual of that denomination and its pastoral supply is always taken from the ministry of that church. The Rev. Dr. J. W. Shackleford of New York City and attached to the diocese of New York was its first pastoral supply, and for many years returned to guide its summer services. It has never been anything beyond a vacation church for the summer visitors, and is open only about three months of each year. The liberality of summer tourists and the non-resident members enables the management to provide attractive musical artists drafted from metropolitan choirs to render the vocal parts of the church ritual, and the singing has always been one of the features of this anomalous church, which survives without any affiliation in the denomination to which it nominally belongs.

At a meeting held Aug. 25, 1883, the building committee reported that it had completed its duty, and the church building was free from debt. The following named persons were then elected as trustees of the society to attend to its secular affairs: J. J. Crane, M. D., J. C. Carey, John M. Crane, all of New York; H. A. Tucker, M. D., Brooklyn, N. Y.; Col. Nicholas Van Slyck, Providence; Holder M. Brownell, New Bedford, and A. J. Burgess of Cottage City. The value of the church building and lot when ready for occupancy was about $5,000, and it has had considerable interior improvements since then. The last report of its communicants gave the number as twenty.

UNION CHAPEL

Certain of the summer residents, not identified with either of the preceding denominations, organized the Oak Bluffs Christian Union Association, in 1880, for the purpose of providing religious services which should be undenominational in character. This body erected a meeting-house which they called Union Chapel, at a cost of about $6,000, and it was opened for service by the late Rev. S. F. Upham, D. D., who for many years after preached the first sermon annually at the beginning of the summer. The musical portion of the services has always been a distinguishing feature, the talent being drawn from the many celebrated singers who make this town their mecca during the vacation period.

SCHOOLS

The earliest reference to educational matters in this section is to be found in 1755, when Peter Norton, Henry Luce and Malatiah Davis were chosen a committee "to determine where the school shall be keept in the farm neck."[1] This was then a part of the school system of Edgartown, and these arrangements were made to accommodate the pupils of the

[1]Edgartown Records, I, 209.

Sanchacantacket and Eastville districts. It is not known where the school-house was located, if one existed at that time, as it is doubtful if any were built so early. Owing to the scattered settlements of Farm neck it is probable that a "moving" school was kept in this section and held in private houses. In 1775 it was voted to hire two schoolmasters, and the town was divided into two districts, and school-houses for each were decided upon. Ichabod Wiswall (1704-82) was probably the first teacher in this district, called the North West and later Homes Hole district, and the usual "tradition" verifies this.[1] The earliest school-house known was situated

OLD SCHOOL HOUSE, EASTVILLE.

about thirty rods southeasterly from a dwelling house on the site where the residence of Isaac W. Norton now stands. In 1771 such a school building existed in the "North West division" and provision was made for its repair and the hiring of a master.[2] In 1776 the school committee for this division was Ebenezer Smith, Samuel Smith and Ebenezer Norton. At this date no settled policy in regard to the maintenance of schools in this section seems to have been adopted, and the records give but little information as to the actual conditions of its educational facilities. The money raised for schools varying from year to year was divided proportionately, and the

[1]Sketches of Old Eastville Houses by the late Constant Norton in "Cottage City Star," 1883.

[2]The town voted, in 1782, to sell this school-house to the highest bidder, the proceeds to be applied "for the use of a school" (Edg. Rec., II, 8).

district committees were empowered to spend it in building or hiring school-houses or teachers as each saw fit.[1] In 1795 Shubael Davis, Ichabod Norton and Samuel Smith, 3rd, were the committeemen for the Homes Hole division. Small appropriations only were available prior to 1810, probably less than $100 annually for this section, and it need not be estimated how much could be done with this amount of money.

The rapid growth of the town, following the Camp Meeting period, necessitated the construction of school houses to accommodate the increasing population. A new building was provided for Eastville at a cost of $850, and another for the Highland section at a cost of $2,300. In 1880 these two schools housed seventy-five scholars, and at that time $700 was allotted for the expenses of maintaining same, two teachers being employed. The appropriations for schools for this district of Edgartown was one of the subjects for the annual wrangle of the taxpayers prior to division of the town — each side claiming that injustice was done in the allotments. The amounts expended in 1810, which we have seen to be about $100 per annum, are an example in contrast to the conditions existing now.

A century later this town had school property valued at $14,000 and appropriated about $5,000 annually for educational purposes.[2]

SETTLEMENT AT MAJOR'S COVE

THE LINE OF NORTON MAGNATES

The acquisition of land about this inlet of Sanchacantackett pond began with a purchase of some meadow by Nicholas Norton, at an unknown date, of Thomas Sissetom, one of the petty chiefs of that region.[3] The transaction is not of record, and the deed is not now known to be in existence.[4] It was about the "Wading Place," probably in the vicinity

[1]In 1800 the entire appropriation for schools was but $300, to be divided among four districts. In 1802 it was but $200, and in 1804 it was increased to $350. In 1816 only $150 was appropriated. In 1825 the money was divided by the number of scholars in each division. In 1832 the sum of $450 was appropriated for schools.

[2]Town Report, 1908.

[3]In his will Norton bequeaths to son Joseph "a tract of land lying at Sanjacantacket joyning to the mill Creke which I bought of Mr. Sam," but the town records give Sissetom. Perhaps there were two purchases.

[4]Information of Medical Director, B. H. Kidder, U. S. N., who states that he had seen the deed, and that it was taken to Boone, Iowa, by this deceased brother, I. N. Kidder, and lost after his death, in 1878.

of Miober's bridge, and was held by him in the same way that many tracts of land were found to be in the posession of the whites, by a private purchase of the natives' "rights." This meadow was thus described in the records:

> The abovesaid land was Layd out at the head of the swamp near Mr Boults farm taking Beginning at a Oak marked by a fut path at the head of the swamp which Joyns to the wading place and runneth in its Southern Line By the said Path towards Wil Lays Plain about 73 Poles; and from said Tree westerly to an old stump on a hill near the old Path that goes to homes hole: which stump is distant from the said tree about 50 poles: and from said stump southwesterly seventy three Poles to a tree marked on the side of an hill: from thence crossing over at the fore said path to a marked tree about seventy poles.[1]

On Jan. 28, 1684, he had "liberty granted to him to purchase a piece of land that lieth against his meadow at Sanchacantackett."[2] This was the beginning of the long and extensive ownership of territory by this family in that section. On Sept. 20, 1686, Matthew Mayhew, as patentee sold one hundred acres at the "Wading Place," which took its first bound mark on the southeast, at Miober's bridge, and for over two centuries "Bolt's Farm" has been a local landmark in that vicinity. Boult sold it in 1703 to Israel Daggett, and it finally came into the possession of Joseph Norton, and has ever since been a part of that ancient inheritance.[3] It is probable that Nicholas Norton utilized the small brook which runs from a marsh into Sanchacantacket pond for a mill site, as the remains of a dam are still visible, and there are references to it in the early deeds of that region.[4] There is no evidence that he resided here, and it is probable that he never did. By his will, 1690, he gave "all my meadow at Sanjacantick" to his son Benjamin, upon certain conditions, which it is quite certain he fulfilled, as in 1726, this property was sold to James[4] Pease, who in turn disposed of it to Matthew Norton in 1731, and on the same day Matthew sold it to Ebenezer Norton.[5]

The first Norton known to have resided on this property was Joseph, son of Nicholas, born in Weymouth, Mass., March,

[1]Edgartown Records, I, 18, 39.

[2]Ibid, I, 30.

[3]Dukes Deeds, II, 3; IV, 114; V, 427.

[4]This brook separates the farms of Henry Constant Norton and B. H. Kidder. There was a mill here, according to tradition, for grinding oak bark for tanning purposes; and as it is surmised that Nicholas Norton was a tanner, the tradition probably has some foundation.

[5]Dukes Deeds, V, 86, 97, 112.

1652, and it is supposed that he built his house here about 1700, perhaps when his son Joseph, Junior, on his marriage, succeeded to the father's house on the Mill path. The new house built by Joseph at Major's cove was about ninety rods northwest of Miober's bridge, and about eight rods northeast of the road, and a part of it was standing one hundred and fifty years later. He was the first of a long line of local magnates who ruled in this domain for two centuries. He was easily one of the most distinguished citizens of Edgartown during his lifetime. Although politically opposed to the ruling family, yet he surmounted these difficult conditions, and held the highest offices in the gift of the government. He was connected with the "Dutch Rebellion" in 1673, but in 1675 had been forgiven, and was made marshall, constable and water bailiff, of the General Court. He was chosen overseer (selectmen), 1682; county commissioner, 1684, 1686, 1695; proprietors' agent, 1687; and when the island came under the Massachusetts jurisdiction, he was recommended to Sir William Phipps, by Simon Athearn, as "being a man of Curag(e) & a good Estate," and the Governor appointed him marshall in 1692, on this recommendation. He was appointed justice of the King's Bench, 1695, and was generally known thereafter as Justice Norton, in the records, although he held the place but a few years. He was again high sheriff in 1699, a position with which he is more particularly identified, one as dignified in those times as that of judge. A number of stories are told of his commanding influence over the Indians, who held him in great awe, on account of his majestic figure and his fearlessness. He lived to the ripe old age of 89 years and ten months, dying Jan. 30, 1742, leaving a large estate. Among the personal effects he bequeathed to his son Ebenezer was a "silver tankard," from which may have been sipped that seductive potion of choice rum which was served to the committee on the bounds of Sanchacantackett. This son succeeded him in the possession of the ancestral acres at Major's Cove.[1]

Ebenezer Norton, born about 1691, was the second to occupy this property, and built himself a house about half way between Miober's bridge and the homestead of his father, probably about 1715, when he married, and during his oc-

[1]Dukes Probate, III, 139. This tankard descended to Peter, son of Ebenezer, who bequeathed it to his son Ebenezer (1741-1805), who went to Maine and it is probably an heirloom among his descendants (ibid., VII, 203).

cupancy of the place until his death, April 11, 1769, he added a part of Felix neck and some outlying land to the original estate. His life seemed to run in less public channels, and but little is found about him on the records. He was selectman, 1738; school committee, 1738, 1739, 1742, 1745, and was prominently identified with the affairs of the church during his lifetime. It is stated by descendants that he was a lieutenant of the militia. It is related that when on his dying bed he saw the winding sheet, which had been prepared for him in advance, bleaching on the lawn in view of his bedchamber. The family hogs were noticed by him rooting around this piece of fine linen, and he called out to the astonished family, "Drive those hogs away from my winding sheet! It will not be fit to bury the Devil in!" He had two sons, Eliakim, the elder, and Peter; and the legendary lore, which is thick about this family and its paternal acres, gives us the further tale of a disagreement which these two brothers had about a cosset lamb, and that Eliakim gathered up his personal belongings, and went to a "far country" settling at the North shore. The younger brother remained at home.[1]

Peter Norton, third of the line, was born Sept. 9, 1718, and renewed in his person the martial spirit of his grandfather, Joseph. His house, probably erected about 1740 when he married, was situated a few rods west of that built by his grandfather, and from it could be seen, in his day, the curling smoke rising from thirty wigwams of the Sanchacantacketts. His property by gradual increase bordered the entire western cove of the great pond, and for him it received the name of Major's Cove, which it has ever since borne. Peter Norton was of a military turn of thought, and in 1756 was captain of the Edgartown company, and on Aug. 8, 1761, was commissioned as Major of the Dukes County regiment, raised during the French and Indian wars.[2] Like his father he was interested in the schools, and served on the school committee many years. When the Revolution broke out he was too old to enter that war, but acted upon committees to prepare for the defence of the town. He was commissioned high sheriff, Oct. 24, 1776, by the Provincial authorities, and held the

[1]The slight value of "tradition" is illustrated by this legend, for it is of record that Eliakim and Peter Norton together bought several pieces of property in Chickemmoo in 1747 and 1748, which would seem to dispose of the reason alleged for Eliakim's departure from the paternal roof at the age of thirty because of a quarrel over a pet lamb (Dukes Deeds, VIII, 12, 13).

[2]Massachusetts Archives, XCIX, 24.

position for many years.[1] When the Baptist sect came to the island after the Revolution, Major Peter became identified with it, and was, by reason of his commanding influence, a leading light in that church. He died Feb. 3, 1792.[2] Five of his sons removed to Maine, and the family homestead fell in 1792 to Ichabod, his youngest son but one.

Ichabod Norton, born Dec. 17, 1762, inherited the northern half of his father's estate, the southern portion having been alienated during the lifetime of his father. He remained a bachelor throughout his long life, and with an

THE "MAJOR NORTON" HOUSE (1752).
RESIDENCE OF HENRY CONSTANT NORTON.

inheritance gradually growing in value by judicious investments, through many years, aided by few personal wants, he became the wealthiest man of his time upon the island, His property was largely in real estate, both here and in Maine, in vessels, and in mortgages, and these conditions of thrift and simple personal habits gave rise to the most conflicting stories, both of his wealth and of his miserly habits. The truth probably lies between the two extremes, for while it was true that he lived in a house that had all the signs of dilapidation about it and the surrounding premises; did not keep a carriage,

[1]This appointment was made upon the recommendation of Chief Justice Joseph Mayhew, who said that Norton preferred to be a Colonel of the militia (Mass. Archives, CXCIV, 208).

[2]Backus, Church History of New England, II, 375; III, 167.

because, as he said, he had to keep a dozen for others, referring to those used by his debtors; exacted the last dollar on notes and mortgages, and all the added attributes of a "close" man, yet it is conceded on the other hand, that he gave much privately to charity, in his own way; was just to the deserving poor; always had a kind word for children and was merciful to all the animal kind. His habits were formed in youth, as he said, from a need for economical living, and being a bachelor, his life at best was a narrow one, which turned for its companionship to a "fool nigger" named Harry, or as the absurd individual explained his full name, John Harry Monus John Peter Tobirus Peter Toskirus Peter Tubal Cain. Whence he came no one knew, but for fifty years he presided in the kitchen of "Uncle" Ichabod, and became one of the characters of the neighborhood. He was a confirmed monomaniac on the subject of wars and martial matters, though perfectly harmless, and his conversation was largely a confabulation of historical gibberish, which led those who knew him to believe he had been in the service of England, probably in the naval forces. He pretended to be in communication with individuals below the surface of the earth, and if halted by a question he would mysteriously repeat it, in a solemn manner, and turn his ear to the earth for the answer. Prompt news service was always to be had, for Harry would answer in a few seconds, "Admiral Hawke fought 'em sir, and has taken forty ships," or some such trivial mummery. There is an excavation on the Ichabod Norton place as large as a good sized cellar, made by him, still known as "Harry's Hole." When he planted melons he would put an old iron pot in the middle of the patch, "for a model for the melons," he would explain.

No refining influence of wife or children came into the life of this lonely man, Ichabod Norton, yet he was very human, and could find it to his taste to cause a legend to be put over his fireplace: "Deal justly, love mercy, walk humbly," and doubtless he tried in his contracted homeless life to do all these three things, and probably succeeded in each of the requirements.[1] His will, dated Sept. 28, 1843, and proven Oct. 18, 1847, is probably the longest on record in the County registry, containing bequests to about all of his relatives, many friends

[1]"Reformation" John Adams gives this picture of Ichabod Norton:—"He has but few of the comforts of this life and lives on coarse food. We ate, prayed and wept over him. He gave us two dollars tribute money." (Autobiography, p. 451.)

and a charitable legacy. At this time there were fifty-two of the grandchildren of his father living, and all were remembered, presumably. After his death, the farm was further sub-divided, and the long line of local magnates was broken.[1]

SETTLEMENT AT POHQU-AUKE (PECOY)

Isaac Norton, elder brother of Joseph, and probably the eldest son of Nicholas Norton, also became one of the early landed proprietors and residents of the Sanchacantacket region, finally settling on the north side of Major's Cove. His first investment was about Squash meadow, with several others, in 1683, and on Jan. 28, 1684, he was granted a lot on the south side of Tacknash's field.[2] About 1688 or 1689 he bought the Indian "rights" to the fertile little neck, since called Pecoy, of Ezekiel Pauknessimmun,[3] and this he added to a lot previously bought of Maquaine, in 1685, "in consideration of an iron pot and other goods."[4]

HOUSE OF THE FIVE ISAACS

He built his house on the north side of the W'Quahti-pog pond, a commanding position, perhaps soon after the purchase, and thus becomes, next to Joseph Daggett, the earliest settler in this region, on Ogkeshkuppe neck. This house was given to his son Isaac (37) in 1713, and he in turn deeded it, in 1721, to the third Isaac (113). Isaac, Jr. had sons Isaac, Stephen, Henry, and Shubael, of whom the first two were bachelors, and lived according to tradition in the east half of the house, and Shubael, the married brother, in the other with his family. By will the shares of the unmarried brothers went to the fourth Isaac, son of Shubael, and he was in turn succeeded by the fifth and last of the name to live in this house of notable family history.[5]

[1]Many of the facts about him have been obtained from a biographical sketch of Ichabod Norton prepared for the press by James Athearn Jones, of West Tisbury, and published in pamphlet form for private distribution, in 1848, by the executor. It was intended as a vindication of Mr. Norton. The historical portion, purporting to give a sketch of his ancestors, is painful in its errors. It does not seem possible to crowd more mis-statements into a few pages devoted to the early generations of Nortons than there appears.

[2]Edgartown Records, I, 34.

[3]Dukes Deeds, I, 88.

[4]Ibid., III, 25. When the neck was divided these purchases were confirmed to him, but he was obliged to make restitution to the other owners of the six-and-twenty shares.

[5]Information given by Mrs. Annie Daggett Lord. The east half becoming dilapitated was torn down, making the building considerably smaller.

EASTVILLE.

SETTLEMENT AT ONKAW AND QUINNIAAMUK.

The extreme northern end of the eastermost chop became a settlement apart and distinctive before the 18th century. The nearest settlers were at Major's cove and Farm pond, and a stretch of several miles separated them from their neighbors. This locality, next to Chappaquiddick, was the last stand of the Indians of the town, and during the following century and a half the smoke from their wigwams rising skyward could be seen from any house in this region.

The sachem Wampamog, in 1669, gave the first tract of land here in severalty to the sisters, Alice and Keziah Sessetom. In the quaint language of the native the sachem deeded to them a tract "at the place called Quannaamuk":

> It is the will of me Wampamog that the eldest called Ales Setum should have the breadth of twenty-five rods and that she that is called Keziah Setum should have the breadth of fifteen rods: both these to have same wedth now said at the pond and so upward as far as Daggetts bounds: I, Wompamog say this is firmly and of right theirs because I have divided this quantity of land to them, even to Alcs and Keziah Setum, the daughters of Thomas Setum: it is theirs I say and all their offspring for ever: or if they fale, to go to their kindred: may they in peace enjoy this land for ever for I will never alter this nor shall any that defend my Sachemship do this; but let these peacefully enjoy the said land even Ales and Keziah.[1]

It will be recalled that this Alice Sissetom (or Setum) was the Vineyard Pocahontas, the Indian wife of Joseph Daggett. Part of this land subsequently descended to Daggett's daughters, Esther and Alice, the half breeds.[2]

THE FIRST SETTLEMENT

There were various early purchases by the whites in this region, Richard Sarson in 1686, Thomas West in 1692, and Isaac and Thomas Norton and Robert Cathcart in 1698, but it is not believed they had houses there.

Edward Cottle, Jr. was the first person who lived at Onkaw, the ancient inheritance of his wife's Indian grandmother, Alice Sissetom. He was there as early as 1695, "where he had a dwelling house," and he may be reckoned as the

[1]Dukes Deeds, VI, 412.

[2]See Court Records, 1690; Joseph Daggett vs. Jacob Norton and James Pease, Jr., suit for trespass with verdict for plaintiff. In 1698 a tract forty rods wide, same quantity as given by Wampamog was sold at public vendue to Jacob Norton. This may be the identical land.

first settler of the region subsequently known as Eastville.[1] Here he was surrounded by Indians of the Sanchacantacket tribe, of which tribe his children were quadroons. It is probable that he was the sole resident of the English race in this place for the ensuing twenty-five years.

Benjamin Smith of Edgartown had been granted, in 1704, a tract of thirty acres, and although he did not settle here he bequeathed it with other property here to his two sons, Thomas and Ebenezer, and the latter settled on the land (now The Highlands) about 1725 and it became an inheritance to succeeding Ebenezers of this family for several generations.[2] A new settler, in the person of John Cunningham, came to Eastville in 1725 and bought land of Cottle at various times[3] for the ensuing ten years until his death, and he was followed by another stranger, John Cousins, about 1730, who acquired land in the same vicinity. Theophilus Pease and Thomas Claghorn moved up here from Edgartown at the same time and settled in Eastville. A third stranger, Malatiah Davis, made the first of his many purchases here in 1744, and his descendents for several generations were identified with the little settlement. He was followed by David Davis in 1759, another stranger to the Vineyard, and not known to be related to the earlier Davis residents. These two families resided here for the next century, intermarried and became specially identified with this settlement.

"BARBARY COAST"

This was a neighborhood full of the romance of the sea, and these new settlers brought to it the additional mystery of family "skeletons" from other regions, as will become detailed in the sketches of their lives. The men of this little hamlet got their living from the deep in all lines of endeavor, and not the least of their sources of supply was that seemingly ghoulish business of wrecking, of profiting by the unfortunate deodants of the storms and tides of the Vineyard sound. Whether justly or in humor this place was known in local parlance as the "Barbary Coast," in token of the avocation of most of its people, and many weird tales are told of the hard bargains driven with luckless skippers who had drifted on the treacherous shoals of these waters.

[1]Dukes Deeds, V, 305.

[2]Edgartown Records, I, 64; comp. Deeds, II, 285.

[3]Dukes Deeds, IV, 76, 116, 118; V, 50, 385.

Annals of Oak Bluffs

THE METHODIST CHURCH[1]

So far as is known, the first individuals here professing to be Methodists, were two colored persons, John Saunders and his wife. They had been slaves in the state of Virginia. By extraordinary efforts and rigid economy they had been enabled to purchase their freedom. They set out in a vessel bound to some port in Massachusetts, which stopping for some cause in Homes Hole harbor, these persons concluded to land at Eastville. They arrived in 1787 and remained in this vicinity several years. John, being an exhorter (having as is understood held this position among his fellow slaves) preached occasionally to the people of color, at "Farm Neck." It is represented that he was highly esteemed by them, but it does not appear that any society was formed as a result of his labors. In 1792, Saunders removed to the adjacent island of Chappaquiddick, where there was also a settlement of colored people, where his wife having died, he remarried, and where he also died in 1795.[2] In the early part of the same year of Saunders' decease, 1795, the justly celebrated Jesse Lee, the pioneer of Methodism in New England, visited Martha's Vineyard. This settlement was the second place he visited and the following entry appears in his journal relating to the event:

> Friday [February] 6th. [1795]. I preached at Shubael Davies' in Edgartown. I had a refreshing season and spoke with faith.[3]

It may be presumed that the host of Lee was a convert to the new doctrine, as in those days of religious intolerance itinerant preachers would not be entertained by those of other denominations. There is, however, nothing of record to show any establishment of regular services here following the visit of this pioneer. The ministers assigned to the Vineyard circuit

[1]For some of the facts in this sketch of early Methodism the author is indebted to the kindness of Mrs. Fanny A. Deane, of Edgartown, who loaned the manuscript of a "Centennial address" prepared by her father, Rev. Hebron S. Vincent, and delivered, in 1884, before one of the annual gatherings of that denomination at Cottage City.

[2]There was an impression, although not a very prevalent one that at sometime late in the eighteenth century, Dr. Thomas Coke, afterwards Bishop, stopped in a partially wrecked vessel at Homes Hole, when passing along the coast. But of the correctness of this tradition there is no substantial evidence. Following him in all his nine voyages to America, there is nothing to indicate that he ever came to our island under any circumstances.

[3]Stevens, Memorials of Methodism, I, 328.

probably held meetings here, and one of the earliest, if not the first, to embrace the faith and teachings of this sect was Joseph Linton, whose house was used for the public services. In 1821 a "class" was in existence, and the itinerant for that year makes numerous references to meetings which he conducted on "the east side of the harbor."[1] Private houses continued to be used until about 1840, when a small structure was built on the old road leading to Cottage City.[2] The leading spirit in this local mission at this time was "Uncle" Jeremiah Pease who drove up from Edgartown every Sunday for years and preached in this rude structure,"without money and without price." His only reward was a bountiful dinner at "Brother" Linton's, after service. In 1842 the Rev. John Adams notes in his journal a visit to Eastville after an absence of twenty years and adds: "I preached in the little Methodist house to twenty-four hearers." This may be an indication of the numerical strength of the society at that date.

The development of the annual camp meeting services about this time and the growth of the settlement about Squash Meadow pond, which subsequently became known as Oak Bluffs, resulted in the abandonment of the building and the discontinuance of services here. After a fitful career this little meeting house passed into the hands of the Ladies Aid Society of the M. E. Church of Cottage City. In 1888 the disused building was purchased by Mr. T. W. Chapman, who moved it to the Vineyard Highlands, where it forms the main part of the house now occupied by his daughter. It still shows the remains of hand hewn shingles and hand-wrought nails on its roof.

THE BAPTIST CHURCH

From all the information obtainable it is not understood that there was any organized church of this denomination in this settlement. The persons holding that belief, resident here, were members of the societies already formed in Tisbury or Edgartown, and merely joined in a temporary manner for convenience of worship.[3] Services were held in private

[1]John Adams, Autobiography, Vol. I, *passin.* The meetings in 1821-2 were all held "at Brother Linton's."

[2]This building had no pretensions to architectural beauty, being without belfry or other ornaments usual in houses of worship.

[3]One of the earliest members of this church was "Daddy" Richardson. His views were characteristically expressed when he said that "Nobody could be baptized in a pint porringer."

houses before 1840, usually conducted by a lay member. About 1845 a small edifice was erected by Mr. Obed Luce from the contributions of the worshippers and their friends, aided by volunteer labor. It was built on the old road leading from Eastville to Cottage City, on land owned by Mr. Shaw Norris, who gave the use of it, free of rent. Itinerant preachers of this denomination held services here from time to time to supplement the regular supply of the laity. Jesse Pease was an early preacher, followed by Tristram Cleveland, Solomon Athearn, and John Mayhew. This chapel was a small unpainted structure without ornamentation. The passing away of these laborers and the improved church privileges at the Wesleyan Grove camp ground caused the abandonment of this primitive structure and the services of these earnest lay exhorters.

The abandoned edifice was sold by the surviving members to Benjamin A. Norton, who dismantled it and hauled it to North Tisbury, where it forms the main portion of his house.

TAVERNS

The only public houses in this town, prior to the growth of Oak Bluffs, in the last half century were situated at Eastville. This place was a hamlet made up mostly of taverns and ship chandlers' shops, where the seafaring man was accustomed to tarry voluntarily, or by force of circumstances. East Indiamen, with their rich cargoes, anchored off this compact village awaiting orders from Boston or Salem, or to recruit their stores with fresh supplies of food and raiment. Beef, mutton, poultry, vegetables, corn, rye and other island produce found a ready sale, for cash, or in exchange for rum, sugar, coffee and other "foreign" luxuries. It was the custom in those early days for the captains and crews of these ships from foreign ports to remain on shore while in the harbor, and these homely taverns gave ample entertainment, with their huge fireplaces, bountiful kitchens and general good cheer. An itinerant tailoress or a cobbler was usually within call to make or repair a depleted outfit, and the housewife, aided by an Indian woman and some of her older daughters, managed this motley household without friction or loss of dignity.

The following named persons were licensed innholders in the precinct of Eastville by the County Court for the years specified:

Thomas Claghorn 1730-83; who was succeeded by his widow, Susannah Claghorn, 1784-6; John Cunningham, 1731-2; John Cousins, 1731-65; Thomas Pease, Jr., 1751-87; David Davis, 1759-67; who was succeeded by his widow, Sarah Davis, 1768-87; Ebenezer Smith, 1786-1806;[1] Malatiah Davis, 1798-1806. Most of these taverns were in one neighborhood, convenient for the shipping interests, which furnished the most of their patronage. That they were the scenes of jollity at night when "Jack" came ashore is evident from what we know of their character. John Cousins was indicted in 1733 "for sufering Disorders in suffering fidling, singing

THE CLAGHORN TAVERN,
BUILT ABOUT 1730.
NOW THE OLIVER LINTON HOUSE.

& Dancing" in his tavern, but the jury acquitted him. The subsequent owners of these houses continued the business of tavern keeping till about the middle of the last century. One still survives, the Eastville Inn (1907), as a last relic of this interesting neighborhood of taverns.

THE FIRST MARINE HOSPITAL, 1798

It need not be said that old "Homes' Hole" is and was the greatest haven for storm- and tide-bound coasters along

[1]It was at the tavern of Ebenezer Smith, during the War of 1812, that Captain James Lawrence, U.S.N., was a frequent guest. During one of these visits, in 1814, a son was born, who was given the name of James Lawrence in honor of this distinguished officer. It is stated that the gallant sailor made a present to his namesake, besides cutting off a gold button from his coat as a token of the event. This boy was the late Capt. James Lawrence Smith of Vineyard Haven.

the New England shores. Then, as now, the sick or disabled sailor was put ashore here for care and treatment, and at the period which we are considering he was "boarded out" at one house or another under the supervision of the local physician. It was often impossible to obtain shelter for them when they were suffering from contagious diseases, for it must be remembered that small pox was then a prevalent scourge, as the practice of vaccination had not become established in this country. The Vineyard had suffered from it in 1738, in consequence of an epidemic introduced by a sick sailor who was put ashore at Homes' Hole in December of that year. No shelter could be obtained for him, and he was sent back again to the vessel, which was bound for Boston, where the man was detained at quarantine until he recovered [Records, Selectmen of Boston, 1738, vol. xv., p. 88]. Several persons died in this epidemic, including the local physician, Dr. Matthews, and many families had two and three of these cases at one time in their houses. Doubtless this incident was repeated often during the last century, and the danger of promiscuous "boarding out" of sick sailors, the inhumanity of turning them away when sick with contagious diseases, stimulated the leading citizens to meet the necessity of establishing a marine hospital at Homes' Hole. The following memorial was presented to the General Court in January, 1798:

To the Honbl. Senate and house of Representatives of the Commonwealth of Massachusetts now sitting in Boston:

The memorial of the Subscribers Justices of the Court of Common Pleas and General Sess. of the Peace in Duke's County shows that they from a sence of their Duty and out of Humanity to their fellow men think it Highly Necessary that a Hospitle should be built on the Island of Martha's Vineyard for the Reception of Such Sick Seafaring men as frequently arrive at the harbour of Holms hole with the Small Pox and other Contagious Distempers who cannot always git received on Shore by reason of the great Difficulty in gitting houses theefor. We should further Suggest that the West side of Holmes-hole Harbour would be much the most Convenient place for such a Building.

Martha's Vineyard,
January, 20th, 1798.

(signed) JAMES ATHEARN,
SHUBAEL COTTLE,
BENJA. BASSETT,
BERIAH NORTON.

In less than a month favorable action was taken by the General Court upon this memorial, and on February 17, the following order was passed:

Resolved. For the reason set forth in said memorial, that an hospital shall be built on the Island of Martha's Vineyard at or near the harbour of Holmes Hole, for the reception of such sick persons as may arrive there from sea, that the same shall be erected at the discretion and under the direction of his Excellency the Governor of this Commonwealth, and that his Excellency be requested to appoint some suitable agent or agents for the purpose of carrying this resolve into effect, and that there be allowed and paid out of the public Treasury, a sum not exceeding seven hundred dollars, to defray the expense thereof.[1]

In accordance with the authority vested in him by this resolve, the Governor, Increase Sumner, appointed two agents for superintending the construction of the hospital, viz:

Council Chamber,
Boston, Feby. 17, 1798.

In pursuance to the above Resolve, I do hereby appoint James Athearn, Esq., of Tisbury, and Beriah Norton, Esq., of Edgartown, agents for the purpose of carrying this Resolve into effect and the said agents are hereby directed to make a return of their doings to me as soon as they can conveniently. (Council Files, 1798).

Notwithstanding the petition asked the General Court to locate the hospital on the west side of the harbor (now Vineyard Haven), the agents purchased one half acre of land bordering on the Lagoon (then a part of Edgartown) of Malatiah Davis, Esq., of Edgartown.[2] From the widow Jane Smith and her son Ebenezer they bought a "low double" house then standing on the Highlands of East Chop for the sum of $210, and from the testimony of an aged man, the grandson of Malatiah Davis, we learn that this house was moved across the fields and set in place upon the site selected.

The account printed below gives the complete expenses of the commissioners, and shows that they were a little over a year completing their task. The account is especially remarkable, however, from the fact that the building was constructed within the appropriation.

DR. THE COMMONWEALTH OF MASSACHUSETTS IN AN ACCT. WITH JAMES ATHEARN & BERIAH NORTON, AGENTS APPOINTED TO BUILD A HOSPITAL.

1798.		
March.	To Cash paid for House for Hospital as per apprizal..	$210.00
	" " " Willm. Jernegan & Thos. Beetle for app'g house	3.50
	" " " for Land for Hospital as per Deed Treasr. office	25.00

[1]Mass. Resolves, IX, 402.

[2]Paying therefor $25.00, and the deed conveying the property to Peleg Coffin, Treasurer and Receiver General of the Commonwealth is recorded in the County registry, Vol. XIII, folio 538.

April.	To Office paid	James Coffin ....pr. Receipt......		$9.00
	" " "	Ichabod Cleaveland... " "		4.00
	" " "	Joseph Claghorn ..... " "		36.22
May.	" " "	Jonathan Fish .... " "		1.00
	" " "	Benjamin Smith ..... " "		19.44
	" " "	Benjamin Smith, Jr... " "		26.92
June.	" " "	Thomas Jones ...... " "		28.33
	" " "	Ebenezer Jones ...... " "		28.33
Augt.	" " "	Thos. Jones, $19.83 pr. Do. Do. Ebenr. Jones		39.66
	" " "	Thomas Pease for Building Chimney ...		13.00
	" " "	Bays Norton for Diging Clay 1.50, Do. rum 25		1.75
	" " "	James Coffin ....pr. Receipt......		5.25
	" " "	Jethro Worth .... " "		16.50
	" " "	Uriah Coffin.......... " "		40.20
	" " "	Timothy Coffin ...... " "		4.47
	" " "	Malatiah Davis ...... " "		20.00
	" " "	Benjamin Davis ..... " "		9.08
	" " "	David Coffin, Jr. .... " "		1.34
	" " "	Rufus Davis.......... " "		5.25
Sept.	" " "	Joseph Holley .... " "		.63
	" " "	Joseph Hammit...... " "		1.75
Jany. 1, '99.	To "	Joseph Dexter .... " "		3.75
	To cash "	Joseph Dexter for Iron Bar		1.10
Nov.	" " "	William Merry ......pr. Receipt......		6.00
	" " "	Malatiah Davis ...... " "		61.63
	" " "	Thomas Jernigan .... " "		2.00
	" " "	for Duck for a cot made by Thos. Jernigan		1.83
	" " "	Black Sam, for clearing & cleaning Hospitle, &c		1.50
	" " "	James Athearn, 4 Days attending Business		8.00
	" 16½ Days Myself overseing & assisting, &c., &c., at $2			33.00
	" Cash paid Samuel Smith, Regester for Record'g Deed			.50
	" 1m. Laths $2, to Elijah Daggett, 38ct., to Elijah Hillman 46			2.84
	" Cash paid Joseph Hammitt for Jos. Dexter pr.Receipt			1.75
				$674.52

To Commission Rec'g & Paying Money & settling, &c.,

CR. 1798. March.	By Cash recd. of Peleg Coffin, Treasurer, by Warrant from the Governor Agreeable to a Resolve of the General Court Past in Febury Last	$700.00
	By an overcharge, pd. Jos. Hammett Rect. once & charged a second time without a voucher	1.75

The aforegoing is a true acct. Errors Excepted

(signed) JAMES ATHEARN,
BERIAH NORTON.

This building was put to immediate use, and adjoining it a little cemetery was early begun by a local physician who had the charge of the institution. A well preserved slate stone records the following epitaph to the memory of probably the first sailor who died in the hospital:[1]

IN
MEMORY OF
SAMUEL LOCKWOOD
OF ST. JOHN, NEW BRUNSWICK,
who departed this life
October 28, 1801,
Aged, 42 yrs., 5 mos., 15 dys.

Unfortunately no records of the hospital are known to be extant, and nothing remains of a period so far back, excepting some few accounts and letters about the years 1826 to 1830 in the files of the Custom House. By that time, however, the old hospital had been abandoned as such, according to the memory of an old resident (Mr. Ichabod Luce), who thinks that it was occupied as far back as 1824 by an old fisherman (one "Daddy" Richardson), as a residence. Others confirm this evidence that it was abandoned as a hospital after a number of years, and after the death of Richardson it remained unoccupied and later was razed to the ground.[2] An old cellar, which still marks its site, and near by a few grave stones, moss covered and out of plumb, are the only existing memorials of the first hospital for sailors built upon the Vineyard, and the second in the United States, specially designed for the sailor in his days of sickness, the pioneer of the system of Marine Hospitals which, for nearly a century, has ministered to his wants.[3]

[1]There is also a stone in this enclosure to the memory of John Gates, of Portsmouth, N. H., "who died at sea April 30, 1828, aged 44." It bears a masonic emblem.

[2]George ("Daddy") Richardson was remarkable for his memory of the Scriptures, and many believed he could repeat the whole Bible as he never hesitated to give without error any chapter called for. He knitted seines and presumably acted as nurse in the hospital.

[3]The honor of its possession belongs to the State of Virginia, which, Dec. 20, 1787 passed a law establishing a marine hospital and authorizing the appointment of a commission by the Governor to select a site in the town of Washington, County of Norfolk, Virginia (Hening's "Statutes at Large," Vol. XII, p. 494). In the "New Hampshire Spy" of Nov. 4, 1788, there will be found a letter from Norfolk, under date of Sept. 24, 1788, which contains a paragraph relating to the laying of the corner-stone of this hospital. It was completed the next year and in 1801 sold to the United States.

Annals of Oak Bluffs

THE STRANGE STORY OF JOHN COUSENS

Over the early settlement of this hamlet the mysterious advent of John Cousens, and his selection of the Vineyard as his permanent home, casts a romantic shadow. To begin with his antecedents and progenitors we must go far away to the Spanish main for a background, and as far back as 1667, see the beginning of his complex ancestry. Capt. William Sanford, an English master mariner, commanding the Pink "Susannah," lay at anchor in the River Surinam, Dutch Guiana, and on March 27 of the year mentioned, married Sarah Whartman on board his craft. The next year he came to New Jersey, bought a large tract of land at New Barbadoes and settled down to the life of a gentleman planter. Here was born to him a daughter, Grace, who grew to womanhood, and when this period arrived there came to the Province of New York to rule it as the Royal Governor, Richard Earl of Bellomont, sent over by King William and Queen Mary. In his suite of officials was Barne Cosens of London, who came as secretary to the Earl and served as Clerk of the Provincial Council. He was the second son of John and Mary (Barne) Cosens of the parish of St. Clement Danes, London, born about 1674, and while it is not known that his father's people were specially prominent, it can be said that the Barnes were of high social standing in the English metropolis. Three of them had served as Lord Mayor of London within the century before the birth of Barne Cosens, and a number of them enjoyed the honors of knighthood. On April 28, 1697, this favored member of the Royal Governor's entourage led Grace Sanford to the altar, and we may assume for the present that there was the usual domestic bliss following the union. At all events three children were born to Barne and Grace (Sanford) Cosens, Mary, John (1700), and Sarah, and then trouble ensued between the parents. What it was we cannot say, but Barne Cosens evidently considered it necessary to leave on public record his last words of condemnation of his wife and the mother of his offspring. After the death of Bellomont, in 1701, Barne Cosens remained in office under his successor and served as Escheator General for three years, and then shortly after returned to England, never to revisit these shores. Before he sailed away he drew up his will, Dec. 5, 1706, as "about to take a voyage to England," and after making bequests to his three children added the provision regarding his wife that she "shall not on any acco't whatsoever have or obtain Letters of Administration of my will or of my estate or have anything to doe with the education of my children or any of them."[1] Barne Cosens left this stigma on his family escutcheon and went home to die. He deceased between that date and late in 1709, when the widow Grace, "of the Cittie of New York widow and Relict of Barney Cousens," made her last will and testament. In it she bequeathed to her daughters "all that my one Third part of my Late husbands estate which ought of Right to belong unto me;" and to her son John is devised the sum of £50, besides other amounts to relatives.[2] She survived until 1721, when her will was probated, and the only son had arrived at his majority. Shortly after he had left the opportunities and advantages of the American metropolis, and before 1725 we find him hidden from the world in the little hamlet on the west shore of Homes Hole.[3] Why did this scion of these gentle families so closely associated with the official court circles of England come to this distant isle of the sea and make it his home? Was it to obtain forgetfulness and oblivion for some family skeleton? We may never know, but the rest of his life is an open book. He married, about 1725, Jemima (102), daughter of Thomas and Hepsibah (Skiff) Norton, and thereafter the couple lived at Eastville, where three daughters were born to them. John Cousens kept a tavern, as was the fashion in those days, for over thirty years, until his death, which occurred Nov. 1, 1765, in the 65th year of his age, and his wife survived him scarcely four years. His daughter Mary married Moses Ogden of Elizabeth, New Jersey, and from her descend many distinguished families of New York, including Pierrepont Edwards, Governor and Senator Edwards of Connecticut, the wife of Eli Whitney the inventor, and John Cosens Ogden, the author and divine. The next daughter, Anne Frances, married Colonel Beriah Norton, and Sarah the third daughter, married David Davis of Eastville. John Cousens was not a tavern keeper nor a wrecker by birth or association, and his life of exile on the Vineyard, away from kith and kin, doubtless conceals some strange secret. It is doubtful if anything more definite will ever be known which can throw further light on the subject. The moss-grown slate over his grave tells us but little, but

[1] N. Y. Surrogate Records, VII, 555.
[2] N. Y. County Deeds, XXX, 178.
[3] Dukes Deeds, IV, 222.

we can believe that it marks the last resting place of a descendant of the Lords Mayor of London.[1] Surely a strange story for this sedate island.

THE WENDELL–DAVISES

Another family of New York origin, possibly related to the Cousens of the same state, became settlers of Eastville about 1750, and for several generations were identified with it. The first of the name in this country is said by family tradition to have been Barné or Barney Davis, a surveyor, who settled in Albany, N. Y., and left a son, Thomas. The further tradition is that this Thomas married Catherine Wendell, but it is evident that the tradition is partially wrong, as the records do not bear out the statement. Catherine, daughter of Evert Jansen and Maritje (Abrahamse) Wendell of Albany, born 1667, married Thomas Millington in 1699, and had among others Mayeke (Mary), baptized April 28, 1700, and she is the one who probably married Thomas Davis. This merely places Catherine Wendell one generation back. Thomas and Mary (Millington) Davis had two sons baptized in Albany, Thomas, Aug. 26, 1722, and David, Sept. 13, 1724, and shortly after the family of seven children removed to North Carolina. They settled at Yeopim on Albemarle Sound in that state, where the two boys, Thomas and David, lived until they were brought North, about 1737, to Plymouth, Mass., to be educated. Thomas remained in Plymouth, married there and became the ancestor of a distinguished family, including Judge John Davis and William T. Davis, the historian of his native town. David later settled on the Vineyard at Eastville, where he engaged in the occupation of pilot until his death in 1768, being lost in Boston bay in a storm. He married Sarah, daughter of John Cousens, Oct. 3, 1750, and two of his children, bearing the names of Wendell and Sanford, and their descendants perpetuate the names of their paternal and maternal ancestors to this day.

Descendants of the sons and daughters who remained in North Carolina are to be found in that State, as well as in Virginia, Kentucky and Tennessee. The name, however, has become almost extinct upon the Vineyard.

[1]The town clerks, parsons and stonecutters of Edgartown, and all who had to record the unusual name of his grandson, Barne Cosens Norton, struggled hard to make it Barnabas, thinking it was a contraction of the biblical name. It is probable the name was pronounced in two syllables.

COL. MALATIAH DAVIS

Melatiah Davis The second family of this name in Eastville, of which Malatiah was the progenitor, is not related, as far as known, to the Wendell-Davises who settled here about the same time. It is said that Malatiah came here before 1740 from Falmouth, but it is possible that Falmouth, England is meant, and that he entered the employ of Thomas Butler in the tannery business of the latter. Davis was then about twenty-three years old (born about 1717), and soon after this he married Jemima Dunham (131), by whom he had eight children. He was prosperous and thrifty in business and became a man of prominence in the community, a large land holder and a leader in town affairs. He was identified with the militia, Ensign in 1761, Lieutenant 1765, and was known as "Colonel" in later life, probably through his promotion to that rank. He died Jan. 9, 1795, in the 79th year of his age. His son Malatiah married Mary Cousens Davis of the other family, and thus united the two houses of Davis in Eastville.

SAMUEL NORRIS.

The first known ancestor of this family, long distinguished in the annals of Eastville, was Samuel Norris, a carpenter of Freetown, 1715, Dighton, 1720, and Bristol, 1721, whose wife was Rebecca [Howes?]. She died in the latter place March 3, 1745, leaving a son Thomas (b. 1726) among others. This Thomas married Patience, daughter of Thomas Harlock, August 11, 1751, in Bristol, and soon after removed to the Vineyard, settling at Edgartown. He was in the French and Indian wars, 1759-60 and died April 10, 1775, aged 49 years. He left eight children of whom Samuel, born 1753, settled in Eastville, married Lucy, daughter of James and Rebecca (Butler) Shaw, and is the ancestor of one of the ablest men ever credited to this town in its recent public life, the Hon. Howes Norris, thrice senator from the Cape District.

SEPARATION FROM EDGARTOWN

EARLY SENTIMENT FOR INDEPENDENCE

The remoteness of Eastville from the village of Edgartown contained the germ of the idea of an independent existence of this part of the town when it should become numerically strong enough to demand this privilege. About 1825, as told by older residents of Eastville, this sentiment took concrete form in an agitation for a separation from the parent town; but no definite details are obtainable, as the matter never proceeded to the point of specific action. The little hamlet did not then have sufficient population nor valuation to justify its establishment as an independent community; and it is probable that the movement was designed to influence some pending controversies between the two sections of the town. Doubtless the northern section suffered then from lack of its share of the town appropriations, as was the case in later years, when it grew to the proportions of a possible township.

The growth of the summer resort around the Squash Meadow region following the development of the camp-meetings, and the general increase of a resident population in that section, accentuated the idea of future autonomy. This took definite form about 1872, when the residents of Eastville and the newer settlement at Vineyard Grove joined together in a campaign for separation from Edgartown. The residents of Eastville, when they were almost the only permanent population of Farm Neck, had no natural affiliations binding them to the old town. They had no decent roads, nor school houses, and felt neglected by the voters of the older village in the distribution of annual favors at town meetings. They were a hopeless and helpless minority, comprising not more than fifteen families, and they chafed under the yoke. It was seven miles by a sandy road to the post office, the town hall and a good school house. As a result of these conditions they traded and received their mail at Homes Hole, and all their interests were in this association with the people of that settlement. The men of Eastville were the original inspirers of every sentiment for a division of the town, and as the feeling for independence grew, its leaders were always found there. It is apparent that the majority of voters of Edgartown village paid but scant attention to these continued murmurs of discontent, and thus annually piled up arguments in favor of a separation by their treatment of this section of the town.

THE FIGHT FOR SEPARATION.

On the date above given (1872) a Representative to the General Court, understood to be favorable to division, was elected through the influence of the people of Eastville, and a petition for separation was circulated among the residents of the northern section of the town. The people of the old village countered this move with a remonstrance against separation, and induced such a considerable number of the non-resident tax payers of Vineyard Grove to sign it, that the petitioners for the new town found it the better policy to defer action at that time. The agitation, however, was kept up continuously, and in the few following years the ranks of the divisionists were recruited from this same non-resident element which had been employed against them previously. No improvement in the relations of the two sections ensued even at this juncture; and such favors in the way of improvements as could be obtained from Edgartown were either grudgingly bestowed or forced by appeals to their sense of justice.

The men most active in the north part of the old town in the various movements for a division were Howes Norris, Ichabod Norton Luce, Joseph Dias, Otis Foss and Samuel Butler. These men finally enlisted the support of nearly all of the non-residents who were incorporated into a separate committee of thirty to carry on the battle. Oliver Ames of Easton, who then owned a fine summer residence at Oak Bluffs, was chairman of this committee of non-residents, and at that time he was yet only a private citizen of large wealth and influence in the business world. When the battle was found to be a strongly contested engagement, and after two successive defeats of the petitioners, Mr. Ames said he "guessed he would go to the Senate to help out," and he did. This divisional fight was undoubtedly the inspiration of his entry into political life, and this service as Senator was the prelude to his promotion to the offices of Lieutenant-Governor and Governor of this Commonwealth.

Among the many non-residents, who devoted much time and effort during the several years of leglisative battling before success was finally reached, were Hon. Nathaniel Wales of Stoughton, at first a Senator and later of the Governor's Council; Hon. Edward B. Gillette of Westfield, a prominent attorney and a director in the Boston and Albany Railroad; Hon. William N. Sage of Rochester, N. Y.; Captain John S. Damrell of Boston, and Mr. N. Sumner Myrick of the same city, then a correspondent of the Boston Herald and a young attorney at law. These and other non-residents proved to be a most efficient factor in the campaign, as their interest and influence ramified throughout all portions of the state, and they were able to appeal to the sources of public influence which affected the opinions of the legislators.

THE CAUSES OF THE TROUBLE

In the statements which follow, detailing the complaints of the petitioners for separation, the author is not expressing his views of the merits of the controversy, but paraphrasing the language of those who entertained these grievances against the dominant authorities of Edgartown. The advocates of division were first aroused to action by the continuous neglect of the interests of their section, both in respect to a share in the civil honors in town management, and in the refusal to provide the ordinary necessities of decent roads and good schools for a growing community. Edgartown village profited by the rapid and unusual increase of taxable improved property in the Camp-Meeting grounds when permanent residences began to dot the landscape, and nothing was given in return to the new community. As an instance of this almost fatuitous disregard for the convenience of the citizens of the north end of the town, may be cited the refusal to build a bridge across the narrow channel emptying the Lagoon. The people residing in this section had no outlet to the westward towns on the Vineyard except by water, while a mile only separated them from the village of Vineyard Haven, where they could have convenient mail facilities and the other benefits that a large settlement affords. Requests for appropriations to build this connecting link were repeatedly voted down. At last the petitioners took the matter to the General Court in the form of a bill compelling the county commissioners to build the bridge, and the responsible leaders of the Edgartown interests fought the measure with great earnestness, but without success. Another instance of this nature was the refusal to build a road through the farms along the Eastville shore, until the residents of that section gave the town bonds that it should not cost the town anything. Temahigon avenue, which runs from the Eastville Inn to New York avenue, and New York avenue itself, two of the finest roads in the present town, were only obtained by the guarantee on the basis above mentioned, of the people of Eastville to the town of Edgartown.

Coincident with the refusal of Edgartown to build a bridge across the Lagoon channel on account of the expense involved, the old town interests projected the present Beach road which should connect them with the new settlement at Oak Bluffs. As usual a short-sighted policy was adopted in the construction of this highway. While competent contractors offered to build a macadam road for $40,000, the Edgartown leaders pushed through a vote to employ none but townspeople in this work and a common dirt road was finally completed at an expense of nearly $60,000. But the object of preventing the citizens of the northern section from going by road to another section of the island had been accomplished. Nor was this wasteful financiering the only ground of complaint with respect to money matters. The old town voted $15,000 more to build a railroad parallel to this Beach road, which could be of no possible benefit to any other section of the town, and it proved to be a total loss, as an investment.

THE STORY OF THE STRUGGLE

For three successive years, 1878, 1879 and 1880, these petitioners for division took their case to the General Court for relief. They were represented by Hon. Charles R. Train, while the old town entrusted its case to the Hon. Selwyn Z. Bowman. With such able counsel on both sides, and the prominent men interested throughout the state among the non-resident petitioners, the case became one of the most noted town division contests ever threshed out in the history of the Commonwealth. The struggle developed exceedingly bitter feelings between the people of the two sections, and before its close the petitioners had practically abandoned attendance at town meetings because of the personal ill-treatment which they claim to have received at the hands of their opponents. Charges and counter charges of dishonesty in the financial management of the town were freely made, and the motives of each side were impugned as selfish or dishonest. The case of the remonstrants was one of general and particular denial of every complaint set forth by the petitioners. Figures taken from the town reports were employed by both sides with equal facility to establish opposite contentions; and amid this arithmetical maze of percentages, the average person might well flounder in his efforts to deduce the real truth from their diametric arguments. The remonstrants claimed that the debt of the town was due to improvements made for the benefit of the new section, and that it would be unjust to the old town to be burdened with a moiety of it, as after the separation an undue proportion of taxable property would be taken into the new town. It appeared from an analysis of the property interests of the petitioners, that, while numerically strong, they represented at first a minority of the taxable realty. This element of non-resident petitioners, while potentially valuable from a political standpoint, constituted a hazardous asset as an argument for division. It can readily be seen that the division of Edgartown was not their concern legally, as they were not voters, and the propriety of their appearance was seriously questioned as a matter of public policy, by the many not immediately interested in the matter. The counsel for the remonstrants dealt with this feature in vigorous terms, and practically demanded their entire exclusion from the case in the interests of justice. He used this circumstance with great effect in an appeal to the sentiment of fair play, picturing the hundreds of wealthy and influential nonresidents throughout the state engaged in a combination against the poor, defenceless island community, struggling against disruption and despoilment.

As was inevitable, this contest entered into the local politics of the Vineyard as a whole, and the elections of the representative to the General Court in the years 1878-80, inclusive, were fought out on the issue of division. In 1878 and 1879 Captain Benjamin Clough of Tisbury was chosen as an opponent of division through the votes of Edgartown and her friends in other sections of the island. This position of advantage accrued to the benefit of the old town in the legislative struggles of those two years, as Captain Clough succeeded in defeating all the active work carried on by the petitioners throughout the state. As representative of the local interests of his district the Vineyard member exercised a controlling influence on a subject which was purely a local affair, in accordance with the unwritten law and custom of the legislature. For the third and last time the contestants waged the usual preliminary skirmish in the election of a new representative to sit in the General Court of 1880, and, after a spirited campaign, Stephen Flanders of Chilmark, an avowed friend of the petitioners, was the successful candidate. The strategic advantage was now with the divisionists, and the influence of the local representative would be against the old town. The tide had turned, but both sides returned to the arena undismayed by previous defeats and the recent election. The old arguments were repeated in favor and the old replies were flung back without much change. The General Court lent a favorable ear, and on February 17, 1880, the Bill incorporating the new town became a law.

At the first meeting of the voters of the new town of Cottage City, in March, 1880, the following named persons were chosen as its officials for the ensuing year:

William H. Davis, Frederick U. Ripley, Otis Foss, Selectmen, Assessors and Overseers of the Poor; Oliver E. Linton, Town Clerk; Joseph Dias, Town Treasurer and Collector of Taxes; Oliver E. Linton, Henry C. Norton, Phœbe A. Norton, School Committee; Edward H. Hatfield, Shubael H. Norton, Albert A. Bosworth, Board of Health.

Its valuation was $1,197,435, with 1,058 taxable buildings, including 15 hotels. It then stood as 142 among the 306 towns in the state, as regards valuation.

CHRISTENING THE NEW TOWN

The name of the new town became a bone of contention during the agitation. The summer residents in various portions of the proposed town desired to give it the name of the section in which each lived. The post office had been called Vineyard Grove and Oak Bluffs at different periods, and the people residing at the Highlands and about the Camp Meeting Grounds favored the former name, while the residents of Oak Bluffs insisted on the retention of this title. Both sides were unyielding in this matter, and the dispute threatened to disorganize the divisionists. At this juncture the Hon. H. A. Blood, a former Mayor of Fitchburg, Mass., and a summer resident, suggested the compromise name which was finally adopted. As general manager of the Fitchburg Railroad he had designated this locality in his advertising matter for summer travelers as the "Cottage City of America," and the suggestion was made by him to the leaders that the new town be called Cottage City. He claimed that through his extensive exploitation of this name throughout the country it was already known as Cottage City to hundreds of summer visitors, and that it would be good policy to adopt it officially.

For a long time the bitterness engendered by the struggle remained, but at this date, a generation after the events above narrated, it can be said that both sections are happier, less contentious, and better off financially and otherwise as a result of the division.[1]

NAME CHANGED TO OAK BLUFFS

The baptismal name of this town never gave entire satisfaction to many of the residents. In many respects it was a ridiculous pretence to call a very small town a *city* and it gave strangers an erroneous impression which became the source of humorous comment whenever mentioned seriously. To reverse the name it would sound equally senseless to speak of the City of Cottage Town. This sentiment grew in strength from year to year and when, in 1906, it was proposed to give the place a dignified name scarcely any opposition was manifested. The large consensus of opinion was in favor of the earlier title of the place, Oak Bluffs, and on Jan. 25, 1907, the General Court incorporated the town of Cottage City under the new name.

The officers elected at the first town meeting following this change were:

Frederick W. Smith, Ezekiel H. Matthews, Elmer E. Landers, Selectmen, Assessors and Overseers of the Poor; Francis P. Vincent, Town Clerk; Edwin R. Frasier, Treasurer; William C. Russell, Auditor; Ezekiel H. Matthews, Collector of Taxes; Samuel G. Rice, George F. Moulton, Osgood N. Mayhew, David J. Barney, School Committee; Manuel S, Bettencourt, Superintendent of Streets; Eli A. Leighton. LaRoy S. Lewis, Constables; Sherman T. Meara, Charles T. Besse, Job H. Gorham, Health Officers; John E. Sandiford, Samuel N. Kidder, Andrew Warren, David J. Barney and Everett Joy, Board of Engineers; John W. McGrath, George P. Briggs, Manuel A. Vincent, Park Commissioners; Job H. Gorham, Sidney H. Hicks, LaRoy S. Lewis, Cemetery Committee; George H. Stratton, Sealer of Weights and Measures; Charles T. Besse, Pound Keeper; Frank W. Chase, Snow Welch, Manuel S. Bettencourt, Fence Viewers; Edwin R. Frasier, Tree Warden.

[1]It is related, as an instance of the animosities aroused, that on an early visit to Edgartown after the bill was passed, one of the principal leaders from Eastville was greeted with a chorus of groans and other uncomplimentary demonstrations from people who had hastily gathered on learning of his presence in the town. They aligned themselves on both sides of the street, the principal thoroughfare of the town, and continued this hostile serenade until his business was completed and he had departed for his home.

U. S. GOVERNMENT SERVICES

LIGHTHOUSE ESTABLISHMENT

There is one lighthouse in the town, situated on the highlands of East Chop. It was built in 1869 by the late Capt. Silas Daggett of Vineyard Haven as a private enterprise. His project had the financial support of marine insurance companies, steamship lines and coastwise commercial interests making use of this great waterway of travel. Anticipating the final disposal of it to the general government he completed the tower, maintained it for a period until its transfer was accomplished. This is probably one of the few instances of such an undertaking on our coast, but the energetic promoter thought that governments moved too deliberately and he went ahead with his project, trusting in subsequent reimbursement. It is a flashing red light.

The tower is circular in form, with a railed gallery around the lantern. The bluff on which it stands is about seventy-five feet above sea level, and in the period 1845–1871 it had receded about seventy-five feet as a result of erosion by wave action, a rate of nearly three feet per annum.

POST OFFICE

The growth of the annual summer population following the establishment of the camp meetings resulted in the necessity for mail facilities, and in 1870 a post office was established with the designation of Vineyard Grove. This was changed, March 25, 1878, to Oak Bluffs, and almost immediately after, June 11, 1878, changed back to its original name. After the incorporation of the town as Cottage City the name was altered March 30, 1880, to that of the new town, and remained so until Feb. 28, 1907, when it was called Oak Bluffs post office.

The following named persons have served in the office of postmaster: Sirson P. Coffin, commissioned March 7, 1870; Charles M. Vincent, July 19, 1871; Frances P. Vincent, May 13, 1873; Henry C. Norton, May 10, 1888; Charles L. Scranton, Sept. 6, 1889 (present incumbent).

There is no public building for the accommodation of the post office in Oak Bluffs, and the postmaster has always established his quarters in rented buildings. For the greater part of the time since 1870 the office has been located on Circuit Avenue.

MISCELLANEOUS ANNALS

NEWSPAPERS

The first newspaper established in the town was the *Cottage City Star*, which was started by Hon. Howes Norris, in 1879, as editor and publisher. It was printed in a four-page blanket-sheet form and printed local news from all the island towns, but made a specialty of Cottage City happenings. It was a weekly issue during the greater part of the year, but when the tourist season was on, a semi-weekly issue was published. The office was located at No. 1 Commonwealth square. This paper existed for six years, and was sold to Charles Strahan, a Southerner by birth and a Confederate soldier during the Civil War, formerly of Baltimore and New Orleans. He had been attracted to Oak Bluffs because he had found it of great beneficial value to his health, and made it his home for the next ten years, during which time he conducted this paper on lines similar to the *Gazette* of Edgartown, but the name was changed by him to *Martha's Vineyard Herald*. He continued as editor and publisher until September, 1900, when he disposed of the plant to Elmer E. Landers of Cottage City and William E. Doane of Taunton. In April, 1902, Mr. Doane retired from the firm, and Mr. Landers continues its publication as surviving partner. The office of publication has been from the beginning at the Herald building, on Circuit avenue. It is issued weekly, except in July and August, when a semi-weekly edition is issued.

TAVERNS

As this town grew up it came to have a conglomeration of boarding houses and hotels for the accommodation of the summer visitors, and it would be an unnecessary task to attempt an enumeration of all the houses utilized as public taverns. It will suffice to enumerate the larger and more pretentious hotels which have maintained a continued existence for many years. They comprise the following:

Oak Bluffs House (erected in 1868); Wesley House (A. G. Wesley), Searell House (W. A. Searell), Prospect House (N. E. Huggins), Norton House (C. L. Scranton), Highland House (J. C. Alden), Vineyard Grove House (Joseph Dias), Cottage City House (Mrs. S. A. Stearns), Island House (Hiram Hayden), Pawnee House (Russell Sturgis), Naumkeag House

(E. H. Fennessy), Central House (Fuller and Field), and the Sea View House (Louis Frenkel). This last named hotel was by far the most famous of all, being the largest and best located. Built and furnished at a cost of over one hundred thousand dollars, with over an hundred guest rooms, spacious dining hall, broad verandah, and situated on the shore at the head of Steamboat wharf, overlooking the arrival and departure of the thousands who came annually, it was, during its existence, the social centre for the "Smart set" which gradually came to measure up in numbers with those who flocked hither for religious reasons. It was burned Sept. 24, 1892, just at the end of the tourist season and was never rebuilt. Efforts were made from time to time to interest capitalists in a plan to provide a successor to it, but the disaster came at a time when the abnormal "boom" of Cottage City had subsided, and the demand for such an elaborate hostelry had passed with the turn of the tide. The existing hotels have enlarged and improved their capacity, and are fully able to provide for the travelers who seek temporary lodgings and board.

PHYSICIANS

This town has not had, with one exception, a practitioner of medicine who devoted his entire time to the residents of Oak Bluffs. The summer season created a demand for the temporary services of physicians, and the practitioners of Tisbury and Edgartown, Doctors Butler and Lane of the former place, and Doctors Walker and Worth of the latter place, have maintained offices here during the tourist season. In latter years permanent offices the year round have been established by them.

William Leach, M. D., the exception above noted, was a well known and highly respected physician of the Vineyard for many years. He was born in the town of Kittery, Me., Sept. 23, 1825, received his elementary education in the district school, and fitted for college in the New Market, N. H., academy. He then turned his attention to the study of medicine, entering, in 1852, the medical department of Harvard University, from which he was graduated in 1856. After practising in Boston, till 1863, he came to Martha's Vineyard and resided here continuously, engaged in the successful practice of his profession, at first in Vineyard Haven, and in the later years of his life exclusively in Oak Bluffs. He died March 31, 1903, nearly four score years of age. He was a member of the Martha's Vineyard Lodge, A. F. & A. M., of the Vineyard Haven Lodge, No. 228, I. O. O. F., and of the Massachusetts Medical Society.

CEMETERIES

There are three burial grounds in the town, the "Cottage City", which contains the oldest grave stone, 1759; the "Farm Neck," whose earliest stone is 1764, and the small ground near Old House pond, where the earliest stone bears the date of 1816.

GRAND ARMY OF THE REPUBLIC

The veterans of the Civil War residing on the Vineyard formed a Post of this organization in 1890, with headquarters at Oak Bluffs. It was christened Henry Clay Wade Post, No. 201, of the Department of Massachusetts, in honor of that gallant naval officer who died at Pensacola. Henry W. Coye of Vineyard Haven was its first Commander, serving for five years in that office. The Post has enrolled about fifty veterans on its roster, and meets the first and third Thursdays of each month in G. A. R. hall on Circuit avenue. It is assisted in its work of fraternal care of the sick and needy of its members by the Woman's Relief Corps, an auxiliary organization.

THE MARTHA'S VINEYARD SUMMER INSTITUTE

This institution was another unique feature of this unique town. Established in 1878 as a normal school for teachers, its object was to afford special instruction in advanced studies, scientific and literary, to teachers who desire to combine such work with their weeks of rest and recreation. The professors in the various departments were those who held high place in institutions of learning in all parts of the country, and, like the students, combine this work with their play. A large, fine building, known as Agassiz hall, built in 1882, was specially designed and built for the business of this summer school, and during July and August for about five weeks it was a busy place. Hundreds of teachers availed themselves of the opportunity, and nearly every state and territory has been represented among its pupils. It had a dormitory and dining halls for the accommodation of the students. The number of the latter had increased from 75 in 1878 to over seven hundred in 1896, and a corps of forty instructors comprised its faculty. Col. Homer

B. Sprague was its first President (1878-82), and he was succeeded by Prof. William J. Rolfe, the well-known Shakesperean critic (1882-7), and Col. William A. Mowry, Ph.D., LL.D. (1887-1905). The Institute was disbanded in 1905 and its charter surrendered.

PRESENT STATISTICS OF THE NEW TOWN

Since its incorporation as Cottage City this township has passed through thirty years of exaggerated and normal periods of growth. At the time of its change to Oak Bluffs (1908) the following statistics taken from the assessors' books show its material condition. Personal estate assessed, $143,375; real estate assessed, $1,806,075, of which two-thirds is held by non-residents; total tax assessed, $38,520, including tax on 293 polls. Acres of land, 3,423; dwelling houses, 1,126; horses, 108; cows, 100; tax payers, 1454, including 110 who pay poll tax only. It will be seen upon comparison with the statistics of the other towns that although the youngest community, it has the largest valuation and raises the greatest tax on the Vineyard.

S. MARY'S CHURCH, GREAT BADDOW, ENGLAND,
WHERE JOHN PEASE WAS BAPTIZED.

ANNALS OF GAY HEAD

ANNALS OF GAY HEAD

DOVER CLIFF, 1602

The discovery and christening of this peninsula has a definite date, in 1602, and an authentic sponsor in the person of Bartholomew Gosnold. "The four and twentieth of May," wrote the journalist of that voyager, after they had left Nomans Land, "we set sail and doubled the cape of another island next unto this, which we called Dover Cliff, and then came into a fair sound." The resemblance of this remarkable headland to the famous high chalky cliffs at Dover on the English channel, doubtless suggested to Gosnold and his companions the appropriation of the name for these new-found cliffs of like character. This name, however, did not survive the pages of Gosnold's journal, and it remained for later comers to apply a name to it of their own conception. Some time before 1662 it was "called . . . by the English Gayhead," and this name has lasted as its title ever since.[1] This name, of course, was given to it as descriptive of the gaily colored cliffs seen from the west when approaching the island from the sea.

The Algonquian names at that period were Aquinniuh and Kuhtuhquehtuet, which are elsewhere considered in their philology.

BOUNDARIES

Under a resolve of the General Court, approved March 9, 1855, three commissioners, appointed by the Governor to establish a boundary between the Indian lands on Gay Head and the lands of the white inhabitants of Chilmark, determined upon the following lines:

Beginning at a rock on Nicodemus' Neck, on Squibnocket pond, thence due south across marsh and beach to the sea. From the same rock S. 55 E, across Squibnocket pond to a rock on Hillman's Point, so called; thence N. 10½° E, crossing said pond to the southern end of a stone wall on Nashawaqueedsee, which parteth that neck from Gay Head; thence N. 25° E, three rods, by said wall; thence N. 47½° E. sixty-seven rods, by said wall; thence N. 26° E. three and three-quarter rods, by said wall to its

[1]Dukes Deeds, III, 12. It is always written Gayhead, as if one word, with a lower case *h* in head.

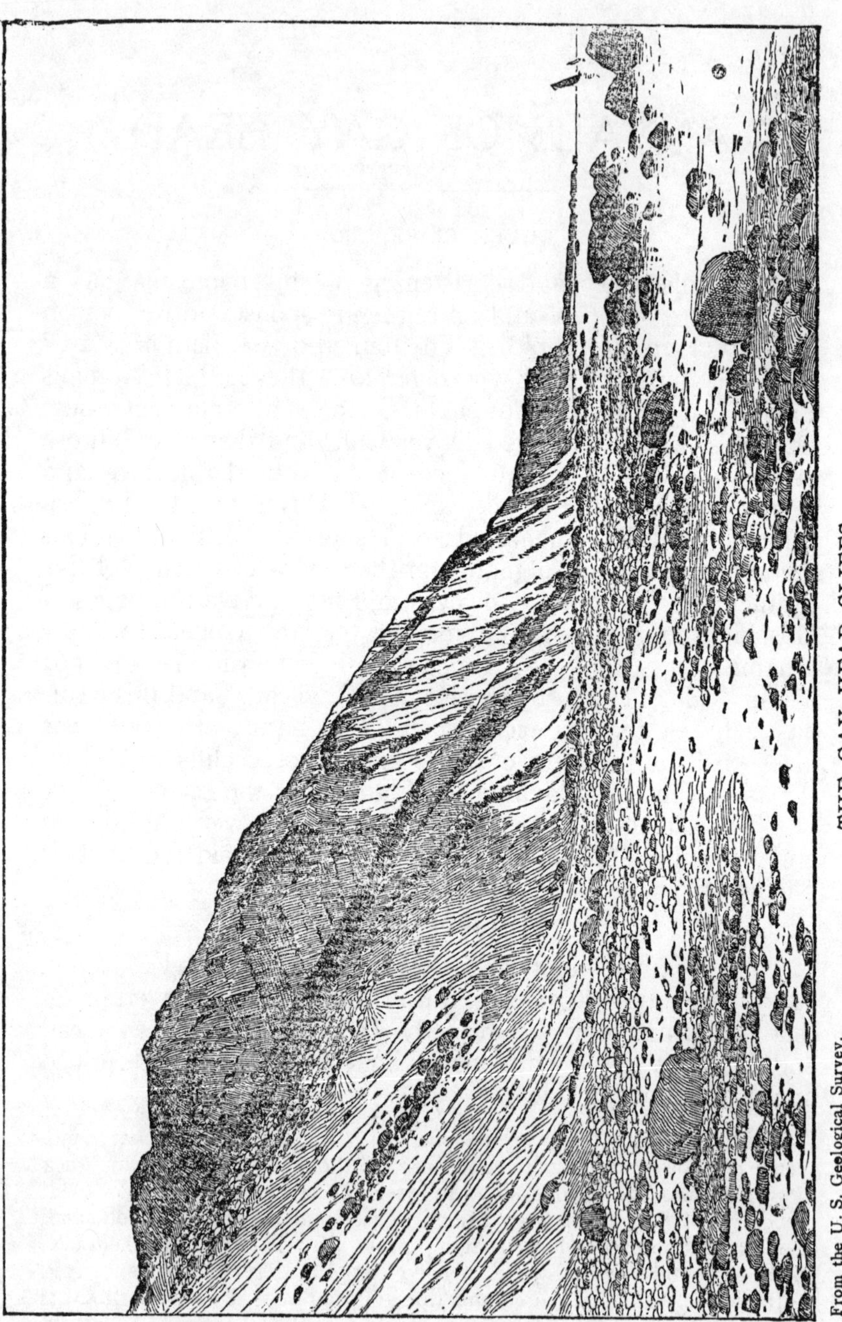

THE GAY HEAD CLIFFS.

From the U. S. Geological Survey.

northern end, by Menamsha pond. Thence N. 51¼° E. crossing said Menamsha pond, in the direction of a rock upon Pease's Point, so called distant about four hundred and fifty rods, until it strikes the middle of the channel or outlet from said pond to the Sound; then by the middle of the said channel as the same now is, or hereafter may be, — the said channel being somewhat subject to change — unto the Vineyard Sound.[1]

On all other sides it is bounded by the waters of the Sound and ocean.

The stone wall referred to has been the dividing line between Nashaquitsa and Gay Head for nearly two centuries. It was first set up in 1714, shortly after "The Corporation" acquired control of the land.[2] The other lines are modern.

POPULATION

There is very little accurate material at hand for a resumé of the population of this town, except within recent years. The inhabitants being of Indian extraction and of a roving disposition, gave but little concern to the census takers before the 19th century. In 1698 there were 260 souls reported as attending church services at Gay Head.[3] There were fifty-eight houses on Gay Head neck in 1712 (Sewall). In 1747 the guardians of the Indians stated that they were "in number about one hundred & twelve, men women and children,"[4] a decrease which is not understood, as shortly before 1786 they numbered 203,[5] and in 1790 there were reported to be 276 Indians living in the peninsula.[6] In 1806 a traveler, visiting the island, states their number to have been 240 that year,[7] In 1838 there were 235 residents in the town.[8] In 1860 an official report states there were 46 families actually resident, comprising 204 souls, of whom 106 were male and 98 female. In addition to these there were 49 persons of the Gay Head "tribe" living elsewhere, temporarily, but claiming tribal rights, making a total of 253 belonging to the town by birth

[1]House Document, No. 48, pp. 8-9. Report of the Commissioners, John Vinson, Asa R. Nye and J. Whelden Holmes. A previous commission had run a division line about 1830 between Gay Head and Squibnocket, but no record of it remains.

[2]Sewall Diary.

[3]Report of Commissioners for Society for Propagating the Gospel.

[4]Mass. Arch., XXXI, 550. There may be an error of 100 in the count. The report states: "the number of houses at Gayhead is 28; we compute four persons to a house which is 112, and of these about 19 Labouring men."

[5]Memoirs of American Academy, II, 153.

[6]Information furnished by Capt. Thomas Jernegan and Benjamin Bassett that year (1st Mass. Hist. Soc. Coll., I, 206).

[7]Kendall, "Travels," II, 196.

[8]Barber, "Historical Collections" (Mass.), 148.

or residence.[1] The oldest was 86 years of age, and six others were over seventy.

Since the incorporation of the town four national censuses give the following figures: 1870, 160 persons; 1880, 161; 1890, 139; and 1900, 173. The state census of 1905 showed a population of 178.

ANCIENT LANDMARKS

ALGONQUIAN PLACE NAMES

Aquiniuh (1662).—This name as applied to Gay Head, is composed of the words, Ukque–adene–auke, or Acqui–adene–auke, meaning "land under the hill," perhaps referring to the shore under Gay Head itself.

Kugh–tuh–quich–e–wutt (1681). — This is the Indian name for the narrow neck of land joining Nashaquitsa and Gay Head. Kuh–kuh–equht–wutt, or Kuh–tuh–que–i–yeu–ut, means "at the going up," as of a hill, and probably refers to the topography of that region, the ascent to the Gay Head plateau. A variation used in 1687 was Catackutcho (Deeds, IV, 128).

Mash–atan–auke.—This aboriginal name has been curiously corrupted into "Shot and Arrow" and "Shot Nigher" hill! It is a compound word, meaning the "great hill land," descriptive of the hilly character of the neck.

Wanummusit. — This name occurs but once (1681) in the records, without any indication of its exact locality. It marked the terminal point of the sachemship of Metaark, starting from Nashaquitsa, and may refer to the Gay Head cliff.

THE EARLY SACHEMSHIPS

Ever since the settlement of the Vineyard, in 1642, Gay Head has remained an Indian reservation and town, and very little of its annals in two hundred and sixty-seven years of existence relates to the white man or the white man's customs and development. Every attempt of the Caucasian to introduce himself with a view to permanent attachment has resulted in his withdrawal from the field, and today this peninsular and insular town is unquestionably Indian in the warp and woof of its very fibre.

[1]Report of Indian Commission to Governor and Council, 1861. Senate Document, No. 96, pp. 30-1.

As usual the English made early efforts to obtain it from its owners. The first occasion was when "Womsuttan alias Alexander, chief sachem of Cossomsett & of the rest of the country thereunto adjacent," sold Gay Head to William Brenton, merchant of Newport, on May 5, 1661-2.[1] This sachem was the elder brother of King Philip and son of Massasoit of the Pokanoket tribe. In this sale he reserved one-twelfth to himself. Nothing ever developed from this grant, as Brenton never made any attempt to claim the rights deeded to him. It may have been that the Sachem of Gay Head, Nohtoaksaet, refused to recognize this transfer made by a chief on the mainland, but for some reason it had the distinction of being recorded in our local land records and in the registry at New York.[2]

After the death of Nohtoaksaet his younger son, Metaark, succeeded to the sachemship in the absence of an elder brother. In 1675 this elder brother returned to the Vineyard and claimed a portion of Gay Head as his birthright. The negotiations are thus recorded:

This was at Gayhead in 1675.

To me Mittark Sachim at Gayhead there came the person called Ompohhannut, and said I am older than thou art, and I ought to be the Sachim, for I am the first born of our father Nohtoaksaet; or otherwise I should have some part of the land of the Gayhead parted off to me, that so I may be still (or quiet) as may be found right by the Indian Sachims and Chiefmen.

Agreeable hereunto I Mettark, Sachim, and my Councel (or chief men) and also the Common Men of Gayhead did appoint a Great Court. We called the Sachims of this Island, and the people as far as the main land to find what might be right with respect to us and Ompohhannut, relating to his claim of land, or of the Sachimship; and we held a Court at that time in Sept. 1675; and we found or did thus in our Court: — we made or sent a jury to judge of the matter of Ompoh–hannuts rights in Gayhead and we gave them, the jury, such proves that what they should determine we would confirm. And these were their names: — Samuel Cashomon foreman, Hosea Manhut, John Hannet, Masquattukquit, Joshua Momatehogin, Stephen Togomasun, Japheth Hannet, Isac Ompany, Samuel James, Pattompan, Matthew Nohnahshesket, Joseph Pemmahchohoo.

And we the jury have found by persons knowing that Ompohhannut speaks true and in the whole, therefore, we now judge that in a division of four parts of the Gayhead, one belongeth to him, and all his heirs forever.[3]

[1]Dukes Deeds, III, 12. This sale was "certified" by Tahcomahhatack, Papamoo, Pessuccook, Poxine, Akeemo, Caleneanute, Teequannum, "natives and Inhabitants on the westermost end of Nope."

[2]It was recorded in 1670 at Fort James.

[3]Dukes Deeds, VI, 369.

In accordance with the decision of the "Sachems and Chief Men" Metaark executed a deed conveying to his brother, Ompohhannut, one-quarter part of Gay Head, and requested the "Great Rulers among the English" to confirm the deed.[1]

Several years after this, on Sept. 11, 1681, Metaark issued a formal declaration, signed by himself and some of his chief-men, that none of the lands in his sachemship should be alienated. In the quaint formulary of the Algonquian language this idea was expressed as follows:

> I Mettack Sachem att Kuhtuhquehtuet and Nashauakquetget as far as Wanummuset:
>
> Know yee all People that I Mettack and my principal men my children & people are owners of this: this our land forever. They are ours, and our offspring forever shall enjoy them:—
>
> I Mettack and we principall men together with our children and all our people are agreed that no person shall sell any Land; but if any person will stealingly sell any Land: take yee your Land because it is yours forever: but if any one will not perform this Covenant he shall fail to have any of this Land at Kuhtuhquehtuut and Nashanaquetget forever:
>
> I Mettack and we principall men and our children say this shall be forever . . . .
>
> I Mettack sachem and my chief men speak this in the presence of God it shall be thus forever.[2]

GAY HEAD SOLD TO GOVERNOR DONGAN

The authenticity of this document was disputed twenty years later, and it was alleged to be a forgery, as will be explained further on. Shortly after this the old sachem died, Jan. 20, 1683, and was succeeded by his son, called Joseph Metaark. Two years later (April 25, 1685) Matthew Mayhew received the grant of the "Manor and Lordship of Martin's Vineyard" from Governor Thomas Dongan of New York, and less than a month after (May 12th) the latter had purchased from the grantee the title and the property appertaining to it, as previously detailed.[3] The property appertaining and remaining was the Gay Head peninsular principally, and in pursuance of the policy adopted by the Mayhews he quieted the Indian "rights" to it by a purchase from "Joseph Mittark Sachim of the Gay Head in Martin's Vineyard, Indian native,"

[1]Dukes Deeds, VI, 370.

[2]Mass. Archives, XXXI, 10. This was signed by Metaark, John Keps, Puttuhquannon and Tasuapinu. The paper was used in 1700 at Barnstable before a committee of which William Bassett was a member. At that time Metaark had been a "praying Indian" for nearly twenty years.

[3]Vol. I, 174-7.

for £30 of all his interest therein. This transaction was dated May 6, 1687, and took place in New York, whither the Sachem had gone, evidently with Matthew Mayhew, who was one of the witnesses.[1]

This sale was in direct violation of the covenant of the old Sachem and his "principal men," made six years previously, and may be taken as an evidence that the document was, as alleged, a forgery. With this transaction began the manorial system in this Indian settlement, and soon the Indians were gravely paying "ears of corn" as quit rents to the Lord of the Manor.[2] As the years passed by the natives found they had no rights in the soil which their ancestors had peopled and which they were now tilling and improving; and after the change of government from New York to Massachusetts had taken place, complaints were made to the new authorities of the injustice of their situation. These complaints were repeated until the General Court, in 1703, appointed a committee to investigate the conditions of the Indians on Gay Head.[3] In their report, dated Aug. 18, 1703, the committee took up the question of this "covenant" of the Indian Sachem offered in evidence by the complainants:

> In the contest about Gay Head it appears to us by deed that Colonel Dongan bought it of Joseph Mataack, sachem; but the Indians object and say that old Mataack by his will did settle it on his sons for the use of Gay Head Indians never to be sold or alienated from them; and to prove it produce an old writing; and upon inquiry into the truth of it, an Indian called Josiah Hosewit, which seemed to be a sober, honest man, came before the committee and owned that he wrote that writing long since Mataack's death; and by the testimony of sundry other Indians we have good reason to think that said writing was forged and not true.[4]

This conclusion was not satisfactory to the Indians, who seemed to have faith in the document as genuine, and two years later (1705) the General Court, upon petition of Moses Will and Samuel Assewit (Horswet), ordered a rehearing. Summonses were issued to Matthew Mayhew, as steward of Lord Limerick, and the Indians affected by the decision and

[1] Dukes Deeds, IV, 128.

[2] "Josias Hosoe [Hoswet] saith that he took up with Gov's Dungans terms, brought a Red Ear of Corn to Mr. Thomas Mayhew to signify it. Terms were to pay a Peck of Wheat yearly for a while and then to pay a Bushel of Wheat *per annum*." (Sewall, Diary, II, 432.)

[3] The members of this committee were Barnabas Lothrop, John Thacher, Stephen Skiffe, John Otis and William Bassett.

[4] Mass. Archives, XXXI, 17; comp., CXIII, 436. This confessed forger was afterwards the native Baptist preacher at Gay Head.

it was ordered that the will of Mataark the Sachem, with the proofs thereof be laid before the Governor and Council.[1]

Meanwhile the steward of Dongan, "by force and virtue of attorneyship," began to make grants or leases of land, "forever," to various natives, by metes and bounds, usually of forty acres each, the consideration being the payment of a quit rent yearly. Some of these unlimited leases were assigned to the English residents of Chilmark later for trifling payments, or in liquidation of debts incurred in business dealings with the whites. This became a source of friction between the natives and their neighbors who had become land owners, and complaints of these irregular transactions reached the agents of the Society from time to time.

THE EARL OF LIMERICK SELLS THE LORDSHIP TO THE SOCIETY FOR PROPAGATING THE GOSPEL

The Irish peer who held the Lordship of the soil in this town was an absentee landlord. It is not of record that he ever visited his domain, and his business interests here had been attended to from the first by his steward, Matthew Mayhew. The quit rents were collected, and leases prepared by the Major until his death in 1710, and this event probably hastened the change of ownership which followed shortly after. The Society for Propagating the Gospel had been for many years looking out for the moral and spiritual welfare of the natives, and its representatives in New England, comprising some of the most influential and wealthy men in the Province, saw that this state of affairs, with a landlord across the ocean, was not for the best interests of their wards. Accordingly they entered into negotiations with Lord Limerick to buy out his interests in the Manor of Martha's Vineyard. This was successfully accomplished, May 10, 1711, and the company, upon payment of £550, "lawful monies of Great Britain," secured the title of Lord of the Manor and the fee of Gay Head. This purchase was made, as Judge Sewall states in his diary, "with the main design of benefitting the aboriginal natives." Livery and seizin was completed Oct. 6, 1712, when Major Benjamin Skiffe and Samuel Sewall, Jr., as agents for Lord Limerick delivered to Penn Townsend, Esq., attorney for "the Corporation," as the society was generally designated here, the lands and hereditaments of the Manor. It was simply a

[1]Mass. Archives, XXX, 501.

change of landlords for the natives, and they were still tenants on the soil once owned by their fathers.

In 1714 a "ditch of four feet wide and two feet deep" was dug across the neck and "set within with Thorns and Barberries," and the Corporation gate erected and closed to signify the exclusion of the public from the reservation. The Corporation, "with the main design of benefitting the aboriginal natives" and to put a stop to the abuses of the indeterminate leaseholds, decided (in 1727) to make a part of this reservation a source of income, and to invest the inhabitants with the sole use and undivided occupancy of the remainder. Accordingly, on May 10, 1727, Abel Hosuit and nine other chief men, "in consideration of the great care, kindness and expense toward us, the inhabitants of Gay Head," executed a quitclaim deed of a tract of eight hundred acres in the northeast corner of the peninsular, bordering on Menemsha pond and the Sound.[1] In consideration of this resignation Pain Mayhew of Chilmark and Samuel Wells of Boston, "attorneys to the Honorable the Company for Propogating the Gospel &c," on the same day, "set off and settled upon the said natives and their posterity, that now inhabit or shall

CHEEPY'S CORN-FIELD.

[1]Dukes Deeds, IV, 199.

inhabit, said Gay Head, while they dwell on said Gay Head, the westerly and southerly part of said Gay Head: that is to say, all the lands of Gay Head aforesaid except what is resigned by said natives to said company."[1] For this residuary tract the tribe was to pay to the Corporation, "as an acknowledgment annually, on the first Monday of November, one ear of Indian corn for each family," with the understanding that the natives and their posterity were to be "always under the direction, government and stent of said Company." The tract of eight hundred acres was immediately leased, the same day, to Ebenezer Allen of Chilmark for a term of twenty-one years at a rental arranged on an increasing sliding scale, which yielded a total of £845 to the funds of the Corporation.[2]

STATE CONTROL OVER THE TRIBE

In addition to the authority of the Corporation in its capacity as landlord over the natives as tenants, and their agreement to be under the "direction government and stent" of this Company, the Province of Massachusetts exercised its sovereign power of supreme control of them as wards of the government. As in all like conditions the wards became restless under the condition of legal restraint over their property and freedom of action, and often, when excited by designing men, would prefer charges of favoritism, malfeasance and other breaches of trust against these guardians. It is difficult to estimate the true situation between charges and counter charges of the one and the other, but when the history of the cupidity of the whites is read in the light of the simplicity of the red men, we can believe that it was not all groundless complaint which the Indians made against the men who had the power over their persons and property. In 1747 this tribe entered two complaints relative to the leasing of their land for a new term, the undesirability of the persons who obtained the leases, the insufficiency of notice to the public, and the various other charges which were answered in detail by the guardians. This answer takes up each complaint and is given verbatim to show the character of the allegations and denial. After stating that they "sett Public notification . . . that on a Certain Day in them Prefixt," bids would be received, they continue:

[1]Dukes Deeds, V, 51.
[2]Ibid., IV, 242.

We Leas'd s'd Land for Four hundred and sixty five Pounds, old Tenor p annum the One half to be paid at the end of every Six Months. As to their Indian built houses to be taken off s'd Land it is no more than what they commonly practice themselves. As for their Fire-wood there is enough for their own use on that part of s'd Neck which is sett off to them which is as good wood as is generally growing on any part of s'd Neck of Land; and the wood that is growing on the Leased Land is very small, Scarcely a stick large enough for a hedge Stake. As to the Article of Complaint: our turning off their Catle and not reserving Feed enough for them it is utterly false, for there is a great deal more Grass growing on the Land sett off to s'd Indians than their Catle can Eat before the Winter will ordinarily spoil the grass, as will appear by the evidence herewith submitted. And as to the Objection made against the Persons to whom the Lease was made we answer it being sett up at a Publick Vandue every Person present had a right to bid for it; and they themselves had but a little time before Let the privilege of Feeding the whole Neck to several of the same persons as appears by a writing in hands of their Com'tee herewith presented, and we doubt not but that the hon'ble Court will Dismiss s'd Petitions as groundless and Vexatious as we humbly apprehend they are, we having acted in the s'd affair with integrity, and with no other view than to serve their Interest and that we have used the likeliest methods, therefore we doubt not but that we could procure the Testimony of every unprejudiced Judicious person in the County.[1]

DISAPPEARANCE OF "THE CORPORATION" AS LANDLORD

Evidence exists of the benevolent control exercised for years by the "Corporation" over the lands in this town, and elsewhere on the Vineyard, acquired by the purchase made of the Earl of Limerick. The political relations of the Province to the Crown, however, becoming more acute as we approach the period of the Revolution, necessarily had its reflex upon the activities of this English Society. The religious and political phases of this subject are considered in another volume of this history,[2] and it will only be necessary to state the fact that it resulted in a gradual withdrawal of contributions and a final loss of interest in the tribe at Gay Head, in common with the other beneficiaries. It is a singular fact that no record has yet been found, if one ever were made, which shows a conveyance of the rights of this corporation to the fee simple of Gay Head, and its other real property on the Vineyard occupied by the Indians. The exact legal status of the reservation during and after the Revolution is therefore a question of ethics and equity. Perhaps it may be held by those who

[1]Mass. Archives, XXXI, 350. Signed by Pain Mayhew, John Sumner and William Hunt.

[2]Vol. I, p. 255.

are learned in the law, that as the corporation was the creature of the crown, all the rights to hold and manage property in this country ceased when the independence of the United States was recognized, and thus the lands escheated to the Commonwealth by arms and the right of eminent domain residing in sovereign power.[1] Whatever the theoretical condition may have been, the state practically assumed control, directly and indirectly, of the property, and in the confusion and antagonisms created by the war, no attempt was ever made afterwards to challenge this authority. The tribe at Gay Head became, in common with others elsewhere, the "involuntary wards of the state." They had no control over their lands and homes. They could make no sale of them to anyone except other members of their tribe; neither could they make a contract binding in law, or sue or be sued except for trifling sums in the the courts of the county.

THE LONG APPRENTICESHIP IN CIVILIZATION

The evolution of the natives from dependents to citizens, after the war, was a slow and retarded process. As an observer truthfully said: "It is hardly to be wondered at that the Indians were 'thriftless and unprovident' for some of the most powerful incentives to elevate man were wanting." They were themselves lacking in initiative by inheritance. There was but one English built house in 1727, but fifty years later they had outgrown their wigwam state. While this was progress in one line there was inertia in others. A visitor in 1786 states that "they burned nothing but bushes, this part of the island affording no wood, and suffered much from cold weather, though peat was procurable in plenty."[2] Twenty years later the condition of the native was discouraging to another visitor, who recorded the opinion that they were intemperate, immoral, and dishonest, though he added that they were more industrious and neater in their person and houses than their people elsewhere.[3] Another traveler of this time said: "We sat by a peat fire, for this fuel is abundant on the

[1]No act of sequestration of this territory as the property of loyalists was passed by the General Court. See House Doc., No. 47, p. 12 (1856). The traveler Kendall, in 1807, says: "One third of the whole peninsula belongs to the Society for Propagating the Gospel etc [the one incorporated here in 1787] by which it is left to the use of the Indians" (Travels, II, 193). There seems to be no other authority for this statement.

[2]Memoirs of the American Academy, II, 153. Letter of Dr. William Baylies.

[3]Rev. James Freeman, in 1st Mass. Hist. Coll., III.

peninsula, and wood is rare." This fuel still furnishes comfort to the present generation in seasons of inclement weather, unless a coal laden vessel unfortunately goes ashore here and jettisons or loses her cargo, when it is washed ashore in sufficient quantities to permit the adoption of metropolitan manners for a temporary period. In 1838 it was stated by an authority that "their dwelling houses, upward of 35, are mostly one story and are comfortably built."[1] Ten years later (1849) the commissioner said of them: "The Gay Headers are, in the main, a frugal, industrious, temperate and moral people; but not without exceptions. In these respects they have greatly improved within the last thirty years and particularly within the last ten or twelve years."[2] In 1861 the commissioners report showed further progress in the refinements of civilization. "They are generally kind and considerate toward each other," he states, "and perform their social and relative duties as well as do other people in whose vicinity they reside."[3] In 1869, at a hearing on Gay Head held by a legislative committee, there was testimony from three clergymen covering a period of seven years, that neither of them had seen a case of drunkeness nor heard profanity among them in that time.[4]

While this satisfactory development had been going on it was reached under conditions of material discouragement. Dependent on the state as wards, improving land they did not own, they were in the same class with aliens, paupers, idiots and the insane in their relations to the body politic. The reservation was still an undivided tract in 1800, and a visitor some years later stated that "each man cultivates as much as he pleases, and no one intrudes on the spot which another has appropriated by his labor."[5] This anomalous condition existed in 1849 according to the commissioner. "While one proprietor has but half an acre and another has over a hundred acres, there is no heart-burning, no feeling that the latter has more than his share. 'I have all I want' says the former, and he is content. This state of things is as happy as it is peculiar; how long it will continue is a problem."[6] He recom-

[1]Barber, Historical Collections (Mass.), 148.
[2]F. W. Bird (House Doc., No. 46, 1849).
[3]J. M. Earle (Senate Doc., No. 96, 1861).
[4]Senate Document, No. 14, 1870.
[5]North American Review, V, 319 (1817).
[6]House Doc., No. 46 (1849), F. W. Bird's Report.

mended strongly the early confirmation of titles in severalty upon an equitable basis. Nothing however was done for a dozen years, and the commissioner, in his report for 1861, makes the following interesting observation upon this peculiar system of occupancy of the soil:

> This law is the unwritten Indian traditional law, which from its apparently favorable working, is probably as well adapted to their condition as any that can be devised. At any rate they adhere to it with great

STONE WEIR.

> tenacity, and are fearful of any innovations upon it. This, probably, is a prominent reason of their jealousy of foreigners, and of the rigorous exclusion of them from any foothold on their domain, except when intermarried with one of the tribe.[1]

THE FINAL STEPS TO CITIZENSHIP

The General Court created this reservation into the "District of Gay Head" in 1862, and shortly after measures were instituted to ascertain and determine the existing boundary lines of such tracts as were held in severalty and the

[1]House Doc., No. 215 (1862), J. M. Earle's Report. About 450 acres were held in severalty, fenced and occupied at this date.

common lands.[1] The person appointed to do this work, the late Hon. Charles Marston, died before completing it, and the General Court of 1866 authorized the Governor to commission "some suitable person" to perform this task. The late Richard L. Pease of Edgartown was appointed by Governor Bullock, and entered at once upon his duties.[2] It was a peculiar and delicate mission. Some of the claimants had the most hazy notions of their holdings. One woman entered a claim for "four rows of corn"! How well he performed it is certified by a legislative committee who visited the reservation during the progress of the work:

> Under his active and judicious supervision, order is being rapidly brought out of chaos, and the limits of each person's lot marked out by stakes and bounds. . . . . . In the performance of his duties, Mr. Pease is obliged, upon such examination and evidence as is accessible, to decide as to the ownership of property, and his decisions are generally acquiesced in with a good grace and with a better spirit of acquiescence, no doubt, than if he were dealing with the ordinary run of white people.

This work covered five years of investigation and research into the family histories of the inhabitants to make a proper apportionment of the shares of each resident or their kin elsewhere, and his report was submitted to the Governor and Council in the spring of 1871, and was ordered printed in full. It was a most valuable document, comprising a mass of valuable historical notes on the people and their lands from the earliest settlement, with a complete census of the inhabitants to illustrate the subject of his report.[3]

INCORPORATION AS A TOWN

While the work of Commissioner Pease was in progress, Governor Claflin, in his annual message to the General Court, called attention to the anomalous political condition of the Indians of the Commonwealth. A joint committee on this subject recommended the enfranchisement of the Indians and the final distribution of the lands of the Gay Head tribe.[4] Both measures were adopted, and the adult male population of the place made the recipients of the glorious privilege of citizenship in this Commonwealth — with a slight drawback. Being neither a town by themselves, nor part of any other

[1]Chapter 184, Statutes, 1862; comp., Resolves ch. 42, 1863.

[2]Resolves, ch. 67 (1866).

[3]Title: "Report of the Commissioner," etc., 8vo, pp. 60. Boston, 1871. His duties did not include a division of the "common" lands.

[4]House Docs., Nos. 483 and 502 (1869).

town, this privilege could neither be exercised nor enjoyed! This political paradox received the attention of the General Court of 1870, which sent a committee here to report on the capacity of the natives for independent existence as a township. This committee made a strong unanimous report in favor of such a conclusion. They said, after reviewing the situation:

> Because they are capable of self-government, as their history since 1862 abundantly shows; because they are worthy and well qualified now as they probably ever will be under the dominion of any neighboring town; because they are far remote from the nearest adjoining town by from four to seven miles; because the people of that town have been and are still strongly opposed to the annexation of Gay Head to them; because the people of Gay Head are (with one exception) unanimous for a separate township; because other things being equal, the wishes of the parties most interested ought to be consulted; and finally, because having already governed themselves in reality for the past few years (since 1862) a continuation of this control, while it would work no injury to any other interests, would be of great benefit to the people of Gay Head — giving them renewed assurance of the confidence of the Commonwealth in them and inspiring them to further effort towards improvement — we unanimously recommend that Gay Head be incorporated as a township by itself.[1]

The recommendation of this committee was concurred in by both houses and the act of incorporation as drawn by them was approved by the Governor, April 15, 1870, by which, after two centuries of retarded development, the last of the Algonquian race on this island became American freemen. Nor were these newly-fledged citizens "without honor in their own country," for under the rotation plan of electing a Representative for the County of Dukes County, Mr. Edwin DeVries Vanderhoop, a native "Gay Header," had the distinction of going to the General Court (session of 1888) to legislate for the white people who had lately enfranchised him. The town is now in its fortieth year of existence, a self-respecting community of people, obedient to the laws, managing its affairs economically, fulfilling all the requirements of an incorporated part of the Commonwealth, and justifying fully the faith of the men who gave it this opportunity for independent development. But it is still an "Indian" town, for the white man has made no invasion here. The words of the Sachem Metaark, spoken in 1681, now seem prophetic:

> Know yee all People that I Metaack and my principall men my children & people are owners of this, this our land forever. They are forever ours and our offspring forever shall enjoy them.

[1]Senate Doc., No. 14 (1870). This was signed by N. J. Holden and G. A. King of the Senate and E. Davis, J. J. Smith and A. G. Hart of the House.

MATERIAL PROGRESS, 1870–1910

The town began its independent career with nothing in the treasury and with only a sandy peninsula to work out its destiny. The first year its receipts were $342.75 and expenses $261.68; ten years later the receipts were $421 and expenses $360.77, but in another decade the showing was rather disappointing. The receipts in 1890 had fallen to $213.90, and the expenditures consumed it all. In the following ten years, however, a marked improvement had taken place, owing to the utilization of town lands, — the famous cliffs. These were leased to a corporation known as the Gay Head Clay Co. in 1893, at an annual rental of $500, and the clay was shipped elsewhere to kilns as material for bricks. The variegated hues of the clay do not resist the heat of burning and disappear in the oven, coming out a uniform color. This added income, doubling their ordinary receipts, enabled the town to increase its expenses for permanent improvement of public property. In 1900 the receipts were $1,025.97, and expenditures $921.67 for all purposes. In the following ten years these sums have also been doubled, the financial condition of the town steadily improving, with annual unexpended balances of generous amounts to its credit. In 1910 the receipts were $2,196.51 and expenses $1,313.06 leaving a balance of over eight hundred dollars.

In 1910 the following record showed the general character of the town's condition: real estate assessed, $30,875.40; personal estate, $9,779.58; total valuation, $40,654.98, after forty years of independence. Number of horses, 8; cows, 22; neat cattle, 56; houses, 48; acres assessed, 1,446.

The principal town officers this year (1910) are: W. H. Morton, Francis Manning, Linus S. Jeffers, Selectmen; Francis L. James, Clerk; Thomas C. Jeffers, Treasurer; Charles S. Hatch, Auditor; Harrison L. Vanderhoop, Tax Collector; Thomas Manning, James F. Cooper, Road Commissioners.

ECCLESIASTICAL AFFAIRS

The natives of this end of the Vineyard were the last to accept the religious teachings of the white men. It was the "last ditch" of the polytheism of the Powwows and the Indians here "had been many Years obstinately resolved" against receiving the Gospel of Christ, "being animated by the neighboring Sachims on the Shores of the Continent." In the year 1663, however, with the assistance of his converts, the elder Mayhew succeeded in convincing the Sachem Metaark of the truth of the white man's religion and he accepted the new theology. The Sachem then became a missionary among his people. In this departure from their ancient belief he was not followed. The influence of the medicine men was still powerful, and he found himself practically ostracised, although a Sachem.[1] He removed to Edgartown, where he lived for the next three years, continuing to preach there, and at the end of that time, when opposition had died out there he returned to his own people. It is recorded then that he "set up a Meeting at the said Gayhead, he himself dispensing The Word of God unto as many as would come to hear him, by which means it pleased God to bring over all that People to a Profession of Christianity."[2] He continued to preach until his death (1683), and was followed by Japheth Hannit. This man was born about 1638, the son of Pamehannitt and his wife Wuttununohkomkooh, and had been brought up in the Christian religion by his parents, who had early embraced its teachings.[3] The Anabaptist schism among the Indians of Gay Head occurred while he was the regular pastor of the missionary church.

FIRST MEETING-HOUSE

How long he preached is not known, but he died in 1712. Doubtless during his ministry he had assistance of other natives. Among them was Abel Wauwompuhque, a brother of Metaark, and Elisha Ohhumuh. In this period, in the year 1698, they were preaching "to at least 260 souls who have here at their

[1]Wuttahhannompisin was one of his first and few converts at this time (Mayhew, "Indian Converts," 131). "This Prince's subjects being resolved to continue in their heathenism, notwithstanding his embracing the Gospel" (Rev. John Mayhew).

[2]"Indian Converts," 22, 299.

[3]His surname was the last half of his father's Algonquian name, and was borne by all his decendants in that contracted form.

charge a meeting house already framed."[1] Abel died in 1713, and was succeeded by Joash Pannos or Panneu, who continued in service till his death (1720) seven years later. The following contemporary account of a native meeting in 1714 during his ministry is here given to show their mode of worship:

> About one hundred Men and Women were gathered together besides Children. Mr. Mayhew directed Joash Pannos, Minister of Gay Head to begin with Prayer; then, Mr. Mayhew preached from Ephes. I. II. — who worketh all things after the Counsel of his own will. Sung 4 verses of the 111th Psalm. Mr. Torrey set the Low-Dutch Tune. Mr. Mayhew gave in the heads of his Sermon in English; a good Discourse. Isaac Ompane concluded with Prayer.[2]

This meeting was a special function at which many visitors were present, but it affords a clear picture of the ceremonies as conducted by them.

SUBSEQUENT ANNALS

In the absence of church records the ministerial succession, if there were any continuous native ministry of the original Congregational mission, remains an unknown quantity. It is doubtful if the natives furnished many preachers after this time as the Corporation encouraged the English pastors of Chilmark and Tisbury to acquire enough proficiency in the Algonquian language to preach to the various assemblies. It is known that Peter Ohquanhut was the "minister of the Gayhead" in 1725,[3] and it is understood, of course, that Experience Mayhew was a general missionary on the Vineyard, and that he preached regularly at each of their meetings in town. Rev. Mr. Torrey of West Tisbury did the same, probably in his own town principally, but doubtless here on occasion, as did the settled pastors of other towns. This condition existed till Experience Mayhew's death (1758), when he was followed, in 1767, by his son Zachariah, and in 1810 by Frederic Baylies. The Baptists practically controlled the religious sentiment of the natives, however, and in 1786 it was stated that "they were seldom favoured with a congregational teacher."[4] A traveler of 1807, while on a visit to the island, says in that year the Congregational church was then taught

[1] Mass. Hist. Soc. Coll., X, 131; comp., Sewall, Diary, III, 397.

[2] Sewall, Diary, II, 432.

[3] "Indian Converts," 100. He was captured by French pirates in 1714 and taken into captivity (ibid., 110).

[4] Memoirs, American Academy, II, 153.

by a native preacher "in orders."[1] It is probable that the missionaries of the several societies were satisfied to have the natives become attached to any form of Christian worship, and did not attempt to discourage the existing Baptist congregation by maintaining opposition meetings in such a small community. The last baby to be sprinkled in baptism was Mary Cooper, b. 1784, later the wife of Johnson Peters.

Shortly after this the old meeting-house, out of repair and untenanted, was abandoned to the elements. It was gradually dismantled, and having failed of its purpose in religious affairs its remaining timbers went to help pay the support of secular teaching, and thus in its last days did quite as valuable service as in its days of pristine strength.

THE ANABAPTIST SECESSION

It is not known when some of the members of the Congregational mission assembly became "converted" to the current Anabaptist doctrines and left their old church to form another. The statements in the existing parish records of this church, prepared by a modern writer, and therein set forth are manifestly misleading as to the origin and responsibility for this schism.[2] That the secession met with the disapproval of the Mayhews there is ample evidence, and its existence was due to the influence of outside proselyting which they could not check. When this began is uncertain. The Commissioners who visited Gay Head in 1698 do not mention this seceding body. The modern church record states "about 1693," but the author has found nothing to fix such a specific date.[3] It is probable that the new influences came from Rhode Island, then a strong Anabaptist colony, as the whites and natives of the west end of this island were in constant business communication with Newport, only a short distance for sailing craft to cover. The first known leader of this sect at Gay Head was Stephen Tackamason, and in 1702 the earliest mention of the existence of such a schism appears. A contemporary authority writes as follows of his visit to this town:

> Japhet [Hannet] Jonathan and Stephen [Tackamason] came to me. I have discourse with them: try to convince Stephen of his Anabaptistical

[1]Kendall Travels, II, 197.

[2]The record states that "this church was gathered under the labors of Thomas Mayhew, Peter Folger and others, and constituted a Baptist church about A. D. 1693." It was, in fact, a secession from the church founded by Mayhew.

[3]Backus (Church History, I, 437) says "In 1694 there was a Baptist Church on the Vineyard among the Christian Indians."

Errors: Mr. Experience Mayhew proposes to me as a thing very expedient that some short Treatise be drawn up and translated into Indian to prevent the spreading of the Anabaptisticall Notions.[1]

This cannot but strike the reader of the generation as an amusing spectacle — a learned Judge of the King's Bench endeavoring to convince an Indian of the theological "errors" of "Anabaptisticall Notions," which involved not only considerations of the mystical origin of the Christian theistic dogmas, but philological excursions into the Hebrew and Greek tongues! It may be doubted whether any Indian of that day had a clear conception of the white man's religion as an abstruse proposition, to say nothing of its various sectarian interpretations. At this time (1702) the same authority states that Josias [Hossuit] and Stephen "have a church of about 30, ten men." The number of souls at Gay Head was then about three hundred, and the extent and importance of the schism may be estimated from these figures.

Stephen died in Chilmark in 1708 and was succeeded by Isaac Decamy, who was described as "a man of sober life and conversation." He came from the mainland with his family.[2] Decamy died about 1720. Following him was Josias Howwaswet (or Horsuit) the younger. He was preaching in 1727, and the congregation was called "a small society of Baptists." The next in succession was Ephraim Abraham and Samuel Kakenehew, the latter of whom, a resident of Chappaquiddick, preached at both places. He died in 1763, and Rev. Zachariah Mayhew, who was a contemporary, said "he was a man of sense and of a regular and Christian life and conversation." In 1763 Silas Paul was ordained as the pastor. He was born about 1738, was baptized in 1758, and at the age of twenty-five began a service as pastor which covered nearly a quarter of a century. He died in 1787, and his gravestone is one of the few remaining stones marking the burial places of Indians on Gay Head. He was the only Baptist minister on the Vineyard during his ministry. According to the church records his pastoral labors do not appear to have been successful. "The church at this time," it is written, "was very low

[1]Sewall, Diary, III, 397. With his well-known fondness for details, as amply illustrated in his voluminous diaries it is improbable that he would have neglected to state that this schism had existed for nine years (since 1693) if such had been the case. The absence of any reference to it in 1698, when commissioners of the Society visited Gay Head, and Sewall's failure to indicate any lengthy existence to it, confirm the view that it was of recent growth.

[2]Backus, Church History, I, 438.

respecting vital piety and practical religion." In 1774 the society had but thirteen members. He was succeeded in 1792 by Thomas Jeffers, a native of Plymouth, born 1742, and a resident of Middleboro in his adult life. He was fifty years of age when he took charge of this church, but it is said he was a man of considerable native ability and well received by his flock. He died Aug. 30, 1818, aged 76 years, after a service of about twenty-five years.[1] He followed farming as a principal

GRAVESTONE OF SILAS PAUL IN GAY HEAD.

means of support as the society could not provide for a clergyman who relied on their contributions for a livelihood. At this date this denomination was worshipping in a meeting-house of its own. It was a plain wooden structure and stood "on the brow of a steep hill," about a mile eastward of the lighthouse.[2] How long the vacancy in the pulpit existed after

[1]A visitor to Gay Head, in 1807, makes the following comment: "The Anabaptist Clergyman is a large farmer and was when young of great promise, but he is now given up to drink" (Kendall, Travels, II, 197).

[2]Kendall, Travels, II, 197.

Mr. Jeffers death we do not learn, but it appears that in 1830 fifteen members of the society became affiliated with the Baptist church at Homes Hole.[1] Whether this occurrence was precipitated by the lack of a pastor is not known. Two years later they were dismissed to form an independent society, April 8, 1832, with Joseph Amos, a Marshpee Indian, as pastor. He was entirely blind, but is described as "a preacher of considerable ingenuity."[2] The first deacons were Simon Johnson and Johnson Peters, and Zacheus Howwaswee, parish clerk. In 1838 there were forty seven communicants; about sixty in 1861 and 40 in 1870. He supplied the pulpit until his death, after which the Massachusetts Baptist Missionary Society began (1855) its supervision over the church and gave it financial support. The following named clergymen have since served as pastors: ——— Bray, ——— Sawyer, Charles G. Hatch, 1861-5; George B. Fitts, 1866-8; Gilman Stone, 1869-71; ——— Snow, 1872-3; Charles Kent, 1874-7; Messrs. Shields, father and son, 1877-87; ——— Thompson, 1887; ——— Allen, 1893; Charles Kent; ——— Engstrom; Louis B. Purmort, 1900-01; William Carpenter, 1902-04; George W. Hawkins (died June, 1906); and Clarence L. Whitman, the present incumbent.

SCHOOLS AND EDUCATION

It may be assumed that after the establishment of the Christian worship in this town some means were taken to provide schools for the education of the Indian children. Of the character, number, location or scope of such school or schools we have no record. Doubtless the preachers could read the scriptures in the Indian tongue, and there were probably others of the quicker-witted sort who could do the same. These preachers usually acted as school teachers with the meeting-house for a schoolroom, and they used the Indian bible, primers and catechisms as text books. A visitor, in 1702, wrote that there were here "two schoolmasters chiefly for winter, Josias Hassawit the Anabaptist preacher and Peter Chavin."[3] It is not probable that English received much attention, if any, and doubtless what little the children learned was picked up by association with the whites. In 1714, in

[1]Records, Baptist Church, Vineyard Haven. In 1827 a Sunday school had been organized.

[2]Barber, Historical Collections of Massachusetts, 148.

[3]Sewall, Diary, III, 397.

an assemblage which numbered nearly half the population, inquiry was made "if any one could read English . . . . . At last only two young men were produced. I set him [Josiah Hosuit Jr] to read in my Psalmbook with red Covers and then gave it him. Promised a testament to the 2d [Abel Sacahcassauet]."[1] We may believe that theological books, catechisms and sermons, however excellent in design, were not calculated to encourage the spirit of learning in these youthful aborigines, and the lack of proper text books suited to their age and capacity prevented the spread of knowledge among them.

The first schoolhouse of which we have any definite knowledge existed in 1807 in the basement of the Baptist church and was described in the following terms: "Beneath against the hill is an apartment of stone called by no better name than the *cellar*, in which, a school master keeps the Indian school. The winter season is the only part of the year in which it is kept . . . . Some of his scholars are remarkably apt and the rest are not below the ordinary level."[2] The person who then taught in this forbidding "apartment" was Ebenezer Skiff, the light keeper, who walked a mile daily over the sandhills to fulfill his task. Frederick Baylies, the missionary, succeeded him for a brief period about 1815,[3] and he was followed by a native, Aaron, son of Cyrus Cooper. Of him a modern authority on local annals writes: "After many years spent in 'furrin parts,' where he learned to speak French and acquired much other information — where he had possessed himself of a set of navigation instruments and many books — Aaron returned home, and his learning soon secured him employment as a teacher."[4] Another returning son of Aquinniuh, fresh from traveling "abroad," Tristram Weeks (b. 1800), was the next teacher, and many of the books used by him are still preserved. He received in part payment for his services the timber that then remained in the abandoned Congregational meeting-house.

At this time, as in the past, and until 1870, the school system was under the control of the state, which paid the expenses, in part, for the Indians were wards of the Commonwealth with a commissioner to govern them. The reports

[1]Sewall Diary, III, 432. Josiah was afterwards a preacher.

[2]Kendall, Travels, II, 196.

[3]A recent writer in referring to this teacher said: "This pedagogue occupied three chairs and spent much of his time in sleeping" (Vanderhoop, "Gay Head Indians, &c.," in New Bedford Evening Standard).

[4]Ibid.,

of these commissioners, regular and special, show an unpromising and generally wretched state of affairs in the school. In 1849, for example, there was an inadequate supply of books for reading and writing according to the commissioner. "But the contemptible and beggarly appropriations (from $50 to $100)," says one of their people who had investigated this subject, "continued to be doled out by the anxious authorities, who never allowed their love of enlightenment and their 'interest in the cause of education' to run away with their parsimonious principles. Is it any wonder that little or no creditable work was ever performed by the natives? Those having the funds in charge always recommended the employment of home talent in order to keep the money at home. Here was a fine example of the blind leading the blind."[1] About this time young ladies from other towns on the island came to teach, one of whom, Mary Jane Tilton (Mrs. Cottle), is most pleasantly remembered for her care and attention to the children under her charge.

The missionary preacher, Rev. Mr. Hatch (1861-5), gave a new impetus to the cause. Those students who had the desire, and those whom he could influence to learn more than was provided in the curriculum, were encouraged to come to his home, where he taught them the higher and more useful branches. His untimely death seemed a blow to the prospects of the scholars, but another, equally as zealous, was found to take up the work, Rev. George B. Fitts of Middleboro. This young man was just out of college (1866), and for nearly three years he was the "guide, philosopher and friend" of these wards of the State, and by the application of methods suitable to the molding of this crude material, the school made a great stride forward.[2] Through his influence philanthropic people in Boston became interested in the work, funds were secured for the modern equipment of a schoolhouse, and visits of these influential patrons gave an added encouragement to the pupils. The school term then comprised eight months, and the expense, about $300, was borne, in part, by the state. A special committee of the General Court appointed in 1869, reported favorably on this appropriation as follows:

In view of the peculiar situation of this people and their circumstances we earnestly hope this aid will be continued. In no better way can the

[1]Vanderhoop, "Gay Head Indians, &c.," in New Bedford Evening Standard.

[2]Some of his pupils became teachers and secured employment in the southern states. One became his assistant after a course at the Normal school.

Commonwealth compensate the long years of degradation to which an unjust denial of the rights of citizenship doomed them, than by generous assistance towards the education of their children.[1]

The recommendations of this committee were adopted and, until 1889, when this state aid was withdrawn, the school had the benefit of twenty years of satisfactory maintenance. Since then the ability of the town to give proper financial support to the school has greatly increased, and a term of nine months is now provided with two teachers. Scholarships have been presented by public spirited friends, and one of the boys has taken a course at the Boston Latin school.

PATHS, HIGHWAYS AND BRIDGES

One hundred years ago a visitor to this town stated: "on the Indian lands there are no made roads, and for the most part only horse paths." This condition existed for about fifty years more, when a continuation of the county road from the Chilmark line to the lighthouse was laid out. Its construction was without design and unscientific, and soon became a continuous sand rut for lack of repairs. In 1870, when the town was incorporated, the act provided that the county commissioners should forthwith "proceed to lay out and construct a road from Chilmark to the lighthouse on Gay Head, and may appropriate such sum from the funds of the county as may be necessary to defray the expense of the same." It was further provided that it should be maintained for five years by the state. This legislation resulted in the construction of the present and only public highway in the town, which since 1875 has been a town charge.

THE GOVERNMENT SERVICES

LIGHTHOUSE ESTABLISHMENT

Only one lighthouse exists in the town, but it is of such an important character that it warrants extended consideration. It was the first one erected on the Vineyard by the general government, and was authorized by an act of Congress approved July 16, 1798, which provided for its construction "As soon as urisdiction of such land at Gay-head . . . . shall have been ceded to the United States." This formality was accomplished

[1]Senate Report, No. 14, 1870, p. 7.

Feb. 22, 1799, by the General Court of this state,[1] and a tract of two acres and four rods passed into the possession of the government. The tower first built was of wood, forty feet high, and the lantern, supported by eight large pine beams,

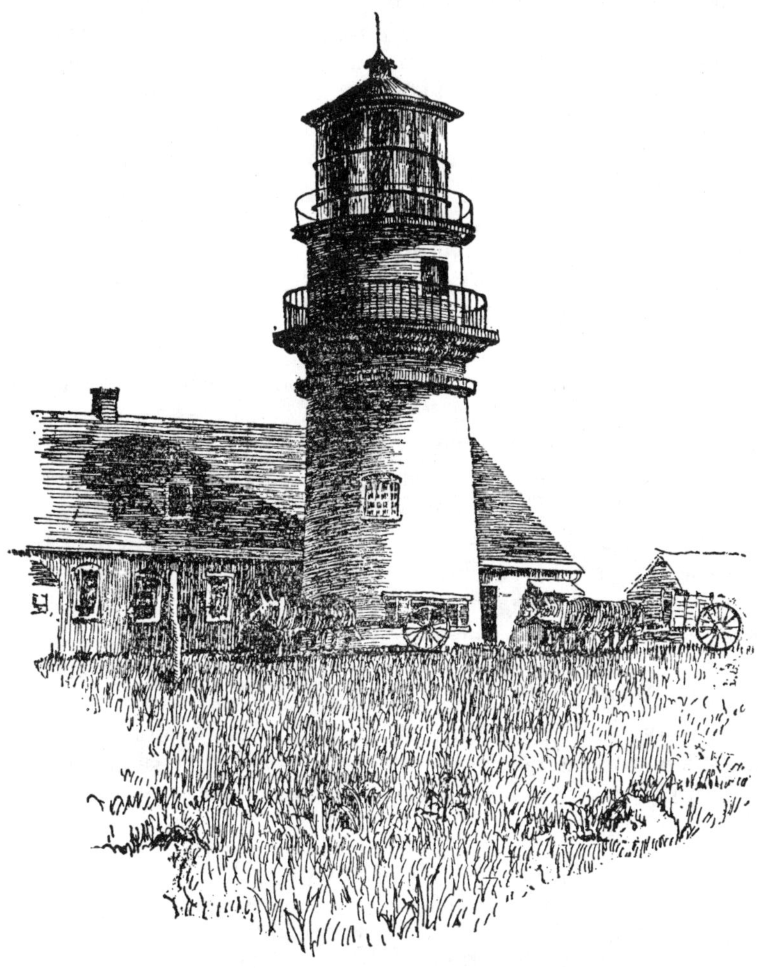

LIGHTHOUSE, GAY HEAD.

was reached by ladders. The light, which was a white flash, was produced by fourteen lamps burning sperm oil, and it is a part of the tradition of the place that there was quite as much smoke as flame resulting from the combustion of this

[1]Laws of Massachusetts, II, 847. The original proclamation of President Adams concerning these acts is preserved at the lighthouse.

illuminant. The keeper was often obliged to wear a veil while in the tower, and the cleansing of the smudge on the glass lantern was no small part of his job. This wooden tower, which had been reduced ten feet in height, lasted sixty years, and the site of it, nearer the brow of the cliffs than the present one, can be seen yet in a circular elevation of the soil. The second and present tower was built in 1858-9, and is of brick construction sixty feet high.[1]

This new lighthouse was placed in the class of the first order and equipped with one of the most powerful illuminators on the Atlantic coast. The compound lens, made by Fresnel, a French expert, consist of 1,003 prisms of the finest cut and polished crystal glass, scientifically arranged in three sections.[2] This results in a refraction of the rays of light from the lamp above and below to the middle of "bull's eye" whence they are projected horizontally in concentrated power. The illuminator is a lamp with five concentric wicks, the largest being five inches in diameter, and it consumes two quarts of oil an hour, or about seven and a half gallons on the longest nights. The distinctive flash effect was retained, but a red one was added. Every ten seconds a white light flashes three times and the fourth is red. This magnificient light sweeps the sea for twenty miles with its great luminous radiants majestically revolving around the tower, affording a sublime spectacle to the beholder standing beneath. A famous writer of a half century ago describes the effect of this during his visit, in the following language: "Of all the heavenly phenomena that I have had the good fortune to witness — borealis lights, mock suns or meteoric showers — I have never seen anything that in mystic splendor equalled this trick of the magic lantern of Gay Head."[3]

> Like a phantom pale, the Gay Head light,
> 'Gainst the blackening cloud of the squall stands out.
> The note of the surf on Menemsha Bight
> Murmurs its warning of "Ready! About!"

This light is visited annually by thousands of people as one of the "sights" of the Vineyard.

[1]The work of construction at this remote point tested the capacity of the contractor. It required eight pair of oxen to transport the iron deck across the island and hoist it into position. In 1903 a new keeper's house, costing $10,000, was built to replace the old one shown in the illustration.

[2]This cost the government $16,000.

[3]Porte Crayon, Harper's Magazine, (1860) Vol. XXI.

The first keeper was Ebenezer Skiff[1] (1799-1834), followed by his son, Ellis Skiff. He was succeeded in turn by Henry Robinson, John Hayden, Samuel Flanders (a picture of whom appeared in *Harper's Magazine* in 1860), Ichabod N. Luce, Calvin C. Adams, Horatio N. Pease, William Atchison, Edward Lowe and Crosby L. Crocker (1886), at present in service.

THE POST OFFICE

Until 1873 this town was served from the Chilmark office at Squibnocket, and on Feb. 14 of that year Isaac D. Rose was appointed the first postmaster of the newly-established office. He served eleven years, and was succeeded by William A. Vanderhoop, Dec. 11, 1884; Paulina A. Vanderhoop, Nov. 14, 1893, and Mary A. Cleggett Vanderhoop, Aug. 13, 1907, the present incumbent.

LIFE SAVING STATION

A fully equipped station of this service was established at Gay Head and placed in commission Dec. 20, 1895, with a crew composed of native surfmen, and the crews have generally been of Indian extraction. The record of the station is that of great efficiency and notably brave work.

MISCELLANEOUS ANNALS

NOTABLE WRECKS

This headland has been the scene of many marine disasters since its settlement by the English, a line of reefs making out far into the Sound, hidden from view, and strong currents setting unwary mariners onto the Devil's Bridge, to be dashed and broken in pieces by the pounding of the waves.

In the night of Jan. 14, 1782, occurred a disaster laden with sorrow for the people of the Vineyard, as the master and more than half of the crew were residents here. The vessel had started from Edgartown under favorable weather conditions, but a severe storm of wind and snow arose towards night and she was driven ashore on the reefs about two miles from the

[1]The Boston Marine Society recommended Capt. Silas Daggett of Homes Hole as keeper "should he find it for his interest to surrender other objects of business to this alone" (Records, Aug. 6, 1799).

cliffs. A contemporary poetic threnody of twenty stanzas thus tells, in part, of what befell them.

The ship was split from stem to stern,
    Which filled their hearts with supprise,
When these poor mortals came to see
    Supprising death before their eyes.

Twelve men hung to the quarter deck,
    If I do rightly understand,
And nine of them was drowned,
    The other three got to land.

There were 15 poor souls in all
    That the rageing ocean proved their grave
I hope they did for mercy call
    Though but little warning seemed to have.

It is a little difficult to follow the mathematics, to say nothing of the metre of this rhyme, but later verses seem to say that twelve lost their lives.[1] Matthew Butler, Samuel Wiswall, Bayes Norton, Samuel Fish, Jethro Norton, and Isaac Bunker were of Edgartown. Four were buried at Edgartown and the rest in Chilmark.

The wreck of the *City of Columbus*, which occurred in the early hours of the morning of Jan. 18, 1884, was the most appalling in the annals of this headland. The vessel was proceeding from Boston to Savannah, and the night was unusually clear with the moon shining, though a heavy wind was blowing; the air was bitterly cold, and the seas were high. As she was passing the Devil's Bridge, about 3:45 A.M., the man at the wheel either misunderstood an order for a change of course or a wrong order was passed, and in a moment she was fast on the treacherous ledge of rocks and careened to port. The sea was soon making a clean sweep of the larger part of the deck. For some reason those on duty in the lighthouse did not discover the stranded vessel until 5 A.M., when the keeper of the light (Horatio N. Pease) called for assistance. Meantime, as the unfortunate passengers, aroused from their sleep, came upon deck they were washed off into the raging surf and either drowned or killed by their injuries. Four men succeeded in reaching the shore in a ship's boat about 7 o'clock, and one of these died from exposure almost immediately after landing. The volunteer crew of Gay Headers, consisting of

[1]This "poem" was evidently written by a survivor. The author of this book has a copy made in 1842 by Betsey Burdsall for "Jane Randal, one of these fatherless children." Parson Thaxter states that fourteen were lost.

Thomas C. Jeffers, in command, Henry H. Jeffers, Raymond Madison, Thomas E. Manning, Charles Stevens, Simeon Divine, and John O. Anthony, could make no headway in launching their whaleboat, as it was stove up in their efforts to clear the breakers, and they barely escaped drowning. At about nine o'clock a life-boat was successfully launched by a crew of Gay Head Indians, consisting of Joseph Peters captain, Samuel Haskins, Samuel Anthony, James Cooper, Moses Cooper, and John Vanderhoop. After battling an hour they were able to bring seven men ashore rescued from the rigging. A second crew manned it, all Indians, except the captain, James T. Mosher. They were Leonard L. Vanderhoop, Thomas C. Jeffers, Patrick Divine, Charles Grimes, and Peter Johnson. They had rescued thirteen men when the U. S. Revenue Cutter *Dexter* arrived to render assistance, having been called to the scene by telegraphic messages. There were passengers still in the rigging, but many had become numbed and frozen, and had dropped off exhausted, into certain death. Lieutenant John U. Rhodes commanded a rescuing party in one of the ship's boats and performed feats of heroism that made his name famous in the story of this terrible wreck. It was impossible to effect a landing on the vessel or get very near to it owing to the danger of being battered to pieces in the heavy seas. The only way men could be helped was to induce them to jump overboard and be picked up. But two men remained in the rigging, and both were fast losing strength. Rhodes, with a line about him, jumped into the chilling, surging waters and swam for the wreck. Some wreckage struck him and he sank, was pulled out, taken to the *Dexter*, revived, and his wound dressed. He insisted on making the second attempt and this time he succeeded. The last two living souls on the unfortunate ship were aided in their leap for life by him and brought to safety. "For heroic exertions at the imminent peril of his own life" the Massachusetts Humane Society presented a gold medal to him, and their silver medal was given to each member of the Gay Head crews.[1] The toll of the sea from this unnecessary wreck was one hundred and twenty-one souls, and is the greatest disaster in the history of the place.

[1]The Squibnocket lifeboat of the Massachusetts Humane Society was brought over before the end of the efforts at rescue. She was manned by Eddy C. Flanders, captain; Benjamin F. Mayhew, E. Elliott Mayhew, William Mayhew, Cyrus C. Look and Seth Walker. They did excellent relief work, and were awarded a bronze medal by the Humane Society.

TAVERNS

There have been no "public houses" in this town worthy of record, as the transient visitor is infrequent except in summer, and private families have always furnished temporary lodging and otherwise cared for the traveler who remains at Gay Head over night.

CEMETERIES

The native population of Gay Head preserved the traditions of their race in the matter of burials, although the town has not proved to be rich in the funeral memorials of its dead. Few graves, which have accidentally been opened, have yielded up much archæological treasure. Small articles, such as stone fishing implements, arrow points, corn, and tobacco, have been found buried with the Algonquians of Gay Head. Naturally they had no well-defined grounds set off for their burials, as this was not an Indian custom, but there is a considerable collection of graves on Abel's neck, and a tradition is that Hiacoomes, the first Indian preacher of the Vineyard, is here interred. This seems quite unreasonable, as he was a resident of Chappaquiddick. On the old Congregational meeting-house lot are many graves, and on Meletiah's hill, in the rear of the site of the Baptist meeting-house, may be seen still more. Most of them are marked with rough stones, and the inscriptions are nearly obliterated. In fact, scattering memorials of the dead are to be noticed all over the peninsula.

The modern burying ground contains the remains of the Indians of this day and generation, as well as some of the white race, and has no special historic interest.

MARITIME TRAFFIC

As showing the extent to which this great marine highway guarded by Gay Head is used the following record, kept by an official of the lighthouse in the year 1870, will testify: number of craft seen passing, 36 ships, 160 barks, 1,541 brigs, 21,642 schooners, 1,989 sloops, and 1,102 steamers, making a total of 26,470 vessels of all classes and rigs.

INDUSTRIES

The principal occupation of the residents has always been the fisheries, and it continues to be so, individually and collectively, for the town derives some income from licensing fish traps and pounds. In addition to this is the shipping of clay from the cliffs, which has continued for nearly twenty years in the hands of the Gay Head Clay Co. and the Gay Head Fire Brick Co., as lessees of the town rights, as previously noted.

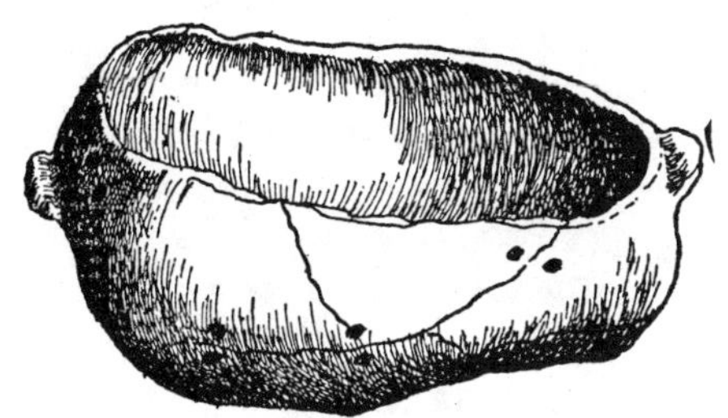

STONE BOWL.
EXCAVATED AT GAY HEAD IN 1907.

ANNALS OF GOSNOLD

THE ELIZABETH ISLANDS

ANNALS OF GOSNOLD

THE ELIZABETH ISLANDS

FORMATION OF THE GROUP

The chain of a dozen islands, large and small, running westward from the mainland of Cape Cod at Woods Hole, between Buzzards Bay and Vineyard Sound, constitute the Elizabeth Islands, known now as the town of Gosnold, an integral part of the County of Dukes County. These islands, varying in size from a few acres to several thousand, now bear the following names, beginning at Woods Hole and going westward in sequence: Nonamesset, Uncatena, Monohansett, Naushon, Weepecket, Pasque, Nashawena, Penekese, Gull, and Cuttyhunk. They have been, since the first purchase by Mayhew in 1641, a part of the political life of Martha's Vineyard and this county, at first forming one of the outlying portions of the Manor of Tisbury, later of Chilmark and for the past quarter of a century as an independent township.

POPULATION

There are but few references at hand for computing the number of persons living on these islands before 1800, and none prior to the middle of the eighteenth century. In 1761 it was stated that there were "near twenty families" here, and we can estimate that this represents about ninety souls. In 1777 there were reported seventeen families and "about 100 souls" (Mass. Arch., CXVII, 758). The census of 1790 gives 13 on Cuttyhunk, 10 on Nashawena, 21 on Pasque, and 59 on Naushon, a total of 103.

No further records of the separate enumeration of people resident here until after its incorporation as a township exist. The decennial censuses of the United States show the population of Gosnold as follows: In 1870 it was 99; in 1880 it was 152; in 1890 it was 135; in 1900 it was 164. The state census of 1905 showed a population of 161 in the entire group.

DISCOVERED AND NAMED BY GOSNOLD, 1602

The voyage of Captain Bartholomew Gosnold and his landfall at Nomans Land in the spring of 1602 has been narrated in this history (Vol. I, pp. 59-65), and it will only be necessary to refer to his landing and settlement on the westernmost of the group, now called Cuttyhunk. Leaving Nomans Land on May 24, 1602, the "Concord" sailed past Gay Head, which was "doubled," in their course, "and then came into a fair sound where we rode all night." This was the Vineyard Sound. "The next morning," the journalist continues, "we sent off one boat to discover another cape that lay northwest of this, between us and the main, from which were a ledge of rocks a mile into the sea, but all above water and

EARLIEST MAP OF THE ELIZABETH ISLANDS, 1610.
FROM THE ARCHIVES OF SIMANCAS, SPAIN.

without danger."[1] Sailing around this they anchored in "one of the stateliest sounds," which was named by them Gosnold's Hope.[2] "This island," near which they dropped anchor, wrote the journalist, "Captain Gosnold called Elizabeths Isle," the one now known by its Indian name, Cuttyhunk.[3] This little Elizabeth's Isle, has thus survived three centuries as one of the landmarks of the early voyagers, and spread itself in the plural form over the entire group.[4]

[1]The "Sow and Pigs" reef.

[2]Now called Buzzards Bay.

[3]At the close of his narrative of the voyage the statement is repeated as to Captain Gosnold naming it, "which he called Elizabeths Island," is the language used. It may be assumed that it was bestowed in honor of the Queen of England.

[4]In 1702 Wait Winthrop, in a letter, spoke of the present Naushon as Elizabeth's Island.

These islands thus taken possession of and named became English soil by right of discovery and occupancy. They were included in the territorial grant of the King to the Council for New England in 1606, but when that corporation dissolved in 1635, and divided the New England coast among themselves they were not assigned by name to either Gorges or Stirling. In the then hazy knowledge of this region it can not be said which of the members of the Council had a definite legal claim to these islands.

PURCHASE BY MAYHEW, 1641

Stirling's agent asserted his right of jurisdiction over them, however, as he had done in the Vineyard and Nantucket, and when he sold those two islands, in 1641, he gave Thomas Mayhew, under date of Oct. 23, that year, a supplementary authorization to "plant" upon the Elizabeth Isles. The agent of Gorges made no pretensions of title to them.

At this time they were probably unsettled, either by whites or Indians. Three years before this (1638) Underhill, in his "Newes from America," stated that the "Elizabeth Ilands all these places are yet uninhabited." It does not appear that Mayhew took any steps to attract settlers or to dispose of his rights to others for many years, nor is there any contemporary evidence of Englishmen living here for the next twenty-five years. The name of Quick's Hole is of contemporary usage (before 1670), and suggests an original form of an English surname of a person who may have lived at that place.[1] This, however, is but a conjecture.

Mayhew and his son began, in 1654, the purchase of the Indian "rights" to these islands, securing Cataymuck first (1654), while Nonamessit "with several other islands" had been conveyed by the Sachem Seayick in various deeds, before 1668, but unrecorded. Coincident with this, in the larger domain of government politics, the proprietorship of these islands was being transferred from Lord Stirling's heirs to the Duke of York, in 1663, although in the Duke's Patent of 1665 they are not mentioned by name. This, however, was of small moment to court politicians, and on Jan. 3, 1667-8,

[1]One William Quick, a mariner, was of Charlestown (1636), and removed to Newport two years later. He left Rhode Island in June, 1644, on account of religious troubles [4th Mass. Hist. Coll., V, 194; VII, 55, 323-4]. His avocation as a mariner would naturally lead him to and fro through the Vineyard Sound when going between Boston and Newport.

Colonel Richard Nicolls, the Duke's representative in New York, wrote to Mayhew that "all the Islands except Block Island from Cape Cod to Cape May are included in my Masters patent." This was sufficiently comprehensive to include the Elizabeth group, and Col. Francis Lovelace, in his notice of May 16, 1670, addressed it "to all Persons concerned who lay clayme or have any pretence of Interest in . . . . . . any of the Elizabeth Isles," among the other places enumerated. By this process of benevolent assimilation these waifs and strays on the map came to be under the jurisdiction of New York. The individual ownership of such indefinite property was of little concern in those times, and transfers of title were seldom recorded. For this reason the early holders of the several islands composing this group have pretty successfully evaded detection. It is known that some of them were purchased before 1671 by William Brenton of Newport, but no record of it has been preserved other than an adjudication of his title in that year.[1]

THE NASHANOW ISLANDS

This group of islands was known as Nashanow to the Indians of the seventeenth century, and the following statements relative to the aboriginal ownership of some of the group establishes the priority of this name. It is the only occurrence of it known to the author, and its similarity to Naushon will be noted. Probably it is the origin of the name of the largest island, Naushon.

The testimony of Old Hope, the Indian of Mannomett, as followeth:—Saith, that hee knew the little island, lying next Saconessett, called Nanomeesett, and a necke of land or little iland called Uckatimest, belonging to the great iland called Katomucke, and another little iland lying between the said great iland and Nanomesett belonging to Job Antiko, his grandfather Comucke, and soe to Jobs father, Thomas Antiko; and said Hope further saith that the said great iland, called Katomucke, and another little iland called Peshchameesett, to belonge to Webacowett.

Washamwatt, Indian of Nanomeesett, witnesseth also to the truth of what the abovesd Hope hath affirmed as abovesaid.

And William Numacke testifyeth that hee hath heard his father, Nanquatumacke, often say the same things as is above testifyed by Hope and Washawatt concerning the ilands comonly called Nashanow Ilands.

And Washamatt further testifyeth that he hath heard the abovesaid

[1]In his will, proved Nov. 13, 1674, Brenton gave to his son-in-law, Peleg Sanford, "all interests in Elizabeth Islands and Gay Head lands." The inventory of his estate includes "my part in Elizabeth Island, £40."

Thomas Antiko to give the above said Iland Nanomeesett, and the said necke and little iland unto his two sons James and the abovesaid Job Antiko, for many year agon, being near the time that Napoitan, sachem of Barnstable died of the smale pox.[1]

The meaning of this word Nashanow is uncertain, but probably signifies the midway islands, between Buzzards Bay and Vineyard Sound.

ABORIGINES AND THE MISSIONS

It is doubtful if there were many Indians who lived on these islands as a permanent abode. They were not fitted for their support on account of their size, with the exception of Naushon, and we may conclude that they were temporary habitations for them during the summer season and when the fishing was good. These Indians seemed to have no tribal connection with those of the Vineyard, but held allegiance to the Sachem of Buzzards Bay, who was a vassal of "a great Sachime upon the Mayne near Pacannakicke." In 1654 Seayick was the local Sachem and in 1666 it was Quaquaquijott.

Few myths and traditions of Algonquian origin relating to these islands have been preserved. Wait Winthrop, Jr., who used to spend some vacations here about 1700 at his father's island (Naushon), has recorded some that he heard. One was to the effect that before the English came to America there was a white whale kept in the great pond at the west end of Naushon. Another relates to the great Indian deity building a stone bridge from the mainland to Nonamessitt, during which he was bitten by a crab. Snatching his hand away suddenly with pain he flung the crab over to Nantucket whence grew all the crabs in that region.

There is a singular absence of Algonquian place names, exclusive of the names of the islands forming the group, and this is a further indication that it was not much more than a place of resort and rather less than an abode. In 1671 Mayhew stated that there were "15 families [of Indians] at Elizabeth Iles 7 whereof praying families."

These islands were likewise in the missionary field of the Mayhews, the work beginning about this date with some native converts as assistants to the elder Thomas Mayhew.

[1]Plymouth Colony Records, VI, 21, 22. The date of this testimony is not given in the record, but it was not far from 1675.

How long the work was continued regularly is not known, but John Weeks was preaching to the Indians in 1700 at a salary of £10 per annum,[1] and later a native preacher, Jannohquosso, held services here. In 1727 another native, Daniel Shohkau, "still preached the Gospel to a few families at Winthrops Island" (Naushon). With the increase of the white settlers the conditions were not favorable nor congenial for the two races to live on these small islands together, and it is probable that the last Indian had left before the close of that century.[2]

INCORPORATED WITH TISBURY MANOR, 1671

When the Mayhews were in New York arranging their affairs with Governor Lovelace in 1671, the charter of Tisbury Manor was created on July 8th, as explained elsewhere, and this group of islands was made a part of that disjointed manor. Its connection with the town of Chilmark thus began and was to continue for nearly two centuries. Again, on Nov. 1, 1683, it was included by name in the establishment of Dukes County as "Elizabeth's Island,"— and when the Lordship and Manor of Martha's Vineyard was created in 1685 the Elizabeth Islands were included in the new dignity.[3] After the transfer of jurisdiction from New York to Massachusetts by the charter of 1691, the Elizabeth Islands were again named in the act confirming the settlement of the County of Dukes County. From these various acts this group came to have a habitation and a name, and henceforth its status was fixed. A curious legal complication occurred in connection with them shortly after the change. A suit for trespass on the island of Naushon had been entered for the October term of the County Court at Edgartown in 1695, and the defendant, Anthony Blaney by his attorney, demurred to the competency of the court to try the case. He contended that the Justices and "the Marshall who a rested him" had no authority "for such action on Ilesabeth Ilands" because their commissions were for "Marthas Vineyard" only. Upon an examination of this allegation the judges were forced to "allow the defendants plea Sufficient

[1]New York Col. Doc., IV, 75.

[2]Mayhew, "Indian Converts", 123, 131.

[3]In the transfer of the Manor back to Governor Dongan, the Elizabeth Islands were not in the "excepted" list and inferentially they remained a part of the Lordship, though never after mentioned in its affairs.

to barre further proceedings." New commissions were accordingly issued the next year in which the words "Dukes County" was substituted for "Marthas Vineyard," and the defect was healed.[1]

ANNALS OF THE REVOLUTION

These islands were not the scene of any conflicts great or small between the British and American forces, but their proximity to the line of water communication made them a sort of frontier post for the rebels and a rendezvous for the ships of the King's navy in search of the enemies' boats.[2] Captain John Linzee of the *Falcon* was an early marauder in this section, both ashore and afloat. Mrs. Elizabeth Bowdoin, wife of the owner of Naushon, sent a communication to the Provincial Committee of Safety, dated Dorchester, June 4, 1775, in which she recites the depredations of landing parties from this sloop of war under his command. Elisha Nye, who was acting as her agent at the island, sent in an account to her amounting to £14:10:0 for sheep, beef, a gun and "riding my horse and use of my well," which represented her losses from this particular raid. Mrs. Bowdoin asked the Committee to send troops to protect her husband's property, as the stock of sheep has been a source of supply to the Province as subsistence and wool.[3] Captain John Grannis and a company of thirty men were immediately sent from Falmouth as a coast guard.[4]

The first military movement of the provincial authorities in connection with these islands was the inclusion of them early in 1776, in the Sea-Coast Defence establishment. Major Barachiah Bassett was the officer in command of this detachment as a part of the Vineyard quota. On March 21, 1776, the town officials of Martha's Vineyard petitioned for seventy-five men to be stationed at the Elizabeth Islands with two cannons mounted at Tarpolin cove. In answer to this, Major Bassett was directed to mount four nine-pounders wherever he thought advisable for the defence of these islands, and they were probably mounted at Naushon. He informed the General Court "that it will not be in my power to afford

[1]Mass. Archives, Council Records, II, 421.

[2]See Vol. I, pp. 331-2.

[3]Ricketson, "History of New Bedford," 353.

[4]Freeman, "History of Cape Cod," II, 452.

protection which is necessary for these Islands westward of Tarpolan Cove Island & the vessels that are constantly parsing without I have at least Ten Whale Boats." These were allowed. In November of that same year, however, the Sea Coast Defence establishment was disbanded by the Provincial authorities, but Major Bassett was directed to retain Lieut. Elisha Nye, two Sergeants and twenty-one men at the Elizabeth Islands as an exception to the general order.[1] Nye was commissioned by the Council as a Captain early in 1777, and rendered excellent service as a commanding officer.[2] The roster of the company which served under him during this year and part of the next follows herewith:

MUSTER ROLL OF THE COMPANY COMMANDED BY ELISHA NYE IN 1777[3]

ELISHA NYE, Captain

STEPHEN NYE, 1st Lieutenant — WILLIAM TOBEY, 2nd Lieutenant

SHUBAEL HATCH, NATH'LL COBB, ISAAC GORHAM — Sergeants

HOWES HALLET, JAMES WIRTHLEY, DAVID TAILOR — Corporals

RICHARD CHURCH, Drummer — NATHANIEL DILLINGHAM, Fifer

Abner Hinkley	Jonathan Lumbert	Jonathan Nye
Jonathan Vincent	Ebenezer Bacon	Joseph Bacon
Lot Bassett	Thomas Bacon	John Wilts
Miller Pain	Elihu Hatch	Isaac Vincant
Samuel Bunch	Isaac Parker	Isacher Nickerson
Eleoney Howes	Christopher Sears	Nathaniel Young
Josiah Crowell	Elisha Hallett	Croker Young
Nathaniel Matthew	Nathan Wing	Nathaniel Ellis
Joseph Hallet	Ebenezer Cobb	Ebenezer Clarke
Jonathan Phiney	William Sanford	Obed Young
George Lewis	Samuel Robinson	Amaziah Harden
Sturgis Howes	David Dunham	James Downes
Edmund Howes	Richard Robins	Robert Hatch
Enos Howes	Uriah Hatch	Eliakim Gibbs
Nymphas Hinckley	Daniel Barse	Ephraim Norris
Andrew Hedge	John Bassett	Jabez Gibbs
Thomas Howes	Edmund Bassett	Noah Howes
Edward Cobb	Nathaniel Bassett	Nathaniel Gibbs
John Cobb	Elisha Smith	Elisha Allen
Barnabas Downs	Isaiah Howes	John Taylor
Silvanus Hinkley	John Bourne	Elijah Howes

[1]See Vol. I, 359-61, for complaint of the Vineyard authorities on the discrimination in favor of the smaller section of the county.

[2]See Vol. I, 364-5.

[3]Mass. Arch. (Rev.), XXXVI, 157.

ATTEMPTED ANNEXATION TO DARTMOUTH

The political connection of these islands with Chilmark, seven miles across the Sound, would not be productive of the best administrative results, and as a natural consequence this disarticulated portion sought relief and improvement, but the means chosen was only a shift of the place but not the burden. In 1788 Holder Slocum and five others describing themselves as "Proprietors of the four Elizabeth Islands (so-called) known by the names of Peskanees, Nashwinnah, Cutterhunker and Pennakees," petitioned the General Court for a separation from Chilmark and annexation to Dartmouth. The reasons assigned by them for this change of jurisdiction were as follows: (1) "There is great Disparity in the assessment of their Taxes, from which they cannot gain any Relief without passing twenty Miles over sea." (2.) — They have not been notified "when a valuation was about to be taken." (3.) — If obliged to "have Recourse to Law . . . . . the Remedy (to use an old Proverb) might be worse than the Disease." (4.) — That "agreeable to the Maxim Taxation and Representation ought ever to go hand in hand," they conceived themselves deprived of one of the "Essential Rights of Freeman as they have no Voice in the Election of Town Officers for said Chilmark." (5.) — They could offer "many other just and weighty Reasons" but concluded that these were sufficient.

The General Court directed that the town officers of Chilmark and Dartmouth be notified of the petition and given an opportunity to be heard thereon.[1] Under date of Dec. 25, 1788, Robert Allen, town clerk of Chilmark, filed the remonstrance of that town in which the allegations of the petitioners are traversed. He stated (1.) that no petitions for relief from taxation had ever been received from the Elizabeth Islands; (2.) "that persons residing on sd Islands have at several times been persuaded by the Inhabitants of Chilmark to have an assessor chosen amongst them but they have ever Refused"; (3.) that the petitioners were "exceedingly mistaken with regard to the situation of the s'd Islands . . . . . as the Distance from Dartmouth to Chilmark is nearer seven leagues and from Chilmark to sd Islands seven miles."

The exceedingly unconvincing terms of the petition seemed to be conclusively answered by the reply of the Chil-

[1]Mass. Archives, Senate Documents, No. 1093. Received Nov. 20, 1788.

mark authorities, though the "many other just and weighty reasons" which remained unspoken by the petitioners might have disclosed unexcepted strength. The house of Slocum, however, was "divided against itself," for under date of Jan. 8, 1789, Christopher and Giles Slocum of Cuttyhunk, calling themselves owners of that island, sent in a remonstrance against the proposed change of jurisdiction, and the petitioners, on Jan. 23, following, were given leave to withdraw. This ended the short campaign for separation.

SEPARATION AND INCORPORATION

For three-quarters of a century the idea of independent existence slumbered, and two generations of people passed out of existence. With a handful of voters and no political influence the prospects of severing relationship with Chilmark were chimerical. The growth of the summer tourist and seashore visitor revived the sentiment, and to this was added the wide personal and business relation of the late John M. Forbes, the "Master of Naushon." In 1863 this sentiment had crystallized, and the inhabitants of the several islands began anew the campaign for separation. Petitions signed by Edward Merrill, John Flanders, John W. Flanders, Benjamin B. Church, George N. Slocum, John M. Forbes, Willard Besse, Otis Slocum, Harry A. Slocum, Joseph Tucker, Charles C. Church, Henry J. Allen, W. R. Veeder, Daniel Hamland, Jr., and Henry P. Macomber, were presented to the General Court, asking that the islands be incorporated by the name of "Monohansett,"[1] They alleged unequal taxation, appropriations, division of town offices, etc., and the usual accompaniments of loss of rights and privileges.

Notice was served on Tristram Mayhew, Samuel T. Hancock, and John Hammett, as Selectmen of Chilmark, and on Dec. 22, that year, they were directed by the town to present a remonstrance. This they did, and state in objection that the proposed town "is a portion of the small town of Chilmark owned principally by non residents and very sparsely populated; and that all the legal voters are but sixteen in number, a part of whom are tenants and laborers, temporary residents, and they are not sensible of unequal taxation."

[1]Printed in *Vineyard Gazette*, Oct. 2, 9, 16, 23, 1863. The original petition has a pencil note, "5 Res. Voters," checked on it.

Notwithstanding the apparent absurdity of incorporating such a few persons into a body politic, yet the great influence of Mr. Forbes prevailed, and the prayer of the petitioners was granted. The name selected, however, was not that asked

CHURCH AND SCHOOL,
CUTTYHUNK.

for, but instead Gosnold was chosen in honor of the first discoverer, and on March 17, 1864, the new town was added to the list of independent communities in the state.

EDUCATIONAL

With such a small, isolated and scattered population it will not be expected that either elaborate measures or complete facilities for instructing the youth have been undertaken here. The records of Chilmark give scanty and irregular information on this subject. The first entry relating to it is under date of 1754, when the town voted £4 "toward procuring a school on the Islands belonging to sd town." The use of the plural indicates that this appropriation may have included Nomans Land as one of the "islands."[1]

In 1789 the sum of £5 was appropriated "for the use of the inhabitants of the Islands for a school,"[2] and in 1790 the sum of £8 was voted specifically "for the use of a school at Elizabeth Islands."[3] The location of this school is not known, but it is probable that it was at Pasque or Cuttyhunk, where most of the inhabitants of the islands were centered.

In 1850 there was one school with fourteen scholars, for which $42 was expended, and in 1863 there were fifteen scholars, and an appropriation of $57.60 for their education.

When the town was incorporated, in 1864, the appropriations for school purposes were doubled at once. In 1864 it was $100; in 1867 it was $260.57; in 1885 it was $439.55; in 1895 it was $501.80; and the present year (1910) it is $571.19, and yet there has been no increase of scholars in all these years. The number this year is fifteen, but the amount expended per capita has increased from $3.80 to $38, a most creditable showing.

In addition to this the town has a public library of about three hundred volumes, which is to be reckoned as an adjunct to the educational privileges of its people.

TAVERNS

The following named persons were licensed innholders in the town of Gosnold by the County Court for the years specified: Zaccheus Lambert, 1755-64; Robert Hatch, 1755-68; Roger Merrihew, 1756-7; John Shreve, 1760; Barnabas Hinckley, 1773; Elisha Nye, 1773; John Nye, 1784-1806. Lambert kept his inn at Tarpaulin Cove and it is probable that all the public houses above licensed were there or on the island of Naushon.

NUNNAMESSETT

This island is the eastermost of the group, and is about two miles long and half a mile wide. It was purchased of the Sachem Seayick by Thomas Mayhew, Sr., prior to 1666,

[1]Chilmark Town Records, I, 105.
[2]Ibid., I, 224.
[3]Ibid., I, 230.

as in that year he sold it to his daughter Martha, wife of Thomas Tupper of Sandwich.[1] It passed into the possession of Wait Winthrop and thence into the Bowdoin family with the transfer of Naushon.[2]

A house was built on the island about 1769 for Paul Robinson, and he was later succeeded in the occupancy by Oliver Grinnell. Governor James Bowdoin died in this house in 1790, and after his death it remained unoccupied for seven or eight years, everything being left untouched.[3]

MONOHANSET

The name of this island was written in 1682 as Monahhanesuh. It is a small island of about twelve acres. It was sold by the Elder Mayhew to John Haynes in 1681, and by the latter reconveyed to Matthew Mayhew the next year.[4] Richard Sarson sold it to Wait Winthrop in 1688, and it then followed the line of possession of the successive owners of Naushon.[5]

ONKATONKA

The modern pronunciation and spelling of this islet is Uncatena. It lies between Nonamessett and Naushon. It was probably one of the "other small islands" conveyed by Seayick to Mayhew whence it passed into the possession of the Winthrop and Bowdoin estates. A house was built on it about 1800 and was occupied by Seth Robinson.[6]

KATAYMUCK

This island, the largest in the group, which is about eight miles long and nearly two miles wide, has had several names attached to it since the coming of the English to this locality. Its Algonquian name was Cataymuck (1654) or Kataymuck, varied as Katamiwick (1666), the translation of which, like that of Cataama on the Vineyard, is "great fishing place." It was called Tarpolin Cove Island as early as 1682, and for many years after; Elizabeth's Island (1702), Naushaun (1717), Winthrop's Island (1727); but the title of Naushon has sur-

[1]Dukes Deeds, I, 55, 329.
[2]Ibid., III, 354.
[3]Ricketson, New Bedford, 355.
[4]Dukes Deeds, I, 358.
[5]Ibid., I, 147.
[6]Ricketson, New Bedford, 355.

vived each of these, and for the past hundred years has been almost exclusively used. It is derived from Nash-chawan, meaning between the tide rips or currents at each end, rather than the sides.

It was purchased from the Sachem of Monument, Seayick, April 20, 1654, by the Rev. Thomas Mayhew, Jr., the only recorded instance of a land transaction made by the young missionary during his lifetime. The deed conveys "one Iland neare Woods his hole Called by the Indians Cataymuck."[1] After his death the title does not appear to have been vested in his children, as on Aug. 7, 1668, the Sachem Seayick executed an instrument in which he validates certain prior grants in which he has "by severall deedes gyven & conveighed unto Thomas Mayhew of Martin's Vineyard the island called Kataymuck * * * * with severall other islands named in the deedes." These earlier conveyances are not of record, but before this confirmation, on Sept. 27, 1666, the Governor had disposed of one-quarter of Cataymuck to Peter Oliver of Boston. This deed gives a few additional particulars and the description of the part conveyed is here quoted:[2]

One full quarter part of the greater Island of Elizabeth Island, beginning at the Western end Called by the Indians Katamiwick, being about eight miles long, lying Northward from Martynes Vineyard & Southward from Monument Bay, being brought & purchased by us of Quajaccset Sachem of Monument & also of Quaquaquijott a great Sachime upon the Maine near Pacannakicke.[3]

CHRISTENED AS SILEBY

In 1671 Governor Lovelace recognized the equity of Matthew Mayhew in the fee of the island as first purchased by Thomas Mayhew, Jr., and "recommended to him (*i. e.*, Governor Mayhew) to give some compensation to the Grand Childe for his consent to his Fathers Right."[4] On Jan. 12, 1681, the Governor, shortly before his death, sold the remaining three-quarters of the island, "being part of the manor of Tisbury," to John Haynes, merchant, late of Boston, and provided in the deed that the place was "to be hereafter called

[1]The original deed is in the collection of the Pilgrim Society at their hall in Plymouth, and one of the witnesses was young Thomas Paine. It is not recorded in our county records.

[2]This deed is also in Pilgrim Hall, but is recorded in our registry, Vol. I, folio 328. The consideration was a debt liquidated by Governor Mayhew to Thomas Daggett.

[3]York Co. Deeds, III, 114. This was also signed by Jane Mayhew, wife of the Governor.

[4]New York Council Minutes, III, 68.

MAJOR-GENERAL WAIT WINTHROP
FIRST MASTER OF NAUSHON

Sileby."[1] The significance of this is not apparent from such investigations as the author has been able to make. Sileby is a parish in Leicestershire, England, but it has no known connection with our Mayhew family, a connection which readily suggests itself because of the predilection of the Governor in bestowing here the names of places with which he was earlier associated in England. The Vicar of Sileby informs the author that the name of Mayhew has not been found in his parish registers, and it can only be surmised that it may be the home of some one connected with the Governor by marriage, possibly his first or second wife's. The new name, however, did not have any "hereafter" and does not appear in subsequent records after the Governor's death.

Haynes did not retain his interest long as the next year he reconveyed it to Matthew Mayhew.[2] The latter sold this for £460 in 1682 to Wait Winthrop of Boston.[3]

THE WINTHROP ESTATE

When this beautiful island passed into the possession of Major General Wait Still Winthrop it became the suburban estate of a man of wealth and culture who made it his playground and proceeded to develop it as such. "It may be worth something in time," wrote Winthrop to his brother, Governor Fitz John, when he announced the acquisition of the property. He began the improvement of it at once, procured tenants to develop and cultivate the land, while he gathered here and there game and edible birds and wild animals to stock the place. As early as 1698 his correspondence shows the installation of a buck and doe moose and wild turkeys. Here the younger Wait Winthrop spent his vacations and amused himself with studies of the aboriginal lore of the islands. Being on the great highway of coastwise commerce it was a frequent port of call for ships to replenish their water barrels at Tarpaulin cove. "Here arrived an English ship from Nevis," wrote young Wait, in 1702, "the master whereof sent my Father a dozen and half of oranges." It is probable that this cove or the "French Watering Place" was the location of the first house on the island. Captain Kidd, the pirate, made harbor here on his last voyage before his arrest. Winthrop writes, under date of July 12, 1699: "Captain Kidd and his crew

[1] Dukes Deeds, I, 45.
[2] Ibid., I, 333.
[3] Ibid., I, 274.

are kidnapt here . . . . . they left som smale matter at Tarpolin with the man there." In 1702 the house "on the east End of Elizabeths Island was raised," as we read in the pages of young Wait's diary, and from these brief glimpses of happenings there we may obtain some knowledge of the life at Naushon under its first gentleman owner.

The western quarter of Naushon, sold to Peter Oliver, became the subject of considerable litigation, though the absence of records obscures the exact conditions. Nathaniel Oliver, son of Peter, in 1695, began suit against Anthony Blaney, "of Elizabeth Iland for entering into and withholding the possession of one full quarter part" of this island, "beginning at the westermost end."[1] Oliver was non-suited on a technicality, as related elsewhere, and nothing further is heard of the case. In October, 1702, in association with James and Daniel Oliver and Sarah Noyes, he again entered suit for the possession of this quarter section, this time against Caleb Ray and Joseph Fuller, "in that they refuse to deliver to him" this tract of land. As there are no records to show what claims Ray or Fuller had to this particular property it can only be surmised that it came into their possession by some purchase or purchases which gave them good title.[2] Through the laxity of jurisdiction over these islands before 1700 the documents covering these transactions may have been recorded at Barnstable, Newport or Plymouth.

THE BOWDOIN FAMILY

From this time on the tenure and occupation of the island is clear. After the death of Wait Winthrop, Nov. 7, 1717, his son John and daughter Ann Lechmere, on Jan. 11, 1717, sold it to James Bowdoin of Boston for £1,500, although it had been inventoried at £2,000, including the stock.[3] By will, dated September, 1713, not executed, he bequeathed to his only daughter Ann, wife of Thomas Lechmere of London, "all my island called by the Indians Katamick otherwise called and known by the name of Elizabeth Island alias Tarpolin Cove Island . . . . . in the present tenure and occupation of John Weekes and [Joseph] Fuller." This bequest was

[1]Dukes Court Records. Anthony Blaney was a tenant of Wait Winthrop as early as 1684, and Winthrop's correspondence indicates that he had much difficulty in collecting the rental (5 Mass. Hist. Coll., VIII, passim).

[2]It is probable that they were tenants rather than land owners.

[3]Dukes Deeds, III, 354.

contingent upon the failure of his son John to pay £2,000 to his sister Ann Lechmere within twenty years, and if done it was to become his. There were legal complications between the heirs and Bowdoin extending over many years, and it was not until 1744 that the new family acquired an undisputed title to their property.[1] Since its acquisition by the Bowdoins, to the present day practically, it has been a country gentleman's demesne, and there is attached to it all the accompaniments of the life of the squire and his tenants from generation to generation. The Bowdoin family were the "Masters of Naushon" for one hundred and twenty-five years, continuing and maintaining the traditional standard of generous living first set by Major General Winthrop. The sons of the first Bowdoin, James and William, stocked it with deer that they might have a park after the manner of the nobility of England, and in 1766 they procured the passage of a law protecting these animals from destruction by the poachers. Descendants of these deer still roam the island, and its subsequent owners have stocked it with English and Scotch game birds and varieties of our native prairie fowl.

Lieutenant Governor James Bowdoin, by his will dated March 23, 1789, proven Nov. 16, 1790, bequeathed this property "to my dear son James Bowdoin, the whole of my share, viz: one half of the Islands Catamock or Naushon, Nanemasset and Ankatarmy (Uncatena)," and this third James Bowdoin, by marriage with his cousin Sarah, an only daughter of his uncle, William Bowdoin, acquired the other half. The new owner enjoyed his inheritance for about twenty years, and by will dated June 4, 1811, bequeathed it to his nephew James, the son of Sir John and Lady Tempe (née Bowdoin), upon condition of his assuming the name of Bowdoin, his mother's family.[2] In default of heirs the property was devised to James Bowdoin Winthrop, and under like default to Bowdoin College as residuary legatee. James Temple Bowdoin died Oct. 31, 1842, and the Trustees of Bowdoin College entered suit for the property, claiming possession to the exclusion of young James Temple Bowdoin, in whom the property was entailed.

The ground of the claim of Bowdoin College involved the question of citizenship of this Temple heir, the intentions

[1]Dukes Deeds, V, 389; VI, 394; VII, 185, 189.

[2]James Bowdoin died Oct. 11, 1811, "at his seat on Naushon Island, aged 59 years."

of the uncle, and sundry nice points of law. Eminent counsel was employed on both sides, including Daniel Webster and Rufus Choate, but before a trial was had a compromise was agreed upon by the parties, who agreed to the sale of Naushon with all the stock and other personal property thereon to William W. Swain of New Bedford and John M. Forbes of Milton for the sum of $20,000, of which Temple received seven and the college three-tenths.[1]

THE FORBES FAMILY

The joint ownership of Swain and Forbes lasted thirteen years, during which time the islands were used for sheep raising and general agricultural purposes in addition to its development as a country estate. Swain sold his interest to Forbes Nov. 7, 1856, and ever since that date it has been in the possession of the family, being inherited by J. Malcolm Forbes, son of John M., and in turn by his heirs, a period of sixty-seven years.[2] In the history of the island it has been the property of but three families; Winthrop, 48 years; Bowdoin, 115 years; and Forbes, 67 years, covering a total of 228 years as a gentleman's suburban estate.

The Forbes family, as the last "Masters of Naushon," has emulated successfully its predecessors in the high ideals of the establishment created by the Winthrops and the Bowdoins, and it bids fair to pass on under their tenure with this unique reputation untainted by commercial exploitation.

WEEPECKET

This small island, lying on the north side of Naushon, contains about four acres. It was acquired by the Elder Mayhew of the Sachem of Monument, and sold in 1682 to Matthew Mayhew.[3] The latter left it to his son Matthew and of him it was purchased, in 1714, by Benjamin Weeks of Falmouth.[4]

PASKITCHANNESSET

The modern name of this island is Pasque, but it is an abbreviation of an Algonquian word which is variously written;

[1]Dukes Deeds, XXIX, 140. The Deed is dated Oct. 30, 1843, and conveys Naushon, Nonamesset and Uncatena.

[2]Ibid., XXXVIII, 295. The consideration was $15,000.

[3]Ibid., I, 239.

[4]Ibid., III, 75.

Pesketennees (1670), Passhikhanneset (1696) Pashketaneset (1713), Pesketineasset (1775), and Pesk (1790). It is on the west end of Naushon separated by Robinson's Hole, being in dimension about two miles long by one wide, and containing about eight hundred acres. This island has a tidal inlet about half a mile long and its name in Algonquian denotes this: Pash–kehtan–es–et, "where the sea breaks through or divides."

The first owner was Thomas Mayhew, who sold it in 1670 to Daniel Wilcox of Dartmouth.[1] The latter sold it, in 1696, in two equal parts, to Abraham and John Tucker,[2] and it was generally called Tucker's island while in their possession.

The following description of present day conditions on the island shows that it is devoted now to pleasure seeking:

> Here we found a club house with appointments calculated to render not only the members of the club and their families comfortable, but all the guests invited by them. The island includes more than a thousand acres which the club has divided into two farms, erected commodious buildings, including club house, ice house, stabling &c. The club has also vegetable and flower gardens, sail boats and row boats, and the river which sets a mile into the island is stocked with a hundred thousand menhaden as bait for the use of the club.[3]

POOCUTOHHUNKUNNOH — CUTTYHUNK

The Algonquian name for the historic isle, as given above, is a compound of Pohqu–etahun–kunnoh, which means an open, cleared (broken up) field, which had been cultivated, a planting field. It may have been bestowed in consequence of the brief cultivation undertaken by Gosnold as related by his journalist, or to similar work done by the natives. It is now abbreviated by the elision of the first syllable and the slurring of the last two, leaving Cutohhunk or Cuttyhunk as now written. Earlier forms of spelling are Catehank (1690) and Cuddahunka (1791).

This island is irregular in shape, enclosing a large fresh water pond with an islet therein, a peculiar conformation not found in any other like situation hereabouts. The land comprises about five hundred acres, some of it very fertile.

A few local place names of Algonquian origin have survived. Quawck is said to have been the aboriginal name for

[1]Dukes Deeds, I, 253; Comp. N. Y. Council Minutes, III, 68.

[2]Ibid., I, 127, 129. They were sons of Henry Tucker of Dartmouth

[3]From "Fishing in American Waters."

Gosnold's island. The lofty promontory running out from the north end was called Cappiquat. The passage between Cuttyhunk and Nashawena bears the name of Canapitset.

Hither, in 1602, came Bartholomew Gosnold, as already described in detail, seeking a suitable place to begin the foundation of a colony under the patronage of the Virgin Queen.

This little island they chose for their abode, and on this spot Gosnold began the foundation of the first settlement of Englishmen in this region. The description of the place is unmistakable in its accuracy:

> On the Northwest side of this island, neere to the sea side, is a standing Lake of fresh water, almost three English miles in Compasse, in the middest whereof stands a plot of woodie ground, an acre in quantitie or not above: this lake is full of small Tortoises and exceedingly frequented with all sorts of fowles . . . . . we determined to fortifie our selves in the little plot of ground in the midst of the Lake above mentioned where we built an house and covered it with sedge, which grew about this lake in great abundance; in building whereof we spent three weeks and more.[1]

GOSNOLD'S ISLAND,
CUTTYHUNK.

This pond still exists with the "rocky islet" in its centre and is now called Gosnold's Island.[2]

According to the journalist of the voyage Cuttyhunk was then "full of high timbered oaks . . . . . cedars straight and tall, beech, elm, holly, walnut trees in abundance, hazlenut trees, cherry trees, sassafras trees, great plenty all over the island, a tree of high price and profit; also divers other fruit

[1]Brereton, "Briefe Relation," pp. 7, 8.

[2]On it was erected, in 1903, through the efforts of a number of patriotic men living in this section, a stone tower as a memorial of the first discovery and settlement of Englishmen on our soil.

trees." This seems almost a fairy tale in the light of present day condition. The "stately trees" either existed mostly in his imagination for colonizing purposes, or else they have melted before the devastating axes of former generations. Fifty years ago not a tree was growing on the island and not even a decayed or decaying stump could be seen above the surface. Even now but a few small shade trees are to be seen, the survivors of many planted, struggling for existence through the cold blasts of winter, and the constant wear and tear of the winds from the ocean.

The voyagers worked on their fort and storehouse, as if they intended to remain, and presumably finished both. While here they visited the mainland in the direction of Dartmouth, and went possibly as far as New Bedford. In all this time their intercourse with the natives was satisfactory, agreeable and profitable, and nothing is recorded to explain their brief stay. In less than a month the company had decided to abandon the settlement and return to England. The journalist thus states the alleged reasons for this sudden change:

> But after our barke had taken in much Sassafras, Cedar, Furres, Skins and other commodities as were thought convenient, some of our company that had promised Captain Gosnold to stay, having nothing but a saving [*i. e.*, money making] voyage in their minds, made our company of inhabitants (which was small enough before) much smaller, so as Captain Gosnold, seeing his whole strength to consist of but twelve men, and they but meanly provided, determined to return for England, leaving this island (which he called Elizabeth's Island) with as many true sorrowful eies as were before desirous to see it.

They sailed for England on June 18th, and after a voyage of five weeks landed at Exmouth.

PURCHASE AND SETTLEMENT

Cuttyhunk remained an uninhabited island after its abandonment by Gosnold for an indefinite period. It came into the possession of Thomas Mayhew, probably by purchase from the Indian Sachem of this region, and in 1668 he sold it to Philip Smith, Peleg Sanford and Thomas Ward, all of Newport, R. I.[1] Sanford acquired the rights of the others and in 1688 disposed of one-half of it to Ralph Earle of Dartmouth.[2] Earle sold this the same year to his son Ralph

[1]Dukes Deeds, I, 249.
[2]Ibid., II, 13.

Earle, Jr., who became as far as can be determined the first permanent settler.[1] In 1693 Ralph, Junior, sold a quarter of the island to his brother, William,[2] and by successive purchases of the holdings of these two brothers and Peleg Sanford's remaining half, all in 1693, Peleg Slocum of Dartmouth became the sole owner.[3] The Slocum family continued to reside here for the next century.

VISITATIONS BY HISTORIANS, 1797, 1817 AND 1903

The fame of this island because of its first discovery and occupancy by Gosnold has been the occasion for a number of pilgrimages hither by persons interested in the history and antiquities of New England. The first of record is that made by the Rev. Jeremy Belknap, one of our earliest historians, who in 1797 came to Cuttyhunk for the particular purpose of identifying the locality where Gosnold built his fort and storehouse. He published his findings of which the following is an abstract:

To this spot I went on the 20th day of June, 1797 in company with several gentlemen (foot-note, Capt. Tallman of New York, John Spooner, Mr. Allen, pilot, of New Bedford) whose curiosity and obliging kindness induced them to accompany me. The protecting hand of Nature has reserved this favorite spot to herself. Its fertility and its productions are exactly the same as in Gosnold's time, except the wood of which there is none. Every species of what he calls 'rubbish' with strawberries, peas, tansy, and other fruits and herbs appear in rich abundance unmolested by any animal but aquatic birds. We had the supreme satisfaction to find the cellar of Gosnold's store-house: the stones of which were evidently taken from the neighboring beach: the rocks of the islet being less moveable and lying in ledges. The whole island of Cuttyhunk has been for years stripped of its wood, but I was informed by Mr. Greenhill, an old resident farmer, that the trees which formerly grew on it were such as are described in Gosnold's Journal. The soil is very fine garden mould from the bottom of the vallies to the top of the hills and affords rich pasture.[4]

In 1817 another party composed of members of the Massachusetts Historical Society made a pilgrimage to examine the site of the Gosnold settlement. Their report states:

In the western end of the pond is a high islet surrounded by a rocky margin and covered with a very rich soil. . . . . The stump of a red cedar stood near the shore, and we brought home a piece of it as a remembrance of our expedition. On the Northern bank of the islet, about ten

[1]Dukes Deeds, II, 8. Ralph Earle of "Catehank" was indicted in our court in 1690 for stealing an Indian boy and was convicted.

[2]Ibid., II, 9.

[3]Ibid., II, 6, 16, 22.

[4]Dr. Belknap's Biography, II, pp.113-5.

yards from the water, we found a small excavation overgrown with bushes and grass, on one side of which were three large stones in a row at the distance of three feet from each other, having under them other stones of the same size lying in the same direction. Between these were smaller stones, which appeared by their form and smoothness to have been taken from the beach. In another excavation twenty yards south of the former, near the centre and highest part of the islet were similar stones, but very few in number and not disposed in any apparent order. On digging in other parts of the islet we found more of the same kind. We conjectured that the first excavation was all that remained of Gosnold's cellar and the latter a part of the trench dug for the purpose of forming the fort.[1]

In the early part of this century these remains, as described, were to be seen, but unfortunately since then the ground of the little island has been ploughed up and cultivated, so that scarcely a vestige remains of Gosnold's work of three centuries ago. Careful excavation might restore it.

The tercentenary of Gosnold's settlement and occupation of this island, occurring in 1902, a number of gentlemen interested in historical research, formed an association to erect a memorial of the event. This took definite form in the shape of a design for a stone tower to be placed on Gosnold's island in the pond, and it was completed and dedicated with appropriate ceremonies in August, 1903. It is a round tower built of rough stone, with circular steps inside to the look-out deck at the top, and it makes a commanding landmark for mariners approaching the Vineyard sound from the west.

NASHAWENA

This island is three miles long and a mile wide. It was originally bought, in 1674, by Peleg Sanford, Philip Smith and Thomas Ward, the latter two owning the eastern half.[2] By various purchases of the heirs of these first proprietors, about 1743, it came into the possession of Holder Slocum and remained in the tenure and occupation of his descendants for the next hundred years.[3]

The origin of the name is undoubtedly from the same root as Naushon. It means "third shell place."

PENEKESE

The earliest form of this name is Puanakesset (1670), and it is also written Penemakeeset (1696), varied with Penekesset, Penuasset (1731), and a modern form is Pune (1870).

[1]North American Review, Vol. V.

[2]Dukes Deeds, I, 249; II, 115. The Mayhews were the grantors.

[3]Ibid., VI., 524-5-7.

The island contains about forty acres, and was bought of the Mayhews, in 1670 by Daniel Wilcox, who sold it to Peleg Slocum and Abraham Tucker.[1] It gradually became the possession of Holder Slocum and his heirs. In 1873 the late Prof. Louis Agassiz appealed to the public and the General Court for the funds to establish a summer school of comparative zoology, and the then owner of this island, Mr. John Anderson of New York, a wealthy tobacco merchant, offered him the use of Penekese and a fund of $50,000, as an endowment for the school. The offer was accepted, work on the buildings was begun, and when complete it was called the Anderson School of Natural History. It was in operation for two summers when a fire destroyed it, and the school was never rebuilt.[2] In 1907 the state acquired the island, and has erected thereon an establishment for the isolation and treatment of patients afflicted with leprosy.

EGG OR GULL ISLAND

This very small island, just east of Penekese, was first in the possession of Ralph Earle, Sr., of Dartmouth, and in 1693 he transferred it to William Ingraham, a shipwright of Swansea who sold it in 1734 to Holder Slocum, and it became an inheritance in this family during the following century.[3]

U. S. GOVERNMENT SERVICES

Lighthouse Establishment: — One of the earliest lighthouses on this coast was erected on Naushon at Tarpaulin cove. It was built in 1759 by Zaccheus Lambert, a tavern keeper resident there, "at his own Cost & Charges . . . . save that the People of Nantucket have found him Oyle out of their meer Courtesy." It was established to the satisfaction of the General Court in 1762 that it had "been a means of Saving many Vessels from being lost & found to be of great advantage to Navigation," and this enterprising citizen was granted a sum out of the Province treasury for his expenses.[4] Ever since that time a light has been maintained there, but it was not till 1816 that the general government assumed control and erected the present building.

[1]Dukes Deeds, I, 253; II, 17-25; V, 410.

[2]"Origin and Progress of the Anderson School of Natural History at Penekese Island," 1874, with illustrations. The trustees were Louis Agassiz, Thomas G. Carey, Alexander Agassiz, Martin Brimmer and Theodore Lyman.

[3]Dukes Deeds, III, 376; V, 409.

[4]Mass. Archives, III, 526.

Six years later the lighthouse on Cuttyhunk was built by the government (1822), and with its mate at Gay Head forms the beacons to the mariners entering Vineyard Sound from the west.

Life Saving Service. — The reefs that make off from the western extremity of the Elizabeth Islands, with the "Sow and Pigs" as a first danger, have made this a disastrous point for ships in bad weather. Many a vessel has gone to destruction hereabouts. This caused the demand for the establishment of a station of the Life Saving Service of the United States, and on Feb. 14, 1890, it was placed in commission, bearing the name Cuttyhunk, on which island it is located.

PRESENT CONDITION OF TOWN

The town of Gosnold is nearly fifty years old, and in that time has made gratifying material progress. Its first appropriation of $400 for town expenses, in 1864, looks small in comparison with the money raised this year (1909). In 1869 the taxes had more than doubled, $872.92, while in 1883 they had risen to $1,445.81. In 1890 they raised $1,678.30, and ten years later $1,850.06, with a little larger balance to their credit each year. The present year (1909) the totals are: receipts, $2,994.35; expenditures, $2,201.15; a seven-fold increase which is an indication of the thrift and prosperity of this little island settlement.

The valuation in 1894 was $222,747, while this year (1909) it has more than doubled, and is classified as follows: Land, $391,268; buildings, $154,895; personal estate, $38,123; total, $584,286. It has 37 residents assessed, 12 non-residents, living in 48 dwellings. Of assessed land there are 8,486 acres, and there are 28 horses, 31 cows, 5 cattle, and 2,220 sheep.

EARLY REPRESENTATION OF THE ELIZABETH ISLANDS 1632.
FROM MAP IN WOOD'S "NEW ENGLAND'S PROSPECT"

INDEX

INDEX TO ANNALS OF EDGARTOWN

NAMES OF PERSONS

Index to Annals of Edgartown

NAMES OF PLACES

INDEX TO ANNALS OF WEST TISBURY

NAMES OF PERSONS

NAMES OF PLACES

Index to Annals of West Tisbury

INDEX TO ANNALS OF CHILMARK

NAMES OF PERSONS

NAMES OF PLACES

Index to Annals of Chilmark

INDEX TO ANNALS OF TISBURY

NAMES OF PERSONS

Index to Annals of Tisbury

NAMES OF PLACES

INDEX TO ANNALS OF OAK BLUFFS

NAMES OF PERSONS

NAMES OF PLACES

INDEX TO ANNALS OF GAY HEAD

NAMES OF ENGLISH PERSONS

NAMES OF INDIAN PERSONS

NAMES OF PLACES

INDEX TO ANNALS OF GOSNOLD

NAMES OF PERSONS

NAMES OF PLACES